Bird Families of the World

A series of authoritative, illustrated handbooks of which this is the 16th volume to be published.

Series editors

C. M. PERRINS Chief editor
W. J. BOCK
J. KIKKAWA

THE EDITOR **Janet Kear** completed her doctoral thesis in Cambridge in 1959, after which she started work as a research scientist at the Wildfowl & Wetlands Trust at Slimbridge. When she retired in 1993, she was Director of all the Trust's eight centres throughout the UK. She served on numerous committees and councils, including the British Trust for Ornithology, Durrell Wildlife Conservation Trust, English Nature, Liverpool Museums, the Royal Society for the Protection of Birds, and the Wildfowl & Wetlands Trust. A past President of the British Ornithologists' Union and editor of *Ibis*, Janet received the Union Medal in 1998, the same year that she was Vice-President of the International Ornithological Congress. An author of many scientific papers on wildfowl, she also wrote a number of important books, including *Man and Wildfowl*, winner of *Natural World*'s Book of the Year award in 1990. In 1993 she was awarded an OBE for services to wildfowl conservation. Janet's lifelong study of ducks, geese and swans took her to many different parts of the world. She retired to North Devon with her husband, John Turner, and continued to write and advise on wetland and wildfowl issues right up to the time of her death in November 2004. A facsimile of this book, the result of thirteen years of work, was given to Janet on the day of her death.

THE ARTIST **Mark Hulme** trained as a freshwater biologist and gained an MSc in Applied Hydrobiology from Cardiff University in 1985. He worked for several years in the Education Department at Arundel Wildfowl and Wetlands Trust Centre and then as an illustrator at the Slimbridge headquarters. Daily access to Trust wildfowl collections and rearing facilities allowed him to follow the development of many species from egg to adulthood. After leaving WWT, this intimate knowledge of ducks, geese and swans allowed him to continue to specialize in wildfowl illustration and he painted the duck plates for the concise version of *Birds of the Western Palearctic*. Away from the constraints of illustration work, he indulges his passion for creating loose, expressive watercolour paintings.

Bird Families of the World

Bird Families of the World

Ducks, Geese and Swans

Edited by
Janet Kear

Illustrated by
Mark Hulme

Volume 1
General chapters
Species accounts (*Anhima* to *Salvadorina*)

UNIVERSITY PRESS
2005

OXFORD

UNIVERSITY PRESS

Great Clarendon Street, Oxford OX2 6DP

Oxford University Press is a department of the University of Oxford.
It furthers the University's objective of excellence in research, scholarship,
and education by publishing worldwide in

Oxford   New York

Auckland   Cape Town   Dar es Salaam   Hong Kong   Karachi
Kuala Lumpur   Madrid   Melbourne   Mexico City   Nairobi
New Delhi   Taipei   Toronto   Shanghai

With offices in

Argentina   Austria   Brazil   Chile   Czech Republic   France   Greece
Guatemala   Hungary   Italy   Japan   South Korea   Poland   Portugal
Singapore   Switzerland   Thailand   Turkey   Ukraine   Vietnam

Oxford is a registered trade mark of Oxford University Press
in the UK and in certain other countries

Published in the United States
by Oxford University Press Inc., New York

A catalogue record for this book is available from the British Library

Library of Congress Cataloging in Publication Data

Data available

ISBN 0 19 861008 4 (Volume 1)
ISBN 0 19 854645 9 (Set)

10 9 8 7 6 5 4 3 2 1

Typeset by Macmillan India Ltd

Printed on acid-free paper by Thomson Press, India

Acknowledgements

The book would not have seen the light of day without huge help from Gaye Callard, who remained cheerful through every setback, from Tim Davis, who took over from Gaye towards the end of preparation and has been quite wonderful, and from Rosie Ounsted who, with characteristic efficiency, assembled the long section of references.

Many authors have been incredibly useful to the editor, to her assistants and to the compiler of the reference list. In particular, we should like to thank Tony Fox, Peter Fullagar, Baz Hughes, Kevin McCracken, John Harshman, Tim Jones and Eileen Rees for help well beyond the call of duty. Glyn Young and Mary Lanyon spent tedious days helping to ensure that the references in the text matched those in the reference list, and provided welcome assistance at many times. We should like to thank *all* authors most warmly for their contributions, and for their patience during what has been a long gestation.

Janet Kear also thanks Cathy Kennedy of OUP, Chris Perrins of the EGI, Nicole Duplaix, Petra Butcher, Dave Coles, Clem Fisher, Errol Fuller, Martin Brown for help with skins, Pat Morris, Clare Lee, Margaret Sage, Mark Stanley Price, Linda Birch and Derek Scott for help with references, Geoff Wilkinson, Phil Trathan and especially John Turner, for help with maps, Carol Colclough and Chris Ellison for their computing skills and Rhonda Washington for assistance with the Long-tailed Duck account. Bjarke Laubek kindly advised on swan damage to crops, Robin Woods on Falkland Island wildfowl, and Glen Chilton on the Labrador Duck. Van Remsen and Edward Dickinson also assisted with taxonomic problems. Nigel Collar has been his usual very helpful self. Mike Moser is especially thanked for allowing the frequent use of his library. David Stroud made many useful suggestions for improving the sections that deal with population and status of geese. Rosie Ounsted is grateful to Colin Poole for help with references to Baikal Teal, David Li for Barheaded Goose references, and Li Lukang for help with Chinese names.

John Bowler would like to thank Peter Fullagar for his comments on Radjah Shelduck, Murray Williams for his detailed comments on the Black Swan, and Eileen Rees for hers on the Bewick's and Whistling Swans. Tommy Michot and his fellow authors are grateful to Milton W. Weller and Stephen E. Adair for helpful comments on the Redhead manuscript and Daryl McGrath for technical editing. Nial Moores thanks Baz Hughes, and Mike Crosby of Birdlife International. The latter very kindly allowed access to the then unpublished Asian Red Data Book, and considerably improved original drafts of his account of Baikal Teal.

Pat Wisniewski thanks S.A. Halse, Des Callaghan, Martin Brown, C. Doyle and W. Boles for information supplied, or help with, the Cape Barren Goose, and Clem Fisher and Louise Wisniewski for assistance in locating papers. Irene Würdinger wishes to express gratitude to Bholu Abrar Khan, Deputy Chief Wildlife Warden at Bharatpur, India for his kind help and for information on breeding pairs of Barheads in Ladakh, and J. Heinze, Hildesheim, Germany for sharing his counts of breeding pairs in the Quinghai Hu Nature Reserve (Kokonur) in 1992.

Gwen Brewer thanks Michael D. Sorenson for information on Orinoco Goose genetic relationships, Fernando Ortiz Crespo for advice on its range in

Ecuador, and David G. Ricalde for information on its nest sites in Bolivia. J.L. Peters kindly supplied data on South American Teal in the wild; and Glyn Young provided the dimensions of Ringed Teal eggs which were, surprisingly, previously unrecorded. Eileen Rees thanks Roberto Schlatter, Tony Richardson, Susan Earnst, Nick Harrey, Richard Phillips, Carl D. Mitchell (i.e. the American Carl Mitchell), Bill Sladen, Arnthor Garðarsson, Ólafur Einarsson, Ævar Petersen, Anna Belousova, Yuri Shchadilov, Murray Williams, A. Meng and David Parkin for help with swan data. John Quinn thanks Jesper Madsen and Tony Fox.

Des Callaghan is grateful to T. Donegan, P. Salaman and Clara I. Bohorquez for information on Northern Screamers in South America. In the Pinkfoot account, Hugh Boyd uses data on linear measurements collected by R.A.H. Coombes in 1930–60, with additional information from the late John Berry. Patrick Claffey's unpublished work was consulted for Hartlaub's Duck distribution. R.E. David kindly provided unpublished figures for the numbers of Hawaiian Geese on the island of Kauai. Malcolm Ogilvie thanks Vanessa R. Anderson and Ray T. Alisauskas for unpublished weights of King Eider ducklings hatched in the wild. Jeff Black thanks Sharmila Choudhury and Myrfyn Owen for their contributions to Chapter 4.

Christian Dau thanks his co-author Sasha Kistchinski for his insight on the biology and distribution of Spectacled Eider and for promoting initial collaborative studies. Additionally, contributions were made by numerous colleagues in the US: J. Brueggeman, F. Fay, P. Flint, J. King, R. King, C. Lensink, E. Mallek, M. Petersen and D. Troy; and in Russia: D. Solovieva, E.E. Syroechkovskiy, Jr and E.V. Syroechkovskiy. Ron Summers is grateful to Ricardo Matus for unpublished information on sheldgeese in Chile.

Glyn Young thanks Frank Hawkins, Richard Lewis, Felix Razafindrajao and Roger Safford for data on Madagascar Teal; Roger Cattermole, Keith Zabell, Kevin McCracken, Judith Rhymer, Lance Woolaver and Rob Wilson helped in many ways, as did Kevin Johnson and Michael Sorenson. Frank McKinney's enthusiasm for Crested Ducks helped greatly in the writing of that account, and Alison Pearce shared unpublished data on Crested Duck behaviour. Baz Hughes thanks Nigel Jarrett for comments on an earlier draft of the manuscript of Chapter 3 and, finally, Colin Pennycuick and John Quinn advised on Chapter 6.

This book is dedicated to **The Wildfowl & Wetlands Trust**, to the memory of **Frank McKinney** (1928–2001), who inspired more than one generation of duck biologists, and to **Hugh Boyd**, who has provided similar encouragement for classical studies of geese.

Frank was the Trust's first doctoral student, and Hugh was the Trust's first Resident Biologist. Their contribution to us, and to the birds that we love, has been incomparable.

Contents

List of colour plates

Colour plates fall between pages 172 and 173.

List of abbreviations

>	greater than
<	less than
†	extinct lineage and deceased authors
AEWA	African-Eurasian Migratory Waterbird Agreement
AOU	American Ornithologists' Union
Apr	April
asl	above sea level
Aug	August
BMR	basic metabolic rate
BOU	British Ornithologists' Union
bp	before present
BSC	Biological Species Concept
BTO	British Trust for Ornithology
c	about
CITES	Convention on Trade in Endangered Species
cm	centimetre
CWS	Canadian Wildlife Service
Dec	December
DEE	daily energy expenditure
DNA	deoxyribonucleic acid
EMR	existence metabolic rate
ENSO	El Ninõ Southern Oscillation
Feb	February
♀	female
FEPC	forced extra-pair copulation
Gr	Greek
ha	hectare(s)
h	hour
IUCN	The World Conservation Union
IWC	International Wildfowl Count
IWRB	International Waterfowl Research Bureau (now Wetlands International)
Jan	January
juv	juvenile (usually a first-winter bird)
km	kilometre
km^2	square kilometre
kHz	kilohertz
L	Latin
LRS	lifetime reproductive success
♂	male
m	metre(s)
Mar	March

min	minute(s)
mtDNA	mitochondrial DNA
mybp	million years before present
ND2	dehydrogenase subunit 2
N,S,E,W	north, south, east, west
n	number in sample
Nov	November
NZ	New Zealand
Oct	October
ppt	parts per thousand
PSC	Philogenetic Species Concept
RSPB	Royal Society for the Protection of Birds
SAFRING	South African Bird Ringing Unit
s.d.	standard deviation
s.e.	standard error
sec	second(s)
Sept	September
SGPP	Shortgrass Prairie Population
SONON	Samenwerkende Organisaties Vogelanderzock Nederland
srRNA	subunit ribosomal nucleic acid
TERA	Troy Ecological Research Associates
UK	United Kingdom of Great Britain and Northern Ireland
US	United States of America
USFWS	US Fish & Wildlife Service
ybp	years before present
WSGCOA	Waterbird Specialist Group of Chinese Ornithological Association
WWF	World Wide Fund For Nature
WWT	The Wildfowl & Wetlands Trust
ZICOMA	Zones d'Importance pour la Conservation des Oiseaux à Madagascar (Madagascar Important Bird Areas Project)

Plan of the book

The book contains two parts spread over two volumes. Part I consists of eight general chapters, contained wholly within Volume 1, while Part II is composed of 165 species accounts split between both volumes.

PART I

After a general introduction, Chapter 2 deals with wildfowl Taxonomy and Systematics. A listing and discussion of fossil Anseriformes can be found in Chapter 2, but the taxonomic status of all extant tribes precedes their treatment in Part II. There are then five chapters dealing with aspects of life history, and a final chapter on Conservation and Management. Figures and tables in Part I are numbered according to the chapter in which they appear, i.e. Figure 1.1, Table 2.2, Figure 3.1 and so on up to Chapter 8.

PART II

The species accounts describe the screamers, ducks, geese and swans in detail but, in an effort to save space, the accounts in Part II have been condensed. A multiple-authored book of this kind is hard to control minutely, and the treatment given to the species is not uniform. Authors obviously differ in the emphasis that they have chosen to give to the various sections—they were encouraged to write at greatest length about those aspects of the bird's biology that they felt were crucial, unusual or where research findings were recent or unpublished. Where information is readily available elsewhere, the reader is referred to that source. In a few cases, where there is a wealth of relatively new information, it seemed sensible to have separate accounts of subspecies, as with the two races of the Tundra Swan (the Whistling Swan and Bewick's Swan), and the South Georgia and Brown Pintails. On the other hand, the Eurasian and American Green-winged Teal was split by the British Ornithologists' Union (but not by the American Ornithologists' Union) into two species while the book was being written and, as relatively little is known about differences between the two, they are dealt with in the same account. Figures and tables in Part II have been given the prefix 9.

Nomenclature

Jim Peters's *Checklist of the Birds of the World* (1931), of which the section on Anseriformes was revised by Paul Johnsgard in 1979, was used as the source of most of the species citations. This citation is given beneath the title of every account; the type locality (where the described specimen was found) is on the next line, plus any comments; the author and date of the genus name (if different from that in the main citation, and if this is the first species within that genus) are on the following line. As an example, the Canada Goose *Branta canadensis*, which is the first *Branta* goose to be dealt with, reads thus:

Anas canadensis Linnaeus, 1758, Syst. Nat., ed. 10, p. 123
Canada; City of Québec suggested
Branta Scopoli, 1769

For the etymology of scientific names, Jobling (1991) was the usual reference, while Lockwood (1984) provided interpretation of vernacular names in the English language. Scientific names of plants and animals that are not wildfowl are given at the first mention in Part I and, again, on first mention in Part II.

Sequence and taxonomy

The decision about which sequence to use in listing the species was not an easy one to make. Current work on DNA is altering earlier ideas on taxonomy, but many of the findings are still not published, nor subject to critical review. We have, in general, followed the sequence and major groupings of Brad Livezey (1997b) except where recent work has suggested other evolutionary pathways, for instance, in the position of the stiff-tailed ducks, Musk Duck and White-winged Duck.

Description

Male and female plumages are described, sometimes rather briefly as full treatments are available in earlier publications. Nonbreeding plumages, usually of the male, are dealt with under MOULT. Immature plumage is also described, as is the downy cygnet, gosling or duckling.

Voice

No sonograms are drawn, but where these have been published elsewhere, the reference is given. Calls that are rendered phonetically are printed in italics.

Measurements

Weights and measurements of wing, bill and tarsus of live wild birds are given where these are available; if captive birds or skins have been used, this is stated. Some of the information on egg size and weight, and on the weight of newly hatched ducklings, was collected from captive birds at WWT, and is previously unpublished—again, it has been used where there is a shortage of data from the wild. Weights are in grammes, dimensions in millimetres and standard errors indicated, unless stated otherwise. Body length measurements in the section on 'Field characters' are from Delacour (1954–64) and Madge and Burn (1988) or, in a few cases, are original.

Displays

As is usual, ritualized displays have their initial let-
ter capitalized.

Conservation and threats

Continuing favourable conservation status was
important to all authors, but the emphasis that
this section has been given varies. Where a species
or subspecies has been listed recently as in danger
of extinction by BirdLife International or the
Threatened Waterfowl Specialist Group, this is
indicated.

References

The references contain the papers, books, theses
and other publications cited in the text. Major publications on the wildfowl group are fairly numerous
and all are referred to; readers should consult them
for details of earlier work.

PART I
General chapters

1

Introduction

Janet Kear

Wildfowl (often called waterfowl in North America) consist of the ducks, geese and swans which, with the screamers and Magpie Geese, make up the avian order Anseriformes. It is a large order, divided unequally into the suborder Anhimae, or screamers, and the suborder Anseres which, in turn, is divided into the unique Magpie Goose within its own subfamily, tribe and genus, plus all the others in a single huge subfamily called the Anserinae (Livezey 1997b). The Anserinae are diverse in form so that although most species, in comparison with most songbirds for instance, are large, they vary from the small pygmy-geese (a female African Pygmy-goose may weigh as little as 260 g) to the swans—among the largest of flying birds. The clearest feature in their evolution is that species within the group seem to become better and better adapted to living in and on water. However, the picture is complicated by the fact that diving, as a method of foraging, has evolved a number of times. The protection that water can give from land-based predators means that, unlike most birds, the Anserinae can manage a simultaneous moult of wing and tail quills that renders them flightless for three to four weeks annually.

A factor that unites wildfowl is their dependence on wetlands at various stages of their lives. These productive habitats are under threat in many parts of the world through the increasing demands of human beings for whom water has become a diminishing and precious resource. Wildfowl are among the most obvious indicators of the richness and diversity of wetland habitats; they are at the top of the wetland food-chain, and are peculiarly susceptible to disturbance, pollution, drainage and development.

Most ancient human communities arose alongside wetlands (Coles and Coles 1989) where the presence of water met a basic need, and fish and fowl were crucial dietary items. Today, wetlands continue to supply food, water storage, flood control, the stabilization of shorelines, retention of chemicals, sediments and nutrients, wildlife habitat, recreation and aesthetics. They are defined in the Ramsar Convention (which is more fully covered in Chapter 8) as 'areas of marsh, fen, peatland or water, whether natural or artificial, permanent or temporary, with water that is static or flowing, fresh, brackish or salt, including areas of marine water the depth of which at low tide does not exceed 6 m'. As a habitat, wetlands occupy only a small part of the Earth's surface but biodiversity and rates of endemism in these areas are high, and many plants and animals live only in freshwater ecosystems. Wetlands are as variable as the wildlife that occupies them; their dynamism means that classification and definition are difficult, and will depend on latitude, altitude, water chemistry and underlying geology (Finlayson and Moser 1991). Definition is complicated further by the fact that American usage often differs from European (Mitsch and Gosselink 1993). Some examples of wetlands and of the types of wildfowl that they support are described below.

The arctic *tundra* of the northern hemisphere is a vast, generally flat, treeless region with underlying permafrost. It is perhaps the wetland type that has been least altered by human activity. Its marshy surface is frozen for much of the year, but the spring snow-melt floods huge areas of low-lying river valleys, and shallow lakes and ponds become numerous. In the warmth and long days of summer, the tundra produces flushes of insects and protein-rich vegetation that are exploited by the young of a number of ground-nesting wildfowl, such as Whistling and Bewick's Swans, some of the smaller geese like the Brent Goose and Lesser White-fronted Goose, and by ducks such as Baikal Teal, Northern Pintail, eiders and scoters. The birds have in common a strong migratory habit and a short breeding season; they enjoy a relative scarcity of mammalian predators while nesting, but their offspring must grow and fledge rapidly in order to fly south, or move to the sea, before winter returns and the land freezes once more. In some years, when the arctic spring comes late, breeding failure is complete and no young are produced, so it is not unusual for population size to fluctuate markedly.

The *taiga* is the mainly coniferous forest that lies between the tundra and the steppes, extending from the Urals to Kamchatka, and across sub-arctic North America. Little that remains of the forest is entirely pristine; it has been felled, replanted and managed, and much has been replaced by agriculture. Predatory birds, mammals and a few reptiles are commoner here, and what trees there are provide nesting cavities that are more difficult for a predator to enter than an open nest on the ground. Breeding ducks of Eurasian woodlands include Mandarin, Smew, goldeneyes and mergansers. The females are smallish in order to make use of holes for incubation, and both sexes can fly among trees with ease, have largish eyes, webbed feet that are adept at perching, and sharp claws that can cling to tree bark. Within the taiga's countless lakes, marshes and bogs are some of the world's famous waterbodies, such as Lake Baikal in the heart of Siberia, and Lake Kanka in the far west. Asia's 'duck factory'—the middle and lower basins of the Ob and Irtysh Rivers in western Siberia, covering about 1.8 million km^2—is a summer home to many of the ground-nesting ducks that winter in the Mediterranean, the Middle East and the western side of the Indian subcontinent, and is comparable in productivity to the prairie pothole region of North America.

Peatlands or *mires* occur throughout the world, often underlying marshes, swamps, floodplains and coastlines. They are particularly common across the northern regions of Canada and Russia, and form when decomposition fails to keep pace with the growth of vegetation. There are two types: nutrient-rich peat swamps that have a water supply that is additional to rainfall, and nutrient-poor bogs that rely only on local rain, are often acidic and dominated by *Sphagnum* moss.

Marshes have good supplies of fresh water and develop in low-lying, flat ground over mineral soils, and are dominated by reeds, rushes and sedges. They are found at all latitudes and were common in temperate Europe until the eighteenth and nineteenth centuries, when vast areas were drained for agriculture. The water level may rise and fall with the seasons, and is deepest after snow has melted on higher ground. Marbled Teal, Red-crested Pochard and Ferruginous Duck are typical European reed-bed nesters. In the US, marshes make up 90% of wetland areas, and the famous potholes of the prairies are depressions left from the last ice age that developed slowly into marshland. The stifftails are also marsh ducks that feed by diving for insect larvae living on the surface of the bottom ooze; these insects are often especially adapted to live with a rather poor oxygen supply and, like chironomids, are rich in haemoglobin.

Swamps are typically flooded for most of the growing season, and form over waterlogged soils. *Phragmites* is the principal plant seen in temperate areas, while large tropical swamps may be dominated by papyrus and cat-tail. American swamps often have trees standing in pools created by North American Beavers *Castor canadensis*, and Buffleheads, Hooded Mergansers and Wood Ducks nest within tree cavities. Screamers wade through the humid, tropical swamps of northern South America, taking emergent plants by grazing. Some deeper swamps of Africa, Asia and Northern Australia are home to the floating water-lilies whose buds and seeds provide food for pygmy-geese. Predators are common in tropical swamps, so many tropical ducks have both parents present to defend the ducklings until they are able to fly. Protein foods may be in short supply, and many young wildfowl grow slowly and are at risk of predation for a relatively long period.

Temperate *watermeadows*, especially temporarily flooded grassland, make valuable autumn and winter feeding grounds for migratory seed-eating dabbling ducks. They dry out during the summer half of the year, and are then invaded by annual plants that grow rapidly and seed prodigiously before dying in the autumn as rainfall increases and the floods recur, thus providing quantities of food for ducks, many of which will have bred further north, such as Northern Pintail, Eurasian Teal and Northern Mallard. Nowadays, much short-term flooding is under human control, and increasing numbers of dabbling ducks of Asia, such as Baikal Teal and many whistling-ducks, use rice paddies, and other temporarily irrigated cultivated land.

Ephemeral tropical wetlands are typical of northern Australia with its unpredictable rains, sudden filling of dry lake beds and the germination of seeds that have lain dormant in the parched soil for years. As in temperate floodplains, plants grow quickly, flower and seed, invertebrates reach maturity and breed, and ducks fly in to make use of both. Australian wildfowl tend to have extended nesting seasons and, often, long-term pairbonds so that male and female remain close and can breed rapidly (within three weeks) if the right conditions occur. They also tend to be nomadic, moving with the rains, like the Wandering Whistling-duck and the Magpie Goose of northern Australia which, since wild rice was one of their natural foods, took to cultivated rice with enthusiasm.

Tropical *rainforests*, where birds in the canopy are particularly difficult to count, are where the cavity-nesting, tree-perching and sedentary White-winged Duck of southeast Asia, wild Muscovy of northern South America, and Hartlaub's Duck of west Africa are found. They are well camouflaged, which suggests that they may have evolved in the presence of aerial predators.

Large *lakes* are usually a sign of glaciation, and so are more common in northern regions than, for instance, in the Mediterranean basin. They are areas in which wildfowl may roost at night, safe from land-based mammals, or in which they moult and replace wing feathers during the flightless phase. If the water is fairly shallow, diving ducks such as Canvasback may find starch-rich roots on which to feed, Tufted Duck will take molluscs from the bottom, while the mergansers catch fish. *Reservoirs,*

dams and *borrow pits* are increasingly common in places where there were originally few stretches of open water, and are used frequently by adaptable species as roosts and feeding sites.

A linear stretch of *river* or *stream* may be claimed by territorial species, such as African Black Duck and Meller's Duck, and the turbulent white waters of the southern hemisphere by the even more aggressive Blue Duck, Salvadori's Duck and Torrent Duck. These ducks all have a disposition that is intolerant of close neighbours, and knobs on the 'wrists' of their wings with which to fight; they dive for an aquatic insect diet that, in the north, would be more likely to sustain fish of the salmonid family. The Harlequin is the only equivalent white-water diver of the northern hemisphere, feeding underwater on blackfly *Simulium* larvae and pupae. The banks of, and islands in, rivers and streams are selected by many riparian ducks that breed surrounded by flowing water, usually at rather low densities, such as the fish-eating Goosander (at 0.16 pairs per km), Red-breasted Merganser (at 0.03 pairs per km) and Brazilian Merganser (at one pair per 9 km) (Holmes and Clement 1996, Silveira and Bartmann 2001).

The interface between the sea and the land is seen in *estuaries* and *deltas, intertidal mudflats* and *saline lagoons* (the last particularly common in the non-tidal Mediterranean). These habitats include the tidal freshwater and saltmarshes that occur along sheltered temperate shorelines and which, by buffering storms, help to protect the hinterland. Saltmarshes are among the most productive of natural systems, with annual productivities that equal the highest levels achieved by agriculture. Tidal estuaries are also rich in organic food particles, and are therefore populated by invertebrate-feeding shelducks, or dabbling ducks taking floating seed from upstream vegetation. Many ducks, like the South Georgia Pintail, breed on freshwater, where their tiny offspring escape the burden of dealing with a high uptake of salt, but move to the coast in winter. Wintering Brent Geese feed primarily on algae and *Zostera* grazed from the intertidal mudflats, the Kelp Goose is another coastal grazer of seaweed, and the Cape Barren Goose feeds on turf kept short by sea spray. They must have active salt-excreting glands (explained further in Chapter 3), at least during that part of the year when they utilize a saltwater environment. In the tropics and subtropics, *mangrove* creates a shrubby and even forested tidal swamp upon which, for example, the West Indian and Lesser Whistling-ducks, and the grey teal group, especially the rare endemic Madagascar Teal, depend for cavity nests. Crocodiles *Crocodilus* are often an essential part of the mangrove habitat (Mitsch and Gosselink 1993), and present a predatory hazard for ducks and ducklings.

Shallow *coastal waters*, including sea bays and straits over continental shelves, are productive habitats that are also relatively safe from duck and egg-eating mammals. Many wildfowl roost at night, or moult their flight feathers, in shallow sea bays. The extinct diving Labrador Duck once fed in the tidal shoals, other divers such as Greater Scaup feed just offshore, and wintering Harlequin, eiders and scoters are found in deeper water—all are animal eaters, particularly fond of crustaceans and molluscs, as also are the steamer-ducks of South America. Again, salt will be taken in in quantity and must be got rid of; its extraction depending not just on the possession of efficient kidneys, but on supra-orbital glands that birds inherited from their reptilian ancestors. Sea-ducks tend to be medium-sized and well-insulated with a thick layer of body fat and dense outer covering of feathers, and take more than one year to reach full size and sexual maturity. They are vulnerable to oil spills and often get caught in fishing nets (Tucker and Heath 1994). A few inhabitants of the coast, such as the steamer-ducks of South America and the flightless teal of New Zealand, have developed permanent flightlessness and never grow their wings long enough to be able to fly (Livezey and Humphrey 1986, Livezey 1990).

Man and wildfowl

Man has interacted with and exploited wild waterfowl populations for many thousands of years. They are conspicuous, and favourite subjects for killing and eating, surveying, education, recreation and research worldwide; their taxonomy is more thoroughly studied than that of other bird groups, as is their ecology, and they are among the most admired for their beauty and for the mystery of

their migrations. Wetlands, the habitat on which they depend, have not stimulated the same degree of interest until recently (Finlayson and Moser 1991).

Domestication and farming

Man's interest in consuming wildfowl, as well as in using their feathers for warmth and their fat for lighting and heating, was behind their early domestication. Two goose species were involved, the Greylag Goose and the Swan Goose, and two ducks, the Mallard and the Muscovy. Features of all wildfowl domestication include large size, a reduced number of tail and wing feathers, flightlessness, rapid maturation, an increased clutch size, long breeding season, loss of 'broodiness' (so that the technique of artificial incubation becomes necessary at an early stage), loss of aggression, a polygamous mating system, and the laying down of abdominal fat.

The domestication of the goose

The goose and the Rock Dove were the first birds to be domesticated some 5000 years ago. All the important domesticated birds are seed-eaters or grazers that had an early association with humans through their raids on crops, and the goose is no exception. The eastern race of the Greylag Goose is likely to have been the ancestor of most domestic types; it breeds further south than the western race, is large, lays early in the spring and over a long period, has a grey cast to its feathers and a pinkish bill and eye-ring—all features of many farmyard breeds of geese. They were kept mainly for meat and oil (as early as the Egyptians, humans seem to have known that they could be force-fed to enlarge their livers), but also for down and feathers; they provided quills with which to fletch arrows, and for pens. Some dozen breeds have been developed; rapid growth is a feature of white breeds such as the Embden and Roman, while epicurean flesh and a larger egg supply come from the brown ones, such as the Toulouse. The Sebastopol Goose was bred for its curly feathers that were useful for filling pillows and quilts (Kear 1990).

Two domestic breeds of goose descend from the Swan Goose- the Chinese and the African. Their flesh is less fat and, as they are more tolerant of warm climates, they are usually the type kept in tropical countries, and are found to be particularly useful as watchdogs, having retained a loud voice and acquired a greater inclination to use it during the course of domestication. Again, white forms are primarily kept for meat production and brown ones for their eggs.

Duck domestication

The Mallard has been domesticated for over 2500 years, the Romans initiating the process in Europe, and the Malays in Asia. Ducks, other than wild ones, were not included in lists of poultry sold in London until 1363 (when they were called 'tame Mallard'—the term 'duck' is not seen until 1528), and did not become common in the British diet until the 15th century. The Mallard has produced about 20 farmyard breeds in Europe, but many more in south and east Asia where 75% of all domestic ducks are kept. Those used for egg-laying are usually brown, while pale-plumaged varieties are farmed for their ability to grow and put on flesh quickly. Only five kinds of domestic Mallard have attained any degree of commercial popularity in the West: the Aylesbury (Figure 1.1), Pekin and Rouen have been developed for meat production, the first two being white, and the Khaki Campbell and fawn Indian Runner are excellent egg-layers. In all cases, the male in breeding plumage has retained the curly tail of his wild ancestor.

The Muscovy Duck was probably domesticated by the South American Indians of Peru as a pet; it had sentimental value but was also useful for its feathers, and for ridding houses of ants, flies, crickets and other insect pests (Whitley 1973). We do not know when it was first farmed but, by the time the conquistadors reached the New World, the Muscovy was already a household animal (Donkin 1989). Both the duck and its eggs were sometimes eaten but, unlike the Mallard, it was not changed much from its wild ancestor. The domesticated Muscovy is larger than its wild cousin and occurs in a variety of colours, although there are no recognized breeds. Muscovy drakes will cross with females of Mallard-type domestic ducks, producing sterile offspring that mature fast. These 'mules' have

1.1 Aylesbury Duck—bred for its white plumage, large size and for its meat.

been bred commercially in France since the middle of the 19th century; they are lean-breasted birds, the males of which can be force-fed for pâté de foie gras, while the females are killed for their breast fillets (Kear 1990).

Farming of the Mute Swan

The Mute Swan was semi-domesticated in Europe for its meat and feathers, and pinioned (the joint of one wing tip being removed before the young could fly) for easy control. Pinioning must have restricted the natural choice of mate somewhat, but humans never interfered to stop particular pairs breeding, never killed adult birds, and seldom selected between cygnets that were taken for the table. Almost all British Mute Swans were grounded for 1000 years or so, and yet maintained healthy populations—the sound of their wings in flight would not have been heard in Britain, and probably not on the continent of Europe, until the beginning of the last century (Birkhead and Perrins 1986). During the 12th and 13th centuries, any wild swans in Britain became 'owned' by persons with freehold land, and strays were pronounced to be the property of the Crown. They were seen as status symbols, whether alive or dead. No medieval feast was complete without a roast swan or two (up to 400 were sometimes eaten). They had to be young birds to have any gastronomic value, and the practice was to take the cygnets from their parents at 'swan-upping' and put them in special pits containing a pond, to be fattened on barley until Christmas or some other great occasion.

Ownership necessitated a system of marking with a lifelong label (Ticehurst 1957), and the soft tissue of the bill was found to grow scar tissue that remained until death. At swan-upping, all swans were counted, and the cygnets pinioned before they were old enough to fly and their bills marked if they were to be left to mature. An elaborate system of dividing the young between the owners of the parent birds was devised and a swan master, appointed by the King, oversaw the whole operation. As many as 630 swan marks were in use between 1450 and 1600; today, when we have different tastes in meat, only three royalties remain, but still any unmarked swans on the Thames belong to the Crown (Ticehurst 1957, Birkhead and Perrins 1986, Kear 1990).

Eider farming

Feather down is unique to wildfowl and only found in those species where the female incubates alone; in the case of some northern breeding ducks, this down is wonderfully soft and has superb insulating properties, so that the clutch retains its heat in the absence of the female and, perhaps as important, its moisture. Eider farming has been practised in Iceland for nearly 1000 years, the birds providing the material from which the finest eiderdowns are made. Common Eiders are firmly protected and nest in large colonies, 'belonging' to the farmer on whose land they breed. As the down is extremely valuable, farmers encourage their visitors in a variety of ways. Stone slab nesting boxes are provided on the ground, with a slight hollow underneath,

and here the female lays her eggs. Predators, such as Arctic Fox *Alopex lagopus* and the introduced American Mink *Mustela vison*, are kept at bay. Flags are erected to flutter in the breeze and indicate the position of the protected area (Doughty 1979). The suggestion is that the flags resemble the wings of gulls in whose colonies wild Eiders often choose to nest because their eggs suffer less predation if they incubate among a mass of other birds. Once the Eider has started to incubate, she pulls down from her breast to line the nest and to cover the eggs on a few occasions that she leaves during incubation. The farmer makes two collections of down, the first fairly soon after incubation has started (the bird replaces the lost down almost immediately), and the second after she has hatched and left with her ducklings. The first collection is the most valuable as the down is largely pristine, the second needs careful cleaning to remove adhering grass, egg-shells and moss (Kear 1990). The annual down harvest may produce a substantial proportion of the farmer's income. The record amount seems to have been collected in 1915 when 4294 kg were gathered—the production of about 280 000 females (Doughty 1979). Currently, about 350 farms produce nearly 3000 kg annually; with prices around 6000 Danish kroner (£512 or US$746) per kilo, which amounts to an astonishing market value of £1 536 325 or US$2 240 422 (Hansen 2002).

Wildfowling

Many wildfowl, being relatively large and good to eat, are the prized quarry of hunters, and are a renewable resource of great economic value (Mitsch and Gosselink 1993). They became quarry many thousands of years ago. Fish-hooks, nooses, pitfall traps, snares, loops, bird-lime and flight-nets were all employed in order to catch wildfowl somewhere in the world. The driving and netting of moulting wildfowl, through the use of duck decoys (see below), and some other methods of catching ducks without the use of firearms, persisted well into the last century. At the end of the 1950s, it was estimated that 1 200 000 ducks were killed in an average winter season in the marshes around the Caspian Sea of northern Iran; shooting accounted for only 9% of them (Savage 1963). The capture was mainly at night, by net, gong and flare. This method involves two boats; in the bow of the first burns a weak, flaring flame. Behind this stands a man with an elongated hand net, and behind him a companion who does the paddling. The second boat travels close by and contains a man beating a brass gong incessantly. Northern Mallard are the ducks most susceptible to this method of hunting; they wait for the boats to approach within a few metres and are caught as they leap into the air; the whole process is dazzling and bewildering, and resembles nothing that they have cause to fear. One team may take 600 birds in a night.

Royal Egyptian carvings and paintings first depicted the thrill and enjoyment of the wildfowling party. Here it was the throwing stick that was aimed skilfully at the neck of the ducks, mostly Northern Pintail, in order to kill them. Hawking has been around since the time of Aristotle, and captive Goshawks *Accipiter gentilis* and Peregrine Falcons *Falco peregrinus* (the falcon that the Americans call the 'Duck Hawk') were flown at wild geese and ducks. As with the Egyptians, this was done mainly for sport rather than for food, and hawking was indulged in only by the wealthy.

Guns did not initially improve man's success in killing wildfowl. The tedious business of muzzle-loading, shoving powder and a projectile down the tube or barrel with a ramrod, tended to ensure that the duck got up and flew away before the wildfowler was ready to fire. The invention of the breech-loading gun, which broke at a hinge and could be loaded near the ignition system, happened during the first part of the 19th century, and was crucial to the evolution of successful wildfowling. Developments in the philosophy of wildfowling gradually produced the idea that the surest way of killing 'cleanly', the hardest and therefore the most sportsmanlike, was to aim at flying quarry.

The modern definition of wildfowling in Britain is precise: it is the pursuit of legally taken ducks and geese below high-water mark with shotguns. Dogs to retrieve the dead and wounded game, especially after dark, are an essential part of this tidal-zone shooting. The wildfowlers' favourite breed—the Labrador—was developed in the 19th century as well. They sit by the hunter's side while the ducks and geese are shot, and are then sent out to collect the birds.

Wildfowling, though predominantly a male sport, is no longer the preserve of the rich. In the UK, membership of the British Association for Shooting and Conservation (BASC) stands at around 120 000 with over 1600 affiliated wildfowling clubs. Wildfowlers take part in wildfowl counts, create reserves and, typically, are far-sighted enough to realize that conservation measures ensure the continuation of their sport. In the US, the recreational hunting industry spends huge sums of money in local economies (estimated at US$58 million for the Mississippi flyway alone) (Mitsch and Gosselink 1993).

Decoys

Before the development and subsequent easy access to guns, many human communities relied on catching wild waterfowl for food by rounding up those that were flightless. Inevitably, their carcases were then in rather poor condition, with reduced muscle and fat. The Dutch decoy, invented 600 years ago but brought to perfection in the sixteenth century, was a sophisticated system for trapping plump and flying birds that depended, for its effectiveness, upon the mobbing response that swimming ducks show towards mammalian predators such as dogs and foxes. The word 'decoy' comes from a contraction of two Dutch words, *de kooi*, that mean 'the cage'. The device was a modification of a shallow pool, usually not more than 2 ha in extent and surrounded by quiet woodland, from which radiated up to eight ditches or 'pipes'—curved extensions of the pool covered with netting hung over semicircular hoops. Along the outside curve of every pipe was a range of overlapping reed screens, higher than a man, that worked on the principle of a 'Venetian blind', concealing birds on the pool but enabling those under the netting to see the decoyman if wished. Connecting these high screens at ground level, and making in plan a zig-zag pattern, were shorter screens known as dog-leaps (Kear 1990, Karelse 1994, Heaton 2001). Considerable skill and knowledge of animal behaviour were required to operate the system. Wild flying creatures had to be persuaded to use the pond and then be enticed beneath the nets so that they could be caught. It must have been common knowledge among country people that ducks on water will swim towards and follow certain mammals moving on land, but it was a clever operator who devised a strategy for putting the birds' behaviour to use. Ducks respond to a range of mammals, and will approach stoats, squirrels, foxes and dogs; but only the domestic dog can be trained by humans to work at a distance. Traditionally, the decoy dog was small, fox-like, reddish in colour, with a bushy tail and a lively gait. The Dutch developed a special breed called a *kooikerhondje* which looks like a red-and-white, long-legged spaniel, and appears on paintings by artists such as Jan Vermeer (1632–75) and Jan Steen (1626–79).

The tendency to swim towards a dog or fox is related to the collective 'mobbing' response of many birds to a predator. The birds' action must have survival value, and an essential part of the performance is that the participants are not in any perceived danger; close pursuit of ducks by the fox is unlikely since mammals are inefficient swimmers and do not fly. Thus, the real hazard is the possibility of being surprised—of not realizing that the predator is there. Mobbing ensures that all members of the group are aware of the danger, teaches the inexperienced what the enemy looks like, and perhaps gets rid of the problem, causing the predator to depart rather than endure the 'embarrassing' attentions of the mob.

The decoyman first checks that there are sufficient wild ducks on the pond and then tests the breeze. Birds take off only into a wind, so disturbance near a pipe into which the wind is blowing means that the ducks turn back towards the pool and fly from under the nets. That is why decoy ponds needed more than one pipe if they were to operate in all weathers. The dog has then to be shown to the ducks at one of the dog leaps, to walk quickly down the pipe away from the ducks and the pool, disappear behind the next screen, and reappear at the next leap and so on until most of the ducks have followed it under the netting. The man in charge of the dog must, of course, remain hidden until the right moment. When as many birds as possible have been drawn in, the decoyman appears at the outermost gap in the screen, behind the ducks. The ducks' retreat to the open pond seeming to be cut off, they fly into the wind down the narrowing pipe with the decoyman in pursuit, visible to them but not to the birds on the pond, until he has them caught in a funnel trap at the end. The method was highly successful. In 1790 Londoners alone were said to be consuming over 200 000 decoyed ducks in a season, and the annual take in Holland as late as 1952 was thought to be 300 000, of which 73% were Northern Mallard, 15% Eurasian Teal, 8% Eurasian Wigeon and 4% Northern Pintail (Kear 1990, Karelse 1994).

Two hundred years ago, decoys were common in many parts of Europe where there was a seasonal flight of ducks, for instance, in Ireland, Bohemia, France, Denmark and Germany, as well as England, Wales and The Netherlands. Modifications of the decoy system were also known as far away as Iran, Pakistan and Japan. A great decline in the use of decoys for obtaining dead birds for food occurred during the 20th century, as guns became readily available. In The Netherlands, the number of decoys dropped from about 1000 to the 118 registered in 1979 (Karelse 1994). In England and Wales, the number fell from 200 used for catching birds for market, to four still operating in 2002, but for a different purpose—research. In 1907, a decoy in Denmark was used for the first time to catch Eurasian Teal, not to kill them, but in order to release them individually marked (see Chapter 6). Four years later, in 1911, the first duck was ringed in a Dutch decoy (Karelse 1994). The majority of ducks ringed in the UK have been caught in restored decoys, starting at Orielton in Wales in 1934. The results obtained have been invaluable, and our knowledge of wildfowl migrations would be far less advanced had those few decoys not remained sufficiently intact into the latter half of the twentieth century (Kear 1993). Similarly, scientists studying duck migration patterns in The Netherlands have employed the country's historic decoys to catch ducks (Karelse 1994).

The word 'decoy', particularly in North America, nowadays refers to the carved or moulded model ducks that float on water and entice birds to join them within reach of a gun. The verb 'to decoy' means to lead into danger, and derives from the flocks of domesticated and tame Mallard that were kept in decoys for this function. They were bred small, were often white so that they could be readily distinguished and passed over at the time of slaughter, and noisy since their task was to call their wild brethren from the skies. A female Call Duck, as the breed is known, is noticeably noisier than her wild ancestors. The Decrescendo call—*QUACK, QUACK, quack, quack*—that all female Northern Mallard give in late summer and autumn, apparently in order to summon an intended or absent mate, is especially loud in Call Ducks and very persistently uttered.

Aviculture

Man's admiration for ducks, geese and swans has meant that for many years they have been kept for their beauty and companionship rather than for their utility. They look better than other birds in captivity, and a cage is usually unnecessary and a pond appears so much their natural element that, even when rendered flightless by feather-cutting or pinioning, they need be neither obviously unhappy nor unsightly. Collections of pinioned wildfowl, such as those of the Wildfowl and Wetlands Trust (WWT), have played an important role in informing the general public about the needs of conservation, thus ultimately helping to ensure the safety of the wetland habitats on which their wild relatives depend. They also provide excellent subjects for investigation, and students have made use of these captive assets for research into displays and preening behaviour, calls, breeding performance, moult, disease, parasites and responses to stimuli such as daylength and temperature. It was aviculturists who first thought of providing hole-nesting ducks with artificial cavities in which to nest; the 13th Earl of Derby who, between 1831 and 1851, bred many wildfowl for the first time in captivity at Knowsley near Liverpool, provided his birds with boxes on poles. The provision of boxes is now commonplace for many wild populations in situations where natural holes are in short supply. Observations made in

wildfowl parks and zoos during the last half century were also fundamental to our understanding of ethology, and courtship displays have been used to determine taxonomic relationships (Lorenz 1951–53, 1979, 1991, Lorenz and Von de Wall 1960, Johnsgard 1965a).

Not all wildfowl are equally easy to keep and, among the keener aviculturists, there was in the past great competition to be the first to maintain and breed the rarest. Screamers and Magpie Geese are still unusual in bird collections, but when Magpie Geese were bred, some observations were made that would have been difficult in the wild; it was only after they had hatched young in captivity that it was realized that the adults fed their goslings—a most uncommon occurrence in any goose (Johnsgard 1961b). The smaller whistling-ducks were early favourites with aviculturists—West Indian and Black-bellied Whistling-ducks were kept in captivity before 1750, and the Fulvous Whistling-duck first bred at London Zoo in 1872. Many of their displays and breeding habits were described initially from studies of tame birds, and they were characterized as preferring to keep apart from other ducks. At temperate latitudes, however, they do not reach their potential life span, being vulnerable to the cold and with a tendency to get frostbitten toes in winter (Hillgarth and Kear 1982a).

Captive swans and geese have settled well and are long-lived, since grass and seeds form their natural diet (most cygnets and goslings are even reared entirely on plant proteins), and all species have bred in confinement. However, not all individuals of the small, high-arctic breeders, such as Bewick's Swan, Brent and Red-breasted Geese, will nest readily at the temperate latitudes of most zoos—the days never quite get long enough to stimulate the hormone cycles that the birds would experience in the wild (Murton and Kear 1973). The near-tropical Hawaiian Goose has problems of a different kind: they lay early when daylengths are short, but when the temperature is still cold at temperate latitudes, and females frequently suffer from egg-peritonitis (Kear and Berger 1980, Hillgarth *et al.* 1983). Gizzard worm *Amidostomum* problems can be fairly common in captive geese and sheldgeese, particularly birds at a juvenile stage, where they are kept on grass swards that have been used for many years. The larvae attach themselves to grass blades and are taken in by the grazing bird. The thread-like nematodes live beneath the horny lining of the gizzard; the lining can become severely damaged with a heavy infestation, and the bird fails to digest its food properly. Fortunately, routine prophylactic measures have been possible and the cycle of reinfection can be broken if the lawns are rested for a while.

Studies of sheldgeese and shelducks in captivity (Hillgarth and Kear 1979b) revealed that females tend to live longer than males, an unusual situation in wildfowl where sex ratios are often skewed towards males (e.g. Owen and Dix 1986, and see Chapter 5) and where, in captivity at least, males have greater longevity. This may be related to the common observation that the female shelduck is the dominant partner of the pair. Longevity seems partly related to body size, with swans on average living longer than geese, which live longer than ducks.

Mandarin Duck and American Wood Duck have such attractive drakes that almost every aviculturist wants to keep them, and they have a long history in captivity; the Mandarin has been kept in its native China and Japan for centuries. However, like the White-winged Duck of southeast Asia, they are particularly susceptible to avian tuberculosis (Hillgarth and Kear 1981) and, in captivity, frequently die before they reach middle-age. Avian tuberculosis is caused by a bacillus to which most humans are immune; however, interest in the disease has intensified recently because it can become pathogenic in those with HIV.

Seaducks, Kelp Geese and steamer-ducks that spend all or part of their lives on saltwater have generally not done well in confinement, and require special care if they are to survive on freshwater long enough to breed (salt is a natural disinfectant for many waterborne diseases). The Common Goldeneye was established as a captive breeder in 1909, Barrow's Goldeneye in 1937, but the Common Scoter, Harlequin Duck and Long-tailed Duck only nested successfully in the 1970s, and none breeds particularly freely in temperate zoos. Of the sawbills, the robust Red-breasted Merganser and Goosander have been more successful than the others. Aspergillosis, renal failure and impactions of the gizzard tend to be commoner in captive seaducks than in other waterfowl; however, many of the internal parasites affecting seaducks in the wild, such as *Acanthocephala* and *Coccidia*, are absent because their secondary hosts do not occur. Even common freshwater parasite 'carriers', such as snails, tend to be eaten out of a waterfowl collection (Hillgarth and Kear 1979a).

Captive Ruddy Ducks bred (in their native US) in the 1930s, but the White-headed Duck, Maccoa, Argentine Ruddy Duck and Black-headed Duck not until the 1970s, so close research on captive birds was not possible until then (Matthews and Evans 1974, Carbonell 1983, Rees and Hillgarth 1984). The stifftails had the reputation of being difficult for the aviculturist, and were particularly hard to hand-rear, so that eggs were often left with their mothers to hatch. This resulted in escapes, as in the case of the Ruddy Duck in Europe which now threatens the genetic purity of the native White-headed Duck. Stifftails were found to be summer breeders in temperate wildfowl collections, with egg-laying seasons similar to the tropical whistling-ducks which tend to produce eggs on either side of the longest day in June, rather than only in the spring as in the majority of northern ducks (Murton and Kear 1978).

Since many wildfowl do adapt and breed fairly freely in captivity, there is potential for allowing the release of some species, whose populations are declining in the wild, back into their original habitats. Such reintroduction programmes are not easy to conduct, and only a few have been successful (some examples are examined in Chapter 8). Most aviculture must be seen as existing for itself; often it brings great pleasure, or provides research possibilities, or gives the public the chance to see the birds and habitats on which their taxes and entrance fees are being spent. Humans seem to find therapeutic value in having pets, and in feeding wild animals from the hand, especially when they are as attractive and responsive as cygnets, goslings and ducklings.

Cultural values

Ducks, geese and swans have inspired cultural expression in song, dance, language, poetry, prose and art (Kear 1990). Their wetland habitat, on the other hand, has often had a bad press, being portrayed as dismal and dangerous, and the source of numerous human ills, including malaria. 'Swamped' and 'bogged down' are not situations that recommend themselves. Our attitudes are ambivalent, but are gradually changing, thanks in part to books on such watery and diverse subjects as Iraq's Marsh Arabs (e.g. Wilfred Thesiger's *Desert, Marsh and Mountain* and Gavin Maxwell's *A Reed Shaken by the Wind*), the European Otter *Lutra lutra* (*Tarka the Otter, Ring of Bright Water*), Water Vole *Arvicola amphibius* (Ratty in *The Wind in the Willows*) and an ugly duckling who was destined to become a beautiful swan. Mother Goose, who features in the title of collections of fairy-stories and nursery rhymes, is a family friend to whom we entrust our children.

Dutch artists of the seventeenth century captured, perhaps for the first time in Europe, the beauty rather than the darkness of wet landscapes. Painters such as Jan van Goyen (1596–1656), Jacob van Ruisdael (1628–82) and Meindert Hobbema (1638–1709) depicted the brightness of flat watery land under a reflected sky with unforgettable brilliance. Across the Channel in East Anglia, artists like John Constable (1776–1837), who lived near the river Stour in Suffolk, and John Sell Cotman (1782–1842) of Norwich, continued the tradition. Constable's watermeadows seem essentially English, yet it is an England that has almost entirely drained away.

Peter Scott, founder of the Wildfowl & Wetlands Trust and himself a convert from shooting ducks and geese, produced many books and paintings that have been an inspiration, and helped to change attitudes. His legacy, in the form of WWT's nine wetland centres spread around the UK, and which have formed the model for similar centres in many parts of the world, continues to demonstrate the value and essential nature of wetlands and wildlife for people. Economically and aesthetically, wetlands and wildfowl are valuable to us and are worthy of study and conservation. This book details the lives of ducks, geese and swans—their travels, social behaviour, breeding and feeding habits, and the way in which their populations are controlled. The last chapter in Part I looks at some of the threats and conflicts that must be resolved if wildfowl and their wetland habitats are to have a future in our modern world.

2

Taxonomy and systematics

Des Callaghan and John Harshman

Members of the Anseriformes are more closely related to one another than to any other birds; the group is recognized by all taxonomists, regardless of their approach to avian systematics.

The discovery and description of ducks, geese and swans have shown noticeable peaks of activity over the past 240 years (Figure 2.1). Linnaeus (*Systema Naturae* 1758) described 35 species, while Gmelin (*Syst. Nat.* 1789), Vieillot (*Nouv. Dict. Hist. Nat.* 1816) and Eyton (*Monogr. Anatidae* 1838) contributed greatly to the number described, so that by the end of the 19th century most living species were known to science. During the 20th century, only three new ducks were discovered: Crested Shelduck on the Naktong River in South Korea (Kuroda 1924), Campbell Island Teal on Campbell Island off New Zealand (Fleming 1935), and White-headed Steamer-duck along the coast of Chubut Province

in eastern Argentina (Humphrey and Thompson 1981).

The arrangement of wildfowl into a system that represents their evolutionary history has been the subject of much debate and extensive study. Early taxonomists constructed classifications on the basis of superficial comparisons of morphology and limited reference material (Eyton 1838, Bonaparte 1856, Gray 1871, Sclater 1880, Salvadori 1895, Phillips 1922–26, Peters 1931). Delacour and Mayr (1945, 1946), however, provided an inspired revision of the classification of the group, excluding the screamers or Anhimidae (Table 2.2). Their work was based largely on comparisons of general habits, displays, skull anatomy and the plumage of the downy young; the system was accepted widely and formed the basis of most subsequent work. Later studies primarily used comparisons of behaviour (Lorenz 1951–53, Johnsgard 1960b, 1961a, 1962, 1965a, McKinney 1975), interspecific hybridization (Sibley 1957, Johnsgard 1960a), the structure of the male syrinx or windpipe (Humphrey 1958a, Johnsgard 1961c), molecular characteristics (Yamashina 1952, Sibley and Ahlquist 1972, Jacob and Glaser 1975, Brush 1976, Kessler and Avise 1984, Patton and Avise 1986, Madsen *et al.* 1988, Sibley and Ahlquist 1990, Sraml *et al.* 1996, Harshman 1996, Johnson and Sorenson 1999, McCracken *et al.* 1999), antigens and antibodies (Cotter 1957), skeletons (Verheyen 1955, Woolfenden 1961), feather lice (Timmermann 1963), and eggshell structure (Tyler 1964). These studies established the wildfowl among the best known of avian groups.

In the 1990s, Livezey (1997b) provided a classification (Table 2.2) based on cladistic analysis of

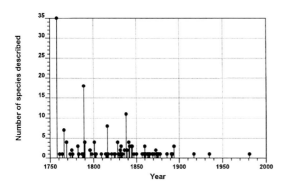

2.1 Temporal distribution of the description of anseriform species currently extant.

2.2 Structure of four previous major classifications of the Anseriformes.

System	Family	Subfamily	Tribe	No. genera	No. species
Delacour and Mayr (1945)	Anhimidae*	None	None	2	3
	Anatidae	Anserinae	Anserini	4	20
			Dendrocygnini	1	8
		Anatinae	Tadornini	8	20
			Anatini	5	40
			Aythyini	2	15
			Cairini	8	13
			Mergini	7	20
			Oxyurini	4	7
			Merganettini	1	1
				42	**147**
Johnsgard (1978)	Anhimidae*	None	None	2	3
	Anatidae	Anseranatinae	Anseranatini	1	1
		Anserinae	Dendrocygnini	2	9
			Anserini	4	21
			Cereopsini	1	1
			Stictonettini	1	1
		Anatinae	Tadornini	5	15
			Tachyerini	1	3
			Cairini	9	13
			Merganettini	1	1
			Anatini	4	39
			Aythyini	3	16
			Mergini	8	20
			Oxyurini	3	8
				45	**151**
Sibley and Monroe (1990)	Anhimidae	None	None	2	3
	Anseranatidae	None	None	1	1
	Dendrocygnidae	None	None	2	9
	Anatidae	Oxyurinae	None	3	9
		Stictonettinae	None	1	1
		Cygninae	None	2	7
		Anatinae	Anserini	14	43
			Anatini	23	88
				48	**161**
Livezey (1997b)	Anhimidae	None	None	2	3
	Anseranatidae	None	None	1	1
	Anatidae	Dendrocygninae	Dendrocygnini	1	8
			Thalassornithini	1	1
		Anserinae	Cereopsini	1	1

2.2 *contd.*

System	Family	Subfamily	Tribe	No. genera	No. species
			Anserini	3	16
			Cygnini	3	8
		Stictonettinae	None	1	1
		Tadorninae	Plectopterini	2	3
			Tadornini	6	15
			Merganettini	3	6
		Anatinae	Malacorhynchini	2	2
			Anatini	11	60
			Aythyini	4	17
			Mergini	10	22
			Oxyurini	4	9
				55	**173**

★The Anhimidae were not treated by Delacour and Mayr (1945) or Johnsgard (1978) but are included to aid comparison.

morphological characters. He included treatment of 30 fossil species and more than a decade of analyses (Livezey 1986a, 1989a, 1989b, 1991, 1995a–c, 1996a–c, 1997a, 1997c, Livezey and Martin 1988). Until DNA studies were undertaken towards the end of the 1990s, this probably represented the most useful arrangement of relationships. It was the sequence adopted by Madge and Burn (1988) who hoped that 'Livezey's review will be a standard reference for many years to come'.

Mayr and Bock (1994) emphasized the need to recognize the distinction between those standard avian sequences that are important for communication among, for example, ornithologists, conservationists and decision-makers, and those provisional classifications that are used in discussions among taxonomists, in an effort to understand phylogenies. As shown above, many classifications are available for the wildfowl group, and these have provided different names for various ducks, geese and swans, and diverse ordering systems. Yet, despite the considerable amount of work that has been undertaken and the rapid development of statistical techniques for investigating phylogenies, a non-controversial classification is not yet available. Even the detailed investigations of Livezey produced some inadequately

resolved relationships, while both earlier and later molecular studies provided results that conflict with his conclusions (Bottjer 1983, Madsen *et al.* 1988, Sibley and Ahlquist 1990, Sraml *et al.* 1996, Harshman 1996, Johnson and Sorenson 1998, McCracken *et al.* 1999).

Species and subspecies concepts
Species

Table 2.2 shows that there has been a gradual increase in the number of recognized wildfowl genera and species, from 42 genera and 147 species (Delacour and Mayr 1945) to 55 genera and 173 species (Livezey 1997b). This has happened despite there being only one new species discovered in the last 50 years (White-headed Steamer-duck). The increase in the number of genera is a result of a growing tendency to assign a separate taxonomic rank to each branch of a phylogeny, and this is a prominent feature of the classification derived by Livezey (1997b). We recognize 52 genera and 165 species; however, the determination of generic limits is still poorly resolved and remains subjective (Voous 1992).

One of the major areas of current taxonomic debate centres on the definition of a species. Zoologists have traditionally held the notion that a species is a group of individuals that forms an interbreeding population such that gene flow can occur freely within the group but hardly ever occurs outside it (Quicke 1993). The most widely known definition based on this notion is the Biological Species Concept (BSC), proposed by Ernst Mayr (1942). Roughly, the BSC proposes that a species is a group of interbreeding populations that are genetically isolated from other groups by reproductive isolating mechanisms such as hybrid sterility or mate acceptability (Quicke 1993). This was later modified so that evidence of a stable hybrid zone allowed two taxa to be recognized still as distinct species (Short 1969, Mayr 1982a, Haffer 1992). While this concept can be applied with ease to overlapping (sympatric) populations, or those in close proximity (parapatric), it cannot be applied to those that are isolated (allopatric). In the last case, the systematist is left effectively having to guess whether two taxa could interbreed—a decision usually based on morphological, behavioural or vocal characters. The ability to hybridize is often of limited value in assessing specific status; this is certainly the case with wildfowl, where interspecific hybridization is exceptionally common and even intergeneric hybridization is not unknown (Johnsgard 1960a). Nonetheless, most of the earlier taxonomic works on the Anseriformes used some form of the BSC.

Recently, the replacement of the BSC with the Phylogenetic Species Concept (PSC) of Cracraft (1983) has been proposed (McKitrick and Zink 1988, Zink and McKitrick 1995, Zink 1996). Under this concept, species are defined roughly as the smallest groups of individuals that possess at least one unique genetically determined characteristic that is present in all members of the group and absent from all close relatives of other groups. Thus, the main difference between the BSC and the PSC is that the latter does not consider present biological characteristics directly, but rather the acquisition of features during evolution (Baum 1992). Clearly, application of the PSC leads to a greater number of species than does the BSC, which is the main reason for the increased number of ducks, geese and swans

recognized by Sibley and Monroe (1990) and Livezey (1997b). Indeed, the PSC has been criticized mainly because of impracticalities imposed by a greatly inflated number of species, and the problem of identifying many of them (Mayr 1992, Collar 1996).

Subspecies

Many ducks, geese and swans differ in size or colour in parts of their range. This can be a gradual change over a large geographic area (a cline) or discrete differences shown by isolated populations, such as those on islands. Such variants are often named as subspecies or races which, in the Linnaean period, were called 'varieties' (Mayr 1982b). Early taxonomists attempted to provide names for every local variant, no matter how slight the difference or how small their sample. Consequently, many of the subspecific names attached to species proved worthless and, unfortunately, many of these persist in the literature.

Subspecies have always generated controversy amongst taxonomists (Lanyon 1982). In an attempt to improve the usefulness of the subspecies rank, the '75% rule' was developed, on the basis of which a local population is given a separate subspecific name only if at least 75% of the individuals can be separated reliably from those of other populations (Amadon 1949). Nineteen anseriform subspecies that have been described in the literature since the work of Delacour (1954–64) do not appear to conform to the 75% rule. However, nearly 30% of the wildfowl species dealt with in this book can be divided into subspecies; most contain just two or three subspecies, but the Common Eider has six and the Canada Goose can be split into 12!

The time required for subspecies to evolve will vary according to generational length, the adaptability of the species and the evolutionary pressures acting upon individuals within the population. In some species of birds, this can be surprisingly short, for example the European Goldfinch *Carduelis carduelis* evolved into a well-marked subspecies within 60 years of its introduction into Bermuda (Lack 1974). Some subspecies are so distinct that it is difficult to decide whether they should be treated as subspecies or species. Among the Anseriformes, at least 14 subspecies seem to be close to achieving specific status, such as the Whistling and Bewick's Swans, Chinese and Indian Spot-billed Ducks, and American and European White-winged Scoters.

Homoplasy

The classification of organisms into a system that reflects their true relationships (or phylogeny) is hindered considerably by the impact of homoplasy. This arises when unrelated species show similarities because they have evolved under similar conditions (known as parallel or convergent evolution), and when the characteristics of some species evolve from a primitive state to a derived state, and then back to a primitive state (known as character reversal). These evolutionary changes can lead to misleading conclusions about relationships.

Homoplasy is common within wildfowl, in particular in relation to convergent evolution of adaptions for diving (Livezey 1986a, Faith 1989, McCracken et al. 1999). For example, although the White-backed Duck is very similar superficially to the stiff-tailed ducks (Oxyurini), and was included within that tribe in most early taxonomic works, it seems that it is a whistling-duck (Dendrocygnidae) highly adapted for diving (Livezey 1986a). The problem of character reversal is also common; for example, Livezey (1995b, 1997b) argued that the stiff-tailed ducks are well within his family Anatinae, and have reverted to constructing nests without female feather down. However, molecular data (Bottjer 1983, Madsen et al. 1988, Sibley and Ahlquist 1990, Harshman 1996, Sraml et al. 1996, McCracken et al. 1999) suggest that they are a much more basal divergence, and so may never have evolved the use of down for lining their nests.

Fossil record

The fossil record has played a vital role in reconstructing the course of evolution (Hallam 1988). The anseriform fossil record is good relative to many other bird groups. This is mainly because of large size and an aquatic environment where bodies

2.3 Temporal occurrence of anseriform families and subfamilies in the fossil record (based on Brodkorb 1962, 1964, Howard 1964a, Olson 1977, 1985, Alvarez and Olson 1978, Cheneval 1984, 1987, Becker 1987, Livezey and Martin 1988, Bickart 1990, Chandler 1990, Olson and James 1991, Livezey 1997a, 1997b). († denotes extinct lineages) (mya = million years ago).

Family Subfamily	Palaeocene (65–56 mya)	Eocene (56–35 mya)	Oligocene (35–23 mya)	Miocene (23–5 mya)	Pliocene (5–2 mya)	Pleistocene (<2 mya)	Holocene (<10 000 ya)
Anhimidae	-	√	-	-	-	√	√
Anseranatidae	-	-	-	-	-	-	-
†Romainvillinae	-	-	√	-	-	-	-
†Cygnopteridae	-	-	√	√	-	-	-
†Paranyrocidae	-	-	-	√	-	-	-
†Presbyornithidae	√	√	-	-	-	-	-
†Cnemiornithidae	-	-	-	-	-	-	√
Anatidae							
Dendrocygninae	-	-	-	√	√	√	√
†Dendrocheninae	-	-	-	√	-	-	-
Anserinae	-	-	√	√	√	√	√
Stictonettinae	-	-	-	-	-	-	-
Tadorninae	-	-	-	√	√	√	√
Anatinae	-	-	-	√	√	√	√

are likely to settle into the sediment and become fossilized. Brodkorb (1964) listed 175 fossil Anseriformes (89 extinct and 86 extant), and the current total is probably over 200. However, two caveats need to be considered when interpreting the record: it is still highly incomplete and patchy in coverage, and the material that is present has not been analysed adequately; for example, Table 2.3 shows that fossils from most major anseriform lineages are absent for much of their history. Also, many fossil species that have been assigned to extant genera, especially *Anas*, need to be treated with caution until restudied (Olson and Feduccia 1980a). For example, *Mionetta blanchardi*, a species abundant in the lower Miocene of France, was placed in *Anas* until recently; studies have shown, however, that it is a primitive anseriform belonging to an extinct subfamily (Dendrocheninae) that diverged after the Dendrocygninae (whistling-ducks) but before the geese and swans (Anserinae) and is, therefore, only distantly related to *Anas* (Livezey and Martin 1988, Livezey 1997b). Moreover, Livezey and Martin (1988) also provisionally included *consobrina* and *natator* within *Mionetta*, both of which are also Miocene species previously put in *Anas*. These authors concluded further that a majority of fossil Anseriformes lack sufficient material to permit confident assignment to any tribe or subfamily.

Origin and relationships

Origin

Birds first evolved in the late Jurassic, approximately 150 million years ago, and the earliest evolutionary divergences among extant birds seem to appear in the late Cretaceous (approximately 80 million years ago) (Cracraft 1986) (Figure 2.4). *Gallornis straeleni* was the earliest fossil assigned to the Anseriformes, described from early Cretaceous beds in France, and was the earliest known fossil bird at that time (Lambrecht 1933). Subsequently, it was linked to the flamingos (Phoenicopteridae) (Brodkorb 1964), but later its affinities were considered impossible to determine owing to the very fragmentary nature of the material (Feduccia 1996). *Eonessa anaticula*, uncovered from late Eocene deposits in Utah, US, was also considered

2.4 The geological time-scale (after Harland 1989) (my = million years).

anseriform (Wetmore 1926a, Howard 1964a). The poorly preserved material, consisting solely of a left wing, was examined subsequently by Olson and Feduccia (1980a), who were confident that it was not anseriform and suggested it may be gruiform (a crane).

The earliest fossil currently considered to be anseriform is *Presbyornis*, known from the Paleocene and Eocene (Olson and Feduccia 1980a, Feduccia 1996, Livezey 1997a) (Figure 2.5). In addition, other early fossils include *Romainvillia*, from the early Oligocene, *Cygnopterus* from the middle Oligocene, and an undescribed anseriform from the early Oligocene of Nebraska, US (Brodkorb 1964, Howard 1964a, Olson and Feduccia 1980a).

On the basis of DNA–DNA hybridization data, Sibley and Ahlquist (1990) concluded that the Anseriformes originated in the late Cretaceous or early Cenozoic. Livezey (1997b) thought that the

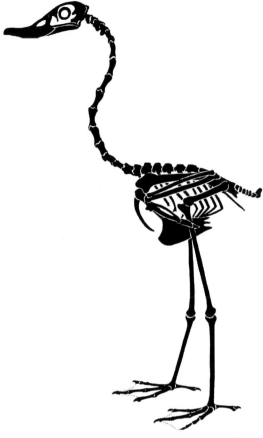

2.5 Provisional reconstruction of the skeleton of *Presbyornis* (from Olson and Feduccia 1980a).

Paleocene/Eocene family Presbyornithidae was more closely related to Anatidae than were the Anhimidae (screamers) and Anseranatidae (Magpie Goose), so that the Anseriformes originated in the late Cretaceous. Olson and Feduccia (1980a) and Olson (1985) also proposed that the anseriform lineage began in the late Cretaceous, based largely on the fossil *Presbyornis* and a number of apparently charadriiform (wader or shorebird) fossils from the late Cretaceous of New Jersey, US. Indeed, a late Cretaceous fossil (*Telmatornis rex*) has duck-like humeri, but it is not certainly anseriform and has been retained tentatively within the Charadriiformes (Olson 1985).

Thus, the Anseriformes were among the first groups of extant birds to evolve; their geographical origin, however, is unclear. It was considered that they originated in the northern hemisphere, probably in the Palearctic, an idea that was based on the large number of fossils collected in the northern hemisphere and the present high species diversity there (Howard 1950, Weller 1964a) (Figure 2.6). However, there is a northern bias to palaeontological research. Also, many extant northern species are of recent evolutionary origin (Livezey 1996b), and the diversity of species may be linked to isolation and differentiation of populations caused by relatively modern glaciations (see Ploeger 1968). Livezey (1986a, 1997b) felt that the majority of the major anseriform groups identified originated in the southern hemisphere, including the oldest lineages. On the other hand, Kear (1970b) suggested that wildfowl originated in the tropics, based, in part, on the response to photoperiod (daylength) of such species as the Magpie Goose and whistling-ducks (Murton and Kear 1973, 1975, 1978).

Relationships

The relationship of the Anseriformes to other birds has been a controversial taxonomic issue in ornithology. Most recent authors have concluded that wildfowl are most closely related to the gamebirds (Galliformes). There is indication of a close relationship in, for example, characteristics of the skull (Bock 1969, Cracraft and Mindell 1989, Dzerzhinsky 1995, Zusi and Livesey 2000), DNA–DNA hybridization data (Sibley and Ahlquist 1990, Bleiweiss *et al.* 1995), immunological distances (Praeger and Wilson 1976, 1978), muscle structure (George and Berger 1966, Cracraft 1981) and skeletal characters (Livezey 1997a, Cracraft and Clarke 2001, Mayr and Clarke 2003). DNA sequence studies have generally confirmed this relationship (Caspers *et al.* 1997, Groth and Barrowclough 1999, van Tuinen *et al.* 2000, 2001, García-Moreno and Mindell 2000, Cracraft *et al.* 2004). All things considered, the relationship between wildfowl and gamebirds is the best supported of all connections between any two orders of birds.

However, not all recent studies have agreed with this conclusion. Some authors have linked wildfowl

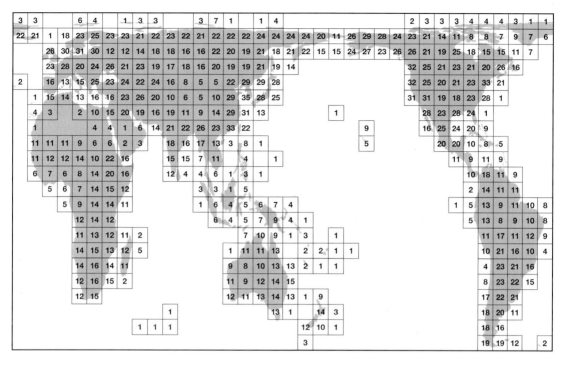

2.6 Species diversity of Anseriformes that survived into the Holocene, showing high diversity in the northern hemisphere. The number of species that occur (or occurred) within each grid-cell is indicated.

to the storks, ibises and spoonbills (Ciconiiformes) and/or to the flamingos (Pheonicopteridae) (Sibley *et al.* 1969, Sibley and Ahlquist 1972, Hagey *et al.* 1990). Relationships with the latter have been based primarily on the structure of the bill and feet, the development of the young, and the similarity of duck and flamingo feather parasites (Feduccia 1996). Based largely on the Paleocene/Eocene fossil *Presbyornis*, it has been suggested that the Anseriformes are closest to the Charadriiformes (Olson and Feduccia 1980a, Olson 1985). Skeletal data analysed by Ericson (1997) contradicted an anseriform–galliform relationship, instead placing their affinities with charadriiform and ciconiiform birds. Ericson *et al.* (2001), on the basis of a combined analysis of morphological and DNA sequence characters, found anseriforms to be equally related to charadriiform, ciconiiform and phoenicopteriform birds (but see their addendum, in which they

accept a relationship to the galliforms as best supported on the basis of more recent data). Olson (1985) stated that 'there is no evolutionary possibility of the Anseriformes having arisen from the Galliformes (or vice versa)', but did not suggest alternative relationships.

Evolutionary patterns

From their early origins, the Anseriformes have evolved into a diverse group of birds that inhabit every continent and major island except Antarctica, from the Arctic to the tips of the southern continents. Many extant species evolved over two million years ago; for example, a number of Pliocene fossils appear indistinguishable from present-day species (Whistling Swan, Greylag Goose, Garganey, Northern Shoveler, Northern Mallard, Gadwall, Eurasian Teal, Ring-necked

2.7 Bill of female Northern Shoveler showing lamellae.

Duck, Common Pochard and Bufflehead) (Howard 1964a).

The key to their success seems to be a unique adaption to filter-feeding. This consists of what is, by analogy, a double-piston suction pump, with the piston (the tongue) in the upper jaw, rather than in the lower jaw as in all other filter-feeding vertebrates (Zweers 1974, Olson and Feduccia 1980a, 1980b). Fluid is drawn in at the tip of the bill and expelled out of the sides past the filter plates (rows of lamellae, Figure 2.7) (Kooloos *et al.* 1989). This, as is discussed in Chapter 3, proved to be an adaptable structure that has been, for example, modified for grazing and for seizing fish (Olson and Feduccia 1980a, Feduccia 1996). In contrast, the filter-feeding adaption of the flamingos, wherein the tongue is located in the lower jaw, has proven to be relatively inflexible; indeed, flamingos have diverged little (six Recent species) and remain dependent largely on alkaline lakes with algal blooms (Olson and Feduccia 1980a, 1980b, Feduccia 1996).

Considering the early origin of Anseriformes (late Cretaceous), Paleogene fossils are surprisingly rare. They do, however, become common during the Neogene. Indeed, the discovery of what Becker (1987) called *Oxyura* cf *dominica* and *Bucephala ossivalis* from late Miocene beds in Florida, US and *Mergus miscellus* from the middle Miocene of Virginia, US (Alvarez and Olson 1978) suggested that all modern anseriform tribes had diverged by the end of the Miocene. Thus, there seems to have been a major burst of radiation during the Oligocene and Miocene (mid-Cenozoic) that remains unexplained.

Major groups

The major anseriform groups are listed below. The taxonomy of extant families and tribes is described in Part II, preceding the relevant species accounts, but fossil species are dealt with here († denotes extinct lineages). The major groupings follow Livezey (1997b), except in a few cases. Stifftails have been removed from Anatinae and given subfamily status (Bottjer 1983, Madsen *et al.* 1988, Sibley and Ahlquist 1990, Sraml *et al.* 1996, Harshman 1996, McCracken *et al.* 1999). The Musk Duck has been removed from the stifftails into an uncertain position (*incertae sedis*) within the Anatidae (Sraml *et al.* 1996, McCracken 1999). The White-winged Duck *Cairina scutulata* has been split from the Muscovy *Cairina moschata* and restored to its own genus *Asarcornis* (Harshman 1996, Sorenson *et al.* 1999). The authors of the species accounts have retained a number of earlier scientific and vernacular names, and have adopted English spelling (Gray Teal becomes Grey Teal, for instance). They differ from Livezey (1997b) in treating the Brent Goose, Tundra Swan, Spot-billed Duck, South American Teal and Versicolor Teal as single species with two or more subspecies. The shelduck are all retained in *Tadorna*, the wigeon, Gadwall, Cape Teal and Falcated Duck in *Anas*, the Pink-headed Duck in *Rhodonessa*, the Rosybill and Southern Pochard in *Netta*, and all the pochards and scaup in *Aythya*.

Order Anseriformes (Wagler, 1831)

Family Anhimidae Stejneger, 1885— Screamers

Three species in two genera *Anhima* and *Chauna*.

Family Anseranatidae (Sclater, 1880)— Magpie Goose

One species *Anseranas semipalmata*.

†Family Presbyornithidae Wetmore, 1926

This extinct family contains at least four, possibly many more, species: (i) *Presbyornis pervetus* from the early Eocene of Utah, US (ii) a slightly smaller, unnamed species from the Paleocene of Utah and Mongolia (iii) the much larger *P. isoni* known from the late Paleocene of Maryland, US, and (iv) *P.* (*Telmabates*) *antiquus* known from Patagonia (Olson and Feduccia 1980a, Olson 1985, Benton 1993, Feduccia 1996). The affinities of *Presbyornis* have been disputed but, following intensive study, there seems little doubt that the genus represents an early anseriform lineage (Olson and Feduccia 1980a, Feduccia 1996, Livezey 1997b, Ericson 1997). *Presbyornis* were medium-sized, filter-feeding birds with long legs (Feduccia 1996). The skull of *Presbyornis pervetus* shows remarkable similarities to that of the extant Freckled Duck, including the unusual upturned bill, and also to the extant Pink-eared Duck (Olson and Feduccia 1980a) (Figure 2.8). The birds inhabited shallow, saline lakes, and seem to have had well-developed salt glands (Feduccia 1978, Olson and Feduccia 1980a). They may have been colonial birds, and at least one nesting colony has been located (Feduccia 1978).

†Family Cnemiornithidae Stejneger, 1885

This extinct family is composed of *Cnemiornis calcitrans* and *C. gracilis*, known from abundant fossil remains in New Zealand (Worthy *et al.* 1997). They were linked with the Cape Barren Goose (Owen 1875, Oliver 1945, Delacour 1954–64) and subsequently placed alongside the sheldgeese (Tadornini) (Brodkorb 1964, Howard 1964a). However, it seems that they had an earlier origin, and diverged between the Magpie Goose and whistling-ducks (Dendrocygninae) (Livezey 1989a). The only fossil material is subrecent (Holocene) (Howard 1964a). They were large, flightless, goose-like birds (Livezey 1989a) that probably grazed on short herbage in grassland and open forest (Holdaway 1989). Their

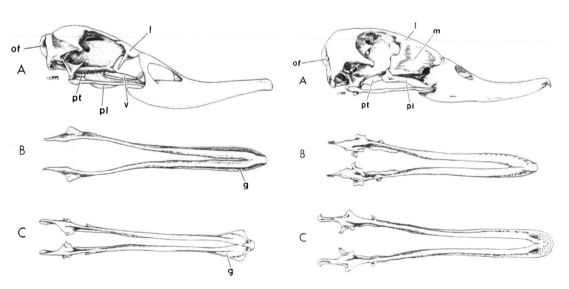

2.8 Left: lateral view of the skull (A) and ventral view of the mandible (B) of *Presbyornis*. Note the characteristic groove (g) in the mandibular ramus. This is also present in the extant Pink-eared Duck. Right: lateral view of the skull (A) and ventral view of the mandible (B) of the Freckled Duck. Note the upturned bill and the long, narrow mandibular symphysis, as in *Presbyornis*, contrasted with the mandible of a typical duck (C), Northern Mallard. Abbreviations: l—lacrimal; m—lacrimal membrane; of—occipital fontanelle; pl—palatine; pt—pterygoid; v—vomer (from Olson and Feduccia 1980a).

extinction may have coincided with the arrival of Polynesians and their commensal dogs and rats (Holdaway 1989).

†Family Romainvillidae Lambrecht, 1933

Little is known of this extinct, early lineage of the Anseriformes. Only one species, *Romainvillia stehlini*, has been described from late Eocene beds in France (Howard 1964a). It had robust proportions, like the dabbling ducks Anatini, but relatively long and sturdy legs like the whistling-ducks Dendrocygnini, and was the size of a goose (Howard 1964a, Olson 1985). Skeletal characters suggest that it diverged between the Anseranatidae and Dendrocygnidae (Livezey 1986a). However, its taxonomic position is tentative pending further examination.

†Family Cygnopteridae Lambrecht, 1931

Three species are known from this extinct family, *Cygnopterus affinis* from middle Oligocene beds in Belgium (Howard 1964a), *C. lambrechti* from the Oligocene of Kazakhstan, and *C. alphonsi* from the Miocene of France (Howard 1964a, Cheneval 1984, 1987). Little is known about them, although they were the size of geese (Olson 1985). They are allied closely with the geese and swans (Anserinae) by some authors (Howard 1964a, Brodkorb 1964, Cheneval 1987), but Livezey (1986a) suggested that they should be given familial rank and sequenced (provisionally by epoch of occurrence) between *Romainvillia* and *Paranyroca*. Thus, again, the taxonomic position remains provisional and awaits further study.

†Family Paranyrocidae Miller and Crompton, 1939

This family is based upon a single species, *Paranyroca magna*, known from two leg bones found in the Lower Miocene deposits of South Dakota, US (Howard 1964a). However, the structure of the bones shows that it was primitive to Dendrocygnidae, but more advanced than Anseranatidae (Livezey 1986a). *Paranyroca* was a large bird, the size of a Whistling Swan (Howard 1964a).

Family Anatidae Leach, 1820
Genus Biziura (incertae sedis)—Musk Duck

One species *Biziura lobata*.

Subfamily Dendrocygninae Reichenbach, 1849–50
Tribe Dendrocygnini (Reichenbach, 1849–50)—Whistling-ducks

Eight species in one genus *Dendrocygna*.

Tribe Thalassornithini (Livezey, 1986)—White-backed Duck

One species *Thalassornis leuconotus*.

†Subfamily Dendrocheninae Livezey and Martin, 1988

This extinct subfamily comprised two genera *Mionetta* and *Dendrochen*, which show close affinities to the whistling-ducks (Livezey and Martin 1988). *Mionetta* presently includes three species (*M. blanchardi*, *M. consobrina*, and *M. natator*), all known from lower Miocene beds in France (Brodkorb 1964, Livezey and Martin 1988). Originally, they were all placed within *Anas* (Brodkorb 1964, Howard 1964a). *Mionetta* were small, duck-like birds, moderately specialized for diving, and were probably sexually monomorphic in plumage and size (Livezey and Martin 1988). It seems that at least one species, *M. blanchardi*, nested in cavities in limestone cliffs adjacent to water (Livezey and Martin 1988). Only one species of *Dendrochen* is known currently (*D. robusta*) from lower Miocene deposits in South Dakota, US. However, *Anas integra* (early Miocene of US) and *A. oligocaena* (late Oligocene of Russia) may belong in *Dendrochen* (Cheneval 1987). *Dendrochen robusta* probably inhabited forested stream margins within subtropical savanna, a habitat quite different from that of *Mionetta* (Livezey and Martin 1988).

Subfamily Anserinae Vigors, 1825—Swans and geese
Tribe Cygnini (Vigors, 1825)—Swans

Seven species in two genera *Coscoroba* and *Cygnus*.

Tribe Cereopsini (Vigors, 1825)—Cape Barren Goose

One species *Cereopsis novaehollandiae*.

Tribe Anserini (Vigors, 1825)—True geese

Fifteen species in two genera *Anser* and *Branta*.

†Tribe Thambetochenini Livezey, 1996—Moa-nalos

This extinct tribe, endemic to the Hawaiian Islands, contained at least four species in three genera (*Chelychelynechen*, *Ptaiochen* and *Thambetochen*). *Thambetochen chauliodous*, the first species to be discovered, was thought to be a true goose (Olson and Wetmore 1976, Olson and James 1982). Following the description of the other moa-nalos, Olson and James (1991) instead considered them either derivatives of the shelducks or dabbling ducks. This conclusion was based on the presence of ossified syringeal bullae, which do not occur in geese. However, cladistic analysis of morphological characters from available fossil material suggests, provisionally, that they belong with the geese and swans (Livezey 1997b). This is supported by an analysis of mitochondrial DNA extracted from subfossil material, showing that the moa-nalos are closely related to the Anserini and share a common ancestor with the Hawaiian Goose (the only extant true goose on the islands) (Sorenson *et al.* 1999). The moa-nalos were large, flightless, goose-like birds, with tortoise-like bills. It seems likely that they were hunted to extinction by the Polynesians (their name in Hawaiian means 'vanished fowl'), since they were extinct before Europeans reached the islands (Olson and James 1991).

Subfamily Stictonettinae (Boetticher, 1950)—Freckled Duck

One species *Stictonetta naevosa*.

Subfamily Oxyurinae (Phillips, 1926)—Stiff-tailed ducks and allies

Seven species in three genera *Heteronetta*, *Nomonyx* and *Oxyura*.

Subfamily Tadorninae Reichenbach, 1849–1850—

Tribe Merganettini (Bonaparte, 1853)—Blue Duck, Torrent-duck and steamer-ducks

Six species in three genera *Hymenolaimus*, *Merganetta* and *Tachyeres*.

Tribe Plectropterini (Eyton, 1838)—Spur-winged Goose and comb ducks

Three species in two genera *Plectropterus* and *Sarkidiornis*.

†Tribe Euryanatini (Livezey, 1989)

As far as is known, this tribe consists solely of *Euryanas finschi*, an extinct endemic of mainland New Zealand (Worthy 1988, Livezey 1997b). It has been placed within various anseriform groups, including the dabbling ducks (Lambrecht 1933), perching ducks (Cairinini) (Howard 1964a), and alongside the Spur-winged Goose within the Plectopterinae (Brodkorb 1964). However, phylogenetic analysis of 50 morphological characters led Livezey (1989a) to conclude that *Euryanas* was a moderately derived 'proto-duck', and a member of a lineage that diverged before the true shelducks but after the geese and swans. This small duck seems to have inhabited forest and scrub throughout mainland New Zealand, had reduced powers of flight and was a cavity nester (Worthy 1988, Holdaway 1989).

Tribe Tadornini (Reichenbach, 1849–50)—Shelducks and sheldgeese

Fifteen species in five genera *Cyanochen*, *Alopochen*, *Neochen*, *Chloephaga* and *Tadorna* (one species recently extinct).

Subfamily Anatinae (Leach, 1820)—True ducks

Tribe Malacorhynchini (Boetticher, 1950)—Pink-eared Duck and Salvadori's Duck

Two species in two genera *Malacorhynchus* and *Salvadorina*.

Tribe Anatini (Leach, 1820)— Surface-feeding or dabbling ducks

Fifty-seven species in eleven genera *Cairina, Asarcornis, Pteronetta, Aix, Chenonetta, Nettapus, Amazonetta, Callonetta, Lophonetta, Speculanas* and *Anas*.

Tribe Aythyini Delacour and Mayr, 1945— Pochards and scaup

Seventeen species in four genera *Marmaronetta, Rhodonessa* (recently extinct), *Netta* and *Aythya* (one species possibly recently extinct).

Tribe Mergini (Rafinesque, 1815)—Seaducks

Twenty species in ten genera *Polysticta, Somateria, Histrionicus, Camptorhynchus* (recently extinct), *Melanitta, Clangula, Bucephala, Mergellus, Lophodytes* and *Mergus* (one species recently extinct).

3

Feeding ecology

Baz Hughes and Andy J. Green

As with all organisms, a duck, goose or swan is designed to reproduce—to survive and prosper throughout the year in order to maximize the quantity and quality of offspring produced, and ultimately to maximize its lifetime reproductive success (see Chapters 4 and 5). The success with which an animal completes this annual cycle is governed largely by its ability to avoid death from natural causes (predation, disease, starvation) and human-induced mortality, most importantly hunting. Once a duckling, gosling or cygnet enters the world (and its species, genetic make-up and life history characteristics are set), its physical condition is determined mainly by the amount of food or energy that it is able to secure. Of course, many other factors have a direct (e.g. weather conditions) or indirect (e.g. mate choice) effect, but none is as immediate as the need to feed. Wildfowl, like all animals, seek to optimize their condition by feeding in a cost-effective and energy-efficient manner. This chapter provides an insight into how wildfowl achieve this by presenting a description of their morphological adaptations for feeding, the food they eat, their needs through the annual cycle, the ways in which they obtain food, and the behavioural strategies they use to maximize their feeding success whilst minimizing predation risk and competition with other animals.

Their food choice and feeding strategies are affected by many factors, natural and artificial, intrinsic and extrinsic. Rather than cataloguing the effects of such factors, we have focused on the unique and interesting aspects of their feeding ecology. For more information on wildfowl feeding ecology, nutrient reserve dynamics and the physiology of the feeding process, readers should consult the comprehensive works of Krapu and Reinecke (1992), Alisauskas and Ankney (1992), and Baldassarre and Bolen (1994), while Owen and Black (1990) gave a succinct overview. Todd (1996) and Johnsgard (1978) provided sources of information on food and feeding ecology of all of the world's wildfowl, whilst the species accounts in this book give detailed global references. We have referenced key publications, both recent and classical. These focus on commoner species from North America and Europe on which the most detailed work has been conducted; however, we also cite pioneering work on species from elsewhere in the world, especially threatened species. Throughout, we have tried to present information in a biologically meaningful way—to have the reader consider things from the bird's point of view—by continually relating factors to the annual cycle (cf Baldassarre and Bolen 1994).

Morphological and behavioural adaptations for feeding

Wildfowl are morphologically adapted to an aquatic way of life in three ways: most have a keratinous, spatulate bill suitable for filter-feeding; most have webbed feet and relatively powerful legs set well back on the body for propulsion in the water; and all have a dense body plumage for insulation since water conducts heat away from the body much faster than air. However, there is marked variation in morphology among wildfowl, and this depends upon their specialized life-styles and feeding techniques.

Bill and tongue

The general feeding apparatus is similar in all species (except the sawbills): a long, flat bill covered by a soft membrane with a nail at the tip and lamellae along the sides of both mandibles to sieve prey items from water (Goodman and Fisher 1962). The number of these lamellae varies between species and individuals; for example, a Northern Mallard has 36–54 on the upper jaw and 72–80 on the lower (Lüttschwager 1955). There are also many touch receptors at the tip and on the upper surface (Gottschaldt 1974, Berkhoudt 1980), presumably to aid in tactile feeding. Wildfowl feed by sucking water in through the slightly open bill tip before forcing it out through the lamellae using a pumping action of the tongue. Any food items trapped by the lamellae are then directed down the oesophagus by special papillae on the sides and rear of the tongue. The number and density of these lamellae are greatest in species like the shovelers (Figure 2.7) and Pink-eared Duck that filter plankton (Crome 1985b, Kooloos et al. 1989)—filter-feeding ducks may have twice as many lamellae as diving ducks that swallow prey whole.

Most wildfowl have this typical bill structure, although modified bills are found in those with specialized feeding habits (Figure 3.1). Large geese such as Greater Snow Geese, Greylag Geese and, most obviously, Thick-billed Bean Geese have powerful bills designed for digging for tubers of marsh plants. Smaller-billed geese, such as the Red-breasted Goose, are adapted for grazing short turf. The Northern Shoveler has a long spatulate bill twice as wide at the tip as at the base, whilst sawbills have long, thin, serrated bills with hooked nails, ideal for grasping and holding slippery fish and eels. Sawbills also have two rows of barbs on the upper surface of the tongue, presumably to assist in holding fish. Other species, such as the New Zealand Blue Duck, the extinct Labrador Duck and the Pink-eared Duck, have special fleshy bill flanges thought to increase the efficiency of their feeding activities and/or to protect the bill whilst foraging amongst stones (Kear and Burton 1971). The flightless Auckland Island Teal is reported to have a hardened gape (the corner of the mouth), perhaps to aid in swallowing spiny isopods (Weller 1975a).

Interspecific (between species) differences in bill and tongue morphology, especially in the size and shape of the bill and the number of bill lamellae and their density, have been used to explain differences in feeding ecology in terms of the type and size of prey taken which enable resource partitioning (Tremblay and Couture 1986). For example, species with longer bills can probe further into the sediments, whilst those with a greater lamellar density, such as shoveler, can filter smaller food items from the water column (Crome 1985b), leading to correlations between lamellar densities and invertebrate prey size and seed size in several field studies (Thomas 1982, Nudds and Bowlby 1984, Nudds 1992, Nummi 1993, Tamisier and Dehorter 1999). However, ducks are highly sophisticated and adaptable in their feeding behaviour, and show great flexibility in their size selection in relation to food abundance. Denser lamellae simply reduce the costs of filtering small items, but increase that of filtering larger items, and may often increase the variance in the size of items taken rather than decrease the average size. Thus, in other studies, lamellar differences do not explain interspecific differences in size selection; Mateo et al. (2000) and Nummi and Väänänen (2001) suggested that this could be due to a superabundance of food causing a high degree of dietary overlap. Ducks have mechanisms for feeding on items smaller than the interlamellar gap, although these mechanisms remain poorly understood (Kooloos et al. 1989, Gaston 1992).

A multivariate analysis of 12 morphological characteristics of the bill and tongue of six species of North American diving ducks supported such interspecific morphological partitioning (Lagerquist and Ankney 1989). Canvasback had long, narrow, deep bills, well suited to probing and grasping plant tubers from the substrate. Greater Scaup, Lesser Scaup and Ruddy Ducks had short, wide, shallow bills enabling them to strain small animal and plant material from the benthos. Redheads and Ring-necked Ducks had bills of intermediate size and shape, suited to straining seeds and grazing leafy

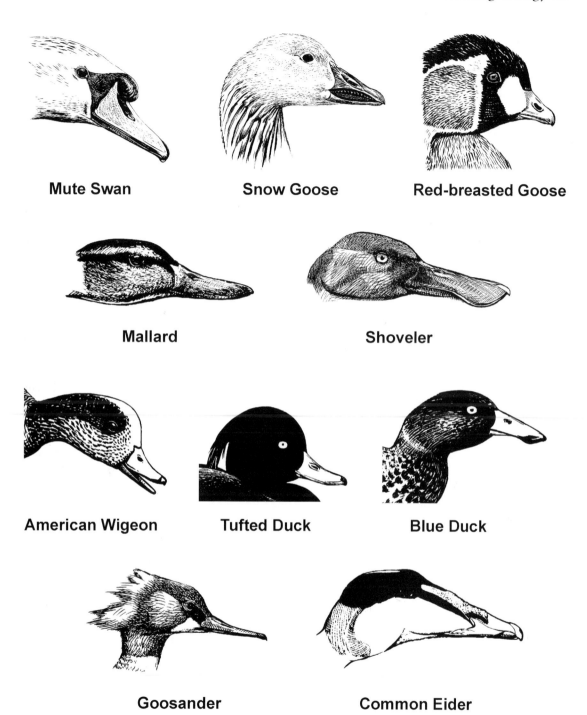

3.1 Adaptive radiation in wildfowl bill structure. Artwork by Joe Blossom, Mark Hulme and Helen Shackleton.

parts of plants. Overall, bill size and shape were more important than lamellar density or tongue characteristics in distinguishing the six species.

Feet

The screamers and three wildfowl species—Cape Barren, Hawaiian and Magpie Geese—do not have fully webbed feet. The Magpie Goose, like the screamers, has almost no palmations and the others have semi-palmations (Figure 3.2), presumably suiting their owners to a mainly terrestrial life-style (Humphrey and Clark 1964). All other wildfowl have webbed feet set well back on the body to help propel them through water. On the surface of the water the feet are used as paddles, moving backwards with the webs expanded and forwards with the foot closed. Whilst swimming on the water surface, wildfowl use alternate leg strokes in the vertical plane, and they use simultaneous strokes in the horizontal plane whilst diving; i.e. when underwater they kick their feet out to the sides (Lindroth and Bergstöm 1959, Weller 1964a, Tome and Wrubleski 1988).

The size and structure of the legs and feet are determined mainly by feeding habits and habitat. Swans, geese and dabbling ducks, which walk and feed on land or in shallow inshore waters, have relatively small feet (Raikow 1973), while diving ducks have shorter legs and larger feet with a more flattened, lobed hind toe or hallux. The larger paddle area of the feet of diving ducks results primarily from a lengthening of the digits and a corresponding increase in web area. Eiders lack an enlarged paddle—their relative size is similar to dabbling ducks—but possess a lobed hallux. Whilst this could imply that the eider is a less efficient diver, this is probably offset by the fact that eiders beat their wings under water (Humphrey 1958b).

Tail

The tails of swans, geese and dabbling ducks serve mainly as aerial rudders which help birds to manoeuvre in flight. This is perhaps most noticeable when geese perform their swift 'wiffling' descents. In diving ducks, the tail is designed more as an underwater rudder (Brooks 1945), not only to steer but also to help maintain position in the water. Stiff-tailed ducks and Musk Duck, the most agile and adept divers, have the longest, most flexible tails (Raikow 1970).

Eye

Diving ducks have eyes that are specially adapted for underwater foraging. They have a more powerful sphincter muscle controlling the iris than do dabbling ducks, and some species, such as mergansers, have a clear, lens-like central window in the nictitating membrane which is said to act as an auxiliary lens to permit close underwater focusing (Walls 1942, Levy and Sivak 1980). The New Zealand Blue Duck is reported to use binocular vision, while most other wildfowl have monocular sight (Brooks 1938).

Gut and internal organs

Wildfowl typically have a narrow, comparatively thin-walled oesophagus, although the eiders and mergansers have a thicker-walled oesophagus, presumably to accommodate their harder or more injurious prey (Humphrey and Clark 1964). The oesophagus leads to the glandular foregut, or proventriculus, and on to the muscular stomach, or gizzard, in which food is ground. Geese, which feed on fibrous plant material, have particularly large gizzards, while the Common Shelduck, which feeds mainly on tiny snails, has a relatively small one. Seaducks have greatly enlarged gizzards to crush the hard calcareous shells of their main bivalve prey (Lack 1974, Guillemette 1998).

Herbivorous wildfowl, with their highly fibrous diets, must extract as much nutrient as possible from plant material and have, on average, larger gizzards and longer caecae than species relying on an animal diet (Kehoe and Ankney 1985, Barnes and Thomas 1987). Caecae are blind-ended tubes that attach to the gut where the small intestine joins the rectum; they are thought to aid in the digestion of plant material (Fox and Kahlert 1999). Intestines are longest in omnivorous species and appear to be influenced by overall diet diversity (Kehoe and Ankney 1985, Barnes and Thomas 1987).

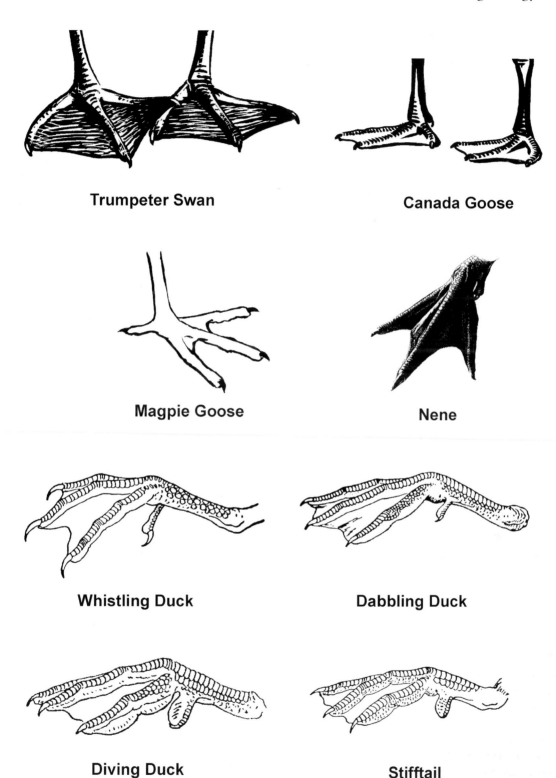

Trumpeter Swan

Canada Goose

Magpie Goose

Nene

Whistling Duck

Dabbling Duck

Diving Duck

Stifftail

3.2 Adaptive radiation in wildfowl foot structure. Artwork by Joe Blossom, Mark Hulme and Helen Shackleton.

Diving ducks have relatively large hearts in relation to other wildfowl, and heart mass increases with average foraging depth (Bethke and Thomas 1987), reflecting the greater cardiovascular demands of diving to deeper depths.

Air sacs

As with all birds, wildfowl have internal air sacs connected to the lungs that extend into the body cavity and into some of their long bones. The Northern Mallard has nine air sacs of which one is single and the rest are paired (Rigdon 1959). The air sacs of some ducks can be inflated or deflated to alter buoyancy (Todd 1996). For example, the Long-tailed Duck expels air from its air sacs while diving.

Body plumage

Wildfowl are well known for the insulative properties of their feathers, especially the thick, warm down feathers which are often used in quilts (see Chapter 1). Extremely soft, light and cohesive, eider down possesses the best thermal qualities of any known natural substance (Todd 1996). The plumage of wildfowl is thick and relatively impenetrable to the elements, thus allowing eiders to exploit aquatic habitats in extreme climatic conditions, such as Siberian coasts during winter. The plumage is waterproofed using oil from the preen gland above the tail. Waterproofing is crucial for survival and the effects of losing it can be fatal. Although wildfowl can survive the condition called 'wet feather', in which contour feather structure is degraded by a fungus (Beynon 1996), total loss of waterproofing, as in birds affected by oil-spills, results in a swift death from hypothermia.

Salt glands

All wildfowl have salt glands, which allow them to sequester salt from their bodies after drinking brine and/or eating salty food. They are most developed in species adapted to life in saline habitats (e.g. Cape Barren Geese, some shelducks, eiders, scoters, and White-headed Ducks). Salt glands are located above the eye, but discharge through the nostrils on top of the bill. These salt glands may secrete a fluid twice as concentrated as seawater (Peaker and Linzell 1975). Common Eiders, which ingest some 50 g of salt per day (Nehls 1996) (more than most seabirds), secrete most within 25 minutes of feeding (McArthur and Gorman 1978) although it takes about four times longer to excrete salt than to ingest it. Active salt excretion, which begins within 10 minutes of salt ingestion, is typified in eiders by head shaking behaviour (Nehls 1996). As in other seabirds (Hughes 1970), wildfowl from saline habitats also have larger kidneys to help in the salt-sequestering process. The cost of excreting salt is low in comparison to the other costs associated with foraging—about 2% compared with 30% for internal processing, such as shell crushing and digestion.

Food availability and content

Energy and nutrient content of wildfowl foods

Wildfowl food has two basic components: water and dry matter made up of inorganic minerals, plus organic protein, carbohydrate, fat and fibre. Each component offers different 'values' relative to the needs of the organism (see Baldassarre and Bolen 1994).

A balanced diet containing a range of minerals and vitamins is just as important to wildfowl as it is to humans. Calcium and phosphorus are particularly important for eggshell production—breeding female ducks need 2.5% calcium in their diet (National Research Council 1977). Ducks are also highly sensitive to selenium and Vitamin E deficiencies (Baldassarre and Bolen 1994). Proteins are required for growth and maintenance—even outwith times of stress, some 4.4% of body protein needs to be replaced every day (Morowitz 1978). Furthermore, wildfowl need to obtain certain essential amino acids that they cannot synthesize themselves. Protein does not, however, provide an efficient source of energy; for this wildfowl rely on carbohydrates and fat. Carbohydrates, stored as glycogen in the liver and muscle tissues, provide the quickest source of energy, but these reserves are small and can be exhausted in less than two days without food (Blem 1990). Wildfowl therefore store most of their energy supplies as fat, which provides twice as much energy as protein (c 38 kJ/g compared with 18 kJ/g) and which can be laid down or mobilized quickly and efficiently. Fibre, because of its high cellu-lose content, is difficult to digest, although both Canada Geese and Brant obtain energy from this food source (Buchsbaum *et al.* 1986, Sedinger *et al.* 1989) (cellulose is not digested, but see Durant 2003). Not all energy contained in food is available to wildfowl. Some may be passed out in the faeces and some needs to be used in actually breaking down food. The 'true metabolizable energy' of a food item may therefore be much lower than the total energy content (Petrie *et al.* 1997), especially for foods that are difficult to digest, such as seeds.

Different food items contain different levels of fats, proteins, carbohydrates, minerals and energy. These can be separated (Table 3.3) into three categories: agricultural plants, wetland plants, and animal matter (Baldassarre and Bolen 1994). Wetland plants can be further subdivided depending on which part of the plant is eaten: seeds, bulbs, tubers, rhizomes and leafy vegetation. Agricultural plants are highest in carbohydrate, native plants less so. Leafy vegetation has a high water and fibre content and, thus, lower nutrient levels (Robbins 1993). Animal food is high in protein and essential amino acids, low in carbohydrates, but high in energy content compared to most plant foods.

The profitability of feeding on these different food items depends on their availability, on how long it takes to obtain them and on the energetic costs in doing so (Table 3.3). Agricultural crops and grains provide an easily accessible, high carbohydrate diet. This has resulted in a major switch in the feeding habits of geese and swans in the northern hemisphere, with most species now visiting agricultural land to a large extent during the winter period (e.g. Pink-footed Goose in the UK—Gill *et al.* 1997). Ducks have also switched to feeding on agricultural grains (Baldassarre and Bolen 1994, Mateo *et al.* 2000), and rice paddies in Asia provide a major food source for globally threatened species, such as the Baikal Teal and White-winged Duck (Allport *et al.* 1991, Green 1992a).

Factors affecting food availability

Throughout the year, wildfowl tend to select habitats that provide them with the best opportunities for obtaining food—i.e. where they can obtain their daily food requirements with minimum effort (Baldassarre and Bolen 1994). Many factors affect the quantity and quality of food supplies available to different species both within and between habitats. Major factors that could affect population levels include climate (and subsequently water levels), the annual growth and energy cycles of the prey items themselves, nutrient levels and water quality, and competition with other wetland animals. Minor factors that mainly cause site-specific or species-specific effects include water depth, water turbidity, salinity, and proximity to safe roosting sites (especially for geese). This section discusses those factors that may impact at the population level.

3.3 The relationships between wildfowl food quality, availability and the feeding ecology of wildfowl (after Baldassarre and Bolen 1994). Availability refers to the ease with which available energy or nutrients are digested and absorbed. Feeding time refers to the time taken to fulfil daily minimum requirements when feeding on such food.

Food Source	Energy (kcal/g)	Protein (%)	Carbohydrate (%)	Availability	Feeding Time
Seeds	4.5	9–15	35–60	Variable	Moderate
Agricultural grains	5.0	9–25	35–80	High	Low
Animal	5.0	40–75	1–20	Low	High
Leafy vegetation	3.5	15–20	15–50	Variable	High
Tubers	4.0	15	75	Mod–high	Low

Climate and seasonal food availability

Climate is by far the most important factor determining the availability of food for wildfowl; temperature and rainfall, especially, determine the overall availability of breeding and feeding sites, and thus the seasonal availability of prey. Late springs in the Arctic delay nest initiation and can lead to complete breeding failures for some species, such as Brant (Barry 1962). Similarly, duck production in North America is severely reduced during drought years, and populations may be affected seriously if drought conditions continue (Krapu and Reinecke 1992, Baldassarre and Bolen 1994). During the great North American drought of the 1930s, when rainfall failed year after year, wildfowl populations declined to their lowest known levels.

Wildfowl tend to exploit different habitats on a seasonal basis in order to benefit from seasonally available foods. Arctic-breeding migrants arrive on their breeding grounds shortly after or just before snow melt so that they and their offspring can exploit the subsequent and immediate flush in new vegetation and invertebrate life. This is perhaps most marked in the prairie potholes of North America where millions of small (< 0.4 ha) wetlands appear after snow-melt (Baldassarre and Bolen 1994). These potholes are teeming with invertebrate life, especially fairy shrimps *Branchinecta*, mosquitoes *Culex* and water fleas Cladocera. Although these potholes represent only 10% of all wildfowl breeding habitat in North America (Smith *et al.* 1964), they can produce up to 50% of the autumn flight of ducks—some 25–50 million birds a year. Indeed, the availability of these seasonal wetlands is the main factor determining the numbers of young produced annually (Baldassarre and Bolen 1994).

Where winter temperatures become low enough to freeze wetlands, wildfowl can no longer feed and are forced to move elsewhere (Ridgill and Fox 1990) or risk starvation. However, cold weather can sometimes make new food items available. For example, Northern Shovelers have been known to feed on fish stunned by extreme cold (Tietje and Teer 1988).

Wildfowl from tropical and arid landscapes are similarly adapted to be able to exploit available food supplies, although these are linked more to wetland availability and abundance (and hence to rainfall) than to season *per se*. Many species can therefore be found breeding throughout the year, but in regions with more predictable wet seasons wildfowl tend to nest during or just after the rainy season when food is most available. Australian wildfowl are nomadic and highly flexible in their breeding habits and will migrate to breed as soon as inland wetlands appear after heavy rains. One such movement followed a flood in the Murray–Darling basin in inland south-east Australia in 1956. In the following year, Grey Teal had scattered in all directions, with ring or band returns indicating that many had reached the coast, some as far as New Guinea in the north and New Zealand to the east (Frith 1962). Unlike most northern hemisphere wildfowl, in which breeding cycles are stimulated by increasing daylengths, Grey Teal and most other Australian wildfowl have no such requirement and can breed at any time of the year (see Chapter 5).

Nutrient levels and water quality

The quantity and quality of many wildfowl foods is affected significantly by nutrient levels. Wildfowl tend to occur mainly on wetlands with high nutrient levels and shun low-productivity oligotrophic wetlands (e.g. Staicer *et al.* 1994). However, this situation is perhaps most obvious when human activity has, either deliberately or accidentally, increased nutrient inputs to wetland or grassland feeding areas.

Sites with artificial nutrient enrichment, such as natural waterbodies suffering from eutrophication (e.g. through fertilizer run-off), or artificial waterbodies such as sewage farms, often hold significant concentrations of waterfowl. Although nutrient input causes eutrophication and an overall decrease in biodiversity, moderate nutrient input causes a proliferation of pollution-tolerant invertebrates, such as oligochaetes, chironomids and isopods. All are favourite foods of carnivorous wildfowl, especially *Aythya* pochards, and these birds can be found in significant concentrations at such sites. For example, the highly polluted Salford Docks is an 8 ha site in northern England that can hold up to 2700 wintering Common Pochard (Marsden and Bellamy 2000).

British estuaries suffering from a high level of nutrient input from sewage discharge have held similarly large wildfowl concentrations. The Firth of Forth in Scotland held up to 25 000 Greater Scaup in the 1960s and early 1970s, but numbers crashed to only 100 birds after sewage treatment was improved (Campbell 1984, Salmon 1988). Given that artificial eutrophication is widespread in wetlands across Europe, it is possible that the current populations of some carnivorous wildfowl are artificially inflated. However, hypereutrophication leads to the loss of submerged aquatic plants which are vital as feeding habitat for many other wildfowl that feed both on the plants themselves and the many invertebrates that live on them (Krull 1970, Wicker and Endres 1995). It will be interesting to see whether wildfowl populations in Europe change following the introduction of the European Union Water Framework Directive in December 2000, which requires major decreases in artificial eutrophication.

Grazing wildfowl also show a preference for the high nutrient content of artificially sown and fertilized grasslands (Owen 1973). White-fronted Geese and Eurasian Wigeon chose to feed on fertilized swards with a higher nitrogen concentration than unfertilized swards (Owen 1976a, Jacobsen 1992) and this food selection is thought to be dependent on the bright colour of the vegetation (Kear 1964, Owen 1972), with brighter, greener vegetation containing more chlorophyll, protein and phosphorus. Grass management regimes currently employed on nature reserves are often designed to provide seed mixes with the most palatable grasses for grazing wildfowl. At WWT's Slimbridge reserve, seed mixes for fields grazed by White-fronted Geese comprise mainly Perennial Rye Grass *Lolium perenne* (50%), Red Fescue *Festuca rubra* (20%), and Bent *Agrostis tenuis* (20%) (Owen 1973). These are subsequently fertilized and grazed (by both geese and cattle) to maximize their protein content and growth of new shoots. There are also examples of geese exploiting naturally fertilized grasslands; for example, Barnacle Geese in The Netherlands chose to feed among gull colonies in which fertilization by gull droppings increased the nitrogen content of Red Fescue above that in surrounding areas (Bazely *et al.* 1991).

Competition

Although difficult to demonstrate, competition for food both between and within wildfowl species and with other animals has the potential to limit populations (Nudds 1992). The level of competition is highest where dietary overlap is greatest, with perhaps the most overlap in wetland habitats occurring between wildfowl and fish. Bottom-feeding fish, most notably Common Carp *Cyprinus carpio*, feed by sucking up the bottom sediments in search of their benthic invertebrate food. In doing so, not only do they compete directly with wildfowl that feed on the same food items, but they often also destroy submergent plant communities, such as pondweeds *Potamogeton* on which other wildfowl feed.

Competition between fish and wildfowl (breeding and wintering) has been suggested by studies revealing negative correlations between wildfowl numbers and fish densities, and by experimental fish removal experiments. Examples include competition between Common Goldeneye, Roach *Rutilus rutilus* and Perch *Perca fluviatilis* in Sweden (Eriksson 1979a), Common Goldeneye and Perch in Canada (Eadie and Keast 1982), Tufted Ducks and a freshwater fish community in England (Giles 1994) and Tufted Ducks and Roach in Northern Ireland (Winfield and Winfield 1994a). Use of a shallow, eutrophic lake in Minnesota by migrating Canvasback and Lesser Scaup also increased significantly after fish removal, apparently due to an increase in both invertebrate and plant food (Hanson and Butler 1994).

In North America, competition for food may be starting to limit some goose populations. For example, after the North American population of Lesser Snow Geese increased to an estimated 4.5–6 million birds, a number of experimental studies on the breeding areas and staging grounds proved that birds were degrading their habitat to levels which could not support their population (Ankney 1996, Ganter *et al.* 1996, Kotanen and Jefferies 1997). They were effectively eating themselves out of house and home! In order to prevent further, possibly irreversible, habitat destruction, North American conservationists have embarked on a population control programme that aims to reduce the population by half by 2005 (Batt 1997). Around 1.4 million geese were subsequently shot during the 1999–2000 hunting season.

Competition between geese has been observed also on moulting grounds in Greenland. In east Greenland, Madsen and Mortensen (1987) found that, in the presence of Pink-footed Geese, smaller Barnacle Geese were forced to feed more on moss than on their preferred diet of sedges *Carex* and grasses (mainly *Poa pratensis*), and thus had to increase their foraging time per 24 hours from 41–46% to 62%. A more worrying example is developing in west Greenland where Interior Canada Geese are expanding their breeding range into that of the endemic Greenland White-fronted Goose. Studies of food choice have proven that, on sites where both species occur together, the larger, more aggressive Canada Geese are outcompeting the Whitefronts for the most nutritious food of meadow grasses *Poa alpina/artica*, horsetails *Equisetum* and sedges, forcing the Whitefronts to feed on nutrient-poor mosses (Kristiansen and Jarrett 2002).

Plant disease

During the 1930s, the Atlantic Brant population in North America decreased when disease affected their major food plant, Eelgrass *Zostera* (Cottam *et al.* 1944). Pacific Eelgrass was not affected and Pacific Brant populations did not decline.

The annual cycle

Adult migratory wildfowl undergo five main periods of annual stress or high energy demand: during spring migration, breeding, moulting, autumn migration and winter. Non-migratory species also potentially suffer high stress during breeding and moulting; their annual cycle is therefore geared to providing the necessary nutrients and energy to survive these traumatic times and, especially, to breed successfully. Overall, wildfowl match their needs according to the demands of this annual cycle, storing nutrients at times of plenty for use during energetically stressful periods.

Energetics

Energetics includes the acquisition, use, storage and conservation of energy vital to drive bodily functions and to enable the physiological processes required for survival and reproduction. Warm-blooded animals, such as birds, also need energy to maintain a high body temperature. An understanding of energetics is important in explaining the strategies wildfowl use to apportion their feeding activities on a daily and seasonal basis.

The metabolic rate of an organism is a measure of the rate at which energy is needed to drive bodily functions. The basic rate, termed the 'basal metabolic rate' (BMR), is the rate at which energy is used when animals are completely at rest. BMR is determined largely by body size, such that $BMR = aW^{0.73}$ where a is the BMR (in Watts) at 1 kg body mass and W is body mass. In wildfowl, a has been estimated at 4.64 (Zar 1968). Birds also need energy to perform their normal daily activities whilst maintaining their body weight; thus the metabolic rate must increase accordingly and this is termed the 'existence metabolic rate' (EMR). Any energy produced in excess of this EMR is termed 'productive energy' and it is this energy that is available to meet the additional demands of the annual cycle, such as breeding and migration.

The amount of energy needed per day is termed the 'daily energy expenditure' (DEE). It is calculated either by determining the absolute consumption of energy over all activities using the 'double-labelled water' technique (see, e.g. Weathers *et al.* 1984) or, more easily but less accurately, by calculating the time spent in each activity over the course of a 24-hour period, by determining the energetic cost of each activity and by summing the products. Unfortunately, the energetic costs of individual behaviours have only been measured empirically for a few species and therefore there are errors in estimating the energetic costs of activities between species (Alisauskas and Ankney 1992). For example, it would be inappropriate to apply flight costs calculated for dabbling ducks to diving ducks or pochards as these tribes have different wing loadings and flight dynamics (Raikow 1973).

Nevertheless, various experimental studies have illustrated that different activities have different associated energetic costs (Butler 1991)—the more strenuous an activity, the greater the relative energetic cost. Flying is by far the most costly activity. For example, for American Black Duck it has been estimated at 12.5 × BMR compared to 2.3 × BMR for surface swimming and 1.4–1.8 × BMR for other daily activities, including feeding (Wooley and Owen 1978). Diving is also an energetically expensive activity, calculated at 3.2 × BMR for Tufted Ducks (Bevan and Butler 1992).

Cold temperatures and high winds (the 'wind chill' factor) can cause significant increases in energy demands. Below a certain temperature—the 'lower critical temperature' (LCT)—wildfowl must increase heat production to maintain their body temperature. The LCT is calculated from the equation: (Body Temperature − LCT) = 4.73 (Body Mass)$^{0.274}$ (Calder and King 1974).

This would suggest a LCT of −20°C for Trumpeter Swans, 1°C for Lesser Snow Geese, 10°C for Steller's Eider and 16°C for Blue-winged Teal (Alisauskas and Ankney 1992). These temperatures, particularly for the ducks, seem rather high (i.e. it is improbable that Steller's Eiders, which habitually spend the winter in subzero temperatures on super-cooled water, would suffer cold stress at any temperature below 10°C). Therefore, calculation of LCT in wildfowl probably needs to take into account the greater insulative properties of their plumage (Alisauskas and Ankney 1992). The rate of heat loss from a duck, goose or swan is affected by whether they are on land or water—resting on water is more costly than resting on land as more heat is lost by convection into the water (Bevan and Butler 1992). Most heat loss occurs from the feet and bill. Indeed, heat loss from the bill in Northern Mallards at 0°C can exceed their basal metabolic rate (Hagan and Heath 1980), although vasoconstriction can reduce this cost tenfold.

Wildfowl offset the energetic costs of low temperatures and adverse climatic conditions in a number of ways, both physiologically and behaviourally. Heat is directly generated by muscle activity during feeding, and by the chemical process of food assimilation. Behavioural adaptations include postural changes, such as facing into the wind, huddling together, seeking shelter on the downwind side of islands or vegetation, fluffing body plumage, placing feet and bills within the plumage, and conducting heat generating activities during periods of cold stress. However, there is a cut-off point below which it is best to conserve energy. At temperatures below −10°C, most wildfowl cease feeding altogether (e.g. Canada Goose—Raveling et al. 1972, Greenwinged Teal—Quinlan and Baldassarre 1984).

For those species that feed by dabbling or grazing, feeding is not energetically very costly as it involves little physical exercise above simply swimming or walking. Some species, especially geese and ducks feeding on agricultural grains, must undertake feeding flights at a relatively high energetic cost; however, this is more than compensated for by the energetic return from their artificial food. For example, field-feeding Green-winged Teal in the Playa Lakes of Texas only needed to feed for 20% of the day compared to 33% for the same species feeding in natural habitats in Louisiana (Rave and Baldassarre 1989). The feeding activities of diving ducks are more costly, especially so in pursuit divers, such as mergansers, which catch their prey through explosive bursts of underwater swimming (Ydenberg 1986). Although there are no published studies on the energetics of diving in white-water ducks, the costs of diving in fast-flowing rivers may be high. For example, to maintain a stable position in a fast-flowing mountain stream for 16 seconds, a Torrent Duck has been estimated to expend the energy equivalent of swimming 50 m underwater (Todd 1996). If seaducks need to maintain their position while diving in tidal currents, they will also suffer higher energetic costs.

Detailed studies of the energetics of diving in diving ducks (e.g. Stephenson et al. 1989, Lovvorn et al. 1991) have proven that most energy is needed to overcome buoyancy, mainly from air trapped in the plumage, but also from air remaining in the respiratory system. Just before diving, most diving ducks therefore exhale and compress their body plumage to minimize the amount of air trapped (Butler and Woakes 1979).

Daily food requirements

In general, the daily dry food consumption of wild-fowl is about 10% of wet body weight (Sincock 1962). Although daily food requirements (DFR) differ in relation to many factors, certain generalizations can be made. For example, larger species (by mass) require more food per day than smaller species, and vegetarians need to eat more of their high-fibre, low-quality food per day than carnivorous species. At the extreme, fish eaters can fulfil their DFR with only one or two meals.

Swans, being the largest wildfowl, can consume large quantities of food. For example, Mathiasson (1973a) calculated that 45 Mute Swans removed a 0.8 ha bed of Sea Lettuce *Ulva lactuta* in a 45-day period. During this time they ate nearly a tonne of this marine alga—around 8 kg per bird per day. The DFR of other herbivorous wildfowl are much lower: Magellan Geese eat about 1.2 kg of grass per day (Summers 1985a) and European Whitefronts about 750 g a day in winter (Owen 1976a). Madsen (1988) estimated that Eurasian Wigeon consumed 74.5 g dry mass per day of *Zostera* (see Michot 1997).

Although there have been many studies of time budgets and energetics of diving ducks, few authors have expressed their results in terms of how much food must be eaten daily. Wintering Ring-necked Ducks need to consume an estimated 3370–4170 Hydrilla *Hydrilla verticillata* tubers per day and Ruddy Ducks 5000–8000 chironomid larvae per hour (or 30–45 per dive) to meet their DFR (Tome 1981, Jeske and Percival 1995). Longcore and Cornwell (1964) found that captive Canvasbacks and Lesser Scaup, fed on natural foods of Wild Celery *Vallisneria americana*, Canadian Pondweed *Elodea canadensis* and various invertebrates, ate 350 g and 220 g of food per day, respectively. Northern Mallards can eat over 100 g of wet weight in grain at one meal (Clark and Gentle 1990). Cornelius (1977) found that Redheads consumed 77.4 g dry mass per day of various foods, while Perry *et al.* (1986) found that Canvasbacks consumed 90 g dry mass per day. Common Eiders in the Gulf of St Lawrence in Canada ate an average of 1.8–2 kg of Blue Mussels *Mytilus edulis* per day, around the equivalent of their own body mass, although more than half of this was shell that was subsequently excreted (Guillemette 1998). A typical meal for a Common Eider wintering in the Wadden Sea would consist of 18 mussels of 47 mm length (Nehls 1996). However, as an extreme example, 1100 small mussels have been recovered from the stomach of one Surf Scoter (Todd 1996). Sawbills eat 15–25% of their body mass of fish per day—around 250–400 g or 2–60 individual fish (Marquiss *et al.* 1998).

In addition to food, wildfowl also need to ingest grit on a regular basis and store it in their gizzard to assist in the mechanical breakdown of food. In general, larger species (with larger gizzards) hold more, larger-sized grit particles than smaller species: Eurasian Teal held 0.9 g of grit compared with 4.5 g in Eurasian Wigeon and 69.8 g in Mute Swans (Thomas *et al.* 1977). The amount of grit varies between species in close relation to gizzard size, herbivorous species having the largest gizzards and containing the most grit. In duck communities, species such as Gadwall or Eurasian Wigeon feeding on plant leaves take in large amounts of fine grit, whereas those feeding on tubers, such as Common Pochards wintering in the Camargue, consume large amounts of coarse grit. The gizzards of seed eaters and invertebrate feeders contain less grit, which tends to be of an intermediate size, whilst those of carnivores tend to have the least grit of all. For a given diet, diving ducks tend to have larger grit than dabbling ducks (Skead and Mitchell 1983, Tamisier and Dehorter 1999, Mateo *et al.* 2000). Grit amount and size sometimes varies between sexes and populations, probably in relation to differences in diet and grit availability (Mateo *et al.* 2000, 2001). For example, Greater Scaup in British Columbia feeding on snails contained less grit than those feeding on plants and algae (Vermeer and Levings 1977).

Nutrient reserve dynamics

Nutrient reserve dynamics, in other words how food is stored and mobilized during the annual cycle, is more fully treated in Chapter 5. However the subject is described briefly here in order to put wildfowl feeding strategies into context.

There have been few studies of the nutrient reserve dynamics of swans, presumably due to the reluctance of researchers to kill such large birds for carcass analyses. In contrast, dozens of studies of nutrient dynamics of geese and ducks were conducted during the 1980s and 1990s (e.g. Afton and Ankney 1991, Gates *et al.* 1993, Alisauskas and Ankney 1994b, Hohman and Crawford 1995) which led to a much better understanding of the way in which wildfowl ingest, store and mobilize nutrients during their annual cycle.

During this annual cycle, wildfowl obtain energy and nutrients from two sources: internal ('endogenous') and external ('exogenous'). In general, they utilize body reserves when they do not or cannot obtain their nutrient requirements from their diet. For example, species that do not feed during incubation must rely on their own fat reserves for energy (see below). Similarly, most choose to feed on high-protein food at stages during the year when they produce body tissue or eggs (e.g. pre-laying females, growing ducklings, full-grown birds in moult). Conversely, the same birds will feed on high-carbo-hydrate food when they need to amass fat stores for migration.

Breeding

Wildfowl reproduction is fundamentally linked to the availability of food, both on the breeding grounds and, for those species that carry their food reserves to their breeding areas, on the wintering grounds and on staging areas. By far the greatest energy demands are on females during the breeding season, due to the additional energy requirements for egg-laying and incubation. Indeed, the energy and nutrient requirements of female wildfowl are among the highest of any bird, especially during rapid follicle growth when eggs are forming in the female's ovary (in most birds, only the left ovary is functional) (Alisauskas and Ankney 1992). Ankney and Alisauskas (1991) reviewed the use of nutrient reserves in 16 species of wildfowl and found that females in all but one species used stored fat for egg production, whilst the use of endogenous protein and mineral stores varied in relation to the nutrient content of foods consumed during egg-laying. Reynolds (1972), and subsequently Alisauskas and Ankney (1994b), suggested that nutrient reserve thresholds for fat, protein and minerals need to be exceeded before rapid follicle growth can begin.

Arctic-breeding geese, swans, and eider ducks depend largely on stored nutrients for their breeding requirements (Ankney and MacInnes 1978, Alisauskas and Ankney 1992), although more recent studies have suggested that foods eaten during incubation and egg-laying may play a greater role in supplying energy and nutrients than previously thought (Gloutney *et al.* 1999). In most of these species, nutrients needed for breeding are collected mainly on the wintering and staging areas; therefore, these species do not spend as much time feeding during the pre-laying and laying periods as other wildfowl. Some geese, such as Lesser Snow Geese, begin egg-laying almost as soon as they arrive on the breeding grounds, and do not feed during incubation, whilst others, such as the Brants (e.g. Ankney 1984), feed for some weeks before breeding commences and take incubation recesses for feeding (Alisauskas and Ankney 1992). The breeding period is not so nutritionally stressful for male geese, although the ganders of many species still mobilize considerable fat reserves to compensate for the costs of mate-guarding and of nest and brood defence. At the extreme, male geese can lose up to 86% of their body mass during the laying and incubation periods (Raveling 1979).

Northern Pintails breeding in Alaska also seem to depend partly on lipid and protein reserves accumulated on wintering grounds for clutch production (Mann and Sedinger 1993). However, most ducks appear to gain their nutrient requirements for reproduction from the breeding ground, building up significant fat reserves that are utilized subsequently, especially in egg production and incubation. Therefore, ducks typically spend more time feeding after arrival on the breeding ground than geese and swans. Most temperate nesting ducks obtain sufficient protein from exogenous sources to enable the production of one egg per day without the need to mobilize protein reserves (Ankney and Alisauskas

1991, Alisauskas and Ankney 1992). Male ducks use considerable fat reserves during courtship and mate-guarding—male American Wood Ducks and Lesser Scaup used 70% of their fat stores by the time females began incubation (Afton and Ankney 1991, Hipes and Hepp 1995).

Wintering

Wildfowl store most of their energy reserves as fat as this provides the highest amount of energy per unit mass. After arrival on wintering areas, feeding activity peaks as birds replenish the nutrient reserves used during migration and lay down fat reserves to tide them through the winter. Some species, such as Green-winged Teal in Texas, can more than double their fat stores between September and January (Baldassarre et al. 1986).

Although it may seem intuitive to suggest that wildfowl should maintain high levels of fat stores throughout the winter until spring migration (as appears to happen in some geese), most of those in northerly latitudes, particularly ducks, experience a characteristic late-winter trough in fat reserves (and feeding activity) before then increasing their feeding activity to lay down fat reserves for spring migration (Baldassarre and Bolen 1994). Some authors have suggested that this is an endogenous cycle of weight loss, mediated by environmental conditions and food supply (e.g. Reinecke et al. 1982, Baldassarre et al. 1986, Perry et al. 1986, Loesch et al. 1992) and that midwinter weight loss reflects an adaptation to, rather than a consequence of, winter conditions (Baldassarre and Bolen 1994). However, the fact that ducks wintering at lower latitudes do not show a midwinter decline in body mass (e.g. Green-winged Teal in Louisiana—Rave and Baldassarre 1991, Canvasbacks in Louisiana—Hohman 1993, Ring-necked Ducks in Florida—Hohman and Weller 1994) suggests that body mass in winter is actually controlled by proximate factors, such as temperature and food availability.

Migration

Given the extremely high energetic costs of flying (see above) and the large distances over which most

wildfowl travel, migration is by far the most energetically challenging part of the annual cycle (see Chapter 6, page 117). Most migrants, therefore, amass fat reserves prior to their spring and autumn migrations via a pre-migratory increase in feeding behaviour and a switch to high-carbohydrate foods (Baldassarre and Bolen 1994). The pre-migratory energy requirements of some female ducks, such as Common Pochard, Redhead and Canvasback, may be further increased by the need for a longer southward migration, as indicated by a latitudinal trend in sex-ratio, with more males to the north and more females to the south (Owen and Dix 1986). Males, nonbreeders and failed breeders in some species of geese and ducks (especially shelducks, seaducks and some diving ducks) need to prepare for additional, generally northward, moult migrations (Salomonsen 1968, see Chapters 5 and 6).

Moult

Immediately after breeding, almost all anseriforms have a complete moult in which all feathers are replaced (see Chapter 5). In all species, except screamers and the Magpie Goose, this includes a period of flightlessness of some 2–5 weeks during which time birds must feed within a restricted area and suffer a higher threat of predation. Swans and geese undergo just one moult per year, while ducks have an additional body and inner wing moult that in the northern species occurs in late autumn and early winter. During the post-breeding moult, up to 25% of a bird's body mass may be shed and regenerated in the form of new feathers (King 1980), leading to the assumption that moulting birds suffer severe nutritional stress (Hanson 1962); that is, 'a situation in which a bird's nutrient demands exceed its nutrient ingestion, resulting in net catabolism in body tissues' (Ankney 1979: 68). However, an increasing number of studies have suggested this is not the case (Hohman et al. 1992, Hohman and Crawford 1995). Wing moult and body moult are covered in greater detail in Chapter 5.

Overall, it appears that moulting wildfowl utilize endogenous fat reserves during moult but not protein reserves (Hohman et al. 1992, Gates et al. 1993, Hohman and Crawford 1995), although protein mass may be lost from breast muscles due to lack of use (Ankney 1979). During moult, some wildfowl, therefore, switch to high-protein foods to provide the nutrients for feather growth. The total protein cost of moult in Northern Mallards is around 84 g over 46 days compared with a protein cost of clutch production of 125 g over 18 days (Heitmeyer 1988).

During moult, many geese and ducks, and males in particular, actually reduce the amount of time spent feeding (Hohman *et al.* 1992). Gadwall in Louisiana spent only 9% of the day feeding during the flightless period compared with 65% beforehand (Paulus 1984a). Although food intake rates in moulting Greylag Geese in Denmark were similar to those before moulting started, the total time spent foraging fell by 58% from over nine hours to less than four. In order to compensate for their reduced food intake, the geese increased the efficiency of their digestion by decreasing the food passage time through the gut, possibly by diverting food into their intestinal caecae (Fox and Kahlert 1999).

Daily time budgets

In order to fulfil the energetic and nutritional requirements of the annual cycle, wildfowl need to spend a certain amount of time feeding each day. The time that they allocate to feeding depends on a multitude of factors, including time of day, season/ stage of the annual cycle, habitat, feeding strategy, foraging technique, food type and availability, daylength, weather conditions, tidal and lunar cycle, disturbance levels, sex, age and physical condition. This section describes how they partition their daily feeding activities, especially with regard to the significance of nocturnal feeding. Detailed reviews of the factors affecting wildfowl feeding ecology can be found in Paulus (1988b), Hohman *et al.* (1992), Baldassarre and Bolen (1994) and Tamisier and Dehorter (1999). Seasonal patterns in the time allocated to feeding are described above.

Ducks, geese and swans differ in the time of day at which they feed and the proportion of the day that they spend in feeding. Herbivorous wildfowl, such as swans, geese and wigeon, spend more of their day feeding than carnivorous species, mainly due to the lower nutrient content and digestibility of their food (Owen 1991). This is most pronounced in the smaller species, such as Eurasian Wigeon and Gadwall, which need to spend 12– 14 hours per day feeding (Mayhew 1988). Diving ducks feed on average for about 5–9 hours a day (Owen 1991), whereas a Goosander, taking a high-energy, high-protein fish diet, may only need to feed for 3–4 hours (Marquiss and Duncan 1994).

Wildfowl may be diurnal, nocturnal or crepuscular in their feeding habits. Terrestrial herbivores, including most geese, are largely diurnal feeders and spend their nights roosting in the safety of large inland waterbodies or estuaries. However, some species, such as Barnacle Geese and Eurasian Wigeon (Ebbinge *et al.* 1975, Mayhew 1988), will feed nocturnally, especially in lighter conditions around the full moon. Furthermore, in predator-free environments, terrestrial feeding geese feed nocturnally even when they are most vulnerable; for example, flightless moulting Greylag Geese on an island off the coast of Denmark fed entirely at night (Fox *et al.* 1995b, Kahlert *et al.* 1996).

Estuarine wildfowl feed both diurnally and nocturnally, their feeding activities being mainly governed by tidal cycles and, thus, to the availability of estuarine foods, such as Eelgrass, which are only accessible around low tide. For example, Dark-bellied Brent Geese and Eurasian Wigeon feeding on mudflats in Denmark and Greater Snow Geese grubbing for roots in intertidal habitats in Canada fed around low tide regardless of the time of day (Gauthier *et al.* 1988, Madsen 1988).

With the exception of ducks that feed by sight, such as mergansers, most ducks can feed at night and many probably prefer to do so (McNeil *et al.* 1992). A lack of nocturnal scientific observations, and perhaps a degree of anthropomorphism, led to suggestions that ducks only resorted to nocturnal feeding when they could not meet their daily energy requirements during daylight. However, a variety of studies during the 1980s and 1990s confirmed that many species, encompassing a range of tribes, food types and feeding strategies, feed predominantly at night (e.g. Eurasian Wigeon—Campredon 1981, Gadwall—Paulus 1984a, Mottled Duck—Paulus 1988c, White-faced Whistling-duck—Petrie and Petrie 1998, Tufted Duck—Pedroli 1982, Ruddy

Duck—Bergan *et al.* 1989). Some ducks, including some of the rarest, are almost entirely nocturnal. Most notable are the three New Zealand teal—the Brown Teal, Auckland Island Teal and Campbell Island Teal. These species, the last two of which are flightless, fill the same ecological niche as small mammals, and feed largely on invertebrates, the flightless species often on amphipods and isopods amongst rotting marine algae (Dumbell 1986, Williams and Robertson 1996). Species exploiting diurnally disturbed habitats may also be largely nocturnal. For example, the Baikal Teal, which congregates in huge diurnal roosts (Moores and Kyoung-Won 2000) of upto 400 000 birds, undergoes spectacular evening flights to feed in rice paddies. (A more recent count in the winter of 2001–2002 estimated a single flock of 265 000 birds).

There have been a number of different hypotheses suggesting why wildfowl feed at night (Owen 1991, McNeil *et al.* 1992). Species that prefer to feed during the day may be forced to do so during the night when their daytime feeding has been inadequate to meet their energy demands. Such a hypothesis is most likely to be true for daytime visual feeders, such as grazing geese, which naturally need to forage for a large proportion of the day in order to acquire sufficient energy reserves from their low-quality diet, and whose food supply does not vary in relation to the time of day. For those species that choose to feed at night, five reasons have been suggested to explain their behaviour, most of which are not mutually exclusive: avoidance of daytime predation (e.g. Tamisier 1974, Fox *et al.* 1994a), avoidance of daytime disturbance (e.g. Owen and Williams 1976), constraints of feeding habits (e.g. visual feeders cannot feed in the dark), increased nocturnal abundance and availability of prey (e.g. Bergan 1986, Jacobsen 1991), or energetic advantages (the concentration of heat-generating feeding activities at night) (e.g. Baldassarre *et al.* 1988). See McNeil *et al.* (1992) for further details.

Some wildfowl show lunar cycles of feeding activity in which nocturnal feeding peaks at the full moon. Barnacle Geese in The Netherlands switched to nocturnal feeding around the full moon (Ydenberg *et al.* 1984). Identical behavioural switches have been recorded in Lapwing *Vanellus vanellus* and Curlew *Numenius arquata* (Spencer 1953, Hale 1980). As these switches were related to the lunar cycle itself and not to moon visibility or light levels, these authors suggested that the geese and waders may be choosing to feed nocturnally in order to exploit invertebrate prey that were more available at that time. A similar explanation was suggested for a lunar cycle of feeding activity in Ruddy Ducks at an inland lake in England (Hughes 1992) in which diurnal foraging was lowest and nocturnal foraging greatest around full moon. Such lunar cycles, with a peak in activity at full moon, are common in a variety of terrestrial and aquatic insects and marine invertebrates (Saunders 1976), therefore it may be expected that wildfowl could adapt to exploit such food resources. However, as far as we are aware, a causal relationship between wildfowl feeding behaviour and lunar cycles of prey availability has yet to be demonstrated.

Food and feeding techniques

Wildfowl diet varies enormously—between habitats, seasons, species, age and sex, and even between and within individual birds; detailed reviews can be found in Krapu and Reinecke (1992) and Baldassarre and Bolen (1994). This section provides a brief description of wildfowl feeding habits, habitats, techniques and food items, including a summary of major seasonal differences in diet.

Most wildfowl are dependent on waterbodies for feeding and/or roosting. Most ducks forage in or close to water, while some species, such as seaducks, pochards and stiff-tailed ducks, only ever forage in water. Swans and especially geese, on the other hand, may feed at great distances from water, only relying on waterbodies for drinking or for a safe roost.

Ducks, geese and swans are able to exploit a wide variety of terrestrial and aquatic feeding habitats and foods. Although most are adaptable and can feed in different habitats, they can perhaps best be separated into the following five classes based on their feeding ecology (some are depicted in Figure 3.4).

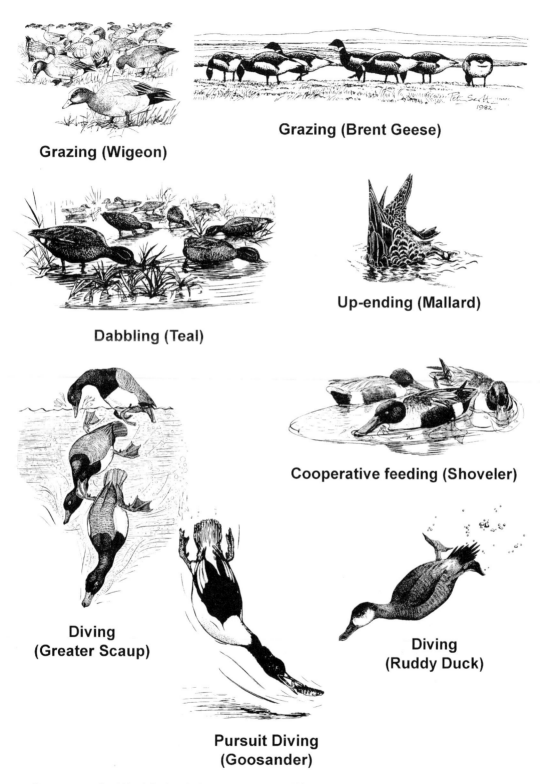

Grazing (Wigeon)

Grazing (Brent Geese)

Dabbling (Teal)

Up-ending (Mallard)

Cooperative feeding (Shoveler)

**Diving
(Greater Scaup)**

**Diving
(Ruddy Duck)**

**Pursuit Diving
(Goosander)**

3.4 Different types of wildfowl feeding behaviour: grazing, dabbling, up-ending, diving, pursuit diving, and cooperative feeding. Artwork by Joe Blossom, Mark Hulme, Barry Stewart and Peter Scott.

Terrestrial grubbers and grazers

Magpie Goose, Cape Barren Goose,
true geese, sheldgeese and wigeon

These herbivorous wildfowl feed mainly on plant material, mostly leafy and below-ground parts, rather than seeds. Animal material is less important, although not absent from their diet. In winter, all must feed for a large proportion of the day in order to obtain sufficient nutrients from their low-quality food. They typically feed in large flocks, which allow a greater proportion of the birds to feed while a small number of birds are alert for predators (Black *et al.* 1992). Most goose feeding flocks normally contain hundreds or thousands of birds; however, at the extreme, and most notably in North America, flocks of Lesser Snow Geese can reach half-a-million or more birds (Todd 1996). The grubbing feeding habits of such large concentrations can obviously cause great damage to habitats, both artificial and natural.

The Magpie Goose, with its strong, hooked bill, is perfectly adapted for digging for tubers in the hard, baked clay of drying swamps, although it also grazes, dabbles and up-ends (Frith 1982). It is one of two species of Australian wildfowl that, uniquely among the order, exhibit parental feeding (Kear 1970b, see below).

Among the northern geese, the small and medium-sized species feed by grazing (i.e. plucking or cutting shoots and stems of vegetation) and the larger species, such as Greylag Goose and Greater Snow Goose, by grubbing (i.e. digging in sediments for roots and tubers). Important food plants for grazers include meadow grasses *Poa*, fescues *Festuca*, rye grasses *Lolium*, whilst Brent Geese specialize on Eelgrass, Common Saltmarsh Grass *Puccinellia maritima* and Sea Plantain *Plantago maritima*. Roots and tubers taken by grubbers include sedges, smartweeds *Polygonum*, bulrushes *Scirpus* and cotton grasses *Eriophorum*. The smaller grazing species, such as Red-breasted Goose and Barnacle Goose, prefer shorter swards than the longer-billed species, such as White-fronted Goose and Pink-footed Goose (Owen and Black 1990). The smaller species also have faster feeding actions (peck and step rates)—Barnacle Geese may clip vegetation at

up to 230 snips per minute. Sheldgeese, with their stubby, short bills, are similarly adapted for grazing on short grass. However, the Kelp Goose, which inhabits the rocky shores of southern South America and the Falkland Islands, feeds mainly on Sea Lettuce and algae.

The three species of wigeon, the Eurasian, American and Chiloe Wigeon, are the only terrestrial grazers amongst the ducks, although many other species feed on leaves, shoots or seeds. The Chiloe Wigeon also feeds in offshore kelp beds. During the breeding season, adult and young Eurasian Wigeon switch from a vegetarian diet to feed largely on emerging adult chironomids (Garðarsson and Einarsson 1997).

Lake, estuarine and riverine dabblers

Swans, whistling-ducks, shelducks, Freckled Duck, Marbled Teal, Black-headed Duck, Brazilian Teal and many *Anas* dabbling ducks including African Black Duck

A variety of herbivorous, carnivorous and omnivorous feeding habits allow these species to coexist (see below). Most feed in freshwater lakes and marshes, although some of the shelducks and pintails are regularly found in saline lagoons and estuaries. Few specialize in coastal habitats, although some island endemics do, such as the Kerguelen and Crozet Island races of Eaton's Pintail, the South Georgia Pintail, and the flightless Auckland Island and Campbell Island Teals, which forage on marine algae and strandline invertebrates.

Swans traditionally feed by up-ending or dabbling on the roots, tubers, stems and leaves of submerged and emergent vegetation, particularly pondweeds (Owen and Kear 1972). In recent years, swans have had a much greater tendency to feed in fields either on arable crops, such as shoots of winter wheat, potatoes and sugar beet (e.g. Kear 1963, Owen and Cadbury 1975, Rees *et al.* 1997b) or on waste grain (e.g. Bortner 1985) (see Chapter 8).

Whistling-ducks are primarily vegetarian, feeding on seeds, tubers, grasses and sedges, berries and fruit (Bolen and Rylander 1983, Petrie and Petrie 1998). In common with dabbling and diving ducks, most species switch to feed more on invertebrates during the breeding season. Some species increasingly feed on agricultural crops; for instance, the White-faced Whistling-duck is said to cause damage to rice fields in Africa (Petrie and Petrie 1998).

Shelducks take a wide variety of animal and plant food, though most prefer to feed on invertebrates that they strain from mud using exaggerated sweeping movements of the head and neck. Common food items include snails, mussels, marine worms, crustaceans and insects. In northern Europe, the Common Shelduck specializes on the tiny *Hydrobia* snail (Olney 1965)—the stomach of one duck contained 3000 such snails—while in the Mediterranean it feeds largely on *Artemia*, blue-green algae and adult beetles (Walmsley and Moser 1981). The globally endangered Madagascar Teal, which filter-feeds in the same manner as shelducks, takes a more omnivorous diet of terrestrial and aquatic insects, seeds and other plant material (Razafindrahanta 1999).

Dabbling ducks either pluck vegetation and 'dabble' it in the bill, or strain small invertebrates, vegetation and seeds from lake margins. Many species also feed from the lake bottom by simply placing the head and neck under the water or, in deeper water, by up-ending. Many, like the Cape Teal and Northern Mallard, occasionally dive for food (Kear and Johnsgard 1968, Miller 1983) and whistling-ducks do so quite commonly; however, these ungainly diving actions demonstrate that diving is not their preferred mode of feeding. The four shoveler species and the Pink-eared Duck have highly spatulate bills specially adapted for straining small invertebrates and algae from the water surface (Crome 1985b). Unlike shovelers, which hatch with a typically duck-shaped bill that later becomes spatulate, Pink-eared Duck ducklings emerge from the eggs with a highly modified bill, implying a specialized life-style from the beginning.

Dabbling ducks take a wide variety of animals and plants during the year. Most are largely vegetarian or omnivorous, with the exception of the shovelers and Blue-winged Teal that take mainly small particles of animal matter (Krapu and Reinecke 1992). Most species, and females in particular, switch to a largely carnivorous diet in spring in order to amass the necessary nutrient and mineral reserves for breeding. Gastropods and crustaceans are a major prey item for some breeding dabblers (e.g. shovelers often feed on water fleas), however insects are by far the most important food source for most species. The most commonly taken insect foods include the larvae and nymphs of the orders Diptera (flies, mosquitoes and midges), Coleoptera (adult and larval beetles), Trichoptera (caddisfly larvae), Odonata (damselfly and dragonfly larvae), Hemiptera (larvae and adults of true bugs) and Ephemeroptera (mayfly larvae) (Krapu and Reinecke 1992, Baldassarre and Bolen 1994). Non-biting midge or chironomid larvae are especially important for many species, both in the larval stages and as emerging adults. Plant foods include pondweeds, smartweeds, spike rushes *Eleocharis*, and some sedges in seasonally flooded areas (Thomas 1982).

The feeding behaviour of dabbling ducks often shows a marked seasonal shift, with feeding occurring at greater depths during the nonbreeding/ wintering period than during the breeding season; that is, in winter, dabbling ducks up-end or immerse their head and neck more often, while in the breeding season they feed more at the surface (Thomas 1980, 1982, DuBowy 1988), probably in response to changes in the distribution of food items. During the breeding season, feeding is concentrated on invertebrates that are found at or close to the surface (e.g. emerging chironomids), whereas in winter, feeding is concentrated at greater depths (e.g. seeds or tubers in the sediments).

For the first few weeks of their lives, once the yolk sac has been absorbed, ducklings feed mainly on invertebrates taken from the water surface—emerging insects, such as chironomid midges, are especially important (Danell and Sjöberg 1982, Baldassarre and Bolen 1994). This high-protein insect food provides the nutrients needed for tissue growth and feather development. Most insects are taken by picking food items from the water surface, although many ducklings are adept at catching flying insects. As ducklings grow, their diet gradually changes to match that of their parents.

Lake and estuarine diving ducks

Stiff-tailed ducks, Musk Duck, pochards, White-backed Duck, goldeneyes and Bufflehead, but excluding Greater Scaup

Lake and estuarine diving ducks are specialized to feed either on plant and animal matter from the bottom of lakes (*Aythyini* and *Oxyurini*) or on swimming invertebrates from the benthos or water column (goldeneyes and Bufflehead). The *Oxyurini* and White-backed Ducks usually specialize on benthic invertebrates, especially chironomid larvae, whilst the pochards are mainly herbivorous, feeding on tubers of submerged vegetation, such as pondweeds and Wild Celery (from which the Canvasback gets its Latin name, *Aythya valisneria*). Some species, including Tufted Duck and Lesser Scaup, often specialize on freshwater molluscs, such as the Zebra Mussel *Dreissena polymorpha* that spread across much of Europe during the early twentieth century and was introduced into North America in the mid-1980s. Most other species take both animals and plants, with the exception of the Australian Musk Duck which is carnivorous, feeding on larger aquatic insects, crustaceans, fish, tadpoles and frogs—a diet actually more similar to that of the White-winged Duck (see below) than to that of other divers.

As with dabbling ducks, most species switch to a largely carnivorous diet in the spring in order to amass the necessary nutrient and mineral reserves for breeding. Food items taken are generally similar to those taken by dabbling ducks, although benthic invertebrates tend to predominate. Ducklings feed mainly on invertebrates (see above), initially taken from the water surface, but within a few days most can also dive to exploit benthic invertebrates.

Diving ducks mainly dive for their food, but most species will also feed by dabbling, up-ending or gleaning insects from vegetation (Weller 1964a, Green 1998a). Most species tend to feed by touch rather than sight, diving to the bottom of waterbodies and sieving food from the benthos by moving their bills in short lateral arcs (Tome and Wrubleski 1988). Some species, such as Lesser Scaup, locate their prey visually in the water column. Unusually, Euliss *et al.* (1997) found Ruddy Ducks fed largely on water boatmen (Corixidae). Diving ducks feeding on bivalves swallow their prey whole rather than crushing it in the bill. Tufted Ducks take larger mussels to the surface for swallowing but swallow small mussels (< 16 mm long) underwater using a 'suction feeding' technique similar to that used by dabbling ducks to filter seeds from water (De Leeuw and van Eerden 1992).

Tome and Wrubleski (1988) studied the diving behaviour of Canvasbacks, Ruddy Ducks and Lesser Scaup and found that all three initiated dives in a similar manner: first they exhaled and brought both feet forward close to the body, before sweeping both feet backwards while arching the neck forward into the water. Upon reaching the bottom, the birds maintained their position with leg strokes directed perpendicularly to the surface. To return to the surface, the birds stopped moving their legs and briefly floated backwards, before a kick of the feet and an upward motion of the head oriented the body towards the water surface. The birds then floated back up with the foot webbing folded so as to offer minimum resistance. Just before reaching the surface the ducks extended both legs laterally and spread the foot webbing to decrease their speed of ascent. During the ascent, Ruddy Ducks pointed their heads forwards, but Canvasbacks and Lesser Scaup pressed their bills down on their chests.

Diving ducks tend to submerge, on average, for about 30 seconds, and up to about 60 seconds at the extreme (Dewar 1924, Streseman 1927–34). Domestic ducks, however, can withstand forced submergence for up to 16 minutes (Schorger 1947). The length of a dive is mainly related to depth (Dewar 1924, Draulans 1982), but also to factors such as body size and composition, and water temperature, as well as the physiological constraints of the species concerned. The *Aythyini* prefer to dive in waters of 1–3 m depth, although they can, and do, dive in much deeper water. In the coastal waters off Sweden, Common Pochard mainly dived to depths of less than 2 m, Greater Scaup to depths of up to 5 m, and Tufted Duck up to 7 m (Nilsson 1972). However, the energetic costs of diving increase with depth, so deep sites are used for feeding only when they hold higher prey densities (Carbone and Houston 1994).

Diving ducks such as Ruddy Ducks and Canvasbacks that feed on clumped animal and plant prey tend to use an area-restricted search technique in which they locate prey patches using exploratory dives over a larger area. Once a food patch has been found, they concentrate on it until the supply there is exhausted (Tome 1989, Lovvorn and Gillingham 1996).

Woodland dabbling ducks

Wood ducks (*Asarcornis, Cairina, Pteronetta* and *Aix*), excluding Maned Goose and Brazilian Teal

A group of tree-nesting and perching wildfowl, the smaller *Aix* wood ducks are mainly vegetarian and feed by dabbling or up-ending. Many have specialized feeding habits: for example, Wood Duck and Mandarin feed mainly in forested habitats on fallen nuts and acorns (Barras *et al.* 1996, Shurtleff and Savage 1996). Wood Ducks are well known for their communal night roosts in forested wetlands that can comprise up to 10 000 birds (Bellrose and Holme 1994). Pygmy-geese, from Africa, southeast Asia and Australia, often frequent open, still waters covered with their preferred food of water-lilies from which they strip seeds and flower heads. Some species, such as Cotton Teal or Pygmy-goose, are found on more open lakes and coastal lagoons where they feed on *Potamogeton*, *Hydrilla* and other aquatic vegetation (Marchant and Higgins 1990). The Green Pygmy-goose is restricted to the floodplains of coastal rivers in northern Australia and southeast New Guinea where they sometimes feed in flooded rice fields. In keeping with other ducks, most of the smaller wood ducks switch to an invertebrate diet in spring.

White-winged Duck, Muscovy Duck and Hartlaub's Duck are all typically secretive rainforest species, inhabiting the waterways and wetlands of tropical forests in southeast Asia, South America and Africa. All are omnivorous, feeding on a wide variety of plant and animal material, including seeds, roots and the green parts of aquatic plants, invertebrates, fish, frogs and snails (Green 1992a). The wild Muscovy Duck eats insects which, as we saw in Chapter 1, may have been one reason behind its domestication. The White-winged Duck is also frequently found feeding in rice paddies. Most of the larger wood ducks are crepuscular, feeding in the morning and evening, and spending the middle of the day and the night roosting in trees.

Coastal and riverine diving ducks: Coastal and estuarine mollusc and echinoderm specialists

Steamer-ducks, Greater Scaup and seaducks (scoters, typical eiders *Somateria* and Steller's Eider)

Steamer-ducks, Greater Scaup, scoters (Fox 2003b) and eiders have stout bills for crushing prey, such as crabs and sea urchins, and for pulling bivalves from rocks which are then swallowed whole and crushed by the gizzard. They breed on islands or freshwater pools, feeding on benthic invertebrates, but spend most of the year at sea, feeding mainly in waters less than 10 m deep. In Norway, Common Eiders feed over kelp beds in water less than 10 m deep, while King Eiders usually dive deeper than 20 m (Bustnes and Lonne 1997). Spectacled Eiders in Alaska regularly forage at depths of 45–70 m (Petersen *et al.* 1998).

All seaducks gather in large flocks in winter. Spectacled Eiders are famous for their huge winter gatherings in which up to 50 000 birds have been found using holes in arctic pack ice over 160 km from land (Petersen *et al.* 1995). Similarly, Common Scoters often moult and winter in huge concentrations—over 1.2 million scoters were seen in the Baltic Sea in 1993, including one flock of 600 000 birds in the Kattegat (Pihl and Laursen 1996).

Steamer-ducks are large, aggressive birds from coastal South America, where they fill the same niche as northern seaducks. The three flightless species are entirely marine, except for infrequent short walks to brackish and freshwater bodies near the coast, whilst the Flying Steamer-duck breeds on inland freshwater lakes (Livezey and Humphrey 1992, Woods and Woods 1997). Steamer-ducks may gather in estuaries and river mouths, where certain food supplies such as bivalves may be greater. Their distribution along rocky coasts is closely associated with kelp beds, where they feed on sea urchins in the same manner as eiders. Although molluscs and crustaceans (particularly crabs) dominate the diet of steamer-ducks, filamentous green algae may also be eaten.

Seaducks and steamers are thought to be both tactile and visual feeders, foraging on bivalves by touch and on items such as crabs and sea urchins by sight. Small prey are eaten underwater while larger items are taken to the surface to be swallowed (Guillemette 1998). The level at which seaducks can sequester salt is not thought to limit the feeding rate of Common Eiders; this is mainly determined by gizzard capacity and the time taken to digest their hard-shelled food (Nehls 1996). During intensive feeding, Common Eiders need to pause for about 20 minutes between feeding bouts and it takes about one hour for food to pass through the gut (Nyström and Pehrsson 1988).

Coastal and riverine diving ducks: invertebrate specialists

Long-tailed Duck and Harlequin Duck

Long-tailed Duck and Harlequin Duck both winter at sea where they feed on a variety of marine organisms, including shrimps, amphipods, small crabs, chitons, bivalves, sea urchins and small fish. A detailed study in Newfoundland found that, in the company of other seaducks, both species fed mainly on benthic amphipods (e.g. *Gammarellus angulosus* and *Calliopius laeviusculus*) and isopods (e.g. *Idotea baltica*) (Goudie and Ankney 1986). Their small, chisel-shaped bills seem well adapted for picking these items from the substrate; however, the daintiness of the Harlequin's bill belies its ability to prise chitons from rocks—a task often impossible for tool-equipped humans (Todd 1996). Along with other seaducks, seabirds and marine mammals, Harlequin Ducks may also exploit the superabundant roe of Atlantic Herring *Clupea harengus* and Atlantic Salmon *Salmo salar* (e.g. Dzinbal and Jarvis 1984).

Both species breed inland, the Long-tailed Duck on tundra pools, where it feeds on insect larvae and small fish (Cramp and Simmons 1977), and the Harlequin Duck on fast-flowing rivers, taking bottom-dwelling invertebrates such as blackfly,

mayflies, stoneflies, and caddisfly larvae (Bengtson 1972a). The Long-tailed Duck has been credited with the deepest dive of any wildfowl, at around 75 m (Alison 1975).

Coastal and riverine diving ducks: riverine invertebrate specialists

Torrent Ducks, Salvadori's Duck and Blue Duck

The three southern hemisphere white-water ducks are highly agile, expert swimmers and divers, with the ability to swim through rapids and traverse waterfalls. All are sedentary, territorial river dwellers that feed mainly by diving.

Blue Duck and Torrent Duck feed in fast-flowing, well-oxygenated torrents where they probe amongst rocks for aquatic insects, such as blackfly, mayfly, stonefly and particularly caddisfly larvae (Kear and Burton 1971, Veltman *et al.* 1995). Blue Ducks and, probably, the less well-studied Torrent Duck also take emerging adult insects, and their diet may include snails, crustaceans, midge and beetle larvae as well as algae, moss and diatoms scraped from stones. As their prey is available all year-round, they show little seasonal variation in diet.

Salvadori's Duck is less specialized than Blue Duck and Torrent Duck, appearing and behaving more like dabbling ducks than the other two species. It frequents a wider variety of habitats, including alpine lakes, ponds and slow-moving rivers, although it breeds mainly on mountain streams (Kear 1975). Most feeding takes place by diving in slow-flowing eddies and pools, although dabbling appears common in this species. The main prey is thought to be insect larvae, especially caddisfly larvae and dragonfly nymphs, water beetles, and water fleas. Tadpoles are apparently regularly taken also.

Coastal and riverine diving ducks: riverine and coastal fish-eaters

Sawbills

Sawbills are super-efficient fish predators with serrated bills for grasping prey. All species breed on rivers, feeding mainly on the smolt (young) of salmon and trout. Wintering sites include inland still waters and rivers in temperate regions, or coastal areas for the more northern species. Fish are the main prey item year-round, although the smaller species, Smew and Hooded Merganser, take fewer fish and more invertebrates and molluscs. Ducklings initially feed on the larvae of aquatic insects, such as caddis-flies and dragonflies. Most sawbills prefer smaller fish of 10–15 cm (Marquiss *et al.* 1998). Girth rather than length appears to determine the maximum size of fish taken, with captive Common Mergansers (Goosanders) taking fish up to a girth of 150 mm (Latta and Sharkey 1966). Small fish are generally swallowed underwater, whilst large ones are taken to the surface (Lindroth and Bergstöm 1959).

Pursuit divers such as mergansers have two methods of feeding: placing their head under the water and using their bill to probe for prey amongst rocks (Salyer and Lagler 1940), and diving. The former technique is somewhat more random than the latter, as all prey items are caught and 'tasted'. Diving may be preceded by a 'head-under search' (Lindroth and Bergstöm 1959, Sjöberg 1988a) in which the birds scan for potential prey items with eyes just below the water before diving to catch their selected prey. Again, small fish will be eaten underwater and larger ones taken to the surface (Lindroth and Bergstöm 1959).

Novel feeding techniques

In addition to these basic feeding techniques, some wildfowl employ novel methods that increase feeding success or minimize the energy needed to obtain food.

Various types of cooperative feeding occur. Mergansers feed cooperatively by gathering in lines or chevrons and driving shoals of fish into the shallows where they are easier to catch (Des Lauriers and Brattstrom 1965). Parental feeding occurs in two Australian species—Magpie Goose and Musk Duck—and in some whistling-ducks (Kear 1970b) (see Chapter 5, page 96). In Magpie Geese, parental feeding is most prevalent in the first week after hatching but persists after the young have fledged at 10–12 weeks of age. Parental feeding by Magpie

Geese may either allow adults to feed young on food they could not themselves acquire, such as tubers from hard ground, or may maximize the numbers of young fledged by allowing adults to feed the most needy offspring. Shovelers and Pink-eared Ducks feed cooperatively by swimming in formations that presumably either channel or concentrate small prey items on the surface film. These formations include lines and chevrons in which successive birds feed in the wake of others, or circles which perhaps create a vortex to draw planktonic food to the surface.

Wild Bewick's Swans feeding at WWT Slimbridge often use foot-paddling as a means of stirring up the benthos to uncover food items. Diving and dabbling ducks benefit from this activity by feeding on items that float to the surface or by diving to feed amongst the foot-paddling swans. The Galapagos race of the White-cheeked Pintail similarly has been seen feeding in association with Caribbean Flamingos *Phoenicopterus ruber roseus* (Todd 1996). Mute Swans dabbling on aquatic vegetation may be accompanied by dabbling ducks that feed on plant fragments and aquatic insects stirred up by the swans. The ducklings of certain diving ducks may similarly benefit from the feeding actions of their mothers; for example, newly hatched Ruddy Ducks in Lancashire, England, fed on detritus which rose to the surface as their parents fed underwater (Hughes 1992).

Some species are kleptoparasites—i.e. they steal food from other birds (Amat 1990). This is perhaps most apparent in birds with high-cost feeding behaviour, such as mergansers, which will steal fish from one another to prevent the need for energy-consuming diving. Among vegetarian species, Gadwall are well known for feeding in association with Common Coot *Fulica atra* and American Coot *Fulica americana* (Chapter 8, page 163), stealing plant material from the birds as they surface (Amat 1990, LeSchack and Hepp 1995). American Wigeon and Eurasian Wigeon similarly feed on aquatic vegetation brought to the surface by foraging swans and diving ducks. Kleptoparasitism on wildfowl by gulls is a common phenomenon (e.g. Chavez-Ramirez 1995), and feeding seaducks, diving ducks and mergansers are often seen accompanied by gulls, waiting opportunistically to snatch a quick meal. Even Bald Eagles *Haliaeetus leucocephalus* have been observed taking fish from Goosanders (Todd 1996). The synchronous diving behaviour of scoters may be an attempt to minimize the effects of such kleptoparasitism (Schenkeveld and Ydenberg 1985).

Some of the decidedly weirder wildfowl feeding habits include carrion feeding, cannibalism, and coprophagy. Carrion feeding is rare, although it occurs in at least three species. The best known example is South Georgia Pintail which feeds on the carcases of Antarctic Fur Seals *Arctocephalus gazella* and penguins. However, Ruddy Shelduck is also reported to feed on carrion at rubbish tips, and Crested Duck on offal at slaughterhouses (Todd 1996). Cannibalism—eating ducklings or adults of their own or, more often, other species—occurs in wildfowl that naturally feed on other vertebrates. Such cannibalistic behaviour is common in captivity; for example, Goosanders at WWT centres have been known to eat Northern Mallard ducklings and to snatch passing Swallows *Hirundo rustica* from the air. While such behaviour is known to occur in the wild, its prevalence is unknown. Musk Ducks have been recorded preying on young Hardhead, Grey Teal and moorhens *Gallinula* in captivity (Todd 1996). Coprophagy (or eating faeces) occurs in swans, geese and ducks (e.g. Black and Rees 1984) and may be more prevalent in those species that take low-quality forage and which must therefore extract as much energy and nutrients as possible from their food.

Sometimes wildfowl can be too greedy for their own good! Millais (1913) reported a Common Eider shot with a 250 mm razor shell stuck in its mouth,

while mergansers are notorious for attempting to eat fish that are too large for them to swallow (Munro 1930, Wick and Rogers 1957). Both captive and wild mergansers have been observed choking to death in such situations (e.g. White 1957). Wildfowl may also swallow foreign bodies, such as metal objects, perhaps as grit (Olney and Beer 1961). An adult Tufted Duck, shot at a gravel pit near London in 1960, was found to have a 40 mm nail piercing its gizzard.

Niche separation

The wide variety of body structure and food choice allow wildfowl to exploit many different habitats and, within each habitat, to coexist by exploiting different ecological niches. There are a number of ways in which niche separation between wildfowl has been illustrated, both scientifically and descriptively. The most simple illustrates the segregation in feeding habitat between the major families, diving ducks diving in deep water, swans up-ending closer to the shore, dabbling ducks up-ending and dabbling along the shoreline, and geese grazing on the bank (Figure 3.5).

The probable feeding habitats of five species of geese in Britain before deforestation were similarly illustrated by Owen (1976b) (Figure 3.6). This showed the small, short-billed Barnacle Goose grazing on offshore islands; the similarly sized Brent Goose specializing on estuarine plants, such as Eelgrass in the intertidal zone and various saltmarsh vegetation; the intermediate-sized Pink-footed Goose feeding on estuaries following the pioneer grass zone; the largest goose, Greylag, grubbing for roots and tubers in *Scirpus* marshes; and the Greenland

3.5 Ecological segregation of wildfowl feeding habits. 1—Grubbing (Greylag Goose), 2—Grazing (Barnacle Goose and Eurasian Wigeon), 3—Dabbling (Eurasian Teal and Shoveler), 4—Up-ending (Northern Mallard and Pintail), 5—Diving (Tufted Duck and Common Pouchard), 6—Pursuit diving (Goosander), 7—Up-ending (Mute Swan). Artwork by Joe Blossom.

White-fronted Goose feeding higher up in bogs, grubbing for roots and tubers.

Lack (1974) described niche separation in ducks in an Australian swamp, with Maned Goose feeding on short-sward grass pastures, Grey Teal on grass, smartweed, and small insects, Pacific Black Duck on the same plants and larger insects, Blue-billed Duck on sedges and midge larvae, Hardhead on large insects and large molluscs obtained by diving, Musk Duck on crayfish, large mussels and deepwater weeds, Pink-eared Duck on minute particles filtered from near the surface, and Freckled Duck on algae filtered from shallow water.

Scientific studies of community ecology in wildfowl have produced a much more complex description of niche separation (see review by Nudds 1992). Focusing largely on ducks (as most geese and swans forage in single species flocks), initial studies described ecological segregation in relation to food, bill and gut morphology, and microhabitat. For example, Pöysä (1983) demonstrated the variation in feeding niche between six species of ducks (Figure 3.7). These rely on a gradient of neck length and bill characteristics that allows them to coexist and reduce competition by exploiting different microhabitats. Pöysä (1983) showed that partitioning of feeding

3.6 Feeding habitats of five species of geese in Britain before deforestation (after Owen 1976b). BA—Barnacle Goose, BR—Brent Goose, PF—Pink-footed Goose, GL—Greylag Goose, GWF—Greenland White-fronted Goose. The European white-fronted Goose (EWF) may not have wintered in Britain in former times.

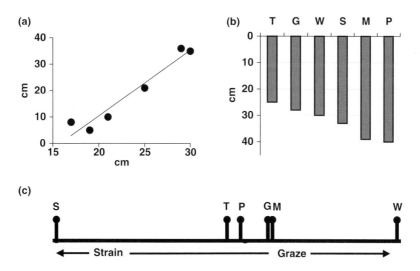

3.7 Separation of six species of dabbling duck in a Finnish breeding area by morphology and feeding behaviours: (a) correlation between mean feeding depth and neck length; (b) maximum depth reached when up-ending; and (c) differentiation on eight measurements of bill morphology, indicating adaptations for straining and grazing. G—Gadwall, M—Northern Mallard, P—Northern Pintail, S—Northern Shoveler, T—Eurasian Teal, W—Eurasian Wigeon (after Pöysä 1983).

methods was more important to dabbling ducks, while partitioning of feeding habitats was more important to diving ducks. At high temperate latitudes, dabbling ducks and diving ducks usually show little or no overlap in feeding behaviour and habitat, forming two clear guilds (Pöysä 1983, Nudds 1992); however, this may not be the case in other parts of the world. In the Mediterranean region, Ferruginous Duck and Red-crested Pochard show characteristics of both dabbling and diving in their feeding behaviour and habitat selection (Amat 1984b, Green 1998a). In studies of dabbling duck communities in Europe and North America, larger species have been found repeatedly to up-end more than smaller ones, possibly because they can do so more efficiently (Pöysä 1983, Green 1998a). It is not known whether this pattern occurs in other continents.

Bill structure was examined in 22 species of North American wildfowl (Kehoe and Thomas 1987), ranging from Snow Goose to Common Merganser (Goosander). The species separated predictably according to the feeding habitats that they chose and the food exploited. They could also be separated by the relative weights of their digestive organs (Barnes and Thomas 1987).

In a study of comparative feeding behaviour and niche organization in a Mediterranean duck community, Green (1998a) found that Marbled Teal fed closest to the surface (mean depth in the water column 8.4 cm), chiefly by bill-dipping (66%) and gleaning (14%). Garganey fed at a mean depth of 9.1 cm, mainly by bill-dipping (57%) and neck-dipping (35%). Northern Mallard fed at greater depths (31.8 cm), mainly by up-ending (46%) and neck-dipping (41%). Ferruginous Ducks fed at the greatest depths (38.4 cm), chiefly by diving (76%). In Baltic coastal wetlands, dabbling ducks with fine lamellar density (e.g. Northern Shoveler) tended to feed in open, offshore areas, and species with coarse lamellar density (e.g. Gadwall) in vegetated, inshore sites (Nudds et al. 1994), perhaps due to the size distribution of their invertebrate prey with smaller invertebrates in the former sites, and larger invertebrates in the latter. However, in most northern European wetlands, body length seems more important in explaining species distribution within and between wetlands, perhaps owing to its effect

on the maximum depth that can be reached when up-ending (Nudds et al. 2000).

Winter diet, behaviour and microhabitat of four coexisting seaducks (Harlequin Duck, Long-tailed Duck, Common Scoter and Common Eider) in Newfoundland were related to body size (Goudie and Ankney 1986). The smaller species (Harlequin and Long-tailed Duck) consumed higher proportions of amphipods and isopods than did the larger Common Scoter and Common Eider, which preferred mussels and sea urchins, respectively. The two smaller species had diets with higher energetic value, but spent more time feeding than did the larger species, partly because they fed in deeper water. Vermeer and Bourne (1984) also demonstrated resource partitioning between three scoter species in coastal British Colombia, with Velvet (or White-winged) Scoter eating more clams Macoma and snails than the others, whose diets comprised mainly mussels. Surf Scoters fed on mussels from fiord walls, whilst the other two species were bottom feeders. Velvet Scoters also selected larger mussels than the others. Anderson and Ohmart (1988) again found strong resource partitioning between different dabbling ducks, diving ducks and mergansers wintering on the Colorado River.

Niches can also be separated in time. A good example is the way that different duck species, whose ducklings tend to rely on similar food resources (e.g. chironomids), emerge from the nest at different times of the year (Toft et al. 1982, Green et al. 1999a).

Feeding site selection and food preference

Although the nutritional requirements of wildfowl are relatively fixed (Baldassarre and Bolen 1994), there is much variation in the quantity, quality, abundance and availability of their food supplies. It is, therefore, a matter of choice—of habitat (both between and within sites), of feeding site and of food item—as to how an individual obtains its daily energy and nutrient requirements. Individuals that exploit their habitats and food supplies in the most profitable way benefit in terms of physical condition and, subsequently, in increased breeding success and survival. Optimal foraging theory

(Krebs and Davies 1987) predicts, therefore, that an animal should forage in such a way as to optimize its gain from foraging (in a trade-off between the costs and benefits of each choice of activity), and this can be exhibited between and within sites, between and within feeding areas (within a given site), and between and within prey species.

Selection of feeding site

Selection of feeding habitat is a hierarchical process influencing the geographical distribution of a given species, the choice of a particular wetland within that area, and the specific point in a particular wetland where an individual feeds (Green 1998b). The choice of wetland is heavily influenced by features such as size, shape, depth, salinity, vegetation and distance to other wetlands. Large wetlands close to others tend to hold more species (Toft *et al.* 1982, Murphy *et al.* 1984, Brown and Dinsmore 1986, Elmberg *et al.* 1994), although Pacific Black Duck and Grey Teal prefer smaller wetlands in southwest Australia (Halse *et al.* 1993). Breeding ducks tend to select wetlands with rich emergent vegetation around the shoreline and a high shoreline to area ratio (i.e. a complex shape), providing good habitat for nesting and brood rearing (Mack and Flake 1980, Elmberg *et al.* 1993, Nudds *et al.* 2000). In winter, when they flock, ducks generally show a stronger preference for large wetlands and a complex shape is less favoured. In Germany, dividing a 20 ha gravel pit into three using dikes reduced the number of wintering wildfowl from 1000 to 170 (Küsters 2000) but increased the number of breeding birds.

In general, birds select feeding sites that are safe from predators, sheltered from adverse weather conditions, and which provide the best food availability (Hildén 1964b). Most studies of feeding site selection have found that wildfowl usually select sites with highest food availability and/or quality, whilst sites with a particular risk of predation, or hunting pressure, tend to be avoided (Tamisier and Dehorter 1999). Gill (1996) showed that Pink-footed Geese wintering on arable land in Norfolk chose to feed on harvested sugar beet fields. Euliss *et al.* (1997) observed that various duck species, such as Northern Pintail, Northern Shoveler and

Ruddy Ducks, fed preferentially during winter on drainwater evaporation ponds in California that provided an abundance of freshwater invertebrates compared to other available wetlands.

The fact that wintering wildfowl select sites with higher food availability is also demonstrated by large-scale shifts from feeding in natural wetlands to exploiting energetically more rewarding agricultural crops (Kear 1990), thus allowing many species to reduce significantly the time spent feeding every day. Globally, this trend has been more apparent in geese, many of which now feed almost exclusively on arable land. Even estuarine specialists, such as Brent Geese in Europe and Brant in North America, have shifted their feeding habits over the past 20 years to exploit farmland once they have depleted their chosen estuarine food plants (e.g. Summers 1990a).

Breeding wildfowl also choose sites with high invertebrate availability. Brood-rearing American Black Ducks in Nova Scotia chose sites with the greatest biomass and density of pelagic invertebrates, and brood density was highest on sites with higher abundance of pelagic and benthic invertebrates (Staicer *et al.* 1994). Parker *et al.* (1992) found that abundance of aquatic insects was the most important factor influencing use of wetlands by insectivorous wildfowl during the breeding season. Variation in pair density of dabbling ducks on inland lakes in Finland was explained by abundance of emergent invertebrate prey (Elmberg *et al.* 1993, Nummi *et al.* 1994), whilst breeding Green-winged Teal in British Colombia chose the most fertile wetlands (Paquette and Ankney 1996). Radio-tracking studies of Common Goldeneye in Finland showed that rearing lakes had more abundant food than hatching lakes (Pöysä and Virtanen 1994). Once brood-rearing areas have been reached, the females of some species, such as American Black Duck (Ringelman and Longcore 1982a), will leave their young to feed elsewhere, presumably to reduce competition for food.

Selection of feeding area

Within a given site, studies throughout the annual cycle have demonstrated that wildfowl seek out and exploit the most profitable feeding habitats and food patches.

In laboratory conditions, Common Pochard select feeding areas offering higher food densities but, for a given food density, prefer shallower areas (Carbone and Houston 1994). In winter, Common Pochard on an inland gravel pit in England chose to feed in shallow areas (99% of feeding occurred in the shallowest 10% of the lake) with highest densities of chironomid larvae (Phillips 1991). Wintering White-headed Ducks in Turkey also selected feeding areas offering the highest densities of chironomid larvae (Green *et al.* 1999b). Greater Scaup, Lesser Scaup and Common Goldeneye wintering on the Detroit River in Michigan selected shallower feeding habitats where highest invertebrate densities were found (Jones and Drobney 1986). Although Common Eiders wintering in the Gulf of St Lawrence in Canada can dive up to 42 m to feed, most chose to feed in shallow water in areas holding the highest densities of their preferred prey of mussels and Green Sea Urchin *Stronglylocentrotus droebachiensis* (Guillemette *et al.* 1993). Goosanders choose feeding sites offering higher densities of fish, and stay longer at such sites (Wood 1985).

Except when feeding on plankton, dabbling ducks are heavily influenced by depth since they cannot reach food in deep water. When up-ending, a Northern Pintail or Northern Mallard can reach about 40 cm, but a Eurasian Teal only about 25 cm (Thomas 1982, Tamisier and Dehorter 1999). Dabbling ducks feed in those areas where they can reach either the lake bottom or submerged vegetation within this range. The depth profile and distribution of such vegetation (which provides plant food for herbivores and houses invertebrates for carnivorous species) thus largely determines the areas of a wetland used by dabblers (Pöysä 1983, Green 1998a, 1998b, Nudds *et al.* 2000). In Californian wetlands, foraging locations used by Gadwall had an average depth of 28 cm, Northern Pintail 26 cm, Northern Shoveler 24 cm and Green-winged Teal 13 cm (Safran *et al.* 1997).

During the breeding season, Eurasian Teal, Northern Mallard and Common Goldeneye broods on lakes in Finland preferentially used *Carex* stands harbouring more nektonic invertebrates and emerging insects than other habitat types (Nummi and Pöysä 1995). Similarly, Barrow's Goldeneye females with broods at Lake Mývatn concentrated in an area at the lake's outlet where the density of blackfly larvae, the principal food item of the young, was highest (Einarsson 1988).

Moulting Greylag Geese in Denmark selected areas that were richest in high-protein Common Saltmarsh Grass (Fox *et al.* 1995b).

Selection of food

Most wildfowl choose food items depending on their nutrient, energy and mineral content rather than selecting given species or genera (Baldassarre and Bolen 1994). Therefore, different individuals may fulfil similar nutrient requirements by feeding on different prey items but with similar overall nutrient content. For example, the species composition of the diets of Ruddy Duck, Northern Pintail and Northern Shoveler feeding on agricultural drainwater ponds in California differed over the course of a winter, but the nutritional composition was relatively stable (Euliss *et al.* 1997).

In general, ducks take a wider variety of prey items than geese and swans. Some species are highly specialized in their choice of food: Brent Geese (or Brants) feed mainly on Eelgrass in winter and exploit it first before moving onto other food items (e.g. Madsen 1988, Wilson and Atkinson 1995), whereas many ducks feed on 40 or more prey species (e.g. Vermeer and Bourne 1984, Sánchez *et al.* 2000). Ducks which feed by sifting invertebrates or seeds from water, or from the bottom mud in wetlands rich in plant and invertebrate species, tend to swallow a diversity of items at one time, and it is sometimes impossible to know which items are taken intentionally and which accidentally.

Many studies of food selection by herbivorous wildfowl have detected dietary preferences for certain nutrients, mainly protein (Sedinger 1997). In general, geese select plant species with the highest nutrient and lowest fibre content (Boudewijn 1984, Madsen and Mortensen 1987), and plant parts of highest quality (e.g. Fox 1993, Kristiansen *et al.* 1998, Therkildsen and Madsen 2000). Where individual plant parts do not differ in quality, geese may select the largest leaves (Kristiansen *et al.* 2000).

Protein requirements for development are highest during spring, summer and autumn, when females need to build up reserves to breed, young need to grow, and adults must moult their body and flight feathers. At these times of year, geese select green leaves and shoots when leaves are actively growing and contain the highest protein and lowest fibre content (Sedinger 1997). Such diet selection has been demonstrated for swans (e.g. Rees 1990) and a number of geese, including Cackling Canada Goose (Sedinger and Raveling 1984), Lesser Snow Goose (Cargill and Jefferies 1984), Pink-footed Goose (Fox 1993) and Brent Goose (Madsen 1988). Before spring and autumn migration, when birds need to store fat for long-distance travel, many geese feed on food high in carbohydrates, such as seeds and tubers (e.g. Alisauskas *et al.* 1988). The quality of food on wintering and staging areas can have subsequent effects on breeding success. Brent Geese that fed on experimental plots with enhanced biomass and protein content in spring were accompanied by more young in the autumn (Teunissen *et al.* 1985).

Various studies have shown that geese flocks grazing on spring growth of vegetation can keep the forage plants in a state of high nitrogen content and low structural cell wall components (e.g. Cargill and Jefferies 1984, Madsen and Mortensen 1987). An increasing number of studies are now reporting that geese can actually 'farm' their food plants by manipulating the quality and quantity of food through cyclical and selective feeding and through fertilizing vegetation with their droppings (Prins *et al.* 1980, Cargill and Jefferies 1984, Bazely and Jefferies 1985, Madsen 1989, Rowcliffe *et al.* 1995). Brent Geese feeding in spring in The Netherlands concentrated on *Puccinellia* and Sea Plantain (Prins *et al.* 1980), visiting the same area of saltmarsh every 3–5 days and eating on average one-third of the young shoots (containing the highest nutrient levels) which stimulated the plants to produce double the amount of foliage as ungrazed plants. Brent Geese feeding on *Puccinellia* in Denmark stimulated vegetation growth by defecation (Madsen 1989), the input of fresh droppings more than trebling primary production of the grass. Wigeon wintering in The Netherlands prefer to graze on Common Samphire *Salicornia europea* than on nearby grasses with a lower energy content, and

select the topmost seedheads with a higher energy and protein content (van Eerden 1984).

Geese and wigeon feeding in terrestrial habitats can be observed easily and their feeding sites pinpointed via concentrations of faeces, which allows diet to be easily identified. In most ducks, studies of prey selection are harder because it is more difficult to determine their exact feeding areas and the true availability of prey items in aquatic habitats (sampling methods used to assess availability are often heavily biased), and because faecal analysis is rarely a viable way of determining diet composition (collection of faeces is difficult, and interpreting the relative importance of soft-bodied invertebrates and harder plant material in the diet is complicated). Furthermore, there is a general lack of data on the nutrient content of duck food items. Nevertheless, studies comparing the availability of food items in feeding areas with the proportion of those items in the diet have suggested that ducks do select certain food items. Michot and Chadwick (1994) found that Redheads wintering off the Louisiana coast preferred the rhizomes of Shoalgrass *Halodule wrightii* to other seagrasses, but that this cannot be explained by a higher nutrient content. Instead, they are preferred because they are an accessible food, more abundant in shallow water than other seagrasses with smaller rhizomes growing closer to the sediment surface. Fulvous Whistling-ducks feeding in rice fields in Louisiana preferentially selected wild millet seeds *Echinochloa* and oligochaete worms (Hohman *et al.* 1996), while Northern Shovelers in Texas preferentially fed on cladocerans and ostracods (Tietje and Teer 1996). Captive Wood Ducks in Mississippi selected Willow Oak *Quercus phellos* acorns over those of three other oak species (Barras *et al.* 1996).

Numerous studies have compared the diet of different duck species in the same wetland and found major differences, showing that differential prey selection occurs even when it is unknown which items are taken at a greater frequency than their availability. Differences in selection between males and females of the same species are sometimes found, while ducks often select certain sizes of a particular prey item. Thus, Northern Mallards wintering in California selected amphipods in relation to their abundance, and selected particularly large individuals both of amphipods and of midge larvae (Batzer *et al.* 1993). Female Gadwall breeding in North Dakota fed more on insects and less on crustaceans and plants than their mates. Females selected algae and submerged plants before laying, then selected chironomid larvae and beetle larvae during egg-laying (Serie and Swanson 1976). Eurasian Teal breeding in Finland and Sweden selected smaller invertebrates and seeds than Northern Mallards, while in terms of prey size selection, Eurasian Teal selected, while Northern Mallard avoided, items below 2.5 mm in length (Nummi 1993, Nummi *et al.* 1995). At Lough Neagh in Ireland, four species of wintering diving ducks, in particular Greater Scaup, selected larger over smaller chironomid larvae, while Tufted Ducks selected larger individuals of the snail *Lymnaea peregra* (Winfield and Winfield 1994a).

As diving ducks feed on discrete prey items, they have been the subject of increasingly elaborate experiments on prey selection and profitability. Draulans (1982), after denuding areas of mussels and replacing them with mussels of known size and density, found that Tufted Ducks concentrated their feeding in areas of high prey density but, at high mussel density, took smaller mussels than predicted. This was thought to be because, at high mussel density, birds could maximize their energy intake by taking two small mussels rather than one large one. De Leeuw and van Eerden (1992) similarly found that, during an individual dive, Tufted Ducks fed selectively on large numbers of small mussels before taking a large mussel to the surface at the end of each dive. Common Eiders feeding in New Brunswick, Canada, also selected smaller mussels than expected in terms of their energy content, but this varied seasonally, with birds taking larger mussels during winter (Hamilton *et al.* 1999). Mussel selection was thought to be related more to minimizing the amount of shell ingested relative to the amount of tissue (the 'shell-minimization' hypothesis of Bustnes and Erikstad 1990b) than to the energy content of the food *per se*.

Common Eiders wintering in the Gulf of St Lawrence, Canada, feeding in beds of the brown algae *Agarum cribrosum*, fed on either the Green Sea Urchin, which is common and easy to find, but of a low energy content, or the crab *Hyas araneus* which is rare and more difficult to find, but of a higher energy content. Beauchamp *et al.* (1992) found that crabs, when encountered, were always taken regardless of how long an eider was submerged, but that urchins were only accepted later in a dive once the chances of finding a crab had diminished.

Captive Goosanders and Red-breasted Mergansers in Sweden showed no food selection when hungry, but satiated birds preferred salmon and Brown Trout *Salmo trutta* (Sjöberg 1988a). Under semi-natural conditions in a stream tank, fish species were taken mainly in relation to their escape behaviour—salmon were caught more frequently than Brown Trout because they tried to escape by swimming through open water rather than hiding. When given a choice, hungry birds always selected the larger fish regardless of species, while satiated birds preferred small fish. These results suggested that hungry mergansers maximize their dietary intake regardless of species (i.e. they take what is immediately available) and are only selective once they have met their basic daily requirements.

4

Ecology of social behaviour

Jeffrey M. Black

Wildfowl are complex creatures that employ a host of behavioural strategies in order to cope with problems related to their food, mates and neighbours in a large variety of geographical settings and environments. Strategies that enable individuals to survive long enough to reproduce will be passed on while less successful strategies are purged. Scientists view animals as making 'decisions' between alternative courses of action; these decisions are made in terms of their usefulness in a cost-benefit analysis (Krebs and Davies 1987). Birds do not consciously solve complicated mathematical calculations, of course, but with care, this style of enquiry can be used by scientists to generate testable hypotheses about the actual mechanisms that lie behind complex behavioural adaptations.

In order to examine their social behaviour, we must begin by considering the birds' ecology—where they live, what they eat, how they cope with enemies, etc. In other words, the wetland environment in all its complexity is the stage on which individual ducks, geese and swans play out their behavioural strategies.

Ducks, geese or swans on their wintering grounds are usually found in groups, and flocks of thousands are common. The gregarious nature of wildfowl is not simply the result of their concentrating in good feeding and roosting areas. Grouping together reduces the risk of predation and increases the possibility of finding and exploiting food. Grouping also provides an opportunity to find and compare potential partners. However, living in groups can also be expensive through the time and energy required to compete for food, mates and nesting resources.

This chapter begins by considering the quintessential form of cooperation, the pairbond, which is initiated during a pair formation process and culminates in the parental care of offspring, that may or may not be the product of the current pairbond. Mating systems are described further in Chapter 5.

Monogamy and the pairbond

Monogamy, involving seasonal or long-term pairbonds, is the primary mating system in most wildfowl (Owen and Black 1990, Oring and Saylor 1992).

Seasonal partnerships are characteristic of migratory Holarctic ducks in which pairbonds are formed on the wintering grounds, and males subsequently desert their mates during the breeding season, leaving the female to hatch and care for the ducklings. This type of pairbond in ducks may have evolved because of the particular requirements of the females in order to breed successfully (McKinney 1986). There are certain periods in the annual cycle where females require male protection, especially during spring fattening and while producing eggs. In many ducks, monogamy may also be influenced by the male-biased sex ratio. By maintaining a pairbond with a single female, a male can be assured of a breeding partner in the face of competition from other males. By attending her closely, he can ensure that she has obtained enough fat/nutrient reserves for the breeding season and he can protect his genetic paternity (McKinney 1986). During incubation, males and females generally go their separate ways. Females have cryptic plumage which helps to hide them from predators, especially while on eggs. The brightly coloured plumage of most male ducks may make his presence unhelpful during the incubation period.

Whereas pair members in most duck species are together for only a short period every breeding season, geese and swans are renowned for remaining with the same mate, all day, every day, each year, often for life. Some ducks, however, also maintain continuous, long-term partnerships; for example, whistling-ducks, shelducks, sheldgeese and certain tropical and southern hemisphere ducks that show biparental care, such as Brazilian Merganser, South American Teal, Chiloe Wigeon, Bronze-winged Duck, the grey teal group, the New Zealand teal group, Blue Duck, Crested Duck and Salvadori's Duck (Williams and McKinney 1996).

Of 17 goose and swan studies where data exist on individually marked birds, mate fidelity (the proportion of pairs in which partners remained paired in subsequent years) ranged from 92% to 100% (Black 1996). Why? Is long-term monogamy advantageous? In two studies it has been shown that a female's build-up of fat reserves, which influences her breeding potential, is related to the effort that her mate puts into providing space in the flock in which she can feed without interruption (Teunissen *et al.* 1985, Lamprecht 1989). Black *et al.* (1996) argued that reproductive success in Barnacle Geese improves during the first seven years due to the pair's enhanced teamwork. They showed that pairs with long pair durations occupied positions on the edge of the flock, where foraging opportunities are best. Perhaps long-term pairs are able to achieve this by fine-tuning their cooperative efforts in encounters and vigilance routines. During incubation, pair members of some goose species need to alternate foraging trips to feeding areas, so that one member remains with the nest at all times to ward off predators (e.g. Prop *et al.* 1984). Developing such partnerships, therefore, could be crucial to the breeding success of geese.

Scientists maintain that the evolution of persistent monogamy is inextricably linked with parental care (Kear 1970b). In geese and swans, a close parent–offspring association usually lasts for most of the first year but, in some species, parents

and offspring can be found in the same locations for five or more years (Evans 1979a, Warren *et al.* 1993). Prolonged parental care facilitates long-term monogamy in Barnacle Geese by enhancing feeding opportunity and subsequent reproductive success of parents due to the goslings' help in family duties. Black and Owen (1989a) argued that, as goslings grow older, they increasingly assist in competing with flock members for feeding space and in scanning for competitors and predators. If this helper effect is real, it is possible that once a pair attains the competitive edge necessary for successful breeding, its chances of succeeding in future years is maintained by prolonging an association with full-size offspring. Once an individual is in this loop (labelled the 'social feedback mechanism', Lamprecht 1986), it is likely to benefit most from preserving a particular mate's collaboration (Black 2001).

The maintenance of monogamy by northern-breeding geese and swans also may be linked to their energetically expensive life-styles (Black *et al.* 1996, Rees *et al.* 1996). In order to attain the condition necessary for successful migration and breeding, these birds have to spend much of their lives feeding. Geese, for example, strive to achieve a threshold in fat/nutrient condition every season. Failure to achieve one threshold may preclude the next, such that an appropriate breeding condition may depend on an individual's foraging performance throughout the year (Prop and Vulink 1992). Under this assumption, females should encourage year-round pairbonds because, by teaming up with a partner, females increase their dominance status, are able to devote more time to foraging, use higher-quality feeding areas and, hence, attain larger body reserves (Black *et al.* 1996).

Both sexes seem to benefit from mate fidelity in terms of reproductive pay-offs. Whereas males profit from access to a mate capable of reproducing on arrival on the breeding grounds (i.e. with sufficient fat and nutrient reserves), females benefit from the male's role in enabling access to food and nest sites (Black 2001).

Williams and McKinney (1996) compared pairbond data from 19 ducks and sheldgeese species. The probability of pairing with the same mate in subsequent years (when both pair members were still alive) was between 66% and 100% (mean of 86%). Species with biparental care were apparently more likely to be faithful (91%) than those with female-only care (81%).

The riverine ducks, including African Black Duck, Blue Duck, Torrent Duck and Salvadori's Duck, maintain pairbonds with the same mates year after year. Most Blue Ducks have one mate in a lifetime, lasting for up to eight years. Reproductive success was found to be highest in the longest-established pairs (Williams and McKinney 1996). In contrast to other river specialists, male African Black Ducks do not contribute parental care to the brood although they remain in contact with the female throughout the year (McKinney *et al.* 1978). Since the habitat of this species is considerably more tranquil than that of the other three river ducks, posing less of a hazard to brood survival, the *Anas* pattern of female-only brood care persists. In contrast, Blue Ducks inhabit dangerous, fast-flowing rivers and both sexes care for the young. This suggests that male parental care, which occurs in some ducks, may be a by-product of year-round territoriality and mate fidelity. If this were the case, male parental care would occur only in those species inhabiting environments hazardous to ducklings, where male participation confers a clear selective advantage (Williams and McKinney 1996). When mate changes occur in Blue Ducks, it is most often a result of one male ousting another (in 39% of cases). The usurping males are usually those on neighbouring territories that have lost a mate through death. These lone males are usually older than victim males. In addition to losing their mate, victim males often lose part of their territory to the usurper.

Pair formation

Before breeding episodes commence, individuals assess and choose mates, and the type of mate acquired may influence whether reproduction is successful. The study of pair formation includes questions related to the process of choosing between prospective partners and the subsequent reproductive pay-off of choosing one type of mate

4.1 High-intensity displays used in social gatherings by Northern Mallard. Displays may have multiple functions and are often directed at specific females (see McKinney 1992). If females respond, they do so by giving calls and swimming in jerking-like fashion (Nod-swimming). When several males are displaying, the female indicates preferences for a certain male by swimming directly behind, pushing him forward and threatening others with sideways head movements in a ritualized performance called Inciting. From Young (1994).

over another. In many ducks, an elaborate series of male attention-getting displays has evolved, and these are often emphasized by brightly coloured plumage that is flashed in a conspicuous fashion (Figure 4.1).

In describing the mate choice process in ducks, McKinney (1986: 169) stated that:

> In winter, females are the limiting sex and they appear to be largely in control of the process of pairing. By their responses to male courtship and their expression of mate preferences, they probably have the last word in deciding which male they will lead back to the breeding grounds. For males, courtship is not merely a matter of monopolizing one female by keeping other males away from her. They must also practise salesmanship to gain female acceptance through the vigour of their displays, the constancy of their attention, and the demonstration of their competence as effective escorts.

Pair formation in geese proceeds in stages (Figure 4.2). The male initiates courtship with loud calls and Neck-stretches, and by herding the female away from other flock members. The female may either reject the male's advances or encourage him (Hausberger and Black 1990). If the female responds positively, courtship proceeds to the next stage of mock attacks and Triumph Ceremonies, initially by the male alone, but gradually by the female as well (Black and Owen 1988). As the pair-bond increases in strength, both birds maintain greater proximity and respond to one another in courtship displays.

In an experiment to identify some of the complexities of the mate choice process, a group of 78 captive Barnacle Geese at WWT Slimbridge were allowed to choose mates freely in large social groups over two years, closely simulating natural pairing conditions (Choudhury and Black 1993). The authors found that geese associated with between one and six potential mates in temporary 'trial' liaisons, or partnerships, that lasted from a few days to a few weeks.

(a)   (b)

(c)   (d)

4.2 The social display during the pair formation process in geese involves: (a) Herding behaviour—the second stage in the pair formation process. The male attempts to position himself between the female and her nearest neighbours; (b) Mock attack with wing display—the third stage in pairing process of new partners. Male runs away from female to attack imaginary neighbours and returns to female, which joins in exaggerated Triumph Ceremony; (c) Triumph Ceremony posture when both male and female hold upright stances while emitting cackling vocalizations as a duet; and (d) Triumph Ceremony posture when male extends his head and neck toward female's head. Female Faces Away before or after male makes contact with his bill. From Black and Owen (1988). Artwork by Joe Blossom.

In 40% of cases, they never returned to a previously sampled bird; in the remaining 60% of cases, instead of leaving one trial partner for the next, they held on to the old partner for a time, whilst assessing the new one. This 'partner-hold strategy' may allow the choosing individual to compare the relative qualities of two mates before making a decision on whether to leave the old partner for the new one. A bird sequentially samples a number of prospective mates, always attempting to stay with the better of the two consecutive ones. The partner-hold strategy should provide the best mate of all those sampled without the need to remember or relocate all previous trial partners.

Some geese also appeared to be more choosy than others; current theory suggests that high-quality birds can afford to spend more time and effort in the mate choice process since they, themselves, are in high demand. Thus, heavy and more vigilant females had more trial liaisons (Choudhury and Black 1993). Since greater body weight means greater fat reserves for breeding and, therefore, a better chance of rearing goslings successfully (see Chapter 3), heavier females may be higher-quality mates. Similarly, increased vigilance of the female may reduce the vigilance burden of the male when protecting the nest and young, thus making the female more attractive as a mate.

There is some indication that geese choose mates from a pool of individuals with which they are already familiar, perhaps birds they were reared with in the Arctic, excluding siblings (Owen et al. 1988, Choudhury and Black 1994). Presumably the benefit of pairing with a familiar bird is that both members 'know' the same set of microhabitats and environments such that making use of those habitats is most effective. A compatible set of genes that cope with a particular environment would also be advantageous.

For geese, once a mate is found, pair members associate every day throughout the year, and for life. When a mate dies, birds tend to choose a familiar replacement mate. It is possible that geese monitor their neighbours, assessing potential mates for the future (Black et al. 1996). It is suspected that ducks also track the suitability of mates for the future during brief forays away from their current mates (McKinney 1985).

The reproductive consequences of mate choice have been described for geese, where small females are more successful if they pair with a small male, and large with large, etc (Choudhury et al. 1996). It is possible that a mismatch in body size could affect a female's ability to cope with the more aggressive nature of the male. In swans, there was no indication that particular size combinations varied in 'compatability' (Rees et al. 1996).

Parental care

The study of parental care includes a bird's investment in eggs, hatchlings and full-grown offspring. After hatching, parental care includes brooding the young, leading them to food and away from predators. Parents may also invest time in fighting with neighbours for feeding space, and scanning for predators and competitors. In ducks, the usual pattern is for the female alone to care for the offspring, whereas in geese and swans both parents are involved. The duration of parental care in ducks is usually until the young fledge at 40 to 60 days.

In some ducks, most notably Common Shelducks, young from different broods mix and form a crèche when they are quite young; the crèches are accompanied by a few adult females (Beauchamp 1998, Eadie and Lyon 1998). The phenomenon is quite common but little is known about its function and evolution. In Common Eider, the risk of predation by gulls on ducklings decreases with crèche size (Munro and Bedard 1977a) (Figure 4.3). In Barrow's Goldeneye that rear their broods on the Laxá River in Iceland, roving females lose or leave their broods to territory-holding females. Movements by the females are linked to the timing of insect emergence which follows a gradient downstream. Territorial females become roving females when insect emergence declines and, in turn, lose their brood to other territory-holding females further downstream (Einarsson 1988). In this way, ducklings are left in areas with the richest food supply. In these studies, it seems possible that females that give up their young to other females benefit by increasing their offspring's chances of survival and by releasing themselves from further parental duties. These females may also enhance their own survival since they

4.3 A crèche of Common Eider ducklings in the care of two adult females.

probably suffer less predation when not accompanying broods. It remains to be determined whether brood mixing comes about by choice, or by accident when two broods cross paths or when families are in dispute.

In geese, it is usual for goslings to remain with their parents for a full 11 months, but many goslings are ousted earlier. Goose parents begin hassling their offspring (with threats and bites) with increasing frequency from mid-February when, at seven months of age, goslings are nearly full-grown. However, parents that keep their goslings benefit from their assistance in encounters and in monitoring competitors/predators. Family members also continue to accrue benefits that come with greater dominance status (Black and Owen 1989b). There is some indication that larger

goslings remain in the family longer than smaller ones, indicating that parents may favour the most able and 'helpful' offspring.

Goslings that leave the family are at the bottom of the pecking order in the flock and are less able to put on fat reserves than those that remain with their parents (Black and Owen 1989b). In order to reduce interruptions to their required foraging bouts, single goslings adopt one of two strategies. When alone, they act as subordinates and direct no time to scanning and fighting; instead they keep their heads down and feed; this risk-prone behaviour is probably driven by their need to maintain daily energy requirements. The alternative strategy is to team up with other single goslings, or tag along on the perimeter of other family groups. By doing so, they may fool some other neighbour who might otherwise displace them.

They may also capitalize on the vigilance of others, thus reducing the risk of predation (Siriwardena and Black 1999).

Paternity

With the advent of molecular techniques, scientists have become aware that 'parents' may also provide care for eggs and young that are not their own. This arises through three intriguing phenomena: when eggs are dumped in or near someone else's nest (intraspecific nest parasitism), by the adoption of offspring, and when birds copulate outside the established pairbond (extra-pair copulation). Nest parasitism in geese is facilitated by the curious behaviour known as egg-rolling: on finding an egg that is not directly in the nest but on the perimeter, the goose tucks the egg under her bill and rolls it into her nest. Adoption occurs after hatching when two or more broods come into close contact and mix together. Birds involved in extra-pair copulations do not normally socialize or cooperate except for the brief copulation event.

Unlike most bird species, male wildfowl are capable of forcefully mating with a female that is not being guarded by her mate. Forced extra-pair copulations occur in many duck species and may be a strategy by which males increase their chances of fathering additional offspring outside their monogamous pairbond (McKinney et al. 1983, Sorenson 1994a, Afton 1985, McKinney 1985, 1986). Forced extra-pair copulation, sometimes involving more than one male, may be stressful and harmful to females (Cunningham 2003).

Data on parentage for wildfowl are quite rare, except for those that maintain continuous pairbonds (Black 1996). The level of extra-pair paternity in Blue Duck, Barnacle Goose, Bewick's Swan and Whooper Swan is negligible. In ducks with more promiscuous social styles, extra-pair paternity is more common.

Some ducks are specialist egg-dumpers, a process that enables them to obtain parental care from individuals of their own or other species (interspecific brood parasites). Laying parasitic eggs is perhaps more common in Redheads than in any other bird. In one study, Redheads laid most of their eggs into nests of Canvasbacks—84% of 564 eggs, compared to only 13% in nests of other Redheads. M.D. Sorenson's (1991) detailed study of this species, in the prairie pothole region of southwest Manitoba, determined that every female was capable of any or all reproductive strategies that were ranked according to their relative energetic effort: not laying any eggs, laying only in others' nests, laying a normal nest on her own, or a dual strategy of laying two clutches, the first as a parasite and the second in her own nest. By marking individuals and photographing egg-laying events at a series of nests, Sorenson found that the three strategies were related to the age of the female and to environmental conditions during the breeding season. In good seasons, with ample water, food and cover, older females employed the duel strategy, while younger birds laid eggs in their own nests. In poor years, with drought conditions, most females switched to tactics of lower reproductive effort: the older females switched from a dual strategy to laying only in their own nests, while younger birds switched from normal nesting to parasitic laying.

In geese, behavioural observations and genetic analyses of parentage have revealed relatively low rates of extra-pair copulations and moderate to high levels of egg dumping and adoption (Black et al. 1996). Lamprecht's (1989) study of a semi-captive flock of Bar-headed Geese showed that proximity of pair members increases in spring and summer when females are forming eggs. Yet, when males were removed for hours at a time during this period, females did not engage in extra-pair behaviour with the numerous other males in the flock, single or paired. Lamprecht also documented a correlation between the males' rate of warding off conspecifics (birds of the same species) and the amount of time females spent feeding. He argued, therefore, that mate-guarding in geese, rather than paternity protection, may have been shaped in evolution to serve the female's build-up of nutrient reserves (Lamprecht 1989). This form of mate-guarding probably also limits the possibility of providing prolonged parental care to unrelated offspring. The situation in colonial Black Brant may be different: during 40 hours of observations, Welsh and Sedinger (1990) observed the highest extra-pair copulation value for any goose species—seven of 26 copulations were outside the pairbond (27%). Further information of this kind will enable an assessment of extra-pair copulation rates that actually vary between species.

Why did geese develop behaviour that accepts foreign eggs (egg-rolling and retrieval) or offspring (brood mixing)? Parents may gain a net benefit from such behaviour because the costs of caring for foreign offspring seem to be low and the benefits high. The costs to the host may include lower hatchability of parasitized broods (Lank *et al.* 1990a, Weigmann and Lamprecht 1991) and increased parental duties with increased brood size (Schindler and Lamprecht 1987, Black and Owen 1989b). Apparently no costs occur after hatch in terms of growth rate or survival of the host's offspring (Williams 1994). Larsson *et al.* (1995) found no long-term costs to hosts in terms of body condition or probability of hatching young in the following year. The benefits of retrieving foreign eggs on the periphery of nests include avoiding total nest failure through predation, because conspicuous dumped eggs attract predators (Lank *et al.* 1990b). Additional eggs and offspring may provide benefits in terms of diluting the risk of predation for host offspring, and gaining dominance status and access to more profitable foraging areas (Eadie *et al.* 1988, Choudhury *et al.* 1993). Cooch *et al.* (1991) showed that goslings in larger broods of Lesser Snow Geese had faster growth rates than those in smaller broods. Additional foster young may dilute the risk of predation to the parents' own offspring in larger broods, as well as facilitate rapid detection of predators (Eadie and Lumsden 1985). Longer-term advantages are more difficult to measure, but it is possible that parents may benefit from sharing foraging or breeding areas with grown-up offspring due to reduced aggressive conflicts and shared vigilance duties by kin-groups (or perceived kin groups, i.e. familiar individuals).

Once paternity is assured by the male's guarding behaviour, any costs of additional offspring to hosts are probably offset by the advantages of a larger family unit. The upper limit to brood size may be influenced by the cost of sharing foraging areas with full-grown offspring. Lessells (1986) showed that Canada Goose females with experimentally enlarged broods initiated clutches on a later date the

following year. Black *et al.* (1996) stressed that much more needs to be discovered about the precise relationship between the individuals involved in extra-pair copulations, egg dumping and brood mixing, as these behaviours might involve kin or partners in reciprocal altruism (see Semel and Sherman 2001). Sherwood (1967) suspected that one brood-mixing event in Canada Geese involved a daughter's brood that was surrendered or taken into the mother's brood, whereas Weigmann and Lamprecht (1991) found that kin nests were not favoured by parasitic Bar-headed Goose females. The subject of brood parasitism is discussed further in Chapter 5.

Avoiding predators

Flocks are thought to be maintained largely in order to share vigilance in detecting predators. Birds that leave an existing flock are probably more vulnerable to aerial predators. Similarly, establishing a new flock with just a few birds would be more risky than remaining in an existing, larger flock. Presumably, the decision to leave depends on past foraging success and expected gains. Different social units have different expectations and pay-offs. The founders of new flocks are often made of dominant family units that come to the end of good-quality food patches and move on to less crowded situations in a new flock. The amount of time that parent birds spend in watching for predators is fairly constant, no matter what the situation. Hungry birds, on the other hand, may establish new flocks even if this involves more risks (Black 1988).

A common feature of goose flocks is that individuals on the edges spend more time scanning their surroundings than those in the centre. Why should birds on the flock edge be more vigilant? Lazarus (1978) examined the concept of the 'domain of danger', where the domain is the area around an individual that is accessible to a predator. The prediction is that the larger the domain of danger, the more time an individual should devote to watching for predators. This was tested on White-fronted Geese by measuring the vigilance of birds with different domains, and the results were found to support the hypothesis. Thus, the evidence suggests an anti-predator function to flocking, where the time spent in scanning decreases with flock size, the relationship being brought about by individuals modifying their vigilance behaviour in relation to their own potential vulnerability.

The anti-predator function of living in flocks was also examined by Pöysä (1987a) in Eurasian Teal by testing two predictions: that flock size should increase with increasing predation risk; and that, when a predator was present, the proportion of time spent scanning by individual Eurasian Teal should decrease with increasing group size. Neither of these predictions was supported by field observations. Instead, Pöysä (1987b) favoured the idea that flocking behaviour in Eurasian Teal evolved to optimize foraging performance in patchy environments. He presented evidence that (a) flock size was related to the abundance of food, (b) feeding flocks attracted flying birds, and (c) arriving birds landed in the part of the flock where individuals were engaged in foraging activity. Predictions of an anti-predator function for flocking were thus not supported for Eurasian Teal.

Food finding

Wildfowl tend to sample a variety of foraging sites and concentrate their efforts in the most nutritious ones first (Owen and Black 1990). The main cues that geese use are the ease with which grass leaves break in their bills, and the colour of the vegetation, both of which co-vary with nutrition (Owen 1981a). However, the behaviour of flock members also strongly influences where individuals choose to feed.

Harper (1982) designed a clever experiment on a pond in the Botanic Gardens at Cambridge that shows that Northern Mallard use a range of cues in deciding where to feed, including the rate that food items appear, the size of the food items, and the amount of competition that is experienced with neighbouring ducks. This last feature concerns the fighting ability, or 'pecking order', of the birds in the flock. The experiment was simple and effective. Pieces of bread were thrown into the pond at precise rates and quantities at two locations. After a few minutes of snapping up the bread, the ducks redistributed themselves between the two provisioned

sites in such a way that all individuals obtained the most bread that was possible. Subordinate birds changed sites when too many dominant birds were present, as dominant birds tended to monopolize the bread. The ducks seemed to be able to adjust their behaviour after assessing the composition of the flock, and their relative ability to obtain the food that was available. Moving to a new site was often more profitable.

Wildfowl also track the behaviour of flock members in order to assess when it may be profitable to enter or leave a flock. By placing different types of Brent Goose decoys in a pasture, Inglis and Isaacson (1978) discovered that when Brent were flying around looking for a place to land, they were attracted to flocks consisting of 'head-down' grazing geese and avoided 'head-up' alert geese. Besides scanning for enemies and keeping track of family members, the head-up posture is held by geese that are involved in conflicts, walking to new positions, or are preparing for take-off to new feeding areas. It seemed, therefore, that the geese preferred to join a flock that appeared more settled, and where the feeding was apparently good.

Drent and Swierstra (1977) went a step further and used models to quantify the lasting 'attractiveness' of Barnacle Goose decoys in different postures. In one trial, they found that geese stayed for a total of 637 hours in a field with 25 decoys in head-down grazing posture and five in the head-up posture, compared to only 34 hours with a decoy flock of the same size containing equal proportions of grazers and sentinels. They suggested that the function of scanning behaviour was not only to detect predators but also to assess the potential profitability of the foraging situation. Wildfowl may also track the position of alternative flocks in the area by monitoring the sight and sound of distant flocks in flight.

The pre-flight signalling of swans also provides suggestive evidence that wildfowl may monitor one another's behaviour so that they obtain information about food (Black 1988). All wildfowl perform a ritualized head and neck movement prior to taking flight, and this has traditionally been thought of as the mechanism that facilitates constant proximity in geese and swans (see below). Black (1988) argued that the signal may be used by individuals to coax flock members to join in their departure to new sites, thus reducing the risk involved in leaving and landing alone or in small flocks—larger flocks contain more eyes to detect danger. Swans that were about to depart to a predictable and rich feeding area (a provisioned site) carried out fewer pre-flight movements, and departed sooner after indicating their intention, than those that were about to depart to poorer and less predictable feeding areas (grass fields). The subsequent departure time from the good area was related significantly to the amount of food that was available initially before it had been depleted. The first leavers were significantly more likely to be subordinate (hungry) birds, yet they invested much more time and energy in pre-flight behaviour than other classes; single birds performed many pre-flight signals over long periods of time until other flock members joined in and eventually left *en masse*. In this way, birds performing pre-flight signals appeared to coax others to join them in moving to new sites.

A resourceful study of food exploitation in geese has revealed that flocking together may be adaptive because of the way a flock of individuals harvests and manipulates the vegetation. Brent Geese visiting a saltmarsh in The Netherlands concentrated their feeding on Common Saltmarsh Grass and Sea Plantain. The geese grazed the same area of saltmarsh in a consistent fashion every three to five days. Prins *et al.* (1980) also found that the length of a visit was related to the time since the previous visit, implying that the geese were responding to the regrowth of the plants. In a companion study, individual plants were marked and clipped at different levels and intervals to simulate defoliation by a goose flock (Ydenberg and Prins 1981). The act of clipping stimulated regrowth, so that the total amount of material produced by lightly grazed plants was almost double that in ungrazed vegetation. Clipping also concentrated growth in the upper (youngest) leaves that were likely to be harvested by the geese on the next visit. Furthermore, clipping every four days, which mirrored the birds' mean visitation interval, yielded the highest productivity by the plants.

These studies suggested that the geese were 'farming' the vegetation, returning to the same area only when sufficient time had elapsed to make another harvest worthwhile. Travelling in flocks and following a pattern of visitation will result in an area of food plants that are growing in phase. It will, therefore, benefit individuals to participate in a flock situation and to save time in relocating plants that are at the right stage of regrowth during a repeat visit.

Competition

Competition for resources is a common feature among gregarious and colonial wildfowl and the way in which birds cooperate influences the outcome of aggressive encounters.

During the winter period, prior to pairing, male ducks often displace females from feeding and roosting positions. This disparity in fighting ability, and the subsequent loss of feeding time for females, is thought to be a mechanism behind large-scale variation in the sex ratio of wintering flocks (Gauthreaux 1978). Choudhury and Black (1992) designed an experiment to test this hypothesis in a flock of Common Pochard. In Britain, this species has a great disparity in sex ratio with only 70% males and 30% females. From Gauthreaux's hypothesis the following predictions were considered: (a) that males dominate females in aggressive encounters; (b) that males monopolize good feeding areas so that females are relegated to poor areas; (c) females that stay and compete with males have poor success in foraging. The experiment entailed casting various amounts of grain onto an experimental water plot and subsequently counting the birds of each sex, as well as their aggressive interactions. Males attacked females more than other males (74% *v* 26%, respectively) even though the sex ratio favoured males five to one. Male dominance appeared to influence the timing of female foraging activity rather than foraging location, females appearing to feed after the requirements of males were fulfilled. The authors concluded that feeding second may be energetically expensive for females, and cause them to migrate further south where food supply may be more abundant and male competition less.

In ducks where both sexes coexist during winter, pairbonds may be established in late winter or early spring prior to migration to the breeding grounds. Once this happens, pair members may act as a team when competing with conspecifics. Males are usually the more active when it comes to actual battles, and in scanning for predators and competitors, while females concentrate on putting on fat reserves. For example, male Northern Mallards increase their vigilant activities and remain closer to their mates, especially during the few days before and during the females' egg-laying period (Goodburn 1984). After pairing, a female benefits from a male's presence by a reduction in the number of interruptions to her feeding (Ashcroft 1976).

A common finding in research on geese and swans that maintain pairbonds throughout the year is that most encounters between neighbours are solved according to the number of individuals in the social unit, so that large families dominate small families, all families dominate pairs, and pairs dominate singles (see Boyd 1953, Raveling 1970). Scott (1980a) demonstrated that Bewick's Swan cygnets from dominant families have greater feeding opportunities than those from subordinate groups, and this is likely to have implications for their survival.

Conflicts are often solved with a minimum of threats and fights. Aggressive effort is tuned according to a bird's perceived level of success. Dominant birds may win an encounter against a subordinate bird with the mildest of threats, whereas two dominant birds may escalate towards actual grappling and wing-beating. Smaller females and young juveniles increase their dominance status when a larger, more aggressive male joins a battle (Black and Owen 1989a).

Aggressiveness is measured by counting the rate at which individuals threaten or chase their neighbours. Gosling aggressiveness is shaped by learning from their father's behaviour and from the genetic predisposition inherited from both parents (Black and Owen 1987). In other words, aggressive parents produce aggressive offspring. The duration and type of parental care that goslings receive in the first year may also influence acquired aggressiveness (Black and Owen 1989b, Marshall and Black 1992). Aggressiveness is also affected to some extent by body size, age and reproductive history (Lamprecht 1986, Black and Owen 1987, 1989b). The most aggressive geese have access to the best food (Black and Owen 1989a) and have the largest territories (Owen and Wells 1979). This means that in some years (but not all) dominant geese reproduce best and contribute most recruits to the population.

In summary, wildfowl are generally gregarious by nature, spending much of their time with mates and neighbours. Most ducks have a varied mating system, ranging from brief copulation episodes to seasonal partnerships. Geese and swans maintain lasting pairbonds, keeping company on a daily basis, often for life. The mate choice process is largely one of salesmanship by males and assessment by females. It involves a series of stages where the potential partners increasingly cooperate in social display. By teaming up with mates, individuals improve their access to resources and safety from competitors and predators. Goose and swan offspring associate as a family for several months, beyond fledging age. Prolonged parental care may benefit the offspring and the help that older offspring provide may improve the parents' future fitness. Living in flocks can be beneficial in terms of avoiding predators and finding food. One of the negative aspects of living in groups is increased competition for resources. Cooperation between pair and family members improves an individual's ability to compete with neighbours.

5

Breeding strategies and biology

John Bowler

Wildfowl demonstrate a wide array of breeding strategies that enable them to inhabit successfully wetlands from the tundra of the high Arctic, through the boreal and temperate zones, equatorial swamps, seasonal wetlands in semi-arid areas, to isolated sub-antarctic islands. This chapter explores the breeding biology of the group, emphasizing the evolutionary pressures that have shaped their remarkably diverse life-styles.

Mating systems

Mating systems can be categorized in terms of the duration of the pairbond and the number of mates obtained by each sex. Of the four main mating systems found in birds (Lack 1968a), three are known in wildfowl. *Monogamy* occurs with exclusive pairing of one male and one female for at least one breeding season or a lifetime, and where parental care is shared by both members of the pair. In *polygyny* a male mates with several females but each female mates with only one male, and parental care is usually given by the female. *Promiscuity* involves mixed reproductive strategies, and males and females may mate with different individuals; in wildfowl, only the female provides care for the young, although in other groups of birds, such as the waders and Jacanas, the male may do so.

The fourth main mating system shown by birds is *polyandry*, in which a female mates with several males, but each male generally mates with only one female; the male contributes most parental care. This form of mating system is most common among waders in productive marshy habitats, where females may lay more than one clutch in a

breeding season. The absence of polyandry in wildfowl is perhaps surprising, since they also nest in marshes, but may be linked to their large eggs relative to body size (see later, *Variation in egg size*). As a consequence, wildfowl investment in a clutch is high, and second clutches in a single season do not usually occur, exceptions being the American Wood Duck and certain Australian and, probably, other tropical ducks (Braithwaite 1976a, Fredrickson and Hansen 1983).

Monogamy

The monogamous mating system is adopted by 90% of all bird species (Lack 1968a). As was described in Chapter 4, it is also the primary mating system of wildfowl where it takes three forms: perennial, annual without re-pairing and annual with re-pairing. For males, the maintenance of a pairbond with a single partner ensures his paternity, and many species actively repel neighbouring males, or 'mate-guard', particularly when the female becomes receptive prior to nesting. The female benefits from the protection afforded by the male in terms of reduced disturbance from other males while she feeds, thus ensuring adequate body reserves prior to egg-laying and incubation. Paired female Bewick's Swans, for example, spend more time feeding, have faster peck rates and slower step rates than single females during the winter (Bowler 1996). Moreover, the dominance rank of the male in the winter flock was found to affect the extent to which his mate could build up fat reserves, as reflected in her abdominal profile (AP) score (Bowler 1994). Female AP score at the end of the winter had a significant positive effect upon breeding success.

Perennial monogamy

Perennial monogamy is well documented in the relatively long-lived swans and geese. Bewick's Swans, for example, may live up to 27 years in the wild, and have pairbonds lasting for at least 19 years (Rees *et al.* 1996). Initial pairbonds are formed in the second, third or fourth winter, depending upon the individual and the species. These initial pairbonds are often only temporary, and first breeding occurs most frequently in the third (most geese) or fourth (most swans) year of life (Johnsgard 1978). Other less intensively studied wildfowl, such as screamers, whistling-ducks, shelducks, sheldgeese, steamer-ducks and other tropical ducks, appear to have permanent pairbonds also (Bolen 1971, Kingsford 1990, del Hoyo *et al.* 1992, Oring and Sayler 1992). In all these species, both sexes show strong site attachment to breeding and wintering areas, while the males take an active role in vigilance, defence of the nesting female and in brood rearing. Extra-pair copulations, polygyny and mate-swapping are rare.

In the northern swans, divorce is extremely rare, although its extent varies between species (Rees *et al.* 1996). There were no cases of divorce among 919 Bewick's Swan pairings that were known to have ended, while annual divorce rates of Whooper and Mute Swans in the same study were 0.7% and 5.8% respectively. Ens *et al.* (1993) postulated that divorce occurs when one member of a pair is able to improve its reproductive success by changing its mate—the 'better option' hypothesis—although a delay before parting may be indicative of the 'incompatibility' hypothesis (Coulson and Thomas 1983, see Choudhury 1995 for a review of divorce in birds). The short-term cost of re-pairing following mate loss was higher for Bewick's Swans than for Mute and Whooper Swans, and the lower level of divorce in this species may be attributable, therefore, to differences in the swans' breeding and/or migration strategies. Bewick's Swans migrate considerably further to reach their breeding grounds than the other two species. This forces them to spend more of their time feeding, while the short summer of their extreme northern breeding grounds further reduces time available for re-pairing (Rees *et al.* 1996).

Similar limitations probably operate among northern geese. For example, Barnacle Goose pairs that re-form in the autumn or winter have a better chance of breeding successfully than those that form closer to the breeding season in spring (Owen *et al.* 1988). Similarly, among Blue Snow Geese at La Pérouse Bay in Canada, females that retained their mate from the previous breeding season had a higher clutch size, on average, than those that did not (Cooke *et al.* 1981). Newly established pairs expend more time and energy in courtship and copulation than do old established pairs, which may have a crucial effect on feeding and fattening rates. Divorce may simply be due to accidental separation and rapid re-pairing of Barnacle Geese (Owen and Black 1990), and most geese of all species probably strive for lifelong monogamy, with consequent advantages for breeding success (Owen *et al.* 1988).

Some southern-hemisphere ducks may also exhibit long-term pairbonds, although data are lacking from the wild. Male Chiloe Wigeon, for example, maintain a strong pairbond with their mate through specialized Triumph Ceremonies, and vigorously defend their mates from other males. They take an active role in brood care and demonstrate strong family bonds, suggesting convergence with the family structure of geese (Brewer 1996). Similarly, the Australian Wood Duck shows extended biparental care (Kingsford 1990). Being relatively small and highly terrestrial grazers, Australian Wood Ducks are vulnerable to predation; by attending broods, males increase duckling survival, and high predation risks may have shaped their biparental care and long-term pairbonds (Kingsford 1990). In other riverine ducks from the southern hemisphere, such as the Blue Duck of New Zealand and the Torrent Duck of South America, pairs defend a territory year-round and have stable and long-lasting bonds (Williams and McKinney 1996). Typically in these species, the male plays no role in incubation, but may defend brood-rearing territories (Geldenhuys 1980b). Males with this mating system may show polygyny as a secondary strategy (Savard 1986b), but not forced copulation (Gauthier 1986).

Annual monogamy without re-pairing

Annual monogamy without re-pairing is the norm among northern-hemisphere dabbling ducks and pochards. These species form new pairbonds every season, and the re-pairing of mates in subsequent years is rare (Oring and Sayler 1992)—although it does happen (Köhler *et al.* 1995, Mitchell 1997). Typically, pairs form on the wintering grounds, or on spring migration, and the male stays with the female until some time during incubation (Sowls 1955). Initial pairbonds may form during the first winter or spring. In many species, females show strong allegiance to their natal area (philopatry), and the males follow them to their breeding site. In some species, such as Canvasback, Redhead and White-cheeked Pintail, males with a firm pairbond may indulge in courtship behaviour towards females other than their mates—so-called 'serial monogamy' (McKinney and Stolen 1982, Sorenson *et al.* 1992). Such behaviour may help to establish beneficial relationships should females subsequently reject their original mates, or if a mate is lost and the female re-nests. Males may simply defend the female from conspecifics, as in the Northern Pintail, or actively defend a distinct breeding territory, as in the Northern Shoveler. They play no direct role in incubation and only rarely provide help with brood rearing. Forced extra-pair copulation (FEPC) is a prominent secondary mating strategy of males and, in northern prairie ducks, this is most frequent in those ducks that do not defend territorial space (McKinney 1985). Territorial behaviour and mate-guarding are strongest among species occupying relatively stable environments (Gauthier 1988). In unstable environments, there is greater variance in male reproductive success, and males tend to adopt FEPC as a secondary strategy, rather than providing extensive mate defence (Oring and Sayler 1992).

Annual monogamy with re-pairing

Annual monogamy with re-pairing occurs in a minority of duck species, being most frequent among the longer-lived shelducks and seaducks. In these species, initial pairbonds commonly form during the second winter, and first breeding usually occurs at two years of age. Both sexes show strong tenacity to breeding and wintering sites. In seaducks, pair members may re-unite on the wintering grounds, reoccupying a winter territory, and subsequently return together to their former breeding territory (see Chapter 6, page 124).

Polygyny

Polygamy of any sort is rare among wildfowl and polyandry is unknown. The best example of a species that exhibits simultaneous polygyny as a primary mating strategy is the Magpie Goose (Frith and Davies 1961b), in which one male associates with two females, both of which lay eggs in the same nest (see later, *Division of labour*). Males of a few, mostly tropical, duck species also exhibit polygyny, although the mating system appears to be largely promiscuous (see below). Opportunistic polygyny probably occurs in many species that are predominantly monogamous. This is most common in cases where females lose mates in species that defend territories, which may allow males to obtain a mate from an adjoining territory. For example, polygynous matings occurred in less than 2% of Barrow's Goldeneye matings (Savard 1986b) when males were beaten in territorial disputes and were unable to defend their territory. Among Eurasian Wigeon in Norway, only one of 52 matings was polygynous (Jacobsen and Ugelvik 1995) and this related to unusually high productivity of a lake in one year, which allowed a second female to stay in the territory of a pair without being excluded by the primary female. Strong attachment to breeding territories by females, after losing or being deserted by a mate, may facilitate a low level of polygyny, even when males normally evict strange females from their mate's breeding site (Oring and Sayler 1992).

Polygyny occurs more frequently in captivity, particularly where there is an imbalanced sex-ratio. Among semi-captive Bar-headed Geese in Germany, a female bias in the population led to over 10% of the dominant males being followed by at least two, and sometimes up to five females (Lamprecht and Burhow 1987), a system known as *harem polygamy*. The males did not protect the secondary females, who were frequently attacked by other geese and spent less time feeding. However, secondary females still fared better than single females, and three such secondary geese became the primary mate of their male after the first female disappeared (see Chapter 4, page 63). This system has not been recorded among northern geese in the wild.

Promiscuity

A few species, notably the Maccoa Duck, Musk Duck, some African Comb Ducks and Muscovy Duck, do not establish strong pairbonds, and males seem to be predominantly promiscuous. All live in tropical climates where the relatively long breeding season may enable males to mate several times, as different females become fertile, and to father several broods. Male Maccoas in southern Africa, for example, defend discrete territories and display to females that are prospecting for a nest (Siegfried 1976c). Each male can have several females in his territory. The extent to which females have promiscuous copulations with other males is unclear, although male Maccoas occupying the fringes of the territory are generally ignored by the females (Siegfried 1976c). Ruddy Ducks nesting in temperate Manitoba are largely monogamous (Siegfried 1976c), whilst those nesting in California, with potentially longer breeding seasons, may demonstrate high rates of forced copulations (27%), at least in some years.

The Black Swan is primarily monogamous in captivity, but pairing arrangements are flexible, and promiscuity is not infrequent. A similar situation is thought to exist in the wild (Frith 1982). First-time breeders may pair only temporarily, either sex may desert its partner after laying (since both sexes incubate the eggs), and usually mate again to rear another brood. In this way, females may lay up to four clutches in a year. Such flexibility may be advantageous in allowing adaptation to a broader range of environmental conditions (Marchant and Higgins 1990).

Mixed reproductive systems

Many wildfowl demonstrate a mixed reproductive strategy in the form of FEPC, which is common among dabbling ducks, some pochards, stifftails and in at least one goose (Owen and Black 1990). This is a secondary reproductive strategy employed primarily by paired males once their mate is incubating (McKinney et al. 1983), although unpaired males were thought to be primarily responsible for forced copulation attempts in a population of African Comb Ducks (Siegfried 1978). Among Blue Snow Geese at La Pérouse Bay, 84% of forced copulations were by paired territorial males, 13% were by males that were thought to be paired and just 3% were presumed unpaired yearlings (Mineau and Cooke 1979a). Most FEPC attempts are directed at females during the pre-laying and laying period, that is, when they are potentially fertilizable, and made in the morning at a time when fertilization is most likely to occur (Cheng et al. 1982, Afton 1985).

Sperm from FEPC is viable; 18% of wild Northern Mallard clutches, assessed by electrophoretic techniques, had multiple paternity (Evarts and Williams 1987). The strategy presumably maximizes individual male productivity (Trivers 1972), since forced copulations are not costly to the male and, for the female, may help assure fertilization, particularly in dabbling ducks such as the Northern Mallard, in which infertility rates may be relatively high (Amat 1987). Gauthier (1988) produced a model to predict which conditions would favour the occurrence of FEPC. The pay-off for the male varied in different habitats, and was highest for species breeding in relatively unstable environments, such as the Northern Pintail nesting in seasonally inundated floodplains, where the risk of total nest failure was high and the male did not defend a feeding territory for the female. The pay-off for the male was lower among Torrent Ducks, nesting on fast-flowing but stable rivers, since the risk of total nest failure was low, and males actively defended large feeding territories for their females (Gauthier 1988). Forced copulations may represent a 'best of a bad job' strategy adopted by males in species that are unable to guard their mates (McKinney et al. 1984, Møller and Birkhead 1993).

Some females may demonstrate a more flexible breeding strategy by laying some or all of their eggs in another female's nest. This is known as egg dumping or brood parasitism (see later, *Brood para-sitism*). A different approach is for females to incubate their own eggs and to leave their hatched offspring to other females to raise, a phenomenon known as crèching or brood amalgamation (see later, *Brood amalgamation*).

Cooperative breeding

Cooperative breeding systems normally include helper strategies, where an individual outside the pair forgoes its own breeding attempt in order to assist another to reproduce. In birds, this usually refers to older offspring helping to feed younger siblings in species in which the young remain with their parents for some time (Brown 1978, 1987). Among precocial wildfowl, such help is not needed, and cooperative breeding is rare. The exception is the Magpie Goose which commonly feeds its young (see later, *Early feeding techniques*), and which typically breeds in polygamous trios where both females lay in the same nest and incubate and rear the young together with the male (Frith and Davies 1961b).

The problem of cooperative breeding in evolutionary terms is that natural selection operates on the individual and, in order to gain genetic representation in subsequent generations, individuals might be expected to behave 'selfishly' (Dawkins 1976). Helpers would appear to be behaving altruistically (Fry 1977), in that they are assisting a breeding pair to raise young whilst forgoing breeding themselves. However, in the case of Magpie Geese, helpers are not only genetically related to those they help—recent testing of birds in a wild colony revealed that the female members of trios were more closely related to one another than were females in general (Horn *et al.* 1996)—but they normally lay some of the eggs, and the gain of helping to rear relatives may offset any reduction in individual fitness (Perrins and Birkhead 1983). Moreover, in many wildfowl, nonbreeding or floater populations occupy marginal habitats that are unsuitable for breeding, whilst breeders occupy the optimal habitat. Cooperative breeding may only evolve in situations where the opportunities for the helpers to reproduce successfully on their own are curtailed, where the habitat is fully saturated (Emlen and Vehrencamp 1985), or where territories

in a local area vary greatly in quality (Stacey and Ligon 1991). By remaining in quality natal territories, young Magpie Geese may increase their chances of breeding through increased survival, and of obtaining eventual breeding space and a mate (Brown 1978). Notably, there is a strong female bias in the sex-ratio which facilitates the develoment of polygamous trios. Provided that the helpers increase the breeding success of the pair without incurring excessive costs (for example, by competing for food in the territory), then cooperative breeding for the Magpie Goose may constitute a life-style in which all parties benefit.

Evolution of wildfowl mating systems

The fundamental difference between male and female wildfowl (and other animals), with respect to the evolution of mating systems, lies in the energetic costs of reproduction. For males, the energetic costs of insemination are relatively low, since sperm are small and cheap to produce. For females, the converse is true; eggs are large and expensive to produce and, in most species, insemination carries a long-term commitment in terms of incubation and post-hatching care (Perrins and Birkhead 1983). As a result, males will, in theory, increase their reproductive success by mating with as many females as possible, while females can only increase their reproductive output by increasing the rate at which they produce eggs. However, male involvement in raising the young may be important for his breeding success, if measured as number of young reared to fledging or breeding age, and this would be a constraint on his reproductive output. Each mating system will represent a balance of high productivity (clutch size) but low parental care versus low productivity but high parental care leading to higher survival of young. Since evolution occurs through natural selection in order to maximize reproductive output, male wildfowl are capable of making more matings than females. Consequently, males will compete with one another for matings, whereas, given an equal sex-ratio, females will not. Females, therefore, may be more selective than males. The success of males, on the other hand, may be more variable than for females, since the best may be very successful, while others fail to mate at all.

As a consequence of these sexual differences, wildfowl exhibit several features that affect their mating systems (Oring and Sayler 1992).

Female-biased parental care

The heavy female investment in the relatively large eggs of wildfowl, together with their greater confidence in parenthood than males (because of FEPC), favours female parental care (Oring and Sayler 1992). The strong female bias in parental care reduces the chances that polyandry will develop, and is a precondition of various types of polygyny. Moreover, the emancipation of males from parental care is a factor allowing for the development of FEPC or serial monogamy as secondary male breeding strategies.

Sex-ratios

Most adult northern temperate ducks, as well as some tropical ducks, exhibit a male-biased sex-ratio (McKinney 1985). This is, in part, a consequence of female-biased parental care, which increases female mortality through higher predation risks, higher body condition stress, reduced access to the best moulting sites and delayed readiness for migration (McKinney 1985). The male sex bias is likely to intensify male–male competition and, hence, sexual selection. Exceptions occur in Magpie Goose, Cape Barren Goose and some of the sheldgeese and shelducks, where longevity seems shorter in the male than it is in the female (Hillgarth and Kear 1979b). In Magpie Geese, a strong female sex bias may facilitate the development of polygamous trios (see above, *Polygyny*).

Female philopatry

Male philopatry generally predominates in birds but not among wildfowl (Greenwood 1980, Blums *et al.* 1996, Garðarsson and Einarsson 1997, Pöysä *et al.* 1997). One exception is the Magpie Goose (Horn *et al.* 1996), the only predominantly polygamous wildfowl, with males entering the breeding population largely at their natal site. The extent of female philopatry is variable in dabbling ducks; young female Gadwall and Northern Shovelers show higher rates of permanent emigration from natal areas than other dabbling ducks such as

Blue-winged Teal, Northern Mallard, American Wigeon and Eurasian Wigeon (Arnold and Clark 1996, Garðarsson and Einarsson 1997). Male philopatry may be important where resource defence plays a prominent role in mate acquisition. This is not the case in most wildfowl, since pairing usually occurs prior to the breeding season (McKinney 1986) and there is, therefore, little selective advantage for males to be philopatric. For females, however, there may be benefits in returning to their natal area in terms of familiarity with food resources and predators. For example, Goosanders may establish their territories along rivers early in the year before many prey species are available, basing their choice on experience of the quantity of food present during the previous year (Wood 1986). Repeat nesting by Common Goldeneye in sites (mainly nestboxes) used successfully in previous years may also allow individuals to exploit gaps in predator home ranges (Dow and Fredga 1983, 1984). Moreover, the predominance of females returning to breed where they were hatched, and the presence of considerable overlap in the home ranges of breeding female Common Goldeneye and their female offspring from previous years (Pöysä *et al.* 1997), suggests that mothers may be more tolerant of offspring holding adjacent territories. Female philopatry is likely to have an important influence on wildfowl mating systems.

Pairbond duration

There is wide variation in the duration of the pairbond in wildfowl (as discussed earlier, and in Chapter 4). Long pairbonds are associated with large body size, low annual mortality and reproductive effort, and slow-maturing young. For males of the smaller duck species, opportunities to pursue alternative reproductive options should be forsaken where long-term mate-guarding or male parental care increases male fitness more than is possible through other options. Males should desert when the relative pay-off from alternative strategies is higher. The trade-off in these factors is likely to be modified by body size and geographic distribution, and their effect upon moult migrations, predator avoidance and access to food resources (Oring and Sayler 1992).

Demographic effects

Among the smaller-bodied ducks that have relatively short life expectancies (Sargeant *et al.* 1984), females may be more prone to accept polygynous relationships, since the costs of postponing breeding may be excessively high. Similarly, the males of relatively short-lived ducks that attempt to remain with their nesting female face much lower probabilities that their mates will survive to breed again. They should, therefore, not be expected to maintain the pairbond without a reasonable chance of a pay-off, and most undergo moult migrations, enhancing their survival and chances of future reproductive success (Oring and Sayler 1992). Larger-bodied wildfowl may have relatively low mortality rates when breeding (e.g. Rees *et al.* 1996), and males, in the short term, face good prospects of enhancing production and the survival of their young by investing in parental care and, in the long term, improved survival of the mate and maintenance of the pairbond.

Timing of pairing

Sexual selection pressures and the male-biased sex-ratios of many wildfowl lead to more intense competition among males for females. Males should, therefore, pair with females as soon as they are willing, particularly those species that nest in relatively homogenous habitats where resource defence is not economic. Females carrying the high energetic demands of producing precocial young are willing to pair early, that is, in the nonbreeding season, since this may help facilitate survival, reduce conspecific interactions, or build body reserves prior to nesting. Protection of females during the nonbreeding season, consequent upon early mating, may be an indirect investment of parental care via the mate (Oring and Sayler 1992). Where females benefit from early pairing, and resources on the breeding grounds are not highly defendable, males may have little option but to pair monogamously in the nonbreeding season.

In some diving ducks, such as Common Pochard and Canvasback, intraspecific competition for food in the nonbreeding season may lead to sexual segregation on both local and larger geographic scales (Choudhury and Black 1992, Woolington 1993, Haramis *et al.* 1994, Carbone and Owen 1995) (see Chapter 6, page 121). In both species, the female proportion of flocks increases towards the southern end of the wintering range whilst, among Canvasbacks wintering in Louisiana for example, the proportion of males is higher at inland sites than in coastal areas (Woolington 1993). Diving is an energetically expensive mode of feeding, which may increase the costs of mate attendance in winter when food is limited and, thus, render early pairing uneconomic. Early pairing is also less advantageous to migratory stifftails such as the Ruddy Duck since their small bodies and high wing loading do not permit females to transport large amounts of stored body reserves to the breeding ground (Tome 1984). Egg-laying by Ruddy Ducks is usually late compared to other ducks, and is timed to coincide with resource peaks in their chironomid food; here, late pairing is probably determined by female bioenergetics and timing of nesting, rather than by male defence of food resources, which might otherwise favour the development of polygyny. Unlike the situation in most sympatric ducks, the gonads of Ruddy Ducks do not regress with long daylengths, and they can continue to lay beyond midsummer.

The evolution of monogamy

Since monogamy is overwhelmingly the norm among wildfowl, and occurs in a wide range of ecological conditions, it may have evolved in more than one way (Wittenberger and Tilson 1980, after Perrins and Birkhead 1983).

When male parental care is essential for female reproductive success

Although the main advantage of monogamy may be that both the male and female leave, on average, more offspring when both help raise the brood (Lack 1968a), male assistance is not always essential for a female to produce some young. Indeed, in many duck species, the male plays no role in incubation, nor in brood care (see later, *Division of labour*). Male assistance is essential only in situations where continuous nest attendance is vital for successful reproduction. Since young wildfowl are precocial, such a scenario is only likely among species nesting in conspicuous colonies where food supply is limiting and rates of predation high, for example, among some arctic-nesting geese. Experimental removal of male and female Blue Snow Geese at various stages of the breeding season (Martin *et al.* 1985) revealed that partnership was essential in order to establish a territory. Females could rear offspring without male assistance, however, but being single was not the best option, at least in a colony situation. Male parental care in wildfowl appears to increase female reproductive success but is rarely essential and is, therefore, unlikely to explain monogamy alone.

Among territorial species, when pairing with an unmated male is always better than pairing with an already mated male

Polygyny probably evolves when differences in the quality of males or territories are large. Conversely, monogamy occurs when resources, such as food, are evenly distributed, and differences in territory quality are too small to merit pairing with an already paired male. Even when differences in territory quality are large (for example, among Bewick's Swans nesting in the Russian Arctic), the benefits of cooperating with a partner to rear young (see above) may outweigh any advantages of polygamy. Monogamy may, thus, have evolved among territorial species for this reason, in combination with the reasons given above (*When male parental care is essential . . .*).

Among non-territorial species, when males can reproduce most successfully by defending one female

This is likely to be the case for most ducks where resources are shared and the sex-ratio is biased towards males. Among most lake and marsh-nesting ducks, males do not establish feeding territories for the brood, and higher female mortality (consequent upon female-dominated parental care, see McKinney 1985) results in a skewed sex-ratio and reduced male competition for females. As a result, male ducks typically pair with females several months before the breeding season and defend them from copulation by other males until egg-laying.

The evolution of polygyny

The factors discussed above, which shaped the evolution of the predominantly monogamous mating systems in wildfowl, largely work against the evolution of polygyny in the group. The two major types of polygyny found in birds require either competition for male status through communal displays at leks, which allows the females to choose their mate on the basis of their dominance (male dominance polygyny), or male defence of resources needed by females (resource defence polygyny).

The male-biased sex-ratio in most wildfowl, and the resultant intensification of male competition for females, would appear to favour male-dominance polygyny, but communal displays among males do not occur, except in Musk Duck. Both forms of polygyny probably evolve where neither the females nor the resources they need are economically defendable by males (Perrins and Birkhead 1983). Such a situation clearly does not occur in many ducks, where males do not defend nest sites or food resources. Even when territories do occur, they are often only nesting, mating or brood-rearing territories, rather than all-purpose territories capable of supporting more than one breeding female and her offspring. Moreover, female–female aggression is strong in territorial river specialists such as Torrent Duck (Eldridge 1986a), which prevents polygynous bonds forming prior to nesting. Opportunities for polygyny amongst wildfowl are, therefore, few, particularly among migrants that breed in seasonally productive environments. Options for increasing reproductive output beyond the monogamous relationship are also few, and include serial monogamy and forced copulations for males, and brood parasitism, re-nesting and double brooding for females.

Where polygyny does occur, it is largely among wildfowl of subtropical and tropical regions. Here, breeding seasons are often longer and resources may be more economically defendable (Musk Duck), variable and extended breeding seasons may allow increased variability in reproductive tactics (White-cheeked Pintail), cooperative nesting by females is advantageous (Magpie Geese), or there is no clear advantage to either sex from early pairbonding (stifftails).

Territorial and colonial breeding strategies

Breeding wildfowl exhibit a wide range of spatial patterns, from the highly territorial Whistling and Bewick's Swans, that typically defend an area of 0.5–1.0 km^2 encompassing several separate pools and intervening tundra (Limpert and Earnst 1994), to colonial nesting arctic geese and eiders that may nest as close as 1 m from one another (Newton and Kerbes 1974). Some coastal and riverine species in temperate and tropical climates—including Mute Swan, Kelp Goose, Orinoco Goose, Radjah Shelduck, the flightless steamer-ducks, Blue Duck, Torrent Duck and Brazilian Merganser—may claim their territories year-round, whereas all migratory species, and most ducks, only defend a territory during the breeding season. Nests may be spaced in a regular, random or clumped manner (Perrins and Birkhead 1983), where even spacing indicates territoriality and clumped spacing indicates coloniality. The scale of spacing is important, however, since many species may be both colonial and territorial. Snow Geese, for example, typically nest in large, dense colonies but, within the colony, pairs will defend a small territory around the nest.

Breeding territories may be defined as an exclusive or defended area (Noble 1939, Schoener 1968) and, in wildfowl, are typically one of two main types (from Hinde 1956):

(a) A relatively large area within which all activities (such as roosting, courtship, mating, nesting and feeding) occur. The territory is occupied by a pair and by their developing young of the year. Territory size is determined by both the size of the bird and the food supply, since larger birds need more food in absolute terms.

(b) A small defended area around the nest and/or female. Nest-site territories, defended only in the pre-laying and laying seasons, are typical of colonial nesters and of many ducks in which the male deserts the female prior to hatch. In some species, such as Giant Canada Goose and Ruddy Duck, the male may defend a small, mobile territory around the female from arrival on the breeding ground until hatch (Siegfried 1976c, Cooper 1978), whilst in other species, such as Common Shelduck, the nest is not defended. Instead, the male defends a separate feeding territory at some distance from the nest, to which the female will fly to feed during the incubation period, and to which they will both bring the brood (Patterson 1982).

Large all-purpose territories

Large all-purpose territories are typical of the screamers, the northern swans, Cape Barren Goose, most of the South American sheldgeese and southern shelducks, the steamer-ducks and river specialists such as Torrent Duck, Blue Duck, Salvadori's Duck and African Black Duck. The last four duck species share with the screamers and Spur-winged Goose the characteristic of spurs on the 'wrists' of their wings which appear to be used in territorial encounters. As mentioned earlier, territories are held permanently by most of these species. All three flightless species of steamer-duck, for example, are sedentary and defend territories aggressively year-round in marine habitats (Weller 1976). Flying Steamer-duck pairs, on the other hand, may migrate to breed on inland lakes where they actively defend territories, but from which they must depart when the lakes ice over in the austral winter.

The northern swans are highly territorial during the breeding season, and will not tolerate the presence of a second pair on small or medium-sized ponds. For Mute Swans, the size of the territory is related to the quality of the habitat and the density of breeding birds. Swan territories near Oxford, England, are smaller in good habitat and larger on poor rivers, while changes in density on the same river stretch may be related to changes in food supply (Bacon 1980). Some Mute Swan pairs may abandon their breeding territory in the winter and return to it the following spring, while others may retain their territories year-round. Their different strategies of territorial defence are also related to food supply; pairs in the best habitat put most effort into defending their territories (Scott 1984).

Regular spacing of territories of riverine ducks, such as African Black Duck, results in a limit to the breeding population, since suitable habitat is scarce, territories are relatively large and boundaries are hotly disputed, with zones of overlap not exceeding 10% (Ball *et al.* 1978). In Blue Ducks, river territories are often bordered by an undefended area that is used by unpaired territorial birds. Densities of river ducks vary from river to river, reflecting the abundance of food and/or pressure from conspecifics (Owen and Black 1990).

Spacing of stifftails during the breeding season is not fully understood. In Maccoa Ducks, and possibly also other stifftail species, males defend territories in which they not only display and attract mates, but in which the females also nest and feed (Siegfried 1976c). This system permits the species to be polygynous, with successful males attracting up to eight females.

Small territories around the breeding site and/or mate

Defence of small territories around the nest site is typical of some geese, most dabbling ducks, the pochards and seaducks, as well as of colonial nesting species (see later, *Coloniality*). Among dispersed solitary nesters, the intensity and timing of territory defence is variable. Males of most northern dabbling ducks, such as American Wigeon, vigorously defend small, well-defined territories centred on their female and nest, from pre-nest selection to at least half-way through incubation, but usually depart prior to hatch. On the other hand, males of southern-hemisphere dabbling ducks, such as Chiloe Wigeon, remain with the brood, contributing towards parental care (Weller 1968b, Brewer 1996).

In some dabbling ducks, notably the blue-winged ducks (McKinney 1970) including the shovelers, Blue-winged Teal and Cinnamon Teal, males show strong site attachment to, and defence of, a small discrete area around the nest, while in others such as Eurasian Teal and Northern Pintail, the male does not defend the nest site and may defend the female only weakly, even during attempts at forced copulation (Cramp and Simmons 1977, Titman and Seymour 1981). The pochards show similar dispersion patterns to Northern Pintail; breeding pairs of Canvasbacks, for example, occupy large and broadly overlapping home ranges

(Sugden 1978), but males show no territorial defence other than of the immediate space around the pair.

The arctic-nesting Long-tailed Duck demonstrates an unusual mix of colonial nesting with defence of small, separate feeding territories. Females from one colony always fed within small (0.5 ha) territories on more distant pools which were defended by the males until the young hatched (Alison 1975).

Evolution of territoriality

As we have seen, wildfowl exhibit a wide range of spacing patterns even within tribes, and it seems likely that no single factor can explain the evolution of territoriality in the group. Competition for scarce resources, however, is important since if resources were superabundant there would be little point in defending them. The main resources that wildfowl defend are food, breeding sites and mates. Costs involved in claiming those resources include time and energy, with the risk of injury or even death, and the economic defendability of resources that will vary with species and ecological conditions. In general, if food resources are predictable in space and time, the benefits of defending a large all-purpose territory are more likely to outweigh the costs, whereas if food is patchy and unpredictable, in ephemeral wetlands for example, the costs of defending a large territory outweigh the benefits and small territories are maintained only around the nest and/or female.

In some colonial arctic-nesting geese, which rely heavily on stored body reserves for breeding, defence of food resources may be less important. In these cases, territoriality may represent defence of the nest and female against the threats of egg dumping and FEPC by conspecifics (Mineau and Cooke 1979b, Owen and Wells 1979). In Blue Snow Geese, for example, the size of the home range of breeding males declines and the overlap between neighbours increases as the risks of brood parasitism and FEPC decline during the breeding season (Mineau and Cooke 1979b). Defence of paternity must be important for all and probably underlies every form of mate defence (Anderson and Titman 1992).

Pairbond duration is also likely to be associated with patterns of spacing. Long-term pairbonds are more closely associated with the maintenance of strong, long-lasting spacing systems, while species with weak or short-term pairbonds are rarely territorial (Anderson and Titman 1992). This relationship may not be cause and effect, but instead may relate to the underlying patterns of resource distribution. In strongly territorial systems, limited defendable and predictable resources may be essential to successful reproduction, and these are defended either continuously or seasonally by long-term mates which must cooperate in territorial defence and have similar interests in the territory (Anderson and Titman 1992).

Coloniality

Colonial nesting is most prevalent among some, mostly smaller, arctic-nesting geese, including Snow, Ross's, Barnacle and Red-breasted Geese. It is also common in Magpie Goose and Common Eider, and occurs frequently in Black Swan at inland wetlands, Red-breasted Merganser nesting on coastal islands, Velvet or White-winged Scoter and Long-tailed Duck nesting on the shores of lakes and pools, and, to a lesser extent, in Black-necked Swan. Colonial nesting is also suspected among at least some of the whistling-ducks (Anderson and Titman 1992). Some dabbling ducks, such as Northern Mallard and Eurasian Wigeon, may also nest in dense concentrations on favourable islands, although the only dabbling duck that nests in true colonies is the South American or Speckled Teal, which sometimes uses the nest holes of the colonial Monk Parakeet *Myiopsitta monachus* (Weller 1967b, Port 1998a, 1998b).

A classic arctic-nesting colonial goose is the Blue Snow Goose of North America, in which pairs nest in close proximity, even in areas of extensive habitat. Although the tundra vegetation may be highly productive, it is distinctly seasonal and the precise timing of highest nutrient levels may vary considerably depending on the timing of the spring thaw. Synchronizing hatching with the timing of peak nutrients in the plants, therefore, may have an important effect on breeding success (see later, *Extrinsic factors*).

An important benefit of colonial nesting and synchronous hatching is the reduction in predation on individual broods. Pairs nesting earlier or later than average have reduced breeding success because of the higher risk of predation outside the peak period (Findlay and Cooke 1982a). Similarly, levels of predation on Brant vary according to colony size, with higher levels recorded at smaller colonies (Raveling 1989).

The Red-breasted Goose of the Siberian Arctic is unusual in that it habitually nests in colonies centred around the nests of predatory birds, particularly Peregrine Falcon. The predator is believed to provide the geese with additional security from ground predators such as foxes (Quinn *et al.* 1995, Quinn and Kokorev 2000, and see later, *Nest location*).

Black Swans may nest solitarily and defend a large feeding territory, but colonial nesting is also frequent, even in areas of superabundant nesting habitat. Onset of breeding is variable and, in many areas, depends on the timing and availability of floods. When floods occur, food for the vegetarian young is unlikely to be limited, and there are presumably no disadvantages and some advantages such as reduced predation, to colonial nesting (Braithwaite 1982). However, where food is patchily distributed and broods from colonial nests are forced to feed together in a small area, brood amalgamation is frequent, whereas in richer, more homogenous habitats, colonial nesters usually rear only their own broods (Braithwaite 1982).

Mute Swans are normally extremely territorial, and may kill intruding swans; however, in exceptional circumstances they nest colonially where there is superabundant food and limited and concentrated nest sites (Perrins and Ogilvie 1981, Bacon and Andersen-Harild 1989). In Denmark, cessation of hunting in 1926 caused a large increase in the national population. Colonial breeding was previously unknown, but its incidence increased as the population rose, from only 1–2% of all pairs in 1943, to 38% (1500 pairs) nesting in over 25 colonies in 1978 (Bacon and Andersen-Harild 1989). A comparison of the breeding success of territorial and colonial pairs revealed that success was always much lower in colonies, even for Mute Swans that had themselves been raised in a territory. The main reason for the difference was lower hatching success due to higher levels of clutch desertion and egg breakage following fights over nesting space in colonies. Since production from the colonies was well below that necessary to replace dead breeders, colonial breeding *per se* was not a viable reproductive strategy. Individual Mute Swans presumably breed in colonies because prime habitats are full, and breeding in suboptimal conditions is better than not reproducing at all, particularly if the prospects of obtaining a territory are low (Bacon and Andersen-Harild 1989).

Evolution of coloniality

The strategy of colonial nesting has evolved in wildfowl largely in situations where food is patchily distributed in space or time, for example in Magpie Geese, or where food is superabundant but nesting sites are localized and concentrated, as with Mute Swans. Benefits of colonial nesting, as opposed to defending small territories around dispersed nests, may be linked to predation and feeding.

Anti-predation benefits

Colonial nesting may lead to more rapid detection of predators—the 'many eyes effect' (Pulliam 1973)—as well as increasing the number of adults present to mob and deter them. Smaller geese are more likely to benefit from coloniality than larger species, since they are at greater risk from predation (Anderson and Titman 1992). There is also likely to be a swamping effect of prey density on predators in colonies, especially when breeding is synchronized. Position in the colony also alters the risk of predation, individuals at the centre being less vulnerable than those at the edge (Newton and Campbell 1975).

Feeding benefits

Colonial nesting in arctic-nesting geese may provide a feeding advantage, since grazing and defecation enhance plant productivity and maintain the quality of tundra vegetation (Harwood 1977). However, although this may be true in certain cases, in others, where goose populations are expanding through decreased mortality, density-dependent effects may operate. The habitat at some Canadian colonies of Blue Snow Geese, for example, has been overexploited by the geese as density has increased, with consequent food-related decline in breeding success (Cooke *et al.* 1995). Similarly, overgrazing of brood-rearing areas in expanding colonies of Greater Snow Geese in Québec have led to reduced size and condition of goslings, and to a decline in their survival on autumn migration (Reed and Plante 1997). Amendments to the Migratory Bird Treaty should increase the harvest of Snow Geese in order to alleviate these problems at the breeding colonies (see page 302).

Costs of coloniality must presumably outweigh the benefits, although the matter has not been studied in detail. Likely costs of colonial nesting identified for Blue Snow Geese include increased competition for resources such as food, breeding sites, nest materials, mates and matings (Mineau and Cooke 1979b). There is also an increased risk of the transmission of disease and ectoparasites.

The nest
Nest types

In comparison to other groups of birds, wildfowl nests are relatively simple structures, often consisting of little more than a depression in the ground or a cavity lined with a variable amount of down from the female's breast (see later, *Incubation*). Material is not carried to the site, but passed backwards, a beakful at a time. Vegetation may be bent or moulded *in situ* by a bird nesting in vegetation, but additional vegetation is rarely added in large amounts, except where both sexes build. This happens in the screamers, Magpie Goose, whistling-ducks, White-backed Duck, Cape Barren Goose and Freckled Duck. The swans, in particular, build very large structures from vegetation obtained close to the nest, both parents helping to provide material. Some species, such as Egyptian and Spur-winged Geese, may use an old nest of a heron *Ardea* or egret *Egretta*, stifftails often adopt deserted coot nests, whilst others, such as Redhead and Canvasback, may simply lay their eggs in the nests of conspecifics

5.1 Black-headed Duck female beside the nest of a Rosybill in which she may lay an egg parasitically.

(see later, *Brood parasitism*). In the extreme case of the Black-headed Duck, an obligate parasite, no nests are built and all females lay their eggs in the nests of other waterbirds (Figure 5.1).

Swan nests typically consist of supporting substrate, mounded material and a nest bowl. They are usually constructed of emergent or submergent aquatic vegetation and rhizomes, although swans nesting on hummocks will use grasses, sedges, tundra heath vegetation and even occasional branches of dwarf bushes such as willow and birch. Nests may be used in consecutive seasons by the same pair (e.g. Rees *et al.* 1997c, Syroechkovskiy *et al.* 2002). Since vegetation may be added every year, a large size can be achieved. Trumpeter Swan nest mounds, for example, are typically 0.4 m high, but may reach 0.91 m (Hansen *et al.* 1971) while, exceptionally, Whooper Swan mounds in the lowlands of northern Iceland may exceed 1 m in height (Einarsson 1996). Annual removal of vegetation around the nest can lead to the creation of a moat around the nest (Hansen *et al.* 1971). Tall nests are beneficial to swans for several reasons. First, they are an insurance against rising water. This is particularly important at low-lying sites in the Arctic and sub-Arctic, where rapid snow-melt during the spring thaw may cause widespread flooding. Even so, severe flooding may still result in the destruction of the majority of clutches of Whooper Swans nesting in some Icelandic valleys (Einarsson 1996, see later, *Extrinsic factors*). Second, tall nests may

become free of snow earlier than lower ones, since snow is blown more readily from the exposed top (Haa-penen *et al.* 1977). This assists early nesting by Bewick's Swans and brings consequent reproductive advantages (see later, *Nest location*).

In most wildfowl, the overriding characteristic of the nest site is safety from predators, since the egg stage is so vulnerable (Owen and Black 1990). However, being relatively large, swans are less susceptible to ground predators, such as foxes, than smaller geese and ducks. Swans can afford to have more conspicuous nests, so their detection of conspecifics and approaching predators may benefit from the elevation of tall nests. Although Bewick's Swan nests are highly conspicuous when an adult is present, they may be difficult to locate when the parent is absent because, being made from local vegetation, they readily blend into the adjacent tundra. A sitting Bewick's Swan can defend the nest and its contents from Arctic Foxes, but not against larger predators such as bears or humans. The approach of a large predator, however, can be observed at distances of over 1 km, and the bird may respond by sliding off the nest to hide behind or in adjacent vegetation. This behaviour, coupled with the cryptic coloration of the nest, may serve to reduce loss of eggs and cygnets to large predators.

As already mentioned, in swans both sexes help with nest construction; male Trumpeter Swans provide the bulk of construction (Henson and Cooper 1992) and male Coscoroba Swans almost all. Bewick's Swan pairs demonstrate a high level of cooperation in nest building, which continues during the laying and incubation period. One bird, usually the male, stands within 2 m of the nest and, facing outwards, pulls up vegetation with its bill, turns and places it closer to the nest. The second bird, usually the female, sits or stands on the nest and reaches down with its bill to pick up the vegetation and add it to the mound. The nest bowl is constructed by the female pressing down with her feet, bill and breast (Rees *et al.* 1997c). Bewick's and Whistling Swans may add additional material after the cygnets have hatched (Monda *et al.* 1994). This may aid brooding on cold 'nights' in the first few days, when the parents will bring the family to the nest. Subsequent addition of material also serves to enhance success in subsequent years by increasing the size of the mound (Monda *et al.* 1994). The mounds survive the erosive forces of ice, spring runoff and wind from one year to the next, and are stabilized by the formation of permafrost cores, as well as by vegetation growth, which is added to by the droppings of the swans and other species using the structure as a vantage point outside the breeding season (Monda *et al.* 1994).

The nests of Magpie Geese are unusual in that they are constructed in two phases: a flat 'stage' built by bending aquatic vegetation *in situ*, followed by construction of the nest on the stage (Davies 1962). This complex floating structure allows nesting in seasonally flooded and vegetated swamps of unpredictable depth, thereby reducing vulnerability to terrestrial predators.

Nest location

The location of wildfowl nests is dominated by the importance of safety from predation. Only the larger swans make little attempt to hide the nest, but even these frequently nest on islands, beaver lodges or floating mats of vegetation, out of reach of land predators (Hansen *et al.* 1971). Where swans nest on shores, they use hummocks or raised ridges that afford good visibility and become free of snow early. On the Russkiy Zavorot peninsula in Russia, experienced pairs of Bewick's Swans were able to produce larger clutches than pairs that had not previously nested at the site, by selecting ridges and laying earlier (Shchadilov *et al.* 1998, see later *The importance of lay date*). The higher reproductive success of experienced pairs was most pronounced in years with an average or late spring thaw. Moreover, there was no evidence that pairs nesting on ridges lost fewer eggs or cygnets than pairs nesting at less conspicuous lower-lying sites, possibly because the pairs nesting on the ridges were more experienced.

Kear (1970b) reviewed the nest sites of wildfowl and divided them into five main types: over water, on the ground, in burrows, in tree holes, and parasitic. The majority nest on the ground and rely on camouflage to reduce risk of predation. Nests are frequently hidden in tufts of reeds or other vegetation, and the plumage coloration of the sitting female is typically cryptic. Dabbling ducks often nest within 100 m of water (Bellrose 1980). In the prairie pothole region of the US, dabbling duck nests were located closer to waterbodies than random sites, but successful nests were located farther from water than nests destroyed by predators (Livezey 1981). There appears to be a trade-off between the benefits of nesting close to water (e.g. better ducking survival through shorter journeys to rearing habitats) and the increased likelihood of nest detection and destruction by predators. One way of nesting close to water and reducing the risk of land predation is to nest on islands. Canada Geese breeding in Ontario, for example, frequently nested on islands (87% of nests), and preferentially chose habitats containing lakes with several islands (Raveling and Lumsden 1977). Large islands are frequently used by several ground-nesting species, and may support high densities of nests. Classically, a 42 ha island on Loch Leven, in the Scottish Lowlands, supports a total of over 1000 nests of six duck species (Newton and Campbell 1975).

Ground nesters also favour cliff sites, particularly some of the smaller *Branta* geese, such as Barnacles, that are unable to defend their nests against foxes. Ledges selected for breeding may be out of reach of foxes, and goslings leaving to reach the relative safety of water are capable of surviving considerable leaps and drops down cliff faces. Where cliffs are absent, small geese nesting on open tundra, such as Ross's Goose, frequently place their nests against rocks or patches of birch (Ryder 1972), which may render them more easily defendable (Owen and Black 1990).

As indicated earlier, the Red-breasted Goose is unusual in that its nests are almost invariably associated with those of predatory birds. The preferred bird of prey is the Peregrine Falcon, although colonies may also develop around the nests of Rough-legged Buzzard *Buteo lagopus* and Snowy Owl *Nyctea scandiaca*, or in association with gull and tern *Sterna* colonies. Nest success was higher in colonies associated with Peregrines than with other species (Quinn *et al.* 1995, Quinn and Kokorev 2000). In a year when lemmings *Lemmus* and *Dicrostonyx* were scarce, Snowy Owls and Rough-legged Buzzards were absent from an area of

Siberian tundra on the Taymyr Peninsula. In the following year, when there were more lemmings, owls and buzzards bred successfully and Red-breasted Geese utilized these new breeding sites (Quinn *et al.* 1996a). The geese are believed to benefit from the defensive behaviour of the birds of prey that chase predators, such as Arctic Foxes, away from their own nest and those of the adjacent geese. The size of the goose colony may be small (*c* 4.4 nests per colony, Quinn *et al.* 1995) and limited by the size of the area that the bird of prey defends. In return, the bird of prey may benefit from the vigilance of the nesting geese, allowing a more rapid response to the approach of large mammals.

Although Red-breasted Goose is the only species to nest habitually with birds of prey (Figure 5.2), others do so from time to time. Long-tailed Ducks, for example, are not infrequently found nesting close to Red-breasted Goose colonies (Quinn *et al.* 1995), while King Eiders sometimes nest in association with Long-tailed Skuas *Stercorarius longicaudus* (Blomqvist and Elander 1988) and Steller's Eider with breeding Pomarine Skuas *S. pomarinus*. Dark-bellied Brent Geese and King Eiders may also nest close to Snowy Owls in lemming years on the Taymyr Peninsula (Summers *et al.* 1994). It has been suggested that Brant on Wrangel Island breed only in association with Snowy Owls, such is the predation pressure from foxes (Litvin *et al.* 1985). Wildfowl may also nest close to colonies of gulls and terns (the

5.2 Incubating Red-breasted Goose with Peregrine Falcon behind.

Swan Goose is an example), and may benefit from the early warnings and mobbing behaviour that help to keep other predators at bay (Vermeer 1968), as recorded of grebes *Podiceps* nesting with gulls in Argentina (Burger 1984). At Loch Leven in Scotland, duck nests within a gull colony were more successful than those outside; and rates of predation inside the gull colony were lower on nests towards the centre of the colony (Newton and Campbell 1975). Ducklings, however, may be taken by gulls after nest exodus (Dwernychuk and Boag 1972). Predation pressure may be so great that ducks take advantage of artificial protection, a classic example being the large colony of Common Eiders that became established around a group of tethered husky dogs in Greenland (Meltofte 1978).

Tree-hole nest sites are widely used by some whistling-ducks, surface-feeding ducks, mergansers and goldeneyes. The American Wood Duck, for example, nests almost exclusively in trees. The amount of forest and openness of the canopy may be the immediate factors in attracting Wood Ducks, but cavity selection and reproductive success seem to be influenced by the availability of suitable enclosed cavities and brood-rearing habitat (Kaminski and Weller 1992). Selection of cavities by Wood Ducks in Indiana was influenced by a vertical entry hole, cavity volume, size of the entrance and the diameter of the tree bole at the entrance (Robb and Bookhout 1995). These features are consistent with those of Pileated Woodpecker *Dryocopus pileatus* nest holes, and it has been suggested that the Wood Duck and the woodpecker co-evolved, since their ranges overlap (Bellrose and Holm 1994). In addition, nest success of Wood Ducks may increase with distance from a waterbody as a result of reduced nest detection and destruction by Raccoon *Procyon lotor* (Robb and Bookhout 1995). Loss of mature trees through commercial logging reduced nest availability in the nineteenth century, and the species suffered. Fortunately, however, Wood Ducks take readily to boxes and the provision of artificial nests has helped recovery, with higher levels of nest success in inconspicuous, purpose-built, predator-proof boxes than in natural cavities (Bellrose 1980). The endangered White-winged Duck of tropical wet forests of southeast Asia is another cavity nester; its continued presence in largely cleared areas of southeast Sumatra has been attributed to its habit of nesting in cavities in rengas *Gluta* trees that are frequently left unfelled in former swamp forest on account of a poisonous irritant in the sap (Green 1992a) that renders the timber unworkable.

Natural availability of suitable nest sites may restrict the breeding distribution of other ducks. African Comb Duck, for example, almost always use the abandoned nests of other species, particularly the large stick nests of Hammerkop *Scopus umbretta* with which it is closely associated (Pitman 1965). Smew typically nest in the abandoned nest holes of Black Woodpecker *Dryocopus martius* and the distribution of the two species is closely matched (Owen 1977), while a similar association is found in North America between the range of Bufflehead and Northern Flicker *Colaptes auratus*. The distribution of woodpeckers and their creation of large cavities would appear to have strongly influenced the distribution of several northern hole-nesting temperate ducks including, probably, American Wood Duck, Mandarin, Scaly-sided Merganser, Goosander, Common Goldeneye, Barrow's Goldeneye in North America, Smew, Bufflehead and Hooded Merganser. The need for a hole in a mature tree has affected the distribution and/or decline of numerous other semi-tropical and tropical ducks, and the subject of nest-site provision as a management tool is discussed further in Chapter 8.

Burrow nesting has been adopted by the shelducks. The Paradise Shelduck of New Zealand traditionally nested in rock crevices, since there were originally no mammals to make burrows. In Britain, Common Shelducks frequently use European Rabbit *Oryctolagus cuniculus* burrows, although the extent of burrow nesting varies considerably. On the Ythan Estuary near Aberdeen, the vast majority of pairs nest in burrows at the Sands of Forvie, where Rabbits are numerous (Patterson *et al.* 1974). On the other hand, on the Isle of Sheppey in Kent, burrows accounted for only 27% of 100 nests located in the early 1960s (Hori 1964). Nests were also found in hollow trees (29%), haystacks (28%), under buildings/objects (23%) and in the open (3%). At Sheppey, loss of Elm *Ulmus procera* trees to Dutch Elm disease, and

reduction in the availability of haystacks through agricultural intensification, resulted in reduced nesting opportunities and major changes in habit. This nest-site constraint led to a predominance of multiple-nesting by Common Shelducks at 'communal' sites in barns, although breeding success was reduced (Hori 1987).

The majority of tropical wildfowl, including the screamers, Magpie Goose, White-backed Duck, Freckled Duck, stifftails, some whistling-ducks and pochards, nest over water. This may represent the primitive condition for the group (Kear 1970b). Freckled Ducks, for example, construct a well-formed cup-shaped platform of finely woven twigs, which is usually placed within shelter but is always located over water (Frith 1965, Braithwaite 1976b); easy access, allowing a direct approach from the water, appears to be a key requirement, and a ramp to the nest is often conspicuous (Marchant and Higgins 1990). Direct access to water presumably reduces vulnerability to terrestrial mammalian predators (Krapu *et al.* 1979). Among Northern Mallard nesting in Manitoba, for example, estimates of nest success were much higher for nests over water (44%) than 'upland' or dry-land nests (12%), despite the increased risk of brood parasitism by other ducks, such as Redheads, at over-water nests (Arnold *et al.* 1993); this was presumed to be due to greater security from terrestrial predators.

The egg and the clutch
Variation in egg size

In common with other precocial birds, wildfowl eggs are large relative to the size of the female and, therefore, benefit from a relatively large reserve of food when newly hatched (Lack 1967). Egg size is dictated to some extent by the size of the bird. The largest eggs, for example, are produced by the largest wildfowl; the Mute Swan's eggs weigh on average 345 g, while African Pygmy-geese produce eggs weighing 27 g. However, there is considerable variation in egg size as a proportion of female body weight. In general, the smaller species tend to lay proportionately heavier eggs, but there are exceptions; for example, although female Barnacle Geese weigh 1.5 times as much as female Canvasbacks, both lay eggs that are on average around 6% of body weight. The stifftails produce extremely large eggs (up to 20% of female body weight) that are particularly resistant to chilling, while the large reserves of fat insulate the newly hatched young in their wholly aquatic environment (Lack 1967, Pelayo and Clark 2002, 2003). A female Ruddy Duck can lay the equivalent of her own weight in a single clutch, and her diving young are self-reliant from an early age; this independence may allow stifftail ducklings that hatch from eggs dumped in the nests of others to survive (Rees and Hillgarth 1984).

Evolution of egg size

Egg size may play a role in population dynamics in that larger eggs produce larger offspring at hatching (e.g. Batt and Prince 1979) which may be more likely to survive, particularly if food resources are limited (Ankney 1980). In some species, egg size increases with the age of the female, for example in Canada Goose (Cooper 1978), Nene (Kear 1973a) and Blue Snow Goose (Cooke *et al.* 1995), although not in others such as Northern Mallard (Batt and Prince 1978) and American Wood Duck (Hepp *et al.* 1987). The condition of the laying female is presumed to affect egg size (Ryder 1970). This was not the case in captive Northern Mallards in one study (Batt and Prince 1978), although, in a separate study, birds on a high-protein diet laid heavier eggs than those on a reduced protein diet (Krapu 1979). Among Blue Snow Geese, variation in egg weight within individuals was small, but mean egg weight varied significantly between years due to environmental effects that acted on the population as a whole. Heritability of egg size was high (0.53), so differences in mean egg mass among individuals resulted, in part, from genetic differences (Cooke *et al.* 1995).

The mass of goose eggs as a proportion of female body mass increases with latitude, and with the severity of the weather when the young hatch, so that large eggs give the young a better chance of surviving poor conditions (Owen 1980). Goslings from larger eggs also develop faster and should, therefore, be able to leave the breeding grounds earlier. This may be particularly important in years when the rearing period is shortened by a late spring and/or an early onset of winter. In swans, proportionate egg size is greatest for the Bewick's Swan, which breeds mostly north of the Arctic Circle, and is lowest for the Mute Swan, which nests in more temperate climes. As with arctic-nesting geese, the female Bewick's Swan invests more in each egg than does the female of a related species breeding at lower latitudes. Smaller eggs may be more appropriate in temperate regions, with moderate climate and predictable food supplies for the young, than in northern areas with harsher weather and more erratic food supplies (Lack 1968b). However, egg mass can vary within the species. Ankney and Bisset (1976) showed that in Blue Snow Geese the lightest eggs weighed only 60% as much as the heaviest, while the heaviest clutches of a particular size weighed more than the lightest clutches of the next largest size. This suggested that the nutrient commitment to a particular clutch size was not the same for all females. There is a heritable component in egg mass (Cooke *et al.* 1995), and heavier eggs may enhance survival of the young under energetically poor conditions (such as in seasons with a late spring), but may be disadvantageous in more average seasons because the extra nutrients could have been used for incubation (sitting females may desert the nest or starve to death if their reserves are depleted). Thus, mean egg mass may be adapted to the average environmental conditions at hatch, but a wide range of egg mass genotypes survive because of the great annual variation in environmental conditions (Ankney and Bisset 1976). However, Cooke *et al.* (1995), in a long-term study of Blue Snow Geese, could find no fitness differences among birds of different mean egg mass, suggesting that selection is currently not operating, or is operating only weakly.

Egg size versus clutch size

Factors controlling egg size seem likely to be linked to clutch size, since together they reflect annual reproductive effort, which in turn will be governed to a large extent by the amount of food available to the female (see Blums *et al.* 2002). Lack (1974) demonstrated an inverse relation between egg size and clutch size in an interspecific comparison of wildfowl. However, his findings were reviewed by Rohwer (1988), who showed only a weak relationship between relative egg size and relative clutch size, and that any correlation was largely driven by a few island species that were not typical. Separate tribal analyses revealed an inverse relationship between egg size and clutch size in only two of the eight wildfowl tribes.

Similarly, intraspecific comparisons (e.g. Rohwer 1988, Cooke *et al.* 1995) have failed to show a consistent pattern of decreasing clutch size with increasing egg size, even when genetic considerations were taken into account (Lessells *et al.* 1989). Indeed, Rohwer and Eisenhauer (1989) found a positive relation between clutch size and egg mass of Brent Geese. Individual species may have evolved to lay large numbers of relatively small eggs or smaller numbers of larger eggs. Wildfowl that are endemic to oceanic islands, such as Laysan Teal, tend to be small and to lay small clutches of eggs that are large relative to body size (Lack 1970, Rohwer 1988). Released Northern Mallards, however, maintain their large clutches and typical egg size on oceanic islands, so changes in relative egg size and clutch size of isolated species are not simple responses to the island environment (Rohwer 1992).

Evolution of clutch size

Clutches may consist of just two or three eggs for Musk Duck (Frith 1982) or a dozen in American Wood Duck and Black-bellied Whistling-duck (McCamant and Bolen 1979, Owen and Black 1990). Although size may vary considerably within a species (e.g. Ankney and Bisset 1976, Raveling and Lumsden 1977, Rohwer and Eisenhauer 1989), there is consistency in mean size within different taxonomic groups and in differing environmental conditions. Most geese and swans, for example, lay clutches of four or five eggs, the stifftails four to six, while the pochards generally produce nine or ten. In others, such as the shelducks, steamer-ducks and mergansers, clutch size within the group is more variable and presumably reflects differences in body size, ecology, and geography.

It has been demonstrated in short-lived passerines that females lay the size of clutch that maximizes their recruitment potential—the 'individual optimization' hypothesis (Perrins and Moss 1975, Pettifor *et al.* 1988). In general, annual breeding effort should be optimized to allow maximum production of young over an individual's lifetime. Clutch size in any year may, therefore, be less than the maximum in order not to reduce the opportunity for future breeding (Williams 1966). Experimental manipulation of clutch size has shown that incubation constraints do not impose an upper limit on brood size when feeding conditions are favourable (Rohwer 1985, Jones 1987). However, substantial weight loss during incubation by Common Goldeneyes, resulting from poor feeding, caused females to desert clutches, probably because they could not maintain a temperature sufficient to hatch their eggs without putting themselves at risk (Mallory and Weatherhead 1994).

A number of hypotheses have been suggested to explain observed variation in clutch size within species (see Klomp 1970, Johnsgard 1973, Rohwer 1992).

Proximate factors

The first theory predicts that clutch size would be the largest number of eggs that can be covered efficiently during incubation. This seems unlikely, in view of the annual variation in clutch size within and between species. The theory predicts that clutches artificially enlarged should suffer reduced success. However, in a large sample of manipulated Blue-winged Teal nests, there were no significant declines in nest success, in the proportion of eggs hatching in successful nests, nor longer incubation periods in enlarged clutches (Rohwer 1985); while in parasitized nests, hatchability does not decline until clutch size is well above normal (Sayler 1992).

The second theory suggests that clutch size is limited by predation pressure. The female of most nidifugous birds starts incubating when the last egg has been laid. As a consequence, the larger the clutch, the longer it is left unguarded and, hence, more prone to predation. However, it seems unlikely that clutch size could have evolved this way, since the rate of predation should be improbably high, even for large clutches (Klomp 1970, Ricklefs 1979).

A third theory is that clutch size is constrained by egg production, and predicts that wildfowl should not be able to extend laying, that there should be an inverse relationship between egg mass and clutch size (see earlier, *Egg size versus clutch size*), and that females should lose weight during laying (Ryder 1970).

Ultimate factors

A fourth theory predicts that brood size ultimately limits clutch size, and that large broods produce fewer surviving offspring than broods of normal size, since they suffer higher mortality rates. Predators may be more attracted to large broods than smaller ones, as demonstrated in Common Shelducks (Williams 1974). As clutch size increases, there will be higher mortality on average, as shown in Blue Snow Geese (Cooch 1961). Other studies, however, have provided conflicting evidence. Among Blue Snow Geese, partial brood loss increased with brood size, but total loss was more frequent among small broods, such that recruitment of young was independent of clutch size (Cooke *et al.* 1995). Survival to flying was independent of brood size in experimental studies of Canada Goose (Lessells 1986) and Blue-winged Teal (Rohwer 1985), while ducklings from large crèches of Common Eider and Velvet Scoter had higher survival rates than those from small broods (Munro and Bedard 1977a, Brown and Brown 1981). These last results may reflect the quality of the attendant female; those attending crèches may be more aggressive and socially dominant (Munro and Bedard 1977b), particularly as females in poor body condition may abandon their young soon after hatching (Erikstad *et al.* 1993). The probability of survival for adult female Emperor Geese increased with larger clutches, suggesting that brood size may also be related positively to survival of the female parent (Petersen 1992a). Rohwer (1992) reviewed the available evidence and suggested that the survival of young is largely independent of brood size, such that large broods tend to outproduce small ones.

Brood size could also constrain clutch size by increasing parental investment to such an extent that the survival or fitness of the adults was lowered (Charnov and Krebs 1974). Parental investment has been shown to increase significantly among larger broods of Bar-headed Geese, Blue Snow Geese and Bewick's Swans (Schindler and Lamprecht 1987, Williams *et al.* 1994, Bowler 1996) so that parental feeding time was reduced. However, dominance rank tends to increase with family size. High rank allows access to the best resources which, in the case of the Bewick's Swan, enabled adult females from the larger families to obtain the highest abdominal profile scores prior to spring migration (Bowler 1994). A reduction in parental survival with increasing brood size, therefore, seems unlikely and, in Blue Snow Geese, the effect of increasing brood size on parental behaviour was not associated with any negative effects on residual parental reproductive effort or fitness (Williams *et al.* 1994).

The number of eggs is limited ultimately by the number of maturing oocytes in the ovary which, in turn, may be determined by the amount of food that the female is able to obtain for yolk and albumen deposition (see Gammonley 1995b). Females examined late in laying do not show a full series of developing follicles in the ovary; instead the last follicle to be ovulated is much larger than any other remaining follicles (e.g. Ankney and MacInnes 1978). Clutch size must, therefore, be determined before and during the egg-laying stage, hence manipulation of clutch size should not alter the number of eggs laid. Among a number of prairie-nesting ducks it has been demonstrated that the addition of eggs during laying does not decrease the number of eggs laid, while egg removal does not increase clutch size (Rohwer 1984). Experimental manipulation of a clutch of Blue-winged Teal showed that neither incubation nor brood rearing constrain clutch size, and that the adaptive limit of size was set by processes occurring in the egg production stage (Rohwer 1985). Conversely, Andersson and Eriksson (1982) found that the addition of large numbers of eggs to the hole nests of Common Goldeneye considerably reduced the number of eggs laid; however, the influence of parasitic females on final clutch sizes was not determined and may have accounted for the unexpected results (Rohwer 1992), while other constraints such as cavity size may also have been operating. Extended laying by wild ducks that have switched to a second nest site and continued laying without interruption has also been reported (e.g. Rohwer 1986). Duncan (1986a) suggested that nest loss restarts a 'physiological egg counter' that enables the female to lay a full clutch in a new nest. If this is true, it casts doubt on the egg production hypothesis (Rohwer 1992). Furthermore, since food availability generally increases as the breeding season advances, the finding of sufficient nutrients to continue laying should be less problematic.

The ultimate constraint, particularly for arctic nesters, is the brevity of the polar summer. Although laying intervals between eggs may decline with increasing clutch size (Watson *et al.* 1993), larger clutches take longer to lay, and since incubation generally does not start until the clutch is complete, time available for the young to hatch and fledge successfully is reduced still further. Probably as a consequence, clutch size declines with lay date in many temperate and arctic-nesting species (see later, *The importance of lay date*).

If clutch size depends directly on the quantity of food available before and during laying, then food shortage should have immediate suppressive effects. There is some circumstantial evidence to support this for Brent Goose and Bewick's Swan, where breeding success is correlated with the spring condition of the female (Ebbinge *et al.* 1982, Ebbinge and Spaans 1995, Bowler 1996). Alternatively, the female could postpone breeding until she had obtained enough resources to produce a 'normal' clutch. This would not be adaptive, however, since lay date is a major determinant of breeding success, and clutch size tends to decrease as lay date increases beyond the median (see later). The diet of breeding females may differ from that of males and nonbreeders, and food quality is also likely to be relevant. Breeding female American Wood Ducks, for example, take a higher proportion of invertebrate prey (59%) than males (34%) throughout the breeding season (Drobney and Fredrickson 1979). Lipid reserve levels may limit the clutch size of Northern Pintails in Alaska by affecting the time of nesting (Esler and Grand 1994). In another study, female protein reserves fell in relation to the number of eggs laid, whereas lipid reserves did not, suggesting that protein may limit clutch size

(Mann and Sedinger 1993). This is not the case in species nesting at lower latitudes. Female Northern Mallard nesting in areas of poor habitat quality in Saskatchewan, Canada, laid similar-sized clutches to those in areas of richer habitat, despite using much less stored fat, suggesting that the amount of stored body fat was not limiting clutch size (Young 1993).

The constraint of egg production on clutch size should lead females to be dependent upon stored reserves for laying. Most laying wildfowl use some reserves (Alisauskas and Ankney 1992), although the extent of dependence varies. In swans, clutch size varies with the distance travelled on migration. The British Mute Swan, which does not undertake long migrations, has the largest clutches (mean = 6 eggs, range 1–12, Birkhead and Perrins 1986, Walter *et al.* 1991), while Bewick's Swan, which travels *c* 4500 km between winter and breeding grounds, has the smallest clutch (mean = 4 eggs, range 1–6, Rees *et al.* 1996). Arctic-nesting geese and swans may begin nesting when little or no food is available and, hence, depend heavily upon stored reserves for laying. The amount of fat that they can store at the end of winter will influence their ability to cope with migration, and the reserves with which they arrive on the breeding ground. This will be modified by the predictability of food on arrival at the breeding grounds. Dusky Canada Geese, for example, nesting at low arctic latitudes (*c* 60°N) can feed at all stages of the breeding cycle; birds on the breeding ground took in all the food needed for their daily energy and pre-laying requirements, and 24% of their requirement during incubation (Bromley and Jarvis 1993).

Female Blue Snow Geese, arriving on the breeding ground with larger reserves, lay more eggs and, irrespective of their original reserves, retained a similar amount for incubation (Ankney and MacInnes 1978). Moreover, peak yearly mass occurred just prior to nest initiation, suggesting that females are unable to carry more reserves on migration. This is not the case, however, for some small migratory ducks. Ruddy Ducks, for example, migrate in North America between southern and coastal wintering sites and breeding areas further north and west. They are small, with high-speed wing-beats that render the accumulation of nutrient reserves for breeding unfavourable in winter and at their spring staging sites (Tome 1984), unlike the larger Northern Mallard, which does accumulate reserves at these times (Krapu 1981). Instead, female Ruddy Ducks need to accumulate food for nesting on the breeding grounds. Only around one-fifth of their basal metabolic requirement is supplied by lipid metabolism (i.e. by using stored fats) during incubation, and they depend almost exclusively upon dietary intake to meet the energy and nutrient demands of reproduction (Tome 1984). However, Alisauskas and Ankney (1994b) found that breeding female Ruddy Ducks had more fat and protein reserves than nonbreeding females at the start of the nesting season, and suggested that the onset of breeding was still related to a nutrient threshold. Nutrients stored in body tissues were found to be important sources of energy needed for clutch formation, whilst clutch size was directly related to mineral resources. Endogenous protein (i.e. protein stored in the body) is not used during laying by Northern Mallard and Cinnamon Teal (Young 1993, Gammonley 1995b), although small, and possibly important, amounts are used by more northerly breeding ducks such as Northern Pintail (Mann and Sedinger 1993, Esler and Grand 1994).

Temperate nesting species use stored reserves for laying and lose mass during the laying period (e.g. Harris 1970). However, Northern Mallard are capable of re-laying with almost no carcass fat (Krapu 1981), possibly because food becomes more abundant later in the season, although a small but important dependence on stored reserves may still exist. A superabundance of food in captive situations would also be expected to allow birds to increase their clutch size by removing the constraint of food availability upon the nutrient stores of pre-breeding females. However, in general, captive wildfowl with unlimited access to high-protein food show similar weight gains to those in the wild and, generally, lay clutches that are at most one egg larger than wild birds (Batt and Prince 1979, Rohwer 1984, Duncan 1986a). This suggests that food availability has a limited proximate effect on clutch size, although nutrient availability may still be an important ultimate determinant (Rohwer 1992, but see Alisauskas and Ankney 1994b).

A final theory concerning clutch size is the 'egg viability' hypothesis (Arnold et al. 1987), which questions why some wildfowl begin incubation before the clutch is complete. The theory suggests that the chance of successful incubation decreases with the length of time that an egg is left unincubated, and that, at some stage, the decreased viability of the first laid eggs will counterbalance the benefit of laying additional eggs. This seems unlikely, since the decline in viability with pre-incubation delay is not rapid. However, predation risks also increase with delayed incubation (see earlier, *Proximate factors*) and the combination of these two factors might be significant. Many ducks spend time at the nest during the laying period, perhaps to keep the eggs warm (Rohwer 1992). The extent of this sitting, together with the extent to which the development rate of eggs can be modified, will affect the synchrony of hatching. There are limits to which developmental inequalities can be overcome (Davies and Cooke 1983b), such that hatching may be prolonged over several hours or even days with an attendant increase of predation. Hence, clutch size may be constrained by a combination of predation risk, declining viability and the limitations of hatching synchrony (Rohwer 1992), which together can account for most of the selection pressure determining clutch size in prairie-nesting ducks (Arnold et al. 1987).

In summary, it seems likely that nutritional requirements for egg production (modified by egg size), as originally proposed by Lack (1967), are indeed an important constraint on clutch size, but that other factors including predation, egg viability and offspring survival also have indirect effects.

Incubation

Incubation is the process of providing heat to an egg after it has been laid in order to encourage embryonic development. Incubation possibly evolved in reptiles; in birds, it relates to the physical requirements of embryos, parental metabolic requirements and predation risks for eggs and parents (Afton and Paulus 1992). Reproductive investment in any year should be optimized to allow maximum production of young over an individual's lifetime (Cody 1966).

Incubation strategies, therefore, should compensate for variable environmental conditions, allow parents to support their body metabolism, and minimize the probability of predation so that the requirements of embryos are in balance with those of the parents (e.g. Jones 1987).

Incubation does not begin upon termination of laying as previously thought (Kear 1970b, Johnsgard 1975) but, instead, begins gradually during the laying period. Females spend increasing amounts of time on nests as laying progresses (Caldwell and Cornwell 1975, Cooper 1978, Wilson and Verbeek 1995, Zicus *et al.* 1995), during which eggs are heated above the minimum temperatures required for incubation (*c* 25–27°C). This may help to maintain embryo viability (Arnold *et al.* 1987), but means that embryonic development will vary by several days upon clutch completion (Caldwell and Cornwell 1975, Cooper 1978). However, eggs still hatch relatively synchronously within clutches, indicating that hatching wildfowl embryos synchronize their activities by calling to one another, as do game birds (Vince 1968, Davies and Cooke 1983b).

Some wildfowl nests contain female down feathers which help to insulate and camouflage the eggs, particularly when the parent is absent. Down is plucked directly from the female's breast which, in turn, exposes an area of bare skin, or brood patch, which is in contact with the eggs during incubation. The habit is best developed in geese and in eiders. Screamers, Magpie Goose, White-backed Duck, whistling-ducks, some swans and stifftails, where eggs are particularly large or there is shared incubation, pull little or no down. Thompson and Raveling (1988) measured the rate of heat loss from eggs of three species of arctic-nesting geese in Alaska. Incubating Brant, which use a lot of down, required less nesting material and needed to be less attentive than the Emperor Goose, which uses little down. Cackling Canada Geese, which use intermediate amounts of down, showed intermediate levels of attentiveness during incubation.

Division of labour

Wildfowl have three incubation strategies (Afton and Paulus 1992): it may be shared between the sexes,

performed by the female only, or brood parasitism may occur, in which eggs are incubated by a host.

Screamers, Magpie Goose, whistling-ducks, White-backed Duck and Black Swan share incubation. As already stated, Magpie Goose is unusual in that trios predominate over pairs. Trios normally consist of one male and two females that are often related in a mother–daughter helper system and which both lay in the same nest. All three members of the trio incubate (Frith and Davies 1961b); in captivity, the male did so mostly at night and the females during the day such that the nest was never unattended (Johnsgard 1961a, Kear 1973b). In tropical northern Australia, with day temperatures often above 45°C, care during the day consists more of shading the eggs by standing over them, rather than heating them. Trios allow every member to spend only a third of the day at the nest and they may, therefore, be less likely to desert; at such temperatures, even a short absence could be fatal to developing embryos (Davies and Frith 1964).

In captivity, incubation by the male has been observed in seven of the eight whistling-ducks and in White-backed Duck, however, data from the wild are sparse (Bolen 1973, Afton and Paulus 1992). Division of incubation time between the sexes is variable. Johnsgard (1978) stated that males of captive Fulvous and White-faced Whistling-ducks, and White-backed Duck assumed most incubation duties; however, wild Black-bellied Whistling-duck pairs spent equal amounts of time incubating (see Afton and Paulus 1992, for a review).

The Black Swan is the only swan in which the male has a well-defined brood patch and actively incubates (Braithwaite 1977, Howey *et al.* 1984). The occurrence of male incubation varied with pairbond strength in a captive colony; males with a strong pairbond shared duties, whereas in pairs with a weak bond, the female carried out most of the incubation (Braithwaite 1981). Incubation by male Black Swans and its effect on reproductive success were studied in detail in an introduced breeding colony in Vienna (Brugger and Taborsky 1993). Males spent more time incubating than females, and the incubation effort of the female was found to limit the reproductive output of the pair by lengthening the interval between the end of incubation and the laying of the second clutch. Male incubation thus increased the productivity of the female and the reproductive success of the pair. The ultimate cause for male incubation in Black Swans may lie in a combination of a monogamous mating system and the species' ability to breed whenever environmental conditions are favourable within its natural range (Brugger and Taborsky 1993).

The evolution of male incubation strategy in wildfowl is a puzzle, but it is perhaps an old phylogenetic trait (Kear 1970b). All species are tropical or subtropical and nest in areas with pronounced, but relatively unpredictable, wet and dry seasons that dictate the onset of breeding (e.g. Siegfried 1973d, Briggs and Lawler 1991), and the reasons suggested for male incubation in the Black Swan could apply to other members of the group.

Female-only incubation is the norm and, in most ducks, the female is left by her mate early in the process and provides little active nest defence (Kear 1970b), although some females will perform distraction displays if the nest is threatened (Figure 5.3). Among geese, sheldgeese and some swans, the male guards the territory, while in Bewick's, Whistling and some Trumpeter Swan pairs (Henson and Cooper 1992) the male also sits on the eggs for periods when the female is absent. Nest sitting by northern swans has been regarded as shared incubation (e.g. Johnsgard 1961a, Hawkins 1986b) and, indeed, male Whistling and Bewick's Swans may sit on the nest for almost the whole period when the female is absent (20–40% of the time), thus protecting the

eggs from predators and reducing heat loss (Hawkins 1986b, Rees et al. 1997c). However, the male does not turn the eggs or shuffle the eggs to warm them as often as the female (Evans 1975, Hawkins 1986b) and, in addition, rarely sits during adverse weather or during hatching, when incubation is critical. Male Bewick's and Whistling Swans do not have a brood patch and, instead of actively regulating the temperature of the eggs, their presence on the nest simply reduces the rate of heat loss. Hawkins (1986b) used dummy eggs to check the rate of egg cooling in the Whistling Swan and found that the eggs did lose heat when the male was sitting. However, when neither swan was present, the eggs cooled 2.5 times more quickly than when covered by the male. Shared sitting allows the female to feed more during incubation and to put more nutrients into the eggs than if she sat alone. Shared sitting duties by Bewick's and Whistling Swans may, therefore, explain in part their proportionately large egg size in comparison with other swans, and may be crucial to their success since they migrate large distances to the breeding areas carrying their reserves with them (Owen and Black 1990).

Using an electronic egg, Howey et al. (1984) demonstrated that the nests of incubating Black and Whooper Swans and Greylag and Barnacle Geese had features in common: there was a slow rise in the temperature of the nest cup with the onset of incubation; a temperature gradient in the vertical plane of the cup throughout incubation; a diurnal rhythm in the temperature and humidity of the cup that was caused by the behaviour of the birds rather than by the ambient environment; and the eggs were turned between 0.59 and 0.95 times an hour, rotated mainly around their long axes.

Egg size and latitude of breeding

Incubation (not including the warming which occurs before the full clutch has been laid) lasts from 22 days (Ross's Goose and Eurasian Teal) to 36 days (Mute Swan and Cape Barren Goose), extending to 44 days in the Torrent Duck and around 45 days in the screamers, and depends in part on the size of the egg. Duration of the incubation period tends to increase with egg size, although there are differences

5.3 Female Northern Shoveler pretending to be injured in order to draw attention away from her nest or young.

between taxonomic groups and between species breeding at different latitudes.

Arctic nesters generally have shorter than 'expected' incubation periods on the basis of egg size, while the incubation periods of tropical species are longer. The adaptive significance of shorter incubation periods at higher latitudes relates to the much shorter season and the rapid development rate of the young if they are to migrate successfully when the climate cools at the end of summer. Ross's Goose, for example, has evolved to breed at latitudes of 72°N in northern Canada and has the shortest incubation period of any goose (22 days). This compares with 25–28 days for the Pinkfoot, a lower latitude arctic-nesting goose breeding at 64°N in Iceland, and 31 days for the subtropical Nene nesting at 20°N (Kear and Berger 1980).

The duck genus *Bucephala* has particularly lengthy incubation periods. All three species are hole-nesters, and the relative safety afforded by their cavity nests may reduce the need for the more rapid metabolism that would shorten incubation. There is a correlation between exposed foraging and sheltered nesting, and there may be a strong selection pressure towards safe (hole-nesting) sites for birds with exposed feeding niches (Alerstam and Hogstedt 1981). Ground-nesting ducks are vulnerable to mammalian predators, particularly at night (Sargeant 1972), and this pressure appears to have resulted in some species delaying the onset of nocturnal attentiveness. Northern Mallard, for example, may remain off the nest for up to five nights after clutch completion (Caldwell and Cornwell 1975), while hole-nesters like Common Goldeneye, and large ground nesters such as Trumpeter Swan which are probably less vulnerable to predation, begin staying on their clutches during laying (Afton and Paulus 1992, Cooper 1979). Delayed nocturnal attentiveness may increase the risk of egg predation and of embryo damage by chilling. However, reduced susceptibility to predation for the female must outweigh the possible loss of eggs, since her death would result in the failure of both current and potential clutches; and freshly laid eggs are cold tolerant (Batt and Cornwell 1972).

Attentiveness during incubation varies considerably. The most 'loyal' goose is the Emperor Goose (Thompson and Raveling 1987). The female takes a recess on average only every two days and sits for 99.5% of the time. The high vulnerability of an unoccupied nest to predation seems the most likely explanation for this loyalty, since an attended nest can be defended from most avian and mammalian predators (Thompson and Raveling 1987). In addition, the goose travels relatively short distances (c 600 km) between winter and breeding quarters (Petersen 1992c). Females arrive with large energy reserves that allow them to lay full clutches and retain enough energy for incubation with minimal feeding (Owen and Black 1990). Ducks are generally less attentive than geese and swans. Female Blue-winged Teal spent around 20% of their time off the nest, and this was mostly used to forage, indicating that their food requirements during incubation were high (Miller 1976). Similarly, only around one-fifth of the basal metabolic requirement of incubating Ruddy Ducks is met by using stored fats, and they depend almost exclusively upon dietary intake to meet the energy and nutrient requirements of reproduction (Tome 1984).

The laying and incubation strategy of most geese is to rely on stored reserves, while ducks devote more energy to egg-laying and then feeding during incubation. This difference between the two groups probably reflects differences in predation rates on occupied and unoccupied nests. Goose nests are normally in the open and are more conspicuous than duck nests, which are usually well hidden in vegetation. The presence of a sitting goose will deter aerial predators and, in the case of larger species, mammalian predators as well. Inglis (1977) showed that nesting Pinkfoot females that were least attentive lost most eggs to predators. The presence of a sitting duck, however, will not reduce substantially the vulnerability of the nest to predation. Swans are intermediate, since shared sitting reduces the risk of predation but, in addition, allows the female to feed (see earlier, *Division of labour*). The exception to this is Common Eider, which breeds on islands inaccessible to land predators. The sitting female is well camouflaged, and the species has evolved to behave energetically like a goose, laying relatively few eggs and being extremely attentive to the nest during incubation (almost 100%) whilst relying entirely on stored fat reserves for maintenance (Milne 1976, Owen and Black 1990).

Incubation behaviour also varies according to environmental conditions. Females tend to leave the nest during the mid (warmest) part of the day, when egg cooling would be slower. The length of absences were correlated with ambient temperature for incubating Blue-winged Teal (Miller 1976); however, attentiveness may also increase during periods of high summer temperatures. Female Northern Mallards in southern Canada spent more time on the nest when temperatures exceeded 32°C, their presence shading the eggs and preventing overheating (Caldwell and Cornwell 1975).

Brood parasitism

Brood parasitism occurs when a female deliberately lays her eggs in the nest of another individual that subsequently cares for the brood. In wildfowl, conspecific brood parasitism is relatively frequent and interspecific brood parasitism infrequent, but egg dumping occurs in all groups and in all geographic regions (Geffen and Yom-Tov 2001). The extent to which it occurs during normal breeding activities varies considerably (Sayler 1992), although many species remain poorly studied. It is relatively common in the whistling-ducks, shelducks, some surface-feeding ducks, pochards, seaducks and stifftails, and seems to occur most in crowded or semi-captive conditions (Titman and Lowther 1975). Advances in genetic testing have revealed that brood parasitism in long-term monogamous species, such as Barnacle Goose, is more common than previously thought; for example, 24% of families were involved in intraspecific brood parasitism in one year (Choudhury et al. 1993).

The nests of Black-bellied Whistling-ducks using nestboxes in Texas are heavily parasitized. At least 70% of all clutches were parasitized in one study (McCamant and Bolen 1979), and time-lapse photography in a later case revealed even higher rates (c 90%, Chronister 1985). Egg dumping is also frequent among pochards. The Redhead exploits congeners when available (Weller 1959), with up to 40% of clutches affected in western Montana (Lokemoen 1966) and up to 75% of eggs being laid parasitically

in Manitoba (M.D. Sorenson 1991), but will also use other diving ducks as hosts. Canvasback nests are regularly parasitized by Redheads and, in areas where Canvasbacks are outnumbered by Redheads, over 95% of their nests may be parasitized (Sayler 1992). Common Shelducks exhibit intermediate rates of parasitism; around 33% of clutches were affected in an area with a relatively dense breeding population, despite a surplus of natural and artificial nest sites (Pienkowski and Evans 1982). Among swans, geese and dabbling ducks, brood parasitism is relatively uncommon except where birds nest in dense colonies, are crowded on nesting islands, for example Chestnut Teal (Norman 1982), or use cavities. Such nests may be easier to find, while competition for nest sites may be relevant among cavity nesters (Clawson et al. 1979). Poor breeding conditions often appear to increase dumping; for example, some 22% of Blue Snow Goose nests at La Pérouse Bay were parasitized (Lank et al. 1989a), but rates were higher in years of poor habitat conditions. Annual parasitism rates correlated more highly with nest site availability than with meteorological variables, suggesting that it was the knock-on effect of climatic conditions upon nest site availability that determined the rate of dumping.

One species of wildfowl, Black-headed Duck, is an obligate brood parasite that never builds a nest and relies entirely on hosts to incubate its eggs (Weller 1968a, Rees and Hillgarth 1984). Captive Black-headed ducklings are not readily imprinted (Weller 1968a), which may be advantageous since they may leave the nest as much as a week before the host's clutch hatches. The remainder of parasitic wildfowl are facultative (i.e. they may choose to make a nest and incubate their own eggs), with individuals resorting to parasitism only on occasion. M.D. Sorenson (1991) suggested that Redhead females employed a flexible, conditional reproductive strategy with four options that included nonbreeding, parasitic egg-laying only (during poor conditions), typical nesting, and a dual strategy of parasitic egg-laying prior to nesting (during good conditions). Parasitic females locate nests by watching and following females from active nests and may even lay eggs when the host female is still on the nest (McKinney 1954). In Common Eiders, parasitic females cue in on areas of high activity by nesting females (Robertson *et al.* 1992). Surreptitious behaviour and nest defence may act as anti-parasitism adaptations, for example in the hole-nesting Bufflehead (Gauthier 1987b), whilst heavy parasitism has been shown to cause nest desertion in Common Goldeneye (Andersson and Eriksson 1982).

The negative effects of brood parasitism on the host include desertion, egg displacement and breakage, and there is some evidence to suggest that the number of eggs laid by the host may also be reduced, for example in Common Goldeneye (Andersson and Eriksson 1982), although not in other species such as the ground-nesting Common Eider (Robertson *et al.* 1992). However, increased brood size generally has a neutral or positive effect on post-hatch survival, for example in Common Goldeneye (Eadie and Lumsden 1985) and Redhead (Austin and Serie 1994) and particularly in species showing extended parental care such as Barnacle Geese (Black and Owen 1989a, Choudhury *et al.* 1993) and Blue Snow Geese (Cooch *et al.* 1991, Cooke *et al.* 1995). Costs to the host females are likely to be negligible in species such as Common Eider, where the number of parasitic eggs laid in each nest is low (1–3, Robertson *et al.* 1992). Although female philopatry makes it possible that the host and parasite are genetically related (Andersson and Eriksson 1982), kin selection is probably not the driving force behind brood parasitism (Sayler 1992), and the net effects of the strategy (pre-hatch and post-hatch) have not been assessed adequately. The hatching success of parasitic eggs is generally low, particularly when females are attempting to salvage breeding opportunities in poor body condition, or when competing for nest sites. Hatching success would be higher in years with good breeding conditions and, in such years, brood parasitism might increase reproductive output.

Sayler (1992) examined the possible origins and adaptive significance of brood parasitism in wildfowl. He suggested that it may allow females to avoid some of the energy requirements encountered during egg production and incubation, since wildfowl tend to lay large clutches of large eggs that require a long incubation period. In addition, since brood size does not appear to regulate post-hatch survival of parasitized broods, hosts have not developed strong anti-parasite adaptations, such as the ability to discriminate foreign eggs (Choudhury *et al.* 1993), and brood parasitism can therefore occur quite easily. Parasitic wildfowl tend to be those that: (a) have limited critical breeding resources, such as hole-nesters; (b) have the opportunity to parasitize, i.e. nests are easy to locate; (c) do not defend nests during the laying period; and (d) have relatively high reproductive effort. Sayler (1992) concluded that brood parasitism was an alternative to normal nesting, which allowed females to increase reproductive output or salvage some breeding success when faced with reproductive impairments. Although parasitic eggs may have low or variable success, such that parasitism produced only 5.3% of Blue Snow goslings (Lank *et al.* 1989a) but 23% of Wood Ducks (Clawson *et al.* 1979), even limited production of parasitic young may be advantageous to individuals in poor breeding years. In good years, reproductive effort may be increased by both parasitizing and incubating a normal clutch for Wood Ducks (Clawson *et al.* 1979) and Redheads (M.D. Sorenson 1991), and thus spreading the risk of losing an entire clutch (Sayler 1992) and increasing fecundity above the limits of normal clutch size (M.D. Sorenson 1991). In the case of the cavity-nesting Wood Duck, both parasitic and host females may derive maximum benefit from limited available nest sites by their mixed breeding strategies (Clawson *et al.* 1979).

Geffen and Yom-Tov (2001) suggested that the large clutches produced by wildfowl increase the period during which clutches are susceptible to parasitism. In comparison with galliforms, where nest parasitism is rare, the larger eggs of anseriforms mean that their chicks are more precocial so that parasitism is less costly in terms of parental care, and less effort is made by nesting females to drive away potential dumpers. Coloniality tends to concentrate nests in a small space, and the lack of cavities means that there is great competition for nesting sites among hole-nesting wildfowl.

Hatching and rearing

Within the eggshell, the embryo is coiled with its head and neck beneath its wing, and the bill pointing into the air cell at the blunt end (Weller 1964b). The first indication of hatching comes between one and three days before the event, when the young start breathing, bill-clapping and calling. Vocalizations from within the egg may synchronize hatching (Vince 1968) and assist imprinting, since the parents respond to the calls (Bjärvall 1968). At the start of hatching, the chick produces a small crack on the surface of the shell with its egg-tooth, and pipping continues for some 3–24 hours until it emerges. Once free of the eggshell, the youngster dries within a few hours and begins moving about the nest. Hatching is generally well synchronized, although there may be some delay in the larger species, particularly where incubation begins before the final egg has been laid. Bewick's Swan broods, for example, may take up to 48 hours to hatch, and the female will continue to incubate infertile eggs even after the remainder of the brood has departed the nest. In Canada Geese, the order of hatch correlates with the order of pipping, and the order of pipping is correlated weakly with the order of laying (Cooper and Hickin 1972). However, among Northern Mallard hatched in incubators, there was a strong correlation between laying and hatch sequence (Prince et al. 1969), reinforcing the view that the early laid eggs hatch first. In Brant clutches, first eggs received up to 48 hours of incubation before the last egg was laid and yet clutches usually hatched within a 24-hour period, suggesting some mechanism for developmental asynchrony prior to hatching (Flint et al. 1994). Synchronous hatching, in combination with incubation during laying, increases fitness by reducing nest exposure and maintaining egg viability, and results in an earlier hatch (Flint et al. 1994).

Recesses by the female during hatching are short, for example in Common Shelduck (Patterson 1982), rare in Snow Geese (Reed et al. 1995) and Bewick's Swans, or do not occur at all, for example in Trumpeter Swans (Cooper 1979). Parental vocalizations increase once pipping begins, and calls given by Common Eider females as their young hatched attracted other females to the nest (Munro and Bedard 1977b). Parental calls are important for early imprinting since the young of cavity and burrow nesters spend their early hours in darkness (Patterson

1982), and all youngsters remain close to the female during this critical period. Subsequently, young Bewick's Swans may move several metres from the nest while the female is still incubating. The male usually moves closer to the nest at this time.

Brood care

Brooding of the young on completion of hatching continues for a few hours or days, depending on the species and conditions. Hole and burrow nesters brood for longer than ground nesters, for up to 96 hours in Common Shelduck (Patterson 1982) probably because of reduced predation risks, and brooding also increases in inclement weather. A few species (swans, geese and some ducks) will return to the nest to warm the young, particularly in poor weather and at night (Scott 1952, Weller 1964b). The newly hatched young of most wildfowl are not cold hardy and require warming for several days or weeks to maintain body temperature. The stifftails are exceptional, since they produce proportionately large eggs and well-developed ducklings that are capable of independent life at an early age. This is particularly important for ducklings of the parasitic Black-headed Duck, which are not brooded after leaving the host nest at one or two days (Kear 1970b, Rees and Hillgarth 1984). The Magpie Goose has taken brooding further and builds small nests around the goslings while they rest (Johnsgard 1965a). In most wildfowl only the female broods, although male swans will take over if their mates are killed.

Departure from the nest

The frequency of parent vocalization increases prior to the young leaving the nest, for example in Blue-winged Teal (Miller 1976), and may serve to coax the young away in a compact group (Cooper 1978, Patterson 1982). Broods tend to leave during the cool of the morning, perhaps to reduce the stress of travel (Afton and Paulus 1992). They are led by one or both parents, often down well-defined routes to rearing areas that may lie at a distance from the nest. Ducklings hatching in tree holes need to drop up to 20 m to reach the ground, while Barnacle Goose goslings may fall as far as 70 m from their cliff nests. However, being light and fluffy, they usually come to no harm.

In general, shelducks, dabbling ducks and pochards move relatively short distances (up to 1 km; Patterson 1982, Talent *et al.* 1982), while Common Eiders and geese move up to 10 km (Munro and Bedard 1977b, Prop *et al.* 1984). Goslings and eider ducklings are relatively large, and have a lower mass-specific metabolic rate which, combined with their larger energy reserves at hatching, allows them to travel further without feeding (Sedinger 1992). Ducklings may be vulnerable to exhaustion, disorientation and predation during overland movement (for example in Wood Duck, Northern Mallard and goldeneye, Ball *et al.* 1975, Savard 1988, Rotella and Ratti 1992), although other studies of Mallard (Talent *et al.* 1983), and Northern Pintail (Duncan 1987b) concluded that overland movement was not an important source of duckling mortality. Mallard nesting in Manitoba and hatching in areas with low wetland density moved further to rearing sites than those that hatched in areas of high wetland density, implying that nests were distributed randomly with respect to distance from water. However, broods that moved further had lower duckling survival, regardless of the density of wetlands (Rotella and Ratti 1992). Since ducks depend on concealment as an anti-predation strategy, and females need to feed extensively during incubation in order to meet a large proportion of their energy requirement (see earlier, *Ultimate factors*), they should nest close to rearing sites. The energy reserves of ducklings and/or risks of predation on long overland journeys may also select for females that nest near rearing areas (Sedinger 1992).

Brood-rearing areas

Brood-rearing areas in most cases tend to have abundant food (see Chapter 3), which may be important for newly hatched young that have limited foraging ability (Talent *et al.* 1983, Einarsson 1988), since nutrition influences juvenile survival (Street 1977). Canada goslings, for example, preferred habitats in which their primary food plants were most available and nutritious (Sedinger and

Raveling 1986). The distribution of broods of Barrow's Goldeneye at Lake Mývatn, Iceland, can be predicted by the distribution and life cycle of the most abundant food, blackfly larvae, although this is modified by the aggressive behaviour of other females present (Einarsson 1988). Ducklings reared in saline lakes in North Dakota were closely associated with inflows of seepage from adjacent freshwater wetlands of low salt content, which affected the availability of aquatic foods (Swanson *et al.* 1989). Ducklings could not tolerate high salt concentrations unless freshwater was also present.

Among Common Eiders in Norway, females that cared for ducklings had similar habitat choice and feeding methods to females without young, suggesting that parental care may not necessarily constrain habitat use (Bustnes 1996). Radio-tracking of Greater Snow Goose broods in arctic Canada, however, revealed that there may be considerable variation in space and habitat use by different families (Hughes *et al.* 1994). Three strategies were identified among pairs with young: *sedentary* pairs had one area of concentrated activity; *shifters* had more than one concentrated area of activity; and *wanderers* had no concentrated activity areas. The habitats used by sedentary broods were richer in pools and lakes than the upland habitats of wandering families, and the young of sedentary pairs hatched earlier, suggesting that they were more experienced parents (Hughes *et al.* 1994). Bewick's Swans in northeast European Russia took their cygnets to pools that the pair had used prior to hatch, while female Long-tailed Ducks undertook exploratory flights before taking their broods to new ponds (Alison 1976). Knowledge of the topography, food supply and predation risks at familiar sites probably enhances brood survival.

Protection from predators

An important function of parental care is protection (Lazarus and Inglis 1978). Alarm calls uttered by the parents when danger is nearby may cause the young to scatter, run for cover, move closer to the parents or freeze (Kear 1970b, Cowan 1974). Isolated ducklings are at greater risk than those in a tight family group. In wildfowl with stable pairbonds (swans, geese, Magpie Geese and some ducks), both sexes actively defend young, assuming threatening postures and sometimes biting and striking adversaries with their wings (Kear 1970b). In most ducks, it is the female parent that is responsible for defence, and she does this mostly by injury-feigning (Kear 1970b). Injury-feigning is less useful, and therefore less common, in tribes such as the pochards and stifftails (in which the young are almost entirely aquatic), in larger birds (such as the swans, geese and Magpie Geese), and among ducks of remote islands where ground predators are uncommon (Kear 1970b). A few species, such as the temperate breeding swans, Musk Duck, Salvadori's Duck and some mergansers, carry their young on their backs, which presumably helps brooding and may remove them quickly from risk of predation (Johnsgard and Kear 1968).

The steamer-ducks of South America are among the minority of ducks in which both the male and female attend the brood. The degree to which males assist in care varies between species and locality. The males of Magellanic Steamer-ducks on the mainland are always with their brood, while Falkland Steamer-ducks are only 91% attentive, and males of Flying Steamer-ducks are only 72% attentive; thus the degree of paternal care is perhaps an adaptation to the harshness of the environment (Weller 1976).

The downy young

The patterns of downy wildfowl have been reviewed extensively (see Fjeldså 1977, Nelson 1993) and are not considered in detail in this chapter, as descriptions appear in the species accounts in Part II. The unusual downy colouring of the Magpie gosling, which includes a cinnamon head and bill, may function to stimulate feeding by the parents (see below).

Early feeding techniques

In comparison with other orders of birds, wildfowl produce well-developed young, although the degree of feeding independence from the parent varies. Emerging from proportionately large eggs, the ducklings of some diving ducks (including stifftails, goldeneyes, New Zealand Scaup, White-backed Duck and Torrent Ducks) are particularly large and are capable of diving for food from an early age. The young of New Zealand Scaup, for example, can dive 2 m to feed, even at a day old (Porter 1940). Newly hatched White-backed ducklings are heavy, averaging 54 g, and weigh a third as much again as a day-old Northern Mallard. Large duckling size, with perhaps associated large reserves of yolk and subcutaneous fat, may be adaptive features associated with vigorous and independent feeding behaviour (Kear 1967a).

The young of geese and dabbling ducks begin pecking at objects immediately upon leaving the nest and must learn to discriminate between food items. Parents assist in finding suitable habitats in which their offspring can feed, but usually do not feed them directly; the exceptions are the screamers, Magpie Goose and Musk Duck, which commonly feed their young, and, to a lesser extent, the whistling-ducks (Kear 1970b). Young Magpie Geese approach their parents to be fed, and have a begging call. The parents feed the goslings directly from their beaks, dropping pieces of food near them, and bending marsh plants so that the seed heads can be reached (Davies 1961, Kear 1970b). The unique cinnamon-red head and bill of the goslings, as in Common Coot, may stimulate parental feeding and inhibit the adult from eating the food itself (Kear 1973b). The goslings make coordinated pecks about 40 minutes after hatching, which increase in intensity during the day and with age if unfed (Davies 1961). In common with most wildfowl (Kear 1964), the goslings orientate their pecks towards high, light, green and yellow objects. This would serve to direct pecks towards the main potential food source, the seed-heads of marsh plants (Davies 1961), but possibly also towards the bills of the parents. Musk Duck females feed their young throughout the pre-fledging period, and the ducklings are very vocal, giving incessant grunt-like begging calls, especially when the parent returns from a dive with food in her bill. Similarly, newly hatched screamers are fed regularly by their parents, which drop food in front of them (Bell et al. 1970). Young of these species tend to be aggressive to one another, and the dominance hierarchy so formed may result in low-ranking young starving when food is scarce (Kear 1973b).

The parents of some other wildfowl aid their young in finding food. Most swans and geese, for example, pull up aquatic plants for their broods that would be otherwise difficult to reach, or break up large food items. 'Trampling' of the feet in swans, geese and in many ducks serves to bring food to the surface that can then be taken by the young, while some pochards may dive beneath their young and force food to the surface (Gillham 1987).

Importance of hatching reserves

Compared to other orders of birds, wildfowl hatch at an advanced stage, and with a substantial food reserve in the form of residual yolk and lipids stored in body tissues that may enable them to survive without feeding for up to seven days (Owen and Black 1990). This is particularly important if weather conditions are poor immediately post-hatch (Slattery and Alisauskas 1995), if the brood have a distance to travel to reach suitable feeding sites, or when the young, such as those of the parasitic Black-headed Duck, receive little or no care from a host (Rees and Hillgarth 1984).

Lack (1968b) examined the proportion of yolk in wildfowl eggs of different size to test whether chicks hatched from larger eggs had the advantage of a proportionately larger food reserve derived from the yolk sac. The average proportionate weight of the yolk did not vary greatly and formed about two-fifths of the weight of the egg. However, in species such as wildfowl that leave the nest upon hatching, the total energy cost of development during incubation is linearly related to initial egg weight (Vleck et al. 1980). Because larger eggs have bigger yolk stores, larger individuals should have a higher energy reserve at hatching. Consistent with this prediction, larger goslings of Blue Snow Geese could survive longer without feeding than smaller ones (Ankney 1980), while Cackling Canada goslings had a shorter predicted fasting tolerance, based on lipid reserves, than Blue Snow goslings (Sedinger 1986). Slattery and Alisauskas (1995) examined the egg composition of arctic-nesting geese and demonstrated that goslings from larger eggs had relatively more lipid reserve. Anderson and Alisauskas (2002) later showed that larger King Eider eggs produced larger ducklings with more lipid and protein reserves, larger breast and leg muscles, higher functional maturity for whole body, leg and breast muscles, and higher tarsal growth rates than ducklings from small eggs.

Hatching reserves also influence thermoregulatory ability. High-latitude nesters have better thermoregulation at hatching than species breeding at temperate latitudes, and this is related to their higher metabolic rates and larger hatching energy reserves (Koskimies and Lahti 1964). Northern Mallard ducklings hatched from large eggs had better thermoregulation than those from small ones (Rhymer 1988). Egg size and corresponding hatching reserves represent an evolutionary compromise between the fecundity of females, the early growth of young and their ability to cope with poor weather conditions post-hatching (Sedinger 1992).

Brood amalgamation

Post-hatch brood amalgamation is common and occurs in at least 41 wildfowl species (Afton and Paulus 1992). It takes several forms. A female or pair may accept foster young (adopt), or aggressively kidnap young into their own brood. A number of adults may collect a group of young that are parentally unrelated (crèche), or several different parents may join together with their broods (gang-brooding).

Brood amalgamations may result in groups that range from only a few young to over 100. Such flocks are relatively uncommon in dabbling ducks, since families tend to avoid contact with one another, although brood mixing occurs more frequently when birds nest at higher densities, especially in urban areas (Titman and Lowther 1975). Amalgamations are also relatively uncommon in geese, possibly because the attentiveness of both parents helps to maintain family cohesion (Afton and Paulus 1992), an exception being Canada Geese. Brood mixing does occur but is infrequent in several other geese, even when nesting at low densities (e.g. Raveling 1969, Prevett and McInnes 1980, Lazarus and Inglis 1986). Amalgamations are frequent in Common Eider and Common Shelduck, particularly where adults feed in areas separate from brood-rearing habitats, or where large concentrations of birds gather late in the season (Williams 1974). Up to 90% of Common Shelduck young may be in crèches after mid-July (Hori 1964). Mixing generally involves birds of similar age, perhaps because adults are less able to discriminate against, and therefore be aggressive towards, young of the same size as their own (Williams 1974, Munro and Bedard 1977b).

There are several possible explanations for the evolution of post-hatch brood amalgamation (see Eadie *et al.* 1988). Crèching may improve survival of young by reducing the risk of predation on any individual and increasing detection of potential predators. For example, Common Eider ducklings survived better in bigger broods when attacked by single gulls (Munro and Bedard 1977a). However, large crèches suffered more attacks than small crèches, and survivorship was very low when crèches were attacked by groups of gulls. Common Shelduck young raised in mixed groups survived less well than those from single broods (Williams 1974). Survivorship of host offspring may be enhanced by the dilution effect of a large crèche (Munro and Bedard 1977a), particularly if foster offspring are displaced to the perimeter of the brood (Eadie *et al.* 1988). In addition, crèches may be tended by females of high rank (Munro and Bedard 1977b) which may allow the young access to better resources. Amalgamation may also improve the survival of adults. Female Common Eiders, which fast during incubation, fed and recouped energy reserves more quickly by leaving young in the care of foster parents (Gorman and Milne 1972). Similarly, Common Shelducks that left the care of their offspring to other adults spent more time feeding and migrated earlier to moulting sites, although their survival rates were similar to those of foster parents (Patterson 1982).

In summary, brood amalgamations are characteristic of species that nest at high densities, hatch synchronously and have limited brood-rearing habitats. Large numbers of young may come into contact early in life under such conditions, thereby increasing the chances of brood mixing (Hines 1977).

Age of independence of young

Timing of independence of the young varies considerably, from the first day of hatching for brood parasites like Black-headed Duck (Rees and Hillgarth 1984) to seven years in the case of some Bewick's Swans that continue to associate with their parents during the winter months (Rees and Bowler 1996). Parental care mostly takes the form of vigilance, which functions in predator avoidance, although avoidance of intraspecific feeding competition may also be relevant. Extended parental care is most extreme in the swans and geese. In Mute Swans, the sexes moult asynchronously so that at least one parent can fly at all times (Birkhead and Perrins 1986), while male Barnacle Geese retain their flight feathers until the goslings are large enough to be safe from avian predation (Owen and Ogilvie 1979). South American sheldgeese behave in a similar way to northern geese, indicating that parental behaviour is an adaptation to ecological conditions such as short breeding season, herbivorous diet and delayed maturity (Owen and Black 1990).

Parental care should reduce as the costs to the parent exceed the benefits of protecting increasingly self-sufficient young. Time spent scanning for predators, for example, declined in Pink-footed Geese (Lazarus and Inglis 1978), Ruddy Ducks (Joyner 1977) and female Common Shelducks (Patterson 1982) as broods matured, whilst time spent away from the young increased in American Black Duck (Ringelman *et al.* 1982) and Northern Mallard (Talent *et al.* 1983). In Ruddy Ducks, the distance between ducklings increased with age, and most broods were abandoned by the female after the fourth week (Siegfried 1977). Declines in parental investment may be less apparent in dabbling ducks that rear broods in secluded shallow-water habitats, where predators are less easy to detect (Afton and Paulus 1992). Ricklefs (1979) argued that there is a compromise between precocity and growth rate in birds, and that the optimum was determined by the potential accessibility of food. If chicks can feed themselves, then selection should favour them doing so. Where young birds can feed themselves, parents are less constrained by the need to provide food and can therefore rear more offspring.

The fledging period

Fledging, the point at which young birds are able to fly, occurs when the primary feathers reach about 85% of their final length (Owen and Ogilvie 1979). In most species, this is when the tips of the growing primaries reach the limit of the coverts above the tail. Feather development occurs rapidly during fledging. In goslings, the first feathers appear on the belly, flanks, scapulars and tail, shortly before the primaries begin to appear, and then spreads to the wing coverts, with the head, neck and back under the wings the last places to feather. No down remains by the time of fledging (Owen 1980).

Different parts of the body develop at different rates. For example, in geese and swans, the legs grow more rapidly than other parts of the body (Würdinger 1975, Bowler 1992). This would enable them to run faster with consequent advantages in escaping from ground predators while still flightless (Owen 1980). Development of the tarsus in relation to other parts of the body of Whooper Swans was more rapid in the wild than in captivity, suggesting that control of the relative growth of different parts of the body may not be simply genetic; exercise and food availability may also be important (Bowler 1992).

Bone growth in geese and swans is almost complete when flight is attained (Owen 1980, Bowler 1992) and, unlike other bird groups, they have not adopted the strategy of fledging before body growth is completed. Mass at fledging, however, is lower than adult mass. Among 20 species of geese in captivity, mass at fledging was on average $87.0 \pm 1.5\%$ (range 75–96%) of lean female mass (Owen 1980), and young birds catch up following their first winter (e.g. Evans and Kear 1978, Owen and Ogilvie 1979).

Variation in the length of the fledging period may be explained by the following factors.

Size of the bird

The fledging period of young geese reared in identical conditions of continuous daylight in captivity depends almost entirely upon body size (Owen 1980), with the smallest species fledging after 40 days when they weigh around 1000 g, and the largest after 65 days when they weigh around 2500 g. Deviations from the trend were small but conformed to the general hypothesis of increasing growth rate with latitude.

Larger species grow faster and, as adult body size increases, flight feathers are completed in a shorter proportion of the post-hatching growth period (Redfern 1989). However, whilst the wings of larger geese grow at a faster rate than those of smaller ones, relative growth in terms of body mass is faster in the smaller species (Owen 1980). Relative growth rate per day is correlated with body size at fledging and, hence, with the latitude of the breeding range.

Latitude of breeding

The latitude of breeding has been shown to have a significant effect upon fledging time in ducks, geese and swans. Briggs and Lawler (1991), for example, showed that ducks inhabiting arid zones of Australia had longer incubation and fledging times than northern-hemisphere species that migrate to breed at higher latitudes. Owen (1980) demonstrated that, among geese, deviations from the trend of increasing fledging time with body size conformed to the hypothesis of increasing growth rate with latitude. For example, the goose with the slowest growth rate in relation to its size was the Nene, which breeds at the lowest latitude (c 20°N), while White-fronted Geese breeding in Russia (at 73°N) had an earlier-than-expected fledging time on the basis of size alone (Owen 1980). High-latitude geese achieve their highest growth rate earlier than low-latitude species (Würdinger 1975), and this may reflect proportionate egg mass which tends to increase with latitude (see earlier, *Evolution of egg size*), thus giving the goslings a good start in growth as well as insuring against cold weather or other unfavourable breeding conditions (Owen 1980).

The effect of latitude may be partly due to the fact that, in summer, the daylight available for feeding increases with latitude. For example, parent-reared Bewick's Swans in captivity at 52°N in England took twice as long to fledge as they would in the Russian Arctic at 70°N (Kear 1972). However, Whooper Swans hand-reared on a high-protein diet in Britain at 52°N developed more rapidly than those in the wild in Iceland at 65°N (Bowler 1992), indicating that the quantity and quality of food available during early development also has an important effect upon growth rate.

Richness of food supply

Growth varies mainly in relation to the quality and availability of food. Among Northern Mallard ducklings given food of varying quality in captivity, there was a close positive relationship between dietary protein and growth, particularly in the first four days after hatch (Street 1978). The growth rate and survival of wild ducklings are likely to be affected mostly by the amount of insect food available, and growth rates of ducklings were significantly reduced in wetlands with a high salt content which, in turn, were relatively short of aquatic foods (Swanson et al. 1989).

The quality of the rearing diet may also affect final size. The wings of late-hatched Redheads were shorter at fledging than those of early broods (Smart 1965a), while the wing lengths of juvenile and adult Northern Mallards were significantly different in different seasons (Owen and Montgomery 1978). These results are consistent with the theory that early breeders benefit by hatching their young when both the quantity and quality of food is highest (Owen and Black 1990). Briggs and Lawler (1991) demonstrated that ducks from arid zones in the southern hemisphere were able to use resource peaks in their environment to produce clutches of similar size to those of northern ducks, and could cope with the variable environment by laying only when conditions were suitable. Garðarsson (1976) showed that the growth curves of Pinkfoot goslings in Iceland closely mirrored the growth of marsh vegetation in their territories. The goslings grew fastest when the vegetation was most productive. However, since the same growth patterns can be seen in artificial conditions in captivity, they can be regarded as an adaptation by the geese, rather than a direct response to the flush of vegetation (Owen 1980).

The importance of the pre-fledging period

The pre-fledging period is critical to the dynamics of populations since young wildfowl are vulnerable to a number of threats, including predation and inclement weather (particularly when their thermoregulatory abilities are underdeveloped), and to starvation. Growth is rapid compared to other precocial birds of similar size; consequently, they require large quantities of highly nutritious food during the growing period and this increases the influence of nutrition on realized growth rate, size at fledging and body composition (Sedinger 1992). Nutrition, through its effect on growth, also affects life-history parameters such as first-year survival (Cooke et al. 1984), age at first breeding and clutch size (Sedinger 1992). For the Blue Snow Geese of La Pérouse Bay (Cooke et al. 1995), gosling growth rate prior to fledging, which largely reflected food availability, was the most important factor affecting juvenile mortality. Food supply in the post-hatch feeding areas determined the condition of the goslings at fledging and their ability to survive autumn migration. For ducklings, the abundance of particular invertebrates in brood-rearing wetlands and, for geese and swans, the availability of nutrient-rich vegetation, will have important effects upon subsequent survival and reproduction. The selection of rearing habitat is therefore critical.

Factors affecting breeding success

Nest success, or hatch rate, is a commonly used measure of breeding success, and is defined as the proportion of nests that hatch at least one egg (Sargeant and Raveling 1992). Breeding success may also be viewed in terms of recruitment to the population. One measure of breeding success is survival to fledging. Early post-fledging mortality, however, may be high (e.g. 35% for Barnacle Geese in 1986, Owen and Black 1989a), and thus fledging rate may not correlate closely with recruitment to the breeding population (Cooke et al. 1984). Among migratory species with prolonged parental care, breeding success is traditionally taken to be the number of young (less than a year old) that appear on the wintering grounds. In the absence of marked individuals, measures of annual productivity may be assessed through censusing the number of juveniles arriving on wintering grounds. When ringed birds return to traditional winter areas, it is possible to record the reproductively successful individuals. Recruitment to the breeding population will be even lower as a result of continuing mortality which, in many ducks, may be density-related in winter (Owen and Black 1990). However, studies of lifetime reproductive success are rare because of the difficulty of following animals over the whole of their lives. In wildfowl, notable studies of lifetime reproductive success have been conducted on Blue Snow Goose (e.g. Cooke *et al.* 1995), Barnacle Goose (e.g. Owen and Black 1989b), Bewick's Swan (e.g. Scott 1988, Rees *et al.* 1996) and Mute Swan (Birkhead *et al.* 1983, Walter *et al.* 1991).

Intrinsic factors

Age of female

Reproductive performance in most animals increases with age and experience and, for some species, fecundity declines in old age (Clutton-Brock 1988). The tendency for clutch size of younger females to be lower has been confirmed for almost all species of wildfowl studied (Rohwer 1992), while senescent declines in average clutch size have been suggested for captive Nene more than seven years old (Kear 1973a) and for Common Goldeneye females after their sixth breeding season (Dow and Fredga 1984).

The age of first breeding by female Blue Snow Geese varies. At La Pérouse Bay, it occurs mostly between Years 2 and 4 (Rockwell *et al.* 1983, Cooke *et al.* 1995) and this was found to increase variation in lifetime reproductive success for the population. The number of eggs laid increased with female age up to Year 5, and there was no evidence for a subsequent decline. Nest failure and total brood loss were both higher among young female breeders than older birds. There was also some evidence for an increase in total brood loss in older breeding females, although this may have reflected cultural and local attachment to degraded habitat (density-dependent effects were a feature of this

study), rather than indicating physiological senescence. Egg hatchability declined with the age of the female parent but this was counteracted by gosling survival, which increased with female age, at least up to six years. As a result of these factors, annual reproductive output in Blue Snow Geese increased with female age up to Year 6 and then declined (Cooke *et al.* 1995).

Improved gosling survival has been noted also for older Canada Goose parents (Raveling 1981), and Barnacle Geese show a similar pattern. Productivity in terms of the number of young brought to the wintering ground increases in the first years of breeding life and then declines after the peak reproductive life of seven to 12 years (Owen and Black 1990). Productivity in ducks also increases with age, although over a shorter time-scale. Among Lesser Scaup, clutch size increases progressively at least to four years of age, while the average number of young produced by a four-year-old breeding female is double that of a one year-old (Owen and Black 1990). Abandonment of nests by Wood Ducks was also more likely in younger females (Heusmann 1984). Nest success was not found to increase with age in Northern Mallard breeding in North Dakota (Cowardin *et al.* 1985), however, and other factors such as dominance may also be relevant, as shown in Common Shelducks (Patterson and Makepeace 1979), since dominance rank may be more closely related to body size than to age (Scott 1980a).

The conventional explanation for increasing reproductive success with age is that lack of experience and staggered maturation *constrain* reproduction in young birds (Curio 1983). However, reproductive *restraint* is also possible, particularly in long-lived species. Young breeders with high future prospects of breeding may refrain from expending maximal parental effort to forestall the associated risk of dying and hence of jeopardizing future reproduction (Curio 1983). Evidence for this theory among wildfowl is conflicting. Among Blue Snow Geese, for example, females had a lower probability of success the year after their first successful nest attempt than after later attempts (Cooke *et al.* 1995), suggesting that they may have invested too heavily in their initial attempt. This was particularly marked among two-year-old breeders, perhaps highlighting their relative inexperience.

Breeding experience

Experience and age are inextricably linked since breeding experience inevitably increases with age. In detailed studies of individual wildfowl the true effects of breeding experience can be assessed, after allowing for the effects of age. In an early study of Mute Swans, the difference in productivity of experienced pairs was greater than would have been expected on the basis of age difference alone (Birkhead *et al.* 1983). Subsequent analyses revealed that female experience (together with mean winter temperature) had a significant effect upon the laying date of the first egg, and since lay date strongly influenced clutch size, which in turn affected fledging success, female experience had a measurable effect upon breeding success (Walter *et al.* 1991). In Common Goldeneyes, female experience of the nest site and its surroundings has been shown to be advantageous; females returning to the same site had greater success than those of the same age that moved to another nestbox (Dow and Fredga 1983), although survival of the young was apparently unaffected by the breeding experience of the female.

In a detailed examination of the breeding success of Bewick's, Whooper and Mute Swans, breeding experience was not found to be significant in influencing the reproductive success of a pair (Rees *et al.* 1996). However, reproductive success did improve in all three species the longer a pair remained together. Together with age, pair duration was a better predictor of reproductive success than breeding experience. The importance of breeding experience may have been underestimated in the study because of strong correlations of experience with age and pair duration, a lack of information concerning failed nest attempts and uncertainty about the previous breeding experience of swans first recorded as adults. The effect of pair duration was more pronounced in some years than in others for the migratory Bewick's and Whooper Swans, suggesting that age and long-term monogamy are more beneficial in some years (poor breeding seasons) than in others.

Inherited characteristics

Some studies have shown that individual females may exhibit high year-to-year repeatability of laying date, for example, Mute Swans (Bacon 1980), captive Northern Mallard (Batt and Prince 1979), Common Eiders (Spurr and Milne 1976) and Common Goldeneyes (Dow and Fredga 1984), suggesting a degree of genetic control. In the study of Blue Snow Geese at La Pérouse Bay, Findlay and Cooke (1982a) determined that variability in lay date and clutch size was derived from two sources: a genetic component—the heritable tendency for females to hatch their clutches at a particular time relative to the colony mean—and an environmental component that influenced the individual genetic component. Repeatability and heritability of lay date were low, suggesting that most differences in lay date among females are due to non genetic differences. Heritability estimates of measures of reproductive success made much later in the breeding cycle declined, probably due to environmentally-based variation, such as predation.

Birkhead *et al.* (1983) showed that a particular female genotype (Esterase polymorphism) had a significant effect upon lay date of Mute Swans nesting in the Upper Thames Valley. However, when female experience was accounted for, this effect was reduced significantly, suggesting that previous experience of breeding, and its interaction with genotypic effects, were more important than genotype alone in determining date of lay (Walter *et al.* 1991). Male and female genotype also had a significant effect on the number of cygnets fledged from a clutch, with males from one class of Esterase polymorphism having a significant advantage and females from the same class having a significant disadvantage. The authors argued that this complex situation could lead to a permanent maintenance of balanced polymorphism.

Extrinsic factors

Flooding

Wildfowl nests are vulnerable to flooding since they are often located close to water. Rising levels frequently affect swan and duck nests (e.g. Lavery 1970b), and flooding was the second most important source of Mute Swan nest loss in England (Birkhead and Perrins 1986). The melt-water produced by a rapid spring thaw flooded all Whooper Swan nests in a valley in southwest Iceland in 1989, although some of the pairs later re-nested (Einarsson 1996). High sea levels in the Yukon Delta of Alaska can devastate goose nests; Brant that selected low areas close to the sea were shown to lose up to 90% of their nests in some years (Mickelson 1975).

Bewick's Swans breeding in low tundra close to the River Pechora in Russia frequently nest on raised hummocks at some distance from water (Rees et al. 1997c). These nest sites are less prone to flooding during the spring thaw and, in addition, become free of snow earlier than low-lying sites. For large species, such as Bewick's Swan, the reduced risk of flooding, and the earlier start achievable on ridges, may outweigh the increased predation risks of a more visible nest located at a greater distance from the waterbody used for feeding and brood rearing.

Weather

Among arctic-nesting species, timing is largely reliant upon snow-melt. Some swans and geese may begin egg-laying with some snow still in the nest, but access to nest sites and food supplies is reduced by snow cover and by the subsequent flooding that accompanies the thaw. Blue Snow Geese, for example, show much annual variation in the onset of laying, which coincides closely with snow-melt (Cooke et al. 1995). The annual clutch size of Canada Geese nesting in the Hudson Bay lowlands varied significantly between years in relation to spring phenology. Clutch sizes were not only larger earlier, but were also larger in seasons with an early thaw (Raveling and Lumsden 1977). Similarly, nesting success (at least one hatched) of Barnacle Geese in Svalbard/Spitsbergen was 15–25% in late years compared with 60–80% in early years (Prop et al. 1984).

In arid areas with marked seasonality in rainfall, timing of nesting is closely connected to the timing of the wet and dry seasons (Lavery 1970b, Briggs and Lawler 1991). The White-faced Whistling-duck, for example, only breeds in southern Africa during the rainy months of October to March (Siegfried 1973d); the Fulvous Whistling-duck, however,

breeds largely during the dry season (April to September) on larger floodplains, where the peak annual floods occur well after the rains have ended. The timing of nesting in both species is related to seasonality in the availability of food (Siegfried 1973d). Similarly in Australia, ducks respond differently to rising water levels in temporary river floods. Dabbling ducks, such as Grey Teal, lay eggs within a few days of the start of rising water, whereas divers like Hardhead delay nesting until there is sufficient deep water for feeding (Braithwaite 1976a). Despite their ability to breed on temporarily flooded wetlands, arid-zone ducks take as long, or longer, to fledge their ducklings as other ducks; during the very brief inundations of some wetlands, they may not breed at all (Lavery 1970b, Briggs and Lawler 1991).

The importance of lay date

Nest initiation is usually highly synchronized, particularly among arctic-nesting geese (e.g. Cooke et al. 1995), and laying may span as little as seven days in high-arctic colonies of Ross's Goose (Ryder 1972, Raveling 1978b). The median laying dates of all non-tropical wildfowl species held in captivity at WWT Slimbridge can be related to the latitude of their native ranges and show a clear relationship with daylength (Murton and Kear 1973, Owen and Black 1990). This suggests that daylength is a strong proximate factor initiating breeding (Murton and Kear 1973). In most temperate and arctic nesters, clutch size declines with later laying dates, for example in Mute Swan (Birkhead et al. 1983, Walter et al. 1991), Bewick's Swan (Shchadilov et al. 1998) and Blue Snow Goose (Cooke et al. 1995). Among Mute Swans breeding in the Upper Thames Valley, clutch size is dependent upon the date of lay, which in turn has a significant effect upon the proportion of cygnets fledged from a clutch (Walter et al. 1991).

We have already seen that the timing of nesting is tuned to the availability of food, such that the young tend to hatch when the quality and quantity of food is highest to allow optimum growth, although this may be modified to some extent by food limitation upon the female in the pre-laying stage (Perrins 1970). Cackling Canada Geese, for example, hatched after most plant foods had reached their peak nitrogen concentration (Sedinger and Raveling 1986); goslings would have benefited from hatching earlier, but since both the initiation of nesting by the adults and the initiation of spring growth by the plants were predetermined by the timing of snow-melt, hatching to catch the peak in food quality was not possible.

Ducks from arid zones where there are marked wet and dry seasons also time their nesting to make use of resource peaks in their environment and may not breed every year (Briggs and Lawler 1991). Among species nesting in tropical and subtropical regions with more constant climatic conditions, lay date would be expected to be less critical, since the window for nesting successfully is wide and selection for laying at the right time less precise. Nene nesting on the Big Island, Hawaii (20°N), for example, have a very long nesting season lasting from September to April and there is no discernible change in clutch size with lay date.

Early nesting birds may face disadvantages. Because nest density may be lower later in the season, the risk of predation on early nests may be higher, while some predators such as skunks *Mephitis* and Polar Bear *Ursus maritimus* may feed on wildfowl eggs early in the season and switch to alternative prey later (Crabtree and Wolfe 1988, Madsen *et al.* 1989). In addition, severe weather and lack of food reserves may cause early nesting birds to abandon their clutch. Early nesting Blue Snow Geese suffered significantly higher pre-incubation failure than late ones (Cooke *et al.* 1995), although birds that failed during laying probably continued to lay the rest of the clutch in a new nest or became nest parasites. Total nest failure and partial clutch loss may be higher in nests initiated later in the season, although these contribute little to overall seasonal differences (Cooke *et al.* 1995). *Per capita* recruitment of offspring into the breeding population was highest among early nesters and lowest among late nesters. Overall selection favours birds that lay and hatch earliest, despite some disadvantages of early laying and, indeed, young hatched early in the season almost always have substantially higher over-winter or post-fledging survival than do young that hatch late (Rohwer 1992), a trend that is independent of parental age (Perrins 1980).

Among Blue Snow Geese, an early nesting bird will recruit as many offspring into the breeding population as a late nesting bird laying one extra egg (Cooke *et al.* 1995).

The negative correlation between clutch size and lay date increases the synchronization of hatch relative to laying, although Cooke *et al.* (1995) suggested that this has evolved in response to energetic constraints of arctic breeding rather than to increased hatching synchrony. The authors postulated that delayed laying implies a longer period over which the female must partition her reserves. Since energy allocation to egg production occurs prior to arrival at the breeding grounds, delayed laying results in the ageing and loss of follicles, with energy regained from reabsorption being channelled back into maintenance reserves (Barry 1962). This leads to further loss of follicles and hence a reduced clutch size as the laying period progresses—the 'nutrient reallocation' hypothesis (Barry 1962, Cooke *et al.* 1995). Dalhaug *et al.* (1996) examined seasonal decline in clutch size of Barnacle Geese nesting in Svalbard/Spitsbergen, and showed that females that arrived first nested first, had the longest pre-laying period, produced the largest clutches, had the longest incubation period and produced larger broods at hatching than late nesters. The authors argued that these results did not support the nutrient reallocation hypothesis and, instead, proposed that geese that arrived late spent relatively less of their reserves on eggs, in order to achieve synchronous hatching with early birds and/or to prevent a late breeding season which might reduce gosling survival, adult survival and/or future fecundity.

Predation

Predation at the vulnerable egg and pre-fledging stages can be high on some species, and result in clutch reduction, clutch loss or abandonment. Among Common Eiders, predation by gulls is such a threat that the female does not feed during incubation, although there may be substantial supplies of food nearby and, instead, depends entirely upon body reserves for laying and incubation (Owen and Black 1990). In a study of Light-bellied Brent Geese (Madsen *et al.* 1989), low nest success (26%) was largely attributable to predation

(62% of all eggs). Polar Bears took the majority of the eggs but they also damaged nests and created disturbance in the colony which allowed aerial predators such as skuas to take eggs from deserted nests. Post-hatching losses were negligible since Polar Bears disappeared later in the season as the pack ice retreated north, and the high pre-hatch predation pressure was the prime factor responsible for the low reproductive output of the population. Similarly, 77% of Magpie Goose nests suffered complete or partial predation in one study (Frith and Davies 1961) where a range of avian, mammalian and reptilian predators was identified, together accounting for 72% of all eggs laid. Predation levels in other studies are lower; for example, predators destroyed 17–22% of eggs laid by Canada Geese nesting in the Hudson Bay lowlands (Raveling and Lumsden 1977), although an additional 2–6% of nests lost a proportion of the clutch to predators.

The effect of predators varies considerably between years. In arctic Siberia, when lemmings, the main food of Arctic Foxes, are in short supply, predators switch to Brent Goose eggs and cause complete breeding failure. Variation in the predation rate has been proposed as a major determinant of cyclic breeding in Brent Goose (Summers and Underhill 1987) and there is circumstantial evidence that Brent Goose success may correlate with the success of other waterbirds breeding in the same area. The matter is discussed further in Chapter 7, page 146.

Predation has been identified as a principal agent of nest loss (Sargeant and Raveling 1992). In prairie regions of North America, nest success is thought to have declined because of increased predation caused, ultimately, by intensive agriculture and habitat change that have allowed predators to converge on dense concentrations of nests (e.g. Boyd 1985, Klett et al. 1988, Johnson et al. 1989), although evidence is conflicting (see Klett et al. 1988). This theory was tested by Beauchamp et al. (1996a) who used data compiled from 37 studies conducted between 1935 and 1992 at 67 sites in the prairie pothole region of Canada and the US. Nest success was found to have declined over time at similar rates among five species of dabbling duck, but nest success among early

nesters such as Northern Mallard and Northern Pintail was lower than that of late nesters such as Blue-winged Teal, Gadwall and Northern Shoveler. Long-term population declines in three species coincided with large-scale temporal declines in nest success. However, since populations of Gadwall and Northern Shoveler had not decreased, the declines in nest success may not be related causally to population change, and factors influencing brood survival were thought to be more relevant. Nest success on islands and in fenced enclosures was higher than at sites where predators were not removed or managed (Beauchamp et al. 1996b), but declined at a similar rate over time. Thus, exclusion of predators resulted in increased nest success but nest loss to mammalian predators did not appear to be the cause of long-term decline in nest success.

Although predation rates may be high early in the breeding cycle, mortality at the nest, and at egg and hatching stages, contributed little to annual variation in recruitment of Blue Snow Geese at La Pérouse Bay (Cooke et al. 1995), suggesting that variability in predation was of minor importance to annual nest success. However, mortality of pre-fledging goslings was important, since some 25% of goslings disappeared at this stage. This occurred mostly during the first days after hatch when predation rates were high, but mortality increased again towards the end of the rearing period, coincident with a decline in food availability (density dependent effects).

Food supply

Food has a profound effect upon breeding success, as described in Chapter 3. Failure in food supplies, for example, may be a major cause of nest abandonment by Black Swans in Australia (Braithwaite 1982). Among Whooper Swans breeding in Iceland, clutch and brood size were larger, juvenile growth rate faster, and post-fledging survival higher at a lowland site compared to a highland one (Rees et al. 1991a). The difference was attributed to a combination of hatching date and habitat quality. Mute Swans in the Oxford area of England hold territories for most of the year and these vary in food availability. On territories with abundant aquatic vegetation and/or a high potential bread supply, females weighed more and laid larger clutches earlier than those on territories where less food was available (Scott and Birkhead 1983). Although there were no direct relationships between territory quality and the number of young fledged, egg volume, or cygnet mass and size, the number of young fledged did relate to clutch size which was itself a function of territory quality.

Arnold *et al.* (1995) showed that nest success of Redheads in Manitoba, Canada, was not related to the late incubation body weight of the female. For both Redheads and Canvasbacks, brood survival and adult survival were unrelated to female weight, suggesting that nutrient reserves were of minor importance in determining future reproductive success. However, northern breeding ducks, particularly dabbling ducks, shifted from poor to more 'luxurious' habitats once the young had hatched (Nummi and Pöysä 1993), suggesting that the limiting effect of food supply may be most important during the rearing phase.

Ducks begin nesting on northern Swedish lakes as soon as the thaw sets in and before chironomid flies emerge. However, peak insect emergence, and thus food abundance, occurs around one month after the thaw, coinciding with the hatching of the ducklings (Danell and Sjöberg 1977). In all duck species breeding at Lake Mývatn, Iceland, production of young was correlated with abundance of chironomid and simulid dipterans (Garðarsson and Einarsson 1994). Breeding productivity varied by an order of 20 in Harlequin Duck, 50 in Eurasian Wigeon, Tufted Duck and Greater Scaup, and over 200 in Common Scoter and Barrow's Goldeneye, and reproductive performance determined subsequent changes in spring population density. Notably, productivity of the one resident species, Barrow's Goldeneye, reacted only weakly to summer food supply, suggesting that for this species the limiting effect of winter food may be important. The results suggest that, for the migrant duck species, summer food was always limiting production (there were no years of superabundance) and therefore population size (Garðarsson and Einarsson 1994).

Among arctic-nesting geese, the all-important effect of lay date on clutch size and breeding success centres on the timing of resource peaks in the environment, such that hatching coincides with, or is slightly after, the peak in the availability of high-quality food (depending on food limitation for the female in the pre-laying stage). Several authors have noted a seasonal decline in the quality of foraging conditions (e.g. Sedinger and Raveling 1986) that would favour early nesting by geese. Lindholm *et al.* (1994) studied the effects of hatch and food supply on the growth of imprinted early and late hatched Snow goslings. They supplemented the diet of half of each group with high-protein pellets, while the remainder foraged only on natural vegetation. They concluded that differences in growth, and possibly survival, between early and late hatched goslings were food-influenced and largely caused by the rapid decline of arctic plants during the summer. Differences of just 5–7 days in hatch date may have important consequences for fitness (Lindholm *et al.* 1994). Sedinger *et al.* (1995) measured the nutritive value and partitioning of energy and protein in green plants by yearling geese. They demonstrated that Blue Snow Geese were more efficient at retaining dietary energy, but possibly lost more of this energy as heat, than the smaller Brant, suggesting a relationship between body size, processing of energy and latitude of breeding in arctic nesters.

Moult

Moult is defined as the periodic shedding of feathers and the replacement of most or all of these by a new plumage (Humphrey and Parkes 1959). In wildfowl, feathers have many functions: they enable birds to fly and to float, provide a protective and insulating covering, and have a signal function in displays. Periodic replacement of worn feathers is necessary to maintain these functions (Payne 1972). Patterns of body moult vary between and among wildfowl tribes, and there is typically a simultaneous replacement of wing feathers during a flightless period (Hohman *et al.* 1992).

Patterns of body moult

Patterns of body feather moult vary greatly, although in many species moult remains poorly studied, particularly in tracts other than the alar tract (the wing feathers). In swans, geese and whistling-ducks, males and females are similar in appearance throughout the year; plumage is replaced only once, and so they are unable to have different plumages that vary with sex and season. Sheldgeese may also moult body feathers only once. Most other wildfowl replace their body plumage at least twice during the annual cycle. Ducks, with multiple plumages and moults, spend more time moulting than other wildfowl (Hohman *et al.* 1992). Moults of wing and body feathers overlap completely in some species, notably northern hemisphere dabbling and diving ducks, but not in others, for example Canada Geese (Hanson 1962) and Brant (Ankney 1984) which have body moult extending into early autumn. Body moult may be prolonged in whistling-ducks and resident geese, relative to migratory species (Hohman *et al.* 1992).

The ancestral pattern of wildfowl is one moult a year (Palmer 1976) and this has been retained by species that are not highly aquatic, have longer periods of immaturity and long-term pairbonds, such as most geese and swans. All highly adapted waterbirds, including the grebes, divers *Gavia*, auks and all highly aquatic wildfowl, have two body moults a year, which ensures good waterproofing. Most ducks have two annual body moults; the exceptions are the more terrestrial species, such as the whistling-ducks, which undergo one, and some deep-diving species such as Long-tailed Duck and the steamer-ducks which moult more than twice a year, probably ensuring that their plumage remains fully waterproof in cold conditions. The fact that most ducks moult at least twice enables them to have two seasonally different coloured plumages.

The addition of an alternate plumage, that differs in colour and pattern from the basic plumage, can confer advantage to birds that undertake two annual moults. The conspicuous breeding dress worn by males, for example, probably evolved under intense sexual selection for mates (Lack 1974). Birds with multiple moults may also benefit from reduced infestation of feather lice, as noted in passerines (Post and Enders 1970). Dull female or juvenile-like basic plumage in male ducks helps to conceal them from predators, a feature which would be less useful to geese and swans that are large enough to defend themselves. Cryptic coloration has obvious advantages for moulting dabbling ducks that spend the day lurking in dense cover while flightless, but is less obvious for pochards and eiders that remain in open water throughout the wing moult (Hohman *et al.* 1992). The adaptive significance of basic plumage may be to minimize abrasion and feather loss of the 'important' alternate plumage (Bailey 1981), while its dark colour may confer a thermal advantage to moulting diving ducks by reducing the temperature gradient between the skin and the plumage, thereby slowing loss of heat (Bailey 1981).

Sexual differences in patterns of body moult

The general pattern of body moult is similar for most ducks, but the timing varies considerably between species and sexes. Females are generally less predictable than males in the timing of their moult (Hohman *et al.* 1992); the key difference is in the timing of the pre-basic moult, which is initiated in northern males when they abandon their mates, and concluded when they shed their wing feathers (Young and Boag 1981). Unpaired males retain their bright alternate plumage longer than breeding males, which may facilitate mating opportunities with late-nesting females (Oring 1968). Male wing moult generally precedes that of females (Hohman *et al.* 1992). This is also true in the Whistling Swan, where the delayed female moult may permit her to replenish energy spent on reproduction (Earnst 1992b). Post-breeding female ducks resume the pre-basic moult (wing feathers) and initiate pre-alternate moult. Completion of the pre-basic body moult before nesting by females reduces their post-breeding moulting requirements, and enables them to begin and complete pre-alternate moult at around the same time as males. Nonbreeding females may even initiate pre-alternate moult before males (Hohman *et al.* 1992).

Among male ducks of northern temperate regions, acquisition of alternate plumage is necessary for pairing, and the timing of pre-alternate moult dictates the timing of pair formation. Northern Mallard, for example, are among the first to complete pre-alternate moult and to establish pairbonds, while Blue-winged Teal may not acquire the alternate breeding plumage until midwinter and are among the last to pair. Pairing chronology is also related to pairing status within species. Male American Wigeon with incomplete alternate plumage pair later than those with complete alternate plumage (Wishart 1983). Moult by males after the establishment of pairbonds either stops or is less intense (Oring 1968); however, pre-basic moult of females is initiated in winter and spring, particularly by paired birds (Smith and Sheeley 1993b), and may continue through spring migration in some species, such as Canvasback (Lovvorn and Barzen 1988), but not in others, such as Ring-necked Ducks (Hohman and Crawford 1995). In female Northern Mallard, moult is apparently not initiated until after pairing (Heitmayer 1987), but this is not true for diving ducks, which do not pair until spring migration. Except for short periods during mid to late winter and summer (egg-laying to fledging of young), males can be found moulting throughout the annual cycle (Hohman et al. 1992).

Physiological control of body moult

Moult may be induced by changes in photoperiod, temperature, food availability, rainfall or disturbance (Lavery 1972, Payne 1972). Regulation of moult is controlled by the endocrine system (Bluhm 1988), but the factors activating regeneration of individual follicles within and between feather tracts are unknown (Hohman et al. 1992). The intensity of moult and rate of feather development will affect the time required to acquire a new plumage, and both vary between feather tracts and species (for a review see Hohman et al. 1992).

Although wildfowl may not be stressed nutritionally during moult (Hohman and Crawford 1995), energy and nutrient costs are substantial, and include nutrients required for synthesis of feather components, increased amino-acid metabolism, changes in water and blood volumes, and altered thermoregulatory capabilities (King 1980). Annual cycles of moult have been described quantitatively for only a few northern temperate wildfowl and, consequently, factors influencing the timing of moult are poorly understood. Food abundance has been shown to influence the timing and duration

of winter moult. Northern Pintail wintering in Texas, for example, were able to moult more rapidly and attain alternate plumage earlier during a wet year, when wetland habitats and food were more abundant, than in a winter of average precipitation (Smith and Sheeley 1993b). The moulting period of Greylag Geese in The Netherlands coincided with a period of rapid growth in their food plant Common Reed *Phragmites australis*. However, food quantity and quality declined during the moulting period, and late arriving geese did not moult at the site but, instead, undertook a reversed migration back to Scandinavia (Loonen et al. 1991). The quality of food, in terms of protein content, during the flightless moult has also been shown to affect directly primary feather length of Northern Mallard (Pehrsson 1987). The lipid reserves of Mottled Ducks in Louisiana provided existence energy for only one-third of the wing moult, and exogenous nutrients appeared to fulfil the bulk of their requirements, emphasizing the importance of habitat quality at moult sites (Moorman et al. 1993). The rate and duration of body moult of Canada Geese in Mississippi were influenced by the trade-off between the amount of energy that they could allocate to feather growth, and the need to replenish nutrient reserves after breeding and prior to the winter. The single moult of Canada Goose may therefore provide more scope for adjusting nutritional demands to environmental costs than the twice annual body moult of most ducks (Gates et al. 1993).

Feathers are composed mostly of proteins, and avian moult results in a net deposition of epidermal protein that can equal a quarter of a bird's protein mass (Murphy and King 1991). However, the amino-acid composition of epidermal proteins (sulphur-rich) differs from the typical amino-acid profile of most food and other body proteins, such that there is a mismatch between the profile of amino acids required during moult and what is available in the food intake. Moulting birds may minimize this mismatch and enhance the efficiency of body protein and amino-acid metabolism by selective feeding, by storing cysteine (an essential amino acid) as glutathione, and/or by altering the dynamics of amino-acid utilization. Alterations of whole body protein metabolism during moult, linked directly or indirectly to cysteine need, may explain why the calorific costs of moult far exceed the apparent costs of keratin synthesis (Murphy and King 1991).

The brown, female-like basic plumage of male Northern Mallard weighs considerably less than that of both female basic plumage and male alternate plumage (Wielicki 1986), and it may be adaptive for males to produce light basic or eclipse plumage since, in many species of northern temperate ducks, it is worn for only a short period (Hohman *et al.* 1992). Scheduling moult so as to minimize overlap with other energy and nutrient-demanding processes, such as migration or egg production, would also reduce the potential nutritional stress of moult (Hohman and Crawford 1995). Moult in Canvasbacks has been shown to overlap with migration, nutrient storage and ovarian follicle development, suggesting that the moulting birds were not nutritionally stressed (Lovvorn and Barzen 1988). This conclusion is corroborated by studies showing that there was no correlation between indexes of moult and endogenous protein reserve (Ankney 1979, 1984, Moorman *et al.* 1993). In Ring-necked Ducks, moulting costs for both sexes were highest during the flightless moult in August. They were also high during winter but were reduced during the spring and autumn migrations (Hohman and Crawford 1995). Although moult remained at low levels during the breeding season among males, females initiated pre-basic moult after arrival on the breeding areas and moulted intensively while acquiring the nutrients needed for reproduction. Although, in general, there was minimal overlap of moulting costs with other energy and nutrient-demanding phases, these results suggested that timing of moult was also influenced by non-nutritional factors such as daylength (Hohman and Crawford 1995).

The flightless moult

Most wildfowl, in common with other waterbirds, moult all their primary and secondary feathers simultaneously, and become flightless for a period. This seemingly risky strategy has evolved almost exclusively in aquatic and marsh-dwelling birds that can feed and escape predation from the land even when they cannot fly. The flightless moult usually occurs soon after breeding, on or close to the breeding grounds. Nonbreeding geese and swans may also travel to and moult in the breeding areas, where they may occupy territories or converge in large flocks. Among diving and dabbling ducks, males leave the females after the onset of incubation, and males of several species may gather together in large moulting aggregations on extensive bodies of water. For example, more than 10 000 ducks of eight species moult on TaksleSluk Lake in western Alaska (King 1973). Among some northern migratory ducks, such as Common Goldeneye and Northern Pintail, many nonbreeders (mostly males) summer and moult in areas north of their breeding ranges in habitats that would be unsuitable for nesting. Many species of northern breeding wildfowl migrate long distances to reach more southerly moulting areas with a milder climate (see Chapter 6).

Timing of wing moult in breeding pairs of Tundra Swans was consistent with the view that females delay moult while replenishing energy spent on reproduction (Earnst 1992b). However, since female body condition increased throughout most of the moult period, and the female hatch-to-moult interval was correlated with clutch size, past energy expenditures did not appear to constrain the timing of moult. In many arctic-breeding geese and swans, moult asynchrony of the flight feathers between males and females is important in facilitating brood protection or territory defence, and these non-energetic demands are probably important constraints on the timing of moult (Earnst 1992b). The flightless moult of adult Grey Teal in north Queensland, Australia, was correlated with climatic conditions (Lavery 1972); birds postponed wing moult during prolonged wet seasons which extended the breeding season, while in dry years with diminishing areas of habitat, indefinite postponement of flightlessness would be advantageous. Plumage development may also vary within age classes. Among Redheads and Gadwall, late hatched young fledged more rapidly than young hatched early in the season (Smart 1965a, Oring 1968). Rates of primary feather growth did not vary between early and late hatched young, but flight feathers matured earlier. Since moult of flight feathers is much less variable than that of body feathers in passerines (Newton 1966), it seems likely that mass of body plumage may also differ between early and late hatched young (Hohman *et al.* 1992). These results demonstrate the ability of wildfowl to make adjustments to meet the energy and nutrient demands of moult, given seasonal constraints and variation in food resources. This flexibility is clearly important for species that occupy highly seasonal environments and have limited mobility while flightless.

Duration of flightless period

The length of the flightless period varies. In southern African wildfowl it has been shown to be correlated positively with wing length (Dean 1978), although differences in relative growth rates between taxa suggest that other factors, such as predation pressure and length of the post-breeding period, may also be relevant. The flight feathers of Mute Swans took 66–67 days to grow to full length in Sweden, although the birds were able to fly before then (Mathiasson 1973a). Eurasian Teal are flightless for around 21 days (Sjöberg 1988b), Barnacle Geese for 25 days (Owen and Ogilvie 1979), Northern Mallard for 32–34 days (Owen and King 1981), and Spur-winged Geese for 42–49 days (Shewell 1959). Wildfowl are capable of flight when flight feathers attain around 70% of their final length (Hohman *et al.* 1992).

Not all wildfowl have an annual simultaneous wing moult. Magpie Geese and screamers moult sequentially and are capable of flight year-round (Owen and Black 1990). This may be of particular benefit to a species that actively feeds its young and which inhabits temporary wetlands under a relatively unpredictable climatic regime of wet and dry seasons. Magpie Geese build their nests at the start of the wet season, and the swamps may be dry by the end of rearing (Davies and Frith 1964) when most other wildfowl undergo their flightless period. Individuals of other species that usually have a wing moult, such as the Magellan Goose of southern South America, may skip a moult and retain their primaries for two cycles (Summers 1983a). Ruddy-headed Geese can also have a partial moult

in which the inner and outer primaries are moulted at different times, probably in alternate years (Summers 1982). This may also happen occasionally among northern species. A Whooper Swan that had its primary feathers dyed during one winter in southwest Scotland returned the following year with the same dyed feathers (Campbell and Ogilvie 1982). This was thought unlikely to be the effect of the dye since many hundreds of swans had previously been marked this way; the singularity of this case points to its rarity, at least among Icelandic Whoopers. Stifftails such as Ruddy Duck may moult wing feathers in late summer after the breeding season and once again in late winter or spring, shortly before, or soon after, spring migration (Siegfried 1973b, but see Hobson *et al.* 2000).

Weight loss during moult

Most wildfowl lay down body reserves that they tend to lose during the flightless period, as described in Chapter 3. This pattern of prior gain followed by weight loss was originally assumed to occur because moult was a stressful process. Andersen-Harild (1981) found that Mute Swans in Denmark lost up to 20% of their body mass while moulting. However, weights varied according to the quality of food available, suggesting that food was the crucial limiting factor. Moreover, in Mute Swans there is a strong positive correlation between body weight and the timing of the start of wing moult (see also Van Dijk and Van Eerden 1991), so that thin swans that begin moulting late survive less well (Perrins and McCleery 1995), and Mute Swans are also capable of making rapid changes in choice of moult site in relation to food abundance (e.g. Ryley and Bowler 1994).

There is increasing evidence to suggest that the loss of weight during moult is adaptive as it reduces the length of the flightless period—i.e. a lighter bird can fly earlier. Douthwaite (1976) found that moulting Red-billed Pintail in Zambia still retained body reserves at the end of the flightless period, despite losing weight while moulting. Similarly, Owen and Ogilvie (1979) showed that most Barnacle Geese lost weight during their annual moult in Svalbard/Spitsbergen, and suggested that birds beginning the moult with large fat reserves would be at an advantage in depleting them, since lighter birds have a shorter flightless period. Eurasian Teal moulting in northern Sweden lost 10–19% of body mass, allowing the birds to escape predators by flying before their primaries and secondaries were fully grown (c 75% of final length, Sjöberg 1988b). Northern Mallards, moulting in predator-proof enclosures and provided with a superabundance of energy-rich food, also lost weight during moult (Owen and Black 1990). Reliance on stored body reserves by flightless Northern Mallards caused their weight to decline, which allowed for reduced activity levels and lowered the risk of predation (Panek and Majewski 1990). However, lipid reserves only met the existence requirements of Mottled Ducks for a third of the flightless period (Moorman et al. 1993); their body size may reflect a balance between the benefits of reduced activity while moulting, and the cost of increased weight, and thus wing-loading, upon the length of the moulting period.

The end of the moult usually coincides with a time of food abundance, so that birds are able to gain reserves quickly before, in the case of arctic and temperate species, the onset of winter. The selective advantage of reducing the length of the flightless period outweighs the small benefit of maintaining body reserves, since the energetic costs of moulting are small compared to other activities of the annual cycle (Payne 1972). Exceptions include some seaducks, such as Common Eider, which remain maritime during wing moult and continue to put on weight (Milne 1976), presumably as the low risk of predation at sea reduces any pressure for early resumption of the power of flight (Owen and Black 1990).

In summary, this chapter has attempted to highlight some of the selective pressures that shape the diverse breeding strategies and lives of wildfowl—strategies that range from the polygynous 'trios' of Magpie Geese feeding their young in colonies in the seasonal swamps of northern Australia; through the long-term monogamous pairbonds of migratory northern swans nesting on the arctic tundra; the annual monogamous pairbonds of northern temperate ducks in which the male deserts the female during incubation and undergoes a separate moult migration; to the Black-headed Duck, a tropical obligate parasite that always deposits its large eggs in the nests of other waterbirds. With such an adaptive range of life-styles, ducks, geese and swans have been able to exploit successfully the majority of Earth's wetlands, where they are among the most conspicuous and best-known of all birds.

6

Movements and migrations

E.C. Rees, G.V.T. Matthews,
C.R. Mitchell and M. Owen

Human interest in the migrations of ducks, geese and swans dates to prehistoric times, but only in the twentieth century were techniques developed to monitor their movements, and to investigate the biology underlying their migratory behaviour. Early studies described the large distances covered by some individuals, which led to further and deeper questions, which Hochbaum sought to address in 1955 in his seminal volume *Travels and Traditions of Waterfowl*. Why did they undertake these journeys? Why did some birds return to the same wintering or breeding sites every season? How is the timing of migration regulated? And how do the birds navigate?

More recently, fine-grained studies have investigated why site fidelity varies between species, why intra-specific variation in dispersal occurs, and what adaptive advantages derive from migratory behaviour. As a family, ducks, geese and swans have shown a wide variety of migratory patterns, ranging from the regular long-distance migrations undertaken every year by species breeding in the high Arctic, to more opportunistic movements in response to local conditions by birds nesting in tropical regions. While the early studies were mainly curiosity-driven, the information that they yielded served to highlight the importance of obtaining an accurate understanding of the reasons underlying site selection when developing conservation plans. As pressures that destroy and degrade the world's wetland resources mount, information gained from migration studies will play an increasingly important role in providing the scientific basis needed if international conventions, species management plans and flyway action plans are to achieve their goals.

Techniques for investigating movements

A fundamental requirement for studying animal movements is to identify individuals; this usually requires that the individuals be caught and allocated a unique marker. Originally, marking techniques were developed to denote ownership which, in ideal circumstances, involved a lifelong label. As described in Chapter 1, in the Middle Ages, Mute Swans were rounded up during their annual wing moult and marked by cutting the soft tissue of the upper bill; the scar tissue that healed the wound remained until death. Netted traps or 'decoys' have been used to catch ducks for the table since the sixteenth century (Kear 1993), but it was not until 1907, when ducks caught in a decoy in western Denmark were fitted with rings and then released, that decoys began to be used to study the migratory behaviour of wildfowl (Mortensen 1950). Very few studies have the luxury of being able to identify individuals by their natural markings. A main advantage of WWT's study of Bewick's Swans at Slimbridge is that every bird can be recognized by its unique black and yellow bill pattern (Scott 1966), which makes it possible to monitor all birds present in the flock. Even here, however, artificial markers are still necessary for obtaining sightings outside the immediate study area, since only trained observers can identify individual swans by bill pattern alone.

The marking of individual birds with leg rings, each engraved with a unique code, has been the basic tool used for monitoring wildfowl migration. Birds are fitted with small metal leg rings, which are more durable than other artificial markings. However, these rings are very difficult to read in the field, so that the information gained is usually limited to a report of the date and recovery site of a bird that has been found dead or recaptured. This was useful for early attempts to estimate survival rates (e.g. Kortlandt 1942), but many observations of a single individual are required to describe the migratory routes and staging sites needed during migration. A major advance in studying the dispersal of larger birds came in the late 1960s with the production by WWT of plastic rings engraved with alphabetical or numerical codes that could be read at distances of up to 300 m in the field with a telescope (Ogilvie 1972). Ornithologists and amateur birdwatchers have since acquired the habit of checking birds for leg rings, but this was encouraged at the start of the Bewick's Swan study by applying yellow dye to the white tail and wing-tips to draw attention to the marked individuals. Bright plumage dyes have also been used on other wildfowl and waders. They can be very useful, not only to provide individual or group marking, but also to increase recovery rates. Handel and Gill (1983) estimated that Western Sandpipers *Calidris mauri* that had been dyed yellow were about 16 times more likely to be seen by observers than birds that had been colour-ringed only. The white undertail coverts of dark-plumaged northern geese (e.g. Barnacle Geese marked on Islay, southwest Scotland) and the white wing covert patches of adult male Eurasian Wigeon also have been dyed bright yellow using picric dye.

Plastic tags attached to the leading edge of the wing have been used on Northern Mallard, Mottled Duck, Common Eider, Goosander and Ruddy Duck, although the presence of the tags has caused problems for some species. For example, Anderson (1963) observed that 3.4% of the Eiders he tagged became solitary, and Bustnes and Erikstad (1990a) reported that tagged breeding female Eiders laid later and produced smaller eggs than untagged birds. Haramis and Nice (1980) described a method of attaching tags to the webs of the feet, and these are thought to cause no harmful effects. A technique to attach web-tags to ducklings in pipped eggs has been described by Alliston (1975). He tested it on seven species of wild ducks (151 ducklings) and no decrease in hatching success occurred; nor did the process affect their survival once they had left the nest.

Leg rings are difficult to read when the vegetation is high or when the bird is on water, leading some researchers to use neck collars on geese and swans. Most studies obtain sufficient information from re-sightings of leg rings only, however, and since the neck collars may have an adverse effect on some species (e.g. they are thought to cause excessive preening by Brent Geese; Ebbinge et al. 1991), leg rings continue to be the method used most commonly for following the movements of individual birds.

Although re-sightings of leg rings, together with seasonal variation in the numbers counted and observations of birds in flight, have served to describe migratory flyways for many species, the development of miniaturized electronics has made it possible to obtain more detailed information about the precise routes taken and the frequency of staging. For many years, the transmitters used on terrestrial and marine animals were too big and heavy to be used on birds, and the early devices, in addition, had a short life-span. The reduction in size and increased reliability of transmitters means that they now provide enormous potential for studying the movements of birds, particularly (since the cost of transmitters remains very high) where substantial information can be gained by tracking a few individuals. Radio-telemetry is used mainly for studying local movements in detail, particularly of birds active after dark, describing the high level of roost-site fidelity by Greenland White-fronted Geese on Islay (Ridgill et al. 1994), or of Pink-footed Geese on Loch Leven (Hearn and Mitchell 1995), and areas covered within a winter by individual Barnacle Geese on the Solway Firth (Phillips et al. 2003). Satellite-tracking is more appropriate for studying movements over long distances and has added greatly to our knowledge of swan and goose migration (see below). Refinements to the satellite transmitters have made it possible to programme them to transmit only at certain times, thus prolonging the life of the battery and ensuring that it remains active throughout the main migratory period. The first transmitters used on swans weighed 100 g (Beekman et al. 1996a, Pennycuick et al. 1996, 1999, Figure 6.1) but, with further miniaturization, transmitters of 20 g, 30 g and 45 g are now used not

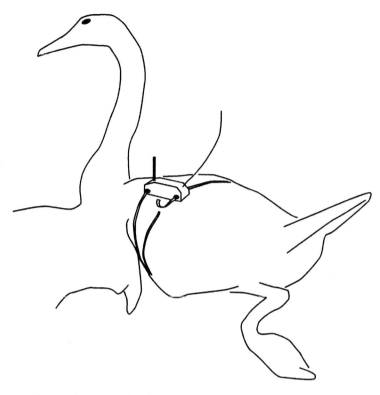

6.1 Satellite-transmitter (box and antenna) fitted to a swan attached with straps passing behind the wings. From Pennycuick *et al.* (1996).

only on swans but on medium-sided geese such as Brent Geese and Barnacle Geese (Butler and Woakes 1998, Clausen and Bustnes 1998, Beekman *et al.* 2002). Solar-powered transmitters can track animal movements over several years, but the cost of recording and retrieving the data over long periods has so far limited their use in studies of migratory wildfowl. Future techniques may include the further development of data loggers, to record air speed, wing-beat frequency and altitude, in addition to giving accurate locations, where the loggers can be retrieved from the birds.

Before the advent of satellite-tracking, broadbrush information on the altitudes of migrating birds, as well as their routes and timing, was provided by radar, although this had to be supported by direct observations in order to identify the species. A combination of radar and ground verification was used to quantify the huge spring passage of about 800 000 Common Eiders through the Baltic region in the early 1970s (Alerstam *et al.* 1974). More recently, satellite imagery has proved a useful tool for describing the habitat and food resources available, thus explaining why birds select certain sites in preference to others. For instance, images from the LANDSAT satellite have been used to detect submerged macrophytes along the Bewick's Swans' migratory route in order to identify potential feeding grounds for birds travelling between arctic Russia and western Europe (Beekman *et al.* 1996b). Analysis of the ratios of stable isotopes in the environment, such as in the food eaten by birds, and relating these to isotope ratios in the birds' body tissues, has proved valuable for studying movements and migration patterns in several avian species (Marra *et al.* 1998, Bearhop *et al.* 1999, 2003, Kelly *et al.* 2002). Stable isotope analysis of feather, blood or claw samples has great potential for elucidating further the reasons underlying migration strategies in wildfowl populations over the next decade.

Calvo and Furness (1992) provided a review of marking techniques and their effects. Chapter 7 reviews the importance of individual marking schemes for the study of wildfowl population dynamics.

Migratory and dispersal patterns

Interspecific differences

Monitoring programmes have discovered a range of migratory strategies that vary both between and within species. These may be grouped into two main categories: the long-distance return migrations of many northern-hemisphere birds, and the less pronounced seasonal shifts in distribution more typical of tropical and low-temperate species. The common factor is that regulation of both short and long-distance movements is influenced mainly by environmental factors, particularly changes in climate and the availability of food in both the breeding and wintering areas.

Long-distance return migrations

The evolution of long-distance migration in geese and swans breeding in arctic regions has been ascribed to the emergence at high latitudes of protein-rich vegetation in spring and the availability of aquatic invertebrates for rapid growth of young (Murton and Kear 1973), although the importance of invertebrates to cygnets and goslings shortly after hatching has still to be assessed. Two duck species that nest primarily in the high Arctic, Long-tailed Duck and Spectacled Eider, also feed on invertebrates (especially the chironomid larvae abundant in tundra pools) during the breeding season, with Steller's Eiders preferring to graze on the fast-growing arctic sedges. Certainly the vast expanses of tundra with their numerous pools, lakes and river channels provide an abundance of nesting habitats in areas still relatively free from human activity. The 24 hours of daylight in the arctic summer also facilitates intensive feeding and the adults' ability to monitor potential predators.

Few animals are adapted to survive the arctic winter, so most arctic-breeding wildfowl fly south to temperate zones, although certain fish-eating ducks such as Eiders, Scoters and some sawbills move to areas of open water on the arctic coast.

Birds nesting in temperate latitudes may themselves fly south in winter or remain in these areas throughout the year. Many Northern Shoveler breeding in Britain winter in France and Spain (up to 60% of the birds present in summer are thought to migrate) and are replaced by Scandinavian and Russian breeders in winter (Mitchell 1990, Kirby and Mitchell 1993). Northern Mallard breeding in Britain, on the other hand, are generally resident but are joined in winter by visitors from northwest Europe (about 20%). The Garganey is the only species breeding in the Western Palearctic where almost the entire population migrates to winter in tropical regions, some even approaching the equator. Northern Pintail, like Garganey, frequent Afrotropical wetlands in winter, but for the Pintail these areas represent an alternative to wintering in the temperate zone (Roux and Jarry 1984).

Southern-hemisphere species do not make such marked return migrations, probably because there is no southern equivalent to the broad expanse of pan-arctic tundra, with its spring bloom of vegetation and mosquitoes that is the breeding habitat for many northern birds. The South American swans and sheldgeese do, however, show seasonal shifts in distribution with seasonal changes in climate, which may include altitudinal return migrations equivalent to latitudinal movements, as well as northward movements in winter. Thus the Andean Goose nests at above 3000 m, but migrates down to about 2000 m to spend the winter (Goodall et al. 1951, Summers and Castro 1988). The Lesser Magellan Goose comprises both migrant and resident populations; birds breeding in Tierra del Fuego may migrate 2000 km to winter in Buenos Aires province, but other populations are resident and may be found wintering in all parts of the breeding range (Goodall et al. 1951, Plotnick 1961b, Summers and Martin 1985).

Interspecific variations in the distribution of long-distance migrants, and the length of migrations undertaken, have been associated with differences in body size, particularly where species are closely related. A comparison of wintering distribution of eight races of Canada Geese in North America showed that the larger races, which are better able to stand cold conditions, tend to winter further north, closer to their breeding ground (Figure 6.2 from Owen 1980). Thus, although Giant Canada Geese lose 50% more heat than Lesser Canadas in absolute terms, differences in the standard metabolic rate mean that heat loss per unit weight of bird is 40% lower in *maxima* than in *parvipes*, resulting in the larger subspecies being more tolerant of low temperatures (Lefebvre and Raveling 1967). Small races of Canada Geese breed further north than large ones, however, and the tendency for the smaller races or species to migrate the longest distances applies to most geese (Owen 1980). The only geese that differ markedly from this trend are the Bar-headed Goose, which breeds at high altitudes in central Asia, and Emperor Goose, the maritime habits of which enable it to remain in Alaska and eastern Siberia throughout the year, although it does disperse southwards in winter. A similar pattern also

occurs in the northern swans, with Bewick's and Whistling Swans breeding at higher latitudes than the larger Whooper and Trumpeter Swans. Thus Whooper Swans, breeding on the taiga lakes across Eurasia, may gain more from breeding close to their wintering grounds than the smaller arctic-breeding Bewick's Swans, by reducing the energetic cost of migratory flight and enabling their comparatively slow-growing cygnets to fledge before the onset of winter.

Several species, such as most Eurasian dabbling and diving ducks, are thought to migrate on a broad front from widespread northern-latitude breeding grounds. For these birds there is no clear-cut relationship between the breeding and wintering areas; flocks wintering in any given region are likely to contain individuals from a range of breeding sites and, similarly, birds from the same breeding areas may often occur in a number of widely separated winter quarters (Scott and Rose 1996). Other populations have a more restricted distribution in summer and/or winter, or follow narrow corridors during the migratory flight. A long-term study of Barnacle Geese has shown that the population breeding on Svalbard winters almost exclusively on the Solway Firth in southwest Scotland (Boyd 1961, Owen and Norderhaug 1977). Further studies of the three Barnacle Goose populations that breed in Russia, Greenland and Svalbard found that, despite the close proximity of their wintering grounds, the populations are in fact now discrete (Ganter *et al.* 1999, Ogilvie *et al.* 1999, Owen and Black 1999, respectively). Distinct populations of Pink-footed Goose have also been described; birds breeding in east Greenland and Iceland winter exclusively in Britain (Mitchell *et al.* 1999), while birds breeding in Svalbard winter in Denmark, The Netherlands and Belgium (Madsen *et al.* 1999b). Wildfowl that undertake long, overseas crossings seem more likely to follow a narrow migratory corridor, presumably because over these ecological barriers they take the shortest distance between each land mass. Transcontinental migrants, on the other hand, may disperse on a broad or narrow front, depending on the distribution of wetlands suitable as staging areas. The Eurasian Whooper Swans are thought to consist of four populations that appear to follow separate,

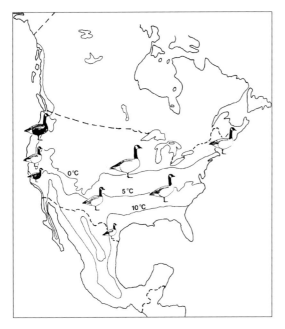

6.2 The wintering areas of eight races of Canada Geese in North America, together with the 0°C, 5°C and 10°C isotherms in January. The drawing of each subspecies is placed approximately in the centre of its wintering range. Large races are better able to withstand cold temperatures than small ones and winter further north, close to their breeding grounds. The small races breed further north than large ones, however, giving rise to the phenomenon known as 'leap-frog' migration. From Owen 1980.

well-defined migratory routes (Mathiasson 1991). The Bewick's Swan's migratory route, from the Russian Arctic across Karelia and the Baltic to wintering grounds in northwest Europe, appears even more restricted (Beekman *et al.* 1996a, Rees *et al.* 1997c, Rees and Bowler 2002). Detailed investigations of the migration corridors used by North American waterfowl (Bellrose 1968, 1980) showed that ducks breeding around the potholes of the prairie regions of Canada and the northern US gather on larger waterbodies in August and September before migrating southwards to the Gulf Coast, with large numbers following the Mississippi Valley to the marshes of Louisiana and Texas. Ducks on the Pacific flyway follow the coast or the central valley of California, and those on the Atlantic flyway follow the eastern seaboard.

Long-distance migrants typically use traditional flyways, and stop at intervals *en route* to rest and feed. Birds crossing the sea, or large areas of unsuitable habitat, must make long non-stop flights, but other species move more gradually. In spring, birds follow the retreating snow-line, which may enable them to take advantage of the best conditions available, but may also delay their onward flights if they encounter freezing condition during their journey north. Studies of migratory swans have suggested that autumn migration may be more direct (Evans 1982), particularly if wind conditions are favourable (Beekman *et al.* 2002), because the birds are unlikely to encounter poorer weather conditions further south, but the timing of migration may still be modified by mild weather conditions met at key staging sites. Thus the Eastern Prairie population of Interior Canada Geese, migrating south through central Canada and the northern US, moves just ahead of freezing conditions in autumn (Vaught and Kirsch 1966). Drent *et al.* (1980) further suggested that the movements of arctic-breeding geese (specifically Barnacle Geese and Brent Geese) are timed to ensure that the birds feed on the most digestible and nutritious grasses as they move during the course of the year, particularly in their selection of sprouting vegetation in spring. An exception may be the Red-breasted Goose, which was thought to arrive on its tundra breeding grounds after the grass has begun to grow. The delayed start to the breeding season was

attributed to its tendency to nest in association with birds of prey (see Chapter 5, page 82), with the later onset of laying enabling it to synchronize with the raptors' breeding programme (Owen 1980, Owen and Black 1990). Recent studies in one breeding area, however, showed that, although Red-breasted Geese may arrive slightly later than other goose species nesting in the region, their arrival might still coincide with the flush of vegetation growth following the thaw.

In the last decade there has been an increasing concern for the suitable spacing of nature reserves that are migration sites, particularly for species migrating on a narrow front. The loss of a critically located wetland, in a narrow migratory flyway, may result in birds being unable to obtain the food and energy necessary for them to complete their journey. The Svalbard/Spitsbergen Barnacle Goose population wintering in southwest Scotland makes a flight of 1500 km to its staging post at the Helgoland archipelago, Norway, in spring. Availability of food in Helgoland appears to be critical in enabling the birds to complete their 1500 km onward migration and to breed successfully (Black *et al.* 1991a). During autumn migration, the same population takes a different route, staging at Bear Island, midway between Spitsbergen and northern Norway, before flying 2000 km overseas to Scotland (Owen and Gullestad 1984). Good feeding opportunities at Bear Island may be particularly important in years when the winter arrives early, since the birds then have a further opportunity to lay down fat deposits after leaving the breeding grounds.

Even transcontinental migrants may be limited in their choice of staging posts, particularly if they are unable to utilize the forested taiga zones. Bewick's Swans can fly some 2000 km non-stop, so the birds have to stop to feed two or three times during their 3000–4000 km journey (Beekman *et al.* 1996a). The availability of food (notably submerged macrophytes such as *Potamogeton*) along the migratory route is therefore important, but eutrophication and drainage of traditional wetland habitat have restricted the Bewick's Swans to a handful of sites. Staging areas in the Baltic countries (particularly Estonia) now harbour most of the northwest European population in spring (Beekman *et al.* 1994, Luigujõe *et al.* 1996, Rees *et al.* 1997c). Body fat accumulated by Snow Geese while staging at James Bay, Canada, is similarly needed if the birds are to make the 1250-km journey to San Lake Refuge, South Dakota, in one flight; some even fly 3200 km direct to the Gulf Coast (Owen 1980). Autumn staging is particularly important for pre-migratory weight gain by young Lesser Snow Geese, which do not have sufficient lipid reserves to complete autumn migration until they have fed at staging sites on the James Bay coast (Wypkema and Ankney 1979). Cackling Canada Geese, which breed in northern Alaska, undertake a 2800-km migration between the Alaska Peninsula and wintering areas in Oregon and California; staging at Ugashik Bay again is thought to be essential if the birds are to complete the journey south (Sedinger and Bollinger 1987). Light-bellied Brent Geese that fly between Ireland and the eastern Queen Elizabeth Islands in northern Canada need to re-fuel in Iceland, and possibly Greenland as well (Merne *et al.* 1999), in one of the longest (if not the longest) migration of any of the geese. Landfall sites in Northern Ireland are also important for this species, with Strangford Lough receiving up to 75% of the population in autumn; there are no comparable pre-migratory staging areas in Ireland in spring (Merne *et al.* 1999).

The extent to which birds in flocks at migratory or wintering sites consist of the same individuals, or whether birds moving out are replaced by new birds moving in (referred to as 'turnover') is an important issue, since a high rate of turnover may mean that the whole population is dependent on several sites during the year. Sightings of colour-ringed and dye-marked Eurasian Wigeon have shown a high degree of within-winter dispersal from marking sites. Turnover rates *per se* are difficult to quantify, although Owen and Mitchell (1988) estimated that up to 50% more than the midwinter peak count of Eurasian Wigeon in Britain pass though sites in eastern England in the autumn months. Many pass on to sites in western Britain and Ireland; others are shot and are replaced by arrivals from Denmark and The Netherlands as the winter progresses. Madsen *et al.* (1998) used

within-winter recovery rates to estimate that some 700 000–1 000 000 Eurasian Teal pass through Denmark in the autumn, although only 34 000 are counted at peak. Likewise, an estimate of bird volume (i.e. the total number of birds using a site) derived from a series of counts and concurrent resightings of marked individuals found that nearly half of the Whooper Swans wintering in Ireland use the Lough Foyle–Lough Swilly region, and confirmed that counts alone underestimated the number of Pink-footed Geese using staging sites in Norway (Frederiksen *et al.* 2001). Sightings of individually marked Eurasian Wigeon suggest strong between-winter site fidelity, and an attachment to key wetlands within discrete pathways during migration (Mitchell *et al.* 1995). Thus, within a broad migration front, individual migratory ducks may visit the same sites year after year.

Recent studies of interspecific differences in life-history strategies have described some consequences of long-distance migration, attributable to various constraints on the birds' migratory and reproductive cycles. A comparison of the benefits of mate fidelity in Bewick's, Whooper and Mute Swans wintering in Britain found that breeding success improved with duration of the pairbond in all three species, but the cost of re-pairing (measured in terms of reduced breeding success) was higher for Bewick's Swans than for Whooper Swans and resident Mute Swans (Rees *et al.* 1996). The 3500-km migration by Bewick's Swans means that they have insufficient time both to find a new mate and to embark on raising cygnets in the short arctic summer, whereas Whooper Swans, with a shorter 800-km flight to Iceland, are able to re-pair and breed in a single season. Divorce occasionally occurs in Mute and Whooper Swans, but has been recorded only once in Bewick's Swans, presumably because maintaining existing pairbonds is particularly important for a species that combines long-distance migration with bi-parental care of the young through the first winter.

Movements of tropical and low-temperate species

Wildfowl that breed in tropical and subtropical regions are more likely than those at higher latitudes to respond to regular cycles of rainfall and to exploit temporary wetlands created by flooding. Periodic flooding in inland Australia, for instance, provides a belt of additional wetland habitats suitable for many ducks and also for Black Swans which move in to breed before retreating to the more temperate coastal zone as water levels fall. Species of the coastal plains, mainly Magpie Goose, Plumed Whistling-duck, Australian Wandering Whistling-duck, Pacific Black Duck and Australian Cotton Teal or Pygmy-goose, move annually from shallow-water to deep-water habitats, which are often located nearby (Lavery 1970a). The movements of Magpie Geese, therefore, are multidirectional, from the shallow-water breeding grounds in the wet season to permanent freshwaters in the dry season (Frith and Davis 1961b, Lavery 1970a). Species of inland Australia, such as Grey Teal, Hardhead and Wood Duck, travel further as evaporation progresses, from shallow waters to more permanent habitat, mostly on distant coastal plains (Lavery 1970a).

The sedentary nature of some endemic island species makes them particularly vulnerable to even short-term changes in their environment. The 1990–91 drought in the Recherche Archipelago, off the southwest coast of Australia, resulted in the death, apparently through starvation, of 40% of the local Cape Barren Goose population, which is now estimated at 250–500 individuals (Garnett 1992, Callaghan and Green 1993). The endangered Laysan Teal, which is restricted to a 370-ha island in the northwest Hawaiian Islands, is at risk from severe droughts or storms that affect breeding success, shifting sands that fill the central lake and, possibly, from sea-level rises associated with climate change; the island reaches only 12 m above sea level (Green 1992b). Other island species and subspecies vulnerable to changing conditions and the introduction of predators include Hawaiian Duck, Eaton's Pintail, Crozet Pintail, South Georgia Pintail and Galapagos Pintail (Green 1992b and see Chapter 8). Other species that are less confined by geographical features, by fragmented populations or by their sedentary habits are better able to adapt to new circumstances. The African White-backed Duck may need to be considered for globally threatened status, but the southern/eastern population undertakes large seasonal movements and numbers can vary greatly from year to year in certain areas. The construction of artificial dams is thought to have resulted in local increases (Callaghan and Green 1993).

Irregular movements and nomadism

Birds may also move in a more erratic manner, often in response to unpredictable localized changes in food availability, which in turn are usually associated with weather. The severe winter of 1962–63, the worst in Europe during the last century, resulted in a massive movement of ducks from areas bordering the North Sea southwards to France and Spain and westwards to Britain and Ireland (Owen and Black 1990). The larger body reserves of geese and swans means that they are better able than the smaller ducks to withstand periods without food, but most of the geese wintering in The Netherlands left for France after a week or two of cold weather (Philippona 1966). Nomadism is more prevalent in areas where the climate is less certain. Arid Australia has an unpredictable environment, occupies about 70% of the continent, and has numerous temporary wetlands ranging from less than 1 ha to 840 000 ha (Lake Eyre). In addition to seasonal movements to the coastal plain, Australian wildfowl may also disperse opportunistically in response to flooding produced by irregular rainfall. There is always wetland habitat somewhere in central Australia, where large numbers of waterbirds occur, but the mechanism by which the birds find these temporary wetlands is still unknown (Kingsford 1996).

Changes in distribution

Adaptation to new conditions may take several generations. In long-distance migrants that show a high level of site loyalty, and in wildfowl that are conservative in their feeding habits, the most common reason for a shift in distribution is habitat change brought about by man. The food selected by wintering geese and swans, and some realignment of the sites selected by these species, have been ascribed to changes in agriculture, notably land drainage and the increase in arable cultivation

(Kear 1963). Migratory swans, which have traditionally fed on aquatic and marshland plants and on flooded pasture, have increasingly moved onto arable land over the last 30 years (Rees *et al.* 1997b, Laubek 1995b, 1998). Similarly, Bean Goose populations underwent considerable changes in distribution in the second half of the twentieth century, as the extensive state farms of eastern and central Europe instigated mass production of maize, corn, rape and sugar beet, which rapidly became attractive to geese, resulting in an increase in numbers in these areas and a corresponding decline in southern Europe (van den Bergh 1999).

The location of suitable roost sites is also important in influencing the distribution of swans and geese. Despite a substantial increase in population size since the 1970s, the early autumn distribution of Pink-footed Geese in Britain is largely the same as in earlier years, with birds being particularly loyal to their roosts (Mitchell *et al.* 1999). The development of reserves in the UK by WWT, which included the provision of large waterbodies to provide secure roost sites, has resulted in a substantial increase in the number of migratory swans wintering at these sites. Although managing reserves for wildfowl could potentially attract birds from other areas (Rees and Bowler 1996), they may also sustain an increasing proportion of a growing population. Thus, the increased population size for Icelandic-breeding Whooper Swans during the late 1990s resulted in both a proportionate increase in existing flock sizes and in the use of new sites for swans wintering in Ireland, whereas British-wintering birds remained at existing sites but with an increasing concentration in key areas, particularly managed reserves (Cranswick *et al.* 2002). Distribution also varies with hunting pressure and recreational disturbance. For instance, hunting and other human activity restricted Whooper Swan breeding distribution to northern parts of Scandinavia and Karelia in the early twentieth century, but the swans' breeding range has since shifted southwards following protection measures in the mid-twentieth century (Nilsson 2002, Hokhlova and Artemjev 2002). Hunting disturbance also redistributes waterfowl within wintering areas (Bell and Owen 1990, Madsen and Fox 1995), and it has been suggested that the development of reserve

networks should be strategic, to ensure that disturbance-free feeding and resting areas are provided along migratory flyways, particularly for species most exposed to hunting and other human activities (Madsen *et al.* 1998). In future years, widespread changes in distribution of all wildfowl groups may result from major environmental changes due to climate alteration.

Species that are traditional in their site selection are generally less able to respond to changing conditions than more nomadic species. The former includes the Greenland White-fronted Goose, which is exceptionally faithful to breeding, wintering and staging sites. Individuals wintering on the Wexford Slobs in Ireland and on Islay return to particular fields, both within and between winters. Elsewhere their distribution has been seriously reduced, due to the combined effects of habitat loss and disturbance, and numbers have declined at many of their traditional haunts (Wilson *et al.* 1991, Fox 2003a). The Gadwall, conversely, has shown considerable range extension in the Western Palearctic during the last century, due to climatic amelioration and human introduction (Cramp and Simmons 1977) and to the increase in suitable habitat such as flooded mineral extraction pits and reservoirs (Fox and Mitchell 1988, Fox and Salmon 1989, and see Chapter 8). It is highly mobile in the north and east of its Western Palearctic range (some 46% of British and Irish-ringed Gadwall recoveries come from overseas), probably due to its preference for shallow eutrophic freshwaters. These are the first to freeze in northern and continental areas during normal winters (Fox and Mitchell 1988). The Low Countries, France and Spain appear to be the main wintering areas for British and Irish-ringed Gadwall recovered abroad; the high proportion of males recovered in France and Spain in winter suggests the involvement of abmigration, in which males pair with 'foreign' females and return with them to the latter's breeding area (Fox and Mitchell 1988).

Competition or coexistence

When two or more species with similar feeding habits occur in the same area, they may also compete for the available food resources, or adapt their behaviour in order to coexist, but either way this may affect their dispersal patterns. A grazing succession has been recorded for White-fronted Goose and Eurasian Wigeon, with Wigeon selecting fields that had been used intensively by geese during the previous month (Rees 1990). The grazing of fields by Bean Geese at Yare Valley, Norfolk, similarly made the grass more suitable for Wigeon, but the Wigeon then rapidly depleted the vegetation to a level which could not sustain the geese. An increase in the number of Wigeon and more intensive sheep grazing are, therefore, thought to account for the shift of Bean Geese from the Yare Valley over the past few decades (Sutherland and Allport 1994). The observation that Whooper Swans dominate Bewick's Swans at sites where both occur suggests that Whoopers may displace Bewick's Swans in these areas (Black and Rees 1984) but, so far, there is no conclusive evidence that competition between the two swans is affecting their distribution except at a local level (Rees *et al.* 1997b).

Intraspecific differences

Variations in migratory and dispersal patterns within species have led to greater understanding of the ecological factors underlying movements. For instance, young birds often migrate earlier and range further afield than adults. Baker (1978) suggested that the main advantage in returning to the breeding grounds for birds not yet of breeding age is the opportunity for exploration and habitat assessment prior to establishing their own territories. This hypothesis could be extended throughout the year, since birds without mates or young do not have to meet the food requirements of their offspring, nor develop nutrient reserves for the next breeding season. Since young and single birds tend to be subordinate, age differences in dispersal patterns may also be due to intraspecific competition. Whatever the reason, Bewick's Swans are certainly recorded at more wintering sites during years when they are single than when paired or in a family party (Rees and Bacon 1996), and two of only three individuals known to have switched flyways were subadult birds (Rees 1991). An age bias in dispersal patterns has also been recorded in the more sedentary Mute Swan (Spray 1981). Young of the

year move sooner and further than adults of several duck species, which may explain why juvenile wildfowl survive less well than adults during their first winter. Young Gadwall ringed in Britain disperse south to France in their first winter, and those from the European mainland move into Britain (Owen *et al.* 1986), perhaps because they compete for food with more experienced birds if they stay in their natal area (Owen and Black 1990). Age affects not only dispersal patterns but also site fidelity, with yearling females returning at lower rates than adult females (after allowing for poorer survival of young birds) of most of the wildfowl species studied (Anderson *et al.* 1992). Homing rates of adult, second-year and yearling Gadwall were calculated at 63%, 47% and 22% respectively (Blohm 1979).

Previous experience of the breeding or wintering grounds also accounts for some intraspecific differences in migration, particularly variation in site fidelity (see below) and return patterns. This is most evident in the long-lived geese and swans, where birds are able to develop and make use of the their accrued knowledge in future years. Bewick's Swans with at least one winter's experience of a wintering site arrive earlier in the autumn than birds new to the area (Evans 1980). This may be due to individuals heading straight for a site that they know has a good food supply close to a secure roost, rather than exploring other possibilities closer to the breeding range. Early arrival may give further benefits by enabling birds to regain condition and competitiveness, allowing them to retain a high position in the social hierarchy when the later swans arrive.

Sex differences in dispersal are found mainly among ducks that, unlike swans and geese, do not usually pair for life. In several European dabbling ducks, where the drake does not take part in brood rearing, male birds generally arrive first at moulting sites and within the wintering range. Later they are leap-frogged by the females which, eventually, have a more southerly distribution. Sex ratios of Common Pochard in Britain are highly correlated with latitude, with a 800:100 male to female ratio at 59°N, and only 150:100 at 50°N (Owen and Dix 1986). Similar trends have been recorded for North American species such as Canvasback,

Ring-necked Duck and Common Merganser or Goosander (Carbone and Owen 1995 review the literature). Reasons put forward to explain sex differences in dispersal include: (a) intraspecific competition for the food available in winter, with males dominating females; (b) the smaller females losing proportionately more heat and so moving to warmer climes; and (c) proximity to the breeding grounds enabling males to arrive early to defend a territory. The most substantial evidence supports the intersexual competition hypothesis, although the other factors may also be relevant. Male Common Pochards show higher levels of aggression than females (74% of male attacks are directed towards females) and this is thought likely to influence the number of females at feeding sites (Choudhury and Black 1992), a possibility already discussed in Chapter 4, page 66.

Differences in the competitive ability of individuals, pairs and family units may also influence the dispersion of wildfowl populations and the carrying capacity of habitat. Intraspecific competition is discussed elsewhere (Chapter 4), but should be considered here since the presence of competitors may result in subdominants moving to less crowded areas. In gregarious species, such as Brent Geese, where interference between individuals is low, birds tend to aggregate and deplete the food supply at the best site and then disperse *en masse* (Charman 1979, Sutherland and Parker 1985). Although dominant male Bewick's Swans with cygnets spend less time feeding and more time in being vigilant than other males, subordinate single birds remain less likely to return to the wintering site in subsequent years (Bowler 1996).

Moult migration

Salomonsen (1968) pointed out that the existence of moult migrations was established in the early 1920s, when the Swedish zoologist Sven Ekman described the phenomenon in Common Eider, Mute Swan and Lesser White-fronted Goose (Ekman 1922). Since then, the movement of birds to areas where they are safe from predation and have a good food supply whilst flightless during the wing moult has been described for several species.

This pre-moult movement cannot be regarded as an early stage of autumn migration because: (a) the moulting site is often in the opposite direction to the autumn migration; (b) certain sections of the population, usually the adult females, do not undertake a moult migration; and (c) the discrete location of the moulting sites and exceptionally high density of birds present, which is consistent from year to year, suggests a highly evolved behaviour.

In many of the dabbling ducks and seaducks, males and nonbreeders congregate on moulting grounds as soon as the females are incubating, whereas the females delay their wing moult until after the young have fledged. The extent to which male dabbling ducks undertake moult migrations is highly variable, both specifically, individually and geographically; they perhaps should not be regarded as 'true' moult migrations since the moulting sites are often within the breeding area or at suitable locations on the autumn migration route (e.g. in Northern Pintail and Eurasian Teal, Salomonsen 1968). Some one-year-old nonbreeding Eurasian Wigeon remain south of the breeding range during the summer and to moult, but the southward movement of breeding males soon after incubation is similar to the moulting dispersal of other dabbling duck species. Diving ducks or pochards usually breed at one year-old, so that there is no distinct moult migration of immature birds. Adult female diving ducks are more likely to join the moult migration, however, usually in smaller numbers and at a later stage than the males, probably because the females sometimes leave the brood before the young can fly (Salomonsen 1968).

The moult migrations of seaducks are better developed and more varied than those of any other group of wildfowl. Male eiders and scoters make long-distance flights to their moulting grounds, accompanied by one-year-old or two-year-old nonbreeders. A varying proportion of the female population also undertakes the journey, although some females remain to look after the ducklings in crèches. The Common Scoter may breed in Scotland and formerly in Northern Ireland, across northern Scandinavia and arctic Russia to the Taimyr Peninsula, but large moulting flocks occur in the North Sea just off the west coast of Jutland

and The Netherlands. Eiders also perform large-scale moult migrations to Danish waters. The entire population of male King Eiders breeding in east Canada (east of Victoria Island) and north Greenland are thought to congregate, with the immatures, in a comparatively restricted area of central west Greenland. Maximum density occurs in the Disko Bay region where up to 100 000 birds moult; the post-breeding males from mid-August until late September, the females remaining well into October (Salomonsen 1968, Frimer 1994). Some females undertake a separate moult migration of a shorter distance and at a later date than the males.

In shelducks, both parents care for the young but, in some cases, males may leave the family before the ducklings are fledged (Patterson 1982). The Common Shelduck has a spectacular moult migration, converging from all parts of its north-west European range to the Helgoland Bight or German Wadden Sea area just off the Weser and Elbe estuaries (Patterson 1982). Here, vast areas of mudflats (especially near the Grosser Knechtsand) afford the food supply and protection against predation required of a major moulting ground (Salomonsen 1968). Bridgwater Bay in southwest England, where soft glutinous mudflats restrict the access of predators, has probably been used by moulting Shelducks since the mid-nineteenth century (Patterson 1982) and remains important despite a decline in numbers in July (i.e. immediately prior to moulting) for the years 1988 to 1993 (Delany *et al.* 1994). In geese and swans, where both parents participate in guarding their young, pairs generally remain together on the breeding territories to moult, and only nonbreeders undertake moult migrations. Moreover, since moulting flocks of nonbreeding swans usually occur only a short distance from nesting pairs, and non-breeders tend to arrive later than breeders in the breeding range, it is not always clear when movements between sites constitute a moult migration. Movements that take nonbreeders away from the breeding areas have been described in 9 of the 15 species of geese, however (Owen 1980 and Figure 6.3), and thus appear to be a genuine migration.

Unlike the situation found in most ducks, which generally moult in areas with a milder climate than

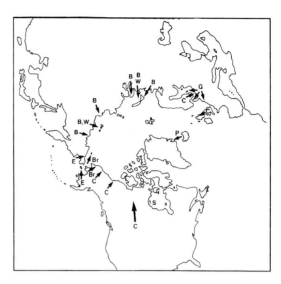

6.3 The moult migrations of geese. Abbreviations: B—Bean Goose; Br—Brent Goose; C—Canada Goose; E—Emperor Goose; G—Greylag Goose; P—Pink-footed Goose; S—Snow Goose; W—White-fronted Goose. Note that the only exception to the rule of northerly movement is that of introduced Canada Geese in the Baltic. Also note that the map is centred on the North Pole. Updated from Salomonsen (1968), reproduced from Owen (1980).

the breeding areas, moult migrations by geese are almost invariably northward (Figure 6.3). It has been suggested that this may be due to the longer daylength at high latitudes enabling the birds to detect predators more easily during the flightless period (Ebbinge and Ebbinge-Dallmeijer 1977), a view supported by the tendency for species breeding in temperate or sub-arctic regions (e.g. the larger Canadas, Bean Geese and the central European Greylag) to show the longest and most well-defined moult migrations. Some species that undertake moult migrations breed north of the Arctic Circle, however, and others, such as the Lesser Snow Geese of Hudson Bay, moult south of the Arctic Circle despite there being suitable areas further north. An alternative hypothesis is that they move to areas with better food quality, associated with the later spring flush of grass in arctic regions (Owen and Ogilvie 1979). This helps to explain the northerly trend in movement and the greater advantage to be gained by the southern populations.

Moreover, a few species, such as Lesser and Greenland White-fronted Geese, move to higher ground to moult since the thaw and the phenology of forage plants are later at higher altitudes (Owen 1980, Owen and Black 1990, Fox *et al.* 1999). The reason why a moult migration appears less obvious in northern migratory swans breeding in arctic or sub-arctic regions remains unclear, but at least in the Bewick's Swan this may be analogous to the weaker movements of high-latitude geese that show less tendency to undertake long journeys prior to losing their wing feathers. Certainly the main moulting sites, both for Bewick's Swans and Black Brant, are in the northern parts of their respective breeding ranges (Palmer 1976, Owen 1980, Mineyev 1991). The Mute Swan, which has a more southerly distribution, undertakes more substantial movements; nonbreeders in the western Baltic and from parts of southern Sweden congregate to moult in the shallow coastal waters of southwest Sweden (Mathiasson 1973b).

Site fidelity

An important feature of the migratory and dispersal patterns of wildfowl is the high level of site fidelity (philopatry) in both the breeding and wintering ranges (Rohwer and Anderson 1988, Robertson and Cooke 1999). The tendency for adult females to return to breed in the place in which they were hatched, and for the male to disperse more widely than the female in search of a mate, is well documented. This is common across species despite the range of habitats and migratory distances involved, with Mute Swans (Coleman and Minton 1979), Lesser Snow Geese (Cooke *et al.* 1975), Long-tailed Ducks (Alison 1977) and Canada Geese (Lessells 1985) all showing male-biased dispersal through the breeding range. The level of natal site fidelity by birds returning to nest does vary between species (Anderson *et al.* 1992 gives a review). Homing by female Blue-winged Teal, for instance, is comparatively uncommon (Johnson and Grier 1988 review the literature), whereas Canvasback and Common Eider females return very frequently (Wakeley and Mendall 1976, Franzmann 1983, Coulson 1984, Anderson 1985).

Johnson and Grier (1988) proposed that homing is generally more pronounced among species (such as Redhead, Lesser Scaup, Canvasback, Northern Mallard, Gadwall and Northern Shoveler) that use stable wetlands, whereas opportunistic settling is more prevalent in Blue-winged Teal and Northern Pintail, which use less predictable habitats.

Since a main advantage of site fidelity is thought to be the birds' previous knowledge of food availability in the area, both sexes may benefit from returning to their natal area to breed for the first time (Greenwood 1980); however, the opportunity to exploit a familiarity with the feeding areas may be particularly important for the female. Females suffer greater weight loss during egg-laying and incubation and, in most duck species, only the female is involved in rearing the young (see Chapter 5). Selection for a high level of natal site fidelity amongst females, therefore, may be particularly strong in ducks that breed at a year-old and where pairbonds last for a single season. Most migratory drakes show little natal or breeding philopatry, although some males without mates may return briefly to familiar breeding areas (Anderson *et al.* 1992 reviews the evidence). The exceptions are mainly seaducks (Anderson *et al.* 1992), with re-pairing of males with former mates, and subsequent breeding philopatry, recorded in Barrow's Goldeneye (Savard 1985), Common Eider (Spurr and Milne 1976), Long-tailed Duck (Alison 1975), Harlequin Duck (Bengtson 1972a), Common Shelduck (Patterson 1982) and Bufflehead (Gauthier 1987a). In the Common Goldeneye, fidelity to the same nest site has been linked to higher reproductive success (Dow and Fredga 1983). Female loyalty to the natal breeding area is also the general rule in monogamous long-lived species, such as geese and swans, where both members of the pair take parental responsibility. Differential dispersal of the two sexes is still considered important to avoid inbreeding (Bateson 1983), however, and any short-term disadvantage to the male of moving to a new area may be offset by the pair returning to that same site thereafter.

Migratory wildfowl may also be highly traditional in their selection of staging areas and wintering sites (see also Chapter 7, page 134). Individual and population loyalty to specific wintering sites is particularly well documented for Holarctic geese and swans. Individual Dark-bellied Brent Geese are loyal, not only to the same estuary, but to the same feeding area within an estuary over several years (St Joseph 1979). Greenland Whitefronts show precise fidelity to their staging sites in Iceland (Fox *et al.* 2002). Satellite-tracking of Whooper Swans between Scotland and Iceland showed that the same birds use the same flightpaths every season, even when crossing the sea (Pennycuick *et al.* 1996, 1999). Not only does the Svalbard Barnacle Goose population use the same wintering site in south-west Scotland, but individual geese use the same tiny parts of the Norwegian staging areas every year (Gullestad *et al.* 1984), and even follow the same tracks—known as 'foraging pathways'—across these fields in Norway both within and between years. (Black *et al.* 2004).

In other goose and swan species, where individual birds also show a high level of winter-site fidelity, the population is more widely dispersed in winter, with pair formation often occurring at migration sites or in the breeding range. A conflict of allegiance is likely to arise, therefore, for newly formed pairs on their autumn migration, since the new mate is likely to have formed an attachment to a different wintering site. A study of the winter dispersal of ringed Bewick's Swans found that males predominated in determining the wintering site of the new pair (Rees 1987). They also maintained their normal time of arrival at their traditional wintering site when accompanied by a new mate, while females did not show such consistency. Further analysis of pre-flight behaviour confirmed that males tended to lead the movement of the pair in autumn. A shift in responsibility within the pair-bond occurred during the winter, however, and flight initiation by the female was more common in spring, supporting the general trend in wildfowl for females to dominate in movements to the breeding grounds. This pattern may be modified also by an individual's previous experience of the different sites. Anecdotal information about Bewick's Swans in winter and Whooper Swans within the breeding range indicates that older females may lead new, younger mates to the wintering sites, whereas older

experienced males may maintain their loyalty to their nest sites upon re-pairing.

Advantages of site fidelity have been described mainly for monogamous wildfowl with long-term pairbonds. In swans and geese, the increase in breeding success with pairbond duration also reflects a pair's experience of the breeding territory, since the pair generally returns to the same nest site every season. Examination of pairbond duration and breeding experience in swans (by considering birds with a succession of mates) found that breeding experience was also associated with increased breeding success, but that it was not possible to determine whether this was due to site fidelity and familiarity with the breeding territory, or to an improvement in the birds' ability to select a mate (Rees *et al.* 1996). In arctic-nesting birds, the shortness of the arctic summer means that the breeding season must follow a tight schedule, leaving little opportunity for exploratory dispersal in the breeding area once individuals join the breeding population. Recent studies of Bewick's Swans nesting in the Russian Arctic confirm that pairs familiar with the breeding area nest earlier in the spring and produce larger clutches than birds new to the site; this was particularly pronounced in late springs when the snow was slow to thaw. The tendency for individuals to follow the same migratory routes every year also means that pairs accidentally separated are more likely to rediscover one another. Similarly, if members of a family become separated during the winter, young birds can find their parents at traditional roost sites.

Mechanisms of migration
Timing

The severity of the arctic winter and the short summer season means that the migratory and reproductive cycles must be synchronized closely, as the birds must breed, moult, develop fat reserves and start migration in the three to four months during which the tundra is habitable. Arctic-breeding ducks, and the eiders in particular, winter at quite high latitudes and appear to move northwards with the thaw. Spectacled Eiders even winter in holes in the pack ice, kept open by the massive numbers present in flocks that feed under the ice on krill and other crustacea. For birds wintering further south, however, different factors must initiate and control physiological and other changes in preparation for migration and reproduction at the appropriate time.

Seasonal migrants have innate 'circannual rhythms' (i.e. a biological rhythm having a periodicity of about one year) of migratory restlessness that are influenced by daylength. Several studies have confirmed that daylength, which is a highly reliable indicator of seasonal change, is the stimulus that triggers the onset of migration in a range of bird species (Lofts and Murton 1968, Murton and Westwood 1977). The photoperiodic response may be modified in the short term by other environmental stimuli, but these usually operate only in concurrence with appropriate photostimulation. Most work on circannual rhythms has been carried out on passerines, but the floodlighting of the Bewick's Swans' roost in the Rushy Pen at WWT Slimbridge provided a unique opportunity for analysing the swans' departure patterns under different light regimes (Rees 1982). The floodlights were installed before the Bewick's Swans started visiting the Rushy Pen and were retained because the artificial illumination did not initially seem to affect their behaviour or welfare. During the 1977–78 winter, however, the swans had all left Slimbridge by 1 February and 18 were identified in West Germany within seven days. When the weather deteriorated later in the month, 14 of the swans identified in Germany returned to Slimbridge and one to WWT Welney in Norfolk (Evans 1982), indicating that the birds had left 'prematurely'. Examination of the effects of the different light regimes confirmed that swans floodlit from dusk until 22.00 h departed on spring migration significantly earlier than those illuminated until 20.00 h, and these in turn left before those receiving a natural daylength. As a result of this study, the floodlights are now dimmed at 19.00 h, and the swans leave Slimbridge at the same time as those wintering in other parts of Britain.

Further consideration of differences in the timing of migration for individual Bewick's Swans wintering at Slimbridge showed that certain individuals always tend to arrive early in autumn or to leave late in spring (Rees 1989). The analyses took account of the swans' previous experience of the site, which also influenced their arrival and departure patterns (Evans 1980). Moreover, full-grown independent offspring had arrival dates similar to those of their parents. It remains to be seen whether consistency in the timing of migration is related to the location of individuals in the breeding range, and thus the time taken to complete their migratory journey, or whether every bird has its own innate response threshold to increasing daylength in the spring.

Once the swans have received sufficient photostimulation to signal the onset of the migration season, the final departure date is determined by weather conditions, particularly wind direction (Evans 1979b, Rees 1982). A major study of the migration of Lesser Snow Geese over central North America found that birds prefer to migrate on following winds, although wind strength did not appear to be important (Blokpoel and Gauthier 1975). Satellite-tracking of Whooper Swans between Britain and Iceland has provided further insight into the birds' migratory strategies under adverse weather conditions (Pennycuick et al. 1996, 1999). Northbound swans that encountered strong head or side winds landed and stayed on the sea for up to 31 hours; two birds forced by gales from their flightpath recovered their position and eventually made landfall in a direct line with their original flightpath. Transcontinental migrants use staging areas to rest and accumulate body reserves (Drent et al. 1980), as well as to wait for conditions to improve during the journey north (Rees and Bowler 1991). Theoretically, the autumn migration may be more rapid and direct, since the birds are less likely to encounter adverse weather during their journey south. Certainly, Bewick's Swans are more likely to be reported at migratory sites in spring than in autumn (Evans 1982). Numbers staging in Estonia are usually much higher in spring (Luigujõe et al. 1996), and non-stop flight distances (i.e. where the birds did not stop for more than 2.5 days) were much longer in autumn (on average 1032 km ± 363) than in spring (on average

350 km $\pm$ 166) (Beekman *et al.* 2002). However, autumn passage through Estonia has taken longer than spring migration in recent years, occurring in two waves, with nonbreeders arriving ahead of family parties. The shorter stopovers in spring were thought to be due to the late start to the spring migration due to adverse weather conditions (Luigujõe *et al.* 1996). Food abundance also regulates the use of sites during migration. Dark-bellied Brent Geese, arriving at staging sites in autumn, rapidly deplete the supply of *Zostera*, their preferred food, after which there is little regrowth of vegetation, whereas in spring continuous growth of vegetation regenerates the food supply (Ebbinge 1992).

Since birds have to carry the body fat that provides the energy needed for migration, a further limitation on the timing of migration may be their body condition before departure. Surprisingly, however, there is no evidence to show that the extent of body reserves affects the birds' departure patterns. Brent Geese leave The Netherlands at the same time every year, even though birds in good condition on departure are more likely to have a successful breeding season (Ebbinge 1989). The provision of additional food for Bewick's Swans in winter does not seem to trigger early migration (Rees 1982); other studies have also shown that weights of migrant wildfowl peak in early to midwinter (Matthews and Campbell 1969, Owen and Cook 1977, Evans and Kear 1978, Owen 1981b). Variables other than body condition, therefore, appear to regulate departure, although food shortage may inhibit departure under exceptional circumstances. In the 1977–78 winter, when Bewick's Swans started leaving WWT Slimbridge in January, reached West Germany by 7 February, then returned to the UK because of frozen conditions on the European mainland, it was estimated that the birds would take 24 days to replenish their fuel reserves (Evans 1979b, 1982). They finally departed on spring migration in early March after spending 15–26 days (mean = 23 days for eight swan units) at the site.

It is possible that hyperphagia, where birds feed intensively to build fat reserves for migration and breeding, may be more evident at spring staging sites than in the wintering range, since food intake at these sites is important not only for fuelling migration to the breeding grounds but may also determine reproductive success that summer. Moreover, fat gain may also be easier to achieve at these sites, because there would be newly available food resources following the thaw and longer days in which to feed at higher latitudes. Prompt arrival on the breeding grounds also influences productivity; there is generally an inverse relationship between the date of clutch initiation and reproductive success (Daan *et al.* 1990). Thus the timing of migration involves a trade-off between early arrival on the breeding grounds and the benefits of larger body stores achieved by a longer stay at migratory sites, which in Barnacle Geese was resolved by birds leaving the migratory sites at intermediate dates having the highest breeding success (Prop *et al.* 2003). These decisions concerning the timing of movement from migratory sites are likely to depend on the migratory distances involved, location of staging sites and the ability of the birds to carry additional body stores. For instance, there is anecdotal evidence that Whooper Swans from the Icelandic-breeding population may stop feeding in the days prior to migration, perhaps because they have reached optimum weight for migration and thus avoid carrying excess weight during their long overseas flight.

Mechanical limitations

Several studies have examined the altitude and speed of migration. Results indicate that these vary between species and in accordance with local conditions. Seaducks, for instance, usually skim the waves when migrating along the coast, but Common Eiders migrating in southern Scandinavia gained height upon crossing land and were lost from view (Alerstam *et al.* 1974). Average altitudes of geese flying over land seems to be around 600 m above ground level for both Snow Goose (Blokpoel 1974) and Canada Goose (Bellrose 1968, Owen and Black 1990). Commonly, altitudes varied between 300 m and 1500 m, with one instance of a pilot reporting Snow Geese flying at 6200 m over Louisiana (Owen and Black 1990 review the literature). Bar-headed Geese were heard at 8300 m, migrating over a mountain pass in the Himalayas, but their actual height above ground level was rather low (Owen 1980). Exceptionally, a flock of about 30 swans, presumed to be Whoopers, seen at an altitude of 8200 m off the Outer Hebrides, was tracked by radar until they descended over the coast of Northern Ireland (Stewart 1978), but more recent studies have shown that Whooper Swans usually migrate at between 500 m and 1700 m when crossing the ocean (Pennycuick *et al.* 1996, 1999). When crossing land, none flew any higher than necessary for terrain clearance.

Flight speed generally depends upon wind conditions, and also upon the birds' strength to body weight ratio. Thus eider ducks, which have the highest wing loading, are thought to have the highest stalling speed and to be the fastest flying bird, at 76 km/h in steady flight (Rayner 1985). Mute Swans, amongst the largest of wildfowl, are thought to have only enough muscle power for a marginal rate of climb at sea level when laden with fat (Hedenstrom and Alerstam 1992, Pennycuick *et al.* 1996). Geese generally fly at around 60 km/h in still air, but ground speeds of up to 185 km/h have been recorded for Snow Geese, and 140 km/h for Whooper Swans assisted by a jet stream (Owen and Black 1990). Further estimates for Whooper Swans migrating between Britain and Iceland showed that the commonest air speeds were around 21 m/s (76 km/h), although this varied with wind speed, wind direction and fat loading. The flight of a male Whooper Swan (colour-ringed with lettering to read JAP) was particularly interesting (Figure 6.4). The largest swan caught at WWT Caerlaverock, southwest Scotland, at the upper end of the scale for a species thought to be close to the maximum mass capable of powered flight, his flight-performance calculations indicated that he would be restricted to speeds near his minimum power (17 m/s) until some of his fat reserves were utilized. Tracking of his spring migration to Iceland showed that his air speed did not exceed 21 m/s until the final stages. The swan then encountered a northerly gale which threatened to blow him off course into the mid-Atlantic, whereupon he maintained an average air speed of 27 m/s (97 km/h) for over three hours. It is thought that his leaner condition towards the end of his flight

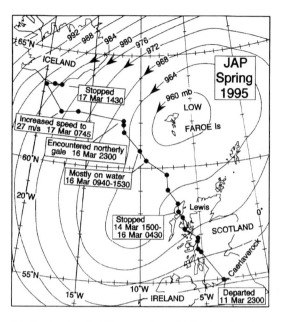

6.4 Track of male Whooper Swan JAP migrating from Scotland to Iceland, 11–17 March 1995. Isobars for 0600h on 17 March 1995. From Pennycuick *et al.* 1996.

enabled him to accelerate and to reach land, probably saving his life (Pennycuick *et al.* 1996). Bewick's Swans are similarly limited in the amount of fuel (fat) that they can carry (24% of body weight), which in turn limits the distance they can travel before needing to feed and replenish their reserves (Beekman *et al.* 1996a). The availability of food resources at regular intervals along the migratory route, therefore, is important for enabling the swans to continue their travels.

Orientation and navigation

Young geese and swans on their first migration remain with their parents all the way to the wintering grounds and return with them in spring to the breeding grounds. Although they split away as the adults settle to breed, there is good observational evidence that the young rejoin their family for at least a second migration. They thus have ample opportunities to learn when, how and where to migrate. It would seem likely that they may learn the general direction of flight from astronomical cues (discussed below) but there is undoubtedly a learning of landmarks and chains of wetlands. In this way, traditions are established and passed from generation to generation. Learned traditions are not rigid but can be adapted to take account of changes in the suitability of wetlands arising from natural changes or human modifications.

Where parent geese and swans are prevented from migrating, for example by wing-pinioning in wildfowl collections and zoos, fledged young show innate restlessness at migration time, but do not fly away. Thus it can be assumed that they do not have innate knowledge of the direction in which to migrate, or of the wintering grounds. However, if other wild geese, even of a different species, pass by, the youngsters may join them and migrate to their winter quarters. Although it seems that goose and swan migrations must be based on learning, there has been virtually no experimental work to establish what exactly is learned.

Ducks are different in that they do not migrate with their parents. Most never see their fathers and leave their mothers soon after fledging. Ringing recoveries indicate that they wander for a while, with some northerly bias, and then set off in a migratory direction appropriate to their population. Such a movement could also be due to them joining experienced birds. Indeed, non-migratory Northern Mallard, fostered with migratory stock, have been recovered 2400 km away (Valinkangas 1933). On the other hand, recoveries of ringed Blue-winged Teal held back until all migrants had passed still indicated a direction normal for their species (Bellrose 1958a); and young birds reared in one area and released in another, where they do not occur, moved in the usual direction (Vaught 1964).

It seems likely, therefore, that ducks, and probably also swans and geese, are equipped with innate 'instructions' to migrate in one general compass direction. This ability has been demonstrated clearly in many species of birds, with strong indications that the distance travelled is also under endogenous, or internal, control. Such distance-and-bearing navigation could enable otherwise unguided young birds to reach the population's wintering grounds, the exact stop-off point being determined by ecological and/or social factors. The underlying innate

migratory controls have not been investigated in wildfowl, but the release of appropriate hormones is probably governed by endogenous rhythms interacting with external factors such as daylength, as in many passerines.

The factors involved in determining a compass direction have been analysed using a well-marked orientation behaviour exhibited by several species of duck upon release (Bellrose 1958b). Matthews (1961, 1968, 1984), working mainly with Northern Mallard, of which he released many thousands, found that their orientation differed in different populations, and was not related to migratory direction, season, sex or age. It broke down soon (20 minutes) after release, and its function did not seem to give birds a better chance of rejoining others, since groups released together show even stronger orientation. Matthews coined the term 'nonsense' orientation but, although not making sense, it does present the opportunity to find the clues that enable a bird to take up the desired direction.

Under heavy cloud, the birds depart randomly whether by day or night (when their tracks can be followed by small leg lamps). This suggests that they are not using a magnetic compass but are relying on astronomical clues. Sun-compass orientation, which has been demonstrated in many species of animals, is confirmed by manipulating their internal 'clocks'. These run on an endogenous circadian rhythm kept in phase with external events by time indicators such as sunrise and sunset. Confined for several days in a closed room in which the light regime is advanced or retarded, their internal clocks are likewise adjusted. On release in sunny conditions, Northern Mallard that normally fly northwest, go southwest when advanced six hours, while those retarded six hours go northeast. Clearly they are flying at a changing angle to the sun, allowing for its apparent movement of 15 degrees per hour. Switched through 12 hours, the birds go southeast when the sun is near the horizon. When the switched 'clocks' indicate that it should be night, the birds go successively from southeast to southwest to northwest to northeast and back to southeast. This is taken to show that the angle-correcting mechanism, having decreased successively through the day as the sun moves from east to west, oscillates in reverse during the night as if the sun moves back from west through south to east. Such oscillating sun-compass mechanisms have been demonstrated in other birds, invertebrates, fish and reptiles. The alternate scheme, to react as if the sun moves on from west through north to south, has also been found in some animals. If that were so in this instance, the Mallard would have gone southeast whatever the time.

At night, when only the stars are available as clues, time shifting has no effect on the northwest orientation. This indicates that the birds are not relying on certain stars, altering their angle of flight with time. Instead, they have presumably observed the movement of constellations round the sky and established the axis of their rotation, the north point, marked by Polaris. This astonishing conclusion has been confirmed by planetarium experiments with Northern Mallard and Eurasian Teal (Wallraff 1972). The ducks were restrained on a rotating turntable and given a mild electric shock whenever they were facing in the training direction. This produced an increase in heart-rate. After training, no shocks were needed for an anticipatory increase to occur. The ducks were able to indicate the required direction in this way under natural starry skies and under the planetarium dome, where the stars are simulated by pinpricks of light. Even completely artificial constellation patterns could be learned provided they were rotated so that the axis reference point could be ascertained. Once this coupling was achieved, orientation occurred under stationary planetarium skies.

In caged tests, the moon either produced a simple phototactic response (i.e. turning towards light) or confusion. In field tests with Northern Mallard, when both moon and stars were visible, time-shifting had no effect on orientation, suggesting that star information predominated. Occasionally, cloud was sufficient to obscure the stars but not the moon, and then time-shifting was effective, six-hour shifts producing the appropriate right-angle changes in orientation. Surprisingly, birds that had been incarcerated out of sight of the moon for a week were apparently able to allow about an hour a day for its eastward slippage; otherwise this would have imposed another right-angle on their orientation.

Twelve-hour time-shifting with the moon produced results that were not conclusive but suggested that moon-compass orientation is subserved by an angle-correcting mechanism as complicated as that for the sun-compass.

Distance-and-bearing navigation, based on sun, star and moon compasses and endogenous rhythms of migratory activity, coupled with the following of experienced birds and the learning of landmarks, would seem to account for much duck migration. But are they able to use some form of true navigation to 'home' on a known goal from an unknown point? The Mallard experiments showed little evidence of this. They appeared very ready to settle in any suitable area. Similar flexibility is shown in 'abmigration', where males pair on the wintering grounds with females coming from other breeding places and return with them. A map of duck recoveries shows broad 'flyways' with the different species not splitting into recognizable subspecies or populations, as do geese and, to a lesser extent, swans. Geese and swans follow more restricted corridors, and often birds from widely separate breeding grounds winter close together without mixing, returning year after year to the same localities. They are the ones more likely to be capable of 'homing' by using more complete navigation mechanisms, but as yet they have not been tested.

Other bird species have been shown to have the ability to home (Matthews 1968), probably 'fixing' their position relative to home on some form of grid, composed of the isolines of two factors that vary regularly across the Earth at an angle to each other. Various candidates for providing such grids have been suggested, such as the positions of the sun or stars, the Earth's magnetic field, forces resulting from the Earth's rotation, or unspecified odours. But none can be said to have been proved beyond doubt. Any grid would have to be 'set' with reference to the surroundings, and this could be done using any of the compasses that have been demonstrated.

Application to conservation

Changes in the distribution of birds pose problems for conservation, since different sites and habitats may be important at different times of year, and all may be crucial for survival. Conservation is particularly difficult where birds cross political boundaries, since a coordinated response is necessary to ensure that protective measures are effective. The Convention on the Conservation of Migratory Species of Wild Animals, known as the 'Bonn Convention' (see Chapter 8), has been revolutionary in addressing the needs of migratory species throughout their range. All migratory wildfowl in northwest Europe are included as Annex II species under the Convention, which requires that 'Range States' (i.e. all countries in which a particular species occurs) be encouraged to conclude agreements for their conservation and management. Article V of the Bonn Convention states that the objective of each agreement should be to restore the migratory species concerned to a favourable conservation status, or to maintain it in such a status. Such agreements should also cover the whole range of the species concerned and should be open to accession by all Range States irrespective of whether or not they are Parties to the Convention.

The African–Eurasian Migratory Waterbird Agreement (AEWA) was drafted under the terms of the Bonn Convention and signed in The Hague in 1995. This sets priorities for the conservation of all waterbirds listed in Annex II of the Convention, and action plans have been developed for some species. AEWA encourages the designation of new protected sites, as well as promoting research programmes and cooperation between Range States (for further information, see Chapter 8.)

Increased international dialogue is also reaping dividends in terms of flyway management plans which, it is hoped, will form the basis for future protection of rare and endangered species. Even before AEWA was developed, those involved in Greenland White-fronted Goose conservation were aware of the need for a conservation plan for the whole population for what is one of the rarest geese in the world. A meeting of representatives of the four Range States (Greenland/Denmark, Iceland, Ireland and the UK) in 1990 led to a Greenland White-fronted Goose International Conservation Plan that described key areas for action in different parts of the range. Unfortunately, although various recommendations included in the plan have been adopted, the plan has not yet been signed and implemented as a whole. More recently, WWT has taken the lead on behalf of Scottish Natural Heritage and the Norwegian Directorate for Nature Management in developing a Flyway Management Plan for the Svalbard Barnacle Goose population, which aims to provide a network of protected sites in Britain, Norway and Svalbard (Black 1998). The Asia–Pacific Migratory Waterbird Strategy for 1996–2000, which provides a blueprint for encouraging cooperation for the conservation of migratory waterbird species and their habitats across the Asia–Pacific region, similarly aims towards developing action plans and establishing a network of key sites. Increased cooperation between Range States generally should lead not only to the development of species management plans, but also help to ensure that those plans are implemented.

7

Population dynamics

Tony Fox

Definitions, flyways, populations

The nature of wildfowl populations

Asked for a definition of a population, a biologist may be forgiven for saying that it is a group of organisms defined in whatever way the observer sees fit for his own purposes! Generally, a population is taken to mean a delimited group of individuals of the same species occupying a particular space in time. This is where the problems begin. A population of Northern Pintail may comprise the entire global 'population' of the species, the 'population' that uses the Western Palearctic at some stage in its life cycle, the 'population' that winters on the Mersey Estuary in northwest England or the small breeding 'population' that frequents a small lake on the Alaskan tundra. All are defined in time and space, but do they have any meaning from the point of view of research, monitoring or conservation?

Many of the pintail in the world are extremely unlikely to encounter each other, simply because of their geographic separation. Hence, it is more relevant to consider the ultimate constituents of a population, which are the individual birds that can potentially interbreed. For instance, Pink-footed Geese are geographically extremely restricted, but we know that there are two discrete populations, one of which summers in Iceland and Greenland and spends the winter in Britain, and the other which breeds in Svalbard and winters in Denmark, The Netherlands and Belgium. Birds from these two 'populations' use different migration routes, and their lives rarely overlap in time and space unless they are deflected off track by severe

weather. Recent marking of birds from both populations confirms that very few birds indeed move between one population and the other, and fewer again make a permanent change between one flyway and the other (see Madsen *et al.* 1999a). The same is true of the Barnacle Goose, which has three such discrete populations nesting in East Greenland, Svalbard, and from the Baltic to arctic Russia. Each of these populations shows differing population trends, in terms of reproductive output and survival rates, faces different nature conservation threats, solutions and legislation in the different countries they inhabit, and uses different chains of habitat networks along their migration corridors. Hence, it makes sense for them to be treated for conservation purposes as separate entities, even if individual birds cannot be ascribed by a bird-watcher in the field to a specific population (since in these examples there are no plumage differences between populations).

These definitions are extremely useful, for example, in ensuring adequate protection for different populations under international agreements. For instance, the criteria used to designate wetlands of international importance under the Ramsar Convention (see Chapter 8) necessitate that 1% of the total flyway population (rather than the global population) uses a site on a regular basis before it is eligible for such recognition and protection. To establish the 1% criterion, it is self-evident that one needs to have some knowledge of what constitutes 100%; that is, the total numbers of birds in a population. This may be relatively easy with geese where different populations are largely separate and discrete, but the problem is more difficult for duck species. These tend to be widely distributed and show more continuous distributions, especially on the breeding grounds. Outside the breeding season, their numbers are highly concentrated into suitable wintering habitat where birds from widely differing breeding provenance mix together. Ringing recoveries of birds captured and marked in different parts of the flyway do at least provide some arguments for segregation of the overall population into separate flyways. A good example is the Northern Pintail of western Europe. This species has been divided into those that winter in North Sea regions and those that winter in the Mediterranean Basin and Africa (Scott and Rose 1996). The North Sea birds are thought to breed in Scandinavia and near parts of Russia, number 60 000 individuals and show relatively stable trends. In contrast, the remainder is thought to originate from breeding areas further east, numbers 1.2 million birds, and is showing signs of decline. In this case, there is a clear need to differentiate these elements in order to tackle their respective conservation problems in an appropriate fashion. Such a pragmatic approach does not rule out further subdivision as better research and monitoring information is forthcoming to define, in more detail, the flyway population structure of these and other duck species.

By virtue of their wetland habitats, wildfowl populations have probably always been patchily distributed in some areas. Human activities in recent decades have frequently resulted in even more fragmentation of formerly more continuous wetland habitats, such that much wildfowl habitat is now discretely distributed. This is true of the White-headed Duck, which favours rather unusual habitats

Below this level of definition, flyway populations can be broken down into increasingly local subdivisions down to the ultimate breeding units (called 'demes' by Krebs 1972). At this level, groups of freely interbreeding birds represent the smallest collective unit of an animal population and are usually defined in terms of their disjunct nature from other such locally breeding units. Nevertheless, such a concept may be rather arbitrary for a species that has a dispersed but continuous geographical distribution, so the definition of such populations is difficult and ultimately subjective.

in Europe and Asia, and which now shows a highly fragmented breeding and wintering distribution. Hence, historically (but perhaps increasingly so in the present) most wildfowl populations have been composed of a number of separate and partly independent sub-groups which are linked by dispersal. This is the classic 'metapopulation' situation, a field that has attracted considerable research interest in recent years (e.g. Hanski and Gilpin 1991, Hanski 1994). A metapopulation consisting of many smaller sub-populations may remain constant over time, whilst the individual sub-populations which make up that larger unit experience a complex mixture of colonization, expansion, stabilization, decline and extinction. Since patches vary in size, quality and physical separation from each other, the processes may be complex and the population processes that occur depend on these features of the patches. Large patches of high-quality habitat may be highly resistant to extinction by virtue of their size and quality and may play a crucial role in maintaining smaller units that are correspondingly more likely to die out. As can be seen, the role of dispersal is crucial, since this provides a mechanism for both recolonization and the propping up of sub-populations that are not self-maintaining.

Interchange between groups

Many goose species underwent considerable expansion in both breeding numbers and range during the second half of the last century. We therefore tend to know more about birds dispersing between groups in increasing populations than in stable or declining ones. Take the Pink-footed Geese that breed in Iceland and Greenland, for example. In the 1950s, it was believed that the majority of the breeding pairs were restricted to the glacial melt river meadows of Þjórsárver in the interior deserts of Iceland. It is now thought that this restricted distribution could have been the result of human persecution earlier last century. However, with restrictions on hunting season and sale of game, the creation of refuges and the increased availability of food from improvements in agricultural practice on the wintering grounds, the population began a sustained increase. In the 1970s, increasing numbers were seen away from the core breeding area, and the species recolonized breeding areas deserted in historical times (see species account in Madsen *et al.* 1999a). Different areas were colonized at different times, and numbers at individual breeding sites often showed increases in numbers far faster than in the population as a whole. As the breeding habitat filled up, so many of these breeding sub-populations reached an equilibrium, after which there was no further increase in breeding numbers. Nevertheless, the global population size continued to increase, despite individual sub-populations showing increasing or stable numbers. The same has been true of Svalbard-nesting Barnacle Geese in newly colonized areas (Prestrud *et al.* 1989). In stark contrast, the Lesser White-fronted Goose has shown increasing retraction and fragmentation of its world range (see species account in Madsen *et al.* 1999a). In this case, the lack of dispersal as a result of shrinking population size leads to isolation of sub-population units, most of which are not robust enough to maintain their own numbers without sustained immigration. In these circumstances, it may rapidly become the case that no single population is self-sustaining and the downward trends of individual sub-populations merely reflect the trajectory of the population as a whole.

It is therefore somewhat ironic that many northern hemisphere wildfowl populations show high levels of site fidelity to wintering (Robertson and Cooke 1999), staging (Reed *et al.* 1998, Fox *et al.* 2002) and breeding areas (Ganter and Cooke 1998). It would appear that, in response to a stable and predictable resource, many species have evolved a strategy of returning to the same network of areas throughout their life cycle. For most female ducks, it is the norm to return to the breeding areas of former years (Anderson *et al.* 1992, Ludwichowski *et al.* 2002). When wetland habitat is predictable, this is a good strategy, but increasingly, human disruption to annual cycles makes this a strategy that is less likely to ensure survival and successful reproduction. Female philopatry is especially evident in breeding geese, so much so that the behavioural trait may become maladaptive. At the extreme, this may result in mature females returning year after year to breed in deteriorating habitat.

This has been well demonstrated by the long-term study of the Lesser Snow Goose colony at La Pérouse Bay in Hudson Bay, northern Canada (Cooke *et al.* 1995). The colony probably did not exist before the late 1940s, but the population increased steadily for many years until the pressure of staging geese and the density of breeding birds themselves began to destroy the very vegetation that they exploit for rearing their young. The results have been marked, with major effects on the breeding output of the colony, a reduction in size of the offspring and the gradual abandonment of central parts of the colony. Females are now forced, by the complete lack of habitat, to search for any suitable nest sites well away from their formerly favoured areas. Here, then, is a case of a wildfowl sub-population colonizing a new breeding area, establishing a sub-population that grows rapidly, then ultimately bringing about its own decline. This, despite the continued expansion of the global population which, all the while, has been colonizing other new breeding opportunities throughout the Canadian Arctic (Alisauskas and Boyd 1994).

Isolating mechanisms

At the global level, most dabbling ducks in the northern hemisphere have identical ecological counterparts in both the Old and New Worlds. Some species, such as Northern Pintail, Northern Shoveler and Gadwall, are common to all northern continents. Although the probabilities of interbreeding between specific individuals vary enormously throughout the hemisphere, there is enough genetic interchange over a long enough period to ensure uniformity of morphology and, to a lesser extent, of ecology. Nevertheless, it is extremely likely that sub-populations do show genetic differences, by virtue of their effective isolation from other sub-groups over sufficient time scales. For some forms, isolation has been sufficiently long for the development of minor differences, such as the differences between Northern Mallard in Greenland and the rest of the northern hemisphere, or between the Green-winged Teal in North America and those of Eurasia. In the case of wigeon, the isolation is such that different species occur in the two land masses and, in the case of many island races or subspecies, physical separation has led to the evolution of distinct genetic entities.

Evolutionary biologists in the 1960s became fascinated with the mechanisms that maintained genetic isolation between species. Since hybridization between ducks and geese in captivity (and in the wild) is common, and their offspring are often fertile, it was argued that plumage and behavioural mechanisms had evolved to maintain the genetic integrity of species (Johnsgard 1963). Hence, it was argued that the reduced coloration of island races of ducks (compared to 'mainland' populations from which they are thought to be derived, Weller 1980) related to the reduced need for species distinctiveness. However, increasingly it is demonstrated that wildfowl are well able to discriminate between subtle differences in calls and plumage (if only because we know that paired birds easily recognize one another), and there seems no good reason to suppose that complex markings or signals are actually necessary to identify conspecifics in order to maintain genetic isolation (McKinney 1992).

Population dynamics
Description and definitions

The overall abundance of a wildfowl species naturally depends on its density in its favoured habitat and the extent and distribution of that habitat. These factors set the overall context for the size of a population and its range but, nevertheless, a great many factors potentially can affect the abundance of a population. Populations show fluctuations in the numbers of constituent individuals in time and space because of changes in four basic parameters. Overall, the size of a population is determined by differences in *recruitment* (i.e. the number of new birds being born) and *mortality* (the number of individuals dying). Hence, if recruitment exceeds mortality, the population will increase, while if mortality exceeds recruitment, the population trend will be downward. Locally, numbers are also affected by the balance of *emigration* (birds leaving an area to move elsewhere) and *immigration* (birds contributing to local numbers by arriving from

elsewhere). It is the changes in numbers of individuals in a given population and the processes that affect the flux in numbers which are generally known as *population dynamics*. If we are to understand the population dynamics of an organism, we need to be able to understand the causes for the observed trends in numbers shown by that particular species. This necessitates an understanding of the factors that affect birth and death rates, and what determines the movements of birds between sites.

Wildfowl have long held the attention of ecologists interested in understanding population dynamics because humans have traditionally exploited them for food. Since many of the most popular hunted quarry species show favourable conservation status (since their numbers currently continue to increase, as is the case in western Europe), it is clear that populations can sustain a level of exploitation which does not cause a decline in their overall numbers. However, not all wildfowl populations have such a happy conservation status. Several show alarming declines and contraction of range and, in these cases, an understanding of the dynamics of a population assumes considerable conservation importance. If we are to understand the reasons for these declines and offer management solutions in order to safeguard them for the future, it is essential that we understand what factors contribute to the regulation of birth and death rates in the population. In this way it may be possible to pinpoint simple mechanisms to enhance reproductive success or to reduce mortality in ways that may restore the population to a favourable situation, where more birds are born than are dying, restoring the population trend to one of increase.

Of particular interest has been the question of whether hunting mortality replaces natural mortality (i.e. weak, injured or otherwise incapacitated individuals are removed by hunting which would anyway have died of other causes)—the concept of so-called *compensatory mortality*. If this were not the case for a population, the hunting kill would remove more individuals than would have died naturally, hunting mortality would be additional to natural mortality (so-called *additive mortality*), and so the banning of hunting would result in an immediate increase in the population. This would not be the case for a population with compensatory mortality, since cessation of hunting would not necessarily show any response in terms of recovery in numbers.

Objectives and techniques for investigating population dynamics

The first question to address in the study of population dynamics is what precisely is the nature of the answer required from any investigation. Generally, the simplest objective is to understand why numbers change from one year to the next. This applies as much to a species showing rapid population growth, which may cause some conflict with land use by humans (as is the perceived case of some goose species and agriculture), as to a threatened species which is declining in abundance. In the former case, the important element may be to determine the factor that has caused the increase in numbers (which may relate to increases in breeding success as the result of colonization of previously unoccupied habitat). However, in order to offer management solutions, it may be that reduction of breeding success (apparently responsible for the upturn in numbers) is not an effective way of reducing the overall population size. For example, finding and destroying nests of geese breeding at very low densities on the open arctic tundra may not be feasible in a practical sense. On the other hand, in long-lived species such as geese, typically the population contains large numbers of immatures and subadults which do not contribute directly to breeding output. Destruction of nests has no effect on these birds, which show high survival and will recruit as breeders in subsequent years. Hence, small changes in annual survival can be far more effective in reducing population size than even large reductions in breeding output of such long-lived organisms.

From a wildlife administration point of view, the best population dynamic is perhaps that of a stable population showing little trend, neither increasing nor decreasing. In this case, the interest is not so much in the dynamics, but rather the stable states that such a population can attain. Here, the greatest interest lies in transferring understanding to

so-called 'pest species' with burgeoning populations, and threatened species that show catastrophic declines. In the latter case, the scarcity of the organism often presents enormous difficulties for the study of individuals, and factors such as loss and fragmentation of habitat, high death rate and poor reproduction may all conspire to create the downward pattern in numbers, such that it is difficult to determine *the* major factor responsible for the decline. Again, even if such a factor were identified, it might not represent a management tool suitable for re-establishing the population to a better conservation status for biological or political reasons.

Hopefully, this discussion demonstrates why it is important that we focus on precisely what information we require when we address questions of population dynamics. It may be more important to look in more detail, seeking to identify a critical stage in the life history (e.g. age at first breeding), or a particularly crucial period of the year (such as the flightless moult period post-breeding). Such parameters may be critical to recruitment or mortality and therefore represent key factors driving population behaviour. Certainly, in ducks, it is well demonstrated that the very young stages of development (just after hatching) are key to survival. Poor duckling survival has a huge impact on the autumn numbers of individuals in a population that may be composed of well over 50% young of the year. By contrast, modelling shows that geese are highly susceptible to small-scale changes in adult annual survival (Tombre et al. 1998). Other species may have different properties affecting their population dynamics in different ways to these extremes. Several ducks show modest peaks in annual mortality among females in the late stages of moult, which may suggest that the combined energetic costs of incubation, raising a brood and replacing flight feathers in succession may place a cost on females not evident amongst males.

Finally, in terms of attempting to explain changes in numbers within a population, we need to identify the factors that modify fitness (i.e. reproductive output and/or survival), and determine whether these are of an intrinsic or extrinsic nature. These distinctions also contribute to our understanding of population dynamics, but may play a key role in determining their importance biologically or politically in affecting, for example, conservation action. We know, for example, that severe weather affects the survival and distribution of ducks in the Western Palearctic (Ridgill and Fox 1990), but we are not in a position to manage the weather. However, we can recommend the establishment of hunting bans to reduce the human level of exploitation in years of severe weather events, and the protection of key refuge areas used by significant numbers of birds only in years of severe weather in northwest Europe (e.g. in France and Spain). Biological agents which cause mortality or reduce fitness (e.g. parasites, disease, predators) are rarely factors which human beings can influence on a scale that can affect population trends but, nevertheless, these may have a dramatic impact on the dynamics of populations. Food abundance and availability also may be critical at certain stages of the life cycle, and here management of suitable habitat offers the potential for enhancement of conditions. Intrinsic factors, such as physiological and behavioural traits, may also play a role. For instance, in most geese, there is a well-demonstrated dominance hierarchy, where particular individuals are dominant over others. This has fitness consequences in so far as dominant geese gain access to the best food, enabling them to obtain optimum body condition. For example, it has been shown that Pink-footed Geese that suffer scaring in spring staging areas by farmers trying to protect their crops fail to build up the same level of fat reserves as geese not subject to scaring that can feed undisturbed. Subsequent analyses showed that the fatter birds were more likely to breed and were more likely to return with larger broods than the geese subject to disturbance (Madsen 1995). Hence, access to good feeding opportunities may affect a goose's ability to reproduce. Similarly, on autumn migration, Owen and Black (1989a) showed that young Barnacle goslings, marked on the breeding areas in Svalbard, were less likely to be seen on the wintering grounds in the subsequent winter if they were lighter than average for their age at capture. So, the better the feeding opportunities, the greater an individual's chances of survival.

What is clear is that the study of individual wildfowl populations is extremely complex and, despite the fact that geese are amongst the most studied vertebrates in the northern hemisphere, we still understand very little about their population dynamics. The numbers of compounding factors are enormous, and there are few opportunities for manipulative experimentation that could increase understanding of some of the key principles. Perhaps our most effective method for understanding the population dynamics of wildfowl is to establish long time series. These are extensive runs of data that, over time, give some clue as to the nature of trends and fluctuations in the numbers of a population, in the hope that the long time perspective will offer some additional insight into how the population functions. So what type of information do we require in order to monitor change in the population? And what additional information do we need to collect to be able to interpret the changes we observe over time?

The most important measure is an annual assessment of the abundance of the population that can be used to measure change from one year to the next. During the breeding season, the numbers of individuals in a population will reach their annual peak as all the young of the year are hatched. However, in the months following the end of the breeding season, especially as birds encounter the hardships of severe weather, mortality increases and the balance of mortality over recruitment means that the population total gradually falls to an annual low immediately before the next breeding season. Given this annual cycle in numbers, when is it best to count the individuals? Since most wildfowl winter in rather large concentrations, it is generally convenient to estimate numbers based on winter counts. This has the advantage of assessing the breeding output of a particular season, and of including that stock in the total. In many goose species, not all birds actually take part in breeding, so surveys of the breeding areas would often fail to locate nonbreeders. Hence, winter inventories have the additional advantage of covering all age and breeding classes, when all birds are mixed together.

In the case of ducks, however, the number of females attempting to breed and doing so successfully is crucial to the number of individuals in the population the following winter, since the adults are swamped in the autumn flight by the number of juveniles produced in the preceding breeding season. In this case, it is important, if it is going to be possible to predict the autumn population, to carry out *breeding surveys* of wildfowl. Both methods have the same object, that is to define an element of the population (whether the entire population or a subset of particular interest) and to collect census information on an annual basis using repeatable standard methods. Over time, it becomes possible to assess the year-on-year changes in this measure to provide a long-term perspective of what is happening to that population.

Given these count data, there is still a requirement to interpret the changes in numbers, to enable an understanding of the causes of population increases or decreases. To understand these sorts of processes, we need to have some measure of the changes in the population parameters discussed above. We need to be able to assess the annual reproductive output in some way, in order to calculate the annual differences in young that recruit to the population. This can be done in a direct manner, by *breeding surveys* prior to autumn migration, or by determination of *age ratios* in the following winter season. It is also important to understand something about changes in survival, and this can be obtained from analysis of *ringing recoveries*, which can be used to estimate annual survival, and hence assess changes over time. Also, several countries collate hunters' *bag statistics* as part of their contribution to management of wildfowl stocks, providing the opportunity to determine the actual kill taken by hunters in any particular season. Since this is a substantial part of the overall annual mortality of a population, the ability to monitor this element of total mortality is important for the effective management of populations.

Winter counts

Generally, most wildfowl species breed at low densities over large areas, but congregate at favoured staging areas and wintering grounds. This has meant that, at least in Europe, the traditional means of assessing population size has been to carry out counts on the wintering areas, when species are most concentrated and easiest to count.

For a number of geese, such as the Greenland White-fronted Goose (Fox *et al.* 1998b), it may be feasible to count more or less accurately all the individuals of a single population. In this particular population, geese tend to be faithful to the same winter sites. Because the vast majority of individuals disperse throughout a known network of sites that have been discovered over the years, and which now enjoy annual count coverage, it is possible to obtain a reasonably accurate annual assessment of the total population. Hence, over the years, a network of largely volunteer counters has been established with the express aim of monitoring the population at all its wintering sites. Such a system has been evolved for most of the goose and swan species that winter in Europe, under the auspices of the Wetlands International Goose and Swan Specialist Groups which coordinate the censuses and maintain databases of the counts.

For many of the abundant and ubiquitous species, however, it is simply not feasible to count every last member of a given population in order to gain a total headcount every year. Nor is it possible to count anything like all the sites where a species occurs, and hence a method of sampling is required. For these species, the object has been to count as many wetlands as possible and to try to assess changes in abundance indirectly. The National Wildfowl Counts were established in Britain in 1947 as a response to the severe declines in wintering wildfowl which had occurred up to the start of the Second World War (Berry 1939). The objective was to cover as many wetlands as possible outside of the breeding season and to count the birds present. Organized by the Wildfowl Trust at Slimbridge, the number of sites counted grew to more than 2000 by the early 1960s and provided the basis for a major national review (Atkinson-Willes 1963). In the mid-1960s, International Wildfowl Counts (IWC) were established by the International Waterfowl Research Bureau (IWRB) to cover the entire Western Palearctic region in January of every year. The IWC initially concentrated on duck numbers, but has been developed and strengthened through the development of other Specialist Groups to cover swans, seaducks and geese. In recent years, a number of reviews have been produced (e.g. Scott and Rose 1996 for duck species and Madsen *et al.* 1999a for geese). The IWC network is now coordinated by Wetlands International, the successor body to IWRB, and count data are now gathered from around the globe. The IWC has a number of objectives, but the prime aim has been to determine the population sizes of all wildfowl species in the world, refining and revising these estimates on a regular basis, and to assess the trends in their population size (e.g. Rose and Scott 1994, 1997). This establishes (to the best of human ability) the total number of individuals in a given population in time and space, which enables the calculation of the 1% criterion. This threshold can then be used to determine which sites throughout the flyway meet the 1% criterion which qualify the site for listing as a Ramsar site (see above, and Chapter 8).

As well as producing population estimates, over time it becomes possible to use counts from large numbers of sites to construct indices of population abundance. These trends identify populations that are showing long-term stability, decreases or increases in number, without knowing the absolute number of individuals in the population (e.g. Kirby *et al.* 1995). Given knowledge of the hunting kill, breeding success and other parameters, these long-term patterns in population abundance can provide a basis for management strategies designed to bring about changes in population trends.

Breeding surveys

Midwinter surveys have become the normal means of censusing wildfowl in Europe because these wintering birds originate from breeding areas in the former Soviet Union, to which Europeans formerly had little access. In North America, the safeguard of migratory waterbirds, which were so obviously a shared resource, led to the first convention on migratory birds signed by Canada and the US in 1916, and joined by Mexico in 1936. In the New World, biologists had access to both breeding and wintering areas and, in order to regulate the harvest of wildfowl coming down the major migratory corridors of North America, it became necessary to assess the breeding distribution of, especially, the common duck species. In particular, because of dramatic year-to-year changes in breeding productivity

(and hence the number of birds in the autumn flight), it became necessary to assess the quality of their habitat on an annual basis. There has, therefore, been considerable effort expended in North America to assess the extent of wetland habitat available to breeding duck populations in spring, and to verify the levels of production by aerial surveys to count broods during the duckling-rearing phase of the annual cycle. In addition, extensive aerial survey and satellite-image interpretation are used to monitor the timing and extent of snow-melt through the American and Canadian Arctic in order to assess its effects on the breeding success of birds nesting and rearing young in these areas. The results are the annual collation of population size and hence trends over time, together with an annual evaluation of the available habitat, both of which can feed into regulation of the harvest as a means of managing wildfowl populations (Cowardin and Blohm 1992) and supporting international management planning procedures (e.g. USFWS/CWS 1986).

The long-term accumulation of numbers of breeding pairs and numbers of birds in the 'fall flight' provides an important barometer of the well-being of these populations (the results of 40 years of annual surveys can be viewed on-line, Southern Duck Hunter 1999). In some areas of North America, the information held on the National Wetland Inventory, aerial survey results and breeding bird densities have been used to map nesting densities of wildfowl over large areas (e.g. in the Dakotas, Reynolds 1995). Between them, these data sources also provide a basis for habitat management and restoration programmes which identify the relative importance and rate of habitat loss in different parts of the continent.

Age ratios (e.g. field determinations, wing samples)

In some wildfowl species, an individual can be assigned to an age class based on plumage characteristics—for example, first-winter Brent Geese show distinctive striations on their backs that differentiate them from second-winter and older birds. White-fronted Geese do not develop their distinctive white forehead or dark belly barring until the December of the year they were hatched, and most other grey geese can be aged during their first winter by careful observation and experience. Despite this, a simple count of the ratio of young birds to adults is not always sufficient to derive a bias-free estimate of production. It has been shown that large family groups of White-fronted Geese are dominant over smaller groups, pairs and single individuals, and hence can gain access to the best food resources (Boyd 1953). This means that successfully breeding pairs are more frequent in the best foraging situations, such as the leading edges of feeding flocks where the food tends to be richest. Where geese may distribute themselves amongst different habitats of different quality, those flocks exploiting the best food resources might be expected to contain the highest ratio of young to adults. These sources of bias need to be borne in mind when compiling age ratios from the field.

Some species, typically the ducks, are almost impossible to age in the field, although this can be achieved in the hand. Hence, age ratios cannot be recorded directly. However, they can be obtained from sampling the hunting bag (assuming the shot sample is a random sample of the population in general). A number of such voluntary schemes operates in Europe, as well as Canada and the US where hunters are requested to send in a sample of wings from their annual bag to experts who can identify plumage differences and ascribe the wing types to age and sex classes. In addition, large numbers of wildfowl are caught in several countries for ringing purposes. Again, based on the assumption that such birds represent a random sample of the population as a whole (which is probably generally not the case when birds are attracted to trapping sites using bait or other incentives), the proportion of young amongst wildfowl captured for ringing purposes may also provide an index of productivity.

But why should we be interested in gathering information on breeding success? Age ratios are important in determining the robustness of the population to perturbations in breeding success and/or changes in survival. The ratio of free-flying young to breeding females provides an important annual assessment of the productivity of the population and can be used to determine long-term changes in this parameter. In species such as the geese, where family cohesion is a feature of the first winter for newly hatched young, it is also possible to determine brood size and the proportions of potentially breeding pairs that have raised young. Based on samples, it becomes possible to assess the numbers of young in a population born in a particular season. By subtracting this statistic from the total population size, it is possible to derive an estimate of the number of birds that have survived from the previous year based on annual population census statistics. In a closed population, this means one can calculate the number of birds hatched and dying every year, the two factors affecting the overall abundance of the population. Hence, these measures of reproductive success and of crude annual adult survival can provide a deeper understanding of some of the factors affecting population trends.

Bag records

For some species of wildfowl, hunting is the major source of mortality. The size of the hunting bag can be used to assess the effects of changes in numbers of birds killed in terms of its effects on death rate and on overall population trends. Where a migratory wildfowl population disperses between different countries, it may also be politically expedient in deciding allocation of bags to different states to be able to demonstrate the magnitude of the hunting off-take in the different states along the migration route. Hence, it is extremely beneficial when considering management options to attempt to assess the extent of the hunting kill at site, local, regional, national and population levels. Given a long-term perspective of the kill and its effect on overall mortality, it may become possible to regulate the size and distribution of the hunting take in order to influence the overall population trend.

In North America, hunting regulations have been designed to be flexible in order to take account of variations in the abundance of wildfowlers' quarry. Based on the abundance of ponds, breeding ducks and broods from aerial breeding surveys, the abundance of different species in the autumn flight can be estimated and a harvest can be shared between geographical areas wanting to hunt the various species. Seasons may be restricted from several months to a matter of hours in order to restrict the harvest in response to falling stocks, and some species may even be temporarily protected and withdrawn from the list of quarry species. The numbers of individuals shot are limited, with the bag limited on a seasonal or individual basis. Unfortunately, in Europe, hunting regulations are not so flexible, and most countries simply implement a close season with little harmonization throughout the flyway. Nevertheless, some countries, notably Denmark since 1947, collate comprehensive records of the annual harvest levels. Despite the lack of any mechanism to incorporate such data into the regulation of hunting seasons throughout the Western Palearctic, the data from such annual surveys provide an assessment of the impact of shooting on different populations. Such information is essential in order to understand the population dynamics of common wildfowl quarry species.

Individual marking schemes

As described in Chapter 6, the use of metal rings fitted to the legs of birds (which bear a return address for the finder) pioneered the study of migration. By comparing the time and place of ringing with the time and position at subsequent finding, it was suddenly possible to interpret the individual movements of birds. However, the reporting of live birds bearing rings is generally rare. More often (especially amongst wildfowl) the bird is found dead, for example when the finder is a hunter who has killed his quarry. Hence, ringing recoveries of wildfowl also provide an assessment of mortality rates, based upon the timing and position of the record. As discussed above, the capture of large numbers of individuals can give an assessment of the production of young based on the ratio of young birds to old in the captured birds sampled, and the recovery of those birds can give an estimate of the mortality rates of different age and sex classes. Hence, ringing has become a valuable tool by which to measure these two parameters in order to give a better understanding of the overall trends in populations (see e.g. Wernham *et al.* 2002).

Unfortunately, the capture and ringing of ducks, geese and swans is time consuming and costly and is, therefore, limited to a few places where there are sufficient resources to carry out such activity. Hence there is considerable geographical bias in the birds ringed (e.g. see Owen *et al.* 1986 for details). The probability of recovery is also highly biased, since most recoveries are the result of shooting, and shooting seasons vary geographically. In Europe, for example, most seasons close in late January, so few recoveries are generated after this time. In contrast, in continental Russia, spring shooting occurs and the hunting seasons in autumn start much earlier than in western Europe. Birds dying from other causes are more likely to be found and returned in the well-populated areas of western Europe than in the vast uninhabited tracts of Scandinavia and Russia.

The use of ringing recoveries to estimate mortality rates is also dogged by the problems of differential reporting rates. The likelihood that a bird killed carrying a ring will be reported depends on a number of factors; the hunter may not retrieve the bird, or may do so and not see the ring; or he may see the ring but choose not to report it. Unfortunately, these factors vary in time and space, because of tradition, weariness of reporting rings from shot birds or deliberately withholding information because of fear of prosecution or revealing your particular favourite hunting area. Despite this, a great deal of statistical effort has gone into the analysis of ringing recoveries and these sources of bias in order to extract the maximum potential information. Again, it is the long-term accumulation of ringing recovery data, generated using constant methods over time, that is most valuable in compiling time series which can contribute to our understanding of population dynamics.

Metal leg rings typically provide two pieces of information about the individual: (a) its capture site, time and age/sex; and (b) its recovery point in space and time. How much more useful to be able to make frequent sequential observations of the same individual! This would enable the compilation of information about its movements, pairing and breeding success, and potentially its death. Sir Peter Scott pioneered this type of approach using natural markers in the form of bill patterns on Bewick's Swans (Scott 1966). The use of individually recognizable marks on geese and swans—such as the fitting of large plastic leg rings or collars (Figure 7.1) bearing codes that can be read at a distance through telescopes—has revolutionized our studies of these birds in recent years. Large rings have enabled the compilation of detailed information about individuals that was never considered possible before. If the loss rate of the markers is known (e.g. how often collars fall off), there are now many analytical techniques available to enable the estimation of survival rates based on re-sighting histories, which take into account the probability of birds being alive but not seen and reported (e.g. Mark software on the internet).

There is no doubt that the use of methods that enable the recognition of individual wildfowl has revolutionized our understanding of population parameters and how they relate to population dynamics. Such markings enable us not only to find out about pairing of individuals, but their age at first breeding, how often they breed and their overall lifetime reproductive output (e.g. Black and Owen 1995). By contrasting differences in reproductive success, it has been possible to understand some of the reasons why some birds perform better than others, based on their competitive ability (Teunissen et al. 1985). This reinforces the idea that

not all birds are the same, and certainly not all birds make the same contribution to breeding output in the population as a whole or to overall mean survival rate. In the future, we are likely to see even more sophisticated techniques applied to the study of the individual and its contribution to population dynamics. We have already seen the use of satellite telemetry to track birds across the globe in order to establish hitherto unknown migration patterns (Clausen and Bustnes 1998), and to measure heart rate and energy consumption en route (Butler and Woakes 1998). Hence, there is no reason to suppose that technology will not extend our horizons further in the coming years.

Factors affecting recruitment
Female condition

Anatidae lay clutches that are large relative to adult body size and of higher energy content compared to those of other bird species. A combination of large egg size and the extended period of incubation enable their offspring to hatch at a relatively advanced stage of development. Young birds are able to leave the nest within a few hours of hatching and can, to some extent, forage independently very quickly. This means that parents invest relatively less time and energy in raising young after hatching (compared to passerines, for example, where parents expend considerable effort in providing food to helpless chicks in their nests). On the other hand, the condition of the breeding female immediately prior to egg-laying and her ability to invest nutrients in reproduction influence her ultimate breeding success more than is the case for passerines.

Despite these basic similarities in all wildfowl, different species have evolved a variety of contrasting strategies to convert nutrients available from their food in the environment into eggs and nutrient stores that sustain the sitting female throughout incubation. At one extreme, the relatively short-lived northern-hemisphere dabbling ducks typically lay 8–12 eggs in a clutch which is incubated by the female alone. Nesting and fledgling mortality is relatively high and, since the males typically desert the females at the onset of incubation,

7.1 Plastic neck collar on a White-fronted Goose.

it is the female who must also protect the brood through to successful fledging. It is generally considered that a female dabbling duck is able to derive most of the essential nutrients for the creation of her clutch and her maintenance throughout incubation at or near the breeding grounds. Furthermore, the ducklings hatch during the period when their food is most abundant, which the attendant parent female can also exploit. In this way, it has been considered that these are 'income breeders' in that it is the quality of the available food in the area of reproduction that has the greatest influence upon the ability to breed successfully.

By contrast, long-lived arctic-nesting geese lay 3–6 eggs in a clutch and, in some cases, may rely heavily on endogenous stores accumulated for egg production, largely transported to breeding grounds from staging areas further south. In this way, geese have been considered to be more 'capital breeders' in that food quality at a point remote from the breeding areas contributes to breeding success. However, most recent research shows that even arctic-nesting geese that breed relatively soon after arrival on the nesting grounds still have the opportunity to acquire significant nutrients, before the laying of the first egg, that make a significant contribution to potential breeding success. During incubation, ganders assist with nest defence, and broods are reared by both parents, the male taking a major role in protecting the family, thus enabling the female to feed and regain reserves depleted during incubation. In this way, the quality of female geese during the prelude to breeding is thought to be more critical than events occurring after hatching. Since a number of widely differing factors may influence breeding female condition, it is worth considering some in more detail.

Parasites

Parasites can affect the reproductive success of birds either by reducing the condition of the female, or by transfer to the young and, in turn, affecting their condition and hence survival. In fact, there are very few reported instances of death from parasite burdens amongst young birds. Because most parasites that kill their hosts almost inevitably kill themselves, it seems likely that the effects of predation on young far outweigh that of parasites. Although there are numerous examples of parasites affecting breeding in many species of birds (see review in Newton 1998), there are relatively few such studies from wildfowl (e.g. Herman et al. 1975). It may be expected that cavity-nesters are more likely to suffer from the attentions of ectoparasites than those laying in open situations, since parasites persist in situations where the number of potential nesting sites is limited. This is perhaps the price that hole-nesters pay for the reduced predation risk. Nevertheless, we know little about the general levels of parasite loads amongst ducks, geese and swans and their effects on reproductive output, and this undoubtedly offers a fertile area for future research.

Body stores and food supplies at laying

The classic study of Ankney and MacInnes (1978) found that the clutch size of the female Lesser Snow Goose was directly related to body weight of the female on arrival at the nesting grounds. They also showed that regardless of clutch size, the weights of females at the start of incubation were the same. Hence, they concluded that the nutrient stores that geese brought with them, in excess of the threshold stores required to maintain the goose through her incubation, were invested in the clutch. This meant that clutch size and quality were dependent mainly upon protein and fat obtained from the wintering grounds and spring staging areas, with little complement made from the food available at the time of laying. We now think that this may have been the case in the particularly late season studied by Ankney and MacInnes but, generally, egg-laying is often delayed after arrival on breeding areas, and that intensive pre-nesting feeding on the breeding grounds may augment existing reserves (e.g. Budeau et al. 1991, Gauthier and Tardif 1991, Gauthier et al. 2003). Hence, rather than being true 'capital breeders', many arctic-nesting geese are thought to exhibit a mixed strategy of storing protein and fats from staging and wintering areas, and supplementing these stores with energy and nutrients available at their breeding grounds prior to nesting. This has even been found to be the case for Lesser Snow Geese (Ganter and Cooke 1996). Hence, the timing of breeding, which has such important consequences for reproductive output in most bird species, is a trade-off between delayed reproduction (to enjoy enhanced food availability during the pre-laying period) and the need to breed as early as possible using the nutrient and energy stores accumulated to date.

Macro-invertebrates make up the dominant proportion of the diet of many northern duck species, especially dabbling ducks that specialize on the larvae of the dipteran family Chironomidae (Krapu and Reinecke 1992). Most breeding ducks exploit the dramatic pulse in invertebrate production in seasonal or ephemeral wetlands, such as steppe regions of Europe and Asia and the prairie pothole country of North America (Crissey 1969). Because of this abundance of prey in time and space, most studies show that female dabbling ducks generally obtain their protein and calcium for egg formation from often intensive bouts of feeding during egg-laying (Krapu 1981, Ankney and Afton 1988). However, not even these species are income breeders, as most of the fat for egg production is derived from stored lipids accumulated by the female prior to nesting (Krapu and Reinecke 1992, Esler and Grand 1994). Hence, in these species, the extent of body stores may also have some influence on the reproductive output of individuals. Nevertheless, it is generally considered that, compared to geese and swans, the abundance of food available to ducks means that breeding productivity is more closely related to conditions experienced at the breeding grounds. Lake Mývatn in Iceland plays host to large numbers of breeding ducks of many different species, all of which exploit the rich production of chironomids and other insects that form the diets of breeding females and, particularly, their ducklings. The relationship is such a good one that there is a high correlation between the production of young and the abundance of the insects in any year. The mean number of fledged ducklings produced in any one year at Lake Mývatn influenced the subsequent change in the spring population density of most of the species (Garðarsson and Einarsson 1994).

We know lamentably little about the breeding ecology and nutrient dynamics of breeding seaducks. It is known that female Common Eiders rarely forage during egg-laying or incubation, laying down stores of fat and protein for egg production prior to laying (Milne 1976), whereas White-winged or Velvet Scoters forage extensively during pre-laying and laying. Nevertheless, the latter species uses fat and protein stores accumulated prior to arrival at the breeding grounds to sustain the female through incubation (Dobrush 1986).

As is becoming apparent, it is difficult to generalize about the influence of female nutrient and fat stores on subsequent reproductive success. Although large species, such as geese and swans, rely upon stores brought to the breeding grounds, it is clear these are supplemented to a greater or lesser extent by feeding during the laying period. Likewise the smaller wildfowl, such as the dabbling ducks and the *Aythya* diving ducks, are not totally reliant upon nutrients obtained from their breeding environment, and may rely to a limited extent on stores to see them through egg-laying and incubation.

Mate performance

The majority of wildfowl are monogamous; that is, a pair remain together for at least one breeding season, sometimes for life. Monogamy confirms paternity for the paired male who can ensure, so far as possible, that no other males have access to his female when she is sexually receptive. In return, his defence of the female assures her of access to feeding resources which may be critical to her breeding attempt. Many ducks are seasonally monogamous, the males deserting the female once incubation starts. There is gathering evidence that at least some pairs may re-pair in subsequent breeding seasons and, for those that do, birds apparently reunite on moulting or wintering areas after the end of the breeding season (e.g. Köhler *et al.* 1995, Mitchell 1997). Amongst these species, it is the male's performance during the prelude to breeding which may affect recruitment. Amongst the swans and geese, many species show long-term, typically lifelong, monogamy, with the male also contributing to nest defence, brood rearing and family protection during the autumn migration and wintering period. In these cases, the performance of the male contributes conspicuously to the pair's breeding success, especially during spring fattening (Teunissen *et al.* 1985, Black and Owen 1987, 1989b). Removal of one or other partner of a Snow Goose pair has demonstrated that both are essential for nest defence, but removal of males during incubation did not result in failed breeding attempts (Martin *et al.* 1985). Nevertheless, it is obviously better to attempt nesting with both members of a pair playing an active part in the reproductive attempt, as shown by the extreme rarity of divorce amongst many species of long-lived wildfowl (Black 1996).

Weather

In many parts of the world, low and unpredictable rainfall has a dramatic effect on ecosystems. Wetlands in many parts of the Middle East, Africa and Australia are ephemeral features of the landscape, and wildfowl must become wandering opportunists, colonizing habitats wherever they are available and abandoning them as they dry out. Australian Grey Teal numbers build very rapidly in years with good rainfall, breeding throughout the continent where suitable habitats occur (Frith 1982), but in drought years the species becomes rare and confined to more predictable coastal wetlands.

Even in the temperate northern hemisphere, variable patterns of precipitation have a profound effect on duck populations. The 'prairie pothole' country of central North America has been called the duck factory of the continent, and consists of over 10 million 'potholes', ephemeral wetlands fed by winter snow and rain. When precipitation is abundant, water tables are high, all hollows are flooded and many millions of pairs bring off young successfully. In years with drought, only the larger, deeper pools retain water and the breeding birds are concentrated, often suffering poor reproduction when they attempt to nest. Water tables start out low and many dry out in the course of the season, killing broods and, in some cases, the flightless females as well. Hence, pothole drought can cause both lost recruitment and increased adult mortality.

In those species dependent upon body reserves for a major investment in reproduction, weather may have a profound effect on the extent of body reserves laid down in preparation for migration and reproduction. Temperatures, and to some extent snow cover, have a considerable impact upon vegetation growth and development of invertebrates.

Hence, a delay in spring thaw can have implications for the quality and availability of food resources to late wintering and spring staging wildfowl as they make their nutritional preparations for migration and breeding (e.g. Nilsson 1979 concerning Whooper Swans). Droughts affecting the feeding conditions of Lesser Snow Geese in the prairies *en route* to northern breeding areas reduced breeding productivity through subsequent lower clutch size and lowered hatching success (Davies and Cooke 1983a).

Predation of eggs and young and anti-predator behaviour

Many wildfowl species have evolved different strategies to reduce the effects of predation on nests and eggs. Several species use nest sites, such as islands, cliffs and cavities in trees, which are inaccessible to predators, and most utilize what cover is available to camouflage the nest as much as possible. Many camouflaged female ducks will sit very 'tight', exploding from the nest only at the very last minute, shuffling through the vegetation as if injured to draw potential predators away from the vicinity of the nest site. In different circumstances, birds may nest in colonies, or at least in close proximity to one another, in order to maximize predator detection and, in some cases, effect mass mobbing of potential predators. Large aggregations of nests may also result in local predator 'swamping' where predator abundance is low, minimizing the maximum potential damage to the breeding population. Equally, where predator densities are high, they are often drawn to high densities of nesting wildfowl and may take a heavy toll of eggs, as occurs in the prairie pothole country.

Effects of age and sex

Reproductive performance tends to increase with age and experience, but may decline again in old age (Ratcliffe *et al.* 1988, Black and Owen 1995). Hence, among geese, reproductive output is highest among 7–12 year-old birds. Relatively little is known about patterns in shorter-lived ducks but, in Lesser Scaup, clutch size increases up to 4 years of age (Afton 1984), such that a four-year-old duck would produce 3.76 duckling compared to 1.64 for first-year birds. In cavity-nesters, such as Common Goldeneye, the nest site is of crucial importance in reproductive prosperity and hence females returning to the same successful sites are more likely to be successful than those that switch nest sites (Dow and Fredga 1983).

Generally, it is the age and experience of the female that affects reproductive output, but in species where the ability of the male to defend a territory determines breeding output, it is the age and experience of the male that is the major determining factor affecting success. In the Mute Swan, young birds may wait several years to occupy a territory, and having established one may not breed successfully immediately (Birkhead and Perrins 1986). Furthermore, the timing of laying is related to the ability of the male to put on weight in spring (and presumably defend the best quality territory, Owen and Black 1990). In Mute and Bewick's Swans, the condition and fighting ability of the male seems to have some effect on the breeding success of the pair (Scott 1988).

Factors affecting mortality

Natural

Unfortunately, relatively little effort has been expended in the study of natural mortality in the regulation of wildfowl populations. Much information from other bird groups comes from radio-telemetry techniques, where tagged birds are followed until the point of death. Long-distance migratory wildfowl do not offer the same opportunities for the use of such techniques as relatively sedentary gallinaceous birds which have commonly been the subjects of such studies. For this reason, perspectives on natural mortality processes in wildfowl may be extremely biased.

Predation (excluding hunting)

Predation is an everyday occurrence for any wildfowl population but, seen from the standpoint of the human observer, the effects of predation on the population dynamics of the organism are very hard to determine. It is only when predators are suddenly introduced, or exterminated in artificial experiments or as a result of unusual natural phenomena, that the effects of change in predation rates can be witnessed. The more normal situations, where predators and prey coexist, is where the overall effects of predation are more difficult to determine, but where long-term coexistence is most likely to persist.

Nevertheless, it is apparent that in many wildfowl species, predation is a major source of egg and chick loss, especially since most species nest on the ground. This rate of loss may vary enormously according to the cover available—hatching success in nesting Northern Mallard was 50% in dense cover compared to almost nothing in exposed areas (Cowardin et al. 1995). Despite what may appear to be high losses, these may not necessarily have severe consequences for the population if breeding pairs are sufficiently abundant. However, if the human management objective is to maximize production of young, such losses can be reduced by relatively simple management techniques. Recent experiments have demonstrated very dramatically the effects that habitat management to reduce predation rates and predator control can have in enhancing breeding populations and reproductive output in the prairie pothole country (Greenwood et al. 1995).

The size of some populations may be influenced by cycles in the alternative prey of shared predators—in particular, the correlations between nesting success of Brent Geese and rodents on their breeding areas have been described widely (Summers and Underhill 1987). Years of high production of young geese (which also coincide with good wader productivity in the same areas, Roselaar 1979) coincide with peaks in lemming numbers, while the years of low production tended to coincide with low lemming abundance or with cold springs. These data tend to support the hypothesis that lemming predators (such as Arctic Foxes and Pomarine Skuas) switch to preying on eggs and young of birds when their primary prey (lemmings) are scarce, causing large variations in the reproductive output of the bird populations. This is manifested on the wintering grounds as variations in total numbers, since the proportions of young vary between 0% and 60% of the autumn flight. In a population of over a quarter of a million individuals, this variation in breeding output has considerable consequences for the absolute size of the population entering the flyway every autumn.

Artificial introduction of predators can have a dramatic effect on species formerly unexposed to such levels of predation. Arctic Foxes and Red Foxes *Vulpes vulpes*, introduced to the Aleutian Islands early last century by trappers, exterminated the Aleutian race of the Canada Goose from all but one island which managed to escape fox introductions. A management programme to rescue this species eradicated the foxes from several islands, and the population has since increased considerably (Byrd *et al.* 1994). Such cases, although artificial in nature, show that, in certain circumstances, predation can have an extremely limiting effect on population size through restriction of reproduction.

By comparison, virtually nothing is known about natural predation rates on full-grown birds. There are instances described of birds being killed by predators trying to defend nests (even nests which were not their own, e.g. Fox *et al.* 1995a). Such predation during the breeding period invariably involves sitting females and consequently may skew sex ratios among the adult population. Foxes kill a disproportionate number of female dabbling ducks in the prairie pothole country (Sargeant *et al.* 1984) and this may be a major contributory factor to the male bias in wildfowl sex ratios (Baldassarre and Bolen 1994). However, the higher vulnerability of males to hunting mortality may counterbalance this effect. In an extensive survey by Stoudt and Cornwell (1976), a mere 0.14% of all mortality could be ascribed to predation on adult wildfowl, the majority being caused by mammalian predators on dabbling ducks.

Food availability and starvation

Starvation amongst wildfowl is generally rarely recorded. Moreover, it is difficult to determine whether a bird falls victim to a predator as a result of undernourishment, in which case the loss is ascribed to predation rather than true starvation. Amongst documented examples, most cases of starvation arise as a result of lack of food at critical points in the life cycle. This may only become manifest when the death toll becomes spectacular, as occurred in

two classic examples. In the first, 14 000 Common Eiders starved to death in the severe winter of 1981–82 (Wrånes 1988) when they were unable to obtain food for prolonged periods. In the second, some 14 000 diving ducks (mainly Common Pochard and Tufted Duck) starved to death in Dutch waters and along the Rhine during the late winter of 1986, a period not normally associated with high mortality. However, these species reach their lowest body weights in February and March and, faced with unusually harsh weather and food shortages at this time (a relatively rare event so late in the winter), their depleted stores of fat and nutrients could not sustain them through even a short period of privation (Suter and van Eerden 1992). There have also been mass starvation events involving Common Eiders in the Dutch Wadden Sea more recently, starting in winter 1999–2000, and thought to be linked to patterns of human shellfish exploitation (Camphuysen *et al.* 2002).

Less spectacularly, incubating females may also succumb to starvation if they have failed to attain the appropriate levels of energy and nutrient stores required to sustain them through their confinement to the nest (e.g. Ankney and MacInnes 1978). In normal circumstances, it might be expected that, for a long-lived bird such as a female goose, it would be a better investment to abandon a nesting attempt that might cost her her life in order to make another nesting attempt in the future. Nevertheless, these examples show that starvation can occur when the balance between accumulated stores and metabolic requirements is not met at critical periods in the life cycle.

It is often considered that food availability represents a density-dependent mechanism for limiting populations at some stage in the annual cycle. However, Owen and Black (1990) considered that, for most quarry species, populations are harvested so heavily that their size lies well below the potential 'carrying capacity' of their environment. In this way, food is rarely limiting, and starvation events are therefore expected to be a rare occurrence. Certainly wildfowl have proved themselves very flexible in the exploitation of a sequence of different food supplies, such that when one source of food is exhausted, birds move on to the next most profitable food source. This is very evident amongst Dark-bellied Brent Geese wintering in southern England. They feed first on the intertidal Eelgrass and algae, moving to saltmarshes and improved grassland during late autumn, but reverting to saltmarshes in the spring immediately prior to migration to the breeding areas (Summers 1990b, Summers and Critchley 1990, Summers *et al.* 1993). These birds actually deplete a finite feeding resource in the case of *Zostera*, abandoning the food source completely when depletion reaches a given threshold (the so-called 'giving up' density, Madsen 1988, Fox 1996).

Food shortage at critical points can be responsible for mortality that may not be linked directly to obvious starvation. At several stages in the annual life cycle, wildfowl may lay down energy and nutrient stores to see them through periods of nutritional stress. The most obvious is autumn accumulations of fat stores to fuel migration to wintering areas and as a source of energy to survive periods of food privation during severe weather. However, where the food supply fails, or where competition results in the failure of individuals to lay down sufficient reserves to sustain them in flights across open sea to ultimate wintering grounds, birds starting the journey in poor condition are less likely to survive than fatter ones (Owen and Black 1989a). The same may be true for other critical periods of the cycle, such as pre-moult fattening by Greylag Geese (van Eerden *et al.* 1997, Fox *et al.* 1998a), where a finite feeding resource may limit the capacity of the moulting habitat to sustain increasing numbers of flightless birds.

Weather

Weather can affect wildfowl mortality in a number of ways, but two major causes predominate. These are: (a) sudden events, such as tornadoes or violent thunderstorms that have been reported to kill ducks and geese (e.g. Roth 1976); and (b) local periods of unusual weather that affect the food supply and/or thermoregulatory demands (such as drought or prolonged subzero temperatures). Since there is little information relating to the first, we concentrate here upon the second.

At northern latitudes, hard weather (typically subzero temperatures) annually forces arctic and sub-arctic breeding wildfowl south to spend the nonbreeding part of their year in milder climes. However, despite the reasonable probability of finding ice-free conditions at a certain point on the globe, in reality, wintering wildfowl witness considerable movements of the zero Celsius isotherm across all continents in the northern hemisphere. Hence, with the onset of subzero temperatures, large-scale movements of ducks are common. In Europe, these most commonly take a south and west direction (Ridgill and Fox 1990). As well as distorting normal distribution patterns, cold weather may also result in higher mortality. In very severe winters, with persistent frosts and deep snow (such as those of 1947 and 1963), more wildfowl than usual were picked up dead and dying, with corresponding effects on breeding populations in the following spring. In addition, many species may experience high levels of hunting mortality, either because they are forced to move to areas where hunting pressure is higher, or because they are more concentrated and often more accessible to hunting because of their need to sustain their energy balance during such times.

The ability of species to cope with prolonged periods of severe weather varies to a great extent with body size. Larger birds (such as swans and geese) have relatively larger reserves and (because of their low surface to body volume ratio) need devote less energy to thermoregulation. These species may be able to last two weeks or more without feeding, so are more resilient to periods of prolonged severe weather. Nevertheless, species such as Mute Swan in Denmark (which lack the tradition of any large-scale winter migration out of the country) face very high mortality in so-called 'ice winters', when the Baltic freezes for several weeks and the swans' energy reserves are depleted. Species may also become the victims of their habitats. Eurasian Teal are typically birds of very shallow wetlands, their small size restricting the depth of water to which they can feed. These waters are of course the first to freeze and, being small, the Teal have relatively high thermoregulatory demands and are probably only able to withstand two or three days without feeding (Boyd 1964). Hence, of all the dabbling ducks, Teal show the most dramatic movements in response to severe weather, and the most obvious increases in mortality as a result of even relatively short spells of subzero temperatures (Ridgill and Fox 1990).

Parasites

As in the case of parasites and their effect on recruitment (discussed earlier), it is generally considered that parasites contribute very few deaths to the overall mortality of birds. Animals already weakened by lack of food may be more susceptible to a parasitic infection, and the parasite is sometimes identified as the cause of death (e.g. the periodic die-offs experienced amongst Magellan Geese on the Falkland Islands reported by Harradine 1982). Again, it is assumed that a parasite that kills its host destroys its own habitat but, nevertheless, outbreaks of death associated with parasites are reported in the literature. The most frequent are amongst seaducks (Ching 1989), especially Common Eider, and involve acanthocephalan worms such as *Polymorphus boschadis* and *Profilicollis botulus* (e.g. Clark *et al.* 1958). The latter species has a common crab species as an intermediary host (Thompson 1985), so the opportunity for constant reinfection is high, suggesting some normal equilibrium in the population. Nevertheless, mass deaths do occur (Clark *et al.* 1958, Garden *et al.* 1964) and have been reported among herbivorous freshwater wildfowl such as Mute Swans (MacDonald *et al.* 1978). It is currently impossible to determine the impact of parasites on wildfowl populations. The impression is that they cause little mortality, and are of far less significance than factors such as predation and food limitation. Occasionally it seems that an epidemic may cause more serious mortality, but the die-off is far less than for some of the diseases discussed below.

Disease

It is remarkable how little we know about the ecology of diseases affecting wildfowl, and about their true impact on population dynamics. Nevertheless, it is apparent that certain conditions favour the build-up of disease, and the effects can be dramatic. It is generally considered that, after hunting, diseases are responsible for the largest proportion of deaths (Bellrose 1980). Avian cholera, in particular,

is responsible for mass deaths of up to 100 000 wildfowl in North America (e.g. Rosen 1971, Brand 1984). The disease is caused by a bacterium, and its effects can be devastating, especially after summer droughts when wintering birds are highly concentrated. During a severe outbreak in early 1950 in the shallow lakes of Texas, up to 0.3% of ducks were fatally affected (Petrides and Bryant 1951). Intriguingly, small species were proportionally more susceptible than larger ones, hence proportionally more Green-winged Teal died of the disease than did Canada Geese. Smaller races of Canada Geese may also be more susceptible to this disease than larger ones (Vaught *et al.* 1967). Variation in susceptibility to viral duck plague has been shown (Woebeser 1981). Amongst other bacterial causes of mass deaths of wildfowl, botulism is perhaps the most serious (although not strictly a disease, since ducks die as a result of ingestion of a neurotoxin produced by the bacterium). Again, it is in North America where the effects are most dramatic, with as many as 4–5 million individuals (mainly ducks) dying (Locke and Friend 1987). Fungal infections, especially Aspergillosis, can also kill a few hundred ducks in local outbreaks (e.g. Adrian *et al.* 1978). Viral infection, particularly avian influenza and duck plague (or duck viral enteritis DVE), can also be responsible for the deaths of many hundreds of ducks (Friend and Pearson 1973, Hinshaw *et al.* 1986).

There is no doubt that populations experiencing very large kills may take some years to recover to previous local population levels, suggesting that infection can play a role in limiting wildfowl numbers under certain situations. However, such events are still rare in the Western Palearctic, suggesting that the impact of disease varies considerably with geography. It is interesting that disease is often associated with stress factors, and it could be that, as wildfowl become concentrated in fewer and fewer refuges, thereby increasing the rate of disease transmission and perhaps increasing their susceptibility, mortality from such sources may increase. This threat may be especially acute for rarer species, where reliance upon refuges is particularly important, and where stress factors operating already make such taxa more vulnerable than commoner species.

Friend *et al.* (2001) warned that vector-borne diseases are likely to affect avian populations in the same way that they are increasingly challenging the health of humans and their domestic stock. If we are to sustain avian biodiversity, conservationists may have to discard the traditional view that disease is not a significant factor in the population dynamics of wild birds, and must manage the environment in such a way as to minimize the probability of disease emergence rather than managing the disease or the affected species only when the pathogen has become established.

Human-induced factors (shooting, pollution, poisoning, collisions and other exploitation)

It has been estimated that hunting in Europe accounts for 11 million ducks and a quarter of a million geese, with a further 15 million ducks and 2 million geese taken in North America (Scott 1982). In addition to direct mortality as a result of shooting, or of wounded birds dying shortly afterwards, must be added the effects of the crippling of individuals that suffer reduced survival (Madsen and Noer 1996, Noer and Madsen 1996). Recent evidence suggests that hunting disturbance can affect stopover schedules, body condition and reproductive effort, at least among geese (Bechet *et al.* 2003, Feret *et al.* 2003, Mainguy *et al.* 2003).

Poisoning of ducks through ingestion of lead pellets was considered sufficiently serious that the use of lead shot was outlawed in North America in 1991. European governments are starting to follow suit, but legislation has been slow to take note of the knowledge that has existed since the 1950s that up to 10% of all wildfowl may die of lead poisoning alone (Bellrose 1959). Poisoning by lead derived from lead weights used by anglers has also caused local extinctions of Mute Swan populations in the UK (Goode 1981), although here changes to legislation have removed this source of pollution from freshwater systems.

Wildfowl (although perhaps excluding the smaller duck species) have generally high wing loadings, which restricts their manoeuvrability, especially of larger birds such as swans and geese. This makes them vulnerable to collisions. For example, Mute Swans in the UK suffer high mortality from crashing into inanimate and moving objects; over half of all Mute Swan deaths result from collisions, the majority with overhead power cables (Ogilvie 1967).

Density-dependence (evidence for additive and compensatory mortality)

It is often argued that mortality from hunting is compensated for by reduced natural losses. This is often explained by the suggestion that birds that succumb to hunting may be those very individuals susceptible to death from other causes (e.g. disease) and so which would have died anyway. Alternatively, if there is some resource (such as the availability of midwinter food) which in some way directly limits numbers surviving to breed in the subsequent year, the removal of numbers of birds in the hunting bag simply removes individuals which would not have survived to breed anyway. Such a mechanism is termed *compensatory mortality* and, clearly, if such a mechanism operates in a population, below a certain threshold, the mortality imposed by hunting would have no depressing effect on either the overall death rate or on breeding numbers. On the other hand, if hunting were to be partly or entirely additive to naturally occurring loss, this extra mortality would be additive—that is, adding to natural mortality and depressing breeding numbers. Compensatory mortality can only occur if the natural loss is in some way linked to population size. The effect is said to be density-dependent because natural losses are related to the numbers of individuals in a specific area, or density. This could occur in situations where a resource limits the number of individuals present in a certain area, but could equally well result from predation (where high densities attract predators and bring about high predation rates) or disease (where large aggregations of birds become susceptible to rapid infection).

The important point is that populations showing a density-dependent response and high reproductive rates offer an apparent surplus that can be harvested. The higher the productivity (and normally higher natural losses), the greater the ability of the population to withstand losses due to hunting. A great deal of effort has gone into trying to detect compensatory mortality in wildfowl populations and to assess the level of compensation where this occurs. The classic study of Northern Mallard in North America showed that, at levels of hunting existing at the time, hunting mortality was largely offset by natural mortality (Anderson and Burnham 1976). Many other species have since been investigated, all showing different breeding strategies, patterns of natural mortality and levels of hunting, but generally it would appear that most species are characterized by reduced natural losses which partially compensate for the hunting take (e.g. Nichols et al. 1984, Nichols 1991). For longer lived species, such as the northern breeding geese, however, evidence suggests that low and relatively constant natural mortality rates do not allow such populations to compensate for additional sources of mortality, such as hunting. The inverse relationship between survival and hunting kill supports this hypothesis in the few studies currently published (Gauthier et al. 2001, Fox 2003a).

Age and sex effects

In general, it is often young and inexperienced birds, rather than older individuals, that suffer higher mortality. In long-lived species, such as the Mute Swan in the UK and the Black Swan in New Zealand, first-year and second-year birds are more than twice as likely to die as adult birds (Williams 1973, Coleman and Minton 1980). Young birds are over-represented in the hunting bag compared to ratios in the wild, apparently again because of inexperience and a greater propensity to disperse from natal areas than that shown by older birds (Owen and Black 1990). Even when competition for limited food resources becomes manifest, it is the younger individuals that suffer from density-dependent regulation. During the severe winter of 1976–77, when the Atlantic coast of North America froze, denying Brant their *Zostera* feeding resource, the proportion of juveniles found dead and dying greatly exceeded their abundance in the population as a whole.

Among geese and swans, there is limited evidence that males are more liable to be shot than females (Imber 1968) and this is certainly the case with many duck species (Owen and Black 1990). However, in many ducks there appears to a preponderance of males in the population for a variety of reasons (Owen and Dix 1986). Competition for food in the more northerly wintering areas can lead to the exclusion of females that apparently have reduced competitive abilities compared to males (e.g. Nichols and Haramis 1980a, Choudhury and Black 1992).

In summary, population dynamics can be seen as the study of changes in the number and composition of individuals in a population, and the factors that influence those changes. In this chapter, we have looked at some of the factors that effect change in populations and the way that we, as observers, can monitor these changes. An understanding of these processes becomes increasingly important as the wetlands upon which wildfowl rely shrink globally and become ever more fragmented as a result of human-induced changes. Large-scale environmental changes, such as climate change and the intensification of land use, are now having widespread effects. If we are to be able to conserve wildfowl populations and their habitats effectively, we need to improve greatly our understanding of how populations 'tick'. In particular, whether we are considering the problems of a pest species, or one threatened because of critically low population size, we need to identify the processes in the annual cycle which regulate the reproductive output and restrict the annual survival of the organism. Such knowledge appears deceptively easy to accumulate, but may take considerable time for waterbirds that may live for perhaps 25 years and breed only periodically. It is also very difficult, without the aid of manipulative experiments, to determine the overall role of different factors affecting vital processes, or the relative strength of density-dependence. The use of modern technology to track and log the movements, behaviour and physiology of individuals has added, and will continue to add, to our understanding of population processes. Nevertheless, there remain many questions to be answered before the population dynamics of wildfowl are truly understood.

8

Conservation and management

Janet Kear, Tim Jones and G. V. T. Matthews

This final chapter considers some sources of conflict between wildfowl and human interests, species and habitat protection, international treaties aimed at wildfowl conservation, habitat creation, breeding in captivity for release into the wild, and future prospects. The discussion has a northern and, indeed, a European bias; however, most basic principles should be applicable in a global context.

Conflicts

Human endeavour often comes up against natural factors, and the interests of wildfowl and wetlands may seem, at times, to be in conflict with economic advance. Birds and their environment frequently suffer as a consequence; strife is not unusual, and most often the birds come off worst. Our throwaway society still leaves anglers' hooks and lines in which birds can become entangled, or discards pieces of plastic which birds can swallow, often with fatal results. The invention of nylon fishing nets, in which diving ducks are caught (Tucker and Heath 1994), has been especially harmful because they are so indestructible. Demand for and ready access to electricity has led to the erection of pylons and power cables which get in the way of flying birds, particularly swans. Pollution can be immensely harmful and oil spills at sea and seed-dressings on farmland take an annual toll.

Agriculture

Accusations of damage to farming interests are not new. Conflict usually involves grazing geese, but complaints are made against swans and ducks as well. The Egyptians worried about the depredations of the Egyptian Goose on emmer (or primitive wheat) crops 3000 years ago, and three Christian saints, who lived between 670 and 770 AD in western Europe, owed their fame to the fact that they could rid farmers' fields of wild geese (Kear 1990, 2001).

Whooper and Bewick's Swans in western Europe are increasingly using agricultural fields. This tends not to concern farmers when the birds clean up sugar beet and potato fields after harvest. However, the birds are unwelcome on young winter wheat and, in Denmark, the winter grazing of Oilseed Rape *Brassica napus* by Bewick's and Whoopers can be damaging in some circumstances (Laubek 1995b). The first reports of Bewick's Swans on Danish fields date from the 1960s and, as the area sown to winter crops increased, so too did the number of grazing swans. While the majority of both Whoopers and Bewick's continued to feed on natural foods, a significant shift to farmers' fields occurred at the beginning of the 1980s, as had happened five to ten years earlier in The Netherlands. The effects of grazing Oilseed Rape vary and depend on a complex interaction between timing, number of swan visits, extent of grazing (whether it is only the leaves that are taken), the weather immediately after the event and that during the following spring and summer. If grazing is followed quickly by a severe frost, then damage is not unusual. Ironically, it was the removal, by selective breeding, of the bitter component in the plant that led to increased grazing when the double-O type rape was introduced in Denmark in 1988. The natural bitterness of 'undomesticated' rape is there to prevent the plant being eaten. Removing it in order to ease the processing of seeds into cooking oil has coincidently rendered the leaves palatable to birds, and complaints of damage have increased dramatically and inevitably (Laubek 1995b).

Parrott and McKay (2001) measured the yield loss caused by grazing Mute Swans on two fields each of autumn-sown Oilseed Rape and winter wheat in three regions of the UK. A 33.7% reduction in total dry weight of seed was found in the rape field subjected to the highest grazing intensity; however, no significant loss was found in the other three fields. As before, yield loss was related to the timing and duration of grazing.

As pointed out in Chapter 3, the trend for wildfowl to feed on agricultural land has been most apparent in geese. Even those coastal specialists, the Brent Geese, have shifted to exploiting farmland grass once they have depleted their littoral food plants (Summers and Critchley 1990). In The Netherlands, Germany and the UK, Brents are increasingly grazing in fields rather than sticking to the tidal zone below high water where they traditionally fed. Scaring them back to this natural habitat is not effective in the long term if the food supply there is inadequate, and shooting merely spreads the damage to neighbouring farms. Brent Geese feeding on Oilseed Rape can cause a loss of up to 27.5% in yield (McKay *et al.* 1993), and the figures for loss from Greylags and Pinkfeet grazing winter cereals range from 0–39%. In addition to a drop in yield, grazing can lead to uneven ripening of the crop (Patterson *et al.* 1989). The grazing sheldgeese of southern South America have likewise taken to feeding on pasture improved by agricultural use, and have suffered terribly because they are thought to compete with introduced sheep (Harradine 1977, Summers and Dunnet 1984, Douse 1987).

Ducks have also switched to feeding on agricultural grains (Baldassarre and Bolen 1994, Mateo *et al.* 2000), and rice paddies in Asia, South America and Madagsgar are important food sources for Baikal Teal, White-winged Duck and Fulvous Whistling-duck among others (Allport *et al.* 1991, Green 1992a, Young 1996b). The White-faced Whistling-duck is regarded as a pest of rice fields

in Africa (Petrie and Petrie 1998), whereas, in Venezuela, Bruzual and Bruzual (1983) found that it was mainly weed seeds of rice cultivation that were consumed. However, many whistling-ducks are poisoned because of their reputation as thieves of young rice.

In countries where swans, geese or ducks that occur on fields are protected, at least for part of the year, the farmer may be expected to scare the birds away rather than kill them. Geese, like many pest birds, flock together but, unlike some other flocking species, they do not have alarm signals that can be used to frighten them; however, they do signal that they are about to fly. As described in Chapter 4, Inglis and Isaacson (1978) showed that simple silhouettes of Brent Geese with their bodies angled upwards and necks extended, and made with heads that oscillated in the wind as if they were ready to fly, were most unlikely to be joined by other geese. The aim of bird scaring, obviously, is to use stimuli that cause birds to leave the area for as long as possible. These stimuli may be novel (man-made), or be natural and related to the birds' efforts to avoid predation. Both types of stimuli can cause approach as well as flight (as in decoying, Chapter 1). However, birds will learn to avoid something that acts as a warning signal of imminent harm; for instance, associating the sound of a bang with being shot at, or with seeing other birds dead or dying. They also eventually discover that the sound alone presents no threat. Thus killing, under licence, may sometimes be needed to reinforce the value of the bangs alone. Man himself remains a potent scaring device.

Schemes giving compensatory payments for the mere presence of birds on crops may need to be expanded, at least in Europe and North America. Such payments are currently made in a few European countries where Bewick's Swan and Barnacle, Brent and Greenland White-fronted Geese (all species of European Conservation Concern) feed on farmland (Tucker and Heath 1994).

Fisheries

There has been growing concern about the impact of the slowly increasing populations of fish-eating

Goosanders and, to a lesser extent, Red-breasted Mergansers (collectively known as sawbills) on commercial fisheries in the UK (Holmes and Clement 1996, Russell *et al.* 1996), US and Canada (White 1957, Wood 1987). It is thought that they remove significant quantities of catchable fish, especially salmon, reduce smolt numbers on rivers, and thus the subsequent salmon harvest. Their daily intake is calculated to be of the order of 20–33% of body weight, and they take prey up to 11 cm long. They might also damage fish, and so lower growth rate and survival, induce stress and disease, cause movement from main rivers into side-streams and, ultimately, make a fishery less attractive to anglers. Investigation has shown that some birds (mainly cormorants *Phalacrocorax* and herons) can cause economic damage in certain circumstances at four kinds of fishery: marine cage farms producing mainly food, freshwater fish farms used for food and for restocking, major rivers fished for sport, and still waters used for sport fishing and restocking—so-called 'put and take' fisheries—(Holmes and Clement 1996). Problems are specific to particular types of fishery, and occur usually where fish are farmed or stocked; neither Goosander nor Red-breasted Merganser are considered serious problems at marine cages or on still waters. More research is needed to establish whether catches by anglers increase as a result of control of sawbills on unstocked rivers (Holmes and Clement 1996), since damage to the health of wild fish populations has almost never been proved.

It seems reasonable that applicants for licences to kill birds should collect data that show that damage is avoided as a result of killing, and that non-lethal methods have not worked. It is insufficient to assume that the presence of fish-eating birds is bound to result in a loss of economically valuable fish. Other predators, such as Northern Pike *Esox lucius* and American Mink, or poachers, may be present, and the incidence of disease is often higher among fish that are stressed in stocked situations. Killing birds may merely leave a gap for newcomers to fill, and continuous control by killing is often ineffective unless reinforced by other scaring methods, as well as being undesirable from a conservation standpoint. Various non-lethal methods of damage alleviation are available, such as scaring, physical exclusion and better fishery design and management. The creation of a stocked food source means that a certain level of loss through predation (in addition to mortality caused by disease and food competition) is inevitable. In unstocked salmon rivers, mortality factors for the fish while at sea are more likely to have significant impact than sawbills; however, conflicts are likely to worsen in the future as sawbill populations grow.

Meanwhile, fish may be causing problems for wildfowl (see later).

Mussel farming

Since mussels have been farmed in the coastal waters of Europe and North America, eiders have been causing complaints. By capitalizing on an easily obtained food, as do sawbills at fish farms, they have become unpopular and, in Scotland for instance, licences have been issued to kill them. Eiders are long-lived, quick to learn, mobile and adaptable. Unlike oysters *Ostrea* and salmon, Blue Mussels are not seeded, penned or fed; they are free food for both wildlife and people. The mussel farmer looks for a clean sea loch and for the presence of mussel predators—where there are plenty of eiders, there must be a liberal supply of shellfish. The young mussel spat need only ropes hanging from rafts to cling to and, within a couple of years, can be hauled in and sold. Rope-grown shells are never uncovered by the tide, so have high feeding and growth rates and high flesh content; they are thin-shelled and free of barnacles, and eiders like them as much as the clients of city restaurants. Common Goldeneyes are a Scottish concern only in Loch Etive, while in Atlantic Canada, eiders are again a major problem, with scoters and Long-tailed Ducks responsible for the loss of newly settled spat. A common way of reducing damage is chasing by boats, although this is costly in terms of time and fuel, and effective for only a short time. However, chasing in conjunction with underwater recordings of boat engines can reduce eider numbers on mussel farms by 50–80%. Laser lights have also proved to be good deterrents (Ross and Furness 2000, Ross *et al.* 2001).

Species protection

Protection is not a new concept; where wildfowl in the past have been regarded as useful, they have been preserved. As early as 1165, Reginald of Durham was recording that Common Eiders were known as *aves Beati Cuthbert*, or birds of the blessed St Cuthbert, a designation that reflected their value as down-producers and, thus, the need to give them protected status.

Bird protection has many roots, including sentiment. In Europe, for instance, swans are protected in every country, often with special penalties; however, this has more to do with feelings than a knowledge that their populations could not sustain an open season. Which species should be protected from any harvest whatsoever? If the only consideration were the amount of meat obtained, then killing a swan makes more sense than catching a teal, but it will take many more years to replace the larger bird (Sladen 1991) and, in general, species that have a long period of immaturity, or where breeding fails completely and regularly, as in some arctic nesters, are not obvious candidates for harvesting. Plenty of migratory wildfowl of the northern hemisphere do produce a surplus of juveniles that can be eliminated before the next breeding season without affecting the replacement capabilities of the stock. But rare species with small populations are often unable to withstand the pressure of added mortality due to hunting. Sometimes hunting is curtailed and protects a species that resembles another, more uncommon, kind; for instance, numbers of the endangered Aleutian race of the Canada Goose rose largely by closing hunting, just before the Aleutians arrived in the fall, of any small Canada Geese in that part of California in which they wintered (Byrd 1998). Sometimes protection is temporary; prolonged cold weather may close the shooting season for a while in the UK as food becomes difficult for the birds to find and they lose condition.

Legal moves in Britain against year-round killing started in the 1880s with the passage of the *Wild Birds Protection Act* which gave protection to all birds in the breeding season between 1 March and 31 July. An act passed in 1939, entitled the *Duck and Goose Act*, extended the closed season a little and ensured that wildfowl could not be shot between 1 February and 11 August, although tidal shooting (below high water mark) was permitted until 20 February. In 1954, another act safeguarded all wild birds at all times except where specified, and removed (in most places) Brent and Barnacle Geese entirely from the quarry list. This was strengthened in 1967 by the banning of market-shooting of geese, and again in 1981 with the advent of the *Wildlife and Countryside Act*. The history of wildfowl protection in the US is well covered in the Redhead account by Tommy Michot and Marc Woodin on page 650.

Market-shooting has been viewed rather differently in the UK and North America. The morality or otherwise of shooting in order to profit from the sale of the bird has exercised the minds of wildfowlers and non-wildfowlers alike. The person shooting for the market is interested in maximum numbers for the least effort and cost, an attitude that runs contrary to the ethos of many sportsmen. Market-shooting of all waterfowl ceased in North America in 1918 (Bellrose 1990), while the sale of dead geese ended in the UK only in 1967, and that move (largely at the instigation of wildfowlers) is thought to have been partly responsible for a great increase in numbers. For instance, Pinkfeet wintering in the UK rose from 35 000 in 1957 to nearly 170 000 in 1988 and to 212 500 by 1999 (although they seem to have reached stability during the last decade) (Musgrove *et al.* 2001). The sale of wild ducks is still permitted in Britain between 1 September and 27 February—those dates having been fixed before the widespread use of deep-freezing to preserve meat—and the only British quarry ducks that are declining somewhat are Northern Mallard and Northern Pintail (Musgrove *et al.* 2001).

There are other great differences between the US and UK in wildfowling regulations, and in public attitudes to the sport. In the US and Canada much of the land is publicly owned and access is free; in Britain most land is private and shooting is allowed only by the owner or his agents. In the US, bag limits are the norm and defined as the maximum allowable daily kill or harvest by a hunter according to regulations set annually by the US Fish and Wildlife Service (Bellrose and Holm 1994); they differ from year to year and are based on reports of duck numbers and expected output. Bag limits are unknown in the UK, where peer pressure tends to regulate excess; equally unheard of are variable open seasons, variable hours (departing from the 'normal' one half-hour before sunrise and sunset) during which shooting is permitted, and systems whereby points are allocated to different species or sexes. For example, male Canvasbacks outnumber females and are scored lower, so that a hunter is permitted to take more of them. One obvious explanation for variation is the difference of scale; North America encompasses a huge latitudinal range, with three main flyways, and includes both breeding and wintering grounds in the jurisdiction of just two countries (three if Mexico is included). In the UK, only a proportion of the ducks shot are home-produced, and the wildfowler has little knowledge of how well any wintering population reproduced in the preceding summer.

The Wood Duck is now the second most popular duck for American hunters after Northern Mallard; there is great interest in the bird (Fredrickson *et al.* 1990) and considerable analysis has been made of the impact of hunting on its populations (Bellrose 1990, Bellrose and Holm 1994). Because of fears for its survival at the start of the last century, a closed season was initiated in 1916 and, in 1990, Bellrose was able to write that the most important single factor in its comeback had been a reduction in kill. In the 1800s and 1900s, the season for waterfowl had run from September to April; for example, Illinois had a season that extended from 2 September to 15 April and, prior to 1918, most American states permitted market-hunting. Complete protection remained in force from 1916 until 1941, when a bag of one Wood Duck was permitted to hunters in 15 states (Bellrose 1990). Thriving populations during recent decades suggest that the regulations restrained the harvest sufficiently, and have allowed numbers to increase in most regions of the US. Problems still emerge; for instance, Wood Ducks are particularly vulnerable to shooting as they fly into an evening roost (Bellrose and Holm 1994). It was also found that early hunting seasons in the southern states could result in unusually large numbers of adult females being killed because of a prolonged attachment to breeding areas

(Fredrickson *et al.* 1990). Unlike the situation in Northern Mallard populations in the US, a Wood Duck harvest can have a depressing effect on survival, and hunting plays a more important role in its population dynamics than it does for the Mallard, which apparently has more flexible compensatory capabilities. However, despite these additive effects of hunting on annual mortality, Wood Duck numbers have increased over most of the species range (Bellrose and Holm 1994).

In both North America and Europe, wildfowl counts, ringing programmes and field research have been shown to be vital to understanding how populations are controlled (see Chapters 6 and 7), and how safe it is to allow a proportion of the birds to be removed in a sustainable harvest. Wildfowl counts are also used, most importantly, in siting reserves in the right places, so that the maximum number of birds will obtain the benefit of good feeding, a safe roost during the entire winter, or a suitable staging post while they are *en route* to destinations north and south. In the UK, a great number and high proportion of wintering wildfowl now depend on the protection of National Nature Reserves or on reserves managed by WWT, the Royal Society for the Protection of Birds (RSPB) and other conservation bodies. The percentage of western European wintering Bewick's Swans that depend on just 15 sites, mostly reserves, is as high as 90% (Beekman 1997). In North America, reserves and habitats are managed for breeding wildfowl, as well as for winter flocks; their requirements have been outlined by Kadlec and Smith (1992). Within reserves, water levels are often regulated, and the type of vegetation will be dictated largely by the water regime selected. Grazing by sheep may be necessary in order to keep grass swards short enough for wintering geese to feed on. Disturbance, for instance from navigation, recreation or wildfowling, that puts pressure on feeding birds can be reduced or eliminated. Disturbance can affect species in different ways—Eurasian Wigeon are particularly liable to desert an area if regularly put to flight, for example—and reserves must be large enough to accommodate the most sensitive species (Musgrove *et al.* 2001).

Species protection often, or perhaps usually, needs an element of human self-interest. Hansen (2002)

suggested that the Common Eider in Greenland, where current declines in bird numbers are appalling, might benefit from an element of private ownership, as happens in Iceland where nesting colonies belong to the farmer on whose land they occur, and who benefits financially from the down collected, as described in Chapter 1. Ecotourism can provide an income from birdwatchers, if the birds are reasonably confiding. Wildfowling also brings money into an area if the annual presence of ducks or geese can be guaranteed by careful husbandry.

Extinction

Thirty-three species of goose or duck and one screamer are on the list of birds threatened with extinction that is maintained by BirdLife International (2000) for IUCN—The World Conservation Union. In addition, 25 subspecies are considered at risk by the Threatened Waterfowl Specialist Group (2001). Five species are classed as Critically Endangered: the first two, Crested Shelduck and Pink-headed Duck, are probably already gone; the third, Madagascar Pochard, was seen as recently as 1991 and may yet be found again; the fourth, Campbell Island Teal, although in very small numbers (perhaps less than 100), is probably no more threatened now than it has been at any time in the last 150 years since rats arrived in the Campbell Islands; and the fifth, Brazilian Merganser, is in a desperate situation, with a population of only 250 individuals left in a river habitat that is seriously damaged through increased turbidity.

BirdLife International (2000) classifies a further seven wildfowl as Endangered, among them the Swan Goose which, in Russia, has dropped to under 1000 birds on only two breeding grounds. Its decline can be linked to its tendency to nest in proximity to humans in easily accessible flood-plains and, where it winters in China, to overhunting. The remaining Endangered species are the endemic Teal and Meller's Duck of Madagascar, the Brown Teal of New Zealand (which is declining rapidly, possibly because of introduced predators), the Koloa of Hawaii, the White-headed Duck, and the White-winged Duck. In the past 50 years, the massive destruction and fragmentation of the White-winged Duck's forest habitat has caused a drastic reduction in numbers, such that the current world population in the wild is estimated at less than 5000 individuals.

Of the two species *known* to have become extinct in historic times (both were seaducks), the last Labrador Duck was shot in 1878, and the last Auckland Islands Merganser in 1902. Extinction is normally caused in one of four ways: by loss of habitat, by overexploitation, by introduced predators and food competitors, or by pollution. Although we cannot be certain in every case, since the biological requirements of rare and vanished birds are often incompletely understood, all these factors seem implicated in recent falls in wildfowl populations. Introduced predators were largely to blame for the loss of New Zealand's only merganser, and for limiting the Campbell Island Teal to a tiny offshore stack (Figure 9.25). Overexploitation was probably behind the demise of the Pink-headed Duck, although habitat destruction was also severe in what is now Bangladesh at the beginning of the last century, and remains so in the home of the Madagascar Pochard. The habitat of the Brazilian Merganser is being destroyed through diamond mining, forest clearance and dam building; fortunately, the species is the subject of a major new conservation initiative by BirdLife International and the Threatened Waterfowl Specialist Group. Hybridization with an introduced close relative, the North American Ruddy Duck, is the main problem for the European White-headed Duck, although habitat destruction and hunting played a large part in its earlier decline. In addition, introduced Common Carp, originally from the Black and Caspian Seas, may now be limiting its population in Spain by taking the chironomid larvae on which the duck depends (Garcia 2001).

Habitat and species protection through international cooperation
The Ramsar Convention

A now familiar and accepted concept, but one that was truly ground-breaking only a few decades ago, is the conservation of wetland habitats through international legal requirements. Many waterfowl are highly migratory and international agreements are therefore necessary to ensure their conservation. Recognizing the crucial importance of safeguarding wildfowl habitats throughout the world, the International Waterfowl Research Bureau (IWRB, now Wetlands International) in the 1960s sponsored a series of intergovernmental and technical conferences to draw up a suitable instrument. These culminated in the signing of the Convention on Wetlands of International Importance Especially as Waterfowl Habitat on 2 February 1971—the first of the modern global environmental treaties. Generally known as the Convention on Wetlands, or the Ramsar Convention after the Iranian town where the text was signed, the treaty has developed into the principal mechanism by which governments cooperate on wetland issues. World Wetlands Day is now celebrated annually on 2 February and is becoming an increasingly important vehicle for increasing public awareness of wetland values (Lyster 1985, Matthews 1993).

Countries joining the Convention are required to designate at least one wetland within their borders for the Ramsar 'List of Wetlands of International Importance' and to take special conservation measures at these 'Ramsar sites'. To qualify for Ramsar status, a wetland must meet at least one of eight technical criteria adopted by the Convention. Amongst these are two criteria dealing specifically with waterbirds and covering those wetlands that regularly support either 20 000+ waterbirds, or at least 1% of the individuals in a population of one species or subspecies of wildfowl. Gathering information to support the application of these criteria is one of the principal functions of the International Waterbird Census (see below) coordinated by Wetlands International.

To date (November 2004), 141 countries are Contracting Parties to the Convention and they have between them listed 1388 Ramsar sites covering over 1.2 million km^2 (roughly the size of the UK, France and Germany combined), with a large number of these having been designated in recognition of their importance for waterbirds.

More generally, Ramsar Contracting Parties undertake to promote the 'wise use' of all the wetlands in their territory. This was a revolutionary concept in 1971 but is now regarded as mainstream and synonymous with the modern concept of 'sustainable use'. The Convention text itself gives only limited interpretation of the meaning and implications of 'wise use'. Consequently, over the years, operational definitions and increasingly comprehensive technical guidelines have been produced. In 2000, the Convention published a series of Wise Use Handbooks, covering such issues as developing and implementing National Wetland Policies, reviewing laws and institutions to promote the conservation and wise use of wetlands, and integrating wetland conservation into river basin management. It is worth noting that the Ramsar wise use provision applies (at least in theory) to more than three-quarters of the world's land surface.

At first, the workings of the Ramsar Convention and the recruitment of new Parties were dealt with on a somewhat *ad hoc* basis by IWRB, which focused on technical aspects, and by IUCN, which took responsibility for legal matters. It was only in 1987 that the Parties agreed to fund a permanent Secretariat based in Switzerland and sharing headquarters with IUCN. Regrettably, the Ramsar Secretariat remains woefully under-resourced, both in terms of the tasks it is expected to undertake and in comparison with the secretariats of other, more recently concluded environmental conventions (e.g. the Convention on Biological Diversity). The principal decision-making body is the Conference of the Parties (COP), which meets every three years, while between COPs the Convention's work is governed by a Standing Committee composed of elected regional representatives. A Scientific and Technical Review Panel was established in 1993 to assist with development of Ramsar's increasingly sophisticated 'toolkit' of technical guidelines. The work of the Convention is also greatly facilitated by its long-standing NGO partners, namely BirdLife International, IUCN, Wetlands International and the World Wide Fund For Nature (WWF).

Of course, legal commitments on paper do not necessarily translate into effective implementation on the ground (see Hansen 2002, for instance, for the problems encountered in Greenland before January 2002). Although Parties have to submit

National Reports to each triennial Conference, these tend for obvious reasons to present an over-optimistic picture. In truth, Ramsar sites, other internationally important sites and wetlands in general continue to suffer loss and degradation, though it is certainly the case that without the Convention this loss would have been more rapid and more extensive. As the servant of the Parties, the Ramsar Secretariat itself can have only a limited 'watchdog' role. It is the national authorities, and more often than not the NGO community, that have the responsibility for monitoring compliance and bringing breaches of the Convention, as well as success stories about its positive use, to light. Since 1990, there has been a register of Ramsar sites where priority conservation action is needed and a mechanism for the Convention to assist at such sites. However, Parties have often been reluctant to register their problem sites and the system has been only partially successful. The COPs provide opportunities for NGOs to castigate publicly shortcomings and infringements, though the norms of international law and diplomacy make it unlikely that strict enforcement measures, such as fines or other sanctions, will ever be developed.

The Bonn Convention

The Bonn Convention on the Conservation of Migratory Species of Wild Animals was concluded in Bonn, Germany in 1979 and entered into force in 1983 (Boere 1989). It provides a global umbrella framework within which the 'Range States' of a given species (or group of species) can establish specific 'Agreements' on the conservation measures to be applied for that species. Perhaps because it is not necessary for a country to be a Bonn Contracting Party in order to join one of the Agreements, the Convention itself has grown relatively slowly. As of February 2004, there were 85 Contracting Parties.

In recognition of the fact that the provisions of the Ramsar Convention apply primarily to the conservation and wise use of wetland habitats, there have been significant efforts under the Bonn Convention to take complementary measures for waterbird species and populations. These culminated in November 1999 with the entry into force of the African–Eurasian Migratory Waterbird Agreement, generally abbreviated as AEWA. This covers 172 species dependent on wetlands for at least part of their annual cycle and applies to 117 Range States, including Greenland and parts of northeast Canada, Europe, western Russia, the whole of the Middle East and parts of western Asia, and all of Africa and Madagascar. By February 2004, there were 51 signatories to the Agreement (though entry into force was still pending for four of these countries).

As its overall goal, AEWA requires parties to take co-ordinated measures to maintain migratory waterbird species in a favourable conservation status or to restore them to such a status. To this end, Parties are obliged to ensure that any use of migratory waterbirds is based on an assessment of the best available knowledge of their ecology and is sustainable for the species as well as for the ecological systems that support them. Parties must also, *inter alia*, cooperate with one another to maintain networks of suitable habitats throughout the entire range of each species; to prohibit the deliberate introduction of non-native waterbird species; to initiate or support research into the biology and ecology of migratory waterbirds; to analyse their training requirements for surveys, monitoring, ringing etc; and to develop awareness-raising programmes concerning conservation of migratory waterbirds. Furthermore, an Action Plan attached to the Agreement (and to be reviewed periodically) sets out specific actions to be taken for priority species, populations and issues. It is hoped that future implementation of the AEWA will be supported through a multi-million-dollar programme submitted to the Global Environment Facility (GEF) at the end of 2003.

Asia–Pacific Waterbird Strategy 2001–2005

The development of this new strategy, which builds on existing waterbird conservation efforts in the region, has been supported by the governments of Australia and Japan, in cooperation with other governments, conservation NGOs and the Ramsar Convention. The initiative is coordinated by Wetlands International and provides an important framework for international cooperation, though without the formal and binding character of a convention. The Strategy focuses on: developing Action Plans for groups of species and for individual globally threatened species; establishing effectively managed networks of sites important for migratory waterbirds; awareness raising, capacity building and improved gathering and sharing of information. An Action Plan for the Conservation of Migratory Anatidae in the East Asian Flyway 2001–2005 has been prepared. This includes, *inter alia*, special action for two priority populations of threatened wildfowl: Swan Goose and Baikal Teal. Priority species for future attention include Lesser White-fronted Goose, Baer's Pochard and Scaly-sided Merganser.

The North American Waterfowl Management Plan

The North American Waterfowl Management Plan—one of the most successful conservation initiatives of its kind in the world—was signed by Canada and the US in 1986, and joined by Mexico in 1994. Its aim is to restore North America's waterfowl populations to the levels of the 1970s, before a combination of habitat loss and inadequately planned and coordinated hunting controls led to major population declines. The plan is based on a broad partnership approach, involving federal, provincial/state and municipal governments, NGOs, private companies and individuals. Since the plan's inception, over US$1.5 billion have been invested in the conservation of more than 2 million hectares of wetlands.

European Union Directives

Another regional driving force for waterfowl conservation in Europe has been the European Union (EU) Directive on the Conservation of Wild Birds (generally known as the 'Birds Directive'). This is a legally binding instrument applicable to all current and future EU Member States and its provisions may be enforced through rulings of the European Court of Justice. A range of penalties, including heavy daily fines, have been imposed by the Court in cases of infringement. The Directive applies to all species of naturally occurring wild birds, their eggs,

nests and habitats, and requires a range of habitat protection, management and restoration measures, together with steps to prohibit or restrict trapping, hunting etc. Special additional measures have to be taken for particularly vulnerable species listed in the Directive's Annex I, together with all regularly occurring migratory species not listed in Annex I. These special measures include the classification of Special Protection Areas (SPA) which, together with Special Areas of Conservation (SAC) designated under the 1992 EU Habitats Directive, form a network of protected areas known as 'Natura 2000'. A number of cases heard by the European Court of Justice, including test cases brought by conservation NGOs, have underpinned the high level of protection enjoyed by SPAs, while many Member States have been reprimanded for their slow rate of SPA designation. But for the Birds Directive, many nationally and internationally important waterfowl habitats would probably have been seriously damaged or destroyed.

Important Bird Areas

Using objective, scientifically based criteria, BirdLife International has taken a regional and national approach to the identification of Important Bird Areas (IBA). This has served significantly to extend knowledge of important waterbird sites, adding to the body of data available through the International Waterbird Census. Although having no legal status, BirdLife International has succeeded in establishing the IBA label as a widely accepted and respected mark of a site's conservation value.

International Waterbird Census

The International Waterbird Census (IWC) was established in 1967 by IWRB, one of the predecessor bodies of Wetlands International. Since then, the IWC has developed into a major tool for monitoring waterbird populations and wetland habitats across Europe, Asia (since 1987) and Africa (since 1991). It provides the baseline information for application of the Ramsar waterbird criteria and enables the monitoring of the health of waterbird populations and wetland sites. However, important gaps remain.

Other international conservation mechanisms

Other international instruments bear to varying degrees on the conservation of wildfowl and wetlands.

The *Convention Concerning the Protection of the World Cultural and Natural Heritage* was adopted in Paris, France in 1972 and, as of June 2002, had 172 Parties. World Heritage Sites (i.e. those sites nominated by governments and accepted for listing through the Convention's strict evaluation procedure) are widely considered to be the 'crown jewels' of the Earth's natural and cultural heritage. While some important wildfowl habitats, such as Campbell Island, feature in the World Heritage List, the fact that many wetlands are subject to multiple human uses—often unsustainably—means that they are unlikely to meet World Heritage criteria.

In 1974 the Man and the Biosphere (MAB) Programme of the United Nations Educational, Scientific and Cultural Organisation (UNESCO) initiated a network of Biosphere Reserves. These are nominated by governments and aim to reconcile biodiversity, conservation and sustainable use. As of May 2002, a total of 408 Biosphere Reserves, including many wetlands, had been designated in 94 countries. Around 70 Biosphere Reserves are also wholly or partly designated as Ramsar sites and there is increasing cooperation between the two networks.

The *Convention on International Trade in Endangered Species of Wild Fauna and Flora* (CITES) was adopted in Washington, DC, in 1973. As of June 2002, it has 158 Parties. However, few wildfowl are included in the lists of species in which trade is restricted or prohibited and subject to close monitoring. These include White-winged Duck, Hawaiian Goose, Laysan Duck, Auckland Island Teal, and the Aleutian Canada Goose.

The *Convention on Biological Diversity* (CBD) was adopted in Rio de Janeiro, Brazil in 1992, and has 183 Parties (as of June 2002). The Convention recognizes that diverse genetic variability within species and ecosystems is vital to the maintenance of such systems. It notes that biodiversity is reduced by certain human activities and commits its Parties to conserving and enhancing biodiversity and to the use of biological resources in a sustainable manner. National Action Plans are to be drawn up to achieve these aims, including the necessary research, the setting aside of special areas, the restoration of degraded ecosystems and the promotion of the recovery of threatened species. The CBD has raised the political profile of biodiversity conservation enormously and a Joint Work Plan has been developed with the Ramsar Convention in recognition of the highly complementary fields of interest covered by the two treaties.

Finally, as climate change, desertification and mismanagement of freshwater ecosystems figure ever more prominently as global threats to biodiversity, the *Framework Convention on Climate Change*, the *Convention to Combat Desertification*, and platforms such as the *World Water Forum* assume growing importance for conservationists. The Ramsar Secretariat has set an admirable example by establishing operational links with these and other bodies, but there remains enormous scope for countries to secure conservation gains by better coordinating their national implementation of multiple international instruments.

Pollution

In many countries, tighter control is needed of effluent discharges into streams and rivers, especially where eutrophication caused by increased nitrate and phosphate inputs can alter the chemistry and the flora of shallow wetlands. Lake Alaotra in Madagascar, like many others, is heavily polluted with pesticides, including DDT. In the UK, the industrial revolution marked the beginning of estuary neglect and, following the Second World War, there was an upsurge in manufacturing based on organic chemicals that were more insidious in their effects on natural systems than earlier organic compounds. Recently, fatty compounds from the edible oil industry have been major pollutants of rivers and estuaries (Jones 2000). Eutrophication in river deltas is thought to be causing the disappearance of *Zostera* in places, reducing the extent of tidal feeding available for Brent Geese, and thus forcing them over the sea-wall onto agricultural fields. Acidification is yet another problem for northern wetlands, as also is climate change—hot summers can make temperate wetlands a breeding ground for botulism, as we saw in the last chapter.

The dumping of bunker oil at sea and cleaning of tanks in international waters continue to put wintering seaducks at risk. Oil tankers pass daily through many narrow northern straits, and major disasters still occur, with many hundreds of birds killed. Eiders, Long-tailed Ducks and Harlequin Ducks are highly susceptible to oiling and many have died in various spills. Major accidents with huge oil tankers still occur, despite public disquiet. Many thousands of Common Scoters were killed in Carmarthen Bay, off the coast of Wales, after the *Sea Empress* oil spill of 1996 (although by February 2000, numbers had apparently recovered, Musgrove *et al.* 2001). Steamer-ducks that live in the oceans around South America similarly suffer from oil pollution.

Lead poisoning was recognized as a hazard for wildfowl more than a century ago and is reported in over 20 countries. Bellrose (1959) estimated that 1.4–2.6 million American birds died each year after ingesting lead pellets from shotgun cartridges. Lead was banned for use in shooting wildfowl in Denmark, Finland, The Netherlands, Norway and the US in the early 1990s, in England by the end of the decade, and by Spain in 2001. In Portugal, scientists are pressing for similar measures to be taken there (Rodrigues *et al.* 2001). Lead was also identified as the major cause of mortality of Mute Swans in Britain in the 1970s, when lead shot used to weight anglers' lines, rather than shotgun pellets, was estimated to cause 30% of all deaths (Goode 1981). After the banning of most lead weights in 1987, the British Mute Swan population recovered sharply.

Not all apparent pollution is to the detriment of wildfowl. As we saw in Chapter 3 (page 35), the installation of a modern sewage system affected the numbers of wintering Greater Scaup in the Firth of Forth in Scotland (Campbell 1984). A study of the Manchester Ship Canal at Salford Docks concluded that its grossly polluted condition, caused by sewage discharge, benefited pochards that fed in areas rich in organic matter where oligochaetes were abundant (Marsden and Bellamy 2000); the authors suggested that improved sewage disposal in the canal might have a serious impact on the wintering ducks by reducing the density of their invertebrate prey.

Habitat creation and management

Most wetlands of the developed world are subject to intensive management. It follows that the distribution of bird populations using those wetlands will be influenced to a greater or lesser extent by human activity. The creation of new wetlands and the reflooding or re-creation of old ones have been fairly recent phenomena that go a small way towards making up for the huge losses.

However, many of these new wetlands are of a different kind, and are not developed for their wildlife conservation value. Over the last half century, dams have transformed the world's major rivers, displaced millions of people, and irretrievably damaged associated ecosystems. Irrigation dams in Africa, Asia and Australia, and hydroelectric schemes everywhere, have provided stretches of water that may support little vegetation but are welcomed by some wildfowl as safe roosts, especially by shelducks and Australian Wood Duck (Kingsford 1992). The wetlands that now surround major cities are typically areas of standing water in reservoirs, borrow pits and ornamental park lakes. For instance, in Greater London, those of greatest importance for wildfowl are reservoirs that were constructed, in the main, at the start of the last century or the end of the nineteenth century. The British of the twenty-first century take the supply of water to their homes and its cleanliness for granted, but only 150 years ago Prince Albert contracted typhoid *Salmonella typhi* from the provision of water to Windsor Castle. It was not until 1873 that any part of London had a permanent water supply, and 35% of the city's supply was still intermittent only a hundred years ago. There are now six large storage reservoirs within Greater London that hold significant numbers of wildfowl in winter, and other sizeable ones nearby in the counties of Essex and Surrey. They are especially valuable for many of the ducks, particularly diving ducks, that migrate from northern Europe in the autumn, one of the most obvious of which is Tufted Duck (Musgrove *et al.* 2001).

The Tufted Duck was known as a regular but very uncommon winter visitor to Britain during the first half of the nineteenth century (Holloway 1996), and did not breed until 1849. It then spread, partly due to climate change (Burton 1995) and to the introduction of the Zebra Mussel, but also thanks to its prompt exploitation of the new deep-water storage systems (Sharrock 1976). By November 1999, 65 800 were counted in Britain, of which just over 5000 were in London's reservoirs (Musgrove *et al.* 2001).

Other useful wetlands in or near London that are too small and shallow to be used for water storage, but were similarly man-made and constructed fairly recently, started as holes in the ground. These include three large gravel pits that, having been worked out and flooded, are often chosen by Gadwall. Like the Tufted Duck, the Gadwall was considered one of England's rarer winter ducks for most of the nineteenth century, and did not stay to breed in the UK before 1850 (Holloway 1996). The Gadwall is not a diver but has profited from the diving abilities of others, and steals food from coots that bring plants to the surface from deeper water (Amat and Soriguer 1984, Knights 1984, Fox 1988, Fox and Salmon 1989, LeSchack and Hepp 1995). There are now, after 150 years of a gradually warming climate, an estimated 15 500 Gadwall in Britain in winter, most of them using flooded gravel pits (Musgrove *et al.* 2001). Good numbers of ducks also winter in London's park lakes and ponds which were originally dug as ornamental waters, and at various sewage farms. In a special category is the new wetland at Barn Elms, developed by WWT from a redundant 110-acre concrete-lined reservoir only 6 km from the centre of London into the London Wetland Centre—a magnificent reserve and tourist attraction.

A few of these new wetlands have been around for a century-and-a-half; more will appear, the human need for water, and for gravel for road building, being apparently insatiable. Meanwhile some novel types of wetland are being created (Merritt 1994). The use of reedbeds—or 'functional wetlands'—for treating sewage, filtering suspended solids and 'stripping' undesirable chemicals from waste water is a concept that is being tried successfully at a number of sites, and should prove of value to smaller dabbling ducks, such as Eurasian Teal and Garganey, as well as to other waterbirds. It is to be hoped that reedbed installation will become routine in association with 'green' housing developments and, particularly, tourism. Wetland creation in the US is at its most advanced, and Mitsch and Gosselink (1993) gave a thorough assessment of the characteristics, management and protection of America's wetlands.

To be useful to wildfowl, habitats must provide food in sufficient quantity at certain times of the year, shelter, security, and meet breeding requirements (e.g. Batt *et al.* 1992). Enhancement of the habitat, therefore, should increase its carrying capacity, usually by increasing the food supply or ensuring greater safety from predation. Provision of agricultural grain, mainly to ensure that migratory birds of the northern hemisphere survive the winter, is not unusual in Europe and North America. It has also been tried successfully for the West Indian Whistling-duck in the Caymans (Bradley 2000). As we saw in Chapter 3 (page 35), a number of ducks, including the Common Goldeneye, tend to avoid lakes where suitable invertebrate foods are reduced by the presence of fish (Ericksson 1983), and it should be possible to manipulate the food supply for ducklings by removing competing insect-eating fish (Kadlec and Smith 1992, Hanson and Butler 1994).

Nestboxes

Secure nesting sites are often scarce, so boxes that can be rendered predator-proof are excellent for increasing local productivity (Zicus 1990a, Ludwichowski *et al.* 2002); in the case of Black-bellied Whistling-duck in Texas, hatching success was 44% in cavity nests but 77% in nesting boxes protected with predator guards (Bolen 1967). Like the diving habit, cavity nesting seems to have evolved more than once among wildfowl; Geffen and Yom-Tov (2001) suggested that hole-nesting has arisen independently at least three times. It will be seen from the species accounts that about a third of all duck species prefer to nest in cavities, and this has a huge influence on their range and life histories. For instance, hole-nesting northern ducks have a breeding distribution that can go no further north than the tree line. They are unable to excavate holes for themselves, and must rely on natural agents to construct them. Thus, in order to conserve Common Goldeneyes, Smew, Bufflehead, Mandarin and Hooded Mergansers, for instance, we must ensure that the woods and forests contain a healthy population of woodpeckers to make the holes that the ducks will use later (Kear 2003). The woodpeckers in turn require a supply of insects that live in or feed on dead and dying timber, so that the woods must be mature (over-mature from the forester's point of view) and not 'tidy' and disease-free. An increase in the number of North American Beavers has been suggested as a factor in the American Wood Duck's comeback, as natural cavities and nestboxes standing in water tend to hatch more ducklings (Beard 1953). The Common Goldeneye was not known as a breeder in the UK and Ireland until 1970 when a pair nested in Scotland. Their absence was, presumably, related to the absence from the British Isles of the Black Woodpecker (Kear 2003). Perhaps because female ducks tend to select nest sites similar to those in which they were hatched (references in Bjärvall 1973), it may take a while for the practice of nesting in boxes to catch on. It was 14 years before nestboxes specifically erected for Goldeneye were accepted (Dennis and Dow 1984), perhaps by a female that had herself hatched in a box on the continent. The small UK breeding population is still largely dependent on boxes rather than on natural holes. Introduced Mandarins are increasing in the same area of Scotland, and threaten to compete with the Goldeneye for nest sites (Coscrove 2003).

Some South American or Speckled Teal nest in ground burrows of woodpeckers *Colaptes* (Nores and Yzurieta 1980) or, in Argentina, choose abandoned chambers in the crowded compound nests of Monk Parakeets. The large enclosed stick nests are 5–20 m up in the tree canopy and provide sites that are safe. Once parakeet nests were placed only in Tala *Celtis tala* trees but, since the beginning of the last century, exotic and much taller *Eucalyptus* gum trees have been introduced and are selected almost exclusively by parakeets and ducks as providing higher nestsites and thus better security from terrestrial predators (Gibson 1920, Hudson 1920, Weller 1967b, Port 1998a, 1998b). In Africa, the native pygmy-goose may nest in disused holes of barbets *Megalaima* and woodpeckers. In Australia and Madagascar, there are no woodpeckers; nevertheless, many of the ducks are cavity nesters, and so storms, fire, fungus, ants and termites must be relied upon to provide holes in rather softer wood (dead and dying trees are still required). Most shelducks use mammal burrows in the ground, except the Paradise Shelduck which, until recently, lived where there were no mammals (the female uses rock crevices instead). The Common Shelduck must have been far less numerous in Britain before Rabbits were introduced by the Normans and kept by monks in special warrens as a ready source of food (Kear 2003). The warrens were bordered by high banks and gorse hedges; the dissolution of the monasteries in the first half of the sixteenth century meant that the warrens were sold into private hands and, eventually, the Rabbits escaped to populate the countryside and construct underground nesting sites for shelducks. The Cape Shelduck uses burrows made by Aardvarks *Orycteropus afer*, which themselves need active conservation as they are becoming rare, as well as those of the South African or Cape Porcupine *Hystrix africaeaustralis* and Springhaas *Pedetes capensis*. The female Ruddy-headed Goose prefers to nest in penguin burrows, as does the Falkland Steamer-duck. The Torrent Duck may use the abandoned burrow of a Southern Ringed Kingfisher *Magaceryle torquata*. Thus, the biodiversity of a whole habitat needs preserving in order to maintain successful breeding populations of these species, and, if a shortage of safe nesting sites is limiting productivity, then artificial ones have to imitate a range of features. In the tropics, artificial nest sites will need to be examined frequently as they themselves may decay, or be swept away in hurricanes.

The tendency for females to dump eggs in boxes that appear identical may increase, making a plentiful supply and careful placing of predator-proof boxes important factors to be taken into account (Bolen 1967, Semel *et al.* 1988). An additional benefit of nestbox schemes is that the construction and erection of

8.1 Male Mandarin at nestbox.

boxes can involve the public and shooting organizations, such as Ducks Unlimited in North America and New Zealand. As well as providing local employment, the construction of nestboxes helps to demonstrate practical conservation techniques (Fredrickson *et al.* 1990). Their use, as was pointed out in Chapter 1, was pioneered by aviculturists who wanted their captive ducks to breed (Figure 8.1); however, the development of structures that are predator-proof has been in the hands of biologists working with wild populations. The wild Orinoco Goose and Scaly-sided Merganser are among species that have benefited recently in taking successfully to artificial sites.

Boxes may seem the answer to many problems of nesting-site shortage, but should not be studied to the detriment of an interest in conserving natural sites. Nestboxes make only a small contribution (4 to 5%) to the juvenile component of the Wood Duck's autumn population (Bellrose 1990), despite some 100 000 boxes being available—more than for any other cavity-nester. A supply of natural cavities must also be ensured by investigation of what best suits the birds, and by careful management of the environment. As pointed out in Chapter 5, the rengas tree of Malaya has resinous sap that is poisonous to humans (although not apparently to monkeys and squirrels who eat the fruit), and so is rejected

by tree-cutters and the timber trade. This is excellent for the rare White-winged Duck that nests in its cavities (Green 1992a), and can survive what would otherwise be clear-felling.

Adverse effects

Deleterious effects, such as excessive disturbance in the northern winter when most of a grazing bird's daylight hours must be spent in feeding, or the release of alien organisms, ought to be counteracted by legislation. It should be illegal to add exotic predators, such as domestic cats, to environments without mammalian predators; food competitors such as Atlantic Salmon, Brown Trout, carp and alien crayfish; destructive elements such as Water Buffalo *Bubalus bubalis* to lily-beds; water plants that smother the native flora; cavity nesters such as Common Starling *Sturnus vulgaris* that compete for the few natural holes; and genetic competitors like Northern Mallard and Ruddy Ducks. Often, indeed typically, the law comes too late and removal of some adverse effect is the only, expensive solution. American Mink escaped from fur farms in Iceland, in Russia, and on islands of the Outer Hebrides as long ago as the 1930s, and have done immense damage. The deliberate release of American Mink, by misguided animal rights activists, unfortunately still occurs (fur farms that house predators outwith their natural range should themselves be closed and moved). Attempts are now being made to rid Scotland's islands of Uist of Mink, and the introduced Hedgehog *Erinaceus europaeus*, before further losses to internationally important breeding colonies of ground-nesting birds occur. Many different fish species, herbivores and carnivores, have been released into the lakes of Madagascar, altering their biodiversity; in particular, the floral composition has been affected greatly. Some fish have competed with waterbirds for food, others have predated them or their young (Young 1996b).

We have yet to see whether the laudable efforts to eradicate the introduced Ruddy Duck from Europe in order to conserve the White-headed Duck will be successful. Can the authorities on Hawaii eliminate the Northern Mallard in order to save the genetic purity of their own duck, the Koloa? The suggestion is made that the same

Northern Mallard should be removed from areas of southern Africa where the introduced bird meets and hybridizes with the native Yellow-billed Duck. Is this a realistic proposal? New Zealand's Grey Duck—a race of the Pacific Black Duck—has widely hybridized with the Mallard that were introduced during the last century (Rhymer *et al.* 1994, Rhymer and Simberloff 1996), but the Mallard in the interim has become an important game bird, and its removal would be very unwelcome to many wildfowlers. New Zealand's Department of Conservation has plenty of experience of ridding offshore islands of mammals that threaten the survival of native birds by eating incubating females, eggs and young, or consuming the vegetation on which the birds depend for nesting cover. In this, the New Zealanders have much to teach the rest of the world, since removal of alien fauna and flora will become more and more necessary in the fight to save rare endemics. Can we think the unthinkable (or merely very expensive and logistically difficult), and propose that many of the Hawaiian islands, and those of the Caribbean, should be freed of their exotic Small Indian Mongooses *Herpestes auropunctatus*? Feral cats *Felis* are also a menace on Hawaii (Banko *et al.* 1999), but attempts to control them are often resisted by the Hawaiian public. Ascension Island in the Atlantic has been cleared of its feral cats; Round Island near Mauritius has been cleared of its Rabbits and goats *Capra*; in the Galapagos, Santiago Island has had its introduced and hugely destructive Pigs *Suf scrofa* eradicated, and foxes have been eliminated from some of the Aleutian chain (Byrd *et al.* 1994). Campbell Island has been cleared, at New Zealand government expense, of rats whose ancestors arrived on sailing ships more than a century ago and its endemic Teal will be reintroduced after captive breeding (Gummer and Williams 1999). And there are current plans to take cats and pigs off the Auckland Islands. Meanwhile, the Kerguelen race of the rare Eaton's Pintail is likewise threatened by rats and mice. Feral cats, introduced in 1956 to control the situation, have spread and are predicted to become a serious hazard to the Pintail if the supply of petrels, the cats' current staple diet, runs out. In addition, Rabbits need removal from Ile du Port in the Kerguelen Island group. Who is going to pay for the control of the Rabbits, rats, mice and cats in these remote places, and which organization will run the programme that gets rid of them? The original 'polluters' are long since dead, and the expense will not be trivial, but countries (UK, US and France, among others) with long associations with these places are not poor, and the satisfaction to be gained, surely, would be immense.

Breeding in captivity for reintroduction

Many ducks, geese and swans, especially those that live gregariously on freshwater as opposed to the oceans, and that do not catch and eat moving prey, take readily to captivity and breed freely (Chapter 1). Thus, there is potential for the captive breeding of those threatened with extinction in the wild for eventual return to their native environment. In practice, this is not so easy as might be supposed and, because reintroduction is seldom successful in establishing a self-sustaining wild population, attempts are sometimes portrayed as wasting scarce conservation resources, and captive breeding as doing more harm than good.

There is no doubt that zoos and bird collections have been extremely useful in providing research material, as outlined in Chapter 1. A few rare wildfowl species would be almost unknown but for studies made in captivity; the Campbell Island Teal, South Georgia Pintail, Madagascar Teal and Meller's Duck have all been bred recently by experienced and dedicated aviculturalists, and much has been learnt about their biology (Gummer and Williams 1999, Martin 2002, Young 2002). Captive breeding will probably be much more difficult to achieve in the case of the extremely rare Brazilian Merganser. We can predict that it will be very choosy about its live fish diet and in selecting a mate; in the wild it has one of the longest territories of any riverine duck, and will need copious quantities of clear, unpolluted, well-oxygenated water. Because it does not flock, it may have little resistance to the pathogens and parasites that are not uncommon in zoos, and against which more gregarious ducks have evolved some immunity. Despite failure in the past (Partridge 1956, Johnson and Chebez 1985), the establishment of a captive breeding population has been recommended (Silveira and Bartmann 2001) as part of a recovery programme, since avicultural techniques have improved considerably in the last few years.

Setting priorities for captive breeding is never simple (Cowling and Davies 1983, Balmford *et al.* 1996), and limitations are not hard to recognize (Snyder *et al.*1996), so the validity of any proposed reintroduction scheme that results from captive breeding must be carefully tested—IUCN (1998) has issued excellent guidelines. The best programmes involve rearing at or near the release site, and release to the wild only after acclimatization in a predator-proof enclosure. Of course, the factors that brought the animal close to extinction need investigation and removal before any reintroduction takes place. In the case of wildfowl, this usually means an end to hunting and the control of alien predators (Kear and Berger 1980). Research after any release is also essential, and satellite-tracking of a proportion of the released birds will almost certainly be necessary; fortunately, such techniques have become much more common and feasible since recent miniaturization of the equipment (see Petersen *et al.* 1995, Pennycuick *et al.* 1996, 1999, Anon 1996b, Kanai *et al.* 1997, Petrie and Rogers 1997a, Staus 1998a). Although expensive, tracking will be but one of many costs in a reintroduction programme that results in useful information, if not in a self-sustaining new population.

Because of a belief in the 1920s that the North American Wood Duck was on the verge of extinction in Connecticut and Massachusetts, this was one of the first ducks to be bred deliberately in captivity for release into the wild. Birds were purchased from aviculturists as far away as Belgium and brought to Lichfield, Connecticut. A gamekeeper was acquired from England and given the task of raising more. By 1939, when the project ended, 2579 had been released, and rings (bands) had been recovered from 15 States and Ontario in Canada (Bellrose 1990). By 1941, the fortunes of the Wood Duck had improved so much that hunting was again allowed; however, Bellrose (1990) suggested that this restoration was due to the protection from

hunting that had been instigated in 1916, and had little, if anything, to do with the releases, or even the nestbox schemes that were running concurrently. Likewise, the migratory Aleutian Canada Goose was saved, as already pointed out, by protection from shooting rather than the elaborate and costly captive breeding of sufficient juvenile geese to be reintroduced onto fox-free Aleutian islands (Byrd 1998).

The reintroduction of a captive-bred flock of Lesser White-fronted Geese, whose numbers are declining rapidly, into a former breeding area of Swedish Lapland has resulted in a flock of about 50 individuals, some of which winter in The Netherlands near Strijen, and stage in spring and autumn near Hudiksvall on the coast of Sweden (von Essen 1991, Callaghan and Green 1993). Hybridization with White-fronted Geese was considered a possible flaw in the programme (Ruokonen 2001), and reintroduction is not thought to be a priority in the species account that deals with the Lesser White-front on page 289, mainly because the reasons behind the decline are so little understood, although habitat loss and hunting mortality are likely to be implicated.

The Hawaiian Goose was the subject of a classic attempt at reintroduction from captive-bred stock (Kear and Berger 1980), and the history and outcome are well covered by Jeff Black and Paul Banko in the species account on page 320. The only part of this reintroduction campaign that worked really well, where the population seems to be self-sustaining, is the unauthorized release of about 25 captives onto the mongoose-free island of Kauai in 1985 (Banko *et al.* 1999); the flock has been augmented with further releases of captive-bred birds, is thriving and currently totals over 750 individuals. The geese released on Maui and the big island of Hawaii continue to suffer from predation by introduced mammals, and must exist in suboptimal upland habitat since the more fertile lowlands, where the geese once bred, are largely converted to farmland and human settlement.

Despite these less-than-perfect successes, the reintroduction of captive-bred Teal to the 11 268 ha of Campbell Island (now a World Heritage Site, and also home to a recently discovered snipe) seems eminently sensible. The Teal were extirpated in the 1800s by rats which, as we saw earlier, have been removed. Two trial introductions in 1999 and 2000 were made to Codfish Island, a 1396 ha reserve 3 km off the west coast of Stewart Island and some 660 km north of Campbell Island. These releases of captive-bred individuals carrying 8 g radio-transmitters should establish, temporarily, a population in the wild; the birds are reported to be thriving (Gummer 2000) and have bred.

Meanwhile, reintroduction programmes are planned currently for the White-headed Duck in Italy and southern France, and are suggested for the White-cheeked Pintail on islands of the Caribbean where they occurred until recently.

Prospects for waterfowl in the modern world

Prospects for wildfowling

Not all species are equally suitable for sustainable harvesting. Large numbers of wild whistling-ducks may be shot; they are apparently easy to obtain because when one of a pair is shot, the other circles its fallen partner and becomes a casualty in its turn. Eiders are shot in some places despite appearing to be ill-suited for wildfowling since they take two to four years to reach breeding age and because success, as measured by young birds fledged, is low in most years. They had a distinct place in the hearts of those who signed the *Migratory Birds Act 1918* between the US and Canada; American Eiders were given special protection, as exploitation had depleted their numbers greatly and, as with the Labrador Duck, extinction was feared. The ducks are protected in most of their European range (but see page 705) and, in some parts, are increasing in numbers. In west Greenland, where thousands are killed every year, numbers are declining (Hansen 2002) and, in parts of Canada, they are still, or again, under severe threat because of aboriginal hunting. Some hunting might be sustained, but not in the spring, nor in combination with down and egg collection (Raveling 1984).

It is clear from the species accounts in Part II that, in nearly three-quarters of wildfowl species, we know little about breeding success and adult survival—essential knowledge if conservation programmes are to be developed that allow a sustainable level of harvesting, as we saw eloquently expressed in the last chapter. The overall decline in North American waterfowl populations since the mid-1970s is a cause for concern. However, habitat degradation on the breeding and wintering grounds, rather than hunting, is considered the major cause for the decrease; hunting is carefully regulated, and suited to local conditions. In the UK, where hunting is also regulated but bag limits are monitored only voluntarily by wildfowling clubs and the British Association for Shooting and Conservation, no duck or goose population seems to be declining as a result of legitimate hunting, although reasons behind the slow fall in Northern Mallard and Northern Pintail numbers are uncertain (Musgrove *et al.* 2001). As many of the species accounts in this book make clear, in some other countries, hunting is still a serious threat. Around the Mediterranean, and in parts of the former USSR (Tucker and Heath 1994), shooting of rare species is all too common, either through misidentification or ignorance of the law.

Certain problems need to be tackled by the wildfowlers themselves. There are worries about the level of wounding—Pink-footed Geese have been found to have reduced survival if they carry shotgun pellets (Madsen and Noer 1996)—and with misidentification of target species, since about 40% of Bewick's Swans X-rayed in the UK had lead pellets in their tissues, and 7% of adult deaths have been attributed to hunting despite the birds being legally protected everywhere (Rees *et al.* 1990, Brown *et al.* 1992). There is evidence, from a small sample, that laws that only lead-free shot can be used for killing ducks in England are being ignored; they may continue to be ignored unless lead is banned from shooting all types of game bird. Releases of reared ducks in order to increase the numbers available for shooting may seem sensible, but Callaghan and Kirby (1996) have identified many environmental concerns.

Integration of wildfowl populations with subsistence societies, that lived by hunting in the recent past, seems culturally important, but experience with the Inuit in Greenland suggests that sustainability following the ready acquisition of modern guns and vehicles may be illusory (Hansen 2002). The same lack of anything to do but hunting, combined with recently acquired leisure time, especially for men, seems to be true also in Alaska (Raveling 1984).

Research needs

Although a few wildfowl species that were enigmatic a decade ago are now better studied (King and Steller's Eider, Harlequin, Musk Duck, Scaly-sided and Brazilian Mergansers among them), there are still very many gaps to be filled. More research is needed into wildfowl that do not live in the Western Palearctic or North America (although the sub-arctic Black Scoter also needs investigation). Some of the missing information seems quite basic; for instance, we know almost nothing of the fairly common Blue-winged Goose of Ethiopia, its nest has never been photographed, and almost all the biological data come from captivity. The wild Hartlaub's Duck is another African duck of which we know very little. The Cotton Teal and Green Pygmy-goose need closer investigation, as do the wild breeding Mandarin of China and Japan, and the Andaman and Indonesian Teals. Some South American species are scarcely investigated in nature, such as the southern races of the Cinnamon Teal, the wild Muscovy, Ringed Teal, Brown Pintail, Rosybill and Bronzewing. How do females of these largely unknown tropical and semi-tropical species convert environmental nutrients into eggs? Our knowledge of the moult patterns of tropical and southern-hemisphere ducks is rudimentary. Typically, species that dive to feed have more than one plumage change a year, some have three; how many does the diving White-backed Duck have, one like its relatives the whistling-ducks, or two as its life-style suggests? Do all stiff-tailed ducks moult their wing and tail feathers more than once, and what adaptive value does a double moult have? From what does the orange colour on the necks and undertail coverts of breeding comb ducks derive? Captive comb ducks at WWT Slimbridge that used to feed on flamingo 'soup', with its high canthaxanthin content, became especially colourful. What is the function of the swollen forehead of the Indonesian Teal; if it isn't housing glands for salt extraction, what is it for?

Ducks, geese and swans are better known than many other wetland birds (the references listed at the end of this book number about 3500); however, more regular counting and wider census coverage are required, especially in Asia, Africa and the Neotropics, areas where population trends are unknown and conservation action is often most urgent (Rose and Scott 1997). Better monitoring of northern seaduck numbers, and their distribution at sea in winter, are also important in view of the catastrophic frequency of oil spills.

Further studies of DNA may alter, yet again, our perception of species relationships and evolution. The Brent and Canada Goose races need to be researched genetically before the populations are irretrievably mixed. The Torrent Duck seems particularly complex in the geographic variability of its male plumage, and might provide another interesting molecular study. The likely subspeciation of the White-winged Duck needs investigation. Other work on taxonomy might include studies of Green-winged Teal. Are the calls of the two species (or subspecies) identical? In Alaska, *Anas crecca nimia* and *A. carolinensis* apparently hybridize readily—if there is assortative mating (*crecca* tending to mate with *crecca*), then we are likely dealing with two species as suggested by the BOU, but if birds choose mates more or less at random, then it is probably one as the AOU supposes.

More research is needed into the situation below the water surface, into water chemistry and the characteristics of eutrophication that make a wetland suitable or otherwise for ducks, geese and swans, and how to change and improve any existing system. Monitoring of the long-term value of newly created wetlands is necessary and not often done. We need to know more about the ultimate fate and breakdown of pollutants and contaminants.

The control of fish populations must be considered desirable in certain places, and fish stocks be manipulated so as to improve the outcome for some species of ducks and ducklings with which they compete for food (Eriksson 1983). Fish stocking is known to reduce the breeding success of Tufted Duck, and can lower overwintering numbers where fish compete for available food supplies (Phillips 1992, Giles 1994, Winfield and Winfield

1994b). The stocking of wetlands with 'sport' or exotic fish should be given much more serious consideration than is often the case (Einarsson 1991); it should be assumed that the ecological balance will change, and the 'stocker' be required to prove that this change will not be harmful. The Madagascar Pochard and a local grebe *Tachybaptus rufolavatus* may have been driven to extinction through the introduction of alien fish. Introduced American Crayfish *Orconectes limosus* have damaged the ecology of marshes in Spain (Tucker and Heath 1994).

We are still encouraging children to examine the unseen habitat beneath the surface by 'pond-dipping'—hauling fish and aquatic invertebrates into an unnatural element to be looked at and handled. It is a messy performance that breaks up a fragile system, and minds should be put to finding a better method of teaching the beauty of, and respect for, underwater wildlife.

Climate change is implicated in the evaporation of wetlands in parts of the steppes with consequent loss of duck numbers. Climate amelioration since 1850 has already resulted in obvious shifts in wildfowl distribution (Burton 1995), and will affect the future success of northern breeding geese and their migratory patterns (Boyd and Madsen 1997). Wild geese can be caught and ringed and, more recently, have radio-transmitters fitted; thus, a great deal of research in Europe and in North America has ensured that we understand more than we did about the regulation of population size, the energetics of migration, and how to manage the vast wintering flocks. Many rising goose populations are in for a rough time in the near future—some are destroying their breeding habitat and fitness is declining. Calls for a reduction in numbers in North America have been heeded and about 1.4 million geese were shot during the 1999–2000 season. A somewhat different problem, that seems to be causing increasing difficulties, is the large number of tame Canada Geese introduced into human-modified environments of Europe. Urban populations of Canada, usually non-migratory, are also a nuisance in their native North America (Kadlec and Smith 1992). How are we to control their populations without upsetting the human populace from whose hands they feed?

Drainage, the lowering of groundwater tables, drought and degradation have caused widespread losses of wetlands around the world. Abstraction of water for agriculture and tourism are continuing threats, as are rising salinity and nitrate levels in the freshwater that we have left. New conflicts between wildfowl and human development arise all the time. The draining of the marshes of Mesopotamia and the exile of the indigenous Marsh Arabs has been a colossal tragedy; a large proportion of the world's Marbled Teal and thousands of other wonderful wildfowl bred in the Iraqi swamps. In Iceland, extraction of diatomite from the Ramsar site of Lake Mývatn started in 1967 and is thought to affect the algal blooms which are the food source for the blackfly larvae and pupae on which the Barrow's Goldeneye depend (Tucker and Heath 1994); because of conservation concerns, dredging will cease in 2010. There are also plans for extensive tree planting in the Icelandic lowlands that will undoubtedly impact on the habitat of the many ground-nesting birds including ducks (afforestation is a popular, green-sounding programme, and one where the potential for damage is not understood by the general public).

The opening-up of the north coast of Alaska in order to extract more oil with which to run the US economy may result in huge interference with the ducks and geese that nest on the tundra. The same is true of parts of the Russian tundra where oil and gas are being sought in a habitat that also has breeding Bewick's Swans. All oil exploration should be subject to environmental impact assessments, but who will carry them out and which international organization will police the conclusions? Efforts to find sources of energy that do not involve oil, or any other fossil fuel, have led to the installation of windfarms offshore in the North Sea. Will the rotating arms affect adversely the thousands of duck that spend the winter on the sea beneath? Research is under way to find out. Perhaps more harm will be done by the helicopters that will need to fly out to service the turbines, and may drive frightened birds up into the rotating arms.

Notwithstanding all the problems, there are some grounds for optimism. Wetland science was unheard of a few decades ago. Developers, engineers and landscape designers are now more fully aware of the possibilities and benefits of wetland preservation and creation (Mitsch and Gosselink 1993, Merritt 1994). University courses are available, there are new scientific journals devoted to the subject, and wildfowl ecology and management are thriving as research topics, especially in North America (Fredrickson *et al.* 1990, Batt *et al.* 1992). The Wildfowl Trust changed its name to the Wildfowl and Wetlands Trust (WWT) in 1989 after it became clear that, for an organization involved in public education, the habitat must be seen to be as important as the birds. The Threatened Waterfowl Specialist Group of the IUCN, based at WWT Slimbridge, now (April 2004) has 939 expert members in 141 countries; although most are in Europe, there are 194 in Asia, 86 in Africa and 75 in South America. There is pressure for wetland preservation from other quarters, since these habitats are often rich in human history. The power of tannic acid, low temperature and oxygen deficiency to keep intact remains of organic material over thousands of years means that wetland archaeology is as endangered by drainage and peat-cutting as is today's wildlife (Coles 1984, 1989). The Ramsar Convention and such initiatives as the North American Waterfowl Management Plan have brought wetland conservation into the international arena.

The species accounts that follow in Part II give detailed and convincing evidence that the world would be a poorer place should any more ducks, geese or swans be brought to extinction through human carelessness.

Plates

Plate 1

Anhima, Chauna and *Anseranas*

---

1. Horned Screamer
Anhima cornuta, p. 176

2. Northern Screamer
Chauna chavaria, p. 179

3. Southern Screamer
Chauna torquata, p. 180

4. Magpie Goose
Anseranas semipalmata, p.182
4a Adult.
4b Juvenile.
4c Gosling.

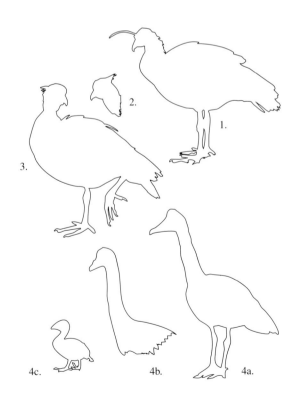

M. HULME

Plate 2

Dendrocygna

1. Spotted Whistling-duck
Dendrocygna guttata, p. 195

2. Plumed Whistling-duck
Dendrocygna eytoni, p. 203

3. Wandering Whistling-duck
Dendrocygna arcuata, p. 205
3 *D. a. arcuata.*

4. Fulvous Whistling-duck
Dendrocygna bicolor, p. 199
4a Adult.
4b Duckling.

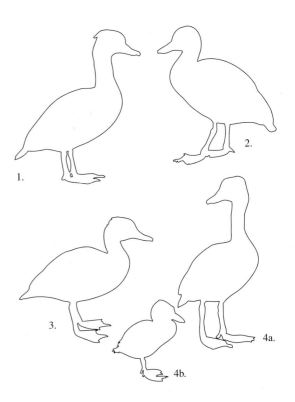

M. HULME

Plate 3

Dendrocygna

1. White-faced Whistling-duck
Dendrocygna viduata, p. 189
1a Adult.
1b Juvenile.
1c Duckling.

2. West Indian Whistling-duck
Dendrocygna arborea, p. 197

3. Black-bellied Whistling-duck
Dendrocygna autumnalis, p.192
3 *D. a. discolor.*

4. Lesser Whistling-duck
Dendrocygna javanica, p.207

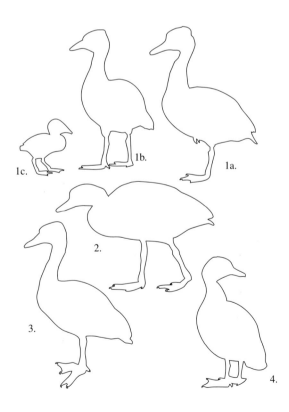

M·HULME

Plate 4

Cygnus and *Coscoroba*

1. Mute Swan
Cygnus olor, p. 231
1 Adult ♂.

2. Black Swan
Cygnus atratus, p. 223
2a Adult.
2b Cygnet.

3. Coscoroba Swan
Coscoroba coscoroba, p. 219
3a Adult.
3b Juvenile.

4. Black-necked Swan
Cygnus melanocoryphus, p. 227
4 Adult ♂.

5. Whooper Swan
Cygnus cygnus, p. 249

6. Whistling Swan
Cygnus columbianus columbianus, p. 238

7. Trumpeter Swan
Cygnus buccinator, p. 234

8. Bewick's Swan
Cygnus columbianus bewickii, p. 243
8a Adult.
8b 1st winter immature.

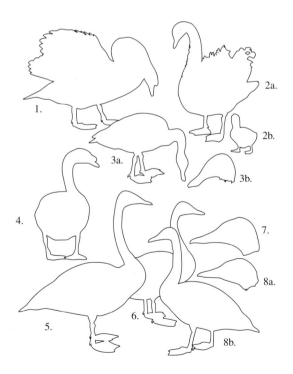

M. HULME

Plate 5

Anser

1. Swan Goose
Anser cygnoides, p. 263

2. Bean Goose
Anser fabalis, p. 266
2a *A. f. serrirostris.*
2b *A. f. fabalis.*
2c *A. f. rossicus.*

3. Pink-footed Goose
Anser brachyrhynchus, p. 270

4. White-fronted Goose
Anser albifrons, p. 281
4a *A. a. albifrons.*
4b *A. a. flavirostris*, adult.
4c *A. a. flavirostris*, 1st winter immature.

5. Lesser White-fronted Goose
Anser erythropus, p. 286
5a Adult.
5b Gosling.

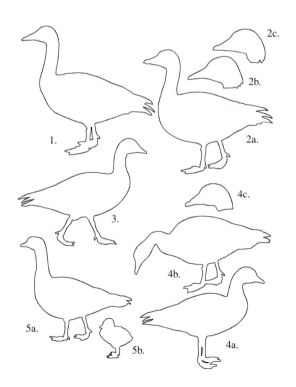

M. HULME

Plate 6

Anser

1. Snow Goose
Anser caerulescens, p. 297
1a *A. c. caerulescens*, adult blue phase.
1b *A. c. caerulescens*, adult white phase.
1c *A. c. caerulescens*, gosling.
1d *A. c. atlanticus*, adult.

2. Ross's Goose
Anser rossii, p.303
2a Adult.
2b 1st winter immature.

3. Emperor Goose
Anser canagicus, p. 293

4. Bar-headed Goose
Anser indicus, p. 289
4a Adult.
4b 1st winter immature.

5. Greylag Goose
Anser anser, p. 276
5a *A. a. anser.*
5b *A. a. rubrirostris.*

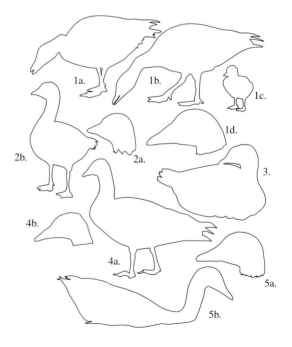

M. HULME

Plate 7

Branta

1. Barnacle Goose
Branta leucopsis, p. 329

2. Hawaiian Goose (Nene)
Branta sandvicensis, p. 316
2a Adult.
2b Gosling.

3. Canada Goose
Branta canadensis, Branta hutchinsii, p. 306
3a *B. c. canadensis.*
3b *B. h. leucopareia.*
3c *B. h. minima.*
3d *B. c. occidentalis.*
3e *B. c. maxima.*

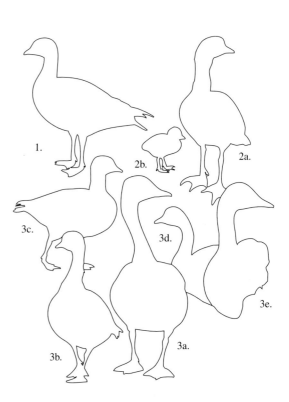

M. HULME

Plate 8

Branta, Cereopsis and *Stictonetta*

1. Brent Goose (Brant)
Branta bernicla, p. 321
1a *B. b. hrota.*
1b *B. b. nigricans.*
1c *B. b. bernicla.*

2. Red-breasted Goose
Branta ruficollis, p. 335

3. Cape Barren Goose
Cereopsis novaehollandiae, p. 257
3a *C. n. novaehollandiae.*
3b *C. n. grisea.*

4. Freckled Duck
Stictonetta naevosa, p. 339
4a Adult ♂.
4b Adult ♀.
4c Duckling.

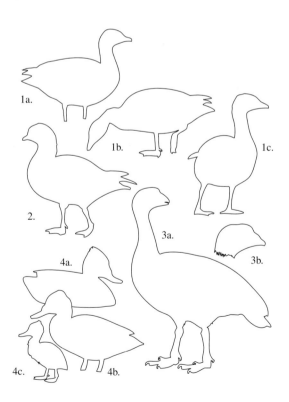

M. HULME

Plate 9

Cyanochen and Chloephaga

1. Blue-winged Goose
Cyanochen cyanopterus, p. 398

2. Andean Goose
Chloephaga melanoptera, p. 410

3. Magellan Goose
Chloephaga picta, p. 411
3a C. p. picta.
3b C. p. leucoptera, adult ♂.
3c C. p. leucoptera, adult ♀.
3d C. p. leucoptera, gosling.

4. Kelp Goose
Chloephaga hybrida, p. 414
4a C. h. malvinarum, adult ♂.
4b C. h. malvinarum, adult ♀.

5. Ruddy-headed Goose
Chloephaga rubidiceps, p. 418

6. Ashy-headed Goose
Chloephaga poliocephala, p. 416

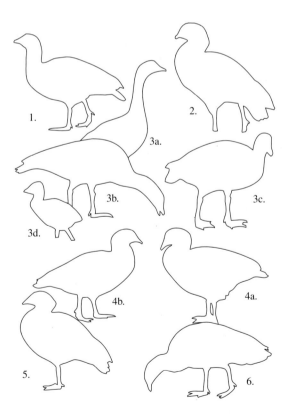

M. HULME

Plate 10

Tadorna

---

1. Cape Shelduck
Tadorna cana, p. 429
1a Adult ♂.
1b Adult ♀.

2. Ruddy Shelduck
Tadorna ferruginea, p. 426
2a Adult ♂.
2b Adult ♀.
2c Duckling.

3. Common Shelduck
Tadorna tadorna, p. 420
3a Adult ♂.
3b Adult ♀.

4. Radjah Shelduck
Tadorna radjah, p. 423
4 *T. r. rufitergum*.

5. Australian Shelduck
Tadorna tadornoides, p. 434
5a Adult ♂.
5b Adult ♀.

6. Paradise Shelduck
Tadorna variegata, p. 436
6a Adult ♂.
6b Adult ♀.

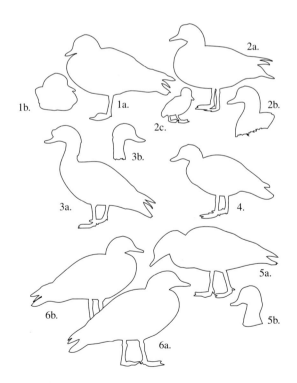

M. HULME

Plate 11

Neochen, Alopochen and *Tachyeres*

---

1. Orinoco Goose
Neochen jubata, p. 408

2. Egyptian Goose
Alopochen aegyptiacus, p. 401
2a Adult.
2b Gosling.

3. Magellanic Steamer-duck
Tachyeres pteneres, p. 381
3 ♂.

4. Flying Steamer-duck
Tachyeres patachonicus, p. 378
4 ♀.

5. White-headed Steamer-duck
Tachyeres leucocephalus, p. 386
5 ♂.

6. Falkland Steamer-duck
Tachyeres brachypterus, p. 383
6 ♀.

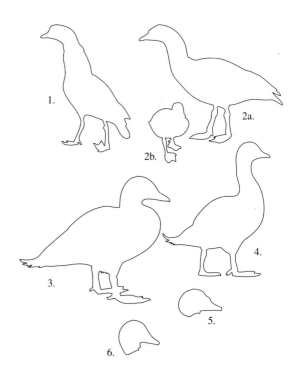

M. HULME

Plate 12

Pteronetta, Cairina, Asarcornis, Sarkidiornis and *Plectropterus*

1. Hartlaub's Duck
Pteronetta hartlaubi, p. 459
1 ♂.

2. Muscovy Duck
Cairina moschata, p. 453
2 ♂.

3. White-winged Duck
Asarcornis scutulata, p. 455
3 *A. s. scutulata* ♂.

4. African Comb Duck
Sarkidiornis melanotos, p 391
4a Adult ♂.
4b Juvenile ♂.
4c Duckling.

5. South American Comb Duck
Sarkidiornis sylvicola, p. 394
5a Adult ♂.
5b Adult ♀.

6. Spur-winged Goose
Plectropterus gambensis, p. 388
6 *P. g. gambensis,* ♂.

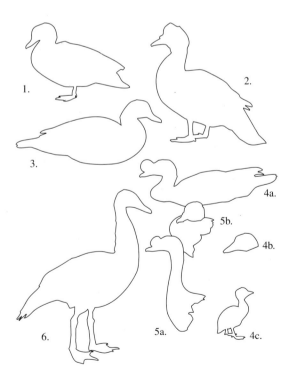

M. HULME

Plate 13

Nettapus, Callonetta, Aix, Chenonetta and *Amazonetta*

1. Green Pygmy-goose
Nettapus pulchellus, p. 477
1 ♂.

2. Cotton Teal (Cotton Pygmy-goose)
Nettapus coromandelianus, p. 475
2a *N. c. coromandelianus*, ♂.
2b *N. c. coromandelianus*, ♀.

3. African Pygmy-goose
Nettapus auritus, p. 471
3a Adult ♂.
3b Adult ♀.
3c Duckling.

4. Ringed Teal
Callonetta leucophrys, p. 482
4a ♂.
4b ♀.

5. Mandarin Duck
Aix galericulata, p. 465
5a ♂.
5b ♀.

6. American Wood Duck
Aix sponsa, p. 461
6a ♂.
6b ♀.

7. Australian Wood Duck
Chenonetta jubata, p. 468
7a ♂.
7b ♀.

8. Brazilian Teal
Amazonetta brasiliensis, p. 479
8a *A. b. brasiliensis*, pale phase adult ♂.
8b *A. b. brasiliensis*, adult ♀.

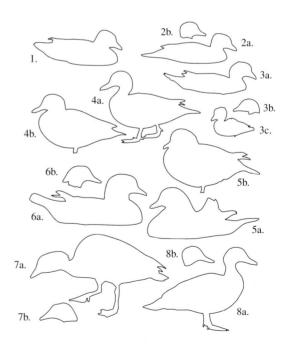

M. Hulme

Plate 14

Merganetta, Hymenolaimus, Salvadorina and *Anas*

1. Torrent Duck
Merganetta armata, p. 373
1a *M. a. armata*, adult ♂.
1b *M. a. armata*, adult ♀.

2. Blue Duck
Hymenolaimus malacorhynchos, p. 370
2a Adult ♂.
2b ♂ duckling.

3. Salvadori's Duck
Salvadorina waigiuensis, p. 445

4. African Black Duck
Anas sparsa, p. 506
4 *A. s. sparsa*.

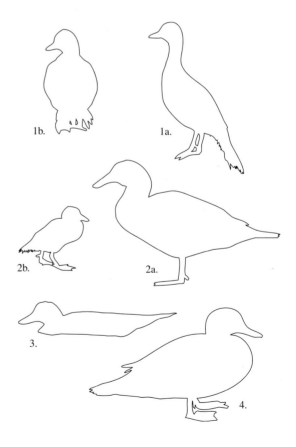

M. HULME

Plate 15

Anas

1. Eurasian Wigeon
Anas penelope, p. 499
1a ♂.
1b ♀.

2. American Wigeon
Anas americana, p. 503
2a ♂.
2b ♀.

3. Chiloe Wigeon
Anas sibilatrix, p. 497
3 ♂.

4. Falcated Duck
Anas falcata, p. 495
4a ♂.
4b ♀.

5. Gadwall
Anas strepera, p. 491
5a ♂.
5b ♀.

6. Baikal Teal
Anas formosa, p. 605
6a Adult ♂.
6b Adult ♀.
6c Duckling.

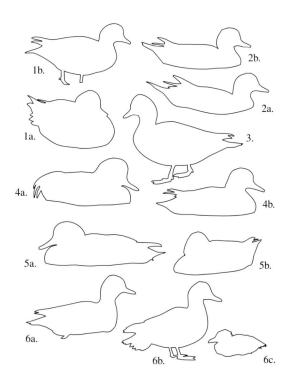

M. HULME

Plate 16

Anas

1. American Green-winged Teal
Anas carolinensis, p. 609
1 ♂.

2. Eurasian Teal
Anas crecca, p. 609
2a ♂.
2b ♀.

3. South American Teal
Anas flavirostris, p. 613
3a *A. f. oxyptera,* adult ♂.
3b *A. f. oxyptera,* duckling.

4. Cape Teal
Anas capensis, p. 488
4 ♂.

5. Madagascar Teal
Anas bernieri, p. 564
5 ♂.

6. Indonesian Teal
Anas gibberifrons, p. 567
6 ♂.

7. Chestnut Teal
Anas castanea, p. 573
7a ♂.
7b ♀.

8. Brown Teal
Anas chlorotis, p. 577
8 ♂.

9. Campbell Island Teal
Anas nesiotis, p. 581
9 ♂.

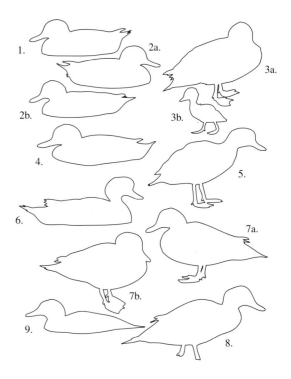

M. HULME

Plate 17

Anas

1. Northern Mallard
Anas platyrhynchos, p. 513
1a *A. p. platyrhynchos,* adult ♂.
1b *A. p. platyrhynchos,* adult ♀.
1c *A. p. platyrhynchos,* duckling.

2. Laysan Duck
Anas laysanensis, p. 528
2 ♂.

3. Hawaiian Duck (Koloa)
Anas wyvilliana, p. 523
3 ♂.

4. Mottled Duck
Anas fulvigula, p. 517
4 *A. f. fulvigula,* ♂.

5. American Black Duck
Anas rubripes, p. 509
5 ♂.

6. Yellow-billed Duck
Anas undulata, p. 541
6 *A. u. undulata*

7. Meller's Duck
Anas melleri, p. 543
7 ♂.

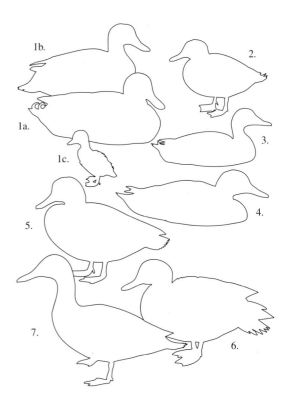

M. HULME

Plate 18

Anas, Lophonetta and *Speculanas*

1. Philippine Duck
Anas luzonica, p. 531

2. Spot-billed Duck
Anas poecilorhyncha, p. 538
2a *A. p. poecilorhyncha*, adult ♂.
2b *A. p. zonorhyncha*, adult ♀.
2c *A. p. zonorhyncha*, duckling.

3. Pacific Black Duck (Grey Duck)
Anas superciliosa, p.533

4. Crested Duck
Lophonetta specularioides, p. 484
4 *L. s. specularioides*, adult.

5. Bronze-winged Duck
Speculanas specularis, p. 487

M. HULME

Plate 19

Anas

1. White-cheeked Pintail
Anas bahamensis, p. 583
1a *A. b. bahamensis*, ♂.
1b *A. b. galapagensis*, ♂.

2. Red-billed Pintail
Anas erythrorhyncha, p. 588

3. Brown Pintail
Anas georgica spinicauda, p. 593
3 ♀.

4. South Georgia Pintail
Anas georgica georgica, p. 590
4a ♂.
4b Duckling.

5. Eaton's Pintail
Anas eatoni, p. 599
5 *A. e. eatoni*, ♂.

6. Northern Pintail
Anas acuta, p. 595
6a ♂.
6b ♀.

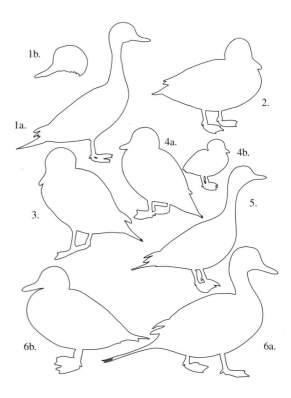

M. HULME

Plate 20

Anas

1. Versicolor Teal
Anas versicolor, p. 616
1a *A. v. versicolor*, ♂.
1b *A. v. puna*, ♂.

2. Hottentot Teal
Anas hottentota, p. 619
2 ♂.

3. Garganey
Anas querquedula, p. 601
3a ♂.
3b ♀.

4. Blue-winged Teal
Anas discors, p. 545
4a ♂.
4b ♀.

5. Cinnamon Teal
Anas cyanoptera, p. 549
5a *A. c. septentrionalium*, ♂.
5b *A. c. septentrionalium*, ♀.
5c *A. c. septentrionalium*, duckling.

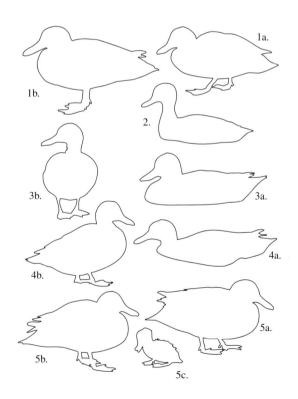

M. HULME

Plate 21
Anas, Malacorhynchus and *Marmaronetta*

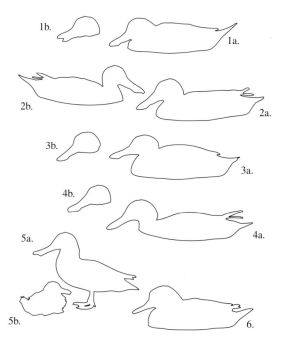

M. HULME

Plate 22

Netta

---

1. Red-crested Pochard
Netta rufina, p. 631
1a ♂.
1b ♀.
1c Duckling.

2. Southern Pochard
Netta erythrophthalma, p. 635
2a *N. e. brunnea*, ♂.
2b *N. e. brunnea*, ♀.

3. Rosybill
Netta peposaca, p. 633
3a ♂.
3b ♀.

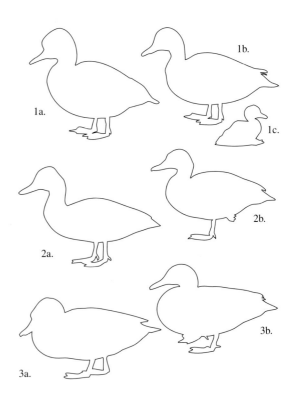

M. HULME

Plate 23

Aythya

1. Canvasback
Aythya valisineria, p. 639
1a ♂.
1b ♀.

2. Common Pochard
Aythya ferina, p. 651
2a ♂.
2b ♀.

3. Redhead
Aythya americana, p. 644
3a ♂.
3b ♀.

4. Ring-necked Duck
Aythya collaris, p. 667
4a ♂.
4b ♀.

5. Hardhead
Aythya australis, p. 655
5a ♂.
5b ♀.

6. Baer's Pochard
Aythya baeri, p. 662
6a ♂.
6b ♀.

7. Ferruginous Duck
Aythya nyroca, p. 659
7a ♂.
7b ♀.
7c Duckling.

8. Madagascar Pochard
Aythya innotata, p. 657
8 ♂.

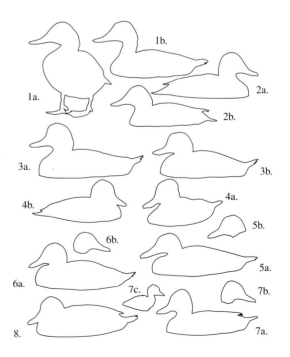

M. HULME

Plate 24

Aythya

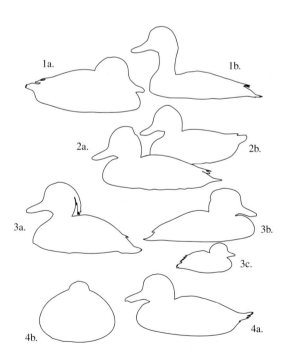

M. HULME

Plate 25

Somateria

1. Common Eider
Somateria mollissima, p. 701
1a *S. m. mollissima*, ♂.
1b *S. m. mollissima*, ♀.
1c Duckling.
1d *S. m. dresseri*, ♂.
1e *S. m. v-nigrum*, ♂.

2. Spectacled Eider
Somateria fischeri, p. 693
2a ♂.
2b ♀.

3. King Eider
Somateria spectabilis, p. 698
3a ♂.
3b ♀.

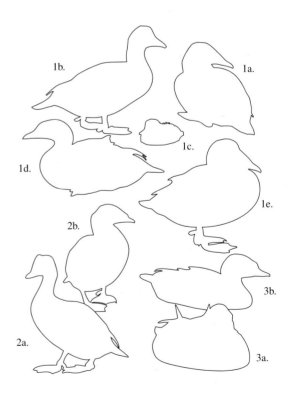

M. HULME

Plate 26

Polysticta, Histrionicus, Clangula and *Melanitta*

1. Steller's Eider
Polysticta stelleri, p. 689
1a ♂.
1b ♀.

2. Harlequin Duck
Histrionicus histrionicus, p. 706
2a ♂.
2b ♀.

3. Long-tailed Duck
Clangula hyemalis, p. 723
3a ♂.
3b ♀.

4. Common Scoter
Melanitta nigra, p. 719
4a *M. n. nigra*, ♂.
4b *M. n. nigra*, ♀.
4c *M. n. nigra*, duckling.
4d *M. n. americana*, ♂.

5. Surf Scoter
Melanitta perspicillata, p. 712
5a ♂.
5b ♀.

6. Velvet Scoter
Melanitta fusca, p. 715
6a *M. f. fusca*, ♂.
6b *M. f. fusca*, ♀.
6c *M. f. deglandi*, ♂.

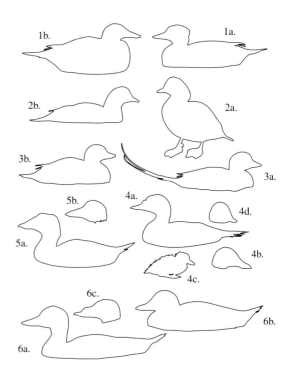

M. HULME

Plate 27

Bucephala

1. Bufflehead
Bucephala albeola, p. 726
1a ♂.
1b ♀.
1c Duckling.

2. Barrow's Goldeneye
Bucephala islandica, p. 735
2a ♂.
2b ♀.

3. Common Goldeneye
Bucephala clangula, p. 730
3a *B. c. clangula*, ♂.
3b *B. c. clangula*, ♀.

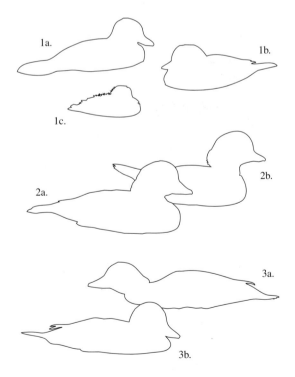

M. HULME

Plate 28

Lophodytes, Mergellus and Mergus

1. Hooded Merganser
Lophodytes cucullatus, p. 744
1a ♂.
1b ♀.

2. Smew
Mergellus albellus, p. 739
2a ♂.
2b ♀.

3. Common Merganser (Goosander)
Mergus merganser, p. 752
3a *M. m. merganser*, ♂.
3b *M. m. merganser*, ♀.
3c *M. m. merganser*, duckling.

4. Red-breasted Merganser
Mergus serrator, p. 755
4a ♂.
4b ♀.

5. Scaly-sided Merganser
Mergus squamatus, p. 759
5a ♂.
5b ♀.

6. Brazilian Merganser
Mergus octosetaceus, p. 749

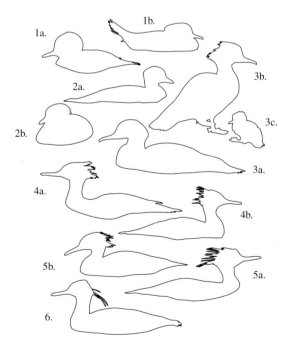

M. HULME

Plate 29

Oxyura and *Nomonyx*

1. White-headed Duck
Oxyura leucocephala, p. 364
1a ♂.
1b ♀.

2. Ruddy Duck
Oxyura jamaicensis, p. 351
2a *O. j. jamaicensis*, ♂.
2b *O. j. jamaicensis*, ♀.

3. Maccoa Duck
Oxyura maccoa, p. 361
3a ♂.
3b ♀.
3c Duckling.

4. Argentine Ruddy Duck (Lake Duck)
Oxyura vittata, p. 355
4a ♂.
4b ♀.

5. Masked Duck
Nomonyx dominicus, p. 348
5a ♂.
5b ♀.

6. Blue-billed Duck
Oxyura australis, p. 358
6a ♂.
6b ♀.

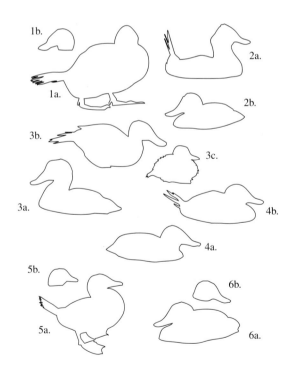

M. HULME

Plate 30

Heteronetta, Thalassornis and *Biziura*

1. Black-headed Duck
Heteronetta atricapilla, p. 346
1a ♂.
1b ♀.

2. White-backed Duck
Thalassornis leuconotus, p. 210
2a *T. l. leuconotus*, adult.
2b *T. l. leuconotus*, duckling.

3. Musk Duck
Biziura lobata, p. 213
3a ♂.
3b ♀.

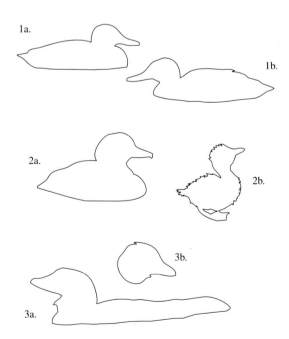

1a.

1b.

2a.

2b.

3b.

3a.

M. HULME

PART II

Species accounts

The screamers

The screamers bear little resemblance superficially to ducks, geese and swans, but there are anatomical similarities that link them to that primitive-looking bird, the Magpie Goose. Flight feathers are moulted gradually so that, like the Magpie Goose but unlike most other wildfowl, screamers do not pass through an annual flightless stage.

Screamers are mainly marshland birds, but found also in open savannas and on the banks of ponds and slow-moving streams. Shallow water is used for roosting and they can swim, although do so reluctantly; chicks swim more frequently, especially when with their wading parents. Screamers fly strongly once airborne and can soar to considerable heights; they look even more like Magpie Geese when on the wing. The Southern or Crested Screamer, in particular, grazes in open grassland along with farm stock, but they and the other species feed mainly on marsh plants while wading through, or walking on, floating vegetation.

♂ and ♀ look alike and seem to pair for life. Courtship displays are inconspicuous, consisting mainly of antiphonal calling or duetting, rapid opening and closing of the bill, and mutual preening of the head and neck feathers. A long breeding season is probably influenced by temperature and rainfall. Nests are placed in shallow water within 80 m of the shore, built of sticks and vegetation. Material is not carried but passed back in the bill so that the nest is constructed of items within easy reach. Both sexes build, and both incubate the large white eggs. On hatching, the chicks are covered in dense yellow down and follow their parents from the nest (Figure 9.1). Like the Magpie Goose, but to a lesser extent, both parents supplement feeding with items placed in the open gape of the chicks, and they also pick up and drop food items, apparently to bring them to their chicks' attention. Another unusual feature is that the young are sometimes oiled from the parent's preen gland.

Pairs establish territories before breeding and flock only in winter. Two sharp spurs protrude from the wrist of each wing and are present as tiny

9.1 Screamer chick.

thorns at hatching. These are used to attack intruders, and broken spurs have been found buried in screamer breast muscle. All species have loud, carrying voices with which they announce their possession of a territory and from which they derive their common name. ♂ calls are lower-pitched than ♀♀, and young birds are first heard screaming at about 8 months of age. A unique feature is that beneath the loose skin lies a network of small air sacs, so that the bird 'crackles' when it is handled. All produce rumbles by vibrating their air sacs, sounds that seem to function as a close-range threat.

Janet Kear

Taxonomy

The Anhimidae (screamers) may represent a link between the more typical ducks, geese and swans and the gamebirds (Galliformes), possessing some of the derived characters of wildfowl, but retaining some derived characters, uniting the two orders, that have been transformed or lost in wildfowl

(Gysels 1969, Sibley and Monroe 1990, Livezey 1997a). The strongest evidence of a close link with other anseriforms is the presence of lamellae (not particularly well developed) on the inside of the upper jaw of *Chauna*, and also in the lower jaw of *Anhima* (Olson and Feduccia 1980a), but there is much additional skeletal evidence (Livezey 1997a, Mayr and Clark 2003).

Presently, anhimids occur in the lowlands of northern and central South America, reaching highest diversity in the northwest. During their evolution towards a terrestrial life cycle, they have differentiated little and comprise currently only three species in two genera. Until recently, the earliest known fossils were of the Southern Screamer from Pleistocene beds in Argentina, dated to about 20 000 years ago (Brodkorb 1964, del Hoyo *et al.* 1992).

Remains of what may be anhimids have been recovered recently from Lower Eocene deposits in the US and Great Britain, suggesting that they were once more widely distributed (Benton 1993, Feduccia 1996). The fossils from the US, however, may represent a new family intermediate between the Anhimidae and Anatidae (Feduccia 1996).

The anhimids possess a number of features unusual in wildfowl, including a gamebird-like bill, only partial webbing between the toes, sequential moult of primaries, and a thick layer of air cells beneath the skin (DeMay 1940, Olson and Feduccia 1980a). They also lack uncinate processes, which are the rib projections that cover and reinforce the rib-cage (del Hoyo *et al.* 1992).

Des Callaghan

Horned Screamer *Anhima cornuta*
PLATE 1

Palamedea cornuta Linnaeus, 1766, Syst. Nat., ed. 12, **1**, p. 232
'Brasilia, Guiana'; eastern Brazil
Anhima Brisson, 1760

Etymology: *anhima* native Brazilian name for screamer; *cornu* L. for horn.

Other names: Portuguese: Anhuma; Spanish: Aruco.

Variation: no subspecies.

Description

ADULT: sexes similar; most plumage greenish black, though white speckling on crown (sometimes extending below eye), white barring on foreneck and plain white on belly and undertail coverts. In addition, large buff-coloured patch on forewings, and white underwing coverts white. 'Horn' is long (to 150 mm), slender black-and-white (sometimes white) cartilaginous appendage protruding forward from forehead. Two spurs protrude from near carpal joint, of which proximal is prominent (up to 50 mm). Beak dark brown to black; legs and feet pale greyish brown; iris yellow to orange. Only small membrane between toes.

MOULT: no seasonal change in colour, and probably only one moult of body feathers annually. No flightless period; moult of primary feathers gradual, although feathers not replaced in simple descending order (Haffer 1968). Uncertain whether horn moulted.

IMMATURE: duller, with shorter horn.

DOWNY YOUNG: greyish yellow above and white below.

MEASUREMENTS AND WEIGHT: ♂ ($n = 10$) wing, 482–585 (545.1); tail, 214–293 (256.4); culmen, 49–55 (52.2). ♀ ($n = 9$) wing, 504–590 (548.7); tail, 216–305 (260.4); culmen, 49–55 (51.7) (Blake 1977); weight, *c* 3000–3150 (del Hoyo *et al.* 1992, Sick 1993).

Field characters

Large, turkey-like bird, 800–940 mm long. Buff patch on upperwing conspicuous in flight (Hilty and Brown 1986). Unlike any other bird in range.

Voice

Three basic vocalizations: *moo co*, Honking and Trumpet (see Gill *et al.*1974 for sonograms). *moo co* disyllabic with second syllable distinctly lower frequency than first; usually repeated at 3–10 sec intervals, and varies greatly in melody and volume. ♂♂ appear to emit harsher, almost barking tone. Pairs of birds often duet this call, producing syllabic vocalization *ha moo co*, or sometimes *ha moo-o co*. Such duets consist of overlap of one bird's second note with mate's first note, and probable that trisyllabic call never emitted by single bird (Gill *et al.* 1974).

Honking is disyllabic, goose-like call of 2 distinct patterns, given in various combinations including in alternation. One pattern has 7–8 strongly developed harmonics, with 1st, 3rd and 5th more amplified than others; other pattern lower, with only weakly developed harmonics. Typical Honking sequence lasts 30 sec, and *moo co* and Trumpets sometimes inserted. Trumpet is loud, disyllabic bugle-like call that carries over longer distances than other calls; consists of low, diffuse introductory note followed by inflected note and 4–5 well-developed harmonics (Gill *et al.* 1974). Gill *et al.* (1974) found *moo co* tended to indicate alarm or disturbance by potential predators or relocations of other screamers, but was also included in distance calling and greeting. Honking used in both greeting and distance calling. Trumpets used primarily in distance calling but occasionally in high intensity greeting. In addition, *ugh* call, produced by sudden collapse of subcutaneous air sacs, associated with pair-bonding and family contact. Low intensity sound given in repetitive sequences occasionally leads to double or trisyllabic sound as intensity and frequency increases (see Barrow *et al.* 1986 for more details).

Nothing published on calls of young.

Range and status

Endemic to South America. Widely distributed in lowlands east of Andes from north Colombia to eastern Bolivia and south central Brazil. Probably many small, isolated populations, as in Cauca and Magdalena valleys (western Colombia) (Hilty and Brown 1986, Naranjo 1986), and Guayaquil/Babahoyo region of west Ecuador (Ortiz Crespo 1988).

Although widespread and common locally, scarce in many areas. Extinct in Trinidad (Scott and

Carbonell 1986), and possibly also in Guyana from where last record was in 1909 (Snyder 1966). Rare in Surinam (Haverschmidt 1968), local in Colombia (Hilty and Brown 1986) and Venezuela (de Schauensee and Phelps 1978), and seemingly also in French Guiana (Tostain *et al.* 1992). Described as frequent in east Peru (Parker *et al.* 1982) and remains locally common in Brazil (Forrester 1993, Sick 1993). Hilty and Brown (1986) described it as numerous in suitable habitat in Amazonia, but rare or absent from blackwater rivers and lakes in Vaupés and Guainía region (eastern Colombia).

Population estimated crudely at <100 000 individuals (Ellis-Joseph *et al.* 1992); overall trend seems continuing slow decline (Rose and Scott 1997).

Habitat and general habits

Inhabits tropical wet savannas, and freshwater lagoons and lakes in open or forested zones. During non-breeding season, also on uncultivated plains, where often gather in small flocks (del Hoyo *et al.* 1992). Pairs occupy well-defined territories consisting of large floating mats of vegetation and adjacent trees. In Colombia, territories ranged 100–240 m² ($n = 6$) (Barrow *et al.* 1986).

In Colombia, Naranjo (1986) reported on almost 17 h of time-budget behaviour. Standing was predominant occupation, and increased from morning (59.5% of activity) through midday (66.9%) to evening (71.1%). Preening next commonest behaviour, and declined from morning (27.9%) through midday (10.9%) to evening (5.9%). During standing or preening, shaking movements included Wing-shake (duration = 3.6 ± 0.7 sec, $n = 5$), Head-shake (3.9 ± 1.01 sec, $n = 7$) and Tail-wag (3.5 ± 0.0 sec, $n = 2$). After long sessions of preening or standing, 3 stretch movements seen: Jaw-stretch (2.8 ± 0.2 sec, $n = 11$), Wing-and-leg stretch (6.5 ± 3.0 sec, $n = 7$) and Both-wings stretch (5.25 ± 0.7 sec, $n = 10$).

Feeding showed progressive increase from morning (9.0%), through midday (17.0%) to evening (20.4%). Most frequent feeding behaviour grazing (97% of feeding time), which occurred while walking or wading across territory. Plants consumed and proportion of occurrence of each (% of grazing time) were *Hydrangea* (56.4%), *Eichornia crassipes* (14.9%), *Polygonum hispidum* (5.6%), *Paspalum dilatatum* (5.1%), *Artemisia absinthium* (3.1%), *Aeschynomene ciliata* (1.4%), *Pistia stratiotes* (1%), *Cardiospermum carendum* (0.4%) and unidentified plants (12.1%) (Naranjo 1986). Small amounts of insects also taken, particularly by chicks (del Hoyo *et al.* 1992). Next most common feeding behaviour, though only 2.6% of total feeding time, was digging, when birds waded slowly through shallow water and moved bills into mud with rapid backward strokes of head. Naranjo (1986) also reported daily activity dedicated to locomotion was small, including flying (5 ± 0 sec, $n = 8$), and walking and wading (22.2 ± 20.0 sec, $n = 23$).

Reported to be extremely tame in some areas (e.g. Haverschmidt 1968) but, if alarmed, readily seeks tops of tall trees. Flies with slow, strong wing-beats, with outstretched neck and legs (Haverschmidt 1968, Hilty and Brown 1986). Soars infrequently (Gill *et al.* 1974, Barrow *et al.* 1986, Naranjo *et al.* 1986). Populations apparently sedentary, with local movements outside breeding season, mainly of juveniles and nonbreeders (del Hoyo *et al.* 1992). Pairs usually remain on breeding territory year-round. However, small, wandering groups gather, possibly of nonbreeders (del Hoyo *et al.* 1992). Local movements occur when wetlands dry out (Sick 1993).

Displays and breeding behaviour

After sunrise, pairs give territorial declaration calls in response to calls of neighbouring pairs, often from one or two trees within territory (Barrow *et al.* 1986). Calls may elicit response from pairs up to 1.5 km away (Gill *et al.* 1974). Second peak of vocalizations occurs prior to roosting. During vocalizations, head bobbed upward and, during more intense situations, buff-coloured wing patches, normally hidden by long contour feathers, exposed and tail lowered and partially spread. Calls and displays performed at greater intensity when conspecific enters territory. Body postures made conspicuous during aggressive attacks; body turned parallel to opponent, buff patches on wings and shoulders exposed, and wings held to side displaying spurs. Attacks consist of jabbing thrusts of wings with spurs erect (Barrow *et al.* 1986, Naranjo 1986).

Modified feather forming horn may be characteristic that displays quality of mate or potential mate (Barrow *et al.* 1986), and length has been linked with age (Spence 1959).

Several appeasement behaviours known: non-aggressive stance held while Bill-clicking, when head pointed upward, and wing-shuffling and preening behaviour cover buff wing patches and hide wing-spurs. Suggests that wing patches act as signals of threat when exposed and submission when covered (Barrow *et al.* 1986).

Pairbond behaviour closely associated with *ugh* call, and includes Mock-preening, allopreening and Head-arching directed toward mate. Copulatory sequence occurs on land and is simple; entails precopulatory calling, nest building movements, side by side walking, short flights to nest, crouching and, very occasionally, Head-flicking (Barrow *et al.* 1986, Naranjo 1986). While ♂ stands on ♀'s back, he nibbles her neck, treads and shuffles tail (Barrow *et al.* 1986). No post-copulatory behaviour observed. Solitary nester with long-term pairbond.

Breeding and life cycle

Breeding protracted throughout year, though occurs mainly during austral spring and summer. ♂ assists in building (Lint 1956) large nest of plant matter and debris in shallow water. Eggs white to buff, mottled cinnamon brown; 83.5 × 58.1 with calculated fresh weight of 155 (Schönwetter 1960–66). Clutch size 3–5 (2–7), eggs laid at 2-day intervals and incubation shared by parents. Naranjo (1986) reported diurnal sessions averaged 65.6 min ($n = 7$) for ♂ and 194.2 min ($n = 6$) for ♀, and nocturnal sessions lasted 830 min ($n = 3$) for ♂ and 934 min ($n = 1$) for ♀. Lint (1956) reported artificially incubated eggs hatched in 44 days, while Naranjo (1986) estimated wild clutch took 40–47 days. Chicks brooded for only few days (Hilty and Brown 1986) but remain with parents for year at least (Naranjo 1986). No data on breeding success, adult survival, nor on longevity.

Conservation and threats

No specific conservation measures have been taken. Main threats seem to be habitat destruction and degradation, and heavy hunting in some areas (del Hoyo *et al.* 1992, Tostain *et al.* 1992).

Des Callaghan

Northern Screamer *Chauna chavaria*
PLATE 1

Parra Chavaria Linnaeus, 1766, Syst. Nat., ed. 12, **1**, p. 260
lakes near Río Sinú, south of Cartagena, Colombia
Chauna Illiger, 1811

    Etymology: *Chauna* from Gr. *khaunos*, silly or foolish, in reference to noisy and clumsy behaviour of screamers; *chavaria* is native Brazilian name for bird, perhaps a woodpecker.

    Other names: Black-necked Screamer. Spanish: Chafa Chicaquire.

    Variation: no subspecies.

Description

ADULT: sexes similar; crown grey, also prominent occipital crest of pointed feathers (to 70 mm long). Sides of head behind eyes and upperpart of throat white, forming broad chin-strap contrasting sharply with broad black neck collar. General body coloration dark grey, but underwing coverts white. Pair of wing-spurs located near each carpal joint. Bill pale grey, and bare skin of orbital area red; legs and feet reddish orange; iris brown. Only small membrane between toes.

MOULT: no flightless period.

IMMATURE: as ♂, but duller.

DOWNY YOUNG: thick greyish yellow down above and white below.

MEASUREMENTS AND WEIGHT: ♂ ($n = 10$) wing, 465–529 (495.8); tail, 185–229 (210.7); culmen, 40–51 (46.3). ♀ ($n = 7$) wing, 460–524 (492.1); tail, 196–211 (206); culmen, 44–50 (46.7) (Blake 1977); weight unrecorded.

Field characters

Large, heavy-bodied bird, 760–910 mm long (del Hoyo *et al.* 1992), unlike any other in range, though may be confused with raptors when soaring high.

Voice

Very vocal, but voice inadequately recorded. Hilty and Brown (1986) described calls as powerful bugled *kleer-a-ruk, cherio*. No published sonograms.

Range and status

Endemic to Colombia and Venezuela. In Colombia, found in lowlands (up to 200 m) of Caribbean watershed, from base of Atrato Valley (close to border with Panama, from where unrecorded) east to base of Santa Marta Mountains and south to middle reaches of Magdalena Valley (Hilty and Brown 1986,

Resident

Ridgely and Gwynne 1989). In Venezuela, restricted to lowlands of Lake Maracaibo basin, in provinces of Zulia, Mérida and Trujillo (de Schauensee and Phelps 1978). Within restricted range, remains locally common; substantial populations remain in northern Colombia, even near dense human populations. The population of northern Colombia and northwest Venezuela declining and estimated at 2000 (Delany and Scott 2002).

Habitat and general habits

Inhabits tropical marshlands and swamps in forested or open country, and often occurs in drier grassland habitat (llanos). Primarily sedentary, though small, loose flocks congregate frequently; feeds by grazing, taking roots, leaves, stems and other green parts of succulent plants (del Hoyo *et al.* 1992).

Displays and breeding behaviour

Unrecorded.

Breeding and life cycle

Very little studied. Breeds throughout year, but eggs laid mainly Oct–Nov (del Hoyo *et al.* 1992). Eggs 91.1 × 61.0 and calculated fresh weight 184 (Schönwetter 1960–66). In early May near Lake Maracaibo (western Venezuela), several nests consisted of large mass of vegetation and contained 2–7 white eggs (Osgood and Conover 1922); del Hoyo *et al.* (1992) gave 3–5 eggs as usual clutch. Incubation, shared by parents, 42–44 days. Chicks brooded for 1st few days, during which time fed from bill by both parents (Bell *et al.* 1970). Fledge in 8–10 weeks and fully independent at 12–14 weeks. No data on breeding success, adult survival, nor on longevity.

Conservation and threats

No specific conservation measures taken, but required in view of low numbers. Population no doubt declining from effects of wetland drainage and degradation, especially through agriculture. Human pressures increasing within range (del Hoyo *et al.* 1992) and, although hunting does not seem acute threat, has caused declines in some areas, e.g. Costa Caribe in Colombia. At least in northern Colombia, captured commonly and kept as pet. Designated Near-threatened in BirdLife International (2000).

Des Callaghan

Southern Screamer *Chauna torquata*
PLATE 1

Chaja torquata Oken, 1816, Lehrbuch Naturgeschichte, pt. 3, sec. 2, p. 639
'in Paragai, um Plata'
   Etymology: *torquata* L. for collared.
   Other names: Crested Screamer. Portuguese: Tachã; Spanish: Chajá.
   Variation: no subspecies.

Description

ADULT: sexes alike. Prominent occipital crest of pointed feathers; head and upperparts grey, darkening to fuscous on flight feathers and tail. Foreneck, breast and body sides pale grey, lightly mottled and streaked white, and abdomen uniform grey to whitish. Underwing coverts white, and 2 large white patches on upperwing (one on base of primaries and primary coverts and other on secondary coverts at wing base). Prominent black neck collar of velvety feathers at base of neck bordered above by narrow white band. Pair of wing-spurs located near each carpal joint. Iris brown; bill reddish brown; legs and feet reddish orange; bare skin of orbital area red. Only small membrane between toes.

MOULT: primary feathers moulted gradually, though feathers not replaced in simple descending order (Haffer 1968). Wing-spurs replaced periodically (del Hoyo *et al.* 1992).

IMMATURE: as adult, but duller. Black collar faint and spurs stunted or absent.

DOWNY YOUNG: head, neck, breast and underparts rusty brown, grading to medium brown on upperparts. Bill brownish black; legs and feet brownish orange; iris dark brown.

MEASUREMENTS AND WEIGHT: ♂ wing (*n* = 7), 525–568 (549.7); tail (*n* = 7), 226–265 (238.4); culmen (*n* = 10), 41–48 (44.6). ♀ wing (*n* = 8), 498–562 (530.8); tail, 216–232 (226); culmen, 40–54 (46.1) (Blake 1977); weight, *c* 4400 (del Hoyo *et al.* 1992, Sick 1993); 3 weighed in captivity of unknown sex 2700, 3000 and 3420.

Field characters

Large and stocky, 800–950 mm long, often seen perched on tops of bushes and low trees. White patches on upperwing conspicuous in flight. Unlike any other bird in range, though may be confused with raptors when soaring high.

Voice

Extremely vocal, but calls inadequately described. Sick (1993) stated voice audible at distance of over 3 km. Double-noted trumpeting call emitted frequently (see Gill *et al.* 1974 for sonogram), including when in flight, and is responsible for local names Chajá and Tachâ (del Hoyo *et al.* 1992). Stonor (1939) noted threatening bird emitted rumbling noise from chest, presumably caused by collapse of subcutaneous air sacs. Also, Hudson (1920) reported birds singing loud duet, sometimes involving all pairs in flock. Sick (1993) described duetting as *GRYa-graGRA*. Also emits *shlarew* when suspicious, and ♂ cries low *ta-HAH* and ♀ high *tew-tew* in flight (Sick 1993).

Range and status

Endemic to South America. Widespread east of Andes from northwest Bolivia and central Brazil south to central Argentina. Remains common throughout most of range (Scott and Carbonell 1986, del Hoyo *et al.* 1992, Hayes 1995) and, although no census data available, estimated to total 100 000–1 000 000 individuals, and stable (Rose and Scott 1997).

Habitat and general habits

During breeding season, inhabits tropical or subtropical wet savannas and freshwater lagoons in open country. During nonbreeding season, drier habitat, such as cropland and meadowland, used; flocks of several thousands may occur, and graze alongside livestock in open country (del Hoyo *et al.* 1992).

Diurnal; gathers in large groups to roost, usually standing in shallow water. Often spends long periods perched at top of trees and shrubs during day and, when alarmed, flies to trees for safety (del Hoyo *et al.* 1992). In some areas, however, tree-perching uncommon, and mounds of vegetation gathered to act as loafing sites and vantage points (Weller 1967b).

Almost entirely herbivorous, diet based on leaves, flowers, seeds and roots of various succulent plants. Crop plants also important in agricultural areas. Small amounts of insects may be taken, and fed to chicks, or taken by chicks themselves. Usual feeding method grazing, sometimes while wading half submerged amidst floating aquatic vegetation.

Powerful flier regularly soaring to great heights with feet and neck outstretched, sometimes in groups of up to 60. Swims infrequently, slowly and with difficulty. During bathing, feathers become thoroughly soaked, and birds dry themselves with wings outstretched (Weller 1967b).

Mostly sedentary, although large flocks congregate during winter and move apparently in response to weather and food availability (del Hoyo *et al.* 1992). Flocks of nonbreeders occur even during peak of breeding season (Weller 1967b, Sick 1993).

Displays and breeding behaviour

Virtually undocumented. Stonor (1939) noted little courtship beyond mutual preening. Copulation takes place on land. Change-over during incubation accompanied by mutual calling and preening (Stonor 1939).

Serious fights between conspecifics seem infrequent, though horny wing-spurs recovered from breasts of birds (Weller 1967b) and pairs defend breeding territory vigorously. Pairbond long-term.

Breeding and life cycle

Little studied. Both sexes construct nest, which consists of large pile of vegetation, collected in area immediately around nest. Located in shallow water, but occasionally on dry land close to water edge. Breeding occurs throughout year, but concentrated around southern springtime, with first eggs usually Sept–Oct (Weller 1967b). Eggs laid at 2–3 day intervals, relatively large, white sometimes with darker spots and granulated shells (Weller 1967b), 91.1×61.0 with calculated weight of 160 (Schönwetter 1960–66). Clutch size 2–7, though 4–5 usual; in Argentina, 4.7 (3–5) ($n = 18$ nests) (Weller 1967b). Sexes incubate in turn, and eggs covered with vegetation when nest left unguarded (Weller 1967b); little down. Stonor (1939) noted ♂ incubating during day, 19.00–17.30 h. Eggs hatch in 42–45 days and chicks leave nest immediately (can swim quite buoyantly); one hatched in captivity weighed 92. Brooded for 1st few days and fledge in 8–10 weeks, becoming independent at 12–14 weeks (Weller 1967b). No data on breeding success, adult survival nor on longevity.

Conservation and threats

No specific conservation measures taken. Habitat destruction and degradation biggest threats, although screamers show some adaptability by foraging on cropland. Since mix regularly with farm birds and other livestock, sometimes in large numbers, persecution by farmers common in areas where thought to compete for food with stock, damage crops or spread disease. Flesh said to be unpleasant to eat, so rarely hunted for meat (del Hoyo *et al.* 1992).

Des Callaghan

Magpie Goose

Taxonomy

The Magpie Goose is the sole member of the family Anseranatidae (Sibley and Monroe 1990, Livezey 1996b, Sraml *et al.* 1996); as yet, no fossils have been uncovered (Brodkorb 1964, Howard 1964a) and no hybrids with other anseriforms recorded (Johnsgard 1960b). The primitive status of the bird is well recognized, and it has often been described as a link between the Anhimidae and the

Anatidae (Delacour 1954, Johnsgard 1961a,c, 1978, Woolfenden 1961, Brush 1976, Olson and Feduccia 1980a, Livezey 1986, 1997b, Madsen *et al.* 1988). Although Sibley and Ahlquist (1990) thought it a sister to the Anhimidae, re-analysis of their data shows it to be a sister to the Anatidae (Harshman 1994). Some earlier authors suggested links to the Spur-winged Goose (Peters 1931, Delacour and Mayr 1945), while others considered it an aberrant true goose (Anserini) (Davies and Frith 1964, Frith 1967).

Magpie Geese are endemic to tropical Australia and New Guinea, and largely terrestrial. They have many peculiarities that set them apart from other anseriforms. Most obvious are: (i) the long (1.5 m) coiled trachea that lies, in part, external to the breast muscles of the male; (ii) the partially webbed feet; (iii) the strong hooked bill with small lamellae; (iv) the cinnamon and grey plumage of the gosling; (v) sequential moult of the primary feathers; (vi) they mate on land; and (vii) the many characters of the skeleton and behaviour (Boetticher 1943, Johnsgard 1961a, 1961c, Woolfenden 1961, Frith 1967, Olson and Feduccia 1980a, Marchant and Higgins 1990). The immature moult sequence is unique among anseriforms (Johnsgard 1961c), and adults exude a strong musky smell said to be similar to that of certain parrots (Delacour 1954). Their habit of parental feeding is exhibited only by one other wildfowl species, the Musk Duck.

Des Callaghan

Magpie Goose *Anseranas semipalmata*
PLATE 1

Anas semipalmata Latham, 1798, Trans. Linn. Soc. London, **4**, p. 103
Hawkesbury River, New South Wales
Anseranas Lesson, 1828

Etymology: *Anseranas* L. for goose *anser* plus *anas* duck; *semipalmata* L. for half-webbed.

Other names: Black-and-white, Pied or Semipalmated Goose. Australian Aboriginal: Gurrmattji, Kuramutchi, Muldrie, Nag, Nagieg, Newalgang; French: Canaroie semipalmé; German: Spaltfussgans; Spanish: Ganso Urraco.

Variation: no subspecies.

Description

ADULT: sexes similar, but ♂ more than 30% heavier than ♀. Distinctive knob on crown larger in ♂ than ♀ (Johnsgard 1961b, Whitehead 1998, 1999). Head and neck black, most of body white including upper forewing coverts and all underwing coverts. Flight feathers, tail and feathering of upper leg region black. Bare area surrounding eye extends to cover three-quarters of bill length. Bill long and large with facial skin usually flesh-coloured or reddish ('pale parchment' in nonbreeding condition) but colour intensifies to claret-red in ♂ when aroused (Marchant and Higgins 1990). Bare skin on bill finely wrinkled with tiny black tubercles creating irregular mottled areas especially along lower anterior portion. Bill tip robust and hooked with distinctive pale grey to ivory nail; legs and feet pale yellow to bright orange; iris brown. Toes more or less free of webbing (semipalmate) and hind toe unusually long. Extraordinarily elongated trachea (Latham 1798, 1824, Eyton 1838, Forbes 1882a), looped under skin of breast and belly of ♂, easily palpable with bird in hand (Frith and Davies 1961b, Whitehead 1999). Feathers often stained russet.

MOULT: body moult of adult largely undescribed. No flightless period but complete annual moult occurs after breeding season *c* May–June (Marchant and Higgins 1990). Moult to immature plumage starts at *c* 4 month old, progressing, as wave, from head back; tail feathers replaced from *c* time of fledging and juvenile wing feathers replaced in moult at 7–8 months; this, and all subsequent flight feather moult, gradual, so that primaries moulted in sequence outwards while secondaries moult in sequence outwards from elbow towards carpal joint but slightly behind primaries. Adult plumage assumed after moult occurring at one year (Johnsgard 1961b).

IMMATURE: lacks knob on head and bill off-white. Plumage generally darker with most of white areas on forewings and mantle absent, and white of underside flecked with dark edged feathers particularly on flanks. Legs and feet pale yellow. Forewing not completely white until at least 2nd year (Marchant and Higgins 1990).

GOSLING: unique among waterfowl in having cinnamon head, neck and upper breast with dark grey-brown upper body, fading to light grey below. Bill, legs and feet initially orange to dull claret but fading to yellow then leaden grey by 2 weeks of age (Davies 1957, Johnsgard 1961b). Tail feathers emerge rapidly from *c* one week (Johnsgard 1961b). For growth rates, including weight gains, see Lavery (1970b) and Whitehead *et al.* (1990a). Juvenile feathering greyish black replacing downy condition by 6–8 weeks and plumage fully grown by 3 months.

MEASUREMENTS AND WEIGHT: ♂ (*n* = 165) wing, 368–450 (419); tail, 170–190; bill (*n* = 74), 72–92 (80); tarsus (*n* = 42), 106; weight (*n* = 402), 1838–3195 (2766). ♀ (*n* = 177) wing, 356–418 (389); tail, 130–160; bill (*n* = 56), 63–82 (73); tarsus (*n* = 43), 93; weight (*n* = 359), 1405–2770 (2071) (Delacour 1954, Frith and Davies 1961b, Marchant and Higgins 1990).

Field characters

Large, long-legged and pied. No similar bird within range. Noisy honking calls; flocks making steady hubbub of sound. Slow steady flapping flight on broad wings, *c* 3 beats/sec in steady flight (Davies 1963). Will land and perch in trees. Upright stance, long yellow or orange legs, long black neck, large bill and head with prominent cranial knob and massive bill distinctive. Floats high in water and walks easily on land. Gregarious and often in flocks that may be large (up to 80 000 birds).

Voice

Loud resonant honks of adults given in form that depends on circumstances (for details see Davies 1963, and sonograms in Marchant and Higgins 1990). Honks of ♀ higher pitched than those of ♂ (Whitehead 1999). Territorial and advertising honks, almost exclusively given by ♂♂, termed Uplift Call, usually uttered standing with sleek feathers; each honk given with upward tilt of bill (Davies 1963). Uplift Calls recognized by members of family, and often elicit Uplift Calls from neighbouring families within flock. Alarm Call single loud honk, resembling Uplift Call but more insistent and given in alert posture, becoming penetrating shriek when distressed (Marchant and Higgins 1990). Concert calling with rapidly repeated honks, sometimes almost trilling, uttered during threat display, during pair formation, in pairbond behaviour, after copulation, as greeting and also in Triumph display by family members following threat encounter. Concert calling often takes form of duetting between family members and duets may occur when birds reunite and before take-off (Davies 1963). Goslings have high sibilant whistle when begging for food or being fed (Johnsgard 1961b, Davies 1963). Honking develops at 6–8 months of age (Johnsgard 1961b). Sonograms of gosling calls in Kear (1968).

Range and status

Endemic to Australia and southern New Guinea. Present distribution concentrated within northern tropical areas of Australia and vast delta areas of Digoel and Fly rivers of Trans-Fly region in southern New Guinea (Jepson 1997). Widespread and often abundant locally within coastal areas (never common beyond 300 km inland) from Broome, West Australia east to Brisbane, Queensland. (Marchant and Higgins 1990). Formerly in southeastern Australia, and well known to settlers of first fleet after arrival in 1788 in Sydney region. Formerly occurred in many coastal swamps, in some places in abundance, from New South Wales through eastern Gippsland, Victoria, to southern South Australia. Recent attempts at reintroduction often successful, with established colonies in several regions of New South Wales and southeastern South Australia, but shooting pressure limits consolidation of population in places (Blakers *et al.* 1984, Marchant and Higgins 1990), and ingestion of lead shot causes high mortality (44% of population in one year) at one release site, Bool Lagoon, South Australia (Harper and Hindmarsh 1990).

Estimates of numbers in Northern Territory 1983–85 suggested population of 3.9 million ±

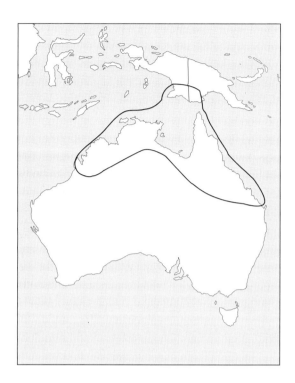

1 million (Bayliss and Yeomans 1990). Numbers in New Guinea unknown and there is no comprehensive survey of northern Queensland. Notwithstanding these deficiencies, seems reasonable to assume total world population > 5 million.

Habitat and general habits

Primarily found on coastal wetlands with suitable feeding sites and safe nesting areas. In Northern Territory, concentrates in dry season at high densities at several swamp refuges with necessary permanent water and food. Disperses widely in wet season to breeding areas on floodplains (Bayliss and Yeomans 1990). Dry season concentration occurs in Alligator Rivers region (Kakadu National Park) where average of 1 600 000 individuals gather (Morton *et al.* 1990a); important sites are Boggy Plain on South Alligator River and nearby swamp draining from Nourlangie Creek (Bayliss and Yeomans 1990). These dry-season concentrations represent 60–70% of Northern Territory population, although area does not provide sufficient breeding habitat; thus, most geese disperse west during wet season to nest,

mainly on Mary River floodplains (Whitehead *et al.* 1990b). In north Queensland, most movements local but some interchange with New Guinea across Torres Strait evident (Marchant and Higgins 1990).

Feeds on grass seeds, especially wild rice *Oryza*, and tubers of rushes and sedges, especially tubers of *Eleocharis dulcis*. Although will filter food from water and can graze and strip seed heads, predominant technique is digging roots and bulbs of swamp plants. Staining of plumage evident with increased digging in swamps, especially as floodplains dry. Details of diet summarized in Marchant and Higgins (1990). ♂♂ feed on larger tubers of *Eleocharis* than ♀♀ (Whitehead and Tschirner 1992). Needs tall erect vegetation for nest building (Davies 1962). Usually roosts communally in trees at night; will roost on areas of bare earth on plains or on elevated platforms of swamp vegetation close to colony when only incubating birds remain on nests (Marchant and Higgins 1990).

Displays and breeding behaviour

Adopts upright posture when Alert and surveying surroundings. Pre-flight signal, especially evident when alarmed, given in Alert posture with side-to-side shaking of head together with trampling, raising and lowering of alternate feet; followed by Bob, when body lowered and legs flexed before bird jumps into air. Flock members behave in characteristic way when alarmed, clustering together and walking rapidly away, all taking flight if alarmed sufficiently (Davies 1963).

Threat signified by fixing gaze and walking towards opponent. Uplift Call has territorial and advertising function and most often given by ♂♂. Fighting, usually initiated by ♂, often breaks out between individuals; takes form of lunging and chasing sometimes leading to both taking flight and attempting to beat one another with wings while also trying to claw one another (Marchant and Higgins 1990). Fighting usually followed by rapid Wing-shake, sometimes followed by stretching neck forwards in Neck-shake, side to side Tail-wag and drinking (Davies 1963, Marchant and Higgins 1990). Family will often gabble together (concert) after aggressive encounters, in manner resembling Triumph display of true geese (Johnsgard 1961b).

Squatting may be used in submission (Marchant and Higgins 1990).

Pair formation accompanied by varying amounts of mutual Concert calling. Allopreening and Courtship feeding occur. Copulation usually performed on nest but mostly quiet, inconspicuous and without elaborate associated displays, except followed by Concert calling (Johnsgard 1961b, Marchant and Higgins 1990).

Predominant breeding unit is stable polygynous trio of ♂ and two ♀♀; with one ♀ dominant over other (Whitehead 1999). Possibility that ♀♀ within family group related suggested by DNA studies (Horn *et al.* 1996). Young of previous season remain with parents forming family entity, as in *Anser* and *Branta* geese, and families group into loose flocks (Davies 1963). Bonds between breeding birds seem lifelong, usually in form of trios but sometimes pairs; larger groups include auxiliaries and can include more than one ♂ (Davies 1963, Marchant and Higgins 1990). Auxiliaries often offspring of family. Nesting occurs synchronously and communally (Whitehead and Tschirner 1990a). Some colonies huge with largest reported 46 km² on Daly River, Northern Territory (Frith and Davies 1961b). Nesting densities up to 1000 nests per km² (Whitehead and Tschirner 1991).

Breeding and life cycle

In northern Australia and southern New Guinea breeding season Feb–Apr, but in southern Australia usually lays Aug–Oct (Marchant and Higgins 1990). ♂ does most nest building; nest is large floating pile of vegetation, and many built before one used (Davies 1962). Nest has deep cup not lined with down. One or more ♀♀ of family lay, all adults in family incubate and all feed goslings (Marchant and Higgins 1990). Parasitic laying suggested by some field observations (Whitehead and Tschirner 1991), but unclear whether these eggs laid by auxiliaries. In captivity, ♂ said to take night shift during incubation (Kear 1973b) but reverse observed in wild, except ♂ and ♀ equally present in daytime nearer time of hatching (Whitehead 1999). Nest never left unguarded once incubation started. Generally, eggs laid daily by individual ♀♀ (Marchant and Higgins 1990, Whitehead 1999) but longer intervals (up to 36 h)

reported in captivity (Kear 1973b). Eggs chalky white when laid but soon stained (Whitehead and Tschirner 1991); also described as glossy with pitted surface, elliptical and pale cream to yellowish white (Marchant and Higgins 1990); 72 × 53 (64–84 × 46–63) (*n* = 692 in 132 nests) (Frith 1982); weight of 232 eggs averaged 110 (76–138) (Marchant and Higgins 1990) while another sample of 541 fresh eggs gave average weight of 104 (Whitehead and Tschirner 1990b). Clutch size difficult to determine because of variable input by more than one ♀. Sample of 172 clutches gave median of 8 (1–16), but 17 single ♀ clutches contained 8.6 eggs compared with 9.4 where 2 ♀♀ laid (Frith 1982, Marchant and Higgins 1990, Whitehead 1999). Incubation 25 days (Frith and Davies 1961b, Whitehead 1999) but reported as 28 days (26–30) in temperate climates (Johnsgard 1978, Whitehead and Tschirner 1990b, Todd 1996). Longer incubation periods (and heavier eggs) reported in some captive situations (Kear 1973b). Laying in different colonies and different years not always synchronous, with 1st eggs sometimes laid months apart (Marchant and Higgins 1990). Young usually leave nest within 24 h of hatching but sometimes remain up to 4 days and total nesting period (start of egg-laying to departure of goslings from nest) 31–33 days (Whitehead 1999). Weight of 118 hatchlings 75 (56–92) (Whitehead and Tschirner 1990b). Goslings fed by adults dribbling food from their bills, allowing small goslings to be fed items otherwise unavailable or out of reach (Johnsgard 1961b, Davies and Frith 1964, Kear 1973b). All members of family defend and guard young fiercely. Young aggressive to one another, especially when begging for food (Kear 1970b). Goslings fledge at 3 months (Johnsgard 1961b) but young may still be fed by adults after fledging and may continue dependent until at least following breeding season (Marchant and Higgins 1990). No crèching recorded.

♀ may lay at 2 years but ♂ not mature until 4 (Marchant and Higgins 1990). Recruitment rate of young generally low with up to 77% loss of eggs (Frith and Davies 1961b, Frith 1977, Whitehead and Tschirner 1990a). Erratically variable wet-season flooding can cause catastrophic drowning of nest sites, possibly occurring as often as 1 year in 7

(Whitehead and Tschirner 1990a). Few data on adult survival but small sample of band returns (72 individuals from 2728 marked adults; excluding birds recovered near banding site in 1st year) included 11 that had lived more than 11 years and 2 that had survived 19 years (Frith 1977). Has lived for 26 years in captivity (Johnsgard 1968a).

Conservation and threats

Specialist feeders that are, in general, only locally nomadic (Frith 1977), showing strong attachment to particular places. Seasonal movements in some parts of northern Australia dictated by annual wet–dry cycle; in these situations, critical that able to concentrate on few suitable feeding areas in dry season. Preferred sites must also provide protection from predation. In wet season, needs abundant food and necessary swamp habitat for nesting. Widespread view in late 1970s that numbers in Northern Territory had been in decline for some time (Frith 1977) but aerial counts suggested that population had recovered by early 1980s (Tullock and McKean 1983). Degradation of tropical coastal wetlands by feral Water Buffalo *Bubalus bubalis* implicated (Frith 1977) but unlikely that these introduced herbivores have limited goose populations (Tullock and McKean 1983). Likewise, seems that impact of livestock not serious (Bayliss and Yeomans 1990). Feral buffalo reduced to very low densities in most major wetlands in Northern Territory recently and now appear unlikely to present significant threat (Bayliss and Yeomans 1990). No evidence that feral Pigs *Sus scrofa* have adverse effects. On other hand, rapid spread into goose breeding habitats of invasive plant *Mimosa pigra* may prove dangerous, particularly because difficult to control (Bayliss and Yeomans 1990).

Make up 80% of bag taken during recreational duck hunting in Northern Territory (Whitehead *et al.* 1988), *c* 3% of Territory goose population. Disappeared from most of southeastern Australia following European colonization in 1788. By 1920, no longer present in South Australia, Victoria or New South Wales (Marchant and Higgins 1990). Attempts over last 50 years to reintroduce geese to southern regions only partly successful because many poisoned or shot before local populations established (Cowling and Davies 1983, Harper and Hindmarsh 1990, Marchant and Higgins 1990). Recent signs of breeding groups in New South Wales, southeastern South Australia and adjacent regions of Victoria, but populations tiny in comparison with vast flocks present in north of continent and in southern New Guinea.

Peter Fullagar

The whistling-ducks

The scientific name *Dendrocygna* means, literally, 'tree swan' and the eight species of whistling-duck resemble the swans in a number of ways. Although they are not always associated with trees, they spend much of the day in small groups, perched on the branches of partially submerged logs.

Like the swans and geese, but unlike other ducks, whistling-ducks moult their body feathers only once a year. They are small—seven species average under 850 g, and the eighth, the West Indian, averages 1150 g. Male and female are similar in size, with the female often heavier in the breeding season. In this, the whistling-ducks differ from most other wildfowl. This may be because both sexes incubate, often in cavities, although it might be that they are able to nest in holes because both sexes are equally small. Nest sites vary; the commonest is a bulky, well-hidden nest built over water with a ramp to it. Nests on the ground, some distance from water, and in tree holes (where they are less substantial, as no duck carries nesting material) are also common, and sometimes the discarded nests of other birds are used. Presumably because the eggs are seldom left uncovered, no feather down is used to conceal the clutch while the parent is away, and there is no defeathered area on the breast of the incubating adult, although vasculation of the abdominal skin develops in both sexes before incubation begins. Unlike the young of swans and geese, the ducklings are conspicuously marked. Their parents seem to help them find food by dabbling beakfuls of seeds in the water, and allowing some of the seeds to leak out to the ducklings which gather round their heads. The ducklings grow slowly on a mainly vegetarian diet, and are able to fly at between 8 and 14 weeks of age. A dull first plumage is worn for only a few months; most species seem to mature quickly and are able to breed at 1-year old.

Both sexes utter loud whistles that are important in keeping family and flock together and, outside the breeding season, whistling-ducks are very gregarious. Mutual preening of the face and neck of mated pairs, and even of flock members, is frequent, and it is notable that a common species of head louse found in other wildfowl is absent from whistling-ducks. Food is usually plant material obtained by wading in shallow water while dabbling or, occasionally, by diving.

Most whistling-ducks inhabit tropical latitudes where daylight lasts for just over 12 hours, and any seasonal changes in daylength are slight. In captivity outside the tropics they may lay clutches of eggs at any time from early spring until autumn and, presumably, only stop then because days become too short to stimulate their sex hormones. The Fulvous Whistling-duck has laid in England as early as 24 February and, as more than one brood may be reared, may lay again in early August and hatch another brood in September (Murton and Kear 1975). In the wild, also, they tend not to have nesting peaks unless the onset of the rains is a regular, predictable event; instead, only a small part of the population begins laying at any one time. Pair formation occurs after aerial chases, but displays between the sexes are inconspicuous except after copulation—in those species that mate while swimming, the pair may then engage in a lively Step-dance, raising the wing furthest from their partner and treading the surface of the water vigorously; others that copulate while standing at the edge of shallow water have only an abbreviated Step-dance. Threat plays an important part in courtship and in pair and family maintenance; it involves holding a Head-down-and-forward posture with the bill open and pointing at the opponent, and with the feathers of the shoulders lifted away from the body.

Janet Kear

Taxonomy

The Dendrocygnini or whistling-ducks form a closely related group. Sexual behaviour is very similar in all species, and hybridization within the group is frequent in captivity; however, there are no confirmed instances of hybrids between whistling-ducks and other wildfowl (Johnsgard 1960a, 1961a).

Whistling-ducks are most closely related to the White-backed Duck, together forming the subfamily Dendrocygninae (Johnsgard 1967, Kear 1967, Raikow 1971, Brush 1976, Livezey 1995a, 1996b, Harshman 1996). Dendrocygninae is the sister group of all the remaining ducks, geese, and swans (Bottjer 1983, Madsen *et al.* 1988, Livezey 1995a, 1996b, Harshman 1996). Prior placements of the group within Anserinae (e.g., Johnsgard 1961a) were not intended to reflect recency of common descent (cf. Johnsgard's fig. 9).

The earliest fossil assigned to the whistling-ducks is *Paracygnopterus scotti* from the lower Oligocene of Great Britain, but its precise affinities are unclear and it may be related to the swans (Harrison and Walker 1979, Cheneval 1987). *Dendrocygna eversa*, from Lower Pleistocene beds in Arizona, US, was also assigned to the whistling-ducks (Brodkorb 1964), but may belong in the Dendrocheninae (Livezey and Martin 1988); however, an undescribed *Dendrocygna* has been uncovered from late Miocene beds in Florida, US (Becker 1987).

The distribution of whistling-ducks is centred around the equator, although the range of some species extends to about 38° in the temperate zones (Figure 9.2). They are highly gregarious and vocal; the ducklings have a unique downy pattern, and the adults a unique tracheal structure (Johnsgard 1960a). A number of apparently primitive characters are retained, including a lack of sexual dimorphism, long-term monogamous pair-bonds, and the participation of the male in brood rearing and (at least in most species) in incubation (Delacour and Mayr 1945, Delacour 1954–64, Johnsgard 1961a, 1962, 1965a, Murton and Kear 1975, Scott and Clutton-Brock 1989, Livezey 1995a).

Species relationships within the genus have been problematic (Delacour 1954–64, Johnsgard 1961a,

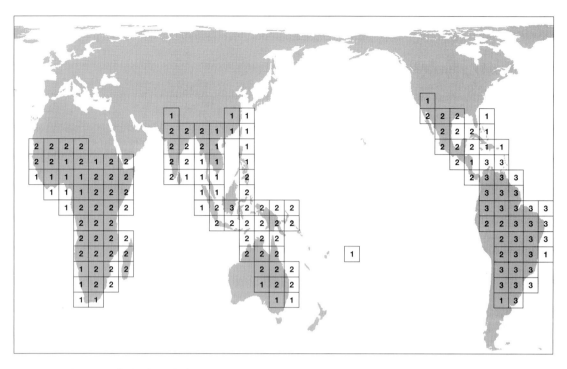

9.2 Species diversity of whistling-ducks (Dendrocygnini) that survived into the Holocene. The number of species that occur (or occurred) within each grid-cell is indicated.

Livezey 1995a). Based on behaviour, Johnsgard (1961a) proposed three groupings: (a) Spotted and Plumed Whistling-ducks; (b) West Indian and Black-bellied, in turn closely related to the White-faced Whistling-duck; and (c) Fulvous and Wandering Whistling-ducks. This sequence was adopted subsequently by most workers (Johnsgard 1978, Madge and Burn 1988, Sibley and Monroe 1990); however, recent analysis of 68 morphological characters (Livezey 1995a) suggested quite different linkages: (a) Black-bellied with White-faced;

(b) Spotted with West Indian; and (c) an unresolved grouping involving Plumed, Fulvous and the sister species of Wandering and Lesser Whistling-ducks. Analyses of DNA sequences (Harshman 1996) defined two groups, agreeing partly with Johnsgard (1979) and partly with Livezey (1995a): (a) West Indian and Black-bellied; and (b) the rest, within which Wandering and Lesser are sisters, but other relationships were ambiguous.

Des Callaghan

White-faced Whistling-duck *Dendrocygna viduata*
PLATE 3

Anas viduata Linnaeus, 1766, Syst. Nat., ed. 12, **1**, p. 205
Cartagena, Colombia
Dendrocygna Swainson, 1837

Etymology: *viduata* L. from *viduus* meaning widowed, in reference to black and white face pattern that resembled a widow's 18th-century head-dress.

Other names: White-faced Tree-duck (this and other *Dendrocygna* known as tree ducks in older literature from North America; hyphenation of 'whistling-duck', adopted by AOU in 1983, followed here). French: Dendrocygne veuf; Malagasy: Tsirriri; Spanish: Yaguaso Cariblanco.

Variation: no subspecies, although Livezey (1995a) suggested variation within the species might warrant further study.

Description

ADULT: sexes similar. Front part of head from behind eyes, chin and throat white (often stained yellow or orange). Rest of head and upper neck black; black line bisects white of chin. Lower neck, chest and upper breast rich chestnut. Underparts from lower breast to tail, black. Sides of breast and flanks white (washed ochre) and boldly barred black. Lower back, rump, uppertail coverts and tail black. Back olive brown, feathers edged buff brown. Scapulars grey brown. Lesser wing coverts dark chestnut, rest of wing feathering bluish grey to black. Bill black with bluish grey, transverse sub-terminal bar on upper mandible; legs and feet bluish grey; eyes brown (Brown *et al.* 1982).

MOULT: adults undergo complete body and wing moult post-breeding, and are flightless for 18–25 days (see Petrie 1998). One body moult annually.

IMMATURE: lacks white face and black head and belly but this replaced by adult-like plumage from 3 months. Feathering duller than that of adult and white face mask sometimes not so distinct. Wing feathers retained, and these show increasing signs of wear until renewed at 12–15 months (Brown *et al.* 1982).

DUCKLING: brown above, yellow below. Dark cap, whitish supercilium and pale line under eye to back of head (Brown *et al.* 1982). Nelson (1993) illustrated specimen from Madagascar.

MEASUREMENTS AND WEIGHT: ♂ (*n* = 6) culmen, 47.0–49.1 (47.7); wing, 216–222 (219); tarsus, 48.1–55.0 (52.6); weight (*n* = 12), 637. ♀ (*n* = 6)

culmen, 45.3–48.9 (47.4); wing, 221–225 (223.3); tarsus, 52.0–55.2 (52.9); weight (*n* = 15), 614 (Brown *et al.* 1982).

Field characters

Long-legged, long-necked, erect-standing duck, 430–480 mm long, slighter in build than Fulvous Whistling-duck. Black and white head, rich chestnut breast, and barred flank diagnostic. On water floats high. In flight, similar to Fulvous, but white face and lack of white on tail or rump noticeable.

Voice

Vocal. Usual contact call sibilant 3-syllabled whistle *swee-swee-sweeoo*, repeated after brief pauses while feeding or flying. Single *wheee* note given by alarmed birds. Individual differences in whistles, that may differ between sexes. Sonogram of duckling distress call in Kear (1968).

Range and status

Tropical central and south America from northwest Costa Rica, south through Panama, and Colombia to north Argentina. Paraguay and Uruguay (Gómez-Dallmeier and Cringan 1990). Was extirpated from Trinidad and Tobago early last century as result of overhunting (ffrench 1973) but now returning. Population of Americas probably > million (Rose and Scott 1997).

Also widely distributed in Africa south of Sahara (except lowland forests of Cameroon and in deserts of southwest) and occurs in Madagascar and on Comoro Islands. Three populations recognized, west African one numbering 250 000, east and south African population of 1–2 million and between which there is some movement during wet seasons, and sedentary Madagascan population of 20 000–50 000; all probably increasing except in Madagascar (Rose and Scott 1997).

Habitat and general habits

Gregarious, foraging in flocks up to several thousand and often associating with sympatric whistling-ducks. Flocks use many kinds of wetland, including freshwater lakes, swamps, flooded lands and estuaries,

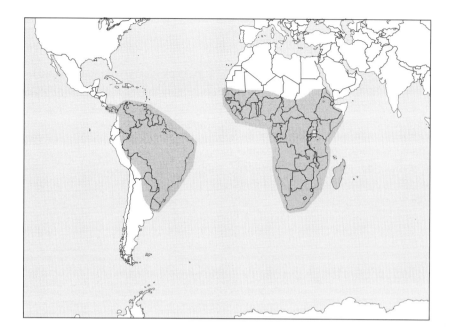

and commonly encountered feeding in rice fields. Feeding activity most intense at dawn and dusk (Petrie and Rogers 1997c, Petrie and Petrie 1998). In middle of day, loafs and sleeps (Brown *et al.* 1982).

Diet correlated with plant phenology; includes tubers in dry season, and seeds during rainy season (Petrie and Rogers 1997b). Insect consumption highest during rains, when animal food abundance and diversity increases, and protein requirement prior to breeding becomes greatest. Range of foraging techniques employed but prefers to feed while standing or wading in shallow water. Bruzual and Bruzual (1983) found that, in Venezuela, less rice taken than by other whistling-ducks and that seeds of *Oryza perennis* and *Cyperus rotundus*, 2 weeds of rice cultivation, consumed in quantity.

Displays and breeding behaviour

Mutual preening of white area of face and throat between pairs common within flock. Courtship simple. At pre-copulation, engages in mutual Head-dipping while swimming. ♂ mounts ♀ with wings outstretched. After copulation, Step-dance display followed by wing flapping and preening (Brown *et al.* 1982). Life-long pairbonds.

Breeding and life cycle

Gómez (1979) has linked size of gonad with precipitation—largest after maximum rains passed. In Venezuela, nests July–Sept. In Africa, timing of wet season seems to regulate breeding (Brown *et al.* 1982). Nests later than congeners, peak laying coinciding with maximum flooding once rains over (Gómez-Dallmeier and Cringan 1990). Nests placed at varying distances from, but sometimes over, water, usually in stands of dense vegetation (long grasses, sedges, rice) and occasionally in open crevices in trees. Nest constructed of surrounding material—leaves and stems of plants—and usually well concealed; none or small quantities of down and contour feathers deposited in nest cup, and unattended eggs left uncovered. Eggs smooth shelled, regular ovate; creamy white tinged pinkish when fresh; 48.7 × 36.9 (45.5–52.7 × 35.0–41.5) ($n = 75$) (Brown *et al.* 1982); in captivity weigh 35.3 (27.5–43.0) ($n = 100$); usually laid one per 24 h. Clutch size in Zambia 7.4 (4–13) ($n = 65$) (Brown *et al.* 1982); compound or 'dump-nests', where more than one ♀ lays in same place, recorded in Africa. Sexes share incubation for 26–28 days, period depending on nest attentiveness. Day-old ducklings hatched in captivity weigh 22.1 (16.5–27.0) ($n = 100$); leave nest 48 h post-hatch and escorted by both parents to wetland with lush emergent vegetation. Defence of young includes Broken-wing display from one or both parents while ducklings seek dense cover; ducklings dive to escape predators if emergent vegetation sparse. Fledge in 60–70 days and usually remain with family well into nonbreeding season. Across range, eggs and ducklings subject to predation by egg-eating reptiles, birds and mammals, including humans. Survival of juveniles varies between seasons but highest in summers of good rains (Brown *et al.* 1982). Become gregarious in post-breeding dry season.

Can breed at one year. No data on breeding success, adult survival, nor on longevity.

Conservation and threats

Abundant. During annual wing moult are particularly vulnerable and seek cover of densely vegetated wetlands. Readily uses man-made wetlands (water storage dams, rice paddies) and in Africa undoubtedly benefits from protection of extensive National Parks and game reserves.

Nigel Jarrett

Black-bellied Whistling-duck *Dendrocygna autumnalis*
PLATE 3

Anas autumnalis Linnaeus, 1758, Syst. Nat., ed. 10, p. 127
America

Etymology: *autumnalis* means of the autumn, apparently in reference to autumnal colours of plumage.

Other names: Red-billed Whistling-duck or Tree Duck. French: Dendrocygne à ventre noir; Portuguese: Asa-branca; Spanish: Pato Pijije Aliblanco.

Variation: 2 subspecies, separated at Isthmus of Panama and based on size and breast colour. Northern form is comparatively larger and described below, southern race is slightly smaller with grey collar on otherwise chestnut mantle and lower breast (Livezey 1995a, James and Thompson 2001). Until recently, northern subspecies was known as *D. a. autumnalis* and Southern Black-bellied Whistling-duck as *D. a. discolor* P. L. Sclater and Salvin, 1873. Friedmann (1947) subdivided Northern Black-bellied Whistling-duck into 2 subspecies *D. a. fulgens* for Texas and northeast Mexico and *D. a. lucida* for remainder of Mexico and Central America, based on shading and coloration of belly plumage. James and Thompson (2001) have reviewed the literature, and determined that southern form is nominate *autumnalis*, and *fulgens* is northern race, with individual variation and possible intergrading.

Description

ADULT: sexes similar. Fawn-cinnamon with distinctive black abdominal and side plumage; upper breast and neck cinnamon. Black stripe on back of neck runs to crown. Wings with broad white strip running almost full length of upper surface, leaving black margin; dark beneath. Tail black, white with black speckling beneath. Neck plumage without striations present in some other *Dendrocygna*. Bill pink to red, with blue nail and yellow saddle at nostrils; feet and legs pink to red (legs and bill pale rapidly at death), legs project, heron-like, beyond tail in flight, tarsi have reticulate scale pattern; eyes dark red-brown. Slightly darker abdominal plumage in ♂, but this cannot be determined under field conditions and not fully reliable in hand.

MOULT: one annual wing and body moult.

IMMATURE: grey, lacking obvious black sides and abdomen, but with white on wings. Feet, legs, and bills also grey. Flight attained at 53–63 days; adult body plumage at 34–35 weeks, with 1st wing moult at 19 months (Cain 1970).

DUCKLING: bright yellow with black facial markings and black vertical stripe on back of neck.

Nelson (1993) illustrated 2 colour variants from Texas.

MEASUREMENTS AND WEIGHT: northern race (*n* = 21) sexes combined, wing, 229–248 (238); tarsus, 58–66 (62); culmen, 49–56 (53) (Bolen 1964). Southern race (*n* = 160), wing, 227–259 (242); tarsus, 47–59 (52). Significant difference between sexes in mean total length (♂ = 471, ♀ = 465) and wing length (♂ = 244, ♀ = 239), but overlap makes measurements unreliable for distinguishing ♂ from ♀ (Bourne 1979). See Bolen and Rylander (1983) for discussion of these data in relation to Bergmann's Rule. Weight in Texas, ♂ 680–907 (816); ♀ 652–1021 (839), with heavier ♀♀ reflecting advanced ovarian development (Bolen 1964). Weights of southern race (Bourne 1979) showed no statistical differences between ♂ 530–890 (741) and ♀ 530–890 (725); however, for further weight data, see James and Thompson (2001).

Field characters

Medium-sized duck, 465–500 mm long, easily distinguished from other species by black sides and abdomen, broad white wing stripe, long neck and legs. Erect posture when standing; white on folded wings forms striking sash against black sides. Slow in flight; flocks lack distinctive formation. Lands on posts and trees with legs and neck bent downward in distinctive inverted U-like posture.

Voice

Unmistakable whistling *pee-chee-chee*, particularly vociferous when flying (sonogram in James and Thompson 2001), and almost constant chattering in resting flocks. Nelson (1993) reported on calls of ducklings; sonogram of distress call of duckling in Kear (1968).

Range and status

Restricted to Americas. In North America, common in southern Texas, especially near Corpus Christi, but expanding markedly in recent decades. Regular breeding in San Antonio area, east to Houston (some in Louisiana), and west to Del Rio,

but observed with increasing frequency and numbers outside this region (Schneider *et al.* 1993). Northward breeding range may be limited to latitude of Dallas, Texas, by bioenergetics (Cain 1973). Shows migratory tendencies in Texas, but some remain, apparently depending on local food availability; flocks wander elsewhere. Occurs throughout Mexico in coastal areas (excepting western deserts), Central America, and into South America, where southern range ends in northern Argentina (where also somewhat migratory), also on some Caribbean islands. Extralimital records include California, Michigan and Kansas.

Population status unknown for much of range, but seems healthy in Texas, where numbers clearly increasing and now hunted legally. Rose and Scott (1997) estimated populations of 100 000–1 000 000 for northern, and > million for southern race.

Habitat and general habits

Occupies lakes, reservoirs, stock ponds, and various kinds of wetlands, but less common on creeks and rivers. Often at low elevations above sea level on coastal areas, but also on plains well inland (e.g. llanos of Venezuela); rare in mountains or dense forests. Flocks rest on mudflats, and feeding flights to grainfields at dusk may involve large numbers. Open wooded areas with tree cavities typical breeding habitat, but some nests on ground in grassy cover or under shrubs.

Largely granivorous; diet in Mexico, in season, includes corn *Zea*, sorghum in Texas, as well as seeds of Bermuda grass in cattle pastures. Native food includes seeds of smartweeds *Polygonum*, and millet *Echinochloa*, and aquatic plants (e.g. *Heteranthera liebmanni*). Overall, 92% of diet in Texas plant material (Bolen and Forsyth 1967); Bourne (1981) and Bruzual and Bruzual (1983), respectively, recorded similar results from Guyana (97%) and Venezuela (97%). Ducklings consume more animal material, chiefly insects and spiders, but apparently not in so much volume as occurs in many other young wildfowl (Bolen and Beecham 1970, Bourne 1981). Relatively light endoparasite loads (George and Bolen 1975) seemingly reflect diet of plant foods (for ectoparasites, see McDaniel *et al.* 1966); parasite infestation low in captivity in all whistling-ducks (Hillgarth and Kear 1982a).

Displays and breeding behaviour

Spring sex ratios 50:50 for adults (Bolen 1970), and pairbond seems lifelong (Bolen 1971). Courtship not obvious, but post-copulatory behaviour involves showy, side-by-side mutual posturing (Meanley and Meanley 1958). Mutual preening uncommon in adults, but Nelson (1993) reported such behaviour in ducklings.

Breeding and life cycle

First eggs laid late Apr–early May in Texas, but nesting continues into late Aug–early Sept. Eggs ovate, white to creamy white; 52.7×38.9 ($n = 538$); in captivity, those of southern race weigh 41.0 ($n = 45$). Clutch averages 13 eggs, but 'dump nests' common, ranging up to 101 eggs (Delnicki *et al.* 1976). Nest

lacks down, perhaps because of alternating attendance of both ♂ and ♀ (Bolen and Smith 1979), but surviving parent of either sex will not continue incubation alone when mate lost (McCamant and Bolen 1977). Both sexes have vascularized incubation patches (Rylander *et al.* 1980). Incubation lasts 28–31 days. Captive day-old ducklings of southern race weigh 26.0 (22.0–31.5) ($n = 100$) (at 12 days, 15 averaged 55.5), and northern ones almost identical at 26.1 (20.0–30.0) ($n = 100$).

Cavities selected for nest may be in several tree species; suitable cavities occurred at density of one per 7.8 ha in southern Texas (Delnicki and Bolen 1975). Nesting cavities usually formed by tree damage or disease and seldom involve those initiated by woodpeckers. Hatching success 44% in cavity nests in Texas, but jumped to 77% in nesting boxes protected with predator guards (Bolen 1967). Important egg predators in tree nests included Rat Snake *Elaphe obsoleta* and Raccoon *Procyon lotor*. Some pairs re-nest following loss of earlier clutches (Delnicki and Bolen 1976). More than 80% of nestboxes used during 12-year period, and 75% of incubated clutches produced ducklings, but compound clutches and their abandonment reduced overall hatching success of 746 nests to 28% (McCamant and Bolen 1979). In El Salvador, Gómez Ventura (1985) recorded 83% occupation of 557 boxes during 5 years; 36% of nests hatched. Ground nests on islands in Mexico had mean density of 16 per ha and 42% hatching success; compound clutches common (42%), and desertion most common cause (58%) of failure (Markham and Baldassarre 1989). Feekes (1991) cited nests at base of fronds atop palm trees in Mexico, but hatching data not collected. Breeds at one year. Bolen and Rylander (1983) provided information on ecology and zoogeography of this and other whistling-ducks.

No data on adult survival, but have lived > 20 years in captivity (Mitchell 1911).

Conservation and threats

Nest boxes, if protected against predators, enhance production (Bolen 1967). Birds quickly nest at sites, such as stock ponds or other wetlands, if boxes provided where trees with cavities unavailable; however, compound clutches lessen production, hence nestboxes may need spacing and be hidden in ways that lessen dump nesting, as shown by Semel *et al.* (1988) for Wood Ducks. Feekes (1991) considered species suitable for sustainable management in Mexico's rural development programmes, including restricted exploitation for food, both eggs and meat, and 'wild duck breeding farms' as means of assuring stable populations.

Shot in Texas and Mexico, where local harvests may be heavy at times, but overall mortality from shooting may be sustainable. Large numbers poisoned with pesticides, likely intentionally, in Venezuela because of alleged depredations in rice fields. Mainland populations apparently not in jeopardy, but those on Caribbean islands may suffer heavy exploitation although reliable data lacking for most of range.

Eric G. Bolen

Spotted Whistling-duck *Dendrocygna guttata*
PLATE 2

Dendrocygna guttata Schlegel, 1866, Mus. Hist. Nat. Pays-Bas, Rev. Méthod. Crit. Coll., livr. 8, Anseres, p. 85
Celebes

Etymology: *guttata* L. means spotted from *gutta*, a drop.

Other names: Spotted Tree Duck.

Variation: no subspecies.

Description

ADULT: sexes similar. Eye-patch, crown, hind-neck and collar dusky black. Face, throat and upper neck pale grey. Breast and lower neck rufous brown, heavily vermiculated with darker brown. Underparts and flanks white with rufous brown scaling. Upperparts and tail dark brown with narrow rufous brown edges to feathers. Bill dark grey, but heavily mottled fleshy-pink, giving dusky red appearance; legs and feet medium grey, with fleshy pink tones, and webs dark grey; iris dark brown.

MOULT: no seasonal plumage changes. One wing and body moult annually.

IMMATURE: in 1st plumage duller than adult, with scaling on belly and flanks not so bold.

DUCKLING: head ashy-grey, with blackish brown cap and 2 prominent stripes on face. Upperparts blackish brown, with 2 white bands on back, and underparts ashy-grey tinged brown.

MEASUREMENTS AND WEIGHT: data from captives, ♂ (*n* = 2) wing, 224–226 (225); culmen, 39.1–43.8 (41.5); tarsus, 51.3–51.6 (51.5); weight, 590–650 (620). ♀ (*n* = 7) wing, 214–224 (220); culmen, 40.2–42.2 (41.2); tarsus, 48.6–52.8 (49.9); weight, 610–860 (740).

Field characters

Frequently occurs in mixed flocks with Wandering Whistling-duck, which is much paler above and lacks grey face and white spotting on flanks. Length 430–500 mm. In flight, pale whitish belly of Spotted Whistling-duck diagnostic.

Voice

Most common vocalizations are nasal, one-syllable call *gack* and simple whistle *whee'-ow*, with occasional more complex *whe-a-whew'-whew* (Johnsgard 1965a). Beehler *et al.* (1986) described wheezy, nasal *zzeou*, breaking into series. Coates (1985) stated typical call is coarsely-whistled *whu-wheouw-whi* or *wu-wheouwhi*, and others included simple whistled *whee-ow*, piping *ti-ti-ti*, various single nasal notes, and drawn-out shrill reedy notes. Pairs in captivity converse in low tones almost constantly. Outermost primary, being deeply notched, produces whirring noise in flight (Johnsgard 1965a).

Range and status

Resident, but locally nomadic, found on most islands from Mindanao (Philippines) southwest to

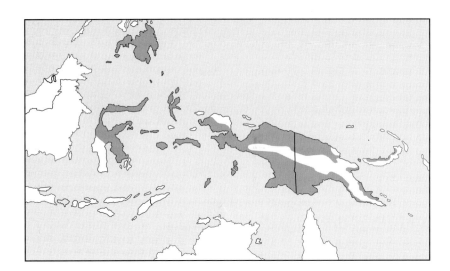

Sulawesi (Indonesia) and southeast to Papua New Guinea (White and Bruce 1986, Madge and Burn 1988, del Hoyo *et al.* 1992). Overall, seems to remain relatively common. Widespread throughout lowland New Guinea and on Aru Island (Coates 1985, Beehler *et al.* 1986); how-ever, has become scarce on some islands, e.g. in Philippines (Dickinson *et al.* 1991), for unknown reasons. Total number uncertain, but probably 10 000–25 000, and remains stable (Rose and Scott 1997).

Habitat and general habits

Little studied. Inhabits most lowland freshwater, including marshes, ponds, lakes, swamps, creeks, banks of rivers and also mangroves (Coates 1985, Beehler *et al.* 1986, White and Bruce 1986). Relatively gregarious, occurring in flocks ranging from few to hundreds (Coates 1985). Roosts in trees (Beehler *et al.* 1986) and frequently associates with Wandering Whistling-duck and Pacific Black Duck.

Little known of diet, but food recorded includes grass seeds and small snails (Coates 1985). Seems to feed mainly at night and twilight by dabbling, grazing and diving (Coates 1985, Beehler *et al.* 1986). Most of day spent loafing in flocks, perched in waterside trees and swamp vegetation, or on shaded grassy banks near water (Coates 1985).

Displays and breeding behaviour

Poorly known. Mutual preening common social behaviour. Johnsgard (1965a) noted only aggressive display was Head-back posture. Coates (1985) described what is probably this display, and also Head-low-and-forward posture commonly performed by other whistling-ducks. Coates (1985) also observed copulation, but noted only prone position of ♀.

Breeding and life cycle

Very little information. In southeast New Guinea, reported to nest in tree hollows (Phillips 1922–26, Coates 1985) although, in captivity, ♀♀ do not invariably choose to lay in boxes. Breeding season seems to correspond with rains, with nests found Sept, Dec, Mar and Apr in New Guinea (Phillips 1922–26, Coates 1985). White eggs laid in captivity measure 52×38 ($n = 11$) (Johnstone 1960), and weigh 41.6 ($n = 48$); Schönwetter (1960–66) gave 53.5×40.8 and calculated weight of 50 for 6 eggs. Clutch 10–11. Incubation lasts 28–31 days, captive ducklings weighed 17.5 ($n = 8$), and Johnstone (1960) reported fledging in captivity at 7 weeks. Downy young seen on Buru Island in Oct, and in Nov at Ambon, although latter not identified with certainty (White and Bruce 1986). Coates (1985) noted increased aggression in flocks in early part of breeding season, which he associated with increased sexual activity as prelude to breeding. He also observed copulation in Nov.

No data on breeding success, nor on adult survival; ♀ lived in captivity for 14 years (Hillgarth and Kear 1982a).

Conservation and threats

No specific conservation measures taken. Doubtless habitat loss, and possibly also hunting, affect numbers. May have exploited expansion of rice production within range, but this presumed change in feeding behaviour undocumented.

Des Callaghan

West Indian Whistling-duck *Dendrocygna arborea*
PLATE 3

Anas arborea Linnaeus, 1758, Syst. Nat., ed. 10, p. 128 America = Jamaica

Etymology: *arborea* from L. *arbor* meaning a tree.

Other names: Black-billed Whistling-duck, Cuban Tree Duck, Cuban Whistling-duck, West Indian Tree Duck, Whistler. French: Dendrocygne des Antilles, Canard siffleur; Puerto Rico: Chiriría, yaguaza.

Variation: no subspecies.

Description

ADULT: sexes similar. Occipital tuft on crown and back of neck black, body and wings mostly brown, with light edging to feathers. Cheeks and sides of neck off-white, throat white. Breast paler than rest of body and speckled. Flank feathers and underparts white with dark brown or black markings giving speckled appearance. Rump, uppertail coverts and tail blackish. Bill heavy and black; legs long, heavy and dark grey with large feet; eyes black. Some ♂♂ exhibit distinct swelling under tail, presumably attributable to phallus (O'Brien 1995). ♀ shows no obvious plumage differences; indistinguishable in field except by behaviour and lack of undertail swelling mentioned above.

MOULT: one plumage worn year-round in both sexes. Nothing known of timing of wing or body moults.

IMMATURE: smaller and lighter coloured than adult. Flank feathers white with light brown down

middle of feathers giving distinctly striped, rather than speckled, appearance. Breast much lighter and rarely speckled.

DUCKLING: blackish above and buffy white below, with dark grey spot on foreneck, and white spots on upperparts (Delacour 1954–64); illustrated in Nelson (1993).

MEASUREMENTS AND WEIGHT: data from Long Island, Bahamas population, ♂ (*n* = 18) wing, 250–284 (268); culmen, 50.0–55.5 (53.4); bill, 55.5–59.9 (56.9); tarsus, 65.2–75.3 (71.4); keel, 81.6–96.0 (88.2); weight, 760–1240 (984). ♀ (*n* = 11) wing, 243–274 (264.74); culmen, 47.7–54.3 (52.0); bill, 51.9–60.5 (56.4); tarsus, 65.9–73.0 (69.8); keel, 75.4–89.0 (84.6); weight, 860–1320 (1064).

Field characters

Large, long-legged, goose-shaped duck. Largest of whistling-ducks, 480–580 mm long; size and black and white flank markings diagnostic and distinguish from other whistling-ducks found in range. Nocturnal habits make it unlikely to be seen with other species of wildfowl.

Voice

Shrill 5-syllable whistle given in flight and when feeding. Also utters harsh high-pitched *peep* continuously when nervous or alarmed, particularly when brood present. Low level of chittering usually audible when in group.

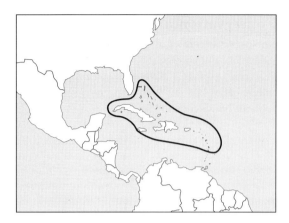

Range and status

Smallest range of any whistling-duck, but widely scattered throughout West Indies. Historically found throughout Bahamas, Turks and Caicos, Cuba, Caymans, Jamaica, Haiti, Dominican Republic, Puerto Rico, Virgin Islands, St Croix, St Kitts-Nevis, Dominica, Guadeloupe, and Antigua and Barbuda, but may have been extirpated from several of these islands as few recent sightings in Haiti, Virgin Islands or St Kitts-Nevis (Collar *et al.* 1992). Wetlands International (2002) estimated a declining population of > 10 000.

Habitat and general habits

Mostly nocturnal and secretive in habit, except seen throughout day when with brood. Adults seldom seen on water but, with broods, spend much of day swimming. Found singly, in pairs, or in flocks of few to one hundred during day in mangroves and swampy areas where roost, often perched on partially submerged trees, and possibly feed. Flies into ponds or ephemeral wetlands to feed at dusk, usually in small flocks and family groups. Preferred habitat shallow fresh, brackish or saline ponds, surrounded by dense vegetation (usually Mangrove *Rhizophora mangle* or Buttonwood *Conocarpus erectus*) in Bahamas, and ephemeral wetlands produced after heavy rains. Radio-marked birds on Long Island preferred mangroves and ponds over 5 other available habitats (Staus 1998a). Feeds throughout night, returning to roosting sites just before dawn. Reported to up-end or dive when feeding (Johnsgard 1965a).

Adults on Long Island fed by walking in shallow ponds and dipping bills in water, grazing in grassy areas, and up-ending occasionally when swimming with broods. Also observed feeding during day in small pools of water on tidal flats near mangroves. Ducklings feed by diving and dabbling at edges of pond.

Diet little known, but assumed to be exclusively vegetarian, including grasses, seeds, pigeon plum fruits, aquatic plants/algae and fruit of royal palm *Roystonea* (Todd 1979). Also feeds on crops such as corn and rice, and considered agricultural pest in some areas (Buden 1987). Stomach contents of adults collected in Isle of Pines were grass (Todd 1916) and, in Dominican Republic, small seeds mostly of grasses (Danforth 1929). Analysis of 6 faecal samples on Hog Cay, Bahamas in 1995 revealed small seeds and aquatic vegetation, but no invertebrate parts (Staus 1998b). Ducklings may feed on vegetation and/or invertebrates in benthos.

Generally considered non-migratory although may move between islands in Bahamas. Radio-transmittered birds on Long Island flew long distances (up to 40 km) between favoured roosting, feeding and nesting sites; showed strong site fidelity to home range area, consistently using same 2 or 3 roosting/feeding sites throughout summer. Radio-marked birds did not leave Long Island, but dispersed up to 15 km from banding site (Staus 1998a).

Displays and breeding behaviour

Aggressive nature well documented in both captive and wild populations, especially when feeding or with brood (Todd 1979). Aggressive displays include Head-low-and-forward (after Johnsgard 1965a) and Jump-flap (described in Clark 1978). Other displays include pre-flight Head-bobbing and raising of occipital tuft (usually accompanied by alarm vocalization) when nervous. Only one instance of allo-preening observed in Long Island population.

Courtship behaviour unknown. Assumed to breed monogamously. Two cases of atleast 2-year pairbonds recorded on Long Island (Staus 1998b). No records of forced extra-pair copulation. Parents appear to defend small brood-rearing areas on ponds, and aggressively evict intruding waterbirds of any species. Appear to use several ponds sequentially during brood development. Parents raise occipital tuft and utter alarm call repeatedly when nervous.

Breeding and life cycle

Breeding season varies from island to island throughout range. Nesting peaked Apr–June on Long Island (Staus 1998b); however, reported to occur nearly year-round, which is case for most islands in which breeding observed (Collar *et al.* 1992). Nests found in tree cavities, on branches, in clumps of bromeliads and on ground (Allen 1961, Paterson 1972, Downer and Sutton 1990). On Long Island, nests consisted of small leaf-lined depression on ground beneath Thatch Palms *Thrinax microcarpa* and other dense bushes, often situated far (up to 1.2 km) from suitable brood pond. Reported to nest on small offshore cays and swim ducklings across several km of open ocean (not always successfully) to brood ponds on Long Island. Eggs cream, smooth shelled; 58.1×42.4 (56.4–61.0×40.7–43.4) ($n = 2$ clutches); weight in captivity 62.2 (54.5–71.0) ($n = 100$). Clutch size 7.7 (6–10) ($n = 3$ nests) on Long Island, Bahamas, and 6.9 ($n = 11$ nests) on Little Cayman (Bradley 2000), although reportedly 10–16 (Collar *et al.* 1992). ♂ assists in incubation, alternating 24 h shifts with ♀ (Staus 1998a) for 30 days in captivity (Johnstone 1957); captive day-olds weigh 36.6 ($n = 34$).

Family bonds strong. ♂ assists in care of young which stay with parents for several weeks, and possibly several months, post-fledging. Family groups behave as geese, feeding together and threatening other individuals and family groups.

No data on breeding success nor on longevity. Mean adult survival rate of .64 (s.e. 0.15) in Long Island population (Staus 1998b).

Conservation and threats

Once common and abundant throughout range, now scarce and status precarious. Classified as Vulnerable by BirdLife International (2000), declines usually attributed to extremely high hunting pressure, habitat loss through wetland drainage, and predation by introduced mammals such as Small Indian Mongoose *Herpestes auropunctatus* and Raccoon (Kear and Williams 1978). Other threats include pollution from domestic sewage, industrial waste and pesticide runoff (Scott and Carbonell 1986), and natural catastrophes such as drought and hurricanes.

Although protected from hunting throughout most of range, poaching widespread. In Bahamas, locally common on islands containing inaccessible duck habitat, and on Hog Cay and northern Long Island where abundant supplementary food provided. Would benefit from establishment of nature reserves in which hunting laws enforced, and possibly from predator control programmes on islands with Raccoons and Small Indian Mongooses.

Recently, public education campaign in Cayman Islands resulted in slow increase in population there. Feeding stations set up to benefit wild birds seem to be successful (Bradley 2000); however, still considered Vulnerable, and not yet returned to former habitats.

Comprehensive range-wide survey needed to estimate total population of West Indies, and individual populations should be closely monitored on every island to determine which conservation strategies are most beneficial.

Nancy Staus

Fulvous Whistling-duck *Dendrocygna bicolor*
PLATE 2

Anas bicolor Vieillot, 1816, Nouv. Dict. Hist. Nat., nouv. éd., **5**, p. 136
Paraguay

Etymology: *bicolor* L. means of 2 colours.

Other names: Fulvous Tree-duck, Large Whistling Teal, Mexican Squealer, Squealer, Tee-kee. Kortright (1942) listed 3 colloquial names that are shared with Black-bellied Whistling-duck, Cornfield Duck, Long-legged Duck and Summer Duck. French: Dendrocygne fauve; Spanish: Pato Pijije Alioscuro.

Variation: no subspeciation nor variation across huge and broken range.

Description

ADULT: sexes similar. Underparts tawny cinnamon to fulvous. Side and flank feathers that overlap folded wing elongated with white upper vane, dark central stripe and brownish grey lower vane. Upperparts blackish brown, mantle feathers broadly rounded with tawny buff ends. Rump black, sides of rump and uppertail coverts pale buff. Tail blackish. Wing blackish except dark reddish brown of middle and lesser coverts. Face tawny, chin white and crown almost chestnut. Rear crown and nape blackish forming stripe, interrupted at back of head. Buff feathering of side of neck furrowed with broken dark lines. Bill dark slate blue; legs and feet deep bluish grey; iris dark brown. ♀ has less vivid colouring and blackish nape stripe continuous.

MOULT: adult undergoes complete wing moult post-breeding and, during vulnerable period of flightlessness, seeks cover of densely vegetated wetlands. Congregations of several hundreds occur in favoured feeding areas once flight regained and, depending on food availability, traditional (local) movements occur. In migratory populations, wing moult delayed until after return to nonbreeding areas. Moult of body feathers may be continuous, although only one plumage change per year (Hohman and Lee 2001).

IMMATURE: paler and more muted than adult, with light edging on mantle feathers narrower and either poorly delineated or lacking. Generally feathers narrower, and with loose texture, apparent when in hand. Wing feathers become duller and variably worn with age.

DUCKLING: white and dark grey. Upperparts (silver grey) paler than other whistling-ducks. Two to 4 white back spots sometimes lacking; illustration of 2 colour variants in Nelson (1993).

MEASUREMENTS AND WEIGHT: ♂ wing in Africa (*n* = 12), 202–242 (216), in N America (*n* = 8), 209–220 (217), in Trinidad (*n* = 10), 209–238 (228); skull Trinidad (*n* = 11), 94.6–106.2 (99.9); culmen Africa (*n* = 12), 43.1–48.1 (46.2), N America (*n* = 8), 44–50 (46); tarsus, Africa (*n* = 12), 52.1–57.2 (54.2), N America (*n* = 8), 54–60 (57.5), Trinidad (*n* = 11), 54.6–59.9 (57.7); weight N America (*n* = 1), 747.7, Trinidad (*n* = 11), 790–1050 (921.4). ♀ wing in Africa (*n* = 15), 203–235 (217), in N America (*n* = 4), 212–220 (216), in Trinidad (*n* = 10), 212–238 (224.3); skull Trinidad (*n* = 11), 94.5–105.4 (98.1); culmen Africa (*n* = 15), 41.5–50.0 (46.1), N America (*n* = 4), 45–49 (47); tarsus Africa (*n* = 15), 50.1–58.9 (54.0), N America (*n* = 4), 54–59 (55), Trinidad (*n* = 11), 52.1–59.4 (56.5); weight, N America (*n* = 3), 712–771.4, Trinidad (*n* = 11), 770–1000 (905) (African data from Brown *et al.* 1982, North American from Palmer 1976).

Field characters

Long-legged, long-necked duck, appearing almost goose-like, 450–530 mm long. Short tail makes body appear dumpy, and flattened crown and longish bill gives head distinctly odd profile. On land, stands erect and walks without waddling. At distance, appears uniformly dark but, at close quarters, pale areas of some flank feathers combine to form cream stripe along sides separating tawny brown of chest, breast and belly from dark brown-black of back, mantle and folded wings. Unlike other whistling-ducks, does not perch much. Wing-beat generally slow, and flies at low altitude in loose bunches rather than in formation. Wings broad and rounded and, with long and sometimes sagging necks and feet trailing behind tail, appears ibis-like. Uppertail coverts form distinctly pale crescent.

Voice

Upon taking wing, squealing whistle uttered, hence American vernacular name 'squealer'. High-pitched 2-syllabled whistle *pit-tu, kit-tee* or *peee-chee*, higher pitched in ♀, given on ground or in flight. Standing birds stretch neck and sometimes lift head and bill to vertical with each call. Conversational *cup-cup-cup-cup* of variable duration and intensity also produced (Palmer 1976). Sonograms of duckling calls, including whistles, in Kear (1968), and description of calls in Nelson (1993).

Range and status

Unique distribution on 4 continents. Occurs in northeast India, Bangladesh and Myanmar (Burma)

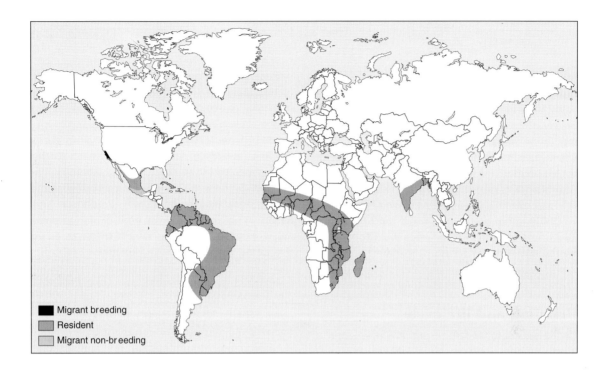

Migrant breeding
Resident
Migrant non-breeding

and occupies belt that extends across central and down eastern Africa, including Madagascar. Absent from coastal and forested regions of west and central Africa and southwest arid region. Also resident in South America, south to northern Argentina and Columbia and, in North America, occurs in Mexico, West Indies and Gulf states of US. Continental populations estimates are 1 million and decreasing for Neotropics and North America (Rose and Scott 1997); 1.1 million in Africa (Rose and Scott 1997); and 20 000 in south Asia (Perennou 1992).

Appear locally migratory across range. Birds of US Gulf coast winter in southern Mexico and, although migratory patterns poorly understood in Africa, southward movement into southern Africa apparent during austral summer, with return movement after breeding season and before winter (Brown *et al.* 1982). In US, numbers waxed and waned; almost disappeared from Texas *c* 1900 but, by 1912, increasing populations and expanding range coincided with increase in rice cultivation (Hohman and Lee 2001). Bond (1971) stated that spread to West Indies only recently, breeding 1st in

Cuba in 1964. Increasing reports on and around islands of Caribbean led to Bellrose (1980) surmising series of invasions along Atlantic Seaboard of US, increasing after 1949, originated in South America.

Habitat and general habits

Flocks most often encountered on shallow fresh or brackish wetlands with extensive contiguous tall grass habitat or rice cultivation. Active day and night-time feeders, foraging noisily in packs numbering tens, hundreds occasionally thousands and often in association with sympatric whistling-ducks. During hottest parts of day, quieter, tending to loaf and sleep in smaller groups.

Diet almost exclusively vegetarian (seeds and structural parts of aquatic plants plus cultivated grains), with some aquatic animal food taken by ducklings (Hohman and Lee 2001). In wet grasslands or marshes, food obtained by walking and dabbling or by stripping grain heads of plants. In shallow water, wades or floats and pecks or sieves items from surface; on deeper water, food collected by swimming with head immersed, sometimes by up-ending and occasionally by diving to depths of 1 m (Palmer 1976).

Display and breeding behaviour

Mutual preening less common than in White-faced Whistling-duck. Courtship inconspicuous. Mating usually occurs on water and, as pre-copulatory display, both engage in mutual Head-dipping and, when equally stimulated, ♂ mounts quickly with wings outstretched almost totally submerging ♀. After dismounting, pair perform Step-dance side by side and treading water; they raise bodies to near vertical position and, with breasts puffed out and necks held in tight S-shape, each holds out wing away from partner. Wing-flapping and preening follows (Meanley and Meanley 1958). Nonterritorial. Pairbond permanent with life-long monogamy.

Breeding and life cycle

Laying period extended, lasting mid May–Aug in North America and coinciding with wet season in Neotropics (Gómez-Dallmeier and Cringan 1990) and South Africa (Siegfried 1973d). Nest usually placed in dense vegetation, often over water. When egg-laying begins, nest frail and little more than trampled platform; 1st laid eggs may be lost during subsequent nest construction. Nest fashioned by both sexes from leaves, stems and uprooted plants, and often has canopy and ramp to water. Very small quantities of down and contour feathering deposited in nest-cup, and unattended eggs left uncovered. Eggs usually laid one per 24–36 h. Eggs bluntly ovate and white to buff-white shells rough when fresh, appearing pitted after period of incubation; 53.4×40.7 ($n = 212$) (Bent 1923); weight in captivity 50.4 (41.5–59.0) ($n = 100$). Egg equivalent to 6.5% of incubating ♀ (Hohman and Lee 2001). Reported clutch size variable because of nest parasitism, but 9.6 (6–16) ($n = 11$) noted by Cottam and Glazener (1959) in Texas; dump nests of 21, 23 and 62 eggs reported (McCartney 1963). ♂ and ♀ share incubation duties and usual for ♂ to take greater part (Delacour 1954–64). Incubation lasts 24–29 days, depending on nest attentiveness, which in turn depends on ambient temperatures—will leave clutch unattended during warmer parts of day, spending longer uninterrupted period on nest near to hatching. Captive day-old ducklings weigh 29.4 (22.0–38.0) ($n = 100$) or 27.8 ± 0.47 ($n = 24$) (Smart 1965b); once dry, leave nest (usually 24–36 h post-hatch) and escorted by both parents to wetlands with lush emergent vegetation. Hatching success 83% in Texas (Cottam and Glazener 1959). Both parents assist with brood care and remain with young at least until fledging. Across range, nests and ducklings subject to predation by egg-eating reptiles, birds and mammals (Hohman and Lee 2001), including humans. When brood approached by possible predator, one parent performs Broken-wing display as other leads young to cover. Fly after 63 days (Palmer 1976). Can breed at one year old. No data on breeding success or adult survival. Maximum life span for ringed adult 6.5 years (Hohman and Lee 2001). Particularly susceptible to cold stress in captivity at temperate latitudes (Hillgarth and Kear 1982a).

Conservation and threats

Biology still not well understood. Regional declines in late 1960s attributed to poisoning from eating aldrin-treated rice. Between 200 and 4600 shot annually in US. Mortality also occurs as result of lead poisoning and collision with powerlines. In southern US, opinions vary as to economic effect on rice cultivation; damage recorded to newly sown rice, and to rice in early stages of growth; however, known to consume considerable quantities of rice field weed seeds (Hasbrouk 1944, Meanley and Meanley 1959, Landers and Johnson 1976, Hohman and Lee 2001). Rice field feeding also reported from Venezuela (Bruzual and Bruzual 1983, Gómez-Dallmeier and Cringan 1990).

Nigel Jarrett

Plumed Whistling-duck *Dendrocygna eytoni*
PLATE 2

Leptotarsis Eytoni Eyton, 1838, Monogr. Anatidae, p. 111
northwestern Australia

Etymology: *eytoni* named for T.C. Eyton (1809–80), British author of *Monograph of the Anatidae or Duck Tribe*.

Other names: Eyton's Whistling or Tree Duck, Plumed Tree Duck or Whistler, Grey or Red-legged Whistler, Grass Whistle Duck, Monkey Duck, Wood Duck. Aboriginal: Yuliya; French: Dendrocygne d'Eyton; German: Tüpfelpfeifgans, Gelbfuss-Pfeifgans; Spanish: Pato silbdor adornada, Suirirí Australiano.

Variation: no subspecies.

Description

ADULT: sexes similar. Pale buff with pale chestnut or cinnamon sides to breast, boldly striped black, together with very prominent, pale yellow, lanceolate plumes on flanks. Head pale buff, slightly darker on crown and palest on face and throat; neck and upper breast pale buff shading to darker buff on hindneck. Underside darker buff-brown merging to pale chestnut on sides of breast where prominent vertical black stripes in front of mass of large, dark edged, pale lanceolate plumes pointing upwards and backwards. Belly and undertail dull white. Mantle, back and scapular feathers pale brown with buff margins. Rump dark brown. Upperwing pale buff-brown, flight feathers darker; underwing coverts off-white with numerous grey spots. Uppertail coverts pale buff; tail dark brown. Bill pale pink irregularly marked with numerous dark freckles; legs and feet pale pink; iris orange-yellow.

MOULT: no seasonal plumage changes, and no information on timing of moults (Marchant and Higgins 1990).

IMMATURE: compared with adult, much paler and lacks any bold stripes and cinnamon colour on sides to breast, and lanceolate flank plumes paler and shorter. Bill, legs and feet flesh-white rather than pink and bill unspotted; iris pale brown.

DUCKLING: similar in head pattern to that of Wandering Whistling-duck but general tone yellow and brown rather than grey and white. Upperside yellow-brown and underside off-white. Strong pattern on face formed by prominent pale yellow supercilium over narrow dark brown eyestripe extending from nape almost to base of bill. Yellowish colour of cheek extends as pale stripe from side to side across nape above another narrow dark brown stripe from upperneck to ear coverts. Prominent pale stripe each side of lower back and broad pale edging present along rear edges of wing stubs. Pale grey bill, legs and feet.

MEASUREMENTS AND WEIGHT: mostly from Frith (1982), tail and tarsus from Marchant and Higgins (1990), ♂ wing ($n = 59$), 222–242 (232); tail ($n = 7$), 65–73 (69); bill ($n = 65$), 37–48 (40); tarsus ($n = 8$), 55–62 (60); weight ($n = 63$), 600–930 (788). ♀ wing ($n = 57$), 215–245 (228); tail ($n = 8$), 64–84 (71); bill ($n = 65$), 37–49 (43); tarsus ($n = 9$), 50–58 (55); weight ($n = 65$), 580–1400 (792).

Field characters

Pale whistling-duck with prominent, flexible, pale yellow lanceolate plumes on flanks. Length 400–450 mm. These features, combined with pink legs and feet and black spotted pink bill, sufficient to distinguish from all other whistling-ducks. In flight, distinguishable from Wandering Whistling-duck by general paleness including upperwing coverts pale buff and uniform with colour of back and mantle. Also underwings paler and spotty compared with uniformly dark underwing of Wandering.

Voice

Loud, high-pitched whistle *wiss-threew* most distinctive call; is more penetrating than whistles of Wandering Whistling-duck. Also utters softer twittering whistle, usually heard at roost, or when flying, and often interspersed with more distinctive single whistle mentioned above. Soft whistling sound also made by wings in flight.

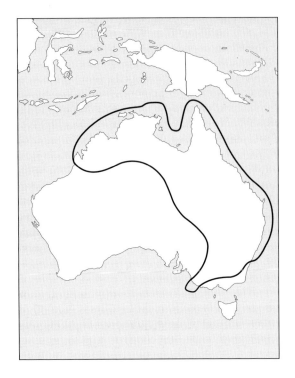

Range and status

Endemic to Australia with wider distribution on that continent than Wandering Whistling-duck. Range extends from lower Kimberley across northern Australia, throughout most of Queensland and south into New South Wales and Victoria, where found mostly within upper regions of Darling River basin and Murray, Murrumbidgee and Lachlan River catchments. Not common in more arid regions and absent from southwest. Stable population of 100 000 to >million suggested (Rose and Scott 1997).

Habitat and general habits

Usually found on tropical and temperate grasslands within reach of freshwater. In northern Australia concentrates in dry season at permanent waterholes and along watercourses on floodplains, dispersing widely in wet season. Not dependent on water for feeding but typically roosts alongside water, on sandbanks or other bare or sparsely vegetated areas near or surrounded by water. Usually avoids coastal or tidal regions. Commonly found in flocks when not breeding, and at these times usually roosts during day in dense flocks near water. Flocks fly out at dusk to grazing areas on grasslands, sometimes at considerable distances from daytime roost and then feed all night (Lavery 1971a, Marchant and Higgins 1990). Usually seen on water only when alighting from flight and then swim buoyantly.

Diet almost entirely herbivorous. Feeds by plucking grass, goose-like, from sward but will dabble when taking food in shallow water (details in Marchant and Higgins 1990).

Displays and breeding behaviour

Highly gregarious. Sometimes forms large dense communal roosts and often mixes with Wandering Whistling-duck. Monogamous and probably forms lifelong pairbond (Marchant and Higgins 1990).

Threat indicated, as for most whistling-ducks, by Head-back and Head-low-and-forward postures, performed by both sexes (Johnsgard 1965a). Fighting occurs between ♂♂ especially at onset of breeding (Frith 1982). Pair formation may involve prolonged chase in air, on and under water, usually ♀ pursued by several ♂♂ (Lavery 1967c, Marchant and Higgins 1990). Mutual nibbling or preening presumably reinforces pairbond. Copulation behaviour similar to that of Fulvous and Wandering Whistling-ducks (Johnsgard 1965a).

Breeding and life cycle

In north, breeds during or towards end of wet season but nesting occurs in south most often in spring or summer. Breeds solitarily, nesting on ground, usually in long grass and some distance from water (Marchant and Higgins 1990). Eggs oval, small for size of duck, smooth, slightly lustrous, milky white, slightly tinged cream (Marchant and Higgins 1990); 48 × 36 (44–55 × 33–38) (*n* = 112 eggs from 14 clutches) (Frith 1982); in captivity weigh 34.7 (*n* = 67). Clutch size *c* 8, but no reliable data. Incubation shared by both sexes, probably in equal proportions, said to last 28–30 days (Marchant and Higgins 1990); captive day-olds weigh 21.9 (*n* = 15). Brood tended by both sexes, with young probably fledging at 56–65 days (Todd

1996). No data on growth of young, age at 1st breeding, breeding success nor adult survival, but have lived in captivity for > 13 years (Hillgarth and Kear 1982a).

Conservation and threats

Abundant and not globally threatened.

Peter Fullagar

Wandering Whistling-duck *Dendrocygna arcuata*
PLATE 2

Anas arcuata Horsfield, 1824, Zoological Researches in Java, pt. **8**, pl. 64 and text
Java

Etymology: from *arcuatus*, L. for bow-shaped or curved, in reference to flank feathers.

Other names: Whistling Teal, Wandering or Whistling Tree Duck, Black-spotted Tree Duck, Diving or Water Whistling-duck, Lesser Fulvous Whistling-duck, Red or Water Whistler, Water Whistle-Duck. Aboriginal: Chipala, Djudiya, Enjep-ere, Walathu; Dutch: Zwervende Fluiteend; French: Dendrocygne de l'Inde, Dendrocygne à lunules; German: Bogenente, Indische or Celebes Ente, Wanderpfeifgans; Java: Meliwies, Meliwis kembang; Philippines: Balinio, Gakit, Naga; Spanish: Pato silbador errante, Suirirí Capirotado.

Variation: 3 subspecies recognized, nominate East Indian Wandering Whistling-duck *D. a. arcuata* from Philippines and parts of Indonesia (west as far as Java and Borneo), Australian Wandering Whistling-duck *D. a. australis* Reichenbach, 1850 from southern New Guinea and northern and northeastern Australia, and Lesser Wandering Whistling-duck *D. a. pygmaea* Mayr, 1946 from northern New Guinea (material in Australian National Wildlife Collection), New Caledonia (or possibly *D. a. australis*) and formerly New Britain and Fiji.

Description

ADULT: sexes similar. Plumage buff to pale brown, merging to chestnut on sides and belly with prominent, lanceolate, white flank feathers broadly edged dark brown. Upperparts heavily scalloped dark brown, particularly on lower back. Scaly appearance merges to uniform colour across lower neck and breast. Pale face and throat but crown, nape and hindneck dark brown. Wings, above and below, dark grey-brown with rich chestnut forewing coverts on upperwing. Undertail coverts and outer uppertail coverts white. Rump and tail dark brown. Bill black; legs and feet dark grey; iris red-brown.

MOULT: no seasonal plumage change. No reliable information on moults.

IMMATURE: plumage duller and paler than adult; lanceolate feathering on flanks not so large; mantle and scapulars more uniform, lacking prominent edging. Undersides and wing coverts less chestnut. White uppertail coverts speckled.

DUCKLING: generally dark grey-brown with prominent pattern on face and pale grey underside. Grey bill, legs and feet. Face, throat and upper foreneck white with crown dark brown. Strong pattern on face formed by prominent white supercilium over dark brown eyestripe extending from nape to base of bill. White cheek extends as stripe from side to side across nape above another dark brown stripe from upperneck to ear coverts. Pale rear edging to wing stubs and pale stripes each side of lower back not distinct.

MEASUREMENTS AND WEIGHTS: *australis* mostly from Frith (1982); tail and tarsus from Marchant and Higgins (1990), ♂ wing (*n* = 287), 196–230 (214); tail (*n* = 12), 50–61 (55); bill (*n* = 24), 39–52 (48); tarsus (*n* = 12), 46–55 (52); weight (*n* = 287), 741–948 (866). ♀ wing (*n* = 86), 201–231(214); tail (*n* = 6), 52–59 (54); bill (*n* = 47), 39–50 (47); tarsus (*n* = 8), 50–55 (52); weight (*n* = 293), 453–976 (732). Subspecific differences relatively slight and based largely on size. *australis* largest (see above, but Delacour (1954–64) gave wing, 200–222; tail, 52–57; bill, 42–48; tarsus, 43–45). *arcuata* slightly smaller, wing, 180–203; tail, 50–55; bill, 42–48; tarsus, 43–45 (Delacour 1954–64), but said to be somewhat larger in south of range (Madge and Burn 1988), and *pygmaea* smallest, wing, 173–183; bill, 41–44 (Delacour 1954–64).

Field characters

Typical whistling-duck with long neck, long legs and upright stance, 400–450 mm long. Rusty looking. Hunched posture in flight with broad wings and dangling legs. Distinctive whistling calls usually given when flying in flocks. Often found on water and dives freely. Looks darker and stockier than Plumed Whistling-duck. Dark bill and legs useful additional features and, in flight, chestnut upper forewing helps to distinguish from Plumed Whistling-duck. Lesser Whistling-duck very similar, including chestnut upper forewings but lacks defined lanceolate flank feathers and has chestnut rather than black and white uppertail coverts, visible particularly in flight. Spotted Whistling-duck much darker with rather uniform plumage, except for distinctive large white spots on underside and flank feathers.

Voice

For whistling-duck, not particularly noisy. Usual call shrill multi-syllabic twittering *wi-wi-wi-wi-wi-wi-whew*, described as rapid descending whistle (Johnsgard 1965a). Sometimes utters whistle as single note; heard usually in alarm or when in flight or at roost. Wing feathers produce whirring sound in flight.

Range and status

Found in northern Australia, New Guinea, Philippines, Borneo, Java and islands within region, also in New Caledonia. Abundant in many areas; particularly numerous in Philippines and parts of Indonesia; common in New Guinea and large concentrations frequently found on coastal wetlands in northern Australia (Marchant and Higgins 1990, del Hoyo *et al.* 1992). In Sepik region of New Guinea *pygmaea* occurs but now seems absent from Fiji and New Britain. Distribution overlaps with

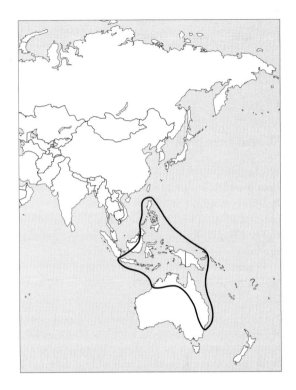

Lesser Whistling-duck in south Borneo and Java, and with Plumed Whistling-duck in Australia. Assumed that breeding occurs throughout main range. Rose and Scott (1997) suggested population of 100 000 to >million for New Guinea and Australia.

Habitat and general habits

Probably sedentary or dispersive rather than migratory over most of range. Known to move from dry season refuges beside permanent water to ephemeral inland wetlands and coastal sites following rains in Australia (Marchant and Higgins 1990). Gregarious when not breeding, often congregating in large flocks. Favours wetlands on floodplains, particularly in northern Australia (del Hoyo *et al.* 1992).

Feeds almost entirely on aquatic vegetation and seeds. Food obtained by dabbling or diving and, in Australia, said to feed mostly at night, roosting in flocks during day (Frith 1982). Details of diet summarized (from Australian data) in Marchant and Higgins (1990). Gregarious, forming large nonbreeding season flocks composed of mated pairs and immatures. These flocks increase in size as concentrate at remaining wet-lands with progression of dry season and, in Australia, often forms mixed flocks with Plumed Whistling-duck (Marchant and Higgins 1990).

Displays and breeding behaviour

Monogamous with pairbond probably maintained lifelong; both sexes select nest site, incubate and care for young (Frith 1982). Generally shy and wary. Holding head erect before taking flight with much calling indicates alarm, and pre-flight signalled by lateral Head-shaking (Johnsgard 1965a). Threat indicated by Head-back and Head-low-and-forward postures (Johnsgard 1965a). Fighting inten-sifies with onset of breeding season (Frith 1982).

Pairbond reinforced by Mutual nibbling (Johns-gard 1965a). Pair formation display not observed and probably inconspicuous. Copulation occurs on water involving pre-copulatory Head-dipping, after which ♂ suddenly mounts. Copulation brief and followed by post-copulatory calling from both birds while side by side, facing same direction, then each treads water and rises in Step-dance with wing on side opposite partner lifted and partly outstretched (Johnsgard 1965a). Following copulation, both swim to shore and bathe and preen vigorously. Soli-tary when breeding.

Breeding and life cycle

Nests on ground in shelter of vegetation and gen-erally away from water but sometimes in marshland (Marchant and Higgins 1990). Nest usually flimsy platform formed by treading and weaving sur-rounding vegetation. No down added. Strong paternal care. Eggs elliptical, smooth, finely tex-tured, slightly glossy and creamy-white (Marchant and Higgins 1990); 51×37 $(47–53 \times 35–39)$ ($n = 114$ from 15 clutches) (Frith 1982); calculated weight 40 ($n = 23$) (Schönwetter 1960–66). Clutch size said to average 10 (6–15) but few reliable data (Marchant and Higgins 1990, Todd 1996) and mean of 8 suggested ($n = 15$ clutches). Incubation, shared by sexes, said to be 28 (Frith 1982) or 28–30 days (Todd 1996). Frith (1982) reported that captive young weigh c 20, and broods fledge at 45–65 days (Todd 1996); however, also reported that, despite being fully feathered by 10 weeks, cannot fly until 12–13 weeks of age (Marchant and Higgins 1990). Young may be capable of breeding at 7 months (Lavery 1967c). No data on breeding success or adult survival; Johnsgard (1968a) noted captive individual > 15 years old.

Conservation and threats

Abundant, and not globally threatened except pop-ulations on some islands, e.g. New Caledonia. Pre-sumed extinct in New Britain (Rose and Scott 1977) and on Fiji following introduction of ground predators such as Small Indian Mongoose, but see Young *et al.* (1997).

Peter Fullagar

Lesser Whistling-duck *Dendrocygna javanica*
PLATE 3

Anas Javanica Horsfield, 1821, Trans. Linn. Soc. Lon-don, **13**, p. 199, pl. 1
Java

Etymology: *javanica* means of Java where type specimen taken.

Other names: Indian Whistling-duck, Javan Whistling-duck, Lesser Whistling Teal, Lesser Tree Duck.

Variation: no subspecies.

Description

ADULT: sexes similar. Overall dark rufous-brown. Head buff-brown with dark grey-brown cap; flanks rufous-brown with creamy streaks. Neck and breast buff-brown to greyish buff. Back dark grey-brown with chestnut bars. Upperwing and uppertail coverts chestnut. Undertail coverts whitish; tail dark-brown. Flight feathers blackish. Bill dark grey to black; legs and feet dark grey, webs and claws blackish; iris dark brown and eyelids bright yellow.

MOULT: no seasonal plumage change. No information on timing of moults.

IMMATURE: duller than adult. Feathers on mantle bordered fulvous. Underparts pale dull brownish.

DUCKLING: dark grey-brown and whitish grey with large whitish spots on back.

MEASUREMENTS AND WEIGHT: both sexes; sample size not known, wing, 170–204 (187); tail, 53–55 (54); bill, 38–42 (40); tarsus, 40–50 (45); weight, 450–600 (525) (Ali and Ripley 1987).

Field characters

Length 410–420 mm; smallest whistling-duck with long neck, elongated body and broad rounded wings. Can be confused with closely related Fulvous and Wandering Whistling-ducks. Slightly smaller size and chestnut uppertail coverts (*contra* creamy-white in Fulvous and whitish in Wandering) major distinguishing characters; moreover, lacks less conspicuous buff collar round middle of foreneck of *bicolor* and black spots on breast of *arcuata*.

Voice

Utters shrill high pitched *tsee-tsee, tchee-tchee* while on wing and also when rising from water. Not very different from calls of Fulvous. Sonogram of duckling distress call in Kear (1968).

Range and status

Pakistan, all over India including Andamans and Nicobars, Nepal, Bhutan, Bangladesh, Sri Lanka, Myanmar (Burma), Thailand, Malaysia, Indonesia (Sumatra, Java and Borneo), Cambodia, Laos, Vietnam, southern China including Hainan, Taiwan, and Riyu Kiu islands of Japan (Smythies 1940, King *et al.* 1975, Ali and Ripley 1987, Choudhury 1990, Lekagul and Round 1991, Sonobe and Usui 1993).

Still abundant through most of range, and commonest resident duck of Indian sub-continent. Used

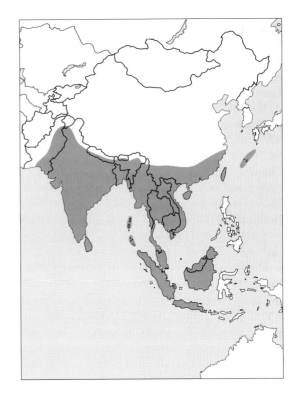

to be widespread in Myanmar (Burma) also but, due to regular shooting, was rare as long ago as late 1930s (Smythies 1940). In Thailand, common resident and winter visitor (Lekagul and Round 1991). Vagrant to Hong Kong (King *et al.* 1975), and frequent elsewhere in range (Sonobe and Usui 1993), usually at low elevations. Although comprehensive population estimate unavailable, Asian waterfowl census 1987–91, in some selected sites, suggested at least 181 000 ducks (Perennou *et al.* 1994); however, in view of coverage of sites in India, assumed that this count represented < 10% of potential world population. Rose and Scott (1997), following Perennou *et al.* (1994), estimated declining population of 100 000 to million for both southern Asia and for eastern and southeastern Asia.

Habitat and general habits

Least studied whistling-duck in field. Inhabits water bodies in forests as well as in villages and countryside. Favoured wetlands include reedy and vegetation-covered tanks, ox-bow lakes, ponds, jungle pools, flooded fields, marshes, swamps and also larger lakes, mangroves and coastal lagoons. Usually found in small parties of 10–20. Mostly seen in pairs during breeding season, while large loose flocks of > 100 nonbreeders encountered in winter. Huge congregations of up to 5000 recorded in Assam. Occasionally associates with Fulvous Whistling-duck. Feeds at night, in early morning and in evening; daytime feeding rare and mostly occurs during breeding season when *c* 20% of diurnal time devoted to foraging (Raj 1991). During daytime, often flocks together on water, or roosts in trees where perches freely on branches.

Feeds in shallow water on vegetable and animal material. Aquatic weeds, tender shoots, grains of wild and cultivated rice, small fish, frogs, snails and worms taken (Ali and Ripley 1987). Can dive easily. Studies of activity pattern show that spends *c* 53% of day resting and 23% preening, especially when in nonbreeding flocks (Raj 1991).

Displays and breeding behaviour

Courtship display not conspicuous. ♂ initiates by dipping and raising head in water followed by swimming around ♀ in Head-down Tail-up posture. This is followed by swimming together for short distance, then ♂ mounts (Raj 1991).

Breeding and life cycle

Breeding activity starts in May and may continue to Oct depending upon arrival of monsoon and raised water levels. In Sri Lanka, breeding occurs chiefly Dec–Jan, and July–Aug (Ali and Ripley 1987). Two broods may be raised in single year. Nests found in holes and other natural tree hollows, including cavities in broken tree trunks, and in fork and boughs of large branches. These holes occur because of rot and other natural causes, local woodpecker holes being too small to be of use; mammals, such as Palm Civet *Paradoxurus hermaphroditus*, may excavate rotten parts of larger and older trees, but no record of such holes being occupied. Nesting on ground near tanks, marshes and reedbeds also common. Twigs and grass main nesting materials used in trees (although do not carry material); deserted nests of kites *Milvus*, crows and herons also used. Tree nests usually not > 7 m from ground, but can be well away from water.

Eggs smooth and ivory-white becoming stained brownish during incubation; 46.9×36.8 ($n = 100$); in captivity weigh 35 ($n = 16$); clutch 10 (7–17). Both sexes incubate for 22–30 days (Baker 1922–30, Smythies 1940, Ali and Ripley 1987); in captivity, incubation lasted 29 days. Ducklings tended by both parents; 2 hatched in captivity weighed 18.3 and 20. There are instances of adult ducks being preyed upon by birds of prey, and diving simultaneously to escape attack. Young birds occasionally fall prey to monitor lizards *Varanus* and to snakes. Probably breeds at one year. No information on breeding success, adult survival, nor on longevity.

Conservation and threats

Being common, not on any priority list for conservation measures, and significant population protected in various national parks and wildlife sanctuaries. Hunted for food over whole of range, although not considered 'good' gamebird. Catching of live birds by various crude methods also not uncommon, and numbers often caught in nets for eating. Collection of eggs as well as ducklings also reported from many areas; eggs either eaten or incubated under domestic ducks or hens, and ducklings reared as pets. Survives well in captivity on Indian sub-continent; at higher latitudes, as in the UK, shows considerable cold sensitivity (Hillgarth and Kear 1982a). Apart from hunting, little information available on causes of mortality.

Anwaruddin Choudhury

White-backed Duck

Taxonomy

The White-backed Duck is the sole member of its tribe Thalassornithini (Livezey 1997b), no inter-specific hybrids have been recorded (Johnsgard 1960b) and it is absent from the fossil record. It was placed within the stiff-tailed ducks (Oxyurini) traditionally because of superficial similarities arising from extreme specialization for diving, and large egg size (Delacour and Mayr 1945, Delacour 1954–64, Johnsgard 1961a, Woolfenden 1961).

Studies of morphology, behaviour, feather proteins and DNA sequences have revealed a relationship to the whistling-ducks (Johnsgard 1967, Kear 1967, Raikow 1971, Brush 1976, Harshman 1996). Livezey's (1986a) study of skeletal morphology found weak support for a contradictory relation-ship but, in later studies (Livezey 1995a, 1996b), he found moderate support for the relationship to whistling-ducks.

Des Callaghan

White-backed Duck *Thalassornis leuconotus*
PLATE 30

Thalassornis leuconotus Eyton, 1838, Monogr. Anati-dae, p. 168
Cape of Good Hope (Cape Province, South Africa)
Etymology: *Thalassornis* Gr. *thalassa* means sea, and *ornis* bird (however, does not readily enter the sea); *leuconotus* Gr. *leukos* meaning white and *notos* back.

Other names: Afrikaans: Witrugeend; French: Erismature à dos blanc; Malagasy: Beloha, Dana-mona (Lac Alaotra).

Variation: 2 subspecies recognized, nominate *T. l. leuconotus* from sub-Saharan Africa, and *T. l. insularis* Richmond, 1897 from Madagascar.

Description

ADULT: sexes similar (see Bell 1997a for discus-sion). Mottled brown with conspicuous white patch at base of bill and white rump best seen in flight. Bill large and blackish, sides mottled fleshy; legs and feet greenish grey; iris dark brown. *insularis* smaller than nominate, crown and breast darker, appearing almost chestnut, all black markings more intense and buff areas greyer.

MOULT: no seasonal plumage changes. Parents moult wings when young 7 weeks old (Brown *et al.* 1982). Limited information on body moults and their timing.

IMMATURE: generally darker, less distinctively marked, face and neck more heavily spotted, white patch at base of bill smaller and duller (Brown *et al.* 1982). Immature *leuconotus* may resemble adult *insularis*.

DUCKLING: distinctive. Upperparts black with large rufous patches on back and wings, underparts whitish grey to black. Head and neck rufous, crown, patch below eyes, chin and band on hind neck black (Delacour 1954–64). Large for size of adult, dumpy and capable of diving as day-old.

MEASUREMENTS AND WEIGHT: *leuconotus*, sexes combined ($n = 16$) wing, 163–171 (169.7); tail, 47.5–53 (49); bill, 32–39 (37); tarsus, 36.5–39 (37) (Brown *et al.* 1982). *insularis* wing, 135–150; bill, 32–37; tarsus, 32–36 (Phillips 1922–26); specimens at British Museum, sexes combined ($n = 10$) wing, 140–150 (145); bill, 33–38 (35). Weight *leuconotus* ♂ ($n = 3$), 650–790; ♀ ($n = 4$), 625–765 (Brown *et al.* 1982).

Field characters

Quiet and unobtrusive, often tame and approach-able. Medium sized, 380–430 mm long, mottled brown diving duck, sitting low in water and appearing 'hump-backed'. May rest with feet turned up and exposed on back. Tail often completely submerged, may be vibrated, particularly before diving. Large head obvious when sitting partially submerged in open water or among floating vegetation. May appear similar to swimming and foraging (diving) Fulvous Whistling-duck, although this duck seldom sits so low in water and has longer neck and more uniform, reddish, plumage. Rarely comes ashore. Runs across water to take off and, when in flight, lack of wing speculum, white rump and trailing feet obvious.

Voice

Usually silent. Both sexes have range of whistling calls and 2 note *curvee* call. May use soft, flute-like trills at nest. Whistles given in flight resemble *Dendrocygna*

(Brown *et al.* 1982). Parents hiss in nest defence. Sonogram of adult *leuconotus* calls in Maclean (1993), and of duckling distress call in Kear (1968).

Range and status

leuconotis resident throughout eastern and southern Africa from Ethiopia to Cape. Second population occurs in western Africa south of Sahara from Gambia and Senegal through Mali and northern Nigeria to western Chad. Breeds Zanzibar. *insularis* widespread in Madagascar up to 1300 m, although rare on deforested Central Plateau. Semi-nomadic habits, caused by natural fluctuations of water level and salinity, make accurate surveying difficult. At lakes such as Antsamaka and Andranolava, western Madagascar, high salinity for much of year makes water unsuitable; however, during wet season,

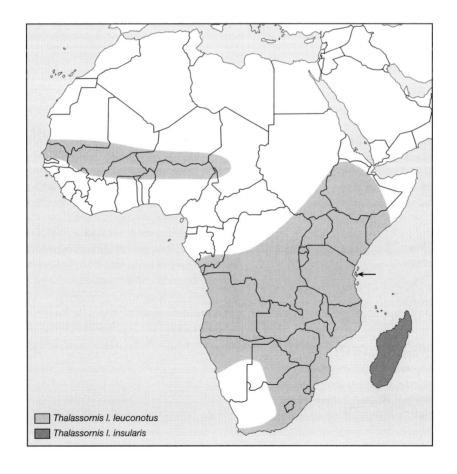

Thalassornis l. leuconotus
Thalassornis l. insularis

numbers may gather—for instance, 118 at Andranolava in Jan 1998 (African Waterfowl Census). Has been recorded at new sites in Madagascar, suggesting degree of adaptability which may help survival. Obvious reduction noted in many areas, although *leuconotus* still reasonably common. Wetlands International (2002) estimated declining 2500–5000 in Madagascar, <1000 in west Africa and 10 000–25 000 in eastern and southern Africa.

Habitat and general habits

Mostly crepuscular. Favours quiet, well vegetated pools and lakes, marshes and dams. Generally remains in cover of emergent and floating vegetation, especially water-lilies *Nymphaea*, where can hide and sleep during hottest parts of day. In Madagascar, often inhabits forested lakes. If chased or threatened, will dive to avoid attack, and may 'kick' spray of water 1 m into air in Splash-dive. Feeds almost exclusively by diving. Diet of aquatic vegetation, seeds and vegetative parts of water-lilies. Young feed on insect larvae and other aquatic invertebrates.

Displays and breeding behaviour

Poorly known. ♂ seen swimming parallel to another presumed ♂ calling loudly. Another ♂ seen swimming alongside smaller bird presumed ♀, both with heads held stiffly, partly raised; presumed ♀ dived and was joined by ♂ on re-surfacing, pair then swam off heads erect, bill-dipping. Pairs recorded swimming together in small circles, bill-dipping frequently. Following copulation, *Dendrocygna*-like Step-dance observed with both ducks treading water, bodies held vertically and opposite wings raised. ♂ bowed forward 3 times almost touching water during this display (Clark 1969). Threat posture similar to whistling-ducks. Breeding pairs do not appear territorial; nests found few m apart (Clark 1979a). May remain paired for several seasons.

Breeding and life cycle

In Africa, nesting recorded throughout year, exact season dependent on rainfall, most nests occurring when water levels highest. Breeds Apr–July in Madagascar (Rand 1936, Langrand 1990); nests found at Antsamaka in May. Disperses following breeding season, as water levels drop, gathering in small flocks on more stable lakes and marshes. Rafts of up to 100 seen on open water in Madagascar (Rand 1936).

Nest built by both sexes, floating in emergent vegetation, or at water's edge with ramp; no down added, but birds pull down vegetation to produce canopy. At Antsamaka, 2 active nests in 2001 found directly beneath nests of Purple Swamphen *Porphyrio porphyrio*. Eggs unique among ducks in being milk chocolate brown; large (*c* 12% of ♀ body weight), ovate and smooth; *leuconotus* 61.9 × 48.7 (55–68.8 × 44.9–51.7) (*n* = 85) (Maclean 1993); weight in captivity 81 (77–94) (*n* = 31) (Brown *et al.* 1982); no data on *insularis*. One parent, of either sex, sits on incomplete clutch but does not incubate. Clutch in southern Africa 6.8 (4–10) (*n* = 74) (Brown *et al.* 1982) or 4.4 (1–7) (*n* = 40) (Clark 1979a); *insularis* at Antsamaka 4.85 (1–8) (*n* = 20). Incubation by both sexes, ♂ principally during day, 29–33 days. Captive day-olds weigh 53.8 (*n* = 8); fledge in 55 days (Brown *et al.* 1982). Juvenile development described in Kear (1967).

No information on breeding success, adult survival nor longevity in wild. Captive ♂ lived for 12 years (Hillgarth and Kear 1982).

Conservation and threats

Able generally to adapt to urban and agricultural areas where suitable conditions exist and is not hunted; however, usually unwilling to fly and easily netted. Modification of wetlands, particularly if aquatic flora affected, poses serious threat. In Madagascar and parts of Africa, introduction of herbivorous fish has altered lake ecosystems and reduced suitability of many areas. No longer occurs on Lake Alaotra, where once considered common.

Semi-nomadic, so protection, and management in pristine state, of many wetlands necessary. Large eggs much prized as food by people living near wetlands, especially in Madagascar where resident subspecies now listed as Endangered by Threatened Waterfowl Specialist Group (2003). Further introduction of exotic fish, and pollution, must be avoided.

Glyn Young

Musk Duck

Taxonomy

The Musk Duck traditionally has been classified as a true stifftail (Delacour and Mayr 1945, Raikow 1970, Johnsgard 1978, Livezey 1986a, 1995b, Johnsgard and Carbonell 1996), but bizarre courtship displays, a fleshy gular lobe, lack of sexual difference in colour, extreme sexual size dimorphism, lekking behaviour, maternal feeding of young, absence of facial and dorsal markings on the duckling, and many unique skeletal characters render it quite unlike other stifftails (Johnsgard 1965a, 1966a, Fullagar and Carbonell 1986, Marchant and Higgins 1990, Johnsgard and Carbonell 1996, McCracken 1999, 2000c). Molecular analyses (Harshman 1996, Sraml *et al.* 1996, McCracken *et al.* 1999) indicated that it is not a true stifftail at all, but an independent, monotypic lineage. Morphological similarities between Musk Duck and stifftails are probably the result of convergence, largely in the hind limb, imposed by diving as a primary means of foraging. Behavioural similarities may reflect shared ancestral traits (McCracken *et al.* 1999). The only Musk Duck relative known to have become extinct during the Holocene is *Biziura delatouri* Forbes, 1892 from New Zealand (Horn 1983, Cassels 1984, Holdaway 1989).

Des Callaghan and Kevin McCracken

Musk Duck *Biziura lobata*

Plate 30

Anas lobata Shaw, 1796, Shaw and Nodder, Nat. Misc., **8**, pl. 225 and text
King George Sound, Western Australia
Biziura Stephens, 1824

Etymology: *Biziura* Gr. *buzen* means thick and *oura* tail, apparently in reference to pincushion-like undertail coverts of ♂ exposed in display; *lobata* L. means lobed.

Other names: Diver, Diving Duck, Lobed Duck, Mould Goose, Steamer Duck. Australian aboriginal: Go-da-ra, Goojuk, ♂ Nanawuli, Peldi, Tanik, ♀ Tarip, Tilmari; French: Canard à membrane; German: Lappenente.

Variation: no subspecies, although possible separation into 2 races requires assessment. Subspecies *B. l. menziesi* of southeast Australia (Mathews 1914), said to have smaller lobes than western *B. l. lobata* and white feather barring rather than buff, unconfirmed by Parker *et al.* (1985). Acoustic variation (Robinson and Robinson 1970, McCracken 1999, McCracken *et al.* 2002) suggests low levels of gene flow between eastern and western populations.

Description

ADULT: sexes differ markedly in size, more so than any other duck (McCracken *et al.* 2000c). ♂ blackish brown. Head and neck with black diamond-shaped cap and collar. Body contour feathers, back and flanks vermiculated with buff or white bars, breast and abdomen lighter pale grey-brown. Wings, dark brownish grey, no speculum; underwings, pale grey. Wing-spurs in some adult ♂♂. Black tail. Bill, wide and tall at base, no perforated septum, black pendant lobe below lower mandible, leathery texture, size varies with age (Gamble 1966); short legs, dark grey, set back on body, tarsi laterally compressed for swimming, large well-developed feet; iris dark brown. Pungent musky odour, presumed to originate from uropygial gland, reported from adult ♂ collected by Vancouver (1799). Subsequently postulated as sex attractant by Darwin (1871) '. . . can be detected long before the bird can be seen'. Strong odour confirmed (Gamble 1966); subtle musky odour evident in wild ♂, dissipates rapidly after capture (McCracken 1999).

♀ smaller and lighter, rudimentary pendant lobe in most, no odour (McCracken 1999).

MOULT: complete simultaneous wing moult finished Apr–Jun in post-breeding ♂, by May in ♀ (Frith 1982, Marchant and Higgins 1990); however, pre-nuptial wing and tail moult observed Sept–Nov in both sexes, suggesting complete moult twice annually (Frith 1982, McCracken 1999). In pre-breeding adult, partial replacement of body feathers, Dec in ♂, Oct–Dec in ♀ (Frith 1982, Marchant and Higgins 1990). Post-juvenile moult completed Feb– July (Frith 1982, Marchant and Higgins 1990).

IMMATURE: as adult, and increases in size over several years.

DUCKLING: head, neck, and back blackish brown; breast and abdomen off-white. Black upper mandible, light orange lower mandible. Small pendant lobe present in embryo by late stages of incubation.

MEASUREMENTS AND WEIGHT: ♂ wing ($n = 26$), 205–240 (226.3 ± 8.6); tail ($n = 27$), 91–130 (117.1 ± 9.0); culmen ($n = 29$), 37.3–42.1 (40.19 ± 1.00); tarsus ($n = 29$), 57.7–69.8 (63.05 ± 2.90); lobe length ($n = 29$), 37.7–102.4 (71.17 ± 18.18); lobe depth ($n = 29$), 11.6–99.5 (62.42 ± 21.48); lobe breadth ($n = 29$), 21.7–39.7 (31.93 ± 4.00); weight ($n = 29$), 1700–3100 (2560.2 ± 331.3) (McCracken *et al.* 2000c). Unusually high wing loading suggests that heavy ♂, not in wing moult, may be unable to fly (Phillips 1922–26, Humphrey and Livezey 1982a). ♀ wing ($n = 13$), 175–190 (183.7 ± 4.7); tail ($n = 12$), 75–110 (96.2 ± 9.4); culmen ($n = 17$), 32.7–37.0 (35.01 ± 1.23); tarsus ($n = 17$), 49.1–60.4 (53.66 ± 2.88); lobe length ($n = 6$), 31.0–36.0 (33.13 ± 1.80); lobe depth ($n = 6$), 5.0–8.0 (6.87 ± 1.22); lobe breadth ($n = 6$), 18.7–21.1 (20.22 ± 0.84); weight ($n = 17$), 1150–1910 (1560.9 ± 245.3) (McCracken *et al.* 2000c). ♀ mass increases 24% between pre-breeding and pre-laying (Briggs 1988). Nonbreeding ($n = 98$), 1346 ± 223.51; pre-breeding ($n = 144$), 1338 ± 210.6; pre-laying ($n = 21$), 1665 ± 200.60; laying ($n = 13$), 1641 ± 120.24; incubating ($n = 4$), 1397 ± 175.20; brood rearing ($n = 21$), 1223 ± 191.21 (Braithwaite and Frith 1969).

Field characters

Unmistakable; powerful, heavy-bodied, short-winged, blackish brown diving duck unlikely to be confused with any other. Adult ♂ large, 610–710 mm long, up to 3 times mass of adult ♀ at 530–580 mm long (Frith 1982, McCracken *et al.* 2000c). Large, distinctly triangular-shaped head and bill; ♂ has black lobe under base of lower mandible. Long, stiff tail, rests flat on water or cocked over back. Generally sits low in water, dives readily, reluctant to fly. Flies primarily at night; laborious take-off requires great distance; shallow, rapid wing-beats. Rarely seen on land, but adults and young walk upright with surprising agility and speed (McCracken 1999).

Voice

Described by Robinson and Robinson (1970), Fullagar and Carbonell (1986), Marchant and Higgins (1990), Johnsgard and Carbonell (1996), McCracken (1999) and McCracken *et al.* (2001a). Except for ♂ advertising calls, and begging calls of young, generally silent. No known flight or alarm calls, although live birds in hand punctuate attacks on investigators with grunts and high-pitched squeals. In captivity, adult ♂ advertising call consists of non-vocal *kerplonk* sound produced by feet with vocal *whirr* component, sharp *cuc-cuc* call, high-pitched whistle, followed by grunt. One captive hand-reared ♂ mimicked phrase 'you bloody fool' and squeaky door. Advertising calls of wild ♂ differ substantially from those of captive birds (McCracken 1999, McCracken *et al.* 2002). ♀ calls rarely heard, but wheezy grunt may be given as distress. ♀ has contact call, begging call and soft trill in presence of young (Frith 1982). Ducklings vocal, giving incessant grunt-like begging calls, also soft contact calls and distress calls similar to those of ♀.

Range and status

Endemic to southeast and southwest Australia. Queensland; widespread southeast, Fraser, Moreton, Stradbroke Island, rare in southwest. New

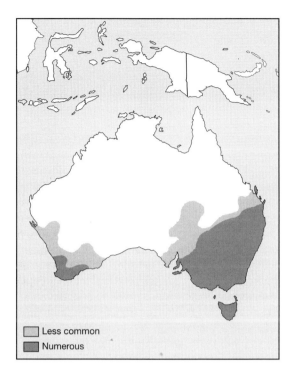

Less common
Numerous

Aerial transect surveys over 12% of eastern Australia, 1983–88, counted 334, 355, < 200, < 100, < 80, and 199 (Braithwaite *et al.* 1985a, 1985b, 1986, 1987, Kingsford *et al.* 1988, 1989).

Habitat and general habits

Almost entirely aquatic, uses terrestrial wetlands, estuaries, and protected coastal waters. Nomadic, long-distance movements undertaken to colonize ephemeral waters such as Lake Eyre (Frith 1982). Breeds in freshwater swamps, marshes, lakes, billabongs, rivers and farm dams; requires dense vegetation for nesting (Frith 1959, 1982, Lowe 1966, Brown and Brown 1981, Fjeldså 1985, Marchant and Higgins 1990), also uses coastal marine lagoons with freshwater upwellings. Birds inhabiting permanent freshwater are probably sedentary. Winter flocks form on larger bodies of water, fresh and saline lakes, reservoirs, rivers, estuaries and protected coastal waters (Frith *et al.* 1969, Corrick and Norman 1980, Gosper 1981, Jaensch *et al.* 1988, Marchant and Higgins 1990), and probably consist of juveniles and post-breeding adults dispersing from ephemeral waters. Winter areas may support small numbers of breeding birds (Lowe 1966, Marchant and Higgins 1990).

Feeds principally by diving in water up to 6 m deep; dives of short duration, 25–30 sec or less (Frith 1982, Marchant and Higgins 1990, McCracken 1999). May also take food from surface or by dredging in shallow water (McCracken 1999). Feeds day and night, generally alone, ♀ occasionally in pairs.

Diet consists of insects, crustaceans, molluscs, and plant seeds (Gamble 1966, Frith *et al.* 1969). Of 544 gizzards collected at Barrenbox Swamp, New South Wales (Gamble 1966), 98% contained animal matter and 74% plant material. Animals included crustaceans (*Cherax albidus*, *Caridina mcullochi*), molluscs (*Physastra*, *Glyptanisus, Corbiculina permena*), insects (hemipterans, odonata, trichopterans, ephemeropterans, coleopterans, dipterans), fish (*Gambusia affinis*, *Tandanus tandanus*), acarines and frogs. Seeds came from plant families Marsileaceae, Leguminosae, Ceratophyllaceae, Polygonaceae, Najadaceae, Boraginaceae, Cyperaceae, Gramineae, Compositae and Rosaceae. See also Cleland (1911), Vestjens (1977),

South Wales; widespread, Murray-Darling basin primarily (Morris *et al.* 1981, Marchant and Higgins 1990). Victoria; throughout, widespread in north and southwest. Tasmania; widespread in east, also King and Flinders Islands (Green 1977, Thomas 1979, Sharland 1981, White 1985, Marchant and Higgins 1990). South Australia; widespread in southeast, Kangaroo Island, west to Fowlers Bay, absent from west (Parker *et al.* 1985, Marchant and Higgins 1990). Western Australia; widespread in southwest, Rottnest Island, vagrant to Gasgoyne and interior (Carter 1904, Serventy and Whittell 1976, Saunders and de Rebeira 1985, Storr and Johnstone 1988, Marchant and Higgins 1990).

No continental population estimates, although population declines evident, particularly in Southeast Regional Surveys (see also Marchant and Higgins 1990). Victoria summer wetland surveys, 1987–89, counted 974, 1947, and 1546 birds on 332, 472, and 626 wetlands (Hewish 1988, Martindale 1988, Peter 1989), while southwest Australia counts, 1986–88, found 4497, 4992, and 4247 birds on 872, 1201, and 1398 wetlands (Jaensch and Vervest 1988a, 1988b).

Lubbock (1980), Barker and Vestjens (1989). Activity-time budgets and foraging dive characteristics summarized by McCracken (1999).

Displays and breeding behaviour

♂ biased sex ratio, > 20 ♂♂ per ♀ at some locations, varying with season (McCracken 1999). Promiscuous, lek-breeding system, classic arena and dispersed leks where numbers permit; no pairbond (Johnsgard 1966, 1967, Lowe 1966, Frith 1982, Marchant and Higgins 1990, Johnsgard and Carbonell 1996, McCracken 1999). Twenty or more ♂♂ and fewer ♀♀ observed at single lek (McCracken 1999). Existence of ♂ territories improbable, other resource defence strategies unlikely (McCracken 1999).

Pugnacious and belligerent. In captivity, attack and kill other birds unless separated, ♂ sometimes kills ♀ (Ogilvie 1975b), young fight and siblings killed; in hand, birds attack investigators (McCracken 1999). In wild, ♂ observed chasing other ♂♂ across water and initiating underwater attacks against both sexes (Lowe 1966, McCracken 1999); breeding ♀ hostile to intruding ♀ (Fitzgerald 1906). Alarmed birds Splash-dive; submerge quickly, producing loud splash and spray of water (Fullagar and Carbonell 1986, McCracken 1999).

♂ breeding display described for captive birds by Fullagar and Carbonell (1986); see also Marchant and Higgins (1990) and Johnsgard and Carbonell (1996). Consists of Paddle-kick, Plonk-kick, and Whistle-kick, may last 32 min, average 12–24 min. Paddle-kick, low intensity, 0.57 sec duration, accounts for 44.3% of total display activities; head and bill aimed forward, pendant lobe inflated, feathers on head and neck erected, wings folded, tail spread on water; at same time wings lifted over centre of back and feet kick sideways and backwards, quickly propelling bird forward, creating loud splash of water up to 2 m high. Plonk-kick, mid-intensity, 0.67 sec duration, accounts for 10.8% of total display activities; head and neck stretched forward with feathers erected, pendant lobe fully inflated, tail held vertically spread open. With each Plonk-kick wings lifted, tail returns to surface, no forward motion, rather ♂♂ rotate or remain stationary. Whistle-kick, high intensity, 0.57 sec duration, accounts for 44.9% of total display activi-

ties; posture similar to Plonk-kick, except tail held fully cocked against back, high-pitched whistle delivered with each kick. Paddle-kick generally precedes Plonk-kick, Plonk-kick generally precedes Whistle-kick (McCracken 1999). Breeding displays of ♂ wild birds described in McCracken et al. (2001a). Pendant lobe inflated by blood pressure (Frith 1982), no oesophageal connection. Two additional post-pelvic caudal vertebrae and well-developed *Musculus levator coccygis* enable dramatic movements of tail (Raikow 1970).

Copulation similar to that of other wildfowl, rarely observed despite extensive observation (Johnsgard 1966, Lowe 1966, Frith 1982, Fullagar and Carbonell 1986, McCracken 1999); no mutual precopulatory displays. Copulation may occur at night, apparent forced copulation attempts observed by McCracken (1999). ♂ possesses small intromittent organ (Forbes 1882b). For additional behavioural information see Lowe (1966), Johnsgard (1966, 1978), Frith (1982), Fullagar and Carbonell (1986), Marchant and Higgins (1990), and Johnsgard and Carbonell (1996).

Breeding and life cycle

♂ display and testes increase in size from Apr, peaks Sept–Oct, testes smallest in Jan–Feb; oocyte development generally coincides with testis cycle, minimum diameter Jan–Feb, maximum oocyte diameter Jul–Aug (Gamble 1966). Egg-laying Jun–Dec, usually Sept–Oct (Frith 1982, Braithwaite and Frith 1969, McCracken et al. 2000a). Nests in dense vegetation over water, *Typha*, reeds, rushes, *Muehlenbeckia cunninghami*, tea-tree branches or hollow logs (Marchant and Higgins 1990). At Murray Lagoon, South Australia, large number of nests ($n = 35$) in flooded Coast Saw-sedge *Gahnia trifida*; water depth 27.1 ± 9.4 (4–42); height above water 32.1 ± 12.4 (16–78); outer diameter 38.4 ± 5.0 (27–51); inner diameter 21.2 ± 3.0 (16–27) (McCracken et al. 2000a). Well-developed hood conceals top of nest, and one or more ramps lead to nest bowl, lined with light grey down after clutch completion (McCracken et al. 2000a). Eggs relatively large, elliptical, thick-shelled, somewhat pointed at both ends, and pale greenish white or buff; 83.73 ± 3.82 × 53.8 ± 1.71 (74.0–91.1 × 48.5–59.0) ($n = $ 130) (McCracken *et al.* 2000a); weight 117 (*n* = 3) (Hindwood 1971) or, calculated from dimensions of 27, 128 (Schönwetter 1960–66). Clutch 3.7 ± 1.8 (1–9) (*n* = 31), no successful clutches larger than 6; larger clutches probably dump nests (McCracken *et al.* 2000a). Inter-specific nest parasitism fairly common; Musk Duck eggs found in nests of Dusky Moorhen *Gallinula fenebrosa*, Blue-billed Duck, Pink-eared Duck, Grey Teal, Pacific Black Duck and Hardhead (Attiwill *et al.* 1981); Bluebill eggs also found in nest of Musk Duck (McCracken *et al.* 2000a). Incubation, by ♀ 24 days in captivity (Marchant and Higgins 1990). Newly hatched young measure length, 171.7 (165–180); culmen, 15.37 (14.7–16.2); tarsus, 25.03 (22.2–29.5); lobe length, 12.50 (10.7–13.8) and weigh 81.7 (80.0–85.0) (*n* = 3). Egg success 2.8 ± 1.2 (2–5) (*n* = 6 clutches) (McCracken *et al.* 2000a). Brood size appears to decline with age, rarely more than one in older broods (Braithwaite and Frith 1969, McCracken 1999). Kear (1970) suggested that brood often reduced to single duckling because dominance hierarchy occurs in which one offspring receives most food.

Young fed by ♀ (Brown and Brown 1997, McCracken 1999); 1460 g ♂ reported still being fed by ♀. Young ride on back of ♀ and may cling to neck when she dives to escape danger. Fledgling period, growth rates and age at first breeding unknown (Marchant and Higgins 1990). Probably does not reach sexual maturity in 1st year.

Conservation and threats

Loss of breeding habitat, caused by agricultural practices, drainage, grazing, burning, increased salinity and inundation due to clearing, main threats (Riggert 1966, Corrick and Norman 1980, Corrick 1981, 1982, Jaensch *et al.* 1988, Marchant and Higgins 1990). Destructive impacts of European Carp *Cyprinus carpio* introductions in river systems, especially in southeast, also may be a problem. Birds occasionally drown in fishing nets. Popular smoked food in Western Australia in 1890s (Serventy and Whittell 1976). Presently protected from hunting, but no management plan yet proposed.

Kevin McCracken

The swans

The swans' nearest relatives are the grazing geese with whom they share a number of behavioural features including a well-developed family life and a firm pairbond between male and female. Swans and geese are therefore classified together in the same subfamily; both are considerably larger than ducks. Whereas geese are confined to the grasslands of the northern hemisphere, swans are more widespread and found in many lowland fresh waters, being rare only in the tropics and absent entirely from equatorial and southern Africa.

Differences between swans and geese are mostly matters of degree—a relatively larger foot or longer neck—but all swans are larger than geese, and, except for the Coscoroba Swan of South America, the adult birds have bare, unfeathered skin between the eyes and the bill. They incubate their eggs for longer (the Black Swan of Australia for 36–40 days), take longer to mature to the flying stage and seldom

breed until they are three years old, while geese lay readily at two years. The male swan helps build the nest, something that only the male Cape Barren Goose does among geese. Swans also provide food for their newly hatched young by plucking underwater or overhead vegetation, and by foot-paddling to raise edible items to the surface. They fly, as do geese, in diagonal lines or V formation.

Of the eight swans, the Trumpeter, Whooper, Whistling and Bewick's Swans are clearly more closely related than the rest; indeed, the Whistling and Bewick's Swans are usually treated as races of the Tundra Swan. These are the so-called northern swans of Europe, Asia and North America; all are white when adult and have black or yellow-and-black bills with no bill knobs. They are migratory, highly territorial when nesting, yet gregarious in winter, and have loud voices. The Whooper Swan's counterpart in North America—the Trumpeter—is the rarest; it is larger and has a similarly flat profile to its head. The Whooper, Bewick's, and semi-domesticated Mute Swan of Eurasia sometimes winter together and may be difficult to tell apart at a distance; indeed, the Bewick's Swan was only generally recognized to be different from the Whooper after a description was published in the *Journal of the Linnean Society*, written by London businessman William Yarrell, in 1830.

Janet Kear

Taxonomy

The tribe Cygnini consists of two genera *Cygnus* and *Coscoroba*, although a third, *Olor*, is erected sometimes to separate the northern swans (Woolfenden 1960, Livezey 1986a, Harshman 1996), but was reduced to a subgenus by Livezey (1996b) (Figure 9.3). Following Livezey's (1986a) suggestion that *Cygnopterus* deserves familial rank between Anseranatidae and Dendrocygnidae, the earliest fossils assigned to Cygnini are *Cygnavus formosa* (collected from early Oligocene beds in Russia) and *Guguschia nailiae* (of the

Oligocene of Azerbaijan) (Cheneval 1987, Bickart 1990); however, both appear to be distinct from modern swans, and Bickart (1990) concluded that the earliest swans referable to Cygnini are from the late Miocene of North America *Cygnus mariae* and *Paracygnus plattensis*. All fossil swans, with the exception of *Cygnus sumnerensis* from New Zealand, are from the northern hemisphere (Brodkorb 1964). Holocene species diversity is also clearly highest in the northern temperate region, particularly in the Palearctic (Figure 9.3). However, Livezey (1996b) argued that the tribe had its origins in the southern hemisphere on the basis that the oldest swans occur in the south, Coscoroba, Black and Black-necked Swans, plus the extinct *C. sumnerensis*.

Swans feed by grazing on submergent plants and also frequently use terrestrial vegetation. The sexes are alike and their plumage lacks any metallic sheen. They have protracted monogamous pairbonds, male participation in nest building and paternal attendance on broods (Delacour 1954–64, Kear 1970b, Johnsgard 1965a, 1978, Scott and Clutton-Brock 1989,

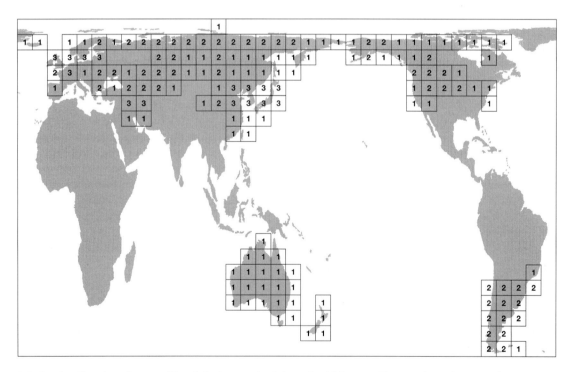

9.3 Species diversity of swans (Cygnini) that survived into the Holocene. The number of species that occur (or occurred) within each grid-cell is indicated.

Livezey 1996b). They also possess, as do geese, a ritualized Triumph Ceremony performed by mated pairs after territorial encounters (Johnsgard 1961a, 1962, 1965a, Livezey 1996b).

The relationship of the Coscoroba Swan, in particular, has been a subject of debate. Based primarily on sexual behaviour, Johnsgard (1960b) suggested that it was a link between the true geese (Anserini) and whistling-ducks (Dendrocygnini); the shape of the head and bill, the feathering between the eyes and the bill, and the markings of the cygnets are all fairly similar to whistling-ducks', although the white plumage and long neck are reminiscent of swans. Other studies, including behavioural (Johnsgard 1978), molecular (Tyler 1964, Brush 1976) and morphological (Woolfenden 1961, Livezey 1986a, 1996b, 1997b), support a close relationship between *Coscoroba* and the other swans, with the former invariably considered older. Immunological and mitochondrial srRNA analyses indicated an early split from the ancestral swan/goose lineage (Bottjer 1983, Zimmer *et al.* 1994). Further molecular analysis (sequencing mitochondrial cytochrome *b* gene and control region) suggested its position as a sister species to the Cape Barren Goose (Harshman 1996, Harvey 1999, Donne-Goussé *et al.* 2002) and agreed with Zimmer *et al.* (1994) in removing *Coscoroba* from a close relationship with swans. Livezey (1996b), after morphological analysis, proposed a sister relationship between Black-necked and Black Swans, which he put in a subgenus of austral swans called *Chenopsis*. Molecular studies were contradictory. Harvey (1999) grouped the Black Swan as the sister of other *Cygnus* swans, while Harshman (1996), using longer sequences but fewer species, agreed with Livezey's grouping. Studies also disagreed about the relationships of the Mute Swan, with Livezey (1996b) and Harvey (1999) making it the sister of the northern swans, while Harshman (1996) placed it as sister to the two austral swans.

There has been disagreement also about the relationship between the four northern migratory swans. The Whooper Swan is sometimes classified as conspecific with the Trumpeter Swan (Delacour 1954–64, Johnsgard 1974), although subsequent assessment of morphological characters suggested that it is most closely related to the Eurasian Bewick's Swan (Livezey 1996b). Whistling and Bewick's Swans are known to interbreed in the wild (Evans and Sladen 1980), and molecular studies of the commonly sequenced cytochrome *b* gene have confirmed the difficulties of resolving relationships, probably because the four lineages separated at about the same time, with interbreeding between Bewick's and Whistling Swans indicating that speciation is still underway (Harvey 1999). Whistling Swans have also bred with Trumpeter and Whooper Swans (Gray 1958) in captivity, and the hybrid offspring are sometimes known to be fertile.

Des Callaghan, Eileen Rees and
John Harshman

Coscoroba Swan *Coscoroba coscoroba*
PLATE 4

Anas Coscoroba Molina, 1782, Saggio Storia Nat. Chili, pp. 234, 344
Chile
Coscoroba Reichenbach, 1853
    Etymology: Chilean name, derived from bird's call.
    Other names: none in English. Portuguese: Capororoca; Spanish: Coscoroba, Cisne blanco, Ganso blanco.
    Variation: no subspecies.

Description

ADULT: sexes alike, ♂ larger than ♀. Plumage white except for black tips to primaries. Rounded head shape with feathering extending well beyond eye to cover face, as in whistling-ducks. Wings short and broad compared with northern migratory swans; tail also short and rounded (Delacour 1954–64). Bill bright red, spatulate and up-turned, without any basal knob, nail pale pink; legs long and sturdy, legs and feet reddish pink; iris dark brown.

MOULT: assumed to have one moult of body and wing feathers annually. Captive adults in northern hemisphere (*c* 52° N) moult flight feathers late July–Aug. In southern Brazil, most moulters noted Aug–Nov (Nascimento *et al.* 2001). A few adults without broods moulted Jan, and some parents with broods moulted Oct and Jan in central Chile (Silva-Garcia 2003). In southern Chile, Vuilleumier (1997) reported some moulting birds late Apr. Duration of flightless period for individual birds unknown.

IMMATURE: develops white adult plumage by 8 months, except for some grey-brown flecking of feathers on top of head, back or wings. Mottled plumage on fledging reminiscent of patterning of cygnet. Body feathers mainly lighter than other swans of same age but with grey-brown patches on neck and back; black on head and around eye. Blue-grey bill becomes red by 5 months, but may remain duller than in adult.

CYGNET: mainly greyish white but, unlike all other swans, with dark patterning on crown, back and wings. Bill grey, pink at tip; feet pale pink tinged grey.

MEASUREMENTS AND WEIGHT: ♂ wing ($n = 5$), 440–498 (465); skull length ($n = 4$), 131.7–138.3 (135.8); tarsus ($n = 5$), 89.0–108.7 (97.9); weight ($n = 3$), 3.8–5.4 (4.5). ♀ wing ($n = 9$), 415–477 (445); skull length ($n = 7$), 122.1–136.0 (129.3); tarsus ($n = 10$), 87.6–99.2 (92.6); weight ($n = 4$) 3.1–4.5 (3.6) (Scott 1972, WWT data). In southern Brazil, ♂ wing ($n = 5$), 375–390 (381); culmen ($n = 26$), 63.3–74.0 (70.1); tarsus ($n = 26$) 98.5–126.0 (110.2). ♀ wing ($n = 4$), 350–358 (354.5); culmen ($n = 92$), 53.0–73.0 (66.2); tarsus ($n = 93$), 84.0–127.5 (102.7) (Nascimento *et al.* 2001).

Field characters

Smallest swan, 900–1150 mm long, with relatively short neck. Distinguished from Black-necked Swan (only other swan in Neotropics), and from sheldgeese, by white plumage (except black wing-tips) and rounded head with duck-shaped bill. Neck longer than sheldgeese, and shorter than Black-necked Swan. Call diagnostic.

Voice

Idiosyncratic *cos-cor-oo*, usually given when threatening intruders. Also monosyllabic hooting note used in contact between paired birds, often uttered by ♂ and ♀ alternately. Notes similar in ♂ and ♀, but noticeably higher-pitched in ♂ (Boyd *in* Scott

1972). In other swans, ♀ tends to have higher voice. Immatures give loud chirping calls and trills when approached by parents.

Range and status

Native to South America; range overlaps that of Black-necked Swan, but has slightly more southerly and patchier distribution. Seems to prefer coastal areas. Occurs in Tierra del Fuego and Falkland Islands north through Chile and Argentina to Paraguay, Uruguay and southern Brazil (Ogilvie *in* Scott 1972). Breeds in southern parts of Argentina and Chile, from Tierra del Fuego to *c* 33° S in Chile in west (breeding range on Pacific coast expanded northwards in recent years, Vilina 1994), and to Paraguay and southeast Brazil in east (Woods 1975). Pair with 3 small cygnets seen at Mare Harbour, Falkland Islands, May 1860 (Abbot 1861, Woods 1988, Woods and Woods 1997); influx of *c* 25 birds in Nov 1998, recorded as singles or groups at several locations, resulted in pair remaining on Pebble Island which, *c* 20 Oct 2000, laid and subsequently hatched 6 eggs of which 4 fledged (White and Henry 2001). In southern part of range, mainly migratory, moving to lower latitudes during austral fall (to *c* 25° S), although those in Magellanic region considered permanent residents (Venegas and Jory 1979). Northwestern Isla Grande (Tierra del Fuego), for instance, important wintering area (Fjeldså and Krabbe 1990), but not found in other parts of that island (Delacour 1954–64, Humphrey *et al.* 1970). More northerly birds tend to be sedentary. Marked movement, with Black-necked Swans, into Uruguay in 1988–89, plus increased mortality, attributed to drought. Most birds seen moving into Uruguay apparently arrived from Argentina (Vaz-Ferreira and Rilla 1991). Otherwise, little known of migratory routes.

Considered rare winter visitor to Chile in early part of 20th century (Hellmayr 1932). Several hundred now in southern and central Chile, and also widespread in Argentina, although distribution tends to be patchy and localized. Up to 500, including breeding pairs, occur in southeast Uruguay, where regularly found in mixed flocks with Black-necked Swans (Vaz-Ferreira and Rilla 1991). Coordinated census of 40 sites in Argentina and

Krabbe 1990). Does not up-end as often as other swans, since fine serrations lining broad bill adapted for straining particles from water surface. Normally feeds on submerged aquatic vegetation and aquatic invertebrates whilst dabbling or wading in shallows, and also comes ashore to graze on waterside pasture, since relatively long legs and upright stance makes walking on land relatively easy (Madge and Burn 1988). Diet and food selection not studied in detail. Birds feeding along coast thought to ingest marine invertebrates (Todd 1996), and young cygnets seen picking insects off water surface. Also flies more easily than other swans, rising directly from land or water (Delacour 1954–64).

Displays and breeding behaviour

Highly territorial during breeding season, and some pairs maintain territories throughout year in water bodies with permanent water levels in central Chile (Silva-Garcia 2003). Aggressive birds (of either sex) call and advance, raising primaries and secondaries of folded wings, in manner reminiscent of threat display of other swans. In this posture, both sexes may advance towards intruder with head down and neck bent, moving head slowly out and back. Adults flap wings with body raised from water after some aggressive encounters. Adults repeatedly chase younger birds from territory, skittering across water in pursuit (Weller 1967b), although captive ♂♂ may tolerate own young even into 2nd nesting season (Griswold 1973) and young rarely chased away in central Chile. When juveniles approached by aggressive parents, give loud chirping call and display dark spot on forehead in apparent appeasement display. No Triumph display between pair members following aggressive encounters except, perhaps, for *Cos-cor-oo* call which may be uttered by ♂ and ♀ alternately.

Pre-copulatory display simply Head-dipping or Bill-dipping by ♂ or both sexes, after which he flies on to her back and grasps nape with bill. Unlike other swans, copulates while standing in shallow water, rather than while swimming. After mating, both stretch head and neck vertically and call, and ♂ or both sexes raise closed wings (Johnsgard 1965a). Three forced extra-pair copulation attempts seen when ♂♂

Uruguay, which included Laguna Blanca and Laguna Mar Chiquita wetlands in Argentina and Laguna Rocha in Uruguay, found 4036 in late May–early June 1998 (Seijas 1999). Population estimated at < 25 000 birds, and thought to be stable (Rose and Scott 1997, Wetlands International 2002).

Habitat and general habits

Less gregarious than Black-necked Swan, but flocks of up to 400 individuals recorded at coastal lagoon in southern Uruguay (Vaz-Ferreira and Rilla 1991), and some 15 000 seen on single marsh in Mendoza Province of Argentina Apr 1990 (Todd 1996). Vuilleumier (1997) noted 1000–2000 offshore from Puerto Natales in southern Chile in late autumn (Apr). Inhabits shallow lagoons, lakes and freshwater marshes with abundant vegetation (Fjeldså and Krabbe 1990). Occurs mainly at lowland sites, but may be found on lakes and pools up to 1000 m (including some nesting pairs) in Andean foothills of Santa Cruz, Argentina (Fjeldså and grasped and mounted unaccompanied paired ($n = 2$) or unpaired ($n = 1$) ♀♀ in their territories.

Breeding and life cycle

Breeding season, June–Dec in wild, is *c* one month earlier than Black-necked Swan, although precise timing varies with location. In northern hemisphere (*c* 52°N), captives conversely breed *c* one month later than Black-necked Swan, usually laying 1st eggs mid-March. Nest building mainly by ♂, up to month before laying (Todd 1996) although in central Chile ♂ and ♀ spent similar proportion of time building (Silva-Garcia 2003). Nests cone-shaped and (unlike nests of other swans) well lined with down; usually situated close to water, at edge of lakes or ponds, on small islands or in marshes, sometimes on floating mass of aquatic vegetation. Breeding density quite high in prime habitats, with nests as little as 18 m (Gibson 1920, Weller 1967b) and 10 m (Silva-Garcia 2003) apart. Territory size in central Chile *c* 0.25– 7.00 ha ($n = 38$). Found nesting in Black-necked Swan colony at Llancanelo reserve, Mendoza, Argentina (Darrieu *et al.* 1989).

Onset of laying mainly June–July, although Darrieu *et al.* (1989) reported pairs sitting on nests at Llancanelo in Sept and Dec. In southeastern Brazil, laying commences July–Aug (Nascimento *et al.* 2001), in central Chile Aug–Nov for 1st broods. Second nesting in central Chile ($n = 2$) initiated when 1st broods 40–50 days old in Oct, cared for by ♂ while ♀ incubated (Brewer and Vilina 2002). Reported to double-brood regularly in southeastern Brazil (Wilmore 1979). Few young hatched Feb also noted in central Chile. Eggs smaller and more rounded than other swans', matt white when fresh, becoming stained during incubation (Delacour 1954–64); 89.2 × 60.4 (82.0–94.5 × 52.9–67.0) ($n = 50$); weight in captivity 167.3 ($n = 43$); clutch 5–9 eggs, with mode of 7 (Scott 1972). Incubation normally 35 days, similar to Black, Black-necked and Mute Swans; arctic-nesting swans have slightly shorter incubation periods (Kear 1972). ♀ incubates while ♂ guards territory, and offspring remain with both parents until fledging, with some family groups persisting for at least another month (up to 8–12 months in central Chile). Cygnets brooded on land, occasionally on old nest, and not carried on parents' back, probably because of adults' relatively short wings. Grow slowly, taking up to 8 months to reach adult size, although fly earlier (Todd 1996), captive-reared cygnets fledging at *c* 14 weeks, and wild cygnets able to fly at 13 weeks. No data on hatching success in wild. Mean brood size 5.32 (1–10) ($n = 41$) in central Chile, with one brood amalgamation noted (Silva-Garcia 2003). Newly hatched broods at risk of predation by Kelp (Southern Black-backed) Gulls *Larus dominicanus*.

Normal age of 1st breeding uncertain, although captive ♂ and ♀ bred at 3 years and, exceptionally, at one year (Kojima 1978). Pairs monogamous and pairbond seems long-term. Average life expectancy in captivity 7.3 years, with some individuals reaching 20 years. Annual survival and longevity in wild unknown.

Conservation and threats

Historically, little evidence of extensive exploitation; not highly sought after as gamebird and, although sometimes shot, hunting does not appear intense (Todd 1996). Patchy distribution makes for vulnerability to habitat loss, particularly since biology underlying distribution poorly understood. Listed as Endangered for Chile as whole, Endangered and Threatened in central and southern Chile (Glade 1993) and as insufficiently known and probably in danger of extinction in Brazil (Bernardes *et al.* 1990). Large concentrations in Magellanic region of southern Chile suggest area particularly important in winter (Vuilleumier 1997). Although entire population not thought to be declining, needs extensive internationally coordinated counts to assess distribution and population levels, and to determine factors influencing site selection.

Eileen Rees and Gwenda L. Brewer

Black Swan *Cygnus atratus*

PLATE 4

Anas atrata Latham, 1790, Index Ornith., p. 834
lakes of Australia
Cygnus Bechstein, 1803

Etymology: *atratus* L. for clothed in mourning, i.e. black.

Other names: none in common use. Australian Aboriginal: Coolecha, Gunawar, plus > 30 others listed in Marchant and Higgins (1990).

Variation: no subspecies, and no geographical variation. Has hybridized with Mute Swans in captivity, but offspring appear infertile.

Description

ADULT: sexes alike, but ♂ generally larger, heavier and longer-necked than ♀. Almost completely sooty black with slightly greyer fringes to body and wing feathers, especially above. Primaries, outer secondaries and alula white, strikingly in contrast with rest of plumage in flight but concealed when on water. Remarkable crinkled edges to inner wing coverts and tertials. White-banded red bill; black legs and feet; eye red.

MOULT: one body and wing moult annually. Moulting can occur at any time of year but non-breeders tend to moult towards end of nesting season, before breeders.

IMMATURE: greyer with dusky-tipped flight feathers and greyish bill. Eye brown.

CYGNET: light brownish grey, rather darker on back. Bill nearly black with light grey tip; lateral feathering on bill curves back towards eyes and lores unfeathered. Feet dark grey tinged brown (Nelson 1976b).

MEASUREMENTS AND WEIGHT: ♂ wing ($n = 111$), 425–550 (511.7); tarsus ($n = 111$), 82.3–113.6 (100.3). ♀ wing ($n = 76$), 440–530 (487.5); tarsus ($n = 76$), 86.6–102.7 (93.4). Weight in Australia ♂ ($n = 247$), 4600–8750 (6270); ♀ ($n = 219$), 3700–7200 (5100); in New Zealand ♂ ($n = 111$), 3800–7700 (6093); ♀ ($n = 76$), 3900–6900 (5090) (Marchant and Higgins 1990).

Field characters

Unmistakable; long gracefully curving neck, and only largely all black swan, 1150–1400 mm long. Striking white primaries and crinkled edges to wing feathers. Juveniles greyer but still much darker than young Mute Swans, only other swan to occur within range. Magpie Goose also pied in flight but pattern reversed, with white abdomen and under-wing coverts and black remiges.

Voice

Large vocabulary. Adult call soft, musical high-pitched bugling (sonogram in Marchant and Higgins 1990), uttered both in flight and on water, which probably functions as contact call. Conversational notes and whistles used between birds on water, and loud hisses when defending nest or young. Wings produce whistling sound in flight.

Cygnets' calls consist of series of cheeps, louder for family greetings, slower, more regular and higher pitched when in distress, loud and high-pitched shriek when alarmed, and trilling sleepy call when tired.

Range and status

Unique to Australasia. Widespread across western part of Western Australia, east and southeast Australia, and Tasmania. Disperses across whole of continent but rare in central regions and north; vagrant to Lord Howe and Norfolk Islands, occasionally reaches southern Papua New Guinea and Irian Jaya (Beehler 1980, Parry 1989). Breeds widely through main range wherever and whenever conditions suitable, but particularly common in south and east New South Wales, Victoria, Tasmania, southeast South Australia and southern Western Australia. Blakers *et al.* (1984) claimed that range expanded northwards since 1951, but this may reflect improved recording and/or vagaries of dry and wet weather (Marchant and Higgins 1990). Introduced to New Zealand 1864–68, increased rapidly, possibly with wild birds arriving at same time, widespread and common on both islands by 1900. Spectacular concentration in

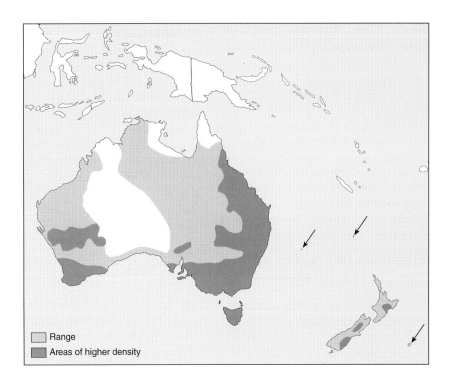

Range
Areas of higher density

1960s of *c* 70 000 at Lake Ellesmere, brackish coastal lagoon on South Island, until storm in 1968 uprooted aquatic vegetation, causing food shortage, breeding failure and serious long-term decline in numbers (Williams 1979). Reached Chatham Island by 1865 and well established before 1922. Wandering escapees from collections not infrequent in western Europe; has bred in wild in UK, and individuals even reach Iceland.

Annual indices of abundance from aerial transects in eastern Australian wetlands 1983–88 ranged 13 800 to 156 000 (Marchant and Higgins 1990); see also Kingsford *et al.* (2000). Some 60 000 in New Zealand plus 3000 on Chatham Island in 1980 (Williams 1981a). New Zealand 1995 estimate of 35 000.

Habitat and general habits

Widespread in temperate and tropical terrestrial wetlands, sheltered estuarine and maritime habitats. Breeds in fresh, brackish or saline (but not tidal) wetlands with enough soft vegetation for nest building and feeding young, islands or tall vegetation for security, shelter and support for nests and open water for feeding (Marchant and Higgins 1990). Readily exploits ephemeral wetlands; during periods of widespread flooding, nests in any shallow water collected in depressions, swamps, pastures or even roadside drains (Frith 1982). Outside breeding season also found on flooded agricultural land, coastal lagoons, estuaries and sheltered bays, wherever aquatic plants, emergent vegetation or soft terrestrial herbage can be reached. Dry ground avoided (Briggs 1979). Can tolerate salinities from fresh to hypersaline, although usually limited in Australia to threshold of tolerance of aquatic food plants *Ruppia* and *Lepilaena* (Corrick 1982). In New Zealand, *Zostera* exclusive food of moulting pre- and nonbreeders at large estuarine and marine sites in summer, and also taken in winter in some regions when wetland water levels high. Gregarious; huge concentrations, reaching tens of thousands, seek safety of large open water bodies during moult. Adults sedentary in permanently suitable habitat, but young and adults from ephemeral habitats nomadic, dispersing widely. Young birds gather regularly in flocks after breeding season. Movements not clearly understood, but probably connected with search for new breeding areas following local rains, although counts in southeast Queensland showed no correlations with environmental variables (Marchant and Higgins 1990). Congregates on permanent water during drought (White 1987). Birds banded in southeast New South Wales dispersed widely through southeast Australia, reaching South Australia and Tasmania (Frith 1982). Birds banded at Lake Whangape in New Zealand were mostly recovered within 50 km of lake, but there was also interchange between North and South Islands, especially by pre-breeders at estuarine moulting sites (Williams 1977).

Feeds primarily in shallow water by submerging head and neck, also dabbles, up-ends in deeper water and grazes on wet pastures. Almost entirely herbivorous, taking leaves and shoots of aquatic plants; can also subsist on agriculture. Winter populations in New Zealand lakes directly correlated with winter biomass of submerged aquatic macrophytes (Mitchell *et al.* 1988, McKinnon and Mitchell 1994). Contribution of faecal phosphorus to nutrient dynamics of shallow lake in New Zealand slight (Mitchell and Wass 1995). Detailed studies of diet at Barrenbox Swamp, New South Wales (Frith *et al.* 1969) and Queensland (Lavery 1967b, 1971a) showed plants taken included *Vallisneria americana*, *Potamogeton* (55% of volume of gizzard contents in Queensland), *Typha*, *Azolla*, *Chara* and *Chlorophyta*. In New South Wales, *Azolla* particularly important autumn and winter food, but proportions of deep water and pasture plants varied with swamp levels. Less than 1% animal matter in diet, including aquatic insects, crustaceans and molluscs, probably ingested by accident. At Lake Ellesmere, took mostly *Ruppia megacarpa* with *Myriophyllum* and *Potamogeton* (Adams 1971), but now grazes on pasture grasses (Williams 1979); at Lake Whangape *Egeria densa* dominated diet but *Glyceria*, *Ranunculus*, *Potamogeton*, *Juncus* and pasture grasses also taken. Reported to take small flounders (Wilson 1957). Cygnet diet dominated by floating seeds since unable to reach deep food (Lavery 1967b); adults seen to pull down young willow leaves for cygnets (Bloomfield and Black 1963).

Found in pairs, family parties or very large flocks throughout year. In New Zealand, *c* one in 5 pairs attempts nesting in any year. Families may move as unit after breeding (Marchant and Higgins 1990). Wide range of social behaviours shown. Birds trumpet to one another in contact, and use black-and-white plumage to signal interactions including take-off when alarmed. In colonies, pilfer nest material, often destroying nests; eggs scattered from destroyed nests scraped into own nests by neighbouring swans and incubated (Miers and Williams 1969).

Aggression common in flocks and increases with flock size (Tingay 1974). Nonbreeders exhibit threats, Wing-lifting and Pecking, the latter rare except when high flock density.

Generally monogamous in captivity with some promiscuity, but pairing arrangements flexible. Sustained monogamy in wild (Frith 1982), although banding suggests pairing associations vary as in captivity. Flexible social relations may be advantageous in allowing broader use of environmental situations. First-time breeders may pair only temporarily, either sex may desert partner after laying and usually mate again to rear another brood; in this way ♀♀ occasionally lay up to 4 clutches a year. In New Zealand, divorce among territorial, solitary pairs appears rare and change of mate normally follows death of partner (Williams 1981a). Age at which attain sexual maturity and breed varies between populations, but normally 18–24 or 33–36 months and within 1–2 years of attaining adult plumage. Estimated annual survival rates of adults in New Zealand $0.84 \pm 0.03\%$ with no apparent difference between sexes, although varies through time (Barker and Buchanan 1993).

Displays and breeding behaviour

White plumage of wings appears important in display which includes Wing-lifting, Pecking, Parading, and Trumpeting (Tingay 1974). Significant difference between sexes in amount of white plumage on wings may be factor in recognition and display (Braithwaite 1981). Crinkled wing coverts and tertials may also figure in display. ♂♂ of adjacent territories Parade, by approaching to within 1 m of one another on boundary, wings lifted and bills pointing down; may touch breast to breast and head to head, and swim back and forth along boundary either keeping breasts together or turning backs and swimming back along border. May last 10 min, interrupted by Pecking, beating of wings and, more rarely, actual fighting (Marchant and Higgins 1990). Pairing arises out of aggressive behaviour, ♀ usually Inciting ♂ (e.g. by Trumpeting) to Parade towards or Chase ♂ rival. When rival repelled,

♂ faces ♀ and Greet, in which ♂ lifts wings and calls whilst extending neck and Chin-lifting (Kear 1972). At end of display, ♂ gives 2–3 rapid wing-beats that expose white primaries. Pairbond reinforced by repetition and tempo increases, evolving into Triumph Ceremony, used for pair-maintenance by established couples. By contrast, first-time breeders perform Greeting less often and with less vigour. Individual recognition by calls. Prior to copulation, pairs display for up to 25 min by ducking, usually in deep water close to nest site; neck and body parallel to surface with brief immersions of head, neck and body, repeated rapidly with short breaks, wings held close. Head-dipping noted as pre-copulatory display (Johnsgard 1965a), treading effected when ♀ outstretched and immobile, often after manoeuvring beneath ♂. Post-copulatory display may include Greeting or Triumph Ceremony, Bill-dipping and Parade, or Chase if other birds nearby. ♂ homosexual pairs not infrequent; indulge in Greeting Ceremony, extended pre-copulatory display and mounting.

Breeding and life cycle

Nesting recorded in all months, and breeding season varies according to local conditions, normally June–Aug in Western Australia and Feb–May in northeast Queensland (Lavery 1967b). Breeding influenced by photoperiodic and, more importantly, nutritional factors (Braithwaite and Frith 1969). Nests in colonies and solitarily, depending on habitat, usually close to water on small islands or in fringe vegetation. In colonies, nests located just outside pecking range of neighbours. Eggs elliptical, slightly glossy pale green to dull greenish white, becoming stained and scratched; 105.0×67.3 ($95–117 \times 60–72$) ($n = 1555$); weight 264 (200–320) ($n = 123$) (Braithwaite 1977). Second laid egg largest on average. Clutch c 5 eggs (Marchant and Higgins 1990) but varies with location and date (Braithwaite 1977). Mean clutch size in Tasmania highest during years of poor breeding, since only experienced breeders lay (Guiler 1970). Mean clutch at Lake Ellesmere declined steadily 1975–79 from 5.0 to 4.0 as habitat deteriorated (Williams 1979). No evidence for smaller clutch size at lower latitudes (Frith 1982). Eggs laid at intervals of 1–2 and 2–3 days in Australia, added daily in New Zealand colonies where laying

highly synchronized: rarely more than 3 weeks between 1st and last eggs. Only swan in which ♂ incubates to any extent; may indulge in elaborate nest relief ceremonies. Incubation during day shared in 3–4 h shifts, mainly by ♀ at night. ♂ spends more time incubating than ♀. Incubation effort of ♀ limits reproductive output of pair by lengthening interval between end of incubation and laying of 2nd clutch (Brugger and Taborsky 1993). By taking greater share of incubation, ♂ may increase productivity of ♀ and thereby own reproductive success. ♂ incubation may ultimately result from combination of monogamous mating system and capacity to breed whenever environmental conditions favourable (Brugger and Taborsky 1993). Prolactin concentrations high in both ♂ and ♀ during incubation (Goldsmith 1982). Incubation period in New Zealand 36.4 (32 43) ($n = 495$) (Miers and Williams 1969), and in Australia 40.5 (35–48) ($n = 89$) days, but significantly different seasonally (longer in winter than in summer) possibly due to ambient temperatures (Braithwaite 1977). Hatching somewhat asynchronous, within 24–48 h (Frith 1982). Young brooded in nest for < 24 h, then led to water. Feed within 24 h of hatching and imprinted on parents and surroundings within 48 h. In solitary pairs, both parents attend and guard young. Amalgamation of broods of varying age occurs in colonies where food patchily distributed and many broods feed within small area. Where food more evenly distributed, colonial nesters seem to rear in family groups. Fledge in 95–140 days in New Zealand according to availability of food. Cygnets remain associated with parents, and amalgamations do not disband until near end of fledging period.

Conservation and threats

Protected by law and sentiment in Australia (Madge and Burn 1988). Reservoirs, farm dams and irrigated crops provide additional feeding habitat but many densely vegetated wetlands affected by drainage, clearing, grazing and burning (Marchant and Higgins 1990). In agricultural areas, manipulation of water levels causes loss of nests by flooding (Tingay *et al.* 1977). Eutrophication of wetlands reduces macrophyte foods (McKinnon and Mitchell 1994), thus driving birds onto pasture where conflict with farmers creates demands for lowering of population in New Zealand (Williams 1981b). There is short hunting season in Victoria and Tasmania because of crop damage caused by large concentrations. Regarded as minor gamebird in New Zealand with 6–8% of population shot annually in 1970s (Williams 1981b); now hunted on considerably smaller scale. Number on Lake Ellesmere so large prior to 1968 that commercial egg-collecting and organized shooting undertaken as control measures. Shooting over nesting areas in Tasmania had adverse effect on breeding, upsetting pair formation; subsequent restriction of shooting resulted in greater cygnet production (Guiler 1966). Reconstruction and raising of favoured breeding islands suggested to improve breeding success by reducing effects of flooding and destruction of habitat by nesting birds (Guiler 1966).

John Bowler

Black-necked Swan *Cygnus melanocoryphus*
PLATE 4

Anas Melancoripha Molina, 1782, Saggio Storia Nat. Chili, pp. 234 (*Melancoripha*), 344 (*Melanocorypha*) Chile

Etymology: *melanocoryphus* Gr. *melanos* black, plus *koruphe* the head.

Other names: none in English. Spanish: Cisne cuello negro.

Variation: no subspecies and no known geographical variation. Hybridization with other swans or geese not recorded.

Description

ADULT: sexes alike, although ♂ generally larger than ♀. Long narrow body and pointed tail; wings relatively short. Black head and neck, from which the bird derives name, form striking contrast to white body. White feathering in black plumage forms eyebrow from above eye towards back of head. Ring of white around eye of some individuals. Bill slate-grey, spatulate-shaped, with pale pink nail, extensive frontal-lobed scarlet-pink caruncle at base of bill of both sexes; pale flesh-coloured legs and feet, legs set well back on body increases swimming efficiency but makes birds clumsy on land (Todd 1979).

MOULT: adults moult flight feathers Aug–Dec in wild or June–Aug in northern hemisphere collections at 52°N (Kear 1972). Duration of flightless period for wild swans unknown.

IMMATURE: head and neck dark brown or black at one year, sometimes with pale grey flecks. Body mainly white but retaining some brown feathering on back and wings; wing tips black. Pink-grey bill. Full adult plumage by 18 months. Frontal caruncle present but smaller and paler than in adult, becoming fully developed at 3–4 years (Navas 1977, Seijas 1997). Juvenile has brown-grey plumage on fledging; bill blue-grey. Quickly develops adult plumage as body whitens, head and neck become darker, and bill acquires reddish colour. Duller coloration of bill and plumage distinguishes young birds from adults throughout 1st year.

CYGNET: white, faintly tinged pale grey, with bluish grey bill, legs and feet. Lateral feathering on bill extends along edges and over top of upper mandibles nearly to nostrils (Boyd *in* Scott 1972, Nelson 1976b).

MEASUREMENTS AND WEIGHT: in captivity ♂ adult wing (*n* = 1), 436; skull length (*n* = 1), 139.3; tarsus (*n* = 2), 91.9–93.1 (92.5); weight (*n* = 9), 4.6–8.7 (5.3). ♀ adult wing (*n* = 1), 418; skull (*n* = 1), 128.3; tarsus (*n* = 2), 77.9–82.5 (80.2); weight (*n* = 8), 3.5–4.4 (4.1) (Scott 1972, WWT data). At 9 months, ♂ wing (*n* = 1), 424, skull length (*n* = 1), 134.9, ♂ tarsus (*n* = 1) 90.3; weight (*n* = 1), 4.3. ♀ wing (*n* = 3), 395–405 (401); skull (*n* = 3), 125.4–127.2 (126.5); tarsus (*n* = 3), 83.7–86.3 (84.7); weight (*n* = 3), 3.3–4.0 (3.7) (WWT data). Immatures in wild ♂ (*n* = 6) wing, 400–430 (418); tarsus, 87.7–93.8 (90.6); ♀ (*n* = 3) wing, 374–400 (388); tarsus, 81.3–89.2 (84.9) (Seijas 1997).

Field characters

Unmistakable in field; typical swan shape, although smaller than northern swans, 1020–1240 mm long.

Plumage white with striking black head and neck. Largest of South American waterfowl, and unlike any other. Wings make swishing noise in flight.

Voice

Soft musical whistle *Whee-whee-whee*, with emphasis on first syllable. Uttered repeatedly when threatening intruders, and as Triumph display by paired birds. Also used as contact call, both on water and in flight. Calls similar in two sexes. Cygnet calls similar to those of other swans, but more goose-like and lighter in tone than those of northern swans (Kear 1972). Sonogram of cygnet's sleepy call in Kear (1968).

Range and status

Native to South America; almost continuous distribution below 25°S, extending from southeast Brazil and southeast Paraguay, through Argentina and Chile, to Tierra del Fuego (54°S) and Falkland Islands (Schlatter *et al.* 1991a). Coordinated census of 40 sites in Argentina and Uruguay found 3028 in late May–early June 1998 (Seijas 1999). Combination of national and regional counts puts total population at

< 100 000, of which 20 000 thought to be in Chile, 50 000 in Argentina, at least 20 000 in Uruguay, 2000–3000 in southern Brazil and 750–1500 on Falklands (Schlatter *et al.* 1991a, Rose and Scott 1997, Woods and Woods 1997). Most in Uruguay occur in Banados del Este wetlands of southeastern lowlands, including up to 10 000 on Laguna de Rocha (Vaz-Ferreira and Rilla 1991). Breeds mainly towards southern end of range, from *c* 30°S, including Falkland Islands (Schlatter *et al.* 1991a, 1991b, Vaz-Ferreira and Rilla 1991). Tends to occupy same range throughout year, although distribution varies as birds in south disperse north in Mar–Apr, to winter at more northerly latitudes. Some movement into northern Paraguay occurs at this time. Thought to be sedentary in Falkland Islands, though local movements onto favoured estuaries occur; no evidence of influx from continental South America, apart from that quoted in Woods (1975). No evidence for change in population size but, following drought in late 1980s, perhaps declining (Rose and Scott 1997). Recorded as vagrant to Juan Fernandez, South Shetland and King George Islands and Antarctic peninsula (Madge and Burn 1988, Todd 1979, 1996, Olavarría *et al.* 1999).

Habitat and general habits

Occurs on variety of wetlands, including shallow lakes with abundant aquatic vegetation, coastal lagoons, shallow inlets, harbours and swampy river basins, often in close proximity to human habitation in South American continent (Schlatter *et al.* 1991a), but remaining shy on Falkland Islands (Woods and Woods 1997). Is not restricted to low altitudes, but also nests near small lakes in upland areas of Chile (Hellmayr 1932). Historical distribution uncertain; Schlatter *et al.* (1983, 1991a) suggested that, like other waterfowl, may have spread from wetlands of Parana and Paraguay rivers to areas south and west of Andes. Earthquakes in southern Chile in 1960, which resulted in sinking of Rio Cruces and coastal valleys from Valdivia south to Ancud (Isle de Chiloe), with subsequent growth of submerged and riparian vegetation, enabled birds to colonize this region (Schlatter *et al.* 1991a).

Feeds mainly by immersing head and neck to take submerged vegetation, by surface feeding in open areas with abundant floating vegetation, and occasionally by up-ending (Vaz-Ferreira and Rilla 1991). Water levels have major effect on feeding site selection, with swans being present in greater numbers and for longer periods when water levels high (Schlatter 1997, Silva and Vilina 1999). Grazing in meadows observed only during drought (Vaz-Ferreira and Rilla 1991), probably because move awkwardly on land. Diet thought to consist mainly of *Chara*, *Potamogeton* and other pondweeds (Fjeldså and Krabbe 1990). Preliminary results of ecological studies at Rio Cruces, Chile, found fed primarily on leaves of *Egeria densa*, which was dominant submerged waterplant (Schlatter *et al.* 1991b). May need more varied diet, however; mortality levels at Rio Cruces were low, but *c* 20 dead juveniles had wing deformities (angel wing), low calcification of skeleton, and nematode infestations, indicating poor nutrition perhaps due to limited range of food available, combined with low calorific value of *Egeria densa* (Schlatter *et al.* 1991b). Other sites frequented in Chile abundant in *Myriophillum* and *Lemno-Azolletum* (Schlatter *et al.* 1991a). Food choice at Banados del Este, Uruguay, unrecorded, but plants available include *Scirpus*, *Typha*, *Potamogeton* (*Coleogeton*) and algae such as *Aphanotece*, *Rhyzoclonium* and *Enteromorpha* (Vaz-Ferreira and Rilla 1991). *Scirpus* and *Typha* are unlikely to be taken when mature, but shooting buds may perhaps be eaten. Feeding on algae on coast recorded both in Uruguay (Vaz-Ferreira and Rilla 1991) and Tierra del Fuego (Owen and Kear *in* Scott 1972). Animal matter, such as aquatic insects and fish spawn, may also be ingested, and cygnets thought to take same food as parents (Owen and Kear *in* Scott 1972).

Tends to disperse in response to climatic conditions, particularly drought; severe drought of 1988–90 resulted in influx of > 4000 to Rio Cruces reserve in Chile (Schlatter *et al.* 1991a, 1998). Major changes in weather conditions, and thus water levels, have in turn been linked to effects of El Niño Southern Oscillation (ENSO) on South American climate (Silva and Vilina 1999). Seasonal fluctuations in water levels similarly account for local movements, as smaller wetlands dry out in summer, encouraging swans to concentrate on more major waterbodies (Schlatter *et al.* 1991). Lower water levels at larger lakes and lagoons in summer also make it easier to reach submerged vegetation. There are seasonal shifts in distribution, as swans from southern part of range move northwards. Migratory distances not known, although re-sightings of swans marked with plastic neck collars indicate possibility of long journeys, a view reinforced by appearance of swans on Antarctic peninsula during 1988–90 drought (Schlatter *et al.* 1991a).

Displays and breeding behaviour

Performs only limited range of displays, particularly in comparison with other swans. In aggression, swims rapidly towards intruder, neck arched but extended forward and neck feathers ruffled, without raising wings. Like northern migratory swans, calls repeatedly during aggressive encounters. Triumph Ceremony, performed by both members of pair after displacing intruder, also has no Wing-raising, and consists mainly of calling, Neck-stretching and Chin-lifting (Kear 1972). Pre-copulatory behaviour similar to other swan, consisting of cob and pen alternately Dipping head and neck in water before mating. No obvious display after mating; partners bathe (Haedo Rossi 1953, Kear 1972).

Breeding and life cycle

Onset of laying and duration of nesting season probably related to latitude of breeding range, and controlled by species-specific response to photoperiod (Murton and Kear 1973). Breeding season thus extends over longer period than that of northern swans, and is similar to others nesting at low latitudes as breeding season unconstrained by long migrations and short arctic summer. This consistent with slow growth rates recorded compared with rapid development of northern swans (Kear 1972). In mainland South America, breeding season usually extends July–Jan, and may continue to Mar–Apr (Schlatter *et al.* 1991a). On Falklands, breeding season shorter and starts later (Aug–Jan). Rainfall, which influences distribution in South America, also affects breeding cycle. Study of ENSO, and subsequent increase in rains, on abundance and breeding success at Estero El Yali Ramsar site in Chile found that, in non-ENSO years, swans reached maximum numbers in winter and were absent in summer but that, during ENSO years, remained throughout year and bred (Silva and Vilina 1999, Vilina *et al*. 2002).

Although breeding pairs normally territorial, nests may be grouped, indicative of colonial breeding. Average distance between nests at Rio Cruces, Chile, 13.6 (1.7–32.0) m (*n* = 39), but extent to which this due to lack of suitable nesting habitat elsewhere in vicinity unclear (Schlatter *et al*. 1991b).

Laying occurs mainly July–Aug, although some pairs may start in June. In northern hemisphere collections (such as WWT Slimbridge at 52°N) nests earlier, in Feb–Mar, or even in Jan in mild winters. Nests situated in or adjacent to shallow lakes, sometimes in reedbeds, or on small islands in lake. As in other swans, both sexes build nest (Haedo Rossi 1953). Eggs oval, cream coloured and glossy, more rounded at one end than other; 101.2 × 66.4 (95.0–106.2 × 63.6–69.5) (*n* = 19) (Scott 1972); in captivity weight 225 (172.5–273.5) (*n* = 57). Clutch 4–6 eggs, although 7 recorded in Falklands (Woods 1975). Incubation, by ♀, 35 (34–36) days; she develops brood patches. ♂ guards nest closely, particularly when ♀ away feeding, and she returns rapidly when ♂ gives alarm call; ♀ can become dangerously emaciated if alerted persistently by mate. Newly hatched cygnets spend much time on backs of parents (usually ♂) until 2–3 weeks old, where warm and relatively safe from predators. Kelp (Southern Black-backed) Gulls suggested egg predator on Falkland Islands (Todd 1979). Predation by Crested Caracara *Polyborus plancus* on eggs and cygnets may have major effect on breeding success (Schlatter *et al*. 1991b). Adult aggression towards cygnets (presumably not own offspring) resulted in high cygnet mortality at some sites (Schlatter *et al*. 1991b). Pairs with downy young seen at same time as pairs with half-grown and full-grown cygnets in Tierra del Fuego in Apr, suggesting that breeding season started late for some pairs, or that few had 2 clutches (Humphrey *et al*. 1970). One pair also seen with 12 chicks, probably through adoption. Cygnets in Argentina fly by early Jan (Weller 1967b), captive-reared birds fledge in *c* 16 weeks.

Age at 1st breeding in wild unknown, but captive-reared birds nest successfully when only 2 years old (Kear 1972). Demographic studies in 1980s and early 1990s indicated that only 7.6–16.2% of population breeds every year, with mean brood sizes ranging 1.5–2.8 cygnets per pair depending on site and year, but annual adult mortality also thought to be low (Schlatter *et al*. 1991b). Extent of monogamy in wild also uncertain, but likely that, like other swans, form long-term pairbonds, particularly since both parents involved in rearing, at least until fledging. Maximum life-span recorded in captivity 20 years.

Conservation and threats

Thousands trapped for skins and feathers in late 18th and during 19th centuries; these used to adorn female clothing in Europe, and as powder puffs (Chapman 1943, Dawnay *in* Scott 1972, Todd 1979). Exploitation now thought to be minimal, although egg collection, hunting, and disturbance have limited population growth at Chilean wetlands. Legal protection of sites in Chile since early 1980s, and wardening of reserves, resulted in major increase in numbers at Laguna El Peral, Laguna Torca and Rio Cruces (Schlatter *et al*. 1991a). Current main problem is high mortality in droughts, including during dispersal in search of suitable wetlands (Schlatter 1998), with human activity, such as development programmes, affecting particular sites (Seijas 1999). Distribution of wetlands to provide a network of sites is also an issue; the few re-sightings of banded swans suggest a tendency to localized movements, and only three Neotropical sites have been identified as sufficiently stable to support regular breeding (Rio Cruces, Llancanelo and Laguna Blanca; Schlatter *et al*. 2002). Aspects of migration currently remain obscure, such as extent of seasonal return migrations as opposed to opportunistic dispersal, whether both breeders and nonbreeders migrate, and level of site fidelity. Important to discover where populations move to in droughts, in order that these sites might be protected. Not currently under threat in Falklands, but would be vulnerable to drainage of extensive wetlands (Woods and Woods 1997).

Eileen Rees

Mute Swan *Cygnus olor*
PLATE 4

Anas Olor Gmelin, 1789, Syst. Nat., **1**, p. 502
'Russia, Sibiria, Persico etiam littore maris Caspii' (Russia)

Etymology: *cygnus* L. for swan, *olor* is also L. for swan. Common name contrasts with strident voice of Whooper Swan and dates from 1785.

Other names: Tame Swan. French: Cygne tuberculé; German: Höckerschwan; Dutch: Knobbelzwaan.

Variation: no subspecies; 2 colour morphs. In 'Polish' phase named *Cygnus immutabilis* by Yarrell in 1838, cygnets and immatures lack melanin and appear white; character sex-linked and commoner in ♀♀ than ♂♂, and in eastern than western Europe (Kear 1972).

Description

ADULT: sexes alike, but ♀ averages smaller and has smaller bill knob. Plumage white. Bill orange with black base, cutting edges, nostrils and nail; black fleshy knob on upper mandible joins triangular area of black skin in front of eye; legs and feet black; eyes hazel. Head and neck may be stained reddish brown.

MOULT: one moult of body feathers annually. Complete adult post-breeding wing moult results in 6–8 weeks of midsummer flightlessness. ♀ of successful nesting pairs moults while cygnets small, followed by ♂, whose moult starts when flight feathers of ♀ well-grown.

IMMATURE: dull greyish brown with black-based dark grey bill, plumage becoming whiter and bill pinker as 1st year progresses. Brown feathers shed gradually; becomes completely white in full moult during 2nd summer. Immature 'Polish' morph white, retaining pink or yellowish legs and feet into adulthood.

CYGNET: pale silver-grey with white underparts; bill black, feet dark grey. Lateral feathering on bill extends upwards in nearly straight line; lores feathered. 'Polish' morph hatches white, with pink or yellowish feet and bill (Nelson 1976a, 1976b, 1993).

MEASUREMENTS AND WEIGHT: ♂ wing ($n = 12$), 580–623 (606); tail ($n = 6$), 205–246 (224); bill ($n = 12$), 74–88 (80.6); tarsus ($n = 12$), 107–118 (114). ♀ wing ($n = 10$), 533–589 (562); tail ($n = 13$), 69–79 (74.2); bill ($n = 13$), 69–79 (74.2); tarsus ($n = 10$), 99–114 (104) (Cramp and Simmons 1977). Weight ♂ 1st winter ($n = 159$), 8.1–12.1 (9.7); 1st summer ($n = 42$), 9.3–13.5 (10.9); adult winter ($n = 59$), 9.2–14.3 (11.8); adult summer ($n = 21$), 10.6–13.5 (11.9). ♀ 1st winter ($n = 221$), 5.5–9.5 (7.8); 1st summer ($n = 36$), 6.4–9.7 (8.3); adult winter ($n = 35$), 7.6–10.6 (9.7); adult summer ($n = 6$), 8.3–10.8 (9.6) (Reynolds 1972). See Brown *et al.* (2003) for sexing by discriminant analysis.

Field characters

Large, 1450–1600 mm long, and conspicuously white. Takes off with laborious, noisy run across water, and gains height only gradually. Landings equally spectacular. Unique singing sound produced by wings in flight. Best separated from all arctic breeding swans by prominent, pointed tail, black-based orange bill, and tendency to arch wings above back while carrying neck curved. Other northern hemisphere swans differ in having silent wingbeats, black and yellow bills, wedge-shaped heads, straighter necks, inconspicuous tails and ringing calls. Immatures browner than arctic breeding swans, whose young appear considerably paler and greyer.

Voice

Despite common name, far from voiceless. Adults utter variety of grunts and snorts, mainly during courtship, and hisses associated particularly with aggressive encounters and threat displays. Cygnets have high-pitched peeping voices until well fledged. Powerful downbeat of wings in flight produces characteristic, far-carrying, throbbing notes, *waou-waou-waou-waou* . . . at a rate of *c* 4 beats per sec. Sonograms of adult hiss, and of wing-beats in Cramp and Simmons (1977), and of distress note and hiss of cygnet in Kear (1968).

Range and status

Found from western Europe to central Asia, whence southerly migration, especially to Black

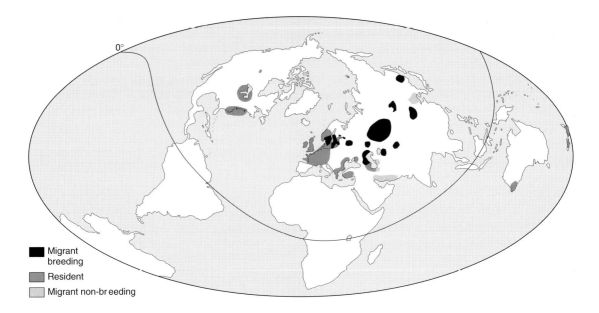

Migrant breeding
Resident
Migrant non-breeding

and Caspian Seas, induced by freezing winter conditions. Recently bred in Mongolia at Gobi Lakes (Robson 2000). Considered native to Britain (Ticehurst 1957). Introductions to many countries of central and western Europe occurred 16th and 17th centuries onward, with marked increases in numbers and expansion occurring through European range after 1950 (decline during war years caused by hunting for food). Sedentary, introduced population in US and southern Canada (nearly 13 000 individuals on US Atlantic flyway and 1700 on the lower Great Lakes in 2000; Petrie and Francis 2003) and smaller ones in Australia and New Zealand. Former exotic populations in South Africa and Zimbabwe extinct (Harrison *et al.* 1997); report of introduced group in Egypt (Brown *et al.* 1982) erroneous.

Most numerous swan species. Winter population estimates in northwest mainland and central Europe 250 000, Britain 37 000, Ireland 10 000, Black Sea 45 000, west and central Asia to Caspian Sea 250 000, central Asia 10 000–25 000, and eastern Asia 1000–3000 (Wetlands International 2002). Most populations continue to increase.

Habitat and general habits

Native to steppe lakes, rivers, freshwater and brackish marshes. Habitat preferences of introduced populations, shallow lakes and slow flowing rivers, often closely associated with humans, and sheltered coastal sites, especially brackish lagoons.

Wide variety of aquatic vegetation obtained by up-ending, by dipping head and neck below water surface, and by dabbling in shallow water. Can feed for up to 30 sec on vegetation as much as 90 cm below surface, though up-ending bouts of half this duration in shallower water normal (Scott 1972). Terrestrial grazing of grasses and cereals also occurs, particularly in late winter when aquatic vegetation may be depleted. In winter, feeding activity peaks *c* 3 h after sunrise and continues until shortly after nightfall (Owen and Cadbury 1975). Daily requirement of moulting adults up to 4 kg of wet vegetable food (Mathiasson 1973b). Demand for food by ♀ increases during spring due to energetic expense of egg formation, and because she hardly feeds during incubation and needs to lay down reserves. Many flocks, especially in urban situations, semi-domesticated, and survive on food, particularly bread, provided by public.

Cygnets eat aquatic vegetation, assisted by parents at first, though are not fed directly. Up-ending begins at 10 days and, after 4 weeks, can submerge head for 6 sec (Dewar 1942).

Displays and breeding behaviour

Characteristic display associated with courtship and aggressive defence of territory. In most frequent courtship display, pairs engage in close, slow mutual Head-turning while facing one another on water with neck feathers and secondaries raised (Figure 9.4). Copulatory behaviour also ritualized and plays important role in maintaining pairbond. Main threat display of both sexes is Busking, when neck feathers and wings raised, head thrown back, and intruder advanced upon with powerful, jerky swimming action. Busking occasionally develops into Wing-flapping, chasing, accompanied by noisy slapping of feet on water, and even direct attack in which bill and carpal joints used to good effect.

Proportion of most populations comprises flocks, often large, of sexual immatures, joined by failed breeders and families during and after midsummer moult; these gatherings play vital role in pair formation (Minton 1971). Breeding birds highly territorial, and territory may be maintained all year. Average distance between nests on rivers near Oxford, England, 2.4–3.2 km, with 90 m minimum (Perrins and Reynolds 1967). Once pair formed, all activity normally confined to territory until young fledge. At few coastal sites in Denmark, Poland, Loch of Harray, Orkney and at Abbotsbury, England, colonial nesting occurs (Kear 1972).

'Polish' colour phase common in parts of north-central Europe and in US but scarce in most populations (Wieloch and Czapulak 1991). Were likely bred selectively for trade in swan skins, possibly in The Netherlands. White cygnets seem disadvantaged in that apparently adult plumage provokes parental aggression, and are driven from territory earlier than grey-brown immatures. Separated from family,

9.4 A pair of courting Mute Swans.

survive less well; however, obtain mates and breed at younger age, so that gene concerned imparts compensatory advantage (Conover *et al.* 2000).

Breeding and life cycle

Well studied (Birkhead and Perrins 1986). In England, early eggs laid mid Mar. Nests on large mound of aquatic vegetation, close to or in shallow water. Base of nest up to 4 m diameter when built in water, 1–2 m if site chosen onshore. Shallow depression in top 5–15 cm deep, lined with softer vegetation and sparse down. Both sexes build for *c* 10 days. Eggs pale green when fresh, laid at 48 h intervals, 112.5 × 73.5 (100–122 × 70–80) ($n = 88$) (Schönwetter 1960–66); weight 345 (294–384) ($n = 80$) (Cramp and Simmons 1977); clutch 6.0 (1–11) ($n = 102$) (Perrins and Reynolds 1967). Incubation 36 (35–41) days by ♀ only, although ♂ may sit on nest while ♀ away. Hatching synchronous, young precocial and nidifugous, weight at day old 220 (180–248) ($n = 17$).

Cygnets have yolk reserves that sustain them for several days while becoming adept at feeding. Parents, particularly ♀, protect small cygnets from aquatic predators, such as Northern Pike *Esox lucius*, by carrying them on back between wings, and assist feeding by foot-paddling and by pulling up underwater vegetation. Fledge in 120–150 days, depending on growth rate. Family may stay together in flock for winter, or young may be driven off parental territory.

Breeding usually starts in 3rd or 4th year, and long-term monogamy normal. Hatching success varies, and in studies in UK, 29–49% of clutches lost before hatching, many through human vandalism. In Oxford area, *c* half hatched young survived to fledging, with most mortality occurring in 1st 14 days (Perrins and Reynolds 1967). In increasing introduced population in Connecticut, US, flooding rather than vandalism main cause (46%) of failure to hatch; clutch size (6.6) tending higher than in UK, as also hatching success (61%) and proportion of cygnets that fledge (69%) (Conover and Kania 1999). Survival rates of immatures improved over 1st 4 years of life and reached 82–90% after year 4 in 3 studies in England (Birkhead and Perrins 1986). Oldest recorded in UK ringing scheme attained 26 years 9 months (Clark *et al.* 2001). Hard winters cause serious mortality, particularly in north continental Europe and Asia, but commonest recorded cause of mortality in UK is flying into human artifacts, especially power cables (Ogilvie 1967, Perrins and Sears 1991, Brown *et al.* 1992).

Conservation and threats

Introductions in Middle Ages, and semi-domestication, were probably for culinary purposes, whereas recent introductions are for birds' ornamental qualities. Close association with humans both beneficial and detrimental. Benefits include large-scale feeding, provision of suitable habitat such as artificial lakes, and existence of veterinary facilities. Human-induced mortality serious, however, and includes

vandalism of nests, hunting, collision with man-made objects, pollution and lead poisoning. Lead identified as major cause of mortality in UK in 1970s, when anglers' weights estimated to cause 30% of all deaths (Goode 1981). After banning of most lead weights in 1987, British population recovered sharply, increasing to record estimate of 37 500 in 2002 (Kershaw and Cranswick 2002). Recent population growth in US and southern Canada giving cause for concern, due to potential for displacing native migratory waterfowl from breeding sites and depleting their food supplies, and control measures are being advocated (Petrie and Francis 2003).

Simon Delany

Trumpeter Swan *Cygnus buccinator*
PLATE 4

Cygnus buccinator Richardson, 1832, in Swainson and Richardson, Fauna Boreali-Americana, **2** (1831), p. 464
Hudson Bay

Etymology: *buccinator* from *bucina*, L. for military trumpet.

Other names: Trumpeter. French: Cygne trompette.

Variation: no subspecies, and little evidence for morphological variation between populations; Alaskan-breeding swans thought to have larger feet than those in Idaho and Montana, but results need verification due to inconsistent measuring techniques (Drewien and Bouffard 1994). Comparison of 3 sub-populations (Alaskan, Canadian and Montanan) at molecular level found little genetic variability. This may be due to bottleneck in Montana population, once reduced to 69 birds, but reason unclear for other groups that did not suffer such serious declines (Barrett and Vyse 1982). Has bred with Mute, Whooper, Bewick's and Whistling Swans in captivity; Trumpeter × Whistling Swan hybrids fertile (Mitchell 1994).

Description

ADULT: sexes alike. Plumage white in both sexes; frequent russet staining on head and neck due to

feeding in iron-rich waters. Characteristic long heavy bill, high and straight along culmen, and totally black except for line of red along anterior part of lower mandible in some individuals; legs and feet black; iris brown. Leucistic adults may have pale yellow or olive lores, and yellowish legs and feet (Kraft 1991, Mitchell 1994).

MOULT: adult wing moult takes 30–40 days June–Sept, with breeding pairs moulting asynchronously. Individuals flightless for *c* 30 days; ♀ moults 1st in Montana, Alberta and Wisconsin, and ♂ generally 1st in Alaskan population. Mitchell (1994) gave detailed summary of moults and plumages.

IMMATURE: predominantly white but may retain traces of juvenile grey feathering on head and neck and on secondary coverts. Bill predominantly black, but may have pink or reddish streaks, particularly around nostrils; legs and feet pinkish grey or olive-grey, becoming black later. Juveniles mainly grey with variable amounts of white upon fledging.

CYGNET: pale grey, with darker areas on rump, shoulder and nape of neck. Bill mainly pink on hatching (in bill of all northern swans, nail appears colourful because translucent and colour of blood shows through), becoming grey-pink, particularly at base and edge of bill. Lateral feathering markedly sculptured, horns of bill never feathered. Legs and feet pale orange or flesh coloured. (Nelson 1976b, 1993). Leucistic cygnets white upon hatching, with pink bill and yellow legs and feet. Leucistic gene apparently occurs only in Tristate population (see below), where 1.8–13.0% of cygnets white; leucism not recorded in wild birds elsewhere (Banko 1960, Mitchell 1994).

MEASUREMENTS AND WEIGHT: ♂ adult wing ($n = 5$), 545–680 (618.6); bill ($n = 18$), 104.0–131.0 (118.2); tarsus ($n = 84$), 121.0–145.2 (132.2). ♀ adult wing ($n = 3$), 604–636 (623.3); bill ($n = 15$), 101.5–127.0 (114.2); tarsus ($n = 64$), 115.1–138.0 (127.0). Weight in Alaska summer, ♂ ($n = 10$), 9.5–13.6 (11.97); ♀ ($n = 11$), 9.1–10.4 (9.6); in Montana winter, ♂ ($n = 152$), 9.1–14.5 (11.9); ♀ ($n = 120$), 7.0–12.5 (10.3) (Banko 1960, Hansen *et al.* 1971, Drewien and Bouffard 1994, Mitchell 1994). 1st winter ♂ anterior nostril to bill tip ($n = 40$), 47.3–57.8 (54.0); tarsus ($n = 108$), 119.5–141.2 (130.1); ♀ nostril to bill tip ($n = 38$), 47.7–57.7 (52.5); tarsus ($n = 86$), 115.3–136.2 (124.7). Weight in Montana winter, ♂ ($n = 167$), 6.8–12.2 (9.9); ♀ ($n = 147$), 6.1–11.3 (8.7) (Drewien and Bouffard 1994, Mitchell 1994). Immature ♂ bill ($n = 8$), 109.8–132.0 (117.6); imm tarsus ($n = 8$), 108.0–125.0 (116.0); weight in Alaska summer, ♂ ($n = 8$), 9.9–12.7 (11.39). Immature ♀ bill ($n = 7$), 99.9–116.9 (109.7); imm tarsus ($n = 8$), 106.0–116.2 (111.2); weight in Alaska summer ($n = 8$), 7.7–10.8 (9.52) (Hansen *et al.* 1971, Mitchell 1994).

Field characters

Largest of all swans, 1500–1800 mm long, although exceptional ♂ Mute Swans may be heavier. ♂ generally larger than ♀ in every age category, but substantial overlap in range means that sex cannot be determined by size alone.

Conspicuous large, white, long-necked bird, with short legs set well back on body. May be confused in field with smaller Whistling Swan, but distinguished by greater size, longer neck and massive black bill with no traces of yellow near eye. Whistling Swans have more rounded head in profile, and comparatively slender bill; however, still difficult to identify at distance. Sonorous bugling call also distinctive.

Voice

Characteristic deep bugling call, from which name derives; emphasis on 2nd syllable (sonogram in Mitchell 1994). Vocalizations may vary with social context; loud open-mouthed calls associated with aggressive encounters and Triumph display, whereas softer, more nasal contact calls used to maintain family cohesion. Younger birds have higher-pitched calls, developing more basal adult tones at *c* 6–8 months (Banko 1960). Sonogram of cygnet's sleepy call in Kear (1968).

Range and status

Historically numerous and widespread, breeding over wide area from central Alaska across Canada to Newfoundland, and south to Carolinas in eastern US, and to Idaho, Oregon, and perhaps California in west. Wintering range equally extensive, ranging from southern Alaska to southern California, central Florida and Gulf of Mexico. Numbers and distribution severely reduced during 19th century, as hunted for skins and feathers. Thought only 69 remained in 1935, although birds surviving in remote parts of Canada and Alaska were not counted.

Numbers partially recovered due to conservation measures in recent years (see Banko 1960). Continental survey in 1990 found 15 630 birds in wild (King 1992, Mitchell 1994), rising to *c* 19 700 by mid 1990s (Rose and Scott 1997). Most recent estimate, in 2000, in excess of 23 000 (see below). Nevertheless, occupy only limited part of original range, and still occur in small isolated flocks in some regions. Three main populations occur: Pacific Coast Population (PCP), which breeds in Alaska and winters from southern Alaska south to Washington State; Rocky Mountain Population (RMP) of Canada and northern US; and Interior Population (IP) consisting of restored flocks in north-central US (South Dakota, Minnesota, Wisconsin, Michigan and Ontario; Mitchell 1994). RMP consists of 2 sub-populations that mix in winter. Migratory Interior Canadian sub-population breeds in Rocky Mountains from Yukon and northwest territories south to Alberta and British Columbia. Swans of mainly sedentary Tristate sub-population, which breed in Idaho, Montana and Wyoming, descend

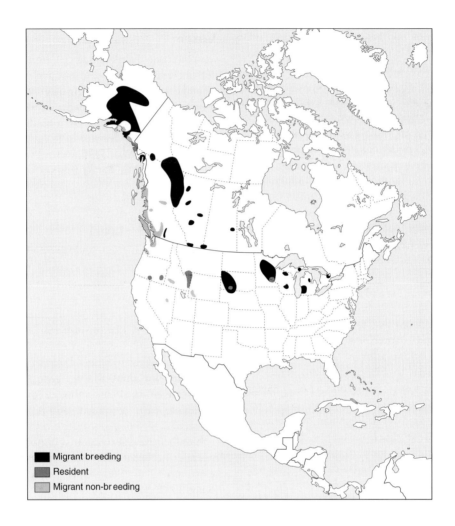

Migrant breeding
Resident
Migrant non-breeding

from survivors of hunting that lived in remote areas. PCP increased from 2847 (including cygnets) in 1968, to 7696 in 1980, 13 337 in 1990, 15 823 in 1995 and 17 155 by 2000 (Conant *et al.* 1991a, 1991b, 2002). Interior Canadian sub-population of RMP also increased from 200 birds in 1974 to *c* 1000, by mid-1980s and 3494 in winter 2000/01 (Hawkings *et al.* 2002), but Tristate sub-population remains at 500–600 following initial increase from 69 in 1932 to 627 by 1954 (Mitchell *et al.* 1991, Rose and Scott 1997). In 1993, IP estimated at 629 free-flying birds, with 148 scheduled for release by 1996 (Mitchell 1994); numbers in IP population thought to be 900 by mid 1990s and reached 2430 in 2000 (Shea *et al.* 2002).

Individual seen 3 times in Japan (Murase 1993); otherwise not recorded outside Americas (Mitchell 1994).

Habitat and general habits

Frequents wide variety of wetland habitats in both summer and winter. Nests mainly in freshwater marshes or near shallow ponds or lakes, preferring sites with abundant invertebrates and aquatic vegetation (Lockman *et al.* 1987, Squires 1991, Mitchell 1994). Uses larger marshes and lakes and brackish estuaries during migration, particularly ice-free areas where able to feed (Gale *et al.* 1987). Habitat selection in winter again dependent upon availability of ice-free water; in inland Tristate area, uses ponds, lakes, streams and rivers (including limited number of sites kept open by warm water from hot springs), whereas those in British Columbia, Washington and Oregon also use estuarine situations.

Adult diet mainly aquatic vegetation. Selects sites with abundance of *Chara* and *Potamogeton* when nesting (Squires 1991), but feeds on range of other plants including waterweed *Elodea canadensis*, Eelgrass *Zostera marina*, sedges *Carex*, milfoil *Myriophyllum* and horsetail *Equisetum* (see review in Mitchell 1994). Studies in Alaska found adults feeding mainly on *Equisetum*; cygnets took invertebrates in 1st 2 weeks after hatching, and vegetation (again mainly *Equisetum* stems and seeds) thereafter (Grant 1991). Regional variation in food selection in winter may reflect availability. In Wyoming, for instance, feeds mainly on *Chara*, *Elodea* and *Potamogeton pectinatus* (Squires 1991) whereas in Washington and British Columbia more likely to move to pasture and arable land, where takes corn, cereals (barley and wheat) and root crops (potatoes and carrots) (Mitchell 1994). Supplementary winter feeding by humans at Red Rock Lakes, Montana, discontinued in 1991 to encourage dispersal to other sites.

Displays and breeding behaviour

Gregarious in winter, and in nonbreeding flocks in summer, although aggressive interactions to establish dominance hierarchies common. Breeding pairs territorial during breeding season. Uses range of displays in aggressive encounters, similar to those of other northern migratory swans, usually accompanied by trumpeting calls. These include Neck-stretching, Neck-pumping, Raising-wings (half-open or fully-extended) and Chasing. Paired birds usually join forces and display together to drive off others. Breeding pairs also raise wings to defend territory against intruders, including aircraft (see Mitchell 1994 for review). Aggressive encounters frequently followed by Triumph display, where pair face one another, quivering raised half-open wings, Neck-pumping, and calling loudly.

Pre-copulatory display limited to Bill-dipping and Head-dipping, reminiscent of bathing, by both sexes. Synchronized movements last few sec before ♂ crosses neck over that of ♀, she extends her neck and lowers her body on water, and ♂ mounts (de Vos

1964, Kear 1972). Post-copulatory display also subtle; after mating, both call in softer voice than usual trumpeting, then rise in water, flap wings in unison, tail-wag several times and bathe.

Like other swans, monogamous; only one case of polygamy recorded in wild (Malcom 1971). Divorce not recorded, but may occur occasionally. Pair formation usually occurs late Mar–mid May (Lockman *et al.* 1987), with pairs remaining together throughout year thereafter.

Breeding and life cycle

Nests situated in, or surrounded by, water; sites include Muskrat *Ondatra zibethicus* or North American Beaver *Castor canadensis* lodges, exposed hummocks, small islands and floating platforms (Hansen *et al.* 1971, Mitchell 1994). Pairs may work on several platforms, but will lay in only one (Banko 1960). Nesting density variable, with size of territory 1.5–>100 ha. Usually one pair occupies pond, depending on complexity of shoreline and amount of food available (Mitchell 1994). Some 30% of Alaskan population and 33% in Montana gain territories every year, of which 67% and 90% respectively laid at least one egg (Bart *et al.* 1991a).

Lays usually late Apr–May. Re-nesting not recorded in wild (Mitchell 1994). Eggs creamy white to dull white, sub-elliptical; 113.9×73.4 $(101.0–126.0 \times 62.8–71.1)$ $(n = 522)$ (from review in Mitchell 1994); those laid by Alaskan breeding population significantly heavier than those from Montana, 363.1 (281.0–410.0) $(n = 104)$ and 336.0 (239.0–395.0) $(n = 72)$ respectively. Intraspecific variation in egg size attributed to inherited factors in Mute Swans (Bacon and Mountford 1990), but further study needed to determine whether this due to genotype, breeding latitude, food supply, interval between egg-laying or other factor in Trumpeters. Clutches usually 4–6 eggs in wild, although up to 9 recorded for Rocky Mountain Population (Gale *et al.* 1987), and 11 in captivity (Lumsden 1988). Although high proportion in Montana breed, compared with those in Alaska, clutches tend to be smaller (4.7 and 5.4 respectively, Bart *et al.* 1991a). Incubation, 32–38 days, mainly by ♀, although ♂ may sit on eggs (1.0–1.75% of his time, Mitchell 1994). Usually ♀

covers eggs with nest material before leaving, and ♂ remains close to defend clutch.

Hatches late May–July; not well synchronized; eggs from same clutch hatch 3–36 h apart (Ripley 1984). Cygnets brooded for 1–2 days after emerging, and at intervals thereafter until several weeks old. Adults help young to feed by treading water and muddy bottom of pond to bring invertebrates and vegetation to surface, particularly during 1st week after hatching. Brood amalgamation relatively frequent; 11.5% of broods monitored in Rocky Mountain population involved adoptions, and adoption rate did not vary between years (Mitchell and Rotella 1997). Fledge in 90–122 days, but typically 99–102 (Mitchell 1994). Offspring usually remain with parents during 1st winter.

Like other swans, potentially long-lived. Maximum longevity in captivity 32.5 years (Kortright 1942), and swans at least 24 years old recaptured in wild (Kennard 1975). Survival rates estimate >80% of adults survive from one year to next (Mitchell 1994). Substantial variation in number of cygnets recorded in population every year, and between breeding areas, attributable to local weather conditions and food supply.

May pair as young as 20 months, but usually not until 3rd or 4th winter (Lockman *et al.* 1987). First breeding typically at 4–7 years (Gale *et al.* 1987).

Conservation and threats

Intensive hunting for skins and feathers nearly resulted in extinction by early 1900s, although Alaskan-breeding (PCP) population less seriously affected. Protected under Migratory Bird Treaty Act of 1918, numbers increased steadily, particularly over last 20 years (Conant *et al.* 1991a), enhanced by recent conservation efforts including habitat protection and reintroduction programmes (Shea *et al.* 2002). Rocky Mountain Population (RMP) remains vulnerable to adverse winter conditions, since apparently lacks ability to find and use suitable habitat outside current range (Shea *et al.* 1991). Attempts to expand wintering range of Tristate sub-population, by relocating birds to historic sites with suitable habitats in Idaho and Wyoming, initiated in 1986. Loss of winter habitat to development also of concern; agriculture provides food, but drainage of wetlands associated with water pollution, and potential for conflict with farmers exists (Mitchell 1994).

Breeding habitat mostly secure, and extent does not appear to be limiting population growth. Some local problems remain, however, such as pollution, recreational disturbance, and industrial development. In winter, identification during Whistling Swan hunts of management concern, particularly as Trumpeter range expands (Drewien *et al.* 1999). Measurements of swans shot in Utah and Montana found 0.7% and 2.1% respectively were Trumpeter Swans. Lead poisoning from ingestion of lead shot remains major cause of death in winter on southern coast of British Columbia, despite banning of lead shot for wildfowling in main wintering areas since 1990 (Wilson *et al.* 1998). Welfare of population monitored closely by US Fish & Wildlife Service and independent biologists, although total population censuses undertaken by Fish and Wildlife Service discontinued in late 1990s. Results of censuses and research projects coordinated and disseminated through Trumpeter Swan Society.

Eileen Rees

Whistling Swan *Cygnus columbianus columbianus*
PLATE 4

Anas Columbianus Ord, 1815, in Guthrie, Geogr., ed. 2 (Amer.), **2**, p. 319
The Dalles, Oregon
Etymology: *columbianus* after Columbia River, US. Other names: Tundra Swan. French: Cygne siffleur.

Variation: sister subspecies of Bewick's Swan. Numerous and widespread in fossil record from late Pleistocene (0.6 mybp) and Holocene (10 000 ybp) of Alaska to California and Florida (Limpert and Earnst 1994).

Description

ADULT: sexes alike, ♂ generally larger and heavier than ♀. White with straight neck, rounded head, black legs and feet, and largely black bill, yellow on bill restricted to small area in front of eye of most adults, reduced or absent in others. Plumage may become stained yellowish by iron in water (Palmer 1976).

MOULT: one body and wing moult annually. Wing moult in July–Aug.

IMMATURE: juvenile plumage attained by *c* Day 70 (Bellrose 1980); brownish grey, darkest on head and neck, paler below and on rump with pinkish grey bill. During 1st winter, white feathers of adult plumage moulted, head first, and usually completed by late spring; bill and legs become progressively blacker and all black by end of 1st summer (Limpert and Earnst 1994). Second-winter birds retain varying amounts of grey-brown feathers on head, neck and wings. No reported cases of leucism (*cf* Bewick's).

CYGNET: greyish above, whiter below with pinkish bill and legs. Horns of bill frequently feathered (Nelson 1976b, 1993).

MEASUREMENTS AND WEIGHT: in winter in Maryland and North Carolina, ♂ wing ($n = 8$) 501–569 (538); bill ($n = 305$), 90–118 (103.7); tarsus ($n = 290$), 94–146 (115.7); weight ($n = 1447$), 3800–10 500 (7200). ♀ wing ($n = 15$) 505–561 (531.6); bill ($n = 164$), 89–117 (101.1); tarsus ($n = 160$), 92–134 (110.3); weight ($n = 1290$), 4100–9000 (6300) (Limpert *et al.* 1987, Banko 1960).

Field characters

Slightly larger than Bewick's Swan, 1200–1500 mm long, but adults best separated by restricted area of yellow lore pattern (extends to posterior end of nares in Bewick's). Superficially similar to Trumpeter, with which overlaps increasingly in range in winter (Drewien *et al.* 1999), but much smaller and more goose-like in flight, proportions and shape, with shorter neck, stockier body and more rounded head. Trumpeter lacks yellow loral spot, has heavier, more wedge-shaped head and bill, and lower pitched voice. First winter birds similar to Bewick's but generally have darker bills and legs.

Voice

Very vocal, voices of sexes similar, those of 1st year birds higher pitched. Soft contact notes between parents and young, all other calls Triumph, Greeting, flight and pre-flight, variants of *ou*, *oh* and *oo*; sonogram in Limpert and Earnst (1994). Flight calls frequent in evening at large winter roosts producing musical murmuring, audible for miles. Hiss given when defending young or nest from predators and during agonistic encounters (Limpert and Earnst 1994). Calls similar to Bewick's, although variation in tone allows separation of captive individuals by experienced listeners.

Range and status

Breeds across northern arctic tundra of North America from northwest Québec, through northern Ontario, northeast Manitoba, Northwest Territories, Yukon, to Alaska, with highest densities in river deltas; also Aleutian Islands and east Chukota in extreme eastern Siberia where evidence of interbreeding with *bewickii* (Evans and Sladen 1980, Kondratiev 1991). Two wintering populations; western population breeds south of Point Hope in Alaska, winters on Pacific coast from Vancouver Island to central California, also inland valleys in California and locally in British Columbia, Oregon, Nevada, Utah and Montana, rarely Aleutians and southwest Alaska; eastern population breeds east of Point Hope and winters on Atlantic coast mostly from New Jersey to South Carolina, casual north to Maine and south to Florida (Limpert *et al.* 1991). Rare visitor to Mexico, Cuba, Bermuda, Puerto Rico (Palmer 1976), Hawaiian Islands and Newfoundland (Limpert and Earnst 1994). Annually recorded in Japan, vagrant to Sakhalin, accidental Komandorski and UK (Evans and Sladen 1980, Ostapenko 1991). Thought extirpated from nesting areas of south Hudson Bay, although recently re-colonizing along coasts of Manitoba, Ontario and Québec, formerly bred locally Labrador (Lumsden 1984). Wintering population in Chesapeake Bay declined since late 1960s and consequently increased in North Carolina.

Three-year-average population index 1987–89 was 87 065 for eastern and 63 571 for western wintering swans, which represented doubling in overall population since early 1950s (Serie and Bartonek

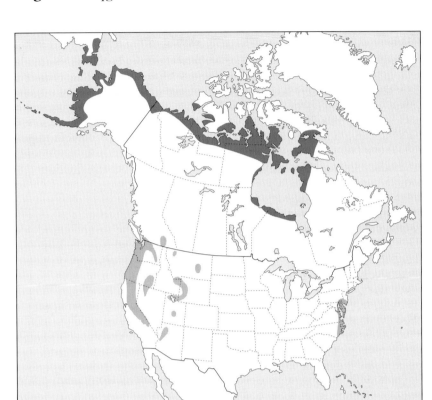

Migrant breeding
Migrant non-breeding

1991a). Numbers in 1980–89 stable overall, with eastern population increasing at 2.3% per annum and western population decreasing at 2.3% annually (Serie and Bartonek 1991b). Eastern population continued to increase during 1990s, with population index at *c.* 100 000 birds in 2000, although long-term growth rates seem to have slowed since hunting was first authorized in 1984 (Serie *et al.* 2002). Current trend for western population also again positive (Trost and Drut 2001). Increase in breeding population index in western Alaska 1965–89 (Conant *et al.* 1991a).

Habitat and general habits

In Nearctic, breeds on tundra lakes and pools, favouring coastal delta areas. Density of nests positively correlated with availability of wetlands, number of lakes and length of shoreline (King and Hodges 1981). Prefers shallow lakes with emergent littoral vegetation and pondweed *Potamogeton*, in areas of little relief with wet meadows (Wilk 1988, Spindler and Hall 1991), also larger lakes in deltas connected to river channels or partly drained, small polygon ponds near lakes, and moist tundra at lake edge (Earnst 1992a). On migration found at shallow ponds, lakes and riverine marshes, also on cereal and harvested agricultural fields. In North Dakota, wetlands containing Sago Pondweed *Potamogeton pectinatus* favoured for foraging, regardless of size or extent of open water; non-foraging swans preferred large (> 1.3 km^2) wetlands with > 95% open water (Earnst 1994). In winter, on rivers, lakes, ponds and shallow tidal estuarine areas, foraging extensively on agricultural fields (Limpert and Earnst 1994).

Feeds throughout day, and at night under full moon, as family group or flock. Dabbles, submerging head and neck, up-ending or grazing in wetlands, using feet to excavate plant parts and molluscs from substrate and bringing food to surface for young to eat. Also grazes winter cereals and forages on waste grains. Diet on breeding grounds mostly sedges *Carex* (37.9% of faecal remains, Colville River Delta Alaska), algae *Nostoc* (23.2%), pondweed *Potamogeton* (22.0%), grasses *Arctophila*, *Puccinellia*, and herbaceous plants *Ranunculus* and *Stellaria* (total = 15.6%), also some arthropods (1.3%) (Bart and Earnst 1991, Earnst 1992a). On migration takes mostly seeds and tubers of *Potamogeton pectinatus* in Utah (Sherwood 1960), tubers of Arrowhead *Sagittaria latifolia* in Minnesota (Limpert 1974) and waste corn *Zea* in Utah, Ontario and Pennsylvania (Limpert and Earnst 1994). In winter, eastern population formerly fed almost entirely on submerged aquatic plants and benthic organisms (Stewart and Manning 1958), but now forages largely on harvested corn and Soybeans *Glycine max* and upon growing winter cereals (wheat, rye and barley). Aquatic feeding upon molluscs *Mya arenaria* and *Macoma baltica*, and submerged vegetation, confined to early winter period until stocks depleted (Munro 1981b, Earnst 1992a). Progression from aquatic feeding to field feeding mirrors that of *bewickii* wintering in northwest Europe. Also feeds on *Lacanthes tinctoria* roots in New Jersey (Castelli and Applegate 1989) and on rice *Oryza stiva* in California (Limpert and Earnst 1994). Gulls kleptoparasitize swans feeding in winter on clams *Macoma* in Chesapeake Bay; are attacked by gulls on average one clam in 3, and lose clam in 52% of attacks (Earnst and Bart 1991).

Parties fly in V formation on migration and local flights, also in loose strings. Rarely flies > 300 m altitude on local flights (Sladen and Cochran 1969), possibly 600–1500 m on migration (Limpert and Earnst 1994). One radio-marked individual had average ground speed on migration of 82.3 km/h (Sladen *et al.* 1969), probably close to limit (Limpert and Earnst 1994). Generally gregarious in winter, often in hundreds or thousands at favoured sites.

Migrates in family groups often within larger flocks, with traditional stopover sites which can differ in spring and autumn (Limpert and Earnst 1994). Departs when winds favourable, travelling longer distances (e.g. 1600 km) over day and night in autumn than in spring, when has more frequent but shorter stops (Sladen *et al.* 1969). Exhibits high degree of site fidelity in winter (Munro 1981a).

Powerful flyer, but takes off with some difficulty from land or water, landings on water followed by slide, on land by running steps. Swims strongly and can dive when pursued. Walks when grazing and can run at speed when flightless during moult. Roosts almost exclusively on land in breeding season but mostly on water during nonbreeding season (Limpert and Earnst 1994). Antagonistic behaviour, of varying intensity but common throughout year, includes Dropped-wings, Raised-wings, Ground-stare, aerial display, Foot-slapping and Wing-flapping. Attacked swan may adopt submissive posture, and victors indulge in Triumph display involving much calling and wing quivering (see Cooper 1979, Hawkins 1986a).

Displays and breeding behaviour

Monogamous; extra-pair copulations not observed and divorce rare. Following behaviours (no major differences from Bewick's) exhibited by pairs (Hawkins 1986a): (a) Forward-call in which bird calls with head and neck extended horizontal to ground; (b) Quivering-wings, Triumph or Greeting display where pair face one another calling and holding out partially extended wings moved rapidly from wrist; often seen when pair re-unite or during aggressive encounters; (c) Head-bobbing in which head vertically raised and lowered whilst emitting single call, used as signal to mate and family members prior to take off (Black 1988); (d) Ritualized bathing when pair repeatedly bounce forward on breasts and dip heads and necks in water before copulation, followed by mutual Head-dipping; (e) in copulation, ♂ mounts partially submerged ♀ from side, and grasps back of her head or neck with bill, extending wings and lowering tail. Copulation lasts < 20 sec and is frequent both prior to and just after egg-laying. After copulation, ♂ slides off ♀ and pair face, partly raise wings and call with heads bowed, followed by extensive preening and washing; (f) Ritualized nest building; both forwards and sideways building may occur away from nest and outside breeding season (Limpert and Earnst 1994). In addition, pairs actively defend breeding territory, chasing away intruders (including geese) up to 1 km from boundary, more rarely pecking intruder's tail in flight or pecking and beating intruder with wrist on ground (Limpert and Earnst 1994). Typically one member of pair stays with nest or brood during encounters, invariably flightless bird during early wing moult. Encounters more frequent prior to hatch and less frequent amongst nonbreeding territorial pairs (Earnst 1992a).

Breeding and life cycle

Pairs arrive on breeding territories mid Mar–late May depending on time of snow melt in relation to latitude (Limpert and Earnst 1994). Territory size 0.5–1.0 km², and typically includes at least part of large water body used for foraging and escape from predators. Pairs may return to same territory as previous year (Sladen 1973), traditional use of foraging sites may enhance grazing by increasing plant production and densities of species that tolerate grazing (Monda *et al.* 1994). Nest from previous year may be re-used or new nest built; building begins 4–9 days before laying. Nests near large water body, on islands, in upland or wet meadow tundra, or on elevated ridges of polygonal ponds, suggesting visibility from site may be important (Earnst 1992a). Nest composed of grasses, sedges, lichens and mosses pulled from within 3 m and constructed by both ♂ and ♀. Three nest-building behaviours recognized (as *bewickii*): (a) forward-building when on nest; (b) sideways-building often involving bird passing vegetation to mate on nest; and (c) scraping (♀ only) when on nest (see Cooper 1979, Hawkins 1986a). Clumps of vegetation, including roots, added to nest and mounds increase in height from year to year with regrowth of vegetation and expansion from permafrost core. Nest mounds may thaw more quickly and have larger buffer of thawed soil than surrounding tundra (Monda *et al.* 1994). Eggs elliptically ovate; creamy white and nonglossy but quickly acquire tan stain; in northern Alaska (Monda 1991) 105.7 × 67.9 (96.1–115.8 ×

62.7–73.9); weight 273 (210–340) (*n* = 320); mean clutch 3.57 (3.09–4.21). Eggs laid every 36–48 h; no re-nesting after clutch loss. Clutch completed in 6–10 days; incubation 31–32 days, and cygnets fledge 65 days later (Limpert and Earnst 1994). Clutch initiation and hatch earlier in years with early snow melt, clutch and brood larger and larger proportion of population nests (Lensinsk 1973, Dau 1981, Monda 1991). Both ♂ and ♀ sit on eggs, ♀ plucks down from breast but brood patch not conspicuous (Hawkins 1986b). During incubation, ♀ spends 60–79% (71%) of time on nest, ♂ 20–38% (27%) (2% no bird on nest). Incubation most intensive when wind chill high. Sitting by ♂ lessens egg cooling, also probably decreases predation risk, shortens incubation period and reduces energy demands of ♀ (Hawkins 1986b). Both ♂ and ♀ turn eggs every 40 min and 'settle' on eggs at start of incubation bout allowing closer contact with eggs. Following nest relief by ♂, ♀ tends to fly directly to feeding site; when relieved by ♀, ♂ often nest builds or loafs near nest (Hawkins 1986b). ♀ incubates for longer bouts close to hatching, and active on nest during hatching.

Eggs and young cygnets predated by foxes *Alopex lagopus* and *Vulpes vulpes*, Brown Bears *Ursos arctos*, eagles, skuas, and Ravens *Corvus corax*; older cygnets and adults by eagles and probably also by Wolves *Canis lupus* and bears (Limpert and Earnst 1994). Young precocial and nidifugous, leaving nest 1.5–3 days after start of hatching and follow either parent. A few families return to nest for brooding up to 3 days after hatching, with brooding continuing during 1st week. Parents treadle submerged vegetation to surface for cygnets which mostly dabble and, more rarely, pass food items directly to cygnets. Cygnets compete directly for food brought to surface and spend more time grazing on land than other swans where they feed more efficiently (Earnst 1992a, 2002). In addition, families have longer feeding bouts than other swans, parents spending more time vigilant and in territory defence, and more time feeding together, thus providing cygnets with increased parental care and allowing efficient foraging (Earnst 1992a, 2002). During 1975–88, mean brood size lower in eastern population (1.9) than in western (2.4) (Serie and

Bartonek 1991b). Pairs with broods in Aug range 15–48%, and on north slope of Alaska, 77% of adults held territories (Bart *et al.* 1991b). Cygnets stay with parents through 1st winter. Continued care reduces foraging competition with conspecifics and kleptoparasitic gulls, and cygnets can exploit foraging behaviour of adults (Earnst and Bart 1991). Families depart together on spring migration but parents arrive on breeding grounds without young. Some offspring probably associate with parents in 2nd and 3rd winters (Limpert and Earnst 1994).

Oldest known swan was at least 21 years (Limpert and Earnst 1994). Annual survival rates estimated at 92% for adults of both sexes, 81% for juvenile ♂♂ but only 52% for juvenile ♀♀ (Nichols *et al.* 1992). Survivorship estimated at 52% on autumn migration for juveniles in eastern population, and 76% during 1st winter (Bart *et al.* 1991b). ♀ can breed at 3 years.

Conservation and threats

Shooting most significant post-fledging mortality factor; over 4000 killed annually in regulated hunting and 6000–10 000 in unregulated hunting (out of season and subsistence hunting in arctic, Bartonek *et al.* 1991). Regulated hunting by permit only allowed since 1962 during autumn migration in west and on wintering grounds since 1984 in east.

Hunting justified because of population increases, concern over crop damage and for trophies (Serie and Bartonek 1991a). Sladen (1991) criticized hunting on biological and aesthetic grounds; including limited data on productivity and recruitment, lack of evidence for serious, widespread crop damage (or that hunting would reduce its occurrence), ethics of trophy hunting and protected status of swans elsewhere. Eastern and western populations managed by US Fish & Wildlife Service and Canadian Wildlife Service, with management plans establishing target population sizes of 80 000 and 60 000 respectively (USFWS/CWS 1986). A drop in 3-year winter average populations to 60 000 in east and 40 000 in west would lead to ban on regulated hunting (Serie and Bartonek 1991a). Mortality from lead poisoning through ingestion of spent shot and fishing weights during migration and on wintering grounds continuing but localized problem (Limpert and Earnst 1994). Loss of arctic breeding habitat to oil and gas drilling and associated activities is increasing threat, as is loss of wetlands through drainage on migratory routes, especially in prairie pothole region. Declines in submerged aquatic vegetation at Chesapeake Bay, Maryland since late 1960s, coincided with shift away from site and increase in field feeding in North Carolina.

John Bowler

Bewick's Swan *Cygnus columbianus bewickii*
PLATE 4

Cygnus Bewickii Yarrell, 1830, Trans. Linn. Soc. London, **16**, p. 453, pl. 24
England.

Etymology: named for Thomas Bewick (1753–1828), English artist, engraver and naturalist.

Other names: Tundra Swan. French: Cygne de Bewick; German: Zwergschwan; Japanese: Kohakucho.

Variation: some geographical variation. Possible clinal increase in bill size (higher at base, wider at tip) eastwards across range. East Siberian population once recognized as separate race *C. c. jankowskyi* Alphéraky,

1904 but probably not justified, since great overlap in measurements and size extremes occur in all populations (Delacour 1954–64). Birds wintering in Japan have, on average, more black on bills than those wintering in England (Scott 1981). Substantial gene flow across Bering Straits suspected between eastern Bewick's Swan and conspecific Whistling Swan of North America, which has significantly less yellow on bill (Evans and Sladen 1980); evidence of mating between individuals of 2 races in US, Japan and Russia (Evans and Sladen 1980, Kondratiev 1991, Syroechkovski 2002) appears to confirm this.

Description

ADULT: sexes alike, although ♂ generally larger and heavier than ♀. All white with straight neck, rounded head, and variable pattern of black and yellow on bill, so much so that birds may be recognized individually (Scott 1966). Legs black; iris usually brown, occasionally blue-grey. Leucistic adult birds with pinkish or yellow legs, and variable amounts of pink on bill, occasionally reported (Evans and Lebret 1973). Head, neck and underparts may be stained rusty.

MOULT: one moult of wings and body plumage annually. Flight feathers moulted late July–Aug, ♀♀ of breeding pairs flightless before ♂♂.

IMMATURE: distinctive in 1st year, largely pale to mid grey, bill highly variable with generally dark tip and pinkish to reddish pink base. During 1st winter and spring, plumage grows increasingly pale as white feathers acquired; black on bill extends over forward pink areas and bill base becomes white, then yellow. Second-winter birds often retain some grey feathers particularly on head and neck, and pink patches may remain on bill.

CYGNET: like Whistling Swan, pale grey with largely pink bill and legs (Nelson 1976b).

MEASUREMENTS AND WEIGHT: in winter in England, ♂ wing ($n = 152$), 480–570 (529.0); tarsus ($n = 111$), 93–119 (106.6); weight ($n = 211$), 4536–8391 (6380). ♀ wing ($n = 133$), 474–542 (509.0); tarsus ($n = 110$), 87–113 (102.4); weight ($n = 189$), 4300–7825 (5642). Skull and tarsus length of 1st winter birds within 97% of adults, but only 80–90% of adult weight; continue to put on weight through 1st winter (Evans and Kear 1978).

Field characters

Superficially similar to Whooper Swan with which range overlaps extensively outside breeding season. Smaller, 1150–1400 mm long, and more goose-like flight, proportions and shape, with shorter neck, stockier body and more rounded head. Yellow base meets black tip of bill on sides with rounded, jagged or square end well behind nostril, never in acute point as in Whooper. Structural distinctions also apply to juveniles, which are generally darker grey than juvenile Whoopers of same age and may show much redder bill bases. Calls also differ, Whooper having louder, lower voice.

Voice

Very vocal throughout year, individually and in chorus, especially on water and in flight. Calls honking or crooning in character, quicker, quieter and less trumpeting than those of Whooper Swan. Sonogram in Cramp and Simmons (1977). Calls used for range of territorial and contact purposes and similar in most contexts. Louder for threat, Triumph Ceremonies and as Lost-call used to relocate partner and young, quieter for Greeting and pre-flight signalling. Loud and sharp single honking note frequently repeated in flight. Resting flock produces quiet babble of musical notes ascending and descending in pitch, louder and more persistent on spring nights immediately prior to migration. Calls of cygnets like those of Mute Swan but gruffer.

Range and status

Breeds only in arctic Russia from Kanin Peninsula west to Chukota sea. Two main populations exist: swans breeding east of Lena Delta, winter mainly in Japan, China and Korea; those breeding west of Urals winter in northwest Europe, mostly in UK, The Netherlands and Republic of Ireland, smaller numbers in Germany, Denmark, Belgium and France (Rees *et al.* 1997c). Important stopover sites in The Netherlands, Germany, and Baltic countries, especially Estonia in both spring and autumn (Luigujoe *et al.* 1996), and White Sea region in spring (Nolet *et al.* 2001). Formerly also wintered commonly in Caspian and Aral Sea areas, now smaller numbers in Iran, Ukraine and Turkey: true size of this smaller third population still uncertain (Syroechkovski 2002). Has declined in Scotland where common in 19th century, particularly on Tiree and South Uist. Also less common than formerly in Ireland and Germany, but numbers have increased dramatically in England where began wintering regularly only in 1920s (Ogilvie 1969, Cramp and Simmons 1977, Robinson *et al.* 2004b).

Migrant breeding
Migrant non-breeding

Western population stabilized at *c* 16 000–17 000 in 1980s (Dirksen and Beekman 1991, Rose and Scott 1994), then increased substantially to 29 000 by mid-1990s (Beekman 1997, Delany *et al*. 1999), but numbers fluctuate due to annual variation in breeding success. Much of recent increase sustained in The Netherlands, where numbers rose from nearly 9000 in 1984 to over 19 000 in 1995 (Beekman 1997). Elsewhere, national trends stable following long-term growth in UK and decline in Ireland, with annual variation probably relating to winter climate. Eastern population larger at 86 000 birds (Wetlands International 2002), but less well known. Only low hundreds counted for Caspian wintering population (Perennou *et al*. 1994), but may exceed 1000 birds (Syroechkovski 2002).

Habitat and general habits

On arctic breeding ground favours open low-lying, sedge-grass, moss-lichen tundra with numerous river channels and lakes, sometimes also broad, slow-moving rivers and backwaters or on islands and coasts. Rarely nests in shrub-tundra, migrants only in forest tundra and taiga. Area of overlap with larger Whooper Swan at northern edge of shrub-tundra restricted, and variable according to climatic conditions in spring that affect northern breeding limit of Whooper. On migration uses small number of suitable lakes, pools and rivers, also shallow saltwater lagoons and coastal waters. Up to 90% of west European winter population occurs at less than 15 sites (Beekman *et al*. 1994). Formerly mostly on shallow lakes and marshes in northwest Europe where fed primarily on aquatic vegetation, but increasingly on flooded pastures and arable land. Depends on open areas of water to roost. Capable of rapid changes in use of wintering sites within range in response to both habitat change and climate.

Feeds by day or night, submerging head and neck in shallow water, up-ending and frequently 'paddling' to raise particles. Also feeds on flooded and dry pasture, and digs with bill for tubers. Diet in

The Netherlands in winter formerly mostly rhizomes of pondweeds *Potamogeton pectinatus* and *P. perfoliatus*, also *Ceratophyllum*, *Zannichellia*, *Myriophyllum*, *Chara*, Common Reed *Phragmites australis* and *Typha latifolia*, with *Zostera* taken in brackish tidal areas (Brouwer and Tinbergen 1939, Bauer and Glutz 1968–69). Depletion of submerged macrophytes through water pollution, drainage and land reclamation forced shift to grass leys and semi-natural grassland, after 1968 and subsequently, to cereals and root crops (Poorter 1991). Limited supply of *Potamogeton* tubers in Lauwersmeer, used up by swans arriving Oct–Nov, caused switch to other foods (Beekman *et al.* 1991). On Ouse Washes in UK, traditionally took soft grasses including *Glyceria fluitans*, *Agrostis stolonifera* and *Alopecurus geniculatus*, plus coarser *G. maxima* later in winter and starchy roots of *Rorippa palustre* but, since 1972–73, increasingly switched to waste crops of potatoes and sugar beet, to cereals (Owen and Cadbury 1975) and to Oilseed Rape *Brassica napus*. At WWT Slimbridge, diet augmented by provision of grain but, during day, grazes meadow grasses on improved pasture, and takes mostly *Lolium perenne* (43.5% of remains in faeces) and selectively grazes for less abundant *A. geniculatus* in damp depressions (Rees 1990). *Chara aspera* traditionally formed major part of diet at spring migratory sites in Estonia, although use of pasture and crops increasing (Rees and Bowler 1991). On autumn migration through Eastern Europe, Beekman *et al.* (1994, 2002) suggested may be energetic bottleneck caused by limited availability of submerged macrophytes at key sites; however, may also make use of pasture and arable crops, as in winter range. On breeding ground (e.g. Russkiy Zavorot peninsula) diet largely shoots of tundra *Carex*, such as *C. aquatalis* and *C. lachenalii*, grasses (including *Dupontia fisheri*, *Arctophila fulva* and *Calamagrostis neglecta*) and soft herbaceous plants (including *Stellaria humifusum*). Tips of *A. fulva* particularly favoured early in spring when little else available. Later in summer, also takes *Carex* seed heads, tundra berries (including *Empetrum nigrum* and *Rubus chamaemorus*) and leaves and shoots of *Potamogeton*, depending on availability in territory. Cygnets eat both adult and immature mosquitoes *Culex* from tundra pools; adults probably do so incidentally. At Slimbridge,

often feed on tide-scoured mudflats in Mar, where only estuarine invertebrates such as amphipod *Corophium* and polychaete worm *Nereis* available, immediately prior to departure on spring migration (Rees *et al.* 1991b).

Flight powerful, as other swans, but with slightly faster wing-beats. Parties may fly in V or diagonal lines, but also in no definite formation. Generally gregarious in winter, often in hundreds or even thousands on ground, where noisier than Whoopers. Typically less wary, except in summer when moulting or during incubation (may leave nest when approached to 20–800 m). Some 67–72% thought to remain in nonbreeding flocks during summer, indicating that recruitment to European population may be based on success of 2000–3000 breeding pairs.

High level of site-fidelity shown by adults and their offspring in winter at favoured sites (Evans 1979a), although singletons less faithful than pairs which, in turn, are less faithful than families (Rees and Bacon 1996). Birds in 2nd and 3rd winters may explore alternative winter sites. Pairs consistent in use of nesting territories (Shchadilov *et al.* 1998), and individuals may also be consistent in use of migratory sites (Rees and Bacon 1996). Birds marked in northwest England and southwest Scotland have more northerly migratory route than those marked in southwest England, while those in southeast England only occasionally extend their range further west (Rees and Bacon 1996). Marked bias in distribution of cygnets in winter, both in terms of geographical location and habitat (Rees *et al.* 1997b); proportion of cygnets higher in The Netherlands than in UK in Jan 1984 (Beekman *et al.* 1985), but lower in Jan 1987 (Dirksen and Beekman 1991), while generally higher at WWT Slimbridge than on Ouse Washes, and lower still in Ireland, at outer edge of winter range.

Displays and breeding behaviour

Wide range of social behaviours shown. Pre-flight signals, which integrate family for take-off, consist of Head-bobbing in which neck alternately bent and stretched while calling; these increase in frequency immediately prior to flight. Members of pair, rejoining after temporary separation, Greet with ritualized

Head-turning on straightened necks while close together with bodies facing obliquely. Antagonistic behaviour common in winter flocks including Head-low threats, Peck, and more prolonged aggression involving quivering of partly or wholly spread wings, Neck-stretching and calling loudly whilst facing opponent. Physical combat involving beak and wings not uncommon, usually between ♂♂. Victor returns to mate or family and indulges in Triumph display, involving Wing-flapping, Neck-stretching and loud calling. Position in dominance hierarchy effects condition in winter as assessed by abdominal profile (AP). This differs between sexes, high-ranking paired ♀♀ have higher AP scores than low-ranking single ♀♀; conversely, low-ranking single ♂♂ have higher AP scores than high-ranking ♂♂; offspring of dominant pairs have higher AP scores than those from less dominant pairs (Bowler 1994).

Agonistic displays between ♂♂ of adjacent territories frequent, particularly at start of breeding season when nesting ridges and feeding sites in short supply due to snow cover, and again in early post-hatching period. ♂ will fly to intruder and stand close by with back arched, Wings-spread, Neck-stretched, calling and shaking body. ♀ may join in or stay on nest and Neck-stretch and call. ♂ may attack persistent intruder with beak and wings, or chase, pecking tail or wings in flight; displays may last for up to 20 min. One fight, resulting in loss of territory to intruder, involved both members of new pair standing on prone ♂ of territorial pair and repeatedly pecking his head, neck, back and wings for over 200 min. Following successful removal of intruder, ♂ typically flies around edge of territory, with slow wing-beats, neck-outstretched and calling, often landing at feeding site on edge of territory.

Pairing does not occur in winter, and must take place either at spring migratory sites prior to arrival at breeding grounds or during summer in non-breeding flocks. Copulation also occurs at spring migratory sites since requires standing water which is frequently absent upon arrival at breeding ground. Copulation observed in early to mid June in breeding areas involved only nonbreeding territorial pairs, presumably reinforcing pairbond. Copulation preceded by ritualized washing, Head-dipping and running water over back by both birds side by side and facing same direction. ♂ mounts ♀ for *c* 10–15 sec holding her neck in beak, then spreads wings, flaps them once and climbs off with head up. Pair then face, in Alert posture, with necks outstretched, calling softly and both Wing-flap. They then move side by side and separate, walking or swimming apart to preen or feed. Process takes 50–90 sec and may be repeated several times daily. In captivity, additional pre-copulatory display of Head-dipping noted, often initiated by ♀ with lowered wings and ruffled head and neck feathers, ♂ joining in with wings slightly raised; when movements synchronized, ♂ mounts (Evans 1975).

Monogamous pairbond of long duration normal; no positive case of divorce in 2220 pair-years amongst established pairs wintering at WWT Slimbridge; one pair at WWT Welney separated after 7 years, having failed to rear any young (Rees *et al.* 1996). If mate lost, bird often re-pairs within 12 months though may remain unpaired for as long as 9 years; mean time taken to re-pair 2.6 years (*n* = 275) (Rees *et al.* 1996). Divorce rate lower than for other swans, and may stem from close synchrony of migratory and breeding cycles that allows only limited time for courtship and pair formation before onset of breeding season.

Breeding and life cycle

Arrives on breeding grounds mid to late May depending on local conditions and begins nesting as soon as site free of snow. May use nest from previous year or build new one. Eggs laid end of May–early June and hatch before end of June. Not colonial but nests closer together in optimum habitat, e.g. 5–16 nests per 10 km[2] on Russkiy Zavorot Peninsula, compared to 1–4 breeding pairs per 10 km[2] (Mineyev 1991, Syroechkovskiy *et al.* 2002) on Vaigach Island. Nest large mound of locally available vegetation, including sedges, grasses, moss, *Empetrum* and even *Salix*, plucked from around site. Paddling and plucking often forms shallow pool around nest; strandline vegetation also used. ♂ passes material to ♀ sitting on nest, which is often on ridge or hummock at some distance from feeding pool, where snow-free early and not liable to flood. Eggs almost equally rounded at ends; white or yellowish, often slightly lustrous, becoming scratched and stained; in Russkiy Zavorot peninsula, northeast European Russia, 102.7 × 66.4 (89.0–117.4 × 60.5–72.0) ($n = 342$); weight in captivity 290 (252–326) ($n = 44$). Clutch 3.62 (1–6) ($n = 97$), but variable between years depending on climate and food availability. Only one brood; replacement clutches not recorded. Eggs laid at 48 h intervals in captivity (Evans 1975). Incubation 29–30 days; by ♀ only, who covers eggs with down and nest material when off feeding. ♂ sits on nest both during egg-laying and incubation when ♀ feeding, more so on warmer days, less on cooler days and at night.

Eggs and young predated by Arctic Fox mostly when adults absent or separated during hatching period, since capable of defending brood successfully. Eggs also taken by gulls, skuas and possibly Wolverines *Gulo gulo*. Hatching somewhat asynchronous, in 24–72 h. Eggshell of 1st hatched egg sometimes carried from nest, rest left but covered with material upon leaving. Young precocial and nidifugous, although may remain in nest for up to 3 days whilst remainder of eggs hatch; cared for by both parents, ♀ broods young at night when small, ♂ vigorously defends territory from rival swans and other intruders (including geese), chasing and pecking them in flight. Some pairs rear broods away from nesting territory. When alarmed, ♀ leads young into hiding at edge of pool. Young self-feeding but, when small, may take vegetation pulled from banks or from beneath water by parents. Adoption of young from neighbouring broods not uncommon in areas of high nest density, with up to 8 cygnets observed in brood. Fledge in 40–45 days, but few records. Young stay with parents through autumn and 1st winter and leave with them on spring migration; however, pairs arrive alone at breeding grounds. Nonbreeders arrive later than breeders in nesting areas, and include some former offspring who spend summer close to natal area. Offspring may rejoin parents and new cygnets at traditional winter haunt in 2nd, 3rd, 4th and even 5th winter, leaving with them again in spring.

Reproductive success improves with pair duration, together with combination of ♂ and ♀ age, and ♂ and ♀ size (Rees *et al.* 1996). First pairing occurs at 3.41 (2–4) years, ♀♀ earlier than ♂♂, and first breeding by 6th year (mean = 6.61, earliest = 3) (Evans 1979a, Rees *et al.* 1996). Annual survival rate for adults at Slimbridge calculated at not less than 87.1%; however, since some individuals shift wintering site, true figure likely to be higher (Evans 1979a). Oldest documented age 27 years, for ♀ hatched 1971 and last seen WWT Slimbridge Feb 1998. Red Fox seems able to take fully grown birds in winter.

Conservation and threats

Western population threatened by continuing eutrophication and drainage of wetlands which have reduced traditional wetland habitat, and encouraged birds onto arable land and pastures where conflict with farmers. Compensation for damage to crops paid in some countries. Breeding habitat increasingly threatened by oil and gas exploration throughout Russian arctic. Moulting and pre-migratory fattening areas also at risk, e.g. major oil-spill in Pechora delta area could affect some 15 000 birds. Despite legal protection throughout range, *c* 40% X-rayed in UK carried shot (Rees *et al.* 1997c), and 7% of adult deaths attributed to hunting (Brown *et al.* 1992). Collisions with power-lines account for *c* 20% of deaths. Main winter sites well covered by reserve networks, although further protection of roosts required (Beekman *et al.* 1994). Management programmes for restoration of aquatic ecosystems underway, particularly in The Netherlands, may allow birds access to more traditional food. Tighter enforcement of hunting laws would improve winter prospects. Protection of key breeding areas, moulting and migratory sites in Russia now critical, since few reserves currently exist in breeding range. Environmental impact assessments of proposed oil and gas developments by independent international organizations urgently recommended (Beekman *et al.* 1994).

John Bowler

Whooper Swan *Cygnus cygnus*
PLATE 4

Anas Cygnus Linnaeus, 1758, Syst. Nat., ed. 10, p. 122
Europe, North America; restricted to Sweden by Linnaeus

Etymology: L. *cygnus* means swan (*kuknos* in Gr.). Common name, as 'Hooper', known since 1566.

Other names: Wild Swan. Danish: Sangsvane; French: Cygne sauvage; German: Singschwan; Icelandic: Álft (Svanur); Japanese: Ō-hakuchō.

Variation: no subspecies. Swans breeding in Iceland once thought to be smaller than those on continent and classified as *C. c. islandicus* C.L. Brehm 1831, but recent biometric data show substantial overlap with Fenno-Scandian (northwest European) population (Rees *et al.* 1997a). No evidence for any population being genetically distinct (Harvey 1999). Some evidence for genetic cline in bill pattern, swans wintering in Japan having more yellow on bill than those wintering in UK (Brazil 1981), with swans in Finland having intermediate markings (Ohtonen 1988). Whooper Swans interbreed in captivity with Mute Swans, Whistling Swans, Bewick's Swans and Trumpeter Swans, producing hybrid young. Whoopers have bred with native Mute Swans in UK, and 6 Mute × Whooper Swan pairs in Sweden raised cygnets (Mathiasson 1992).

Description

ADULT: sexes alike, although ♀ tends to be smaller than ♂. Plumage white. Bill yellow at base and black at tip, with wedge-shaped yellow markings extending to or beyond nostrils; thin line of red or pink coloration on lower mandible in some individuals; black legs and feet; iris dark brown occasionally blue-grey. No confirmed records of adults with pink legs and bill, or of cygnets with white plumage.

MOULT: adults flightless for *c* 30 days from late July–Aug, with season sometimes extending to early Sept, and moult of body feathers continues thereafter. Breeding pairs moult asynchronously, with ♀ moulting first. Nonbreeders appear to moult at same time as breeding pairs, although tend to congregate in large moulting flocks, whereas pairs with young usually remain on territory (Einarsson 1996).

IMMATURE: grey-brown on fledging, darker on crown; underbody whiter with grey-brown flanks. Individuals become progressively white, at varying rates, during 1st winter, and may be difficult to age in field by spring. Adult bill pattern develops during 1st winter, initially chalk-white, then tinged yellow. Juveniles' white bill more easily discernable, for age-checking at distance, than grey feathering in spring. Many yearlings indistinguishable from adults; traces of grey feathering on head and neck only occasionally present. Legs and feet generally black, but may be pinkish grey, or with pink spots on feet. Bill colour similar to adult in 2nd winter, although yellow may be paler.

CYGNET: pale grey, with slightly darker crown, nape, shoulders and rump. Bill, legs and feet flesh coloured. Lateral feathering on bill extends forwards in single long point, often nearly to nostrils (Nelson 1976b).

MEASUREMENTS AND WEIGHT: ♂ wing ($n = 534$), 553–674 (612); skull length ($n = 630$), 138.0–192.0 (174.6); tarsus ($n = 411$), 106.8–142.2 (123.5). ♀ wing ($n = 589$), 521–674 (596); skull ($n = 678$), 140.0–189.0 (170.4); tarsus ($n = 453$), 102.4–132.8 (118.9). Immature ♂ in 2nd winter, wing ($n = 49$), 550–636 (604.9); skull length ($n = 64$), 155.0–190.0 (176.4); tarsus ($n = 38$), 112.5–130.5 (123.6); weight in winter in UK ($n = 69$), 7.4–12.4 (9.8). Immature ♀ wing ($n = 53$), 548–623 (596.7); skull ($n = 75$), 161.4–184.1 (173.5); tarsus ($n = 58$), 111.5–129.9 (121.1); weight in winter in UK ($n = 85$), 7.3–12.0 (9.2). Juvenile ♂ in 1st winter, wing ($n = 156$), 504–647 (591); skull length ($n = 177$), 144.0–191.0 (175.6); tarsus ($n = 95$), 111.6–129.1 (122.6); weight ($n = 177$), 5.2–12.1 (9.0). Juvenile ♀, wing ($n = 197$), 452–628 (577); skull ($n = 217$), 140.0–187.6 (171.5); tarsus

($n = 136$), 113.0–130.0 (118.9); weight ($n = 220$), 5.6–11.3 (8.4) (Rees *et al.* 1997a). Weight in Iceland in summer, ♂ ($n = 109$), 8.0–12.3 (9.76); ♀ ($n = 99$), 6.4–11.0 (8.19); in UK in winter, ♂ ($n = 655$), 7.2–13.5 (10.2); ♀ ($n = 718$), 5.6–13.1 (9.2) (Rees *et al.* 1997a). Winter weights may be higher than average, since taken at refuge where grain distributed. Summer weights vary with location and breeding status (Rees *et al.* 1991a).

Birds from extinct Greenland population perhaps smaller (mean adult wing 562, tarsus 114, $n = 7$) (Schiøler 1925).

Field characters

May be identified by large size, 1400–1650 mm long, flat profile of head and bill (giving roman nose appearance) and by yellow wedge-shaped bill markings extending beyond nostril. Bewick's Swan smaller, tends to have more up-turned and less yellow bill. Less likely to be confused with Mute Swan, despite being of similar size, since Mutes have distinctive orange-red bill with black knob, heavy build, curved neck, and regular throbbing wingbeats in flight. Whooper Swans have relatively long neck, compared with other 2 species, held erect or with kink at base, particularly when swimming. Can be identified by calls, which are more sonorous and clanging than Bewick's Swan; Mute Swans much less vocal, and voice lacks singing quality.

Voice

Highly vocal with bugling, two-syllabled Whooping call, often used repeatedly; deeper and harsher in tone than more musical Bewick's Swan. Strength and pitch of notes vary with social context, ranging from loud and persistent calls during aggressive encounters and Triumph display, to gentler contact noises used between paired birds and families (review and sonograms in Cramp and Simmons 1977). Calls also used during pre-flight Head-bobbing, becoming louder just before take-off, again to maintain pair and family cohesion, and maybe to encourage other members of flock to follow (Black 1988). Cygnets give high-pitched squeaking notes when distressed, and softer contact calls at other times.

Range and status

Breeds across northern Palearctic from Iceland and northern Scandinavia to Pacific coast of Russia, usually in shrub-forest tundra and taiga zones, south of Bewick's Swans' arctic breeding sites. Four main breeding populations, in Iceland, northwest Europe, central Russia and east Russia (Monval and Pirot 1989). Central Russian population perhaps divided into those wintering in Black Sea/East Mediterranean region and those wintering in western Asia (including Caspian), but extent to which swans move between these areas not known (Scott and Rose 1996, Delany *et al.* 1999). Level of interchange between Icelandic and northwest European populations low. A few ringed in Iceland seen again in Norway, Denmark or The Netherlands, but most migrate to Britain or Ireland (Garðarsson 1991a, Rees *et al.* 2002, Robinson *et al.* 2004a) (Figure 9.5).

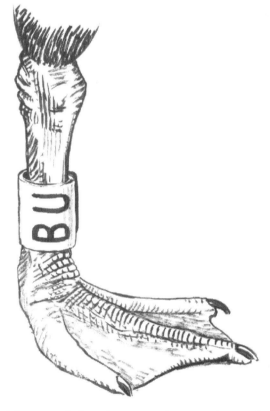

9.5 Engraved plastic leg ring used in research on individual birds.

Similarly, several families ringed in southern Finland in summer 1995 identified in southeast England in 1995–96 and 1996–97 winters (Rees *et al.* 1997a), but most Finnish-ringed birds winter in mainland Europe (Laubek 1998). One report of Icelandic-ringed bird breeding, in 2 successive years, in Finland (Rees *et al.* 1997a). Despite low level of interchange with continental mainland, individuals from Icelandic population move readily between England, Scotland and Ireland in winter, with Loughs Foyle and Swilly being used as migratory sites by swans wintering in UK, as well as by those wintering elsewhere in Ireland (McElwaine *et al.* 1995, Rees *et al.* 2002). May be higher intermingling in populations further east. Small breeding population in Greenland now extinct (Cramp and Simmons 1977); also bred in Faeroes until 17th century, and in Orkney until 18th (Cramp and Simmons 1977). Fewer than 10 pairs breed currently in Scotland and Ireland.

Icelandic breeding population winters mainly in Britain and Ireland, with 500–1300 remaining to winter in Iceland (Black and Rees 1984, Garðarsson and Skarphéðinsson 1984, Cranswick *et al.* 1996, 2002). Total of 20 856 birds recorded during coordinated census in Jan 2000, indicating an increase from the 16 700 seen during 1st international census in Jan 1986 (Salmon and Black 1986, Cranswick *et al.* 2002). Distribution was consistent, however, with some 30–33% recorded in Great Britain, 61–66% in Ireland and remainder in Iceland on each occasion. Distribution in winter, and particularly number remaining in Iceland, varies with weather and food supply. This, together with tendency to disperse into small flocks over range of sites (42% of sites holding Whoopers in 1991 survey had < 10 birds, Kirby *et al.* 1992), makes it hard to monitor population trends except by organizing intensive counts. Nevertheless, seems to be genuine increase in Icelandic population 1960s–mid 1980s. In early 1960s, Boyd and Eltringham (1962) suggested British total in Nov did not exceed 4000, and Hutchinson (1989) put Irish wintering

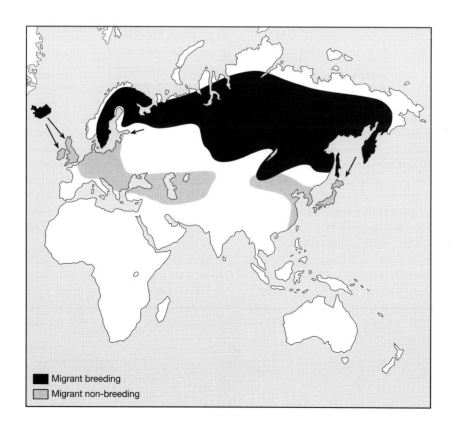

Migrant breeding
Migrant non-breeding

population then at 4000–6000. Population estimates remained in this range until autumn counts in Iceland in 1984 and 1985 yielded *c* 14 000 (Garðarsson and Skarphéðinsson 1984, Garðarsson 1991b).

Northwest European population breeds in northern Scandinavia and northwest Russia, and winters in continental Europe, particularly in Denmark, Norway, Sweden, and Schleswig Holstein, but also in The Netherlands, Baltic countries and central Europe. During cold winters, numbers in Baltic and Sweden fall dramatically, with corresponding increases further south and west (Monval and Pirot 1989). Indices of abundance indicate substantial increase since mid 1960s, and total estimated at 25 000 by 1980s (Rüger *et al.* 1986, Monval and Pirot 1989, Rose 1995). Those wintering in mainland Europe also have scattered distribution, however (Laubek 1995a, Laubek *et al.* 1999), making it difficult to calculate population size and trends by monitoring selected sites. Special survey undertaken in Jan 1995 found > 20 000 in Denmark alone, 14 000 in Germany, 7500 in Sweden, > 5000 in Norway and 3000 in Poland. Over 52 000 counted and total population put at *c* 59 000 (Laubek *et al.* 1999). Few winter as far south as Belgium and France; flock of 22 seen in northwest Spain, Dec 1990, included bird ringed in northern Iceland (Rees *et al.* 1997a).

Numbers and movements of swans wintering around Black and Caspian Seas east to Khazakstan, Turkistan and Uzbekistan unknown or incomplete. Moreover, absence of data on extent to which birds move between wintering areas (particularly between Black and Caspian Seas), or on breeding location of swans from different wintering sites, makes it difficult to determine whether Black Sea/East Mediterranean and Caspian/West Asian swans should be treated as separate populations. If migrate on broad front, however (as suggested by Garðarsson 1991b), likely that Whoopers wintering in Black Sea/East Mediterranean region nest in western Siberia (although may also breed west of Urals), and those wintering between Caspian Sea and Lake Balkhash breed further east, perhaps in central Siberia (Mathiasson 1991, Scott and Rose 1996). Krivenko (1984) reported 9800 pairs breeding in central Russia, including Taimyr peninsula. Midwinter counts in Black Sea and East Mediterranean region put population at 17 000 (including *c* 3300 in Romania), but did not include important Caspian region (Monval and Pirot 1989, Delany *et al.* 1999). Numbers wintering in western Asia (including Caspian) unknown, but may be *c* 20 000 (Scott and Rose 1996). Thought that numbers on Black Sea and in South Caspian region declined recently, although variation in coverage, and effect of weather conditions further north, make it difficult to determine trends (Delany *et al.* 1999).

Eastern population dispersed widely in summer in taiga of eastern Russia (Kondratyev 1991), and in northeast and northwest China (especially in Xinjiang Uigur Autonomous Region, Lu 1990, Li and Yiqing 1996). Midwinter censuses in Japan, China and Korea put population at *c* 30 000 in mid 1990s (Rose and Scott 1997), but more recent data from wintering range suggest *c* 60 000 (Miyabayashi and Mundkur 1999). Up to 15 000 recorded wintering in China (Li and Yiqing 1996), and average of 31 000 in Japan (Albertsen and Kanazawa 2002), although distribution varies between years. Recorded in North America, with small numbers (< 50 birds) wintering on Aleutian and Pribilof Islands, and nesting pair recorded on Attu Island in 1996 and 1997 (Mitchell 1998). Migration routes in Far East still unclear, despite ringing programmes in eastern Russia and Japan. Observations of passage movements identify 2 routes; birds from Anadyr-Penzhina lowlands of far northeast Russia appear to migrate across Kamchatka peninsula and Kuril Islands, presumably to winter in Japan, and those from Kolyma basin thought to follow west coast of Okhotsk Sea (Kondratyev 1991). Kondratyev (1991) reported only 2200 in extreme northeast of Russia (east of River Kolyma, and south to Okhotsk Sea), so some wintering in Japan and China must be breeding further west, perhaps in central Siberia. Three fitted with satellite transmitters at Kominato, North Honshu, Japan, in 1994, and 5 fitted with transmitters in 1995, tracked until midsummer. All 8 remained in easternmost part of range, migrating via eastern Hokkaido and southern/central Sakhalin to mouth of River Amur.

Two remained on lower Amur River, 2 summered on north coast of Okhotsk Sea; remaining 4 flew further north, 3 to middle reaches of Indigirka River and one to lower Kolyma River (Kanai *et al.* 1997).

Habitat and general habits

Eurasian equivalent of Trumpeter Swan of North America. Breeds in diverse range of wetland habitats, adjacent to shallow lakes or pools (often on islets), or in marshes, selecting areas with abundant vegetation. Nesting habitat in Iceland varies from low-lying marsh amidst agricultural fields to upland pools, bogs and lakes set in glacial moraine at altitudes of up to 700 m (Garðarsson and Skarphéðinsson 1984, Rees *et al.* 1991a, Einarsson 1996). In Scandinavia and Russia mainly breeds in swampy wetlands and pools surrounded by forest (including taiga), and reed-fringed lakes in steppe regions (Cramp and Simmons 1977). Expanded north to breed on open tundra in last decade, and now nests regularly in southern part of Siberian Arctic (Syroechkovski 2002). Selects shallow ponds and lakes with abundant emergent vegetation (*Arctophila fulva*, *Equisetum* and *Carex*) in shrub/forest tundra (Gusakov 1987, Kondratyev 1991). Non-breeders tend to remain in separate flocks on lakes, river channels or coastal bays. Lakes, estuaries and sheltered coasts also used as migratory sites. Traditionally winters on freshwater lakes and marshes, brackish lagoons and coastal bays, feeding on aquatic vegetation (Owen *et al.* 1986). Agricultural fields used increasingly for winter feeding in northwest Europe over last 30 years. Areas of open water remain important as secure roosts.

Mostly vegetarian, although breeding pairs seen feeding on emerging chironomids in Iceland in spring, and large numbers ingest marine and freshwater mussels *Mytilus edulis* and *Unio pictorum* during cold weather in Denmark (Einarsson 1996, Rees *et al.* 1997a). Horsetails *Equisetum*, and particularly Water Horsetail *E. fluviatile*, important during breeding season in both Finland and Iceland (Haapanen *et al.* 1977, Einarsson 1996). Sedges *Carex* and Common Cottongrass *Eriophorum angustifolium* also selected in spring by breeders in upland regions of Iceland (Einarsson 1996). Feeds on

variety of other plants, often reflecting regional and seasonal variation in availability and dietary requirements, including *Zostera*, *Ruppia* and *Potamogeton* in Denmark; *Chara*, *Potamogeton* and Canadian Pondweed *Elodea canadensis* in Scotland; and *Glyceria*, *Equisetum* and Marsh Yellow-cress *Rorippa palustre* on Ouse Washes, southeast England (Owen and Kear in Scott 1972). Dietary range similar to that recorded for Trumpeter Swan in North America. Supplementary feeding by public and by local government occurs at most wintering sites in Japan. First recorded feeding on potato fields in northwest Europe during 1940s; may now occur in large numbers on arable land, mainly cereal and potato stubbles, or winter cereals, and occasionally Oilseed Rape. Jan 1995 census in continental Europe estimated 40% of population on aquatic habitats and 60% at arable sites, with birds more likely to feed on aquatic habitats in northern part of wintering range (Laubek *et al.* 1999). Recent surveys in winter in Britain and Ireland found only 7–13% on arable land; although flock sizes were larger for agricultural sites (Cranswick *et al.* 1996, Rees *et al.* 1997b). Most (87%) appeared to be feeding on improved or flooded pasture, or in permanent inland waters, with distribution varying with flood levels.

Autumn migration commences late Sept–Oct throughout range, precise timing determined by weather, particularly at more northerly latitudes. Departure for breeding grounds occurs mainly Mar–Apr. Thus, in areas where Whooper and Bewick's Swans coexist in winter, Whoopers tend to arrive earlier, and to leave later, reflecting shorter distance to nest sites. Whooper Swans migrating between UK and Iceland probably have longest sea crossing of all swans—journey of *c* 800 km. Was thought that flew at great heights, since airline pilot reported flock of swans (presumably Whoopers) at 8200 m off Outer Hebrides (Stewart 1978, Elkins 1979). Those seen migrating along Baltic coast fly just above sea level, however (Alerstam 1981), and 10 tracked between Britain and Iceland remained at low altitudes, maximum height being 1856 m above sea level (Pennycuick *et al.* 1996, 1999). Minimum time taken to cross from Iceland to Scotland in autumn was 12.7 h, and several birds landed on sea, sometimes for long periods. Two tracked during spring migration encountered strong head/side winds when half way to Iceland; one took 31 h to cross, while other spent 4 days at sea. Maximum air speed estimated at 27.0 m/s (97.2 k/h, Pennycuick *et al.* 1996). Adverse weather conditions during migration seem likely to have major effect on survival.

Displays and breeding behaviour

Highly territorial in summer, and generally remain on territory until young fledge. Nonbreeders scattered into small groups (< 10 birds) in Finland (Haapanen 1991), but may occur in large flocks in Iceland (Garðarsson and Skarphéðinsson 1984). More gregarious in winter, although tend to occur in smaller flocks than Bewick's, and families may be seen separately. Aggressive displays, used to defend territories and to establish dominance hierarchies in flocks, similar to those used by other northern migratory swans. Most frequent displays, accompanied by loud calls, include Neck-stretching, Neck-pumping, and raised quivering wings (half-open or, more rarely, fully-extended). Physical combat, where 2 opponents (usually ♂) grapple at close quarters, pecking one another and beating with wings, occurs in only small proportion of encounters. Pairs usually display together against opponents. When defending nest site, one or both members of pair may take off and chase intruder over boundary of territory. Paired birds perform Triumph displays together, usually after winning aggressive encounter, but also upon being re-united.

Courtship and mating occasionally occurs in winter flocks, but more frequently in nonbreeding flocks in spring and summer. Mutual Head-turning, with breasts almost touching, common between paired birds in winter, particularly after temporary separation. Pre-copulatory display by both sexes is ritualized Dipping of head and neck into water (reminiscent of bathing but without wing movements) lasting for only few sec before ♂ mounts. After mating both birds call softly, rise in water, then settle to bathe and preen (Kear 1972).

Although mainly monogamous, and reproductive success improves for pairs that stay together over several years, 5.8% of pairs seen with new mate while original mate still alive (Rees *et al.* 1996); moreover, divorce did not appear associated with poor breeding success; 25% of divorcing pairs had bred in previous year. Divorce rate much higher in Whoopers than in Bewick's Swans, perhaps due to differing constraints on migratory and breeding cycles (Rees *et al.* 1996). Unlike Bewick's Swans, Whoopers may pair with birds in same wintering flock, although pair formation mostly occurs in spring and summer.

Breeding and life cycle

Breeding density in Iceland ranges 1.7–2.5 per 10 km², or 3.9–6.6 per 10 km² when unsuitable breeding habitat excluded (Einarsson 1996). Data on breeding density in Russia scarce, but *c* 28 breeding pairs recorded in 500 km² of Magadan state reserve in far northeast Russia (Kondratyev 1991). Pairs may breed as little as 50 m apart at marshy sites with abundant vegetation, and mean distance between nests in areas with suitable breeding habitat 0.50–0.88 km (Einarsson 1996). Ponds and lakes usually occupied by one breeding pair, although nonbreeders may also gather on lakes to moult. Same nest mound may be used over several years, although refurbished each season (Haapanen *et al.* 1973a). Good-quality territories are occupied in most years, and annual breeding success is higher for pairs on these territories (Einarsson and Rees 2002). Some 60–70% of swans remain in nonbreeding flocks during breeding season (Garðarsson and Skarphéðinsson 1984, Haapanen 1991, Rees *et al.* 1991a, Einarsson 1996). Of territorial pairs, 8–10% fail to lay or hatch eggs (Rees *et al.* 1991a, Einarsson 1996).

Onset of laying depends on thaw, but usually late Apr–May in Iceland and Fenno-Scandia, mid to late May in Russia, and may continue into June across range (Rees *et al.* 1997a). Eggs, usually laid at 48 h intervals, elliptical and creamy white, staining to brownish yellow after few days; dimensions broadly similar across range (Cramp and Simmons 1977), although eggs from Icelandic highlands significantly smaller in volume than those from lowlands (Einarsson 1996)—113.0 × 71.5 (93.0– 126.0 × 61.0–79.0 (*n* = 643) in lowlands, and 112.7 × 70.3 (99.0–121.0 × 64.0–75.0) (*n* = 169) in highlands (Einarsson 1996). Weight 328 (*n* = 26) in Iceland and 331 (*n* = 83) in Europe (Schönwetter 1960–66). Clutch 4 or 5 (2–7) eggs, depending on site (Einarsson 1996, Haapanen *et al.* 1973b). Average clutch sizes recorded in Iceland and Finland similar (4.5 and 4.4 eggs respectively), but smaller (3.4 eggs) and cygnet mortality higher in north Finland than in south Finland (Haapanen *et al.* 1973b, Einarsson 1996). Pairs that lose eggs (particularly after flooding in lowland areas) may lay 2nd clutch (Einarsson 1996). ♀ develops brood patch and incubates for 35 (31–42) days. ♂ remains nearby to defend territory, and occasionally sits on eggs, but normally ♀ covers eggs with down and nest material before leaving to drink and feed.

Most clutches hatch mid June–early July, although occasionally broods emerge late May (Einarsson 1996). Hatching asynchronous (36–48 h). Cygnets brooded by ♀ when small, and mainly self-feeding (Cramp and Simmons 1977). Fledge in *c* 87 days (Haapanen *et al.* 1973b); captive cygnets have faster growth rates than wild birds and fledge in *c* 80 days (Bowler 1992). Cygnets raised in captivity in Britain grew more rapidly than wild birds in Iceland, although growth rates vary with rearing conditions (Bowler 1992). Nesting habitat of pairs breeding in Finland affected the growth rates and subsequent survival of their cygnets (Knudsen *et al.* 2002). Offspring stay with parents during 1st winter. Some families break-up towards end of winter, due to increasing independence of cygnets, but most cygnets remain with parents during spring migration. Most year-old birds remain in non-breeding flocks during summer, and do not try to join parents on breeding territories. No definite evidence of offspring associating with parents in subsequent years, even when in same winter flock.

Long-lived like other swans. Maximum life-span not known but birds ringed in Iceland during 1960s recovered aged at least 22 years, and oldest Whooper in captivity reached 25 years (Scott 1972). Haapanen (1991) estimated annual mortality rate in Finland at 14.9%, and suggested that mean mortality for 1st year, 2nd year and older birds is 30%, 25% and 12% respectively. Einarsson (1996), conversely, found minimum survival rate of 82.6% for swans ringed during 1st winter returning following year. Thereafter, minimum annual survival fell to average 80.1% for swans of 2–6 years, and was 78.3% for swans of unknown age in 8 years after ringing. Lower survival

estimates for Icelandic population may be due to different methods of deriving figures, and more rigorous analyses are required, but long sea crossings could result in higher mortality during migration.

Two swans (both ♀) bred when only one year old, and some 25% seen in 2nd winter (i.e. as yearlings) appeared to be paired, but most birds do not return with mate until 3rd or 4th winter (Einarsson 1996). More ♀♀ than ♂♂ paired by age 2–3 years. Data on onset of breeding scanty, since takes several years for young to breed successfully; 1st breeding usual by 4–7 years, although number still had not bred at this stage (Einarsson 1996, Rees *et al.* 1996). Genetic fingerprinting confirmed that one ♀ bred within 1st year of life.

Breeding success for population varies substantially from year to year; mean percentage of cygnets recorded in flocks wintering at 3 sites in Britain ranged 8.6–22.4% during 1980s (Einarsson 1996). Cold spring weather reduces numbers attempting to breed, and clutch and brood sizes (Einarsson 1996). Biomass of vegetation on territory may influence clutch (Ohtonen and Huhtala 1991), and has significant effect on number of cygnets surviving into 1st winter (Einarsson 1996). Birds from different breeding areas contribute disproportionately to percentage of juveniles reared annually in population (Rees *et al.* 1991a, Einarsson 1996). There is also bias in distribution of family groups in winter range, with marked variation in proportion of juveniles recorded between sites and regions (Rees *et al.* 1997b, Laubek *et al.* 1999).

Conservation and threats

Regional variation in level of conservation and exploitation resulted in increasing populations in some parts, and declines in others. Protection from hunting introduced piecemeal by legislation in countries within range (e.g. 1885 in Iceland, 1925 in Japan, 1927 in Sweden, 1954 in UK, 1964 in Russia), and extent to which law implemented remains variable, particularly in remote areas. More integrated approach to conservation developed under international conventions such as European Community Birds Directive (Annex 1 species) and Berne Convention (Appendix II species). Icelandic, Black Sea and West Asian populations also listed as Category A

(2) in plan for Agreement on Conservation of African and Eurasian Waterbirds under Bonn Convention, requiring preparation and implementation of national Action Plans to improve conservation status. Icelandic population increased from 1960s–mid 1980s (Monval and Pirot 1989, Kirby *et al.* 1992), stable or perhaps declined in mid 1990s (Cranswick *et al.* 1996), but shows further increase to *c* 21 000 in 2000 census (Cranswick *et al.* 2002). Protected in Iceland since 1885; in 1903 this involved protection only during breeding season but, from 1913, again received full protection. Round-ups of moulting swans for food in Arnavatnsheiði, west Iceland, into 20th century was, therefore, illegal. Despite protection from hunting throughout migratory range, some 10% of Icelandic population have lead pellets in body tissue due to illegal shooting (Rees *et al.* 1990). Main cause of death appears to be flying accidents (mostly collisions with overhead wires), followed by shooting, lead poisoning, adverse weather conditions, and predation (Brown *et al.* 1992, Einarsson 1996, Rees *et al.* 2002).

Numbers in Fenno-Scandinavia seriously reduced by human persecution during 19th and early 20th centuries. Illegal hunting and taking of eggs and cygnets brought Finnish breeding birds close to extinction by early 1950s (Haapanen *et al.* 1973b), although numbers increased substantially following protection. Breeding range in Sweden also reduced to latitudes >67°N by 1920s (Fjeldså 1972), but population increased slowly after ban on hunting in 1927, and more markedly from 1950. During last century, estimates of breeding birds in Sweden increased from 20 pairs to 310 pairs in early 1970s and 2775 pairs by 1997 (Nilsson *et al.* 1998). In 1997 survey, breeders found in all areas between coast and mountain chain whereas, in 1970s, were restricted to some core areas in north and to scattered pairs; thus seems to have reoccupied much of original breeding range. Some 30–40 pairs now breed in Estonia, >30 pairs in Latvia, 20–40 pairs in Lithuania and 20–30 pairs in Poland and Germany respectively (review in Luigujõe *et al.* 2002).

The 19th century saw similar declines in Russia, with many breeding sites in southern part of range deserted due to habitat loss and hunting pressure (Dementiev and Gladkov 1952); declines continue in some areas. Agricultural development (including drainage of wetlands) and greater public access contributed to fall in numbers of breeding birds in forest-steppe of northern Khazakhstan during 1970s (Drobovtsev and Zaborskaya 1987). Availability of firearms after 1868 in Japan led to decline in numbers and distribution where formerly abundant as far south as Tokyo; protection in 1925 halted decline but loss of wetlands since 1945 means that once extensive winter range in Japan can never be recolonized (Brazil 2003). Restricted breeding distribution, due to human settlement and increased disturbance in previously remote areas, also recorded in Yamal and Nenetski regions of Russia (Braude 1987, Kalyakin and Vinogradov 1987, Mineyev 1987). Elsewhere, population stable (e.g. central Baraba in Western Siberia; Fyodorov and Khodkov 1987), or increasing due to conservation measures, including development of reserves in far northeastern Russia (Roslyakov 1987) and supplementary feeding in Japan (Albertsen and Kanazawa 2002, Syroechkovski 2002, Brazil 2003).

Efforts at protection made recently in China, following reduction in breeding population due to habitat loss, hunting and taking of eggs and young since 1960s; now ranks 2nd on List of Categories of Protected Birds under China's 1989 Wildlife Protection Law (Li and Yiqing 1996), and reserves established in breeding areas. Nevertheless, small and isolated population in northwest China, where traditionally coexisted with nomadic herdsmen, remains threatened by overgrazing, disturbance and other human activity (Ma and Cai 2000, 2002). Major decline in wintering habitat in Korea during 1960s followed reclamation of coastal and inland wetlands for farm expansion programmes, and for industrial development (Pyong-Oh Won 1981). Current status in Korea unclear, although numbers wintering estimated at 500 in D.P.R. Korea (Pak 1995, Miyabayashi and Mundkur 1999) and at 3500 in Republic of Korea (Miyabayashi and Mundkur 1999). Has long been revered in Japan; artificial feeding in winter widespread, but drainage of important wintering sites remains threat (Ohmori 1981), and changes in agricultural practice may cause future conflict with rice farmers (Albertsen and Kanazawa 2002).

Eileen Rees

Cape Barren Goose

Taxonomy

The aberrant Cape Barren Goose is the only representative of its tribe (Woolfenden 1961, Veselovský 1970, Nováková *et al.* 1987, Livezey 1996b), and no hybrids have been recorded (Johnsgard 1960b). It is absent from the fossil record (Brodkorb 1964, Howard 1964a). Its nearest relatives may have been two extinct flightless geese *Cnemiornis* of New Zealand (Young *et al.* 1996, Worthy *et al.* 1997, Fuller 2001) which also had large salt-extracting glands.

The goose exhibits a number of features that are ancient, including partially webbed feet, the oiling of goslings by their parents, copulation on land, and a pre-copulatory display that lacks any bathing component (Johnsgard 1961a, Kear and Murton 1973). Its affinities to other anseriforms are unclear but it has seemed closest either to the sheldgeese (Tadornini) or the true geese (Anserini) (Delacour and Mayr 1945, Delacour 1954–64, Johnsgard 1965a, Veselovský 1970, Brush 1976, Livezey 1986, 1997b, Sraml *et al.* 1996). It resembles the former in the pied pattern of the downy young, in using the 'wrists' of the wing when attacking opponents, and in performing erect, chest-puffing displays when greeting mates (Veselovský 1970, Kear and Murton 1973). Similarities to the true geese include various displays (especially the typical goose-like Triumph Ceremony performed by mated pairs after an enemy has been repulsed), the reticulated tarsus (scales on the legs arranged in a network pattern), absence of a syringeal bulla (a swelling of the windpipe at the point where it bifurcates into the two lungs) in the male, the similarity in the voice of male and female, the structure of various bones and muscles, and blood plasma proteins (Verheyen 1953, Johnsgard 1960a, 1965a, Woolfenden 1961, Kear and Murton 1973, Livezey 1986, 1996b, Nováková *et al.* 1987). Links to the swans (Cygnini) have been proposed on the basis of a similarly long incubation period, photoperiodic responses and the fact that the male undertakes a prime share of building the nest (Kear 1970, Kear and Murton 1973). Molecular analysis (sequencing mitochondrial cytochrome *b* gene) has, indeed, suggested its position as a sister species to the Coscoroba Swan (Harshman 1996, Harvey 1999), at the base of the anserine clade. Mitochondrial control region sequences (Donne-Goussé *et al.* 2002) also suggested that the Coscoroba Swan is the Cape Barren Goose's closest relative, but showed their sister group to be the swans rather than swans and geese.

Des Callaghan

Cape Barren Goose *Cereopsis novaehollandiae*

PLATE 8

Cereopsis N. Hollandiae Latham, 1801, Index Ornith., Suppl., p. 67
New South Wales = islands of Bass Strait

Etymology: *Cereopsis* Gr. *kerinos* means waxen, plus *opsis* face, in reference to greenish cere at base of bill; *novaehollandiae* after New Holland which was European name for eastern Australia.

Other names: Cereopsis, Pig Goose, Pigeon Goose.

Variation: 2 subspecies recognized: *C. n. novaehollandiae* from islands off southeast Australia; and Recherche Island *Cereopsis C. n. grisea* Storr, 1980 from Recherche Archipelago off Western Australia.

Description

ADULT: sexes alike. *novaehollandiae* medium grey with slightly paler head and upper neck. Crown white. Short scapulars and wing coverts have broad, dark grey sub-terminal bar, while longer ones have similarly coloured oval spot. Primaries and secondaries grey with black tips. Tail and upper tail coverts black. Webbing between toes incomplete. Feet including webs black, legs pale pink to deep carmine with black extending variable distance from feet up legs; bill black but mostly covered by enlarged greenish yellow cere; iris hazel-brown. *grisea* has white of crown reaching top of eye, but less sharply delimited from grey on side of head. Pink of legs duller and less extensive, grey-black extends from feet up front edge of tarsus to hock. Back and wings browner (Storr 1980). Stockier than nominate race.

MOULT: one complete annual body and wing moult usually in Oct following breeding, although nonbreeders and possibly juveniles moult at same time. Flightless during wing moult (Frith 1982, Marchant and Higgins 1990).

IMMATURE: resembles adult but generally paler grey with heavier spotting on wings and scapulars. Cere and legs paler, latter being greenish or blackish; iris dull brown. Cere becomes lime-green at Day 70. Juveniles moult body feathers at *c* 6 months.

GOSLING: top of head, back of neck and dorsal surface dark brown with two broad, parallel, light grey stripes on either side of back. Underside light grey. Face grey with dark brown stripe through eye. Wings dark brown with light grey leading edge. Bill grey-black; legs and feet grey-green; iris black. Gosling of *grisea* stockier and darker, with higher-pitched voice.

MEASUREMENTS AND WEIGHT: *novaehollandiae* ♂ ($n = 14$) wing, 450–490; bill, 48–53; weight, 3700–5100 (Frith 1982). ♀ wing 441–442; tail, 135–169; tarsus, 104.5–106.1 (Marchant and Higgins 1990). In captivity ♂ ($n = 3$) wing, 447–483 (465.7); bill, 44.3–49.4 (46.7); tarsus, 108.7–117.7 (112.9); weight ($n = 1$), 4290. ♀ ($n = 1$) wing, 467; bill, 44; tarsus, 106.2; weight, 3180. *grisea* ♂ wing, 500; tail, 169; bill, 45.7. ♀ wing, 460; tail, 155; bill, 43.8 (Marchant and Higgins 1990).

Field characters

Length 750–1000 mm. Cannot be confused with any other bird within range. Large, grey, long-legged, short-beaked goose with heavy body. Green cere, pink legs and black spotting on wings visible at close quarters. In flight, bulky, uniformly grey except for black tail and trailing edge to broad wings. Flies in loose groups or lines with regular, shallow but powerful wingbeats and glides. Walks with fast, rolling gait and rarely enters water except to escape pursuit, when swims or dives.

Voice

Both sexes produce low, pig-like grunt. ♂ has loud, higher pitched and harsher, usually disyllabic, trumpet. Calls mostly uttered in flight, during display or when alarmed. Both sexes hiss when threatened. Goslings have whistling contact and distress call, latter higher in pitch and uttered with head held high, and coordinate resting periods by emitting long, trilling calls when nestling together; sonogram in Kear (1968).

Range and status

Races separated by *c* 1000 km. *novaehollandiae* occurs on Furneaux Islands (Bass Strait), islands off Wilson's Promontory (Victoria) and adjacent mainland, islands in Spencer Gulf including Investigator Group, Sir Joseph Banks Group and Nuyts Archipelago and adjacent Eyre Peninsula. Vagrant further north and to New Zealand, with unconfirmed sighting in Tierra del Fuego. Introduced to Tidbinbilla in New South Wales, Warrnambool in Victoria, Maria Island in Tasmania, Kangaroo Island in South Australia, and into South Island, New Zealand, where now extinct. *grisea* found on Recherche Archipelago, 240 km long comprising 350 islands and rocks off Western Australia, not all occupied by geese, and islands to west to Red Island (formerly to Albany), mainland near Esperance. Vagrant to Nullabor Plain (Marchant and Higgins 1990, Shaughnessy and Haberley 1994).

Nominate race numbers *c* 17 000 (Robinson and Delroy 1986, Marchant and Higgins 1990); recently *c* 20 000 and rising. *grisea* has population of 650 birds (Halse *et al.* 1995) or 250–500 based on survey Feb 1992 (Garnett 1992). Population of nominate race reduced to 5300 in 1960s (Dorward 1967) due to hunting for sport, and persecution through competition with farming interests (Kear and Williams 1978, Kear 1979, Eberhard and Pearse 1981). Establishment of nature reserves, control of hunting and improvement of grazing allowed population to recover, though declined during drought year of

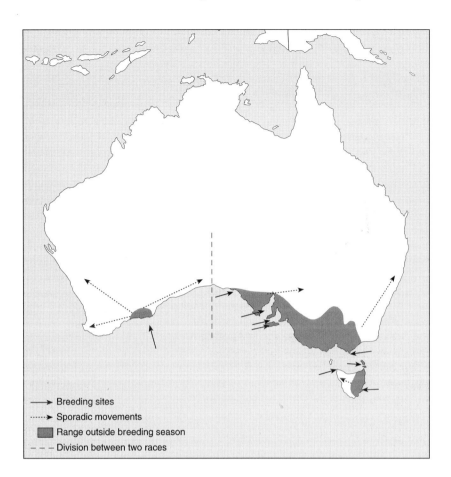

Breeding sites
Sporadic movements
Range outside breeding season
Division between two races

1991 (Garnett 1992) which saw 40% of population die of starvation.

Habitat and general habits

Breeds on small, low islands of limestone or granite (Bass Strait) supporting open shrubland or grassland < 1 m tall. Outside breeding season, occurs on grasslands and freshwater or brackish wetlands on islands adjacent to mainland. Young move in summer to large islands and mainland and prefer flat, open pasture. Roosts on feeding sites, beaches, mudflats, saltmarshes and other wetlands.

Occurs in small flocks, not usually > 300 birds, outside breeding season. Stable dominance hierarchy exists within flocks, although agonistic encounters relating to individual spacing, and position in hierarchy, occur frequently.

Feeds during daylight using characteristic shearing or tearing action to crop vegetation. Diet varies according to season and locality; in Furneaux Group, comprises up to 70% grass during breeding season but Geraniaceae, Plantaginaceae and Asteraceae when grass unavailable in summer. On improved pasture, clover *Trifolium* and cultivated grasses, including cereal crops, eaten; other foods include *Disophyma australe, Juncus, Myoporum insulare, Nitraria schoberi* and alga *Homosira banksii* (Marchant and Higgins 1990). Evidence suggests that feeds non-selectively but chooses swards with high water content, high nitrogen and low fibre. Is unable to digest cellulose (Marriott and Forbes 1970) in common with other geese (Mattocks 1971) but derives nourishment from cell sap. Large salt-extracting glands above eyes (Figure 9.6) allow bird to drink brine during drought.

Moves between islands or to mainland when not breeding and, as pastures dry out, for distances of up to 40 km.

9.6 Skull of Cape Barren Goose showing, above the orbit, mark of large salt-extracting glands.

Displays and breeding behaviour

Pair formation initiated by either sex and begins with one circling other, slowly bowing heads (Waltzing) followed by one or both facing, holding neck high and head down, flapping wings and hissing (Griffin display). Both then face one another with neck outstretched, tail spread and heads raised and lowered while calling in Triumph Ceremony. Copulation preceded by one bird stroking or nuzzling lower back of other, which initiates avoidance response and rotation. ♀ squats and ♂ mounts; mating always occurs on land and followed by Triumph Ceremony. Courtship and mating resemble agonistic behaviour in which one goose faces other, pecks air or lunges, attempting to peck head and neck. During fights, one bird moves behind other after preliminary pushing and wing-beating, and finally jumps on other's back, pecking and beating with wings (Pellis 1982). Monogamous and pair for life. Marchant and Higgins (1990) recorded equal sex ratio; however, in captivity seems biased towards ♀♀. Territorial and aggressive breeders; nests usually over 20 m apart (Frith 1982).

Breeding and life cycle

Territories occupied from Feb and breeding occurs in winter, Apr–Oct, determined by short daylength (captive birds in northern hemisphere at 50°N nest Nov–Mar). Other factors such as rainfall and condition of pasture may influence nesting (Marriott 1970, Delroy *et al.* 1989). *grisea* may lay slightly later. Breeds in pairs or loose colonies with nests well spaced. Nest in hollow on ground, amongst tussock grass, rocks or bushes, often on slope on windward side of island; occasionally in bushes. Sites often traditional. ♂ builds nest of available plant material but ♀ lines with down and maintains structure.

Eggs of *novaehollandiae* from Furneaux Group 82.9 × 55.6, weight 127 (Guiler 1967); from Maria Island 80.9 × 54.6 (Marchant and Higgins 1990), captive *grisea* 78.3 × 53.7, weight 124.5 ($n = 20$) (Crompton 1985). Clutch size *novaehollandiae* 4.24 ($n = 947$) (Marchant and Higgins 1990); captive *grisea* 5 ($n = 7$) (Wooldridge and Wisniewski 1993), wild *grisea* 4 ($n = 16$) (Shaugnessy and Haberley 1994). Eggs elliptical (rounder from captive *grisea*), creamy white with chalky texture; laid at intervals of 1–3 days. ♀ incubates (suffering 20% weight loss) 34–37 days, though 39 days recorded for captive *grisea* (Wooldridge and Wisniewski 1993), while ♂ defends territory. Eggs covered with down when ♀ absent. Hatching synchronous, and young precocial, nidifugous, weighing 70–95, brooded by both parents who lead to water if danger threatens. ♀ may feign injury. Goslings feed within day of hatching. Estimated that 89% of eggs hatch and 54% fledge. Goslings sometimes oiled by parents (Scott 1972). Sequence of plumage development suggests that, although now mainly land-living, derived from goose that reared young on water (Veselovský 1973); however, display has no bathing movements, suggesting that ancestor always copulated on land (Kear 1985), as do Magpie Geese and many whistling-ducks. Fledge within 70–76 days but remain with parents for > 16 weeks. Fledglings form crèches and new fledglings tend to gather in small flocks. Growth complete after 2–3 years (Guiler 1974). Pairs may form at 12 months but normally breeds at 3 years. Captive ♀, reared alone, may imprint on humans, *contra* most geese, where ♂ imprints more readily. No data on breeding success, adult survival, nor on longevity.

Conservation and threats

Population of nominate race probably stable. Active management by grazing may be necessary on some islands. Nature reserve status of Recherche Archipelago protects *grisea* on breeding sites; however, monitoring necessary, especially in droughts and years of high temperature when birds may die of starvation or heat stress (Shaughnessy and Haberley 1994, Halse *et al.* 1995). Although *grisea* common in captivity in Australia and elsewhere, described as subspecies only in 1980; small population size suggested Endangered status to Green (1992), and appears as Vulnerable in recent list of threatened subspecies (Threatened Waterfowl Specialist Group 2003).

Patrick Wisniewski

The true geese

The 15 species of grazing geese, ten grey geese and five black geese, breed from the Tropic of Cancer to the Arctic. Most are migratory, and they fly in V formation in noisy flocks. The loud calls that they make in order to keep in touch, especially at night, have given rise to stories of magic and mystery. As in swans and the Cape Barren Goose, the sexes resemble one another, and both care for their goslings in a prolonged relationship, but the gander is primarily a guardian and neither nest builds nor incubates. Although they swim well, geese are not as aquatic as ducks and have only one change of body feathers a year. They walk easily on land but need water on which to roost at night, and regularly resort to lakes or estuaries; indeed, many species go through the annual wing moult, when they are flightless, on large stretches of water where they achieve safety from land-based mammalian predators, and some undertake a specific migration to secure moult areas. Flocks may remain faithful to these roosts and moulting sites for many generations.

Geese seldom breed before they are at least two years old, and the young wear a juvenile plumage during their first winter which enables observers to age them at a distance. Many are currently subject to great alteration in population levels. This is due to many factors, including changes in hunting practice and in protective legislation, to huge alteration to agricultural regimes that affects both the amount of food available and its quality (and brings birds into conflict with farmers), to global climate change, and to competition with other geese, particularly on the breeding grounds. A few species, such as Hawaiian Goose, Swan Goose, Red-breasted Goose and Emperor Goose, are included in BirdLife International's (2000, 2001) lists of threatened birds, while others have races that are thought to be endangered.

Two grey geese, the Greylag and the Swan Goose, that naturally nest at the same relatively low latitudes as early agricultural man, were long ago brought into the farmyard and domesticated (see Chapter 1).

Janet Kear

Taxonomy

The true geese (Anserini) are generally considered to consist of two extant genera, the grey geese *Anser* and the black geese *Branta*. Often, however, further genera are designated for some, such as *Nesochen* (for the Hawaiian Goose), *Chen* (for the snow geese and Emperor Goose), *Cygnopsis* (for the Swan Goose) and *Eulabeia* (for the Bar-headed Goose) (Delacour 1954–64, Woolfenden 1961, AOU 1983). The recently extinct *Geochen rhuax*, endemic to the Hawaiian Islands (Olson and James 1991), was apparently intermediate between *Anser* and *Branta* (Livezey 1997b).

All Holocene geese are confined to the northern hemisphere, with highest diversity in the Palearctic (Figure 9.7). The earliest fossils are from the Miocene, including many species and genera from Europe (*Anserobranta* [?] *robusta, Anser atavus, A. scaldii, A. cygniformis* and *A. oeningensis*) and North America (*Eremochen russelli, Presbychen abavus, Branta esmeralda, B. howardae, B. woolfendeni, Anser arenosus* and *A. arizonae*) (Brodkorb 1964, Howard 1964a, Cheneval 1987, Bickart 1990). *Palaeopappia eous* and *P. hamsteadiensis* of early Oligocene beds in Great Britain have also been placed in the Anserinae, but their positions are tentative (Harrison and Walker 1979, Cheneval 1987). Despite the obviously strong biogeographic links with the northern hemisphere, Livezey (1996b) argued that the Anserini had their origin in the southern hemisphere, since his analysis showed that the Cape Barren Goose, endemic

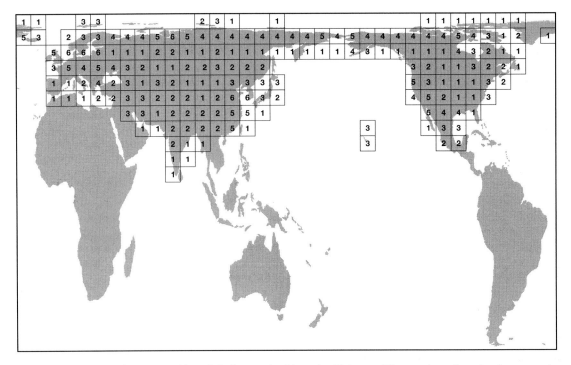

9.7 Species diversity of true geese (Anserini) that survived into the Holocene. The number of species that occur (or occurred) within each grid-cell is indicated.

to Australia, was their sister taxon. Harshman (1996) and Harvey (1999), however, have suggested that the Cape Barren Goose is a sister species to the South American Coscoroba Swan.

Partly due to their great fidelity to breeding and wintering areas, migratory geese have a tendency to subspeciate. Interspecific hybridization is not unusual, including between *Branta* and *Anser*, although hybrids of these genera appear generally to be infertile. Surprisingly perhaps, hybridization between geese and swans is relatively frequent (Johnsgard 1960b), and a close relationship between geese and swans has been recognized by most workers, although there has been disagreement over taxonomic rank and details of composition (Eyton 1838, Sclater 1880, Salvadori 1895, Delacour and Mayr 1945, Delacour 1954–64, Johnsgard 1960b, 1961a, 1962, 1965a, 1978, Woolfenden 1961, Brush 1976, Patton and Avise 1986, Livezey 1986a, 1996b).

Geese retain a number of ancient characters, including similar plumage in male and female, protracted monogamous pairbonds, paternal care of broods and the absence of metallic plumage coloration (Delacour 1954–64, Johnsgard 1965a, 1978, Kear 1970b, Scott and Clutton-Brock 1989, Livezey 1996b). They also show a number of unique characters, including the possession of a ritualized Triumph Ceremony performed by mated pairs after territorial encounters, and striations on the neck feathering that are associated with the vibrating of these feathers in threat (Johnsgard 1960b, 1961a, 1962, 1965a, Livezey 1996b). Black geese appear to have fewer vocal signals than grey geese but more dramatic plumage patterns (especially in the region of the head) (Johnsgard 1960b).

Des Callaghan

Swan Goose *Anser cygnoides*

PLATE 5

Anas Cygnoid Linnaeus, 1758, Syst. Nat., ed. 10, p. 122
Asia
Anser Brisson, 1760

Etymology: *cygnoides* L. for swan-like.

Other names: Chinese Goose, Dry-nosed Goose, Siberian Goose, plus many given to domestic forms such as African, Cape, Knob, Spanish or Guinea Goose. Sometimes placed in genus *Cygnopsis* (Livezey 1996b).

Variation: no subspecies.

Description

ADULT: sexes alike. Upperparts dark chestnut and feathers conspicuously bordered whitish buff. Thin white band borders base of mandible, from where broad dark chestnut band runs over upperpart of head and down hind neck to base. Rest of head and neck pale brown, with chest slightly darker. Flanks barred dark chestnut, becoming heavier towards legs. Anterior lowerparts white except for dark chestnut tail with white border. Bill long, black and swan-like; feet and legs reddish orange; iris reddish brown. ♀ similar but slightly smaller with shorter neck and smaller bill (Delacour 1954–64, Johnsgard 1978).

MOULT: one moult of body and wing feathers annually. Nonbreeders begin wing moult as early as beginning of June, while breeding birds moult July–Aug (Dementiev and Gladkov 1952, Nowak 1970, Tkachenko 1995).

IMMATURE: similar to adult, but no white border at base of mandible nor chestnut barring on flanks. Upperparts and iris duller (Delacour 1954–64, Johnsgard 1978).

GOSLING: head, neck and underparts yellowish buff, with broad blackish patch over lores and eyes. Upperparts dusky brown, with pale buff patches on hind wing and sides of back. Bill blackish grey with light tip (Delacour 1954–64).

MEASUREMENTS AND WEIGHT: ♂ (*n* = 4) wing, 460–473 (467.6); culmen, 89.0–98.5 (94.8) (Dementiev and Gladkov 1952); tarsus, 80–82 (Madge and Burn 1988); weight, *c* 3500 (Johnsgard 1978). ♀ (*n* = 4) wing, 437–445 (444.0); culmen (*n* = 1), 87.0 (Dementiev and Gladkov 1952); weight, 2850–3450 (Johnsgard 1978).

Field characters

Large brown goose, 800–930 mm long. Can occur among flocks of other grey geese, such as Bean Geese (Madge and Burn 1988); however, long black bill and two-toned head and neck characteristic.

Voice

Principal call prolonged, resounding, ascending honk; alarm signalled by harsh, short note repeated 2–3 times. Pre-flight call low *ga-ga-ga-ga-ga* (Delacour 1954–64, Johnsgard 1965a, Madge and Burn 1988). Domestic forms retain raucous alarm call and use it, in particular, as territorial signal.

Range and status

Four breeding areas tentatively recognized: first in west and central Mongolia (north of Gobian Altai) (Nowak 1970, Kitson 1978), and possibly also in neighbouring Tuva along River Tes-Khem and on Lake Tere-Khol (Russian Federation) (Borodin 1984) and northwest China (north Sinkiang Province) (see Dementiev and Gladkov 1952); second, in Torei Lakes in Chita Oblast (Russian Federation) (Zubakin 1981, Kolosov 1983, Borodin 1984), northeast China (west Heilongjiang Province, northwest Jilin Province and northern Inner Mongolia Autonomous Region) (see Scott 1989), and possibly eastern Mongolia; third, Khanka Lake (Russian Federation) (Bocharnikov and Gluschenko 1992); and last in Lake Udyl and Schastye Bay (in Lower Amur, Russian Federation) (Poyarkov 1984, Ler *et al.* 1989) and scattered sites on North Plain of Sakhalin Island (Nechaev 1992). In China, currently winters at few sites on coasts of Yellow Sea and East China Sea, and at several large

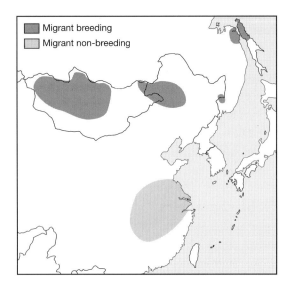

Migrant breeding
Migrant non-breeding

lakes along middle and lower stretches of Chang Jiang (=Yangtze) river (Perennou *et al.* 1994, Lu 1996, Miyabayashi and Mundkur 1999) with at least 15 sites of known international importance. In South Korea, regularly winters on Han gang estuary (Miyabayashi and Mundkur 1999), and in small numbers at other scattered sites.

Historical information suggests that breeding range more extensive in Russian Federation, with sporadic breeding in Minusinsk depression to 54° 31′ N, and more extensive range from southern parts of Baikal and Trans-baikal areas eastwards throughout northern parts of Amur basin and north along coast apparently to Ayan (56° 30′ N) (Dementiev and Gladkov 1952). In east Kazakhstan, formerly bred in Zaysan depression, either sporadically (Dementiev and Gladkov 1952) or quite commonly (Izask 1978), but now extinct as breeder and only occasionally recorded during migration (Izask 1978). Trends in breeding numbers in China and Mongolia unclear.

Although never common in Japan, was formerly regular winter visitor from Hokkaido to Kyushu, although chiefly to Chiba-ken where up to 100 geese wintered annually. Since 1950, however, has become rare winter visitor (Yamashina 1974, Brazil 1991). Historical distribution in winter in eastern China unclear, but does not seem to have altered substantially. Vagrants occasionally reach Uzbekistan and Taiwan (Dementiev and Gladkov 1952,

Izask 1978, Madge and Burn 1988), and frequently recorded in North Korea (Perennou *et al.* 1994).

In general, size of breeding colonies poorly known. In Russian Federation, up to 170 pairs nested at Lake Udyl, but apparently declined to less than 40 pairs (Borodin 1984, Poyarkov 1984, 1992, Bocharnikov 1990b) and nesting in Schastye Bay thought to be infrequent (Ler *et al.* 1989). Numbers breeding at Torei Lakes varies from 6 pairs in dry years to 50–52 pairs in wetter years (Tkachenko 1995). Breeding not confirmed at Khanka Lake since 1976 (Bocharnikov and Gluschenko 1992). In Sakhalin, numbers decreased dramatically with current population estimated at less than 100 pairs (Nechaev 1992) compared to 1200–1300 pairs along 35 km of coast from Cape Tyk to Lakh Cape in 1951 (Gizenko and Mishin 1952).

Status of breeding birds in Mongolia unclear, but Nowak (1970) stated that large numbers breed in west of country and fewer in centre, while Kitson (1978) recorded 1000 birds at Ögii Nor (Arhangay, central Mongolia) on 2 July 1977. Numbers breeding in northeast China unknown.

Winter counts provide 5-year means, 1987–91, of 37 000 individuals of which 25 660 were at Poyang Lake (Jiangxi Province, China) and 10 770 along 300 km of Yancheng shore (Jiangsu Province, China) (Perennou *et al.* 1994). Since 1990, several hundred regularly wintered on Han gang river estuary in South Korea, with 1858 present Mar 1994 (Collar *et al.* 1994) but only 553 during following winter (Miyabayashi and Mundkur 1999). Population estimated at 30 000–50 000 individuals (Miyabayashi and Mundkur 1999), a substantial reduction from previous times (Lu 1996). Most recent estimates by Delany and Scott (2002) give 50 000–60 000.

Domesticated in Asia many centuries ago and varieties farmed, in particular, in relatively warm climates and at low latitudes where annually lay more eggs than geese of Greylag descent (Kear 1990).

Habitat and general habits

On breeding ground, can be found nesting in mountains, valleys and steppes in extremely varied types of terrain, but always in close association with rivers and lakes. Nesting areas vary from mouths of rivers to narrow ravines of upper reaches, and from lakes and floodplain meadows to lowland marshes. Both freshwater and brackish sites utilized, and surrounding vegetation varies from sparse, low communities to forest (Dementiev and Gladkov 1952, Borodin 1984, Nechaev 1992). Typical winter habitat brackish and freshwater lowland marshes, and wet cultivated areas, such as rice fields (Madge and Burn 1988, Brazil 1991, Lu 1996). During migration, occurs in most habitats, including desert steppe far from water (Dementiev and Gladkov 1952).

Flock size varies with season. Spring flocks usually hold *c* 40 birds, while nonbreeding summer flocks contain up to 200, and moulting flocks probably slightly more (Johnsgard 1978, Poyarkov 1984, Nechaev 1992). Winter flocks often consist of several hundred (Perennou *et al.* 1994).

Lu (1996) calculated that daily energy intake for individual on wintering grounds was 308.3 ± 12.6, about twice Basic Metabolic Rate (BMR). Principal food item in winter on freshwater marshes was roots of *Vallisneria asiatica*, while seeds of *Suaeda salsa* most important on brackish sites. Presumably rice selected in some areas. On breeding grounds, grasses thought important, and 10 individuals obtained in Amur basin (Russian Federation) in Aug contained food remnants consisting exclusively of *Carex* (Dementiev and Gladkov 1952). Nonbreeding birds summering along coast of Tyk Bay (Sakhalin Island) fed on coastal meadows, mainly on *Carex subpathacea* (Nechaev 1992), fruits of *Oxycoccus, Vaccinium ovalifolium* and *Empetrum sibiricum*, as well as needles of young *Larix ochotensis* (Gizenko 1955).

Displays and breeding behaviour

Displays do not differ significantly from other grey geese. Both sexes alternately emit low cackle, *gangangangang* during Triumph Ceremony (Delacour 1954–64, Johnsgard 1965a, 1978, Madge and Burn 1988). Pair formation probably occurs in winter, since even earliest arrivals in breeding areas paired (Dementiev and Gladkov 1952, Johnsgard 1978).

Breeding and life cycle

Generally departs winter quarters late Mar and arrives on breeding grounds early–late Apr (Dementiev and Gladkov 1952, Nowak 1970, Poyarkov 1984, Ler *et al.* 1989, Nechaev 1992, Tkachenko 1995). Breeding sites in high mountain areas sometimes not occupied until late May (Dementiev and Gladkov 1952).

Nests shallow depression excavated by ♀; bowl 233 (255–220) mm in diameter and 50 (40–65) mm deep ($n = 9$), and lined with dry grass and down (Tkachenko 1995). Located in variety of areas, in dense vegetation (*Ledum palustre* thickets and stands of *Carex*), on islands (often adjacent to gull colonies), and in steppe grass, but seldom far from water. Although not colonial, many pairs may be located in favoured areas (Gizenko and Mischin 1952, Delacour 1954–64, Nowak 1970, Borodin 1984, Nechaev 1992). White eggs laid from 2nd half of Apr, but May peak laying period (Nechaev 1992, Tkachenko 1995); 82.6×53.9 ($73.0–92.7 \times 45.6–57.5$) ($n = 80$) (Tkachenko 1995); weight 142.3 (117.6–159.0) (Dementiev and Gladkov 1952). Clutch 5.6 (4–8) eggs ($n = 13$); ♀ incubates, but ♂ remains close, defends nest and helps rear young (Delacour 1954–64, Johnsgard 1978). Incubation in captivity 28 days (Johnstone 1970) and, in wild, eggs hatch late May–June (Dementiev and Gladkov 1952, Gizenko and Mischin 1952, Tkachenko 1995). Single broods contain 4 (2–8) goslings (Dementiev and Gladkov 1952, Ler *et al.* 1989, Tkachenko 1995); however, crèches often form, and Poyarkov (1984) recorded group of 60 young at Lake Udyl (Russian Federation), while Kitson (1978) observed 4 pairs with crèche of 20 goslings at Ögii Nor (Mongolia) on 2 July. Broods hatched along river valleys often soon move to lower areas, such as lakes, marshes and coastal bays (Nechaev 1992, Poyarkov 1984, 1992). Most fledge by end of Aug (Ler *et al.* 1989, Nechaev 1992). Breeding chronology in high mountain areas delayed slightly, but most move to lowlands by late Aug. By then, autumn flocks gather in lowlands and migration starts. Most depart by mid-Sept although few stay until early Oct (Dementiev and Gladkov 1952, Nowak 1970, Nechaev 1992, Tkachenko 1995). Time of arrival on wintering grounds unclear.

Probably matures during 2nd winter and begins to form permanent pairbond (Johnsgard 1978). No data on breeding success, survival, nor on longevity.

Conservation and threats

Classified as Endangered by BirdLife International (2000, 2001). Decline in numbers can be attributed partly to massive habitat loss and overhunting in middle and lower Chang Jiang valley in China (Hu and Cui 1990, Callaghan and Green 1993, Lu 1993), while planned construction of Three Gorges Dam will disrupt flow and further reduce wintering habitat (Collar *et al.* 1994). Overhunting, some illegal, has caused declines in Russia, sometimes owing to confusion with Bean Goose (Kolosov 1983, Borodin 1984, Poyarkov 1984, Nechaev 1992). Pziclonskij (1976) suggested that overhunting also problem in Mongolia, but does not agree with observations of Nowak (1970) and Kitson (1978) who considered hunting pressure to be insignificant. Construction of Bukhataminsky Reservoir, flooding Chyorny-Irtysch delta (Kear and Williams 1978), was probably major factor causing extinction as breeding bird in Kazakhstan. More general habitat loss, owing to increasing human populations and economic development in Russian breeding areas, also caused reduction in numbers (Kolosov 1983, Borodin 1984, Ler

et al. 1989). Dementiev and Gladkov (1952) noted, in Maritime Territory (Russian Federation), eggs often taken and placed under domestic birds, while goslings captured and reared for food. Latter practice still frequent on Sakhalin Island (Nechaev 1992).

Creation of reserves and prohibition on hunting conserves wintering and breeding sites in China and Russia (Scott 1989, Tkachenko 1995), while attempts at Lake Udyl (Russian Federation) seem relatively unsuccessful (Poyarkov 1984, 1992). Protected from hunting in Russian Federation, but status needs better enforcement, since poaching frequent (Kolosov 1983, Borodin 1984, Nechaev 1992). A joint Russian–Japanese Conservation Programme has been initiated to coordinate research, study basic biology, create protected areas, reduce shooting mortality and develop a reintroduction programme.

Des Callaghan

Bean Goose *Anser fabalis*
PLATE 5

Anas Fabalis Latham, 1787, General Synop. Birds, Suppl., p. 297
Great Britain

Etymology: from *faba* L. for bean, in reference to bird's diet, or to bean-shaped nail at bill tip.

Other names: French: Oie des moissons; German: Saatgans; Japanese: Hishikul; Swedish: Sädgås.

Variation: 5 subspecies recognized here, Western Bean Goose *A. f. fabalis*, Russian Bean Goose *A. f. rossicus* Buturlin, 1933, Johansen's Bean Goose *A. f. johanseni* Delacour, 1951, Middendorf's Bean Goose *A. f. middendorffii* Severtsov, 1873, and Thick-billed Bean Goose *A. f. serrirostris* Swinhoe, 1871. Sushkin's Goose *A. neglectus* Sushkin, 1895 is colour variant of Russian Bean Goose.

Description

ADULT: sexes alike. Neck and head dark brown, becoming sooty brown on head, sometimes broken by white at base of bill, but never as marked as that on far paler White-fronted Goose. Upper body and mantle uniform medium brown, flank feathers dark centred and white edged. Undertail coverts and tail margin white. Upperwing coverts grey, underwing dark greyish black, flight feathers blackish brown. Bill variously orange and black; legs orange (although variant Sushkin's Goose has pink legs and pink on bill, and some birds may show pinkish coloration of bare parts to varying degree); iris dark brown. Two ecological types recognized, small thick-billed birds breeding in Russian tundra, and larger, longer-billed birds nesting in taiga. Increase in size and length of bill west to east forms basis for further division into populations with differing wintering provenance. *fabalis* large and long-necked, with slender long bill generally more orange than black (Burgers *et al.* 1991). *rossicus* small and stubby with short neck and short bill with strongly curved lower mandible and more saw-toothed appearance to lamellae; bill generally more black than orange (Burgers *et al.* 1991). *johanseni* is considered intermediate between *fabalis* and taiga form of east Asian *middendorffii*, with questionable status (see below). *middendorffii* is largest long-billed form and eastern counterpart of *fabalis*, said to have long, dark-based predominantly black bill, orange restricted to small patch at base of bill. *serrirostris* is largest short-billed form and eastern counterpart of *rossicus*, with dramatically stout bill, black with restricted orange in central portion.

MOULT: one wing and body moult annually.

IMMATURE: much as adult, but head and neck more muted, lighter and less contrasting with rest of body. Lacks white at base of bill. Upperparts more scaly, flank feathers only pale-edged (contrast white of adult); wing coverts appear marbled rather than streaked (van Impe 1973). Orange of bill and legs duller and greyer.

GOSLING: olive brown tinged yellow on face, mantle and nape, with dark streak before eye. Pale below wing which has pale yellow wing bar. Underparts pale yellow. Bill and feet dark grey.

MEASUREMENTS AND WEIGHT: *fabalis* ♂ adult wing ($n = 87$), 452–520 (481); juv wing ($n = 87$), 436–487 (461); adult bill ($n = 93$), 57–70 (63.6); bill depth ($n = 13$), 5.5–7.3 (6.4); tarsus ($n = 21$), 76–90 (82.2); weight ($n = 68$), 2690–4060 (3198). ♀ adult wing ($n = 73$), 434–488 (460); juv wing ($n = 48$), 418–476 (442); adult bill ($n = 75$), 55–66 (60.0); bill depth ($n = 6$), 5.3–7.0 (6.2); tarsus ($n = 11$), 73–80 (76.7); weight ($n = 58$), 2220–3470 (2843).

   rossicus ♂ adult wing ($n = 144$) 430–478 (454); juv wing ($n = 31$) 390–451 (429); adult bill ($n = 142$), 52–63 (57.7); bill depth ($n = 13$), 7.0–10.0 (7.9); tarsus ($n = 13$), 70–81 (75.2); weight ($n = 126$), 1970–3390 (2668). ♀ adult wing ($n = 133$), 405–458 (433); juv wing ($n = 36$), 378–443 (417); bill ($n = 134$), 49–60 (54.6); bill depth ($n = 10$), 6.9–8.6 (7.5); tarsus ($n = 13$), 69–79 (73.9); weight ($n = 117$), 2000–2800 (2374).

   middendorffii ♂ adult wing ($n = 16$), 440–558 (492); bill ($n = 15$), 64–81 (73.3); bill depth ($n = 15$), 7.0–10.5 (8.6). ♀ adult wing ($n = 9$), 465–524 (488); bill ($n = 9$), 63–80 (72.7); bill depth ($n = 8$), 7.0–9.8 (8.6).

   serrirostris ♂ wing ($n = 28$), 440–524 (474); bill ($n = 30$), 59–72 (65.9); bill depth ($n = 26$), 8.0–12.5 (10.4). ♀ wing ($n = 20$), 420–491 (449); bill ($n = 17$), 58–69 (63.3); bill depth ($n = 10$), 8.1–11.3 (9.3) (Cramp and Simmons 1977).

Field characters

Large, long-necked dark-headed grey goose, 660–840 mm long. *rossicus* type may be confused with Pink-footed Goose, but latter smaller, more dumpy with rounder head, shorter bill and more buff-grey underparts, as well as bright pink legs. Size, elongate neck and dark head differentiate from White-fronted Goose, juveniles of which may have dusky orange bills, but never dark head and pale breast of Bean Geese. In flight, long neck and bill characteristic although, again, because of similar call and dumpy proportions, *rossicus* may cause confusion with Pinkfeet. Pattern on upperwing shows less contrast between dark flight feathers and paler coverts than other grey geese.

Voice

Rather less noisy than most geese; flight and contact call *hank-hunk* similar to, although deeper than, 2-note call of Pinkfoot. Sonograms in Cramp and Simmons (1977).

Range and status

Current population of *fabalis* estimated at 100 000 and relatively stable (Madsen *et al.* 1999a), although involving some range retraction in Sweden last century (Mellquist and von Bothmer 1984) and expansion in Finland (Pirkola and Kalinainen 1984). Breeds in Kola Peninsula and taiga areas to west as far as Finland, with tongue of breeding distribution extending down into Norway and Sweden. Nonbreeders begin moulting late June, moult migration northwards being characteristic of both taiga and tundra forms. Moulting subadult *fabalis* remain away from breeding areas, probably in northernmost Lapland or White Sea coasts (Pirkola and Kalinainen 1984). Population breeding in Fennoscandia moves south through southern Sweden to winter there, in Denmark, northern Germany and The Netherlands (Nilsson 1984, Nilsson and Pirkola 1986). This population shows different migration patterns according to breeding area, but high levels of site tenacity to staging and wintering areas (Nilsson and Persson 1989). Numbers decline

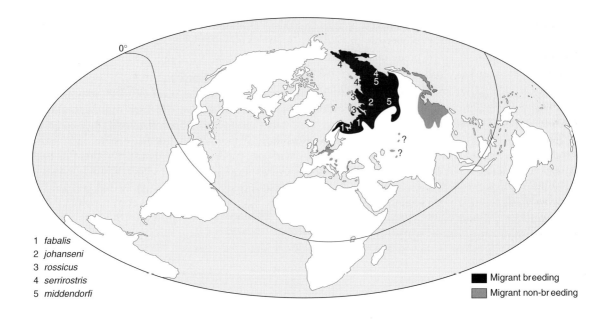

1 *fabalis*
2 *johanseni*
3 *rossicus*
4 *serrirostris*
5 *middendorfi*

■ Migrant breeding
▨ Migrant non-breeding

dramatically in southern Sweden with hard weather, moving first to Zealand in Denmark as in 1982 and 1985, latterly further south and west. Few records of *fabalis* types marked in Fennoscandia being re-sighted or recovered in former East German parts of Baltic. In severe winters, *fabalis* types wintering in The Netherlands, may include some of other origins, since numbers appear to exceed number breeding in Fennoscandia (Burgers *et al.* 1991). Substantial numbers of *fabalis* occur along Baltic coast of former East Germany (e.g. 16 000 in Nov 1995), leaving this area only during severe weather (Nilsson and Pirkola 1986, Rutschke 1987). Ringing recoveries show at least some breed east of Ural Mountains, and most *fabalis* types are recovered in northern half of eastern Germany (Burgers *et al.* 1991). Two flocks, totalling *c* 600 birds, winter in UK, originating from southern Swedish populations (Parslow-Otsu 1991, Hearn 2004a).

rossicus numbers perhaps 600 000, but trends far from clear because of gaps in current count network and confusion between subspecies in some areas (Madsen *et al.* 1999a). Breeding numbers said to have increased in western tundras of Russia (Timanskaya-Yamal), but decreased further east (Gydan, north Yamal and Taimyr, Tomkovich *et al.* 1994, Kalyakin 1995). Large moult gatherings occur

in Novaya Zemlya, Kanin, Yugor, Yamal, western Taimyr, Lena Delta, New Siberia Islands and Indigirka Delta (Uspenski 1965, Mineyev 1990). In winter, differentiated into North Sea element (numbering 275 000 in midwinter) and central European group (325 000) by Huyskens (1986) and, despite changes in relative numbers, thought total more or less stable over last 20 years (Madsen *et al.* 1999a). In autumn, small numbers may migrate through southern Sweden, but majority arrive from breeding areas in northern Germany, Poland, Slovakia, Czechia and Austria as early as Sept, reaching The Netherlands/Flanders Oct, with some continuing on to France and Spain (although population in latter all but extinct, Persson and Urdiales 1995). Studies of collared birds suggest some winter site fidelity to areas in The Netherlands and parts of former East Germany, where may remain for long periods in early winter. More southerly birds penetrate into Poland, but generally use southern areas of Germany, Moravia, Hungary, Croatia and Italy in Oct, ultimately reaching wintering grounds in Greece and Black Sea areas of Ukraine, Romania and Bulgaria. After Jan, start returning, and spring migration patterns even more complex than those of autumn. Individually marked birds seen in The Netherlands/Germany in 1st half of winter, sighted in Hungary in late Feb–early Mar, including bird moving between Rhine and northwest Hungarian Plain in 11 days, showing that winter division into North Sea and Pannonic does not hold.

According to Delacour (1951), *fabalis* types breeding east of Ural Mountains should be of *johanseni* or even *middendorffii* form. Some caught in western Europe do fall within range of measurements for these races (Burgers *et al.* 1991). *johanseni* is supposed to breed in west Siberian lowlands, but racial definition based solely upon 11 ♂♂ and 5 ♀♀ from wintering grounds in Tsinling Mountains of northwest China (race said to winter from Iran across to China). Both yellow-billed and black-billed *fabalis* types recovered in breeding period from west Siberian lowlands, so seems existence of *johanseni* as separate race questionable.

Population of *middendorffii* estimated at 50 000–70 000 (Miyabayashi and Mundkur 1999). Breeds in forest zones of eastern Siberia from Khatanga to Kolyma region, south to Altai and northern Mongolia. Important mass moulting concentrations known from Yana, Indigirka and Lena river deltas (Degtyarev 1995) and 2 sites in western Kamchatka (Makarelskoe and Moroschechnaya River, where 5000–7000 birds moult, but breeding areas unknown, Gerasimov and Gerasimov 1995b). Winters in eastern China (50 000) south to Foochow, North Korea (700), South Korea (6000) and Japan (6000) (Miyabayashi and Mundkur 1999); resightings indicate 90% of 580 birds marked during moult in Kamchatka winter in Japan, reaching northern Hokkaido along east coast of Sakhalin Island, moving south along west coast of Honshu (Kurechi 1991, Brazil 1991, Kurechi *et al.* 1995).

serrirostris population currently 45 000–65 000 and declining (Madsen *et al.* 1996a, Miyabayashi and Mundkur 1999), with tenfold decline in numbers estimated at some breeding areas (Ebbinge 1991). Breeds in tundra zone from Khatanga to Anadyr. Widely distributed in summer on Kamchatka, where modest recovery since 1970s as result of protection, now 12 000 at 3 major roosts on west coast (Gerasimov and Gerasimov 1995b, Kurechi *et al.* 1995). Winters in China (20 000) south to Fokien, South Korea (30 000) and Japan (6000) (Miyabayashi and Mundkur 1999), generally north of *middendorffii*,

selecting more maritime habitats (Miyabayashi 1994). Some Japanese wintering birds, especially those at Lake Keyonuma in northern Honshu, originate from Kamchatka; birds marked in the Kolyma have been seen in Korea (Kurechi 1991, Kurechi *et al.* 1995).

Both eastern forms poorly documented compared to western ones. About 81 000 counted in winter in China, and some 12 000 in Japan (Miyabayashi 1994, Miyabayashi and Mundkur 1999), with increase in recent years under protective legislation. On spring migration, up to 20 000 occur on Kamchatka, mainly in western lowlands (Gerasimov 1990).

Habitat and general habits

Generally less gregarious in winter than other grey geese, flying less between feeding and roosting areas. May also be less subject to severe weather and snow because of habit of probing and rooting, even during mild conditions. Joins mixed goose flocks in central Europe, especially with White-fronted Geese, with which roosts on lakes, rivers and floods (Owen 1980). Confined to agricultural land through much of winter in western and eastern parts of Palearctic. *fabalis* type feeds mainly on grass and clover in Sweden, but generally gleans cereals, sunflower seeds and remains of other harvested crops, including root vegetables such as potatoes but, later in winter and spring, changes to growing winter cereals and grasses which then dominate diet (Nilsson and Persson 1984). Where both races occur together, as in The Netherlands, *fabalis* feeds on grassland claimed from former bog and moorland areas, whilst *rossicus* found on agricultural land, especially waste root crops (Madsen 1987). In Japan, *middendorffii* feeds on lake vegetation, such as fruits of water chestnut *Trapa* and rhizomes of wild rice *Zizania*. By contrast, *serrirostris* found in paddy fields, pasture and agricultural fields (Miyabayashi 1994); habitat use appears similar in Korea, where feeds on *Zizania* and *Trapa* during day at freshwater reservoir sites, as well as gleaning rice from paddy fields harvested by machine (Park and Won 1993).

Displays and breeding behaviour

Strong stable pairbond, probably re-pairing on loss of mate. Timing of pairing and breeding displays little known but, as with most grey geese, little evidence of courtship and display. Copulation similar to other grey geese (Johnsgard 1965a). Families remain intact to subsequent spring (Cramp and Simmons 1977).

Breeding and life cycle

Taiga forms commence spring migration early, arriving in breeding areas late Apr. *fabalis* form nests mainly in minerotrophic aapa mires or spruce boglands, feeding on roots and shoots of cottongrass *Eriophorum* and horsetails *Equisetum*, later switching to fresh green growth, including Timothy Grass *Phleum pratensis* dominated hayfields (Pirkola and Kalinainen 1984). Nests within 400 m of open mire and 2 km of open water, usually 50–100 cm above general bog surface on hummocks that thaw early and are safe from flooding (Pirkola and Kalinainen 1984). Broods led to mires to feed, although feeding ecology unknown; takes *Empetrum* and *Vaccinium* berries during moult, also *Scheuchzeria* (Pirkola and Kalinainen 1984, Filchagov *et al.* 1985). By contrast, tundra forms may not arrive at nesting areas until late May. Nests on dry hummocks on mossy tundra usually close to river floodplain which forms brood nursery area, but above usual flood levels (Dementiev and Gladkov 1952). In Lena delta, densities approach 0.4 birds per km^2 (Pozdnayakov and Sofronov 1995), but nesting occurs in both forms at low densities. Taiga forms lay early May, month later in tundra. Eggs oval but rounded at one end, granular, warm straw-cream; 84 × 56 (74–90 × 53–59) ($n = 75$); weight 146 (Schönwetter 1960–66); weight of captive *fabalis* 148 (133–177) ($n = 31$) and of *rossicus* 145 (122–164) ($n = 53$) apparently differing little. Clutches 3–5 on tundra (e.g. 4.2 in Lena delta, Pozdnayakov and Sofronov 1995), 4–6 in taiga (e.g. 5.15 ± 0.20 ($n = 53$) in Finland, Pirkola and Kalinainen 1984). Incubation 25 and 28–29 days respectively. Goslings fledge in 7–13 weeks depending on subspecies. Mean brood size of *fabalis* 3.0 (Pirkola and Kalinainen 1984), of *rossicus* 3.5 (Pozdnayakov and Sofronov 1995).

Adult survival of *fabalis* 77% based on captured moulting subadults (Tveit 1984). Breeds at 2–3 years in captivity, probably similar in wild.

Conservation and threats

Relatively poorly known throughout range, but especially in east, modification to breeding, staging and wintering habitat constitute threats. Active management of grass swards proved necessary to retain wintering numbers in Yare Valley, UK (Sutherland and Allport 1994), suggesting vulnerability to even subtle changes in agricultural grass sward composition. Very little known about current levels of human exploitation and effects on population, nor about levels of disturbance on breeding areas; however, of X-rayed taiga Bean Geese, 62% of adults and 28% of yearlings carried shotgun pellets in their tissue (Jönsson *et al.* 1985), suggesting significant impact. Good breeding, staging and wintering inventory data from whole range required, together with breeding biology and ecology studies to underpin adequate conservation strategies. Meanwhile, both *middendorffi* and *serrirostris* listed as Vulnerable subspecies by Threatened Waterfowl Specialist Group (2001).

Tony Fox

Pink-footed Goose *Anser brachyrhynchus*

PLATE 5

Anser Brachyrhynchus Baillon, 1834, Mém. Soc. Roy. Émulation Abbeville, sér. **2**, no. 1 (1833), p. 74 Abbeville, lower Somme River, France (outside current range)

Etymology: *brachyrhynchus* Gr. *brakhus* meaning short, plus *rhunkhos* bill. Vernacular name dates from 1839.

Other names: Pinkfoot. Danish: Kortnæbbet gås; French: Oie à bec court; German: Kurzschnabelgans; Icelandic: Heiðagæs.

Variation: no subspecies despite geographic spread. Birds from Svalbard and Iceland/Greenland populations do not differ enough in appearance to be separated taxonomically. On most recent evidence, geese from Iceland and Greenland similar in body size to those from Svalbard, but tend to have longer wings.

Description

ADULT: sexes alike. Head and upper neck dark brown contrasting with paler brown lower neck, chest, mantle, scapulars and rump; flanks dark brown and striated, upperflank feathers white-edged, forming white line; sides of back and rump and some uppertail coverts white. Primaries brown-black with white shafts, secondaries brown-black with narrow white borders, coverts ash-brown, so that upperwing shows clear contrast between pale ashy coverts and dark flight feathers when in flight. Bill short and less massive than in other medium-sized geese, pink and black (sometimes all pink), usually with some white feathers at base; legs and feet pink (rarely orange); eye dark brown. ♂ usually distinguishable from ♀ by larger size and thicker neck. Some individuals have few black-tipped feathers on breast, but less than on many Greylag Geese, and much less than on White-fronted Geese.

MOULT: no seasonal change in plumage, though colours brighter in spring. Single body and wing moult annually. Flightless period 3–4 weeks late June–July.

IMMATURE: in 1st winter smaller, slighter and drabber than adult, upperparts more scaly-looking. Bill and legs duller pink, legs sometimes ochre rather than pale pink. Plumage less distinctive by end of winter, due to gradual replacement of most juvenile body feathers, but flight feathers of young often show greater signs of wear than those of older birds.

GOSLING: green-yellow with darker grey eyestripe, dark crown, back, wings and on front of legs; pattern variable (Nelson 1993).

MEASUREMENTS AND WEIGHT: ♂ adult length ($n = 118$), 680–805 (749), juv 1st winter ($n = 39$), 660–770 (716); adult wing (flattened chord) ($n = 139$), 430–540 (450); juv ($n = 34$), 400–450 (430); adult wing span ($n = 25$), 1470–1620 (1552), juv ($n = 8$), 1470–1620 (1521); adult culmen ($n = 108$), 40–54 (46.4), juv ($n = 41$), 40–51 (45.9); adult tarsus ($n = 84$), 65–86 (74.9), juv ($n = 23$), 71–82 (73.7). ♀ adult length ($n = 84$), 665–736 (719), juv 1st winter ($n = 52$), 630–760 (689); adult wing ($n = 114$), 410–530 (435), juv ($n = 41$), 390–450 (415); adult wing span ($n = 20$), 1420–1630 (1518), juv ($n = 18$), 1330–1490 (1445); adult culmen ($n = 71$), 40–55 (44.8), juv ($n = 41$), 40–59 (43.8); adult tarsus ($n = 62$), 64.5–81.5 (71.0), juv ($n = 31$), 68–76 (71.8). Weight of live birds caught for ringing since 1950, Greenland and Svalbard combined; ♂ adult in winter ($n = 1249$), 1900–3860 (2800), juv 1st winter ($n = 1088$), 1410– 3080 (2431), adult in wing moult in July ($n = 180$), 1990–3120 (2610); adult ♀ in winter ($n = 1307$), 1790–3150 (2409), juv 1st winter ($n = 984$), 1450–2800 (2207), adult in wing moult in July ($n = 125$), 1650–2810 (2332), ♀ juv caught Scotland Oct 1020.

Adults and young usually lightest in Jan, heaviest in Apr when preparing for northward migration. In general, 1st winter ♀♀ and ♂♂ markedly smaller and lighter than older birds; and small samples of 2nd winter birds suggest also tend to be smaller than adults. Some evidence that mean linear dimensions, as well as mass, of UK and Continental wintering geese have varied over time. No evidence that great increases in numbers of both stocks have led to reduction in size of goslings, as reported for several species of Arctic-breeding geese in North America in 1990s, apparently reflecting overgrazing in summer ranges. Mean mass of young of year caught for ringing in UK in early autumn higher in 1990s than in 1950s.

Field characters

Medium-sized goose, ♂ 680–800 and ♀ 660–740 mm long, with round head and short neck. On water at roosts, most easily distinguished from other grey geese within range by shorter neck, small bill and dark head. When feeding, contrast of dark head with greyer body distinctive, while pink and black bill and pink legs usually noticeable. In flight, grey forewing striking; small head, short neck and faster wing-beats distinguish from larger species.

Voice

Higher pitched than Greylag and Bean Geese, but lower than White-fronted Goose. Sonograms from Scotland and Iceland in Cramp and Simmons (1977). In flight, calls (♂ higher pitched than ♀) usually disyllabic *ung-unk* or *ang-ank*, sometimes trisyllabic; softer *wink-wink* or *king-wink* also often heard; alarm call single high-pitched sharp note (Scott 1952). On ground, pairs converse in low murmuring tones; alarm calls abrupt and much louder; loud hisses in threat between ♂♂ and pairs. In 1st year, voice higher pitched, often squeaky.

Range and status

Two groups exist, with little interchange of individuals and no regular overlapping of breeding or wintering ranges. First breeds in Svalbard and winters in Denmark, north Germany, The Netherlands and Belgium, staging in Denmark and central and north Norway on spring migration and on Bear Island and in central Norway in autumn. Second breeds in Iceland and east Greenland and winters in Scotland and England. Though boundaries of distribution altered little during 20th century, large numerical increases in both populations accompanied extensive internal changes in distribution.

Svalbard population numbered < 10 000 in winter in 1930s and 1940s, increasing to *c* 12 000 in late 1940s, then falling to < 5000 in mid 1950s before increasing to *c* 15 000 by 1960 and to *c* 18 000 in early 1970s. In 1980s increased to 25 000–30 000, reaching 32 000–34 000 in 1991–94 and 38 500 in

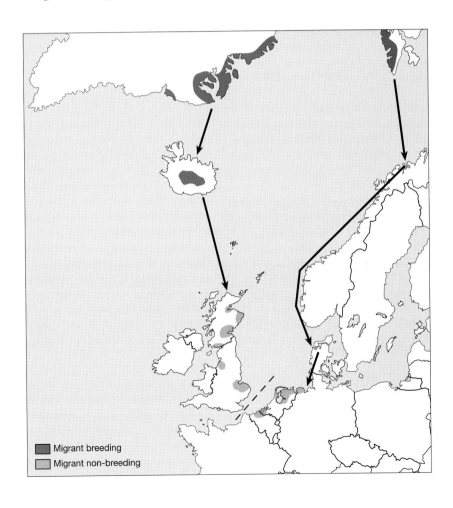

Migrant breeding
Migrant non-breeding

1998 (Ganter and Madsen 2001). Madsen (1987) described changes in numbers on staging and wintering grounds, and alterations in feeding habits that accompanied, and probably caused, increases. Most notable diminution in north Germany, where most wintered in 1950s but where < 1000 seen in recent years due, chiefly, to local changes in agriculture and increased human settlement and activities. In The Netherlands, used to winter in province of Zeeland early in 20th century but abandoned *c* 1920; few seen anywhere until cold winter of 1955–56, then numbers in Friesland built up rapidly to *c* 12000, in parallel with decrease in north Germany. In 1980s began to increase again, to *c* 18000. First used polder areas in Belgium in early 1960s, where up to 4000 found in northwest from mid Nov–early Feb. Some move to northern France in cold winters.

In Denmark, found in narrow corridor along west coast of Jutland, where arrive 2nd half of Sept. In mid-Oct, entire population used to be found there, but increased disturbance from shooting, due in part to attempts to reduce damage to winter cereals, led to many moving to The Netherlands in Oct and, by Nov, only few thousand remain. Their return to Denmark depends on severity of winter; can begin as early as mid-Dec, when they feed on pastures, switching to winter cereals when temperatures fall below freezing although may withdraw again if temperatures drop (Therkildsen and Madsen 2000). By Feb, most may be back, and from end of Mar to beginning of May whole population found in Jutland (Madsen *et al.* 1999b), returning to breeding areas via Norway.

Iceland/east Greenland population proved to breed in Greenland in 1891, but breeding in interior of Iceland not confirmed until 1929. Numbers now breeding in Iceland (40000–50000 pairs) much greater than in Greenland (5000 pairs), and probably always so, although moult migration of some 30000 nonbreeders from Iceland augments numbers in Greenland mid June–late Aug, when return to Iceland following flightless period. Numbers in Britain Oct–Nov increased from 20000–30000 in early 1930s to *c* 260000 in 1994, before falling back to 200000–240000. Increase attributed chiefly to increased adult survival (but see below), resulting

from better protection, partly because many geese shifted to inland roosts, mostly reservoirs, from estuaries where they were vulnerable to shooting and disturbance, and to subsequent establishment of statutory reserves at most major roosts, both coastal and inland (see, however, Fredericksen 2002). Ban on sale of dead wild geese in Britain in 1967 may also have reduced kill. Some increase in adult survival probably due to better food supplies, particularly in late winter, resulting from improvements to grassland (Mitchell and Hearn 2004).

Habitat and general habits

In Svalbard, nests on cliffs, especially near seabird colonies, on rock outcrops, in steep river gorges and on islands, i.e. on sites snow-free early. Later in summer, feeds chiefly in damp sedge-meadows in valley bottoms, as well as near seabird colonies (where vegetation relatively rich). In Greenland, nests on cliffs, riverbanks and hummocks with areas of lush vegetation nearby, where young reared, and migrants from Iceland moult. While flightless, stays close to early thawing lakes or sea, to which can retreat quickly.

In Iceland, formerly concentrated in Þjórsárver, largest oasis in central highlands, where vegetation generally sparse or absent. Þjórsárver held 10700 pairs in 1970, then >70% of entire breeding population. Since 1981, when 10384 pairs, numbers in Þjórsárver declined (6437 pairs in 1996, Garðarsson 1997) and spread from highlands, where some have long nested on cliffs of river gorges or in smaller oases, into uplands and into lowland areas formerly occupied only by Greylag Geese.

In autumn, some from Svalbard stop on Bjornoya (Bear Island) using coastal tundra and grubbing for roots on heaths above cliffs. In spring, on Andoya, north Norway, used to graze on saltmarshes and fens but, since 1980s, moved almost completely to improved grasslands. In Trondelag, central Norway, which, in 1990s, became most important spring staging area, use improved grasslands.

In Denmark in autumn, feeds almost entirely on spilt grain in stubbles; in winter and early spring found on pasture and occasionally saltmarshes, shifting to newly sown cereal fields from late Mar on. In The Netherlands and Belgium, uses fertilized grasslands. In Iceland, most spring arrivals concentrate on farmland in south and east, using potato fields and (scarce) stubbles, as well as fertilized pastures; but some probably continue to go directly to areas of natural vegetation in uplands, which were formerly chief source of spring food. In autumn, most used to remain in uplands to exploit berry crops; increasingly also using improved grass, especially in east. In UK, formerly fed on salt and fresh marshes near estuaries and on inland pastures, but these now largely abandoned for fertilized grass. In 1950s, cereal stubbles most important in autumn, but ploughing soon after harvest has made stubbles scarcer. Largest winter concentrations now feed on sugar beet in Norfolk.

In breeding areas, movements seasonal rather than diurnal. Yearlings, and other nonbreeders, leave breeding pairs and form small roaming flocks that, midsummer, are based on open water (lakes or sea), because of importance of refuge from predators when flightless. In arctic summer, some diurnal rhythms remain, with most adults resting both in coolest midnight hours and in warmest part of day.

Away from breeding areas, usually roosts on water at night, moving out to feed soon after dawn and returning near sunset. Roosts strongly traditional (Giroux 1991). In England, feeding at night at periods near full moon common in 1920s–1950s, but seems less frequent now. In midwinter, nearly all daylight hours spent feeding. In autumn and spring, rest periods at 'parking out areas' often taken on peat bogs, heather moors or rough pastures, or in undisturbed feeding areas.

Diet at all times of year influenced by frequency and kinds of disturbance, as well as by available plants. In spring in Iceland, moves from cultivated land to heaths, to feed on shoots of *Equisetum* and bulbils and rhizomes of *Polygonum* before settling in breeding areas, where those plants and leaves and catkins of *Salix* taken before much new growth available. In summer, feeds chiefly on *Carex*-dominated wet meadows. After completing wing moult, many move from marshes to heaths, feeding on berries of *Empetrum* and other high-energy foods prior to migration. Also used to change diet in Scotland in spring, but less frequent now, with more new grass available.

In wintering areas, improved grasslands used in all months. Barley and wheat stubbles favoured where available, but growing winter cereals, though now common, little used. Potatoes most favoured root crop. In England, carrots in Lancashire and sugar beet in east also eaten (Gill 1996, Gill *et al.* 1997), as were field beans (no longer grown). In Denmark, in areas where tillage crops have replaced grassland, newly sown grain and peas taken in spring. Leaves and stolons of clover and other herbs in grasslands taken. In spring in Iceland, selects most nutritious grasses, especially *Phleum pratensis*. Remarkably efficient at making best use of available plants at all seasons (Fox 1993).

In UK, most newly arrived migrants congregate at few roosts used for many years; Dupplin Loch, Perth, held 63 000 geese Oct 1994. These very large early autumn groups soon disperse, though many roosts hold tens of thousands. Feeding groups usually < 5000, perhaps limited by field size, rather than by social constraints. At all seasons, flocks may include pairs, with or without offspring, single or paired pre-breeders (1–3 years old) and older pairs that failed to breed or lost young. Persistent use of favoured feeding sites, from year to year as well as during one season, common, especially when little disturbed. Flocks seem not to behave as closed groups that discourage newcomers, so that there may be much day-to-day variation in individuals and families using single site.

Displays and breeding behaviour

Most detailed and reliable account of social and sexual behaviour of grey geese is Lorenz (1979, 1991) on Greylag Geese, who makes important point that, because there are many differences in life history of individuals, there are few, if any, standard patterns of pair and group behaviour, even though motor patterns of sexual and agonistic behaviour, similar in all grey geese, show little flexibility. Once formed, pairs may be lifelong, though this does not imply sexual fidelity by either ♀ or ♂.

Pair formation not studied in detail. Three-bird flights, infrequent and apparently provoked by attempted interference by ♂♂ with bonding between pairs, seen in all months Oct–May. Overt sexual activity, including copulation, greatest late Apr–May, at northern staging areas more than at breeding places, where paired ♂♂ primarily concerned with denying other ♂♂ access to mates, both before and after ♀ begins to lay and, second, with protecting ♀, and later eggs, from predators. Gregarious throughout year, though some pairs isolate themselves rather than nesting colonially (may depend chiefly on proximity of suitable nest sites).

Breeding and life cycle

In Svalbard and east Greenland nesting begins late May–early June, completed by mid June. In Iceland laying begins 7–10 May in uplands, and 15 May in central highlands (depending on snow conditions in interior). Main hatching period 1st half July Svalbard and Greenland, from end June in Iceland. Nests on cliffs, rock outcrops and snowfree hummocks, on islands or braided flats in rivers. Nest low mound of grasses and vegetation pulled in by sitting ♀, cup diameter 20–25 cm, depth 5–10 cm. Much down added while laying and through incubation. In Þjórsárver, some nest mounds, used many years, up to 25 cm high. Eggs oval, rough white or pale straw, stained brown during incubation; 78 × 52 (70–90 × 48–58) ($n = 300$); weight 132 (111–149) ($n = 82$); laid daily (Schönwetter 1960–66, Cramp and Simmons 1977). Clutch size Svalbard 'usually 5' (1–7) (Lowenskiold 1964); Iceland 4.4 mode 4 (2–8) ($n = 344$), or 3.9–4.3 (Patterson and Giroux 1990). Incubation, by ♀ alone, 25–28 days, with brief daily feeding breaks when eggs covered with down. ♂ guards, often at distance, close to nest when eggs pipping. Eggshells left in nest, eaten by ♀ next spring. Day-old goslings weigh 86.6 ($n = 9$). In Þjórsárver, nest success 76–79%, mean brood size on leaving nest 2.82, both varying annually with weather and intensity of predation, accounting for c 35% egg losses. Goslings precocious and nidifugous, brooded by ♀ away from nest when cold or wet. Guarded by both parents, chiefly by ♂, as ♀ feeds intensively to gain weight lost during incubation. Fledging period 7–8 weeks during which time parents flightless. Feeds on wet meadows on margins of lakes and rivers, retiring to water to escape predators. Goslings < 10 weeks old sometimes join other broods, but not admitted later after individual identities (voice, appearance) established. Brood size in Iceland falls to 2.59 pre-fledging, 2.32 pre-migration and 2.28 on arrival on wintering grounds (Patterson and Giroux 1990). Mean brood size in autumn in Scotland and England 2.09 ± 0.07 and mean % young 17.9 ± 1.35 (1970–95) (Mitchell *et al.* 1999); mean brood in winter among Svalbard population 2.03 and mean % young 16.9 (1980–95) (Madsen *et al.* 1999b). Little information on hatching and rearing success in Greenland.

Most young remain with parents, first to staging areas, then migrate to wintering places. Young, separated from parents, form groups that may also migrate successfully. Most families remain united through 1st winter and northward migration next spring. Many parents seen to drive off broods when back at breeding site, but occasional families persist with young remaining close though summer and into 2nd autumn (not so frequent nor obvious as in Greenland Whitefronts). Pairs form in 2nd year and most breed in 3rd summer.

Estimates based on census data suggested mean adult survival rate of Svalbard birds at 71% in 1955–74, when population relatively steady, and 85% in 1975–83, when increasing; recoveries of marked birds indicated mean survival rates of 73 ± 3% for adults and 70 ± 4% for 1st year birds (Ebbinge *et al.* 1984). Re-sightings of collared birds in 1990–95 suggested adult survival of 88%. Madsen *et al.* (2002) calculated mean annual survival 1990–99 at 0.829 (0.835 for ♀♀ and 0.805 for ♂♂), declining over period from 0.90 to 0.79; decreasing summer survival main contributor to overall decline, and attributed to increasing mortality on breeding ground. Adult survival rates of Iceland/Greenland population estimated from recoveries of ringed birds showed no significant change from 86% in 1950s to 85% in 1987–91 (Fox *et al.* 1994c); estimates of 1st year survival lower in recent years than in 1950s, though precision of both estimates low. Capture–recapture models, using re-sighting of collared birds since 1987, yielded mean annual survival estimates of 79% for adults and 54% for 1st years, both likely to be somewhat low, due to differences in searching effort and shifts in wintering places (Bell *et al.* 1995). Crude mean annual survival rates of unmarked birds, derived from census data and age-ratio observations, increased from 80 ± 4% in 1950–70 to 86 ± 3% in 1971–80 and 88 ± 2% in 1981–90.

Longevity record in wild 38 years 7 months (Clark *et al.* 2000).

Conservation and threats

Legitimate quarry in all countries in which occurs, though special restrictions in some, notably Denmark, where goose shooting limited to early morning during short autumn season. Recreational shooting in spring everywhere forbidden, but in parts of Scotland and Norway licences to take geese may be issued to farmers, in effort to reduce impact on 'early bite' grass, important for sheep and cattle. Unlicensed (illegal) spring shooting also occurs in Iceland, and geese shot in summer in east Greenland, though apparently with negligible impact (Hansen 2002). When fewer geese and more wildfowlers, as on Solway Firth and Wash in 1st half of 20th century, kill and frequent disturbance created by shooting must have reduced winter survival. No evidence that currents levels of hunting have serious effect in Scotland, but spring disturbance on staging ground in northern Norway has major impact on breeding success. Many geese now roost in protected areas, such as nature reserves created for that purpose; most winter feeding takes place on unprotected farmland.

Þjórsárver, principal breeding place in Iceland, is formally protected by Ramsar designation, but recent overspill across large areas of interior has taken geese into unprotected areas. Principal potential habitat threats in Iceland are development of several new hydroelectric projects on interior rivers, one of which would flood major moulting area, and threat to Þjórsárver itself not finally prevented. Is easier than 40 years ago to take motor vehicles, and thus human disturbance, into interior in summer, but few visit during nesting period and no evidence of detrimental effects on geese. Some breeding areas in east Greenland lie within National Park, but effective protection comes from scarcity of people and abandonment of commercial trapping of Arctic Fox, done on relatively large scale before 1950. In Svalbard, cliff nesting seems effective in reducing human and mammal nest predation, and goose not major quarry.

Principal conservation problem is damage to crops, especially to improved grass in spring. This dealt with so far by local schemes, including organized disturbance by farmers in Norway, at relatively low cost to farmers and agencies responsible for compensation programmes, and to geese themselves. Experimental refuge establishment programme successful in northeast Scotland, but abandoned due to cost. Can peaceful resolutions of conflict continue if Pinkfoot numbers go on rising?

Hugh Boyd

Greylag Goose *Anser anser*
PLATE 6

Anas Anser Linnaeus, 1758, Syst. Nat., ed 10, p. 123 Europe and northern North America (restricted to Sweden by Linnaeus)

Etymology: *anser* L. for goose. Lag appears to be old word used for driving domestic geese.

Other names: Wild Goose, plus many for domestic varieties including Emden, Roman, Toulouse, Brecon Buff and Sebastopol. Danish: Grågås; Dutch: Grauwe Gans; French: Oie cendrée; German: Graugans; Icelandic: Grágæs; Swedish: Grågås.

Variation: 2 subspecies, Western Greylag *A. a. anser* from Iceland and northwest Europe, and Eastern Greylag *A. a. rubrirostris* Swinhoe, 1871 breeding from west of Urals to China.

Description

ADULT: sexes alike, although ♂ larger. Plumage colour uniform grey-brown except for underparts (belly and lower chest) marked with black or dark brown patches, less pronounced than in Lesser White-fronted Geese or White-fronted Geese. Compared to other grey geese, relatively pale blue-grey forewing (revealed in flight). Undertail coverts and tail margin white. Flight feathers dark brown with clear white shaft. Legs pink; bill large and orange or pink depending on race; iris dark brown. Few individuals show pale yellow eye-ring (less pronounced than Lesser Whitefront). Individuals may show narrow white band across base of bill. *rubrirostris* lighter grey, has large pink bill, pink eye-ring and slightly larger than nominate race.

MOULT: undergoes single body and wing moult annually. Flightless period lasts 3–4 weeks.

IMMATURE: sexes alike. Overall plumage almost as adult but more scaly and lacks dark patches on underparts. Bill and legs duller. Retains juvenile plumage until 2nd winter.

GOSLING: varies; olive brown upperparts, wing bar yellow, dark bill and dark greyish legs. Underparts yellow. More or less pronounced light yellow spot on flanks behind wings.

MEASUREMENTS AND WEIGHT: *anser* in Denmark and Bothnia, ♂ adult wing (*n* = 7), 448–480 (465); bill (*n* = 32), 59–74 (66.6), tarsus (n = 32), 78–93 (84.7) juv wing (*n* = 12), 379–455 (430). ♀ adult wing (*n* = 16) 412–465 (442); bill (*n* = 24), 58–65 (61.5); tarsus (*n* = 24), 71–87 (78.8) juv wing (*n* = 3), 400–425 (416). In Iceland ♂ adult wing (*n* = 191), 436–450 (467); bill (*n* = 125), 54–66 (60.0), ♀ adult wing (*n* = 157) 417–480 (447); bill (*n* = 117), 47–62 (56.2). Weight Icelandic population in Oct arriving in Scotland ♂ adult (*n* = 42), 3030–3790 (3454); juv (*n* = 9) 2730–3170 (2900). ♀ adult weight (*n* = 45), 2540–3470 (3039); juv (*n* = 8), 2430–2990 (2722). Winter in Scotland ♂ adult (*n* = 52), 2740–4250 (3793); juv (*n* = 21) 2450–4250 (3297). ♀ adult (*n* = 25), 2070–3960 (3170); juv (*n* = 22) 2810–3540 (3174). Jan–Mar, in Scotland ♂ adult (*n* = 94), 2600–4560 (3509); juv (*n* = 82) 2160–4160 (3083). ♀ adult (*n* = 75) 2160–3800 (3108); juv (*n* = 52) 1980–3220 (2726).

rubrirostris ♂ adult wing (*n* = 16), 435–513 (468); bill (*n* = 19), 59–78 (68.8); weight Mar–May, in Kazakhstan (*n* = 10), 2800–4100 (3455). ♀ adult wing (*n* = 7), 395–470 (448); bill (*n* = 8), 47–73 (63.8); weight (*n* = 7), 2450–3600 (2921) (Cramp and Simmons 1977).

Field characters

Largest of grey geese, 750–900 mm long, distinguished from others by large size, relatively light plumage and lighter neck and head. In flight, easily recognized by pale upper and lower wing coverts.

Voice

Has loud nasal honking voice, deeper than other grey species and similar to most domestic geese (other than Swan Goose types). Sonograms in Cramp and Simmons (1977).

Range and status

Nominate race divided into discrete populations in western part of range. Icelandic population increased since 1950s from 20 000–30 000 to *c* 100 000 in early 1990s, followed by decline; currently estimated at *c* 80 000 (Madsen *et al.* 1999a). Breeds throughout lowlands of Iceland and winters mainly in northeast and central Scotland (Hearn and Mitchell 2004). Apparently no evidence of extensive moult migration among nonbreeding adults as in northwestern population, although few places known to be utilized by *c* 5000 during moult (Skarphéðinsson and Gudmundsson 1990). Arrive in Iceland early Apr (Fox *et al.* 2000). Autumn migration occurs late Sept and majority arrive Scotland mid to late Oct (Mitchell 1995).

Indigenous breeding population of Scotland mainly sedentary and restricted to northernmost part of mainland (Caithness/Sutherland) and Hebridean islands of Harris, Lewis, Uists, Coll and Tiree. Subject to considerable persecution, and dramatic decrease occurred during latter half of 19th and 1st 3 decades of 20th century; reported as in danger of extinction (Berry 1939). Regular counts of breeding population not carried out, but increasing trend since early 1970s and late summer census 1997 found minimum 10 000 (1258 pairs) with main concentrations Uists (3311), Coll and Tiree (2366), Sutherland (1262) and Orkney (1114) (Mitchell *et al.* 2000). This population does not undertake moult migrations but moults close to breeding ground (Madsen *et al.* 1999a).

Reintroduction of birds occurred in UK since 1930s, following extinction *c* 300 years earlier. This largely self-supporting and increasing population *c* 20 000 in 1991 (Delany 1993) and 30 000 by end

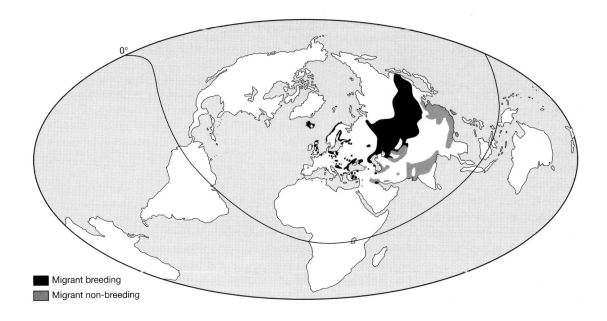

Migrant breeding
Migrant non-breeding

of decade (Rehfische *et al.* 2002), mainly distributed in southwest Scotland, east Midlands and East Anglia, but at many other sites throughout UK. Although some evidence of short-distance migration, majority sedentary, moulting close to breeding sites, although few moult migrations known (Masen *et al.* 1999a).

Since mid 1960s and 1970s, northwest European population increased from *c* 30 000 to *c* 200 000 in 1995 (Madsen *et al.* 1999a). Although usually treated as single unit, can be divided into 2 subpopulations, breeding in either Norway or Baltic. In Norway, breeds almost along entire coast from Finnmark in north to southernmost parts, and consists of *c* 7000–10 000 pairs (Direktoratet for Naturforvaltning 1996). In late summer and autumn, migrates through western part of Denmark where stages for short period, before moving on to The Netherlands (Madsen 1987). Baltic sub-population concentrates in southern Sweden, eastern Denmark and northeastern part of Germany before continuing to The Netherlands. Birds from both subpopulations winter from The Netherlands to southwestern Spain, although few visit France, Portugal and Morocco. Some stay close to breeding grounds especially during mild winters in Denmark, Germany, Sweden and Norway. During

1990s, more have wintered in The Netherlands where 66 000 counted in 1995; however, southwestern Spain remains most important wintering site, holding 110 000 in 1995 (Madsen *et al.* 1999a). Spring migration takes place from mid Jan (Spain) with peak departure during 1st half of Feb. In The Netherlands, numbers staging gradually build up from Feb before onward migration to breeding grounds. Large numbers of nonbreeders and failed breeders of northwest European population undertake moult migrations; main moulting sites found in The Netherlands, Norway and Denmark. In Norway, 22 000 may moult on series of sites scattered through outer archipelagos (Follestad 1988); these birds originate from Norway and southern Scandinavia. In Denmark, moulting site on island of Saltholm discovered in early 1990s; by 1997 were 13 000 birds from southwestern Scania that formerly moulted in Oostvaadersplassen, The Netherlands. Another important moulting site is Oostvaadersplassen, extensive reedbed in The Netherlands, established in 1968. From 1973 to 1992, numbers using this area increased from 1100 to 62 000 (Zijlstra *et al.* 1991, Dubbledam and Zijlstra 1996); however, numbers declined because of lower water levels and, in 1996, *c* 12 000 birds moulted here. In Schleswig-Holstein, northern

Germany, another new moulting site discovered during 1990s and, in 1996, 5000 counted. In Sweden, 2000 moult at lake Tåkern (Madsen *et al.* 1999a).

rubrirostris occupies eastern part of range and divides into 4 populations. Central European and North African birds mostly belong to *rubrirostris*, but types intermediate between *rubrirostris* and *anser* occur. Although count data lacking, trend is upward and numbers reach *c* 28 000 (Madsen *et al.* 1999a) mainly breeding in Hungary, the Czech and Slovak Republics and Austria (Niethammer 1968, Rutschke 1987) but also in Finland, Estonia, Latvia and Lithuania. Predominantly winters in Tunisia and Algeria where arrive from early Nov and depart early Feb. However, few may winter in Balkans and along Black Sea coast (Dick 1993, Vogrin 1996) and some from southern Poland, Bohemia and Czech Republic winter in Spain. Birds from Bohemia recently reported in France. Border between northwestern and central European populations seems to run through Finland (where most belong to central European population), Poland and Czech Republic. Arrive on breeding grounds early Feb–Apr depending on latitude. Autumn migration occurs mid to late Aug–Oct in Finland and Estonia, and Oct–Dec at more southerly part of range. During autumn migration, stopover in Moravia, Neusiedler See, as well as wetlands in northern Adriatic (Dick 1987). Some from this population moult near breeding sites; however, nonbreeders from central Europe migrate to moult in Denmark, The Netherlands, Sweden and Poland. In Finland, move to moulting sites within the country (Madsen *et al.* 1999a).

Black Sea population of *rubrirostris* breeds in Romania, Ukraine, Russian Federation, Syria, Turkey, Greece and Bulgaria, with Danube Delta and Sea of Azov being most important. Little known of movements, and borders between this population and that of southwest unclear. Wintering areas mainly found in Ukraine, Romania and, to lesser extent, Syria and Turkey (Madsen *et al.* 1999a). Population trends largely unknown; midwinter counts in Black Sea region suggest minimum 54 000; however, coverage incomplete (no data from Russian Federation). In Romania, spring migration takes place late Feb–early Apr, and

autumn migration Oct–Nov. Most moulting sites unknown, but nonbreeders from Duni and Dnestr rivers moult in outer parts of Duni Delta and Dnestrovski lagoon. Birds from Orel'Samara rivers moult in breeding areas (Lysenko 1990).

Breeding distribution of southwest Asian (west Siberia and Caspian) population ranges in broad belt from Caspian region in south to Ural Mountains east across Russian Federation in western Siberia. Main wintering sites found in Iran, Iraq, Kazakhstan, Turkmenistan, and along southern part of Caspian Sea. Total population 106 000–183 000, with reliable data needed (Madsen *et al.* 1999a). Suggestion of overall increase since early 1970s. With up to 25 000, Volga Delta is major moulting site, and thousands reported to moult in Kazakhstan. Birds arrive Iran late Oct, with peak arrival late Nov–early Dec; main departure occurs late Feb–early Mar.

Southern Asian population thought to be 15 000 (Perennou *et al.* 1994) and apparently increasing; that of eastern Asia uncertainly estimated at 50 000–100 000, and any trend unknown (Madsen *et al.* 1996a, Miyabayashi and Mundkur 1999). Both populations winter in India and China; Lu (1994) estimated Chinese population at 50 000.

Many types of Greylag exist in domestication, mostly descended from eastern subspecies (Kear 1990) and probably first farmed in 'fertile crescent' of Middle East some 5000 years ago.

Habitat and general habits

Mainly confined to temperate zone, although extends into arctic/sub-arctic areas in places. Breeds in wetlands near lakes or streams. In some countries, coastal islets commonly used for breeding. Nests close to potential feeding sites such as meadows or grasslands. In spring in The Netherlands, prior to migration, feeds on grassland and autumn-sown cereals, and in Iceland, after arrival in spring, feeds on *Phleum pratense* and *Poa pratense* hayfields. During wing moult, nonbreeders and failed breeders gather in areas with good feeding opportunities and access to safe roosts. At Oostervaadersplassen, The Netherlands, feeds mainly on *Phragmites australis* (Loonen *et al.* 1991) and on island of Saltholm, Denmark, main plant taken is *Puccinellia maritima* (Fox *et al.*

1998c). In Denmark in Aug–Sept, uses waste grain from stubble fields, and in Oct predominantly sugar beet, winter Oilseed Rape and newly sown cereals (Madsen 1986). In Germany in autumn mostly found on agricultural land, e.g. sugar beet, maize and cereals, in The Netherlands during Aug–Sept mainly on stubble fields, and in Oct–Nov, on stubble fields, grassland, pasture and saltmarshes. In Austria in autumn takes maize and cereals. During winter in Germany uses grassland, stubble, winter cereals and winter Oilseed Rape, and in The Netherlands mainly rhizomes of e.g. *Scirpus maritimus*, *Phragmites australis* and *Typha latifolia/augustifolia* plus grass and autumn sown cereals. In Spain, geese from Baltic mainly grub-feed on tubers of *Scirpus litoralis* and *S. maritimus*, switching to winter sown wheat if *Scirpus* resource depleted. Norwegian birds largely grazers on wintering grounds in Spain. During winter in Tunisia and Algeria, feeds on *S. maritimus*.

Gregarious, and only during incubation will pairs stay relatively isolated, although may nest at semi-colonial densities (Kristiansen 1997). Feeds largely during daylight hours, most intensely in morning and afternoon; however, moulting non-breeders reported to feed at night (Kahlert *et al.* 1996). Recorded flying more than 10 km from roosts to feeding sites (Nilsson and Person 1992). During Aug–Sept in Denmark, feeds during relatively short periods in morning and afternoon, later increasing time spent feeding (Madsen *et al.* 1999a).

Display and breeding behaviour

Stable monogamous pairbond normally established when birds older than 3–4 years, but may attempt 1st breeding at 2–3 years. Pairing occurs on wintering grounds. Sexual behaviour, including courtship and copulation, best studied of any goose species, illustrated in Lorenz (1979) and described in detailed summary in Cramp and Simmons (1977).

Breeding and life cycle

Nests in variety of habitats out of reach of land predators (Young 1972, Newton and Kerbes 1974,

Kristiansen 1998), hence, typically nests on isolated islands, either coastal or on lakes, and in dense vegetation such as reedbeds. Capable of adapting to nesting in close proximity to humans, such as in parks, but can also be shy. ♀ builds nest using vegetation such as dead reeds in near vicinity. Height of nest 130–600 mm, outer diameter 800–1100, cup depth 50–150 and cup diameter 250 mm (Cramp and Simmons 1977).

Laying date variable due to different latitudes at which breeding occurs. In Continental Europe, eggs laid late Apr with peak mid May, in UK 1st eggs appear late Mar–early Apr, peak mid Apr (Cramp and Simmons 1977). Eggs ovate, creamy-white; *anser* in UK 85 × 59 (78–92 × 54–64) ($n = 60$); weight 149 (122–172) ($n = 60$) (Young 1965); in Czechoslovakia 86 × 58 (77–97 × 53–66) ($n = 230$); weight 164 (151–179) ($n = 113$) (Kux 1963). Clutch size 4–6 (3–12) eggs, laid at *c* 24 h intervals. Incubation, by ♀ only, initiated after last egg laid to ensure synchronous hatching in 27–28 days. After hatching, families often aggregate into larger flocks and tend to remain gregarious thereafter. At hatching, goslings weigh 112.6 ($n = 15$); when 10–20 days old, adults become flightless. Mean brood size in July in Britain 4.1 (3.7–4.6) and in Sept 3.2 (2.8–4.0) ($n = 365$) (Young 1972); in Scania, average clutch 5.36 eggs, mean brood at hatching 4.60 and at fledging 3.14 (Nilsson and Persson 1994). Fledge in 50–60 days; families staying together into subsequent winter. Mean annual survival of birds from nothwest Europe (Scania) 76% for juveniles, 74% for subadults and 83% for adults (Nilsson and Persson 1993).

Maximum lifespan of UK ringed bird > 18 years (Toms and Clark 1998), in captivity, Johnsgard (1968a) reported 26 years.

Conservation and threats

Overall, populations either stable or increasing; however, status of East Asian population unknown (Madsen *et al.* 1996a).

Jens Nyeland

White-fronted Goose *Anser albifrons*
PLATE 5

Branta albifrons Scopoli, 1769, Annus I Hist.–Nat., p. 69

no locality = ? northern Italy

Etymology: *albifrons* L. *albus* white, plus *frons* forehead or brow. Vernacular name first used by Pennant in 1768 in preference to Laughing Goose.

Other names: Greater White-fronted Goose, Laughing Goose, Speckle Belly. Danish: Blisgås; French: Oie rieuse; German: Blässgans; Icelandic: Blesgæs ('Bles' is a horse with a white streak down its nose; *cf* 'blaze' in English); Japanese: Ma-gan.

Variation: 4, formerly 5, races recognized: Russian or European White-fronted Goose *Anser a. albifrons*; Greenland White-fronted Goose *A. a. flavirostris* Dalgety and Scott, 1948; Pacific White-fronted Goose *A. a. frontalis* Baird, 1858; and Interior White-fronted Goose *A. a. gambeli* Hartlaub, 1852. Tule Goose *A. a. elgasi* Delacour and Ripley, 1975 now included in *gambeli*.

Description

ADULT: sexes alike. Head, neck, back and upperparts uniform medium brown, underparts and breast lighter buff-brown, not giving extreme contrast between body and neck of Pinkfoot and Bean Goose. White feathers at base of bill in all adults, with variable black belly barring. Flanks brown, mantle, scapulars and tertials greyish brown with pale fringes. Back, rump and tail greyish brown. Undertail coverts, tail border and ventral region white. Underwing dark grey. Bill variously fleshy pink to bright orange, but depends on race, viewing light and probably condition of bird, nail pale, sometimes almost white; legs and feet orange or yellow-orange; iris warm brown with pale eye-ring, but never so conspicuous as Lesser White-fronted Goose. Greenland Whitefront most morphologically distinct, generally darker brown upperparts and heavy barring on belly, with orange bill.

MOULT: one annual change of body plumage, and one annual wing and tail moult following breeding.

IMMATURE: initially lacks white face patch which develops through 1st winter, especially after Nov. Black belly barring absent until 1st spring. Upperparts more warmly coloured with less patterning. Bill duller than adult, usually with black nail, dark smudging may persist to summer after hatching and into 2nd winter. Legs and feet duller than adult.

GOSLING: green-yellow with dark eyestripe, crown back, wings and outer legs, but variable. Nelson (1993) illustrated goslings from Alaska, Perry River, Adelaide Peninsula and Greenland; Greenland specimen darker than others.

MEASUREMENTS AND WEIGHT: *albifrons* data from I. Kostin, based on birds caught in Taimyr, ♂ ($n = 9$) head length, 103.4 ± 0.9; tarsus, 86.1 ± 1.6. ♀ ($n = 9$) head length, 99.7 ± 1.4; tarsus, 83.0 ± 1.7. Weight in winter ♂ adult ($n = 87$), 2450 ± 29.1; juv (1st winter) ($n = 238$), 2130 ± 11.9; ♀ adult ($n = 92$), 2180 ± 27.1; juv ($n = 287$), 1905 ± 8.4 data from WWT Slimbridge (Cramp and Simmons 1977).

flavirostris data from Greenland White-fronted Goose Study/National Park and Wildlife Service, ♂ adult wing ($n = 226$), 404–460 (436); juv (1st winter) ($n = 272$), 370–450 (413); adult tarsus ($n = 213$), 81–102 (92.2); juv ($n = 255$), 81–100 (91.8); weight in winter adult ($n = 229$), 2050–3600 (2714); juv ($n = 277$), 1900–3510 (2497). ♀ adult wing ($n = 216$), 388–445 (415); juv ($n = 233$), 365–428 (399); adult tarsus ($n = 208$), 76–94 (87.1); juv ($n = 218$), 78–97 (87.2); weight in winter adult ($n = 223$), 1800–2900 (2409); juv ($n = 245$), 1700–2875 (2262).

frontalis data from A. Andreev, based on birds caught in Anadyr, northeast Russian flyway, ♂ head length ($n = 26$), 109.3 ± 0.6; tarsus ($n = 25$), 89.4 ± 0.7. ♀ head length ($n = 31$), 104.0 ± 0.7; tarsus ($n = 29$), 82.4 ± 1.0. Mid-continent flyway in Saskatchewan in Sept, ♂ tarsus ($n = 64$), 91.1 ± 0.3; weight ($n = 66$), 2725 ± 24; ♀ tarsus ($n = 65$), 86.3 ± 0.4; weight ($n = 67$), 2454 ± 22. Pacific flyway in California in winter, ♂ wing ($n = 124$), 440.9 ± 1.1; tarsus ($n = 250$), 89.8 ± 0.2; weight

($n = 407$), 2384 ± 11. ♀ wing ($n = 126$), 420.5 ± 1.0; tarsus ($n = 256$), 89.8 ± 0.2; weight ($n = 384$), 2075 ± 11 (Ely and Dzubin 1994).

gambeli in California in winter, ♂ tarsus ($n = 16$), 81.0 ± 1.2; weight ($n = 54$), 3000 ± 30. ♀ tarsus ($n = 13$), 76.0 ± 0.8; weight ($n = 53$), 2700 ± 30 (Ely and Dzubin 1994).

Field characters

Only Old World grey goose to breed in North America; 660–860 mm long. Orange-legged grey goose separated from similar species by white feathering around base of bill and extensive black belly barring (although both characters usually missing in 1st winter). Shorter, generally uniform pinkish/orange bill, and lighter coloured and squarer head distinguish juvenile from Bean Goose. Smaller and sleeker than paler, greyer Greylag Goose, which has pink legs and heavy bill. Bill colour varies widely with light conditions and populations. In flight, upperwing coverts paler than flight feathers, but darker than Greylag or Pinkfoot and paler than Bean Goose.

Voice

So-called Laughing Goose, very vocal at all times. Flight call ringing *kyow-lyow*, ♀ voice deeper than ♂. Sonogram of flight call in Cramp and Simmons (1977) and of sleepy call of Greenland Whitefront gosling in Kear (1968).

Range and status

Virtually circumpolar, has broader range than any other grey goose. In summer, breeding areas characterized by range of habitats from dry northern systems through wet, boggy tundra in central Canadian arctic, to boreal forest mires in Mackenzie Basin and Russian taiga. In winter, frequents agricultural landscapes throughout range, as well as other wetland biotopes.

Numbers in western Europe and North America generally increasing or stable, those in eastern Palearctic and Asia decreasing. Following data from Madsen *et al.* (1996a, 1999a). Western Palearctic populations: *albifrons* breeds throughout Russian tundra arctic region from Kanin Peninsula eastwards across to Kolyma River delta. In northwest Europe 600 000 and increasing; in central Europe 100 000 and decreasing, but probably much interchange with northwest population and with Black Sea; in Black Sea region 700 000, trends unknown. Important areas in western tundra areas included within Great Arctic Reserve (Syroechkovski and Rogecheva 1994). In eastern Arctic, mass moult concentrations occur in Lena, Indirgirka and Yana river deltas (Degtyarev 1995). *flavirostris* breeds 64–76°N in west Greenland, migrates through south and west Iceland to winter in Ireland and northwestern UK (Fox *et al.* 2003a); numbers 33 000 and recently stable (Madsen *et al.* 1999a).

Eastern Palearctic populations: *albifrons* in Caspian 15 000 and decreasing; major wintering area in Volga delta, where 10 000 congregate (Krivonosov and Rusanov 1990). Only 5 other areas in Caspian region known to hold > 50 — Kirov Bay (Azerbijhan), 3 sites in Iran, and Kerki (Turkmenistan), although other sites in Iran may support such numbers (Perennou *et al.* 1994). In Asia, thought to range from Kolyma Delta (150°E) eastwards (Kistchinski 1973, Cramp and Simmons 1977) and winter in Japan, Korea and China (Brazil 1991).

Eastern Asian *frontalis* breeding in northeast Russia now estimated at 100 000–150 000, only large concentrations occurring in Anadyr lowlands north and south of mouth of Anadyr River, where *c* 7000 breeders occur at densities of 5 nests per 10 km^2 with *c* 4 times as many nonbreeders (Kondratyev 1995, Madsen *et al.* 1996a). Poyang Lake in China held 22 000 in recent years (Perennou *et al.* 1994), national totals for China < 10 000 during 1990–93 (NSGCOA 1994) but recent estimate is 50 000 (Lu *in* Miyabayashi and Mundkur 1999). Some 50 000 wintered in Japan in 1995–96 and 1997–98, plus 3600 in North Korea and 35 000 in South Korea (Miyabayashi and Mundkur 1999). Sites of international importance (holding in excess of 1250 or 1% of population) listed by Miyabayashi and Mundkur (1999) include 17 in Russia, 2 in North Korea, 8 in South Korea, 15 in Japan and 4 in China, although few 1990s data exist at some sites. Of 121 birds marked on Anadyr breeding areas, 18 nonbreeders occurred in Japan and 3 in

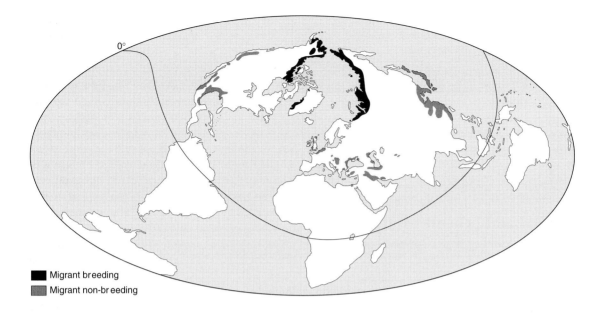

Migrant breeding
Migrant non-breeding

Korea; one bird was satellite-tracked to Neoli River, China (46°N 132°E) (Kurechi *et al.* 1995). Between 10 000 and 15 000 pass through Kamchatka in spring and autumn, with 10 000 recorded on Lake Kharchinsoe alone in spring 1983 (Gerasimov and Gerasimov 1995a, 1995b, 1997a).

North American populations: *frontalis* breeds in low Arctic to fringe of high Arctic in eastern Asia and North America. Pacific population nests only in Alaska, with concentrations on Yukon-Kuskokwim Delta, and winters from southwest British Columbia south through California to Mexico, most common in northern California and southern Oregon. Mid continental population nests from Barrow, interior Alaska and Yukon into central Canadian Arctic as far east as Hudson Bay (north of 60°N). In winter, this element occurs in Mississippi valley, into coastal wetlands of Louisiana and Texas, with some in Mexico. Eastern Pacific birds number 295 000 and increasing. Alaskan birds fly non-stop to Washington/Oregon where pass inland to Klamath Basin (south Oregon, north California) moving into wintering areas in Central Valley and Sacramento Valley in California, many continuing to Mexico. Return migration similar, arriving Yukon-Kuskokwim Delta in late Apr, early May (Ely and Raveling 1984). Only 1.3% of ringed birds

in this flyway recovered in mid-continental flyway and 0.5% in other direction, suggesting little interchange. Mid-continent numbers estimated at 728 000 and increasing; central Alaskan birds migrate through northwest Alberta, rest pass through eastern Alberta, Saskatchewan and Manitoba in Aug, with large flocks aggregating on South Saskatchewan River by late Sept. Most leave on broad front by mid Oct to reach wintering areas in Arkansas, Louisiana, Texas and Mexico. Spring migration starts Feb, completed in Great Plains mid Apr, arriving Alaska in mid-late Apr and late May in central Arctic.

Palmer (1976) included Whitefronts from eastern Alaska and Mackenzie Basin in Canada as separate race *gambeli*, larger and somewhat darker than *frontalis*. Since then, much confusion relates to this form which now taken to refer to large, darker chocolate brown so-called Tule Goose which nests in Cook Inlet region of central southern Alaska and winters in California (Delacour and Ripley 1975, Krogman 1979). Originally referred to as *elgasi* (Delacour and Ripley 1975), but name contended and we use *gambeli* here after Ely and Dzubin (1994). Species in North America shows wide variation from different breeding areas which defies simple classification (Orthmeyer *et al.* 1995) and requires genetic study to relate morphological characters to gene flow between units (Ely and Scribner 1994). Breeds in Alaska, numbers 8000 and increasing (Orthmeyer *et al.* 1992). Uses similar migration routes to Pacific Whitefront in autumn, but remains separate in Klamath Basin. Winters in Sacramento Valley, California, using same roosts as Alaskan *frontalis*, but forages more in flooded marshlands in contrast to open field feeding of *frontalis*. In spring, records from maritime areas of British Columbia suggest coastal route taken north of Washington State.

Habitat and general habits

Breeds mainly on productive lowland and high arctic wetlands created as result of isostatic uplift since last glaciation, although *flavirostris* seems to have colonized upland biotopes as well. Generally feeds on over-wintering subterranean plant storage organs on arrival on breeding areas, such as *Eriophorum angustifolium* stem bases and *Triglochin palustris* bulbils, which may be only forage available. Later switch to new green growth of monocotyledonous plants, following thaw of forage species from earliest available at low altitude.

Moulting nonbreeders and failed breeders may gather in low arctic areas with abundant open water (such as highly productive river deltas of American and Russian arctic) for escape, often remote from major breeding congregations. Following moult, feeds on *Vaccinium* and *Empetrum* berries prior to autumn migration in several areas.

In winter, probably probed for subterranean food resources, since this still occurs where associated with traditional habitats; e.g. *flavirostris* traditionally fed on below ground parts of cottongrass *Eriophorum* and White-beaked Sedge *Rhynchospora alba* on bogland biotopes that rarely froze in winter, being on oceanic fringe of western Europe (Ruttledge 1929). *gambeli* feeds mainly on rhizomes and underground parts of marsh plants in contrast to *frontalis* with which associates. In spring, *gambeli* takes *Scirpus maritimus* rhizomes. However, for most part, species has conspicuously moved into agricultural landscapes during last century, and feeds on range of waste cereals (including rice in US, Japan and South Korea) and seed crops left after harvest in autumn,

as well as roots such as potatoes. Increasingly, grazer of intensively managed agricultural grassland, where highly selective feeder, choosing particular parts of fields to forage in relation to species growing there (Owen 1971) and showing consistent preference for some plants over others (Owen 1976a).

Feeds mainly by day, generally roosting in winter on tidal marshes, sheltered bays, estuaries, brackish and freshwater marshes and floodlands. In US has increasingly moved inland in winter to use lakes and reservoirs. Usually feeds within 20 km of roost site, and may occur in looser flocks and smaller groups than other grey geese, perhaps responding to patchiness of traditional habitats; however, up to 30 000 occur in single flocks in Germany and The Netherlands. May feed at night on flooded fields and on nights of full moon. In some areas, highly winter-site faithful (Wilson *et al.* 1991, Warren *et al.* 1992b). Greenland race also shows strong site fidelity to staging fields in Iceland in spring and autumn (Fox *et al.* 2002).

Unusual in exhibiting long-term associations between parents and offspring and/or siblings (Ely 1993, Warren *et al.* 1993, Fox *et al.* 1995a). Larger family units dominant over smaller families, pairs and individuals, hence fitness advantages to group cohesion due to ability of families to dominate rich feeding patches, at least in winter (Boyd 1953).

Displays and breeding behaviour

Strong, stable pairbond, but will re-pair on loss of mate. Timing of pairing largely unknown, but thought to be spring and summer, very little evidence or observation of courtship display. Aerial 3-bird chases only sign of such behaviour, but confined to spring on nesting areas. Copulation always occurs on water, preceded by ♂ head-dipping and followed by Triumph-type ceremony. Forced and unforced extra-pair copulation recorded despite mate fidelity (Ely 1989).

Breeding and life cycle

Body weight of ♀♀ increases by *c* third prior to spring migration, doubling fat deposits (Ely and Raveling 1989), but this supplemented by feeding on nesting area for up to 3 weeks (Fox and Madsen 1981, Budeau *et al.* 1991). Nests usually amongst vegetation, grass or dwarf shrub heath, often on raised hummocks or on slopes offering safety from unpredictable water tables and/or vantage points overlooking surrounding area.

Eggs ovoid-elliptical, white to creamy white; 53.9 × 80.1 (*n* = 369) Yukon-Kuskokwim Delta, Alaska (Ely and Raveling 1984), 53.7 × 80.5 (*n* = 337) Alaska North Slope (Simpson *in* Ely and Dzubin 1994), 53.0 × 80.6 (*n* = 546) Kent Peninsula, Northwest Territory (Bromley *in* Ely and Dzubin 1994), 54.0 × 83.1 (*n* = 34) Cook Inlet, Alaska, (Timm and Sellers *in* Ely and Dzubin 1994), 54.5 × 79.2 (*n* = 34) in Greenland (Fox and Stroud 1988). Egg weight 128–129, Alaska (Ely and Dzubin 1994), declining by 14% during incubation. Clutch size 4–6 (3–9), large clutches (> 6) probably product of more than one ♀. Mean clutch 4.6 in Yukon-Kuskokwim Delta (*n* = 721), 4.1 in Alaskan North Slope (*n* = 180), 5.6 in Cook Inlet (*n* = 7), 3.8 in Central Canadian arctic (*n* = 185) (Ely and Dzubin 1994), 4.6 in Greenland (Fox and Stroud 1988). Clutch declines with laying date (Ely and Raveling 1984). Incubation by ♀ only, 25 (22–27) days (Ely and Dzubin 1994). ♀ highly nest attentive, sitting 97.1–99.1% of time, and becoming more attentive as incubation progresses (Ely and Dzubin 1994). Attended by ♂ during recesses when normally feeds near nest site (Stroud 1981a, Ely and Dzubin 1994). May also be attended by other adults and subadults that assist in predator distraction and nest defence (Fox *et al.* 1995a). Such birds may associate with pre-nesting pairs, but rarely accompany broods post-hatching, although families may reconstitute on wintering ground (Ely 1993, Warren *et al.* 1993).

Nest success varies widely with site and season (e.g. 2.0–95.7% reported in Ely and Dzubin 1994). Mean brood size declines 3.1–2.8 and marked broods 4.1–3.1 between hatching and fledging in Alaska (Ely and Dzubin 1994) and, in 2 years, 3.7–3.5 and 4.3–3.7 in Greenland (Fox and Stroud 1988). Young fly in 38–45 days. Average age at pairing 2.46 years (Warren *et al.* 1992a), breeding successfully typical in 3rd year (Campbell 1985, Warren *et al.* 1993). Young breeders generally have smaller broods than older ones. Annual survival 65–70% in Pacific Flyway (Timm and Dau 1979, Ely and Dzubin 1994) and 78.5% in Greenland

population (Bell *et al.* 1993). Mid continent birds have higher survival. Longevity record in wild *c* 17 years (Toms and Clark 1998); captive ♀♀ have lived 46–47 years, still laying fertile eggs until death (Rankin 1957).

Conservation and threats

Widely differing conservation challenges exist between different populations, but hunting thought to be major factor controlling most populations (Ely and Dzubin 1994). In North America, numbers increase despite substantial annual kill. Populations of Pacific Flyway increased dramatically in early 1980s after bag limit restrictions and agreements with aboriginal hunters to reduce kill in Alaska (Ely and Dzubin 1994). Similarly, local increases in *flavirostris* winter flock units occurred in response to protective legislation in Britain and Ireland (Fox *et al.* 1998b).

Major oil exploration throughout Russian and North American tundra breeding areas potentially influence habitat selection and possibly reproductive success. Climate change thought likely to affect already highly restricted breeding range. Recent colonization of west Greenland by *interior* race Canada Geese from northern Québec has affected White-fronted Goose behaviour, distribution and abundance in breeding areas where latter formerly only endemic goose species present (Kristiansen and Jarrett 2002, Fox 2003a). On wintering areas, threats of habitat loss and/or modification continue, especially on Gulf Coast of North America (Ely and Dzubin 1994). Roost sites effectively limit foraging areas, so safeguard of roosts offers conservation mechanism for those populations showing high fidelity to favoured roosts. Major shifts in wintering distribution (e.g. of *albifrons* in western Europe) in response to land use alteration and protection from hunting suggest vulnerability to such change (Hearn 2004b). Continued monitoring of numbers, breeding success and hunting kill, through annual life cycle, essential for all populations. Interior White-fronted Goose (as Tule Greater White-fronted Goose *A. a. gambeli*) listed as Vulnerable subspecies by Threatened Waterfowl Specialist Group (2003).

Tony Fox and Myrfyn Owen

Lesser White-fronted Goose *Anser erythropus*
PLATE 5

Anas erythropus Linnaeus, 1758, Syst. Nat., ed. 10, p. 123
'Europa septentrionalis' (northern Europe)

Etymology: *erythropus* Gr. *eruthros* red, plus *pous* foot, meaning red-footed.

Other names: none common in English. French: Oie naine; German: Zwerggans; Swedish: Fjällgås.

Variation: no subspecies.

Description

ADULT: sexes alike, although ♂ slightly larger and may have heavier belly barring than ♀. Head, neck, back and upperparts uniform dusky brown, much darker than underparts and breast which are lighter buff-brown than those of White-fronted Goose. Black belly bars more restricted in extent and less conspicuous than in larger species, confined to lowest part of body with little extension towards flanks. White feathers at base of bill in all adults, normally higher above forehead and extending down towards area behind eye.

Flanks brown, mantle, scapulars and tertials grey brown with pale fringes. Back, rump and tail brown. Undertail coverts, tail border and ventral region white. Underwing dark grey. Bill light and small, pink with nail pale, sometimes almost white; legs and feet orange or yellow-orange; iris warm brown, eye-ring pale yellow and swollen.

MOULT: one body moult annually, and one wing and tail moult.

IMMATURE: initially lacks white face patch which develops through 1st winter, especially after Nov. Black belly barring absent until 1st spring. Upperparts more warmly coloured with less patterning. Bill duller than adult, usually with brown nail. Pale, usually yellow, eye-ring already prominent. Legs and feet duller.

GOSLING: dark brown on back and crown, tinged olive on back. Chin and cheeks yellowish, forehead throat yellow with pale nape and belly. Said to be variable in coloration.

MEASUREMENTS AND WEIGHT: ♂ adult wing ($n = 8$), 370–388 (378); juv ($n = 5$), 360–369 (364); adult bill ($n = 13$) 31–37 (33.6); adult tarsus ($n = 13$) 59–68 (63.7); adult weight in winter ($n = 4$), 1950–2300. ♀ adult wing ($n = 7$), 361–387 (373); juv ($n = 10$), 329–356 (345); adult bill ($n = 17$) 29–34 (31.3); adult tarsus ($n = 15$), 57–65 (61.0); adult weight in winter ($n = 2$), 2100 and 2150 (Cramp and Simmons 1977).

Field characters

Like White-fronted Goose, but has proportionally smaller more rounded head, shorter neck and slighter build. Small size, 530–660 mm long, and clean, uniform nature of plumage distinctive at all times, including immatures. Flies faster, with swifter wingbeats and more direct agile flight than larger, heavier White-fronted Goose, giving more squeaky flight calls. Despite some White-fronted Geese having pale eye-rings, swollen orbital ring of smaller species characteristic at close range. On ground, primaries extending beyond tail, and faster walking peck rates good distinguishing field characters; restricted belly-bars and extensive white forehead not sufficient for separation from occasional small Whitefront.

Voice

Two or three note call much more rapid, squeakier and higher pitched than those of White-fronted Geese. Not loud, but far-reaching and distinctive. Sonogram in Cramp and Simmons (1977).

Range and status

Breeding areas lie in sub or low arctic zone from northern Norway and Sweden across Palearctic to eastern Siberia. In west of range, formerly bred in mountainous areas in Scandinavia (Norderhaug and Norderhaug 1984), but throughout most of rest of range nests in open tundra from Kola Peninsula to Bolshezemelskaya tundra. Range in Fennoscandia contracted dramatically last century and distribution in extreme east and western parts has become

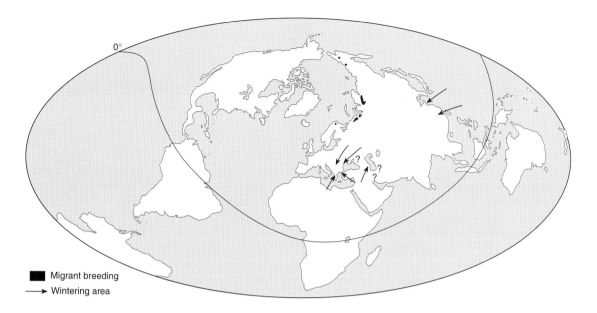

■ Migrant breeding
→ Wintering area

fragmented (Madsen *et al.* 1999a). Finnmark population estimated at 30–50 pairs in 1990s, compared with 10 000 early last century (Norderhaug and Norderhaug 1984, Madsen 1996, Madsen *et al.* 1999a). Swedish population now extinct. Declines on breeding areas linked to increasing tourist activity, angling disturbance and creation of hydro-electric reservoirs in formerly remote areas of Scandinavia (Madsen 1996).

Situation in Russian breeding areas similar (Vinogradov 1990, Rogacheva 1992, Morozov 1999), with drastic reductions in population size and range. Western Palearctic range now comprises 500–1000 individuals in Pechora Delta–Ural/Yamal population and *c* 1000–2000 pairs plus 3000–4000 nonbreeding moulters on Taimyr peninsula (Syroechkovski 1996, Madsen *et al.* 1999a, Romanov 2003). Recent surveys located 3500–4500 in Abyi Lowlands of Yakutia (Artiukhov and Syroechkovski 1999). Limited data on staging areas with 4 internationally important sites known in Russia and one in China. In far east of range, similar dramatic declines recorded in recent decades (Madsen 1996). Counts of 300–7500 in Amur Basin, to 400 in Kamchatka in 1980s and to 15 in Hokkaido, Japan, in mid 1990s (Iwabuchi 1997).

Migration routes poorly understood because of little ringing information. Nankinov (1992) presented census data to suggest possible migration routes, but fragmentation of formerly contiguous breeding range now makes historical analysis impossible. Syroechkovski (1996) reviewed migration routes and Russian ringing data. Satellite telemetry has shown geese from Fennoscandian breeding population may undertake long-distance moult-migration eastwards to Kolgujev Island, Kanin and Taimyr Peninsulas (Lorentsen *et al.* 1998, Aarvak & Øien 2003). In Europe, declines in staging areas in Finland and Hungary mirror those of breeding areas. In Finland, several hundred staged in spring, latterly up to 97 individuals seen (Soikkeli 1973, Aarvak and Øien 1994). In Hungary, *c* 100 000 reported in 1950s, but fell to *c* 5000 by late 1960s (Sterbetz 1982), with 200–600 annually during late 1980s but up to 1200 returned in early 1990s (Farago *et al.* 1991, Madsen 1996). Cultivation of former steppe grassland may have contributed to declines in Hungary (Sterbetz 1968, 1990).

On wintering grounds, > 10 usually reported among large numbers of White-fronted Geese in Romania and Bulgaria during International Waterfowl Census in Jan, although 900 estimated in Romania in 1992 (Madsen 1996). In Greece, up to 1600 reported in 1960s, but by 1980s numbers varied 0–140, although in recent winters small stable group of 140 appear regularly in northeast

Greece. Satellite telemetry in 1990s showed that birds from Fennoscandia move to Kanin peninsula in early Sept, where staged for 3–4 weeks. Three marked birds moved southeast to sites either side of Urals, including one to Kazakhstan (Madsen *et al.* 1999a); however, 2 marked in Norway moved to Kanin Peninsula then to Baltic coast of eastern Germany before migrating to Hungary and thence to Greece, ending up in Evros Delta (Aarvak *et al.* 1996). Finnish and Swedish ringed birds recovered in eastern Black Sea, but only small numbers winter in Ukraine (Madsen 1996). Although recent reports suggested several hundred wintering birds in Crimea (Grinchenko 2001), only 12 found during severe weather in Jan 2002 (Grinchenko *et al.* 2003). Better survey remains priority in this region (Lahti and Markkola 1994). In Azerbaijan, up to 30 000 reported wintering, but evidence suggests only 1500–7000 have since 1960s—special survey in Jan–Feb 1996 found 1058 at most important wintering resorts (Paynter 1996). Knowledge about wintering numbers in Kazakhstan remains patchy, where up to 3500 have been estimated in Kustanay region in autumn (Gurtovaya *et al.* 1999, Tolvanen *et al.* 2001). In Iran, 1970s total varied 4500–7500, but sites there and around Caspian now abandoned.

Population in Western Palearctic declined over 90% in last 40 years; however, in drafting Action Plans, clear how little known of species and of reasons behind rapid decline (Madsen 1996). Factors operating on breeding areas insufficient to explain decrease in numbers since 1950s, and habitat loss and exploitation on staging and wintering grounds more likely explanations. Scott and Rose (1996) estimated population of northern Europe, western Siberia, Black and Caspian Seas at 15 000–35 000.

In Eastern Palearctic, information even scarcer on breeding grounds and wintering areas. Recent information from Chinese Waterfowl Specialist Group and Miyabayashi and Mundkur (1999) identified 6 internationally important wintering sites and one staging site in China, holding whole population. Species still legal quarry. Based on mid-winter counts, eastern element of population was thought to number *c* 6000 (Anon 1994, Madsen 1996), but Iwabuchi *et al.* (1997) counted 13 700 in the East Dongting Lakes, China, in Feb 1997, and

Miyabayashi and Mundkur (1999) revised current population estimate to 14 000, making world population 49 000 individuals or less.

Habitat and general habits

Breeding habitats mostly in scrub ecotone areas close to wetlands in taiga and tundra zone (Uspenski 1965, Rogacheva 1992). In Scandinavia, bred at relatively high altitudes (up to 700 m, Ekman 1922). Feeds on variety of plants along lake and river marshes and in marshes (Lorentsen and Spjøtvoll 1990). Pre-nesting feeding in northern Norway involves foraging on saltmarshes (Aarvak and Øien 1994). Generally arrives on breeding grounds from early May–late June and leaves mid Aug–Sept (Madsen 1996). Siberian geese undertake moult migration to areas north of breeding range (Rogacheva 1992), often exploiting large open waters fringed with sedge *Carex* meadows (Cramp and Simmons 1977), and river valleys with long grass and scrub used for escape from predators. Moulters in Scandinavia moved up altitudinal gradient to exploit young plant growth at higher altitudes (Ekman 1922). Breeders moult 1st week Aug, nonbreeders last 10 days July (Syroechkovski 1996).

In winter, traditionally exploited open short grassland, such as steppe zones and semi-arid biotopes, often selecting short grassy sodic pastures in Hungary and salt steppes (Sterbetz 1968, 1990, Cramp and Simmons 1977). Generally considered more terrestrial in winter habit than many grey geese. Recent habitat preferences hardly known because of rarity of species.

Displays and breeding behaviour

Little studied in wild. Monogamous, lifelong pair-bond in captivity. Behaviour similar to other grey geese, but generally more agitated behaviour and faster movements. Parent–offspring bonds extend through 1st autumn and much of winter, but adults return to breeding area alone (Cramp and Simmons 1977).

Breeding and life cycle

Breeding behaviour and pre-nesting activity virtually unstudied. Nest site usually amongst vegetation, grass or dwarf shrub heath, often on snowfree patch available early in season, such as rock outcrop or prominent hummock. Site often in close proximity to open water or extensive marshy area (Dementiev and Gladkov 1952).

Eggs oval, smooth, creamy white but often stained during incubation; 49 × 76 (*n* = 100) (Schönwetter 1960–66); weight 104 (*n* = 84) (Cramp and Simmons 1977). Clutch size 4–6 (2–8), in Taimyr 5.3 (*n* = 9) (Syroechkovski 1996); single brood. Incubation by ♀ only, 25 days in captivity, 25–28 in wild (Cramp and Simmons 1977) starting 5 June–10 July, mostly mid June (Syroechkovski 1996). Weight at hatching in captivity 66.8 (*n* = 38). Fledge in 35–40 days, 46 in captivity (Owen 1980). Said to remain late on breeding ground, departing mid Aug–mid-Sept (Owen 1980). Pairs may form in 2nd year before breeding, usually at 3 years in captivity (Cramp and Simmons 1977).

Nest success and annual survival generally unknown; however, recorded production of young high at specific breeding areas (e.g. Norway, Aarvak *et al.* 1995, 1996, Yamal, Vinogradov 1990, and Taimyr, Aarvak *et al.* 1997, Tolvanen *et al.* 1998) suggesting breeding output may not be cause of current decline. By contrast, low and declining proportions of young reported on autumn migration in Hungary since 1950s (Sterbetz 1986) and from wintering areas recently (3–6% in winter 1995–96, Paynter 1996) suggest poor survival on autumn migration.

Conservation and threats

Low overall survival rate (as demonstrated by satellite-tagged individuals) probably limits potential recovery of declining and fragmented population that results from high hunting pressure on migration, staging and in wintering areas (Madsen *et al.* 1999a, Lampila 2000). Despite considerable attention in recent years, remains poorly known and requires urgent conservation action, as set out in recent Action Plan (Madsen 1996). Sites of major importance in Russia remain unprotected although actively threatened by industrial and other development (Artiukhov and Syroechkovski 1999). Designated Vulnerable by BirdLife International (2000, 2001), a task force of Wetlands International Goose Specialist Group coordinates research and conservation activities for population identified in Action Plan (Madsen 1996). Habitat loss and hunting mortality identified as most serious threats, operating especially on staging and wintering grounds. Satellite-telemetry proved highly effective in western Palearctic in identifying staging areas and migration routes, but nothing known of situation in eastern part of Palearctic. Conservation challenge is to conserve and manage network of sites, to encourage their use, and ultimately to enable population recovery. Action Plan's highest priority is to identify key sites in Russia, Kazakhstan and Azerbaijan, as well as to minimize hunting kill and disturbance throughout known range. Education and awareness-raising among hunters on staging and breeding areas especially important. Prevention of habitat degradation and loss also flagged as priority for action. So long as wild population persists, reintroduction and restocking programmes need lower priority.

Tony Fox

Bar-headed Goose *Anser indicus*
PLATE 6

Anas indica Latham, 1790, Index Ornith., p. 839
India in winter, and Tibet

Etymology: *indicus* L. means from India.

Other names: Indian Goose. *Hamsa*, Sanskrit for goose, old name of Bar-headed Goose, said to consist of 2 sacred syllables, *Ham* breathing in and *Sa* breathing out (Taube 1957). German: Streifengans. Some authorities prefer *Eulabeia indica*.

Variation: no subspecies. Differs from other grey geese in skull, fatty acid composition (Jacob and Glaser 1975), pattern of aminoacids in haemoglobin (Hiebl *et al.* 1986), post-copulatory display and egg rolling behaviour. No fertile hybrids known with grey or black geese.

Description

ADULT: sexes alike but ♀ averages 10% smaller. Face and head white with two black bars, upper bar circles occiput from eye to eye, lower one half circles nape. Both bars have variable endings and these patterns may serve for individual recognition. Hind neck blackish, lower foreneck deep brown merging into grey, breast grey, upperwing feathers soft grey with white tips, primaries and secondaries black, uppertail feathers white with grey bar, vent white. Bill yellow with black nail; legs and webs yellow, claws black; eyes brown.

MOULT: breeding pairs with goslings start wing moult 24–28 days after young hatch; both adults lose all primaries and secondaries within 24 h. Able to fly 32–35 days later, with young; by then, primaries 80% of normal length and, within 40–45 days, wings fully grown. Moulting of body feathers starts 21–24 days after wing moult and begins with shoulder, followed by wing pocket, back, belly, breast, neck and head, complete within 10 weeks. Breeding pairs with young moult earlier than unsuccessful breeders, non-breeders and subadults. In Altai, breeders start moulting in June, in Pamir in July; by mid Aug all Altai birds flying (Dementiev and Gladkov 1952). Nothing known of moult migration.

IMMATURE: plumage of both sexes like adult but paler and, instead of bars, black streak runs from occiput to back; bill, legs and web greenish yellow.

GOSLING: yellow or greenish grey, with grey patch on head, and yellow patches on wings. Bill greenish grey, nail fleshy. Legs and web greenish grey. Within brood, goslings vary from yellow to greenish grey. Moult into adult plumage starts *c* 115–125 days after hatching.

MEASUREMENT AND WEIGHT: ♂ ($n = 4$), wing, 450; culmen, 47; tarsus, 82; weight, 2600. ♀ ($n = 6$), wing, 419; culmen, 45; tarsus, 72; weight, 2014 (Ma and Cai 1999). Other dimensions and weights in Dementiev and Gladkov (1952), Chi Yen-lang (1961), Delacour (1954–64), Piechocki (1968) and Würdinger (1973).

Field characters

Medium-sized compared with other goose species, ♂ 770 and ♀ 703 mm long (Ma and Cai 1999). Yellow bill, white head with two black bars and light grey body, yellow legs and yellow webs distinguish from all other geese. In flight, appears pale or even white, with black wing tips.

Voice

Adult contact calls consist of 1–3 syllables uttered in social context; greeting has up to 5 syllables with great individual variation and uttered only between pair members, parents and goslings or between siblings; distance call at 1400–1760 Hz is single note given when partner out of sight, or by goslings and juveniles if parent or siblings not seen (Collias 1962); lament call is single note uttered in uncomfortable situations. Adults give 2 different warning notes, one for birds-of-prey and other if land predator, such as fox, approaches. Young and adults hiss in defensive situations.

Goslings give single syllable distress calls (Kear 1968) and lament call (Würdinger 1970). Two or more distinct syllables used in contact (Collias 1962) or as pleasure calls (Kear 1968), and in greeting (Collias 1962). Trill, where syllables recognizable but not separated (Marler 1961), used as sleepy call (Kear 1968). Clicks produced while hatching. Distress call, uttered by lost juveniles, changes at Day 40 into long distance call and adult lament call. Twelve h before hatching, lament call, contact call and trills uttered from within egg; greeting call appears *c* 4 h after hatching, warning calls can be elicited from Day 2.

Range and status

Endemic at high altitudes in central and southern Asia. Breeds discontinuously in Ladakh, Pamir, Altai, lakes of central Asia, China and Mongolia and along upper course of Indus, Brahmaputra, Selenga and other rivers to 5300 m asl (Koslowa-Puschkarewa 1933, Schäfer 1938, Dementiev and Gladkov 1952, Chi Yen-Lang 1961, Kydyraliew 1967, Piechocki 1968, Gole 1982, Ali and Ripley

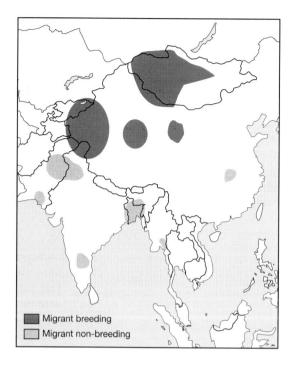

Migrant breeding
Migrant non-breeding

1987, Miyabayashi and Mundkur 1999). Breeding sites hold, at Ladakh 21 pairs, at Karakul (Pamir) 300 pairs (BBC-NDR3, 5 Apr 1994), Kukunor Quinghai Hu Nature Reserve 5520 individuals in 1988 (Lu 1997), 1250 pairs in 1992, and 2000–3000 birds in 1996 (von Treuenfels 1996), > 99 pairs at Bayinbulak Swan Lake, Tianshan, Xinjiang, China in 1992 (Ma and Cai 1999). Other breeding sites in Mongolia and China listed by Lu (1997) and Miyabayashi and Mundkur (1999).

Winters in wetlands, lakes and rivers of Shanzu, Sechuan, Tibet, Yennan, in India, Pakistan and northern Myanmar (Burma). Main wintering areas in China named by Lu (1997). Surveys 1990–91 and 1995–96 (Bishop *et al.* 1997) estimated 13 000–14 500 wintering in south-central Tibet (> 25% world population). Of these, *c* 70% in 2 areas: Shigatse, around confluence of Nyang and Yarlung Rivers, and in Penbo River valley, northeast of Lhasa. Regular counts indicated stable numbers in Tibet in this period. Thirteen internationally important wintering sites known in China (Miyabayashi and Mundkur 1999). Delacour (1954–64) reported, geese 'abundant in northern India, but uncommon

in the south of the peninsula'. Winter censuses by Mundkur and Sridhar (1993) found increasing numbers (1840 in Jan 1991 and 1865 in Jan 1992) in wetlands of Karnataka, South India. In Keoladeo Ghana National Park, numbers decreasing; in March 1981, 41–1544 (Sankhala 1990), in 1985–86, 500–1000 (Middleton and Van der Valk 1987), in Jan 1991 394–420.

Little known of migration routes, but different routes in spring and autumn suggested by Dementiev and Gladkov (1952). Spring migration starts Mar in India and Pakistan; arrives at Koko Nor Mar–Apr, and northern Gobi and Pamir mid May. Autumn migration starts in northern breeding areas end of Aug, Tianshan in late Aug, in Pamir end Sept (Dementiev and Gladkov 1952, Gole 1982). Two ringed in Pamir seen in Kashmir and Pakistan (McClure 1974); 3 ringed at Qinghai Lake in China recovered wintering in Karnataka State southwest India, in northeast India, and in Chittgong, southern Bangladesh (Miyabayashi and Mundkur 1999). Reported over Himalaya at 9000–10 000 m altitude (Swan 1970); peculiarities of haemoglobin enable flying at such heights (Oberthür *et al.* 1982).

Status unclear, but may be threatened and vulnerable, although not IUCN-listed. Two populations recognized, defined by wintering areas, in southern Asia to Myanmar: 16 800–18 900 and (possibly largely sedentary) in China: 15 500–17 500 (Bishop *et al.* 1997, Miyabayashi and Mundkur 1999). Thus world population 32 300–36 400.

Habitat and general habits

In winter areas, can be seen singly, in pairs and families. Families join feeding groups of 2–4 other families. Larger units formed while roosting or before long distance flights (Urfi 1997). Diet in breeding season grasses *Poa*, *Potamogeton pectinatus*, leaves, seeds, berries, small insects and, in water, insects and small crustaceans (Dementiev and Gladkov 1952, Kydyraliew 1967, Gole 1982). If available, takes crops such as beans and peas. In winter eats *Paspalum distichums*, *Pisum sativum*, wheat, other grains, plus 21 other plant species (Middleton and Van der Valk 1987). In Tibet, feeds on harvested barley and spring wheat fields as well as in riverine

9.8 Post-copulatory display of Bar-headed Goose (male behind).

and lacustrine wetlands (Bishop *et al.* 1997). Food items selected by inborn preferences for colour (Kear 1964), form, flavour and tactile information, and by learning from parental tradition. Has high tolerance for otherwise poisonous plants such as *Convallaria majalis* but, compared to other grey and black geese, is 'by far the most selective species' (Wink *et al.* 1993). If not disturbed, flies to feeding grounds at sunrise or shortly before, returning at 11.00 h for roosting, preening, drinking and bathing, and feeds again at 14.00 h (Gole 1982, Würdinger 1998). Uses reservoirs to roost at night in Penbo River valley, Tibet (Bishop *et al.* 1997).

Displays and breeding behaviour

Courtship starts at 2–3 years of age, and consists, in both sexes, of looking at wanted partner using Angle-neck (*Winkelhals*), Head-dipping (*Halseintauchen*) and Imposing-posture (Fischer 1965). Angle-neck is appeasement gesture and helps shorten distance between partners; Head-dipping, seen only on water, is pre-copulation gesture and synchronizes performance; Imposing-posture may show fitness of bird. Greeting ceremony indicates that 2 geese are paired. Lifetime monogamy normal, but 'with a surplus of females, permanent harem groups consisting of one male with one to five females, lasting for up to several years, were

regularly observed' (Lamprecht 1987, Würdinger 1998). Copulation occurs only on water; post-copulatory posture of ♂ unique among geese and more like that of swans (Figure 9.8).

Nesting territory vigorously defended by ♂ while ♀ incubates.

Breeding and life cycle

Pairs recorded breeding singly (Schäfer 1938), in small colonies (e.g. 21 pairs) or large colonies (> 1000 pairs) (Dementiev and Gladkov 1952, Kydyraliew 1967, Gole 1982, Ma and Cai 1999). Nests on islands, on shore of saline and freshwater lakes, and along rivers. Koslowa (1933) reported nests in trees. Tends to return to same nesting place year after year. Density of 184 nests on 4 islands in Tianshan 0.6 per m², similar to reported densities in Qinghai Province and Tibet (Ma and Cai 1999). Building follows laying of 2nd egg; ♀ pulls, with bill, plant material towards belly while sitting or standing on site, and finally lines nest with down. Egg-laying starts Ladakh 2nd week May (Gole 1982), early to mid May in Tianshan (Ma and Cai 1999), in captivity in Europe mid Apr–early May (Würdinger 1973). Eggs 82.1 × 53.8 (78–91 × 47.2–58.3); weight 137 (122–148) (*n* = 70); clutch 5.3 (3–8) (*n* = 22) or, in Tianshan at 2400 m, 4.47 ± 2.19 (*n* = 184) (Ma and Cai 1999). Authors report many eggs dispersed outside nests in colonial situations. Incubation, by ♀ only, begins after 4th or 5th egg laid; lasts 27–30 days. Hatching success 37–51% depending on age and experience of ♀ and successful guarding of ♂. As day-olds, goslings weighed 70.8 ($n = 11$) (Ma and Cai 1999). Two days after hatching, family leaves nest site. Goslings feed themselves from Day 3–4; parents indicate edible plants, and certain techniques of food acquisition (turning stones, etc.) may be learned. Loss of down starts 22–23 days after hatch, at belly. First flights on Days 49–60. In Tianshan, fledge mid Aug–Sept when goslings 65–80 days old, weighing 2000–2400 g and 620–700 mm long (Ma and Cai 1999). Survival seems low (Gole 1982); family size in Bharatpur, India, Jan 1991, 3.4. Pairs migrate with young to winter sites, but not known whether return with them to breeding ground.

No data on adult survival, nor on longevity.

Conservation and threats

Numbers have decreased during last 50 years, and hunting pressure still exists (Green 1992, Gole 1997). Protected Tibet since Feb 1992 but remains unprotected elsewhere in China (Bishop *et al.* 1997); despite protection, hunting occurs in Tibet, although limited by Buddhist wildlife values. Former breeding places (e.g. Lob Nor) are deserted, but Ramsar site and National Park designation, and wetland conservation on breeding (e.g. Koko Nor, Quinghai Hu) and wintering grounds (e.g. Bharatpur, Sultanpur), should be helpful if wise use realized. Second most important site in Tibet partially within Penbo Nature Reserve (9680 ha), but no other Tibetan wintering area protected. Loss of traditional riverine wetlands continues through canalization of major rivers (Bishop *et al.* 1997). Hydroelectric development in Tibet also has scope to disrupt river flows and important goose roosting and feeding areas. Range of conservation measures in Tibet promoted for Black-necked Cranes *Grus nigricollis* will benefit Barheads and Ruddy Shelduck in same area (Bishop *et al.* 1997).

Safeguarded to some extent by sentiment. In Indian myths, Sarasvrati, goddess of learning, associates with a Bar-headed Goose, and a wonderful story, Hamsajataka, connects Buddha and the goose-king, who is his principal disciple (Kear 1990).

Irene Würdinger

Emperor Goose *Anser canagicus*
PLATE 6

Anas Canagica Sevastianov, 1802, Nova Acta Acad. Sci. Imp. Petropolitanae, **13**, p. 349, pl. 10
Kodiak Island, Alaska

Etymology: *canagicus* means from Kodiak Island (Gibson 2002). Common name perhaps derives from old Russian Tzarski Goose or 'goose of the Tsar'.

Other names: none in English. French: Oie empereur; Russian: Beloshey. Placed in genus *Chen* by AOU.

Variation: no subspecies. Taxonomy changed several times since initial description (Rockwell *et al.* 1996). Bannister (1870) erected genus *Philacte* and, primarily because of differences in supraorbital depression (Coues 1884, Miller 1937), remained as *Philacte canagica* until recently. Miller (1937) also discussed structural similarities with *Chloephaga* from South America, but decided these resulted from convergent evolution rather than common ancestry. More recently, Livezey (1996b) identified 2 clades within *Anser*—subgenus *Anser* and subgenus *Chen*—separated by 3 distinct morphological characters; within *Chen*, Emperor sister species to Ross's and Snow Goose. Extending Ploeger's (1968) discussion of effects of Beringian land bridge on distribution, Syroechkovski (2000) hypothesized that formation of this bridge led to speciation of Emperor from blue phase of Snow Goose. He noted that conditions allowing for such an event were coastal-dependent ecology and latitudinal separation between blue and white phase Snow Geese. Some support comes from Shoffner *et al.* (1979), who noted striking plumage similarity between blue-phase Snow Goose and fertile hybrids between Emperor and Ross's Goose.

Description

ADULT: sexes alike. Distinctly bicoloured; head and back of neck white, while chin, front of neck and body dark bluish grey. Body has barred appearance as each grey contour feather medium grey, darkening to grey-black sub-terminal band and then ending with white or light tan distal tip. Exposed tail feathers white but with light to medium grey base. Primaries and foreneck darkest grey. Rachi or shafts of primaries white. Head feathers become stained in spring shortly after arrival on breeding areas, presumably from feeding in ferrous soils, and appear reddish orange. Bill multicolored; upper mandible has small, proximal blue band of variable intensity, then dominating reddish pink band that surrounds dark nares, and then round distal tip that grades from light pink to dark grey; lower mandible dark grey to black. Feet bright yellowish orange with black nails; eye brown. ♀ subtly less plump; staining of head more intense, and feathers, particularly distal tip of greater coverts, seem more tan and less white.

MOULT: remigial moult of adult concludes when young fledge.

IMMATURE: ♂ similar to adult except without white head and neck plumage. Head and neck dark grey. Feathers narrower and more tapered than in later plumages. Moult of head and neck feathers into basic white plumage of adult occurs throughout autumn. Feet continually lighten with age and progress from olive-black to yellowish olive. ♀ similar to immature ♂ but smaller.

GOSLING: forehead, hind neck, and upper body dark, smoky grey; crown and lower body lighter grey. Grades into pale grey with hint of white on throat, breast and front of neck. Small bill and feet dark grey-black (Nelson 1993).

MEASUREMENTS AND WEIGHT: ♂ culmen ($n = 13$), 39.0; tarsus ($n = 13$), 83.8; weight during wing moult ($n = 75$), 2316. ♀ wing ($n = 43$), 372.4;

culmen ($n = 18$), 35.5; tarsus ($n = 18$), 80.0; weight during wing moult ($n = 206$), 1945; data from Alaska Science Center, Biological Resources Division, USGS, Anchorage, Alaska. Adult ♀♀ ($n = 9$) weighed 2337 (Laing 1991) upon arrival at breeding areas, 1685 at hatch ($n = 208$), and then increased in mass by c 17% by fledging (Petersen *et al.* 1994).

Field characters

Medium-sized, 660–890 mm long, stocky, short-necked, bicolored goose. Solid white head and blue-grey body unique. Retrices white with no darker sub-terminal bands, unlike other dark-bodied geese. Confusion with Blue Snow Goose possible; latter has larger bill, longer neck, pink legs, white foreneck and ventral region (see Madge and Burn 1988).

Voice

Less vocal, and readily distinguished from other geese. Emits either strident *kla-ha, kla-ha, kla-ha* or, when alarmed and taking flight, deeper *u-lugh, u-lugh* (Nelson 1887). When alarmed or agitated while on ground, often gives quiet, low groan. All vocalizations more nasal than sympatrically nesting Canada and White-fronted Geese. Sonograms of gosling calls in Kear (1968).

Range and status

Occurs along shores of Bering and Chukchi Seas and Gulf of Alaska throughout life. Breeds primarily on Yukon-Kuskokwim Delta, Alaska, between Askinuk Mountains and Nelson Island (60°15′–61°45′ N). Small numbers also found along Alaska's Seward Peninsula and Russia's east coast (Eisenhauer and Kirkpatrick 1977). During both spring and autumn migration, most spend 1–2 months along north shore of Alaska Peninsula (Petersen and Gill 1982). Some also distributed on south coast of Alaska Peninsula and Kodiak Island. During winter, dispersed through Aleutian and Komandorski Islands, more northerly range than other Pacific geese.

In 1996, 80 000 counted during spring migration, and estimated 31 000 nesting pairs seen on

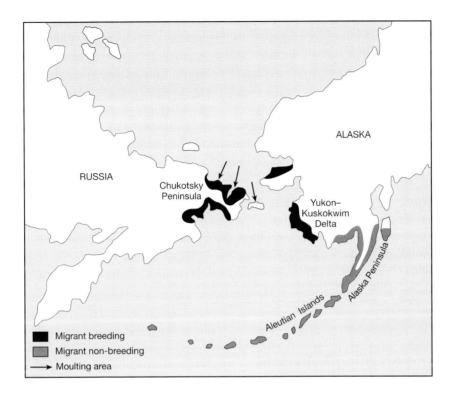

Migrant breeding
Migrant non-breeding
→ Moulting area

Yukon-Kuskokwim Delta (Bowman *et al.* 1996). Numbers breeding in Russia less well known but thought to be < 1000 individuals, nesting primarily in Anadyr region, and using similar migration and, presumably, wintering areas to those breeding in Alaska (Kondratyev 1993, Schmutz and Kondratyev 1995). Vankaremskaya Lowlands (2000) and Kolyuchin Bay Tundra (3500) important Russian moulting areas in 1970s, with 300 at Chukot Peninsula in 1990s (Miyabayashi and Mundkur 1999). Moult migrations of failed and nonbreeders noted (Blurton Jones 1972), with St Lawrence Island being primary site in past (Fay 1961). More recently, failed and nonbreeding geese seen primarily along Chukot Peninsula rather than on St Lawrence Island (Schmutz and Kondratyev 1995).

Comprises single biogeographical population. Rose and Scott (1997) gave total population of 165 000 following Ellis-Joseph *et al.* (1992); however, seemingly too large as greatest known abundance in 1964, when *c* 140 000 observed along Alaska Peninsula in spring. More recently, Threat-ened Waterfowl Specialist Group (2003) estimated 45 000–80 000 based on range of sources.

Habitat and general habits

Predominately nests within 15 km of sea in tidally influenced tundra. Habitat permeated by numerous small ponds, lakes, and tidal sloughs. Halophytic plants dominate as storm tides periodically inundate entire breeding habitat. Nests often along shore of small ponds or sloughs. Island nesting not as frequent as in sympatric Canada geese (Petersen 1990). Herbivorous while on breeding grounds. Consumes *Triglochin palustris* (Laing 1991) and *Elymus arenarius* upon arrival, grubbing shallowly for bulbs of *T. palustris*. Variability of clutch size from season to season (Petersen 1992a), and intense feeding observed upon arrival in early spring, imply that exogenous foods affect reproductive effort. In later spring and summer, adults and goslings graze *Carex subspathacaea, C. ramenskii,* and *Puccinellia phyraganodes* (Laing and Raveling 1993). Goslings spend most (> 50%) of time feeding (Laing 1991). Adults feed less and are alert more, with

♂ spending most time alert. Feeding behaviour and growth of goslings affected by competition with sympatric geese (Schmutz and Laing 2002).

During spring and autumn migration, inhabits shallow, coastal lagoons along Bering Sea, where consumes bivalves, *Macoma* and *Mytilus*, in expansive mudflats exposed by low tide, and roosts on beaches at high tide. Young spend disproportionately more time feeding and often consume green vegetation at high tide instead of roosting (Schmutz 1994). Family associations still evident during migration, although aggregated into flocks of 50–500. Flocks often flush in response to Bald Eagles *Haliaeetus leucocephalus*.

Habitats used in winter resemble those of spring and autumn or are rockier with steeper, more exposed shoreline. Diets poorly studied, but presumably similar to spring and autumn with addition of marine plants *Fucus* and *Zostera marina*. In addition to strong nest area fidelity, faithful to migration and wintering areas.

Displays and breeding behaviour

Once paired, remain together throughout annual cycle. Although dogma says that geese pair on wintering areas (Cooke *et al.* 1995), philopatric behaviour and discreetness of breeding populations have led others to speculate that pairing occurs during spring or summer (Ely and Scribner 1994). As so little studied in winter, timing of pair formation unclear, but copulation and intense mate-guarding observed on Alaska Peninsula during spring migration. Upon arrival on breeding areas, begins nesting within one week (Petersen 1992a). Associations between parents and young sometimes still evident in spring, as year-olds seen near nests of parents.

Breeding and life cycle

Usually initiates nesting mid May on Yukon-Kuskokwim Delta, Alaska (Petersen 1992a) and *c* 3 weeks later in Russia (Krechmar and Kondratiev 1982). Eggs bluntly ovate and creamy white; 79.6 × 51.7 (69–100 × 44–60) (*n* = 2493); in captivity weigh 130.4 (95.0–154.5) (*n* = 100). Average clutch 4–6 eggs, though up to 14 observed as intraspecific nest parasitism common (Petersen 1991); parasitically laid eggs often shaped differently than those of host (Petersen 1992b). Incubation 24.3 ± 1.4 days (Eisen-

hauer and Kirkpatrick 1977). ♀ takes few incubation breaks, spending > 99% of time on nest (Thompson and Raveling 1987). Nest success 60–90%, but highly variable (0–95%) (Petersen 1992a), depending upon Arctic Fox activity. Primary nest predators are foxes and skuas or jaegers. Re-nesting not known, but continuation clutches likely.

Soon after hatch, broods travel to intertidal habitats dominated by *C. subspathaceae* and *C. ramenskii* (Schmutz 2001). Some adoption of goslings occurs. Young grow from hatch to fledging at daily rate of 24.4–26.0 g (Petersen *et al.* 1994). Survival from hatch to fledging 35–71%, with most mortality in 1st 10 days (Schmutz *et al.* 2001). Glaucous Gulls *Larus hyperboreus* principal predators of goslings. Young fledge in 45–50 days. ♀♀ that nest survive less than those that do not; however, of those that nest, those with larger clutches have higher survival (Petersen 1992c). Survival of breeding ♀♀ from fledging to autumn migration areas poorer than ♂♂; otherwise survival of sexes similar (Schmutz *et al.* 1994). Annual adult survival *c* 80% (Schmutz and Morse 2000). Survival of young to autumn migration areas depends on body mass prior to fledging (Schmutz 1993).

Predation pressure may have shifted over time. Gulls primary predators of goslings, and numbers on Yukon-Kuskokwim Delta *c* doubled 1986–95, despite nearly constant numbers of Emperor Geese (Bowman *et al.* 1996, 1997). No noticeable shift in amount of gosling consumption by individual gulls between 1970s and 1993 (Strang 1976, Schmutz and Hobson 1998), thus indicating that larger population of gulls may now consume larger number and proportion of geese. Arctic Foxes and Bald Eagles take adults during breeding and nonbreeding seasons, respectively (Gill and Kincheloe 1993, Petersen *et al.* 1994). Although data lacking, no signs of shift in impact on goose populations. Although data limited, earliest known age of breeding in wild 3 years (Schmutz 2000).

Conservation and threats

Given Near-threatened status by BirdLife International (2000). Annual surveys since 1981 documented decline in early 1980s and subsequent stabilization (Petersen *et al.* 1994). Due to concerns about low population, all legal harvest in North

America ceased in 1986. Has always been important subsistence food in some communities (Klein 1966), and some subsistence harvest still occurs (Wentworth and Seim 1996). In 1985, Yukon-Kuskokwim Delta Goose Management Plan developed cooperatively by various native groups, State of Alaska, and US Fish & Wildlife Service (Pamplin 1986). Plan established guidelines for subsistence harvest and, in particular, called for cessation of harvest of Emperor Geese as were most imperilled of 4 species breeding in Yukon-Kuskokwim Delta. Since 1985, population increased at 1–2% per year and numbered approximately 80 000 birds in 1996. Current management objectives call for increasing population to historic levels (Pacific Flyway Council 1994). To achieve this, growth rate needs to be higher and more similar to that recently experienced by sympatricy nesting Cackling Canada Geese and Pacific White-fronted Geese (Bowman *et al.* 1996). Models indicate population growth rate most sensitive to changes in adult survival (Schmutz *et al.* 1997); thus various mortality factors need assessment.

Most direct human impact on survival is continued subsistence harvest. Approximately 2000–3000 currently harvested every year on Yukon-Kuskokwim Delta, with additional geese taken elsewhere during migration and winter (Wentworth and Seim 1996). Other human impacts more difficult to quantify.

Habitat relatively remote and pristine; however, petroleum pollution may be threat as geese seen in winter in Aleutian Islands with oiled plumage (Byrd *et al.* 1992). Unexpectedly high levels of organochlorines found in other species studied in Aleutian archipelago (Estes *et al.* 1997). Organochlorine presence in Emperor Geese not yet examined. Human-induced climate change may also influence populations by affecting timing of reproduction and subsequent survival. Spring plant phenology in Arctic advanced by nearly week during 1981–91 (Myneni *et al.* 1997), and hatch dates in 1997 earliest yet recorded.

Health status recently studied because of slow population growth and because lead poisoning evident in some species of sympatrically nesting ducks (Spectacled Eider and Long-tailed Duck, Flint *et al.* 1997). No evidence of lead poisoning found, probably as consequence of grazing habit, in contrast to foraging pattern of aforementioned seaducks. Selenium concentrations in blood of adults high (Franson *et al.* 1999), and comparable to levels known to be toxic to captive Northern Mallard (Heinz *et al.* 1990). Not known whether such levels abnormal, but other physiological measures indicate oxidative stress associated with high selenium concentrations (Franson *et al.* 2002).

Joel Schmutz

Snow Goose *Anser caerulescens*

PLATE 6

Anas caerulescens Linnaeus, 1758, Syst. Nat., ed 10, p. 124
Hudson Bay. Blue morph
Anser hyberboreus Pallas, 1769, Spicilegia Zool., fasc. 6, p. 25
northeastern Siberia. White morph

Etymology: *caerulescens* L. means bluish.

Other names: Wavey Goose, Eagle-headed Brant, Blue Goose. French: Oie des neiges. Placed in genus *Chen* by AOU.

Variation: 2 subspecies recognized, differentiated by size, and 2 colour morphs. Lesser Snow Goose *A. c. caerulescens* exists in white and blue (Blue Goose) phases, and breeds over most of range.

Greater Snow Goose *A. c. atlanticus* Kennard, 1927, restricted to islands in north Baffin Bay and northwest Greenland, has rare blue phase.

Description

ADULT: sexes alike. Larger race, *atlanticus*, has heavier bill. Both races exhibit 2 distinct colour phases, dark ('blue', hence Blue Goose) and white (hence Snow Goose). Blue phase variably common (0–100% depending on location) in Lesser, and extremely rare ($< 0.1\%$) in Greater Snow Goose. Plumage polymorphism controlled by simple single locus, two allele system with partial dominance (white phase homozygous recessive). Adult white phase completely white, except for black primaries and generally light grey primary coverts. Adult blue phase typically with head and upper neck white. Lower neck and underparts grey to dark grey. Mantle and scapulars dark grey. Tail plumage variably grey to dark grey, with white fringes. Intergrades (heterozygotes) occur between white and blue phases, generally closer to blue phase in plumage and referred to as blue phase. Most colour variation in blue phase occurs on ventral surface, which ranges from completely grey (generally homozygous blue phase) to completely white, with marginal blue necklace around neck of heterozygote. Bills of both races pink, with dark black 'grinning line' or patch (space between cutting edges of upper and lower mandibles), and white to pink-white nail; legs and feet reddish pink; eyes dark brown. Many, both adult and immature, exhibit ferrous staining of facial feathers. Intensity of staining reflects length of time spent feeding in coastal saltmarshes; birds in interior of North America only lightly stained.

MOULT: yearlings or juveniles (which do not breed), and failed breeders migrate to more northern colonies, where flight feathers moulted; usually occurs before or shortly after completion of egg-laying period (Abraham 1980). Flightless families remain together as unit and typically join loose assemblages of 20–100 families. Successful breeding adults moult remigial flight feathers when goslings 2–3 weeks of age. Regrowth of feathers and return of flight capacity occurs approximately at same time as young fly.

IMMATURE: pre-juvenal moult of gosling begins 2–3 weeks following hatch; juvenal feathers push out natal down, and plumage complete by week 6 with flight attained shortly after. First-year white phase generally white plumage throughout, with black primaries, and greyish feathers about head and neck. Blue phase dark grey, with darker grey or blue feathering on head and neck. Bill, legs and feet dark. Immature plumage persists until Mar of year following hatch, with increasing amounts of white appearing on facial feathers over 1st autumn and spring. Both races reach maximum structural size at 12–18 months of age.

GOSLING: white phase yellow at hatch, blue phase sepia black with yellow gular patch. As with adult, intergrades often detectable, generally characterized by yellow wash on crown and nape of blue phase.

MEASUREMENTS AND WEIGHT: small degree of sexual size dimorphism, with ♂ 2–4% larger than ♀ at all ages; body size of both significantly influenced by early growth conditions, thus difficult to characterize precise average size. *caerulescens* ♂ wing, 380–460 (430); bill (culmen), 50–62 (58); tarsus, 75–91 (84); weight, 1600–2300 (2500). ♀ (same range) wing (420); bill (56); tarsus (83); weight (2280). *atlanticus* ♂ wing, 425–485 (450); bill (culmen), 57–72 (64); tarsus, 83–97 (91); weight, 2700–3800 (3626). ♀ (same range) wing (445); bill (62); tarsus (88); weight (3065).

Field characters

Apart from similar Ross's Goose, unlikely to be confused with any other wild species. Can be told from occasional white domestic Greylag as latter does not have black primaries.

Voice

No formal studies of vocalization exist; general descriptions in Palmer (1976) and Ogilvie (1978). Vocal, as all geese, except during incubation when normally quiet. Almost constant calling by both sexes. Dominant call hard cackling, near-nasal and higher-pitched *la-luk*, similar to small barking dog, made from *c* 1 year of age. Juvenile call similar, but higher pitched. Gosling call short *cheep*; more whistle-like. Large flocks generally audible from considerable distance. Distress calls consist of long bleating wail. Family groups maintained by low guttural grunts with limited range; long series of *uh-uh-uh* notes made in rapid succession. More sustained guttural moan used for warning call to rest of group. Fall flight chorus consists of mix of honks, higher-pitched quacks or squawks, given throughout day and night. Typical sonogram in Mowbray *et al.* (2000).

Range and status

caerulescens breeds colonially throughout Canadian Arctic and Russian north coast and Wrangel Island. Major colonies on Baffin Island (southwest), Southampton Island, West Hudson Bay (North West

Territory), La Pérouse Bay (Manitoba), Cape Henrietta Maris (Ontario), Queen Maud Gulf (NWT), Banks Island, Anderson River delta (NWT) and Wrangel Island. Smaller colonies found in Alaska (particularly along north slope), Akimiski Island (NWT), Kazan Falls and Jenny Lind Island.

atlanticus typically breeds northeast of Lesser. Major colonies at Bylot Island, Admiralty Inlet, Devon Island, Ellesmere Island, with smaller scattered colonies in North Foxe Basin and Greenland. Treated as single population by Rose and Scott (1997).

Winter distribution of Lesser Snow dependent on breeding locality. West Hudson Bay and Baffin/

Southampton Island populations typically winter along coast of Gulf of Mexico, from delta of Mississippi River west to central Texas. Recent expansion northward to include Oklahoma, Missouri, Nebraska and Iowa. Birds breeding in western Canadian Arctic (Banks Island, Wrangel Island) winter in New Mexico, Mexican highlands (Chihuahua), California (Sacramento Valley), and Fraser-Skagit river estuary in British Columbia. Birds breeding in central Canadian Arctic (Queen Maud Gulf) varyingly distributed between Gulf Coast and New Mexico/California. During spring migration, Hudson Bay/Baffin Island and central arctic populations stage in southern Manitoba,

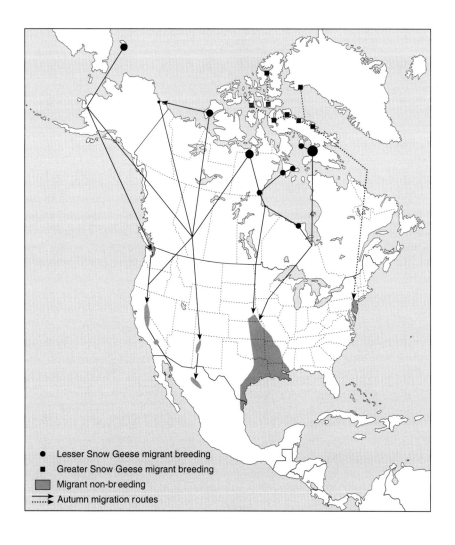

- ● Lesser Snow Geese migrant breeding
- ■ Greater Snow Geese migrant breeding
- ▨ Migrant non-breeding
- ⋯▶ Autumn migration routes

North and South Dakota. Central arctic populations also stage in western Saskatchewan and Montana. Western populations not known to have major staging areas south of eastern Siberia. North Russian birds of northern Far East/east Asian population winter in Korea and China (Miyabayashi and Mundkur 1999); formerly also Japan, but major decline by end 19th century (Takekawa *et al.* 1994).

Virtually all Greater Snows winter in Delmarva peninsula region of US (coastal Delaware, Maryland and Virginia), and stage on St Lawrence River estuary at Cap Tourmente during spring and fall migrations.

Most Snow Goose populations are increasing, and most estimates likely to be exceeded in near future. Estimates for *caerulescens* are $> 1\,000\,000 +$ breeding pairs in Hudson Bay, $> 2\,000\,000$ breeding pairs on Baffin Island, $> 1\,400\,000$ breeding pairs in central Arctic, with additional $> 500\,000$ and $> 85\,000$ breeding pairs in western Arctic and on Wrangel Island, respectively. East Asian population < 300 (Gerasimov and Gerasimov 1995b). Cumulative estimate for *caerulescens*, including breeding and non-breeding individuals, 6–8 million. *atlanticus* thought to number $> 800\,000$ individuals, up from 529 200 estimated in Rose and Scott (1997).

Habitat and general habits

Breeding colonies generally near coast near ponds, shallow lakes, or on islands in river deltas. Both races prefer areas with slightly variable topography, such as knolls and small ridges that clear of snow early and are not flooded during snow melt (Ganter and Cooke 1998). Both races typically nest in habitat consisting of several vegetational assemblages that vary with distance from shoreline. Along shore, coastal saltmarshes, where geese feed but do not nest, saltmarsh plants predominate, such as *Carex* and *Puccinellia*. Zone often followed inland by short grass area, consisting primarily of *Calamagrostis* and *Festuca*. Further inland, short scrub willow *Salix* and dune grasses, primarily *Elymus*, often occur (Cooke *et al.* 1995, Ganter and Cooke 1996). Prior to nesting, arriving geese forage and grub in exposed areas for roots and shoots, frequently causing extensive damage to developing plants (Jefferies *et al.* 1995). With start of nesting, feeds on saltmarsh vegetation as it becomes exposed, increasingly shifting to grasses in vicinity of nesting

area as laying completed, and throughout incubation (Ganter and Cooke 1996, Ganter *et al.* 1996). During brood rearing, feeds early on saltmarsh grasses. As goslings age, switches to alternate food plants (e.g. freshwater sedges), often more abundant but less nutritious (Gadallah and Jefferies 1995). Feeding during brood rearing virtually continuous for goslings, and nearly so for parents. Parental feeding interrupted for care behaviour, more so for ♂ than ♀ (Lessells 1987, Ganter 1994, Williams *et al.* 1994).

Primary productivity of saltmarsh plants often increases in response to moderate levels of grazing (Hik and Jefferies 1990); however, as goose numbers increased in recent years, intensity of herbivory and early season grubbing in several colonies has exceeded capacity of plants to respond, leading to progressive habitat destruction in many areas (Jefferies *et al.* 1995). Following brood rearing, migrates south to wintering areas. Migration saltatory for some populations, more continuous (non-stop) for others. Feeds on variety of plants during migration and over winter, particularly marsh grasses and rice, with increasing use of winter wheat and corn crops (Alisauskas *et al.* 1988). Families typically remain together for 1st year (Prevett and MacInnes 1980).

Displays and breeding behaviour

Mate selection occurs primarily during late winter and early spring, and consists of chase flights and associated displays by ♂, with ♀ selection. Most individuals pair in 2nd winter or on 2nd spring migration (Prevett and MacInnes 1980). Pairbond monogamous over lifetime. Natural divorce occurs, but at low frequency. Strong positive assortative mating based on plumage colour of parents (offspring of white × white pairs choose white mates, offspring of blue × blue pairs choose blue mates, offspring of mixed pairs choose randomly with respect to plumage coloration) (Cooke *et al.* 1995). Mating also thought to be somewhat assortative by age (♀♀ select ♂♂ of similar age; Cooke *et al.* 1995). Some evidence of positive assortative mating by body size (Cooke *et al.* 1995).

Philopatry to natal colony of ♀ (Cooke *et al.* 1995). Nest site typically selected by ♀, close to natal brood rearing area. ♀ responsible for nest construction. Primary role of ♂ defence of nest site from predators and conspecifics, although ♂ and ♀

sometimes share this activity. Territory size generally small ($< 50\,m^2$), varying with colony density.

Breeding and life cycle

Breeding biology similar for both races. Generally dense colonial breeder (densities of 4500 pairs per mile^2 recorded at several colonies), typically starts nesting as soon as snowfree habitat available. Breeders in Hudson Bay/Foxe Basin utilize wet coastal tundra, low-lying river delta habitats adjacent to saltmarsh vegetation for nesting. Many of these habitats newly exposed, as tide line recedes following isostatic uplift of formerly glacially depressed regions. In contrast, breeders in more northern colonies (Banks Island, Wrangel Island, Bylot Island, Queen Maud Gulf) typically nest further inland, generally in floodplain of freshwater river valleys. In such locations, family groups migrate to coast following hatch to feed.

May arrive 7–10 days prior to laying in some years, during which time feed actively (Ganter and Cooke 1996). First-time breeding ♀♀ virtually always return to natal colony. Nest initiation and laying period highly synchronized, generally ranging 7–12 days between 1st and last nest. In most years, ♀♀ start rapid yolk formation at arrival on breeding grounds (Cooke *et al.* 1995). First-time breeders generally nest on periphery of colony, but no evidence that birds progressively move location of nest as they age. Precise nest location influenced by pattern of snow cover, melt-water, and vegetation, as well as presence of old nest cups. Pairs typically absent during early stages of egg-laying. Nest starts as shallow scrape, with increasing amounts of down and other materials added by ♀. Eggs laid at intervals of c 33 h, although considerable individual variation (Schubert and Cooke 1993). Eggs covered by ♀ when ♀ absent from nest. Incubation begins with laying of penultimate egg; occupancy of nest by ♀ virtually continuous from then until hatch (Cooke *et al.* 1995).

Clutch size determined through allocation of ♀'s internal nutrient reserves to egg production and incubation (Ankney and MacInnes 1978). These endogenous reserves may be supplemented to varying degree by reserves acquired prior to laying in some colonies, especially southern colonies (Ganter and Cooke 1996). Re-nesting following early abandonment of clutch possible, although

frequency unknown. Clutch size 3–4 (1–6) white eggs, variable in mass, with most variation occurring among individual adult ♀♀. Average egg weight 105–125 (75–165) (Cooke *et al.* 1995, Mowbray *et al.* 2000). Clutches >6 eggs often seen, but most reflect addition by conspecifics (egg-dumping). Clutch size typically smaller in late seasons; increases with age (1st breeding at 2 years) until 5 years, thereafter constant (Rockwell *et al.* 1993).

♀ alone incubates eggs for 23–24 days, larger clutches for slightly longer than smaller ones. ♀ may leave nest for 1–3 h a day. During incubation, ♂ generally in close proximity; he typically spends 20–30% of incubation period feeding near by; both lose considerable body mass during incubation; ♂ 15–20%, and ♀ 35–40%.

Some eggs lost during laying and incubation, generally to fox and avian predators (primarily gulls, Raven and skuas). Total nest abandonment, intraspecific parasitism (egg-dumping) and heavy nest predation not uncommon in harsh years (Lank *et al.* 1989), especially in northern colonies.

Hatch relatively synchronous, goslings typically leaving nest within 24 h (Findlay and Cooke 1982). Goslings precocial, with shared parental care during brood rearing (Lessells 1987). Hatching also synchronous at colony level, typically more synchronous than laying (Findlay and Cooke 1982). Brood rearing begins when goslings leave nest. In some colonies, particularly high-latitude ones where nesting inland, broods move considerable distances (up to 60 km) during rearing (generally from nesting colony towards coast). During 4–6 weeks of brood rearing, birds spend most time grazing. Goslings grow rapidly, increasing from 85–100 g at hatch to near 1500 g at fledging (Cooke *et al.* 1991). Early hatched goslings typically grow faster and have higher rates of recruitment than later ones (Cooke *et al.* 1984, Cooke *et al.* 1991). Fledge at 6–7 weeks (mid to late July–early Aug), coinciding with regrowth of adult flight feathers. Significant mortality of goslings occurs during rearing, primarily to fox and gull predation. In colonies with increasing habitat degradation, gosling mortality due to starvation significant (Williams *et al.* 1993). In most years, 30–60% of eggs laid result in fledged goslings (Cooke *et al.* 1995).

Family unit maintained through fall migration and 1st winter, and occasionally into 2nd winter (Prevett and MacInnes 1980). By end of 2nd winter, parents drive juveniles from family group. Winter in large gregarious flocks. Primary winter activities are feeding and mate selection by unpaired individuals (Prevett and MacInnes 1980). Little natural adult mortality during migration and over winter. Most annual mortality of adults due to hunting (Francis *et al.* 1992). Adult survival rates 70–85%. Juvenile survival more variable, reflecting additive contribution of natural and hunting mortality (Francis *et al.* 1991). When gosling growth high, and fledging condition good, 1st year survival 40–60%; if gosling growth and condition poor, 1st year survival can be 5–15%.

Conservation and threats

Populations expanding rapidly at most locations, and new colonies being prospected. Population of Lesser Snows (both phases) increased from 600 000 in mid 1950s to *c* 9–10 million in late 1990s, with most increase occurring in Central and Mississippi flyway populations (Abraham and Jefferies 1997). Although precise cause of increase unknown, most researchers (Abraham and Jefferies 1997) believe it reflects: (a) increased overwinter survival due to expansion of agriculture and range of suitable habitats, and reduced harvest on breeding grounds following changes in government policy regarding native harvest; (b) increased survival leading to breeding range expansion and increased breeding success overall as birds began breeding in more productive southern colonies (West Hudson Bay, Cape Henrietta Maria); (c) reduced *per capita* mortality due to hunting.

Prior to 1950, most Lesser Snow Geese in central North America wintered along coast of Gulf of Mexico. As agricultural practices changed, range expanded, increasing number of suitable habitats for overwintering, which likely decreased natural winter mortality, leading to natural increase in numbers. Simultaneously, new regulatory restrictions on native harvest, primarily on breeding grounds, further reduced mortality. As numbers increased, so did their breeding range—new colonies in more southern latitudes (particularly West Hudson Bay colonies and Cape Henrietta Maria in Ontario) originated. Whereas northern colonies experience nonbreeding

seasons at fairly frequent intervals (3–6 years), southern colonies have no failed breeding seasons, and thus contribute new individuals to overall population at more sustained rate than do northern colonies. Migration distances from spring staging areas to southern colonies also significantly shorter than for birds breeding at northern colonies; thus, birds at southern colonies typically have more reserves remaining for egg production. Further, at time of first colonization, southern colonies had abundant vegetation, and significantly extended windows of nest initiation. This led to more numerous and robust young. Recent evidence suggested this advantage now declining under increased density-dependent degradation of southern breeding colonies.

By mid-1970s, production from consistent southern colonies nearly equalled hunting exploitation (mortality). This allowed northern colonies (Queen Maud Gulf, Southampton Island, Banks Island) to begin expanding, compounding problems of overexploitation of habitat caused by staging at southern colonies.

Numbers of sport hunters in North America declined over time (Abraham and Jefferies 1997) which, coupled with natural increase in goose numbers, has led to further reduction of mortality, again accelerating increase in goose numbers. Increasing Lesser Snow Goose numbers have led to increasing habitat degradation of breeding grounds, which has reduced aspects of reproductive success (most notably fecundity and gosling growth and survival) in some colonies. Although this appears to be a 'natural regulatory' response, destruction of habitat virtually permanent, and any population collapse likely to be prolonged. Impact on other species unclear. Loss of east Asian population in 19th century has led to proposed restoration of range (Takekawa *et al.* 1994).

Numbers of Greater Snows also increased from 10 000 in 1900 to nearly 900 000 recently, and also may exceed ability of hunters to have significant impact on population growth in most years. Amendments (1999) to Migratory Bird Treaty (extended spring harvest, electronic calls, increased bag limits) implemented to control increasing numbers of *caerulescens* and *atlanticus* by promoting increased harvest of both.

F. Graham Cooch and Evan G. Cooch

Ross's Goose *Anser rossii*

PLATE 6

Anser Rossii Cassin, 1861, Proc. Acad. Nat. Sci. Philadelphia, p. 73

Great Slave Lake

Etymology: named for Bernard R. Ross, chief factor with Hudson Bay Company and correspondent of Smithsonian Institute (Kortright 1942).

Other names: Ross's Snow Goose, many colloquial names including Scabby-nosed Goose, Wart-nosed Goose, Squealer and Horned Wavey. French: Oie de Ross. Placed in genus *Chen* by AOU.

Variation: no recognized subspecies. Goslings more variable in colour than any other goose. Extremely rare blue phase, which could result from hybridization with blue-phase Lesser Snow Geese (Cooke and Ryder 1971), has steely grey body with white head, neck, belly, tail and vent; wing coverts and tertials dark blue-grey with white edges, but amount of dark coloration variable.

Description

ADULT: sexes alike. Plumage completely white except for black primaries and greyish primary coverts. Less likely to show ferrous staining on head and neck than Snow Geese. Bill pinkish with paler nail and bluish grey warty growths, or caruncles, on base; warts suggested as feature to prevent hybridization with Lesser Snow Geese, or as indicator of dominance to other Ross's Geese; more extensive in ♂♂, and size and extent increases with age; legs pinkish; eye dark brown. ♀ as ♂, but body and head size smaller and neck shorter, reduced warty growths on base of bill, less obvious furrows in plumage of neck and slightly flatter forehead.

MOULT: one body moult annually, no seasonal change in plumage. Wing moult follows breeding.

IMMATURE: white body, neck and head. Smoky grey wash from lores through eye to back of head and crown continues down hind-neck to mantle and sides of upper breast where becomes diffuse. Flanks also greyish with few greyish tertials. Imma-ture ♂ can be separated from immature ♀ by darker, slightly less extensive and neater, more defined areas of brownish grey plumage giving overall cleaner, whiter, more contrasting look.

GOSLING: has unusually dense and fluffy down, short bill, and short toes relative to tarsus length. Colour varies from greenish yellow to grey or white; Nelson (1993) illustrated 8 colour morphs.

MEASUREMENTS AND WEIGHT: ♂ ($n = 22$) wing, 370–400 (385); tail, 110–120 (118); culmen, 37–46 (41); tarsus, 67–74 (70.5); weight in Sept 1962 ($n = 31$), 1320–1880 (1679). ♀ ($n = 20$) wing, 360–395 (370); tail, 110–120 (115); culmen, 34–41 (38.5); tarsus, 62–70 (66); weight in Sept 1962 ($n = 32$), 1270–1660 (1500) (Palmer 1976).

Field characters

White plumage, black wing tips, pale legs and bill, and dark beady eye characteristic. Can only be confused with Greater and Lesser Snow Geese; mostly associates with latter. Appears obviously smaller (perhaps 40%), 530–660 mm long, shorter necked and more rotund; head also smaller and more rounded, and bill much reduced and stubbier with unique grey warty growths. Obvious 'grinning line' of Snow Geese virtually non-existent in Ross's Goose. Feathering at bill base, curved in Snow Goose, forms almost straight vertical line, thus giving 'stuck-on' appearance. Immatures always whiter than similar aged Snow Geese.

Voice

Rather subdued, sad murmuring *mmmmm* or *uuuh-hhh*, similar to lowing cow, uttered as close quarters contact call. When calling loudly, utters repeated *uuggh uuggh uuggh*, ♀ higher *eeggh eeggh eeggh*, similar to Snow Goose but higher in pitch and not so loud or piercing; indeed, appears surprisingly quiet compared to effort expended in calling. Frequency of calls increases when displaying in groups or when in danger. Other calls include high-pitched *keek keek* and occasional harsh *kork* or *kowk* while in flight on migration (Palmer 1976).

Range and status

Numbers breeding in Canadian Arctic increased spectacularly over last half century, from 2000 in 1949 to 188 000 in 1988, probably 500 000 in 1997 (Abraham and Jefferies 1997) and estimated 1 050 000 by 2002 (Wetlands International). Species comprises single biogeographical population (Rose and Scott 1997). Main breeding grounds in Perry River region of North West Territories with Queen Maud Gulf holding most birds (Alisauskas 1992, Abraham and Jefferies 1997); however, large populations now established along west and north coasts of Hudson Bay, at McConnell River and on Banks, Baffin and Southampton Islands (Ryder and Cooke 1973). Other breeding areas may remain undiscovered, while small numbers known to breed in most Lesser Snow Goose colonies in eastern Arctic (Abrahams and Jefferies 1997). On passage, stages at Peace-Athabasca delta in Alberta and Saskatchewan. Most western arctic breeders winter in California, particularly in Sacramento Valley, while perhaps 100 000 birds from eastern breeding populations winter along Gulf coasts of Texas, Louisiana, New Mexico and Mexico. Smaller numbers regularly occur among Snow Geese at other sites throughout US. Recorded in Europe—i.e. Faeroes, Iceland, UK, West Germany and The Netherlands (Lewington *et al.* 1991)—but records clouded by escapes from local captivity. Nevertheless, transatlantic vagrancy may

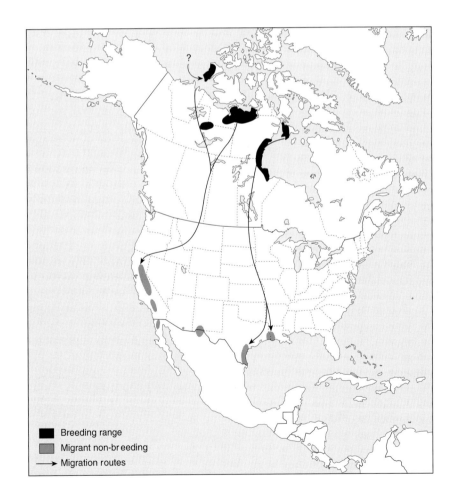

Breeding range

Migrant non-breeding

Migration routes

become more common with expanding North American breeding populations.

Habitat and general habits

Breeding area typically lowland arctic tundra and islands, with nests in close-knit colonies in flat terrain with dwarf vegetation and grassy patches. Highly gregarious both on breeding and wintering grounds. At staging sites, feeds and roosts in shallow, saline waters, but also utilizes agricultural areas, flooded land or potholes. Feeds diurnally on roots, grasses and sedges throughout year and on spilt or unharvested grains in winter. Winter habitat usually wet or marshy pasture, grassy fields and cultivated areas with scattered pools. Roosts on reservoirs and lakes during passage and on wintering grounds.

Displays and breeding behaviour

Breeding displays similar to other goose species with Head-bobbing, Tail-cocking and calling, but ♂ more attentive and persistent in attempts to attract mate, often pushing close to ♀♀ and following every move, calling excitedly with erect, fluffed up neck. ♀♀ always seem completely dominated by ♂♂ which regularly impede their movement and attempt to shepherd them away from other ♂♂. In captivity, ♂♂ often crowd ♀♀ in this manner and show display similar to display walks of flamingos, in which they literally bump into one another, breast first, while clamouring for attention. This comical sight is accompanied by excited calling as birds attempt to 'look proud' by puffing out chests and fluffing up feathers. No information on bonding display of pair in wild.

Mating usually occurs on water, during which ♂ grasps back of ♀'s neck with bill. Copulation brief before ♂ slips off, swims alongside mate, flapping wings, fluffing up feathers and washing vigorously. Pairs formed and copulation probably already taken place by time nesting occurs.

Breeding and life cycle

Due to short arctic summer, begins nest building immediately on arrival on breeding ground; however, this may be delayed by bad weather or cold temperatures resulting in late thaw. Pairs choose new nest site or return to established one. Nests situated amongst boulders or in low scrub constructed of anything immediately available, including twigs, small stones, and even droppings. ♀ carries out most nest construction but ♂ may help.

Eggs white or pinkish when fresh, become dirty and stained during incubation; 73.0 × 47.8 (65.4–80.2 × 44.3–51.4) ($n = 398$) (Ryder and Alisauskas 1995); laid c every 1.5 days in mid June with up to 8 in clutch but 4 on average. Dumping of eggs in nest of other pair or species known, and may explain larger clutches. In common with other arctic nesters, incubation short, at only 22 days.

Precocial young leave nest within 2 days of hatching for safe rearing areas with abundant food source. Closely guarded by both parents, feeding upon tips of grass and sedge, small leaves and insects. Fledge in c 45 days after fast growth. Young remain with parents up to next breeding season unless orphaned or lost. Most breed from age 3; attempts at 2 years occur but probably unsuccessful. In captivity, known to survive 21 years (Klimkiewicz and Futcher 1989) with one captive ♀ at WWT centre still alive at 21 years of age in 1997. Wild birds have life span of c 13–14 years.

Conservation and threats

Has always been hunted, but considered rare and protected in 1931; nevertheless, difficulty in identification means still shot in small numbers. Increased enormously, particularly during last 2 decades, mainly through conservation measures and protection on wintering grounds. In common with much more abundant Lesser Snow Goose, ability and readiness to exploit agricultural land perhaps most important factor in success; however, this massive expansion in numbers (albeit mainly of Lesser Snow Goose) has led to widespread destruction of breeding habitat. North American conservation bodies are, therefore, now encouraging large-scale harvesting (3 times current level) of white goose populations with aim of reducing numbers by c 50% (5–15% per year), to level that can be sustained by arctic breeding habitats.

Martin McGill

Canada Goose *Branta canadensis*
PLATE 7

Anas canadensis Linnaeus, 1758, Syst. Nat., ed. 10, p. 123
Canada; City of Québec suggested
Branta Scopoli, 1769

Etymology: *Branta* comes from Old Norse *Brandgás* meaning burnt goose, and derives from the dark colour of Barnacle and Brent. *canadensis* means of Canada, and this vernacular name was given by John Ray in 1678 following introduction into Britain; Linnaeus described the species from a specimen taken in St James's Park in London.

Other names: Honker. French: Bernache du Canada; German: Kanadagans. Several vernacular names exist, such as Atlantic, Interior, Richardson's, Lesser, Giant, Western, Aleutian, Dusky, Cackling and Vancouver, applied to different groups, based mainly on differences in phenotype, body size, relative proportions of body parts and plumage characteristics, with consideration also to degree of geographic isolation between groups.

Variation: remains controversial, with as few as 8 (Palmer 1976) or more than 186 subspecies (Hanson 1997) claimed. Although Hanson (1997) suggested that the complex consists of 5 species, the AOU (2003) recommended that the group be divided into 2: *B. canadensis* (large) and *B. hutchinsii* (small). Twelve races identified here, including: Atlantic Canada *B. c. canadensis*; Interior Canada *B. c. interior* Todd, 1938; Richardson's Canada *B. h. hutchinsii* Richardson, 1832; Lesser Canada *B. c. parvipes* Cassin, 1852; Giant Canada *B. c. maxima* Delacour, 1951; Great Basin Canada *B. c. moffitti* Aldrich, 1946; Dusky Canada *B. c. occidentalis* Baird, 1858; Cackling Canada *B. h. minima* Ridgeway, 1885; Aleutian Canada *B. h. leucopareia* Brandt, 1836; Taverner's Canada *B. h. taverneri* Delacour, 1951; Vancouver Canada *B. h. fulva* Delacour, 1951; and extinct Bering Canada *B. h. asiatica* Aldrich, 1946. Recent studies of parts of genome of different types, though based on small samples, seem to confirm that assessment, with 7 races large-bodied and 4 small-bodied (Quinn *et al.* 1991, Baker and Marshall 1997, Baker 1998, Shields and Cotter 1998). Baker (1998) analysed material from 10 putative subspecies and was able to distinguish all based on mitochondrial DNA. Scribner *et al.* (2003) exam-ined 7 nominal subspecies in western North America and suggested that, although all were genetically diverged, there is evidence for continuing gene flow. Pearce *et al.* (2000), sampling for both nuclear microsatellite loci and mtDNA, could distinguish *occidentalis* within wintering flocks that included several other dusky-like forms. Introductions, and great increase of most populations, lead to loss of racial identity as ranges overlap.

Description

ADULT: sexes alike. Head and neck black, with white cheek patches usually joined beneath chin. Black neck feathers end abruptly at breast, which varies in colour among races from pale grey through light to darker brown. Mantle colour also quite variable, from grey brown to dark brown, and darker than underparts in all but darkest races. Belly, tail and undertail coverts white. Tail and rump black, separated by white V of uppertail coverts. All races have black bill, legs and feet. Body size declines from south to north. Adult ♂♂ of smallest race, *minima*, c 580–630 mm in length, while those of largest race, *maxima*, may reach 1100 mm. Even individuals of subspecies *interior* decrease in body size from southern part of breeding range, on mainland near southern James Bay, to northern birds on west coast of Hudson Bay (Leafloor and Rusch 1997). Canadas breeding in eastern North America, e.g. *canadensis* and *hutchinsii*, are light-coloured, while dark forms, such as *occidentalis* and *minima* are found in Alaska and British Columbia. Among minor plumage characters that tend to differ among subspecies, *leucopareia* commonly has distinct white collar, also found to lesser extent on *parvipes*. Some races tend to have white feathers on forehead, and some show black stripe through white chins. Shape of head profile differs between races, faces of *hutchinsii, leucopareia* and *minima* are stubby in profile, while bills and heads of *maxima, moffitti* and *canadensis* more elongated. Some subspecies have relatively longer or shorter necks, wings or legs, *minima* has proportionately long legs and wings for small goose.

MOULT: no seasonal change in plumage. One body moult annually and one flightless period when primary and secondary feathers lost simultaneously.

IMMATURE: sparse juvenile plumage worn briefly, largely replaced from Oct, though much of wing retained until following summer. Darker than later plumages, white cheeks tinged brown and less sharply separated from black of head, body feathers small, narrow, rounded (not square) ends, underparts paler and mottled. First winter plumage denser, also smaller-feathered and narrower than adult. Tail feathers narrow, brownish, without sheen, with notched tips; in southern forms may be replaced by end Oct, in small northern forms retained until Jan–Feb. Flight feathers shorter and narrower than adult, less strongly coloured, retained to 2nd summer. Plumage assumed in 2nd year similar to adult, though often duller and flight feathers may be somewhat shorter. Variations between races in timing of moults not well understood.

GOSLING: bright yellow or greenish yellow, with darker brown patch on crown and stripe down nape. Horizontal dark line through eye. Upperparts olive, and underparts yellow-olive. Bill dark slate (all *Branta* geese have dark nail at tip of bill); legs and feet dark greenish. Variation in size, proportions, pattern definition and colour of down and feet parallel, to some extent, those of adult (see Nelson 1993 for weights and measurements of goslings from 14 localities).

MEASUREMENTS AND WEIGHT: although includes largest and smallest of all geese (*maxima* and *minima*) (Delacour 1954–64), no full account of variation in size between breeding groups published. Due to increased mixing in staging, wintering and some breeding areas as most stocks have grown in numbers, increasingly unlikely that thorough treatment will appear. Remarkably few published measurements of many races, including *canadensis*, exist, and there are few samples in which weights are linked to body size, while ranges or other measures of dispersion often omitted. Following generalizations hold with overlapping between classes: ♂♂ larger than ♀♀, and geese more than 2 years old larger and heavier than younger ones. Weights highest before, and at late stages of, spring migration and lowest in midwinter, though ♀♀ entering wing moult after successful incubation often lighter than in winter. Within stocks, small-bodied individuals usually weigh less than larger ones. Larger southern races have relatively large bills; smaller northern breeders have small bills, but relatively long wings. Scale of differences in body size from different breeding groups shown in Table 9.9.

Field characters

So well known that, in North America at least, hardly needs describing. Black head with white cheek patches unique, found in no other goose. Brant lack white cheeks, most of head of Emperor Geese white, and Barnacle Geese have white

9.9 Published linear measurements (mm) of adult female Canada Geese and their mean weights (g) in autumn. Ranked by mean bill (culmen) size. *n* = sample size.

Subspecies	n	Culmen range	Culmen mean	n	Wing range	Wing mean	n	Tail range	Tail mean	n	Weight (g) range	Weight (g) mean
maxima	26	55–63	57	32	472–513	496	22	136–166	154	25		5030
canadensis	7	51–56	54	7	435–488	465	7	134–158	147	7		3450
moffitti	20	51–56	52	20	472–513	478	20	136–159	146	9		3720
interior	90	43–56	50	90	438–509	466	90	132–162	142	36	2590–3990	3330
occidentalis	199	40–50	44	61	408–492	450	60		137	98	2580–4000	3300
parvipes	194		42	194		422				194		2450
hutchinsii	142	32–39	35	24	349–392	371	7		117	25	1610–2330	1950
leucopareia	21		32	20		369	9		120			
minima	11		28	11		354	11		104	24		1310

cheeks that extend across forehead and over throat. In winter, usually found feeding on grass, corn or other agricultural crops, though some, especially in Maritime Provinces and New England, feed on plants in intertidal zone. Roosts on lakes, rivers and coasts.

Voice

North American vernacular 'Honker' derives from ♂ call *ha-honk, ha-honk* of larger races, used in aggressive, territorial and pre-flight signalling, and in Triumph Ceremony of pairs. Second ♂ call, usually monosyllabic, often interspersed with honking call. Chief ♀ call, *hr-ih*, used in same situations, frequently in duets with partner. Quiet growling *urr, ur-eit* used as contact call within pair or family group. Both sexes hiss loudly, with outstretched neck and gaping bill, in defending nest, brood or themselves. Detailed analysis with sonograms of *maxima* in Whitford (1998). Vocalizations of small races not studied in detail but similar although less strident. Contact calls of goslings repeated twittering *wheeo*, distress call disyllabic *peep*, soft trills when sleepy; sonogram of sleepy trill of *moffitti* gosling in Kear (1968). Juvenile voice higher-pitched and weaker than adult.

Range and status

Breeds widely across northern North America (from Aleutian Islands to west Greenland), reintroduced stocks south to *c* 40°N, main range 50– 73°N, reaching Canadian low arctic islands and across mainland Nunavut, Northwest and Yukon Territories, except at high altitudes in west. Adopting classification system used for management purposes by agencies in Canada and US, the maps summarize breeding, staging and winter distribution of 13 stocks, frequently not corresponding to named subspecies. Four management units consist of *interior*, now > 40% of species total. Most *moffitti* and *parvipes* mixed with other races, so numbers cannot be determined precisely. Range and status of a larger bodied form of *fulva* and *taverneri* uncertain. A few *hutchinsii* have bred in west Greenland for many years (Johansen 1956); recently, rapidly increasing numbers of a larger bodied form of *canadensis* have invaded (Fox *et al.* 1996, Malecki *et al.* 2000).

A genetic study shows them more closely related to the *interior* of northern Québec, than to *canadensis* of Labrador (Scribner *et al.* 2003). Small northern forms (*minima* and *leucopareia*) now scarcest, though latter subject of successful recovery programme (Byrd 1998). Dusky *occidentalis*, greatly reduced after earthquake in 1964 damaged breeding habitat in Copper River delta, Alaska, now increasing again (Butler and Eldridge 1998). Mid-sized *hutchinsii* (low arctic) and *parvipes* (sub-arctic, boreal), perhaps 33% of species total, so mixed in winter that status of each hard to determine. Large temperate breeders (*maxima* and *moffitti*), nearly extirpated by shooting, now restored to most of old ranges and beyond, but only *c* 10% of total. Fifty years ago, *canadensis* probably most abundant; decreased greatly until 1980s, and now impossible to count in Atlantic Flyway in winter due to presence of introduced local breeders, but doing well in censused breeding areas. Lost east Asian population of *asiatica* thought to move between breeding sites on Komandorski and Kuril Islands and wintering areas in Japan.

Nonbreeders and failed breeders of many groups undertake northward moult migrations in June, often to areas occupied by smaller breeding birds. On islands in James Bay, local birds less able to compete for limited food, now produce fewer and smaller young (Leafloor *et al.* 1998). In 1980s, *maxima* and other large geese began moult migrations to northern Québec; from *c* 1995 substantial numbers have joined northern spring migration of *interior*. Long-term effects not yet known, but welcomed by Cree hunters for whom geese are important food.

Small northern geese, mainly *hutchinsii*, show 'leap-frog' migration, wintering as far south as northern Mexico and Texas coast while others winter in US, *c* 32–43°N, tending to stay further north than formerly due to agricultural changes that increase winter food, and to roosts on inland waters being kept unfrozen by discharges of warm water from power stations and industrial plants. Some temperate breeders are sedentary, though many move south if winters severe.

Numbers in North America evaluated annually on wintering grounds; in 1940s, *c* 1 million wintered in US (Malecki and Trost 1998). Has increased steadily, to well over 4 million counted

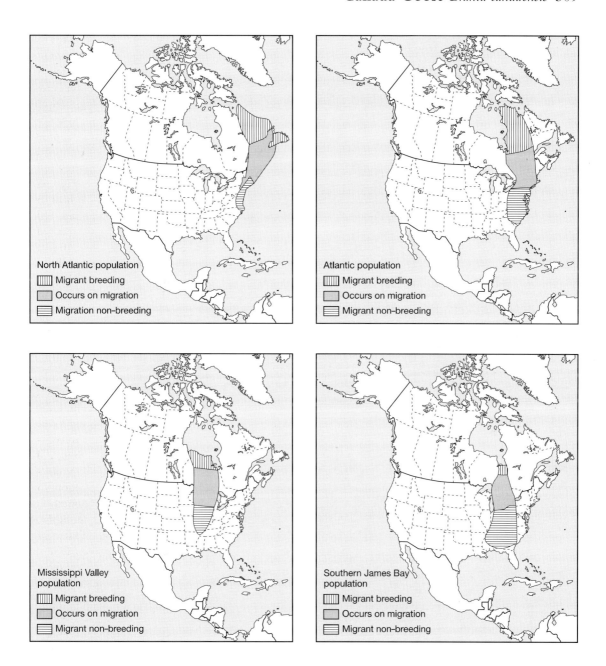

every Jan. These counts, made at major concentration areas, unadjusted to account for geese dispersed elsewhere; there could now be 8 million or more in North America (Dickson 2000). Impossible to produce population index for each subspecies, as cannot be distinguished during aerial surveys, so that most winter counts include mixture of stocks.

First introduced to England in 17th century (subspecies unclear, possibly *interior* and *maxima*), remained scarce and largely based on lakes of country houses until mid 20th century, when efforts to

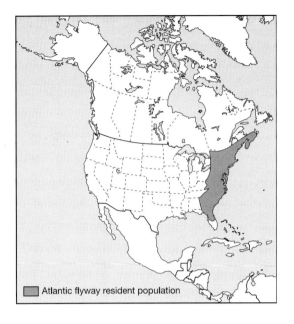

Atlantic flyway resident population

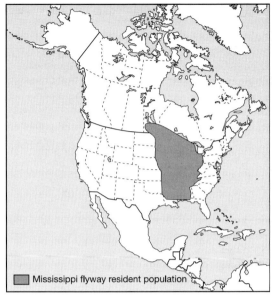

Mississippi flyway resident population

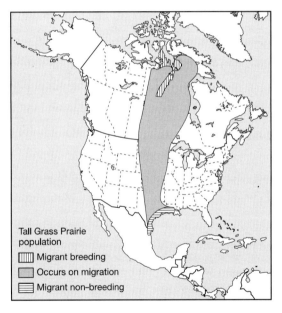

Tall Grass Prairie population

Migrant breeding
Occurs on migration
Migrant non–breeding

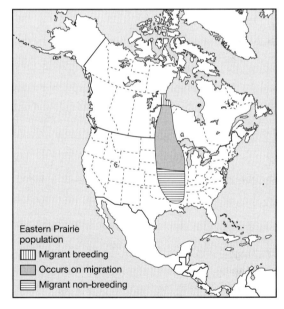

Eastern Prairie population

Migrant breeding
Occurs on migration
Migrant non–breeding

reduce large flock size by translocation of moulters accelerated expansion to *c* 60 000 in 1990s (Kirby 1999). Still increasing rapidly; southern UK may now hold 82 000 (Rehfisch *et al.* 2002). Breeds in nearly all English counties, fewer in north and southwest, and in Wales and Scotland. Some from central England migrate to moult on Beauly Firth 300–400 km north. Those in uplands move to lowlands in winter, some moving to continental Europe, especially during cold spells (Kirby 1999).

Introduced successfully to Sweden (Fabricius 1983) and Norway in 1930s and to Finland in early

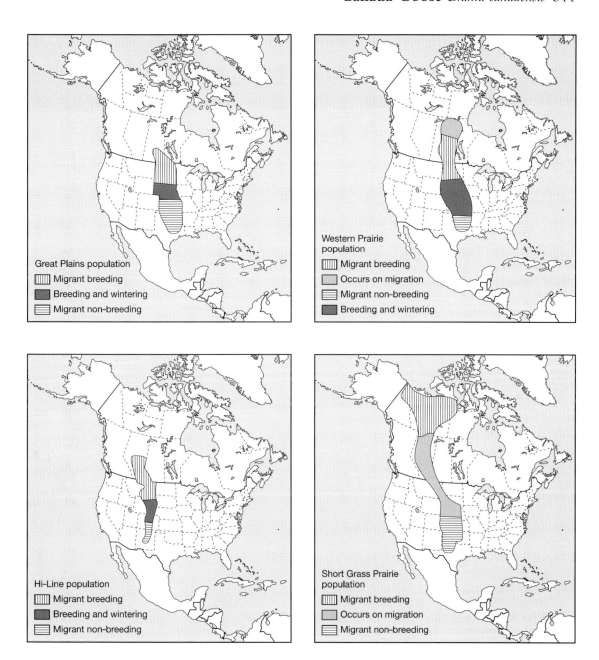

1960s. Free flying populations, mostly small, now also found in Russia, Ukraine, Denmark, Germany, The Netherlands, Belgium and France. In Sweden, increased to 3700 in 1966, 17000 in 1976 and 20000 by 1988. In Finland there were 1500–3000 breeding pairs in late 1990s, and at least 15000 in Norway. Scandinavian geese mostly winter in southern Sweden, Denmark and north Germany where winter numbers reached *c* 50000 in late 1990s (Andersson *et al.* 1999). Most Norwegian birds nearly sedentary. Swedish/Finnish geese winter in southern Sweden or migrate to German

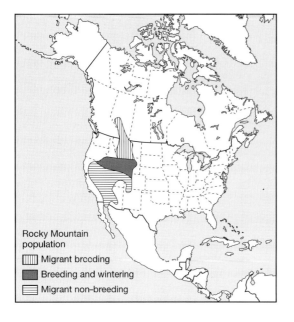

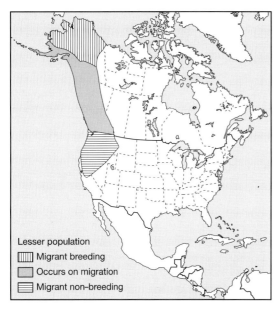

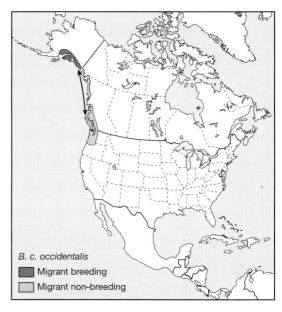

coast, while those breeding in continental Europe largely resident (Andersson *et al.* 1999). In New Zealand, introduced in 1876, and successful breeding population resulted from introductions in 1905; now inhabits grasslands and small ponds of flat valleys extending eastward from Southern Alps; sedentary (Soper 1984).

Habitat and general habits

Wide variation in habitat used for breeding; in North America, range of habitat types probably exceeds that of any other bird. Those breeding in arctic tundra often semicolonial because of clumped distribution of suitable nesting and foraging

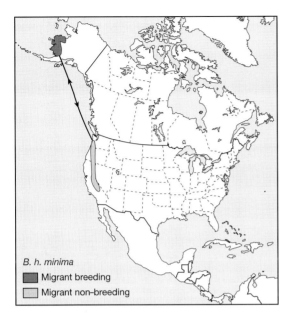

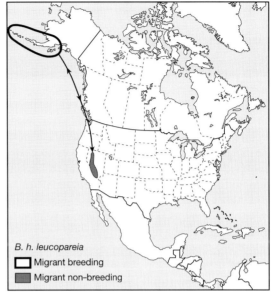

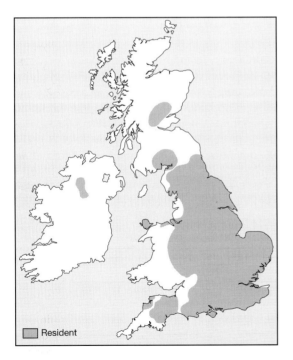

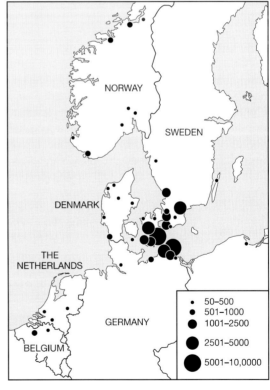

areas. In northeastern part of breeding range (c 67°N), most nests made on raised dry hummocks surrounded by freshwater and distributed over large flat wet plain of short arctic grasses and sedges. In arctic areas, where more exposed rock and rougher terrain (e.g. in central Canadian Arctic or northern Québec), c 75% of nests found near shore of ponds or small lakes, mostly in association with dwarf birch or other small shrubs. Where cliffs occur, nests on ledges, sometimes colonially; cliff nesting also recorded in Colorado, Montana, Aleutian Islands, and northern mainland of Alaska (Palmer 1976).

In Hudson Bay lowlands, occupies flat, poorly drained, swampy plain left after retreat of Wisconsin glacier. Preferred nesting sites on ponds of 0.4–2.0 ha, containing 2 or more small islands or hummocks in fen, and nests commonly found at base of spruce or tamaracks (Raveling and Lumsden 1977). In boreal region of north central Québec, nests almost always on islands in ponds or small lakes, or on moss strips in structured bogs, shores of larger lakes and small ponds without islands being used only occasionally. Dispersed more sparsely in boreal regions than in arctic breeding areas.

Also breeds successfully in agricultural and urban areas of southern Canada (Cadman *et al.* 1987, Dennis *et al.* 2000, Nieman *et al.* 2000, Smith 2000). Campbell *et al.* (1990) reported nests in southern British Columbia in agricultural fields, near irrigation ditches, areas, reservoirs, ditches, dykes and sewage lagoons. In southern Ontario, British Columbia and parts of Alaska occasionally found nesting in trees. (Palmer 1976).

In Europe, nests almost exclusively on islands in water bodies, including rivers, or along coast or in marshes. Feeds mainly on terrestrial plants including grasses and other cereals, and herbs. Moulters feed more on emergent vegetation. In New Zealand, nests located near water; if small islands present, used for nesting (Soper 1984).

In UK, congregates in agricultural fields, feeding on grass, stubble and crop shoots, and many use public recreational areas (Kirby 1999). In Fennoscandia, come together after fledging on nearest arable land. In late autumn, flocks begin to move to winter areas. Not yet known whether significant staging stops used *en route*. In winter in Norway, uses areas near sea, or open water with nearby foraging opportunities (Andersson *et al.* 1999). Those that remain in Sweden during winter restricted to southwest part of country, using coastal bays near arable land (winter cereal grains, sugar beets and potatoes). Important wintering areas also found in eastern Denmark, Germany, The Netherlands and Belgium.

Displays and breeding behaviour

Behaviour of arctic nesters less studied than southern ones. White cheeks against black head and neck add emphasis to all displays which, especially in larger forms, seem more vigorous than in other geese. In feeding flocks, frequent threatening, chiefly by ♂♂ to ensure they, their mates and young have access to preferred food. Main components Head-up, often with pumping (neck repeatedly bent then straightened), Low-coil (running with head lowered forward and bill gaping) often followed by full attack. When tendencies to attack and flee balanced, Coil-down, bent neck retracted above level of carpal joints, bill pointed down, often accompanied by Wing-shaking, producing clapping noise. In pre-flight display, to encourage group members to join in flying, head held high (Erect posture) with increasingly frequent Head-tossing, with lifted chin and head waving rapidly from side to side. Pair formation initiated by ♂ assuming Advertising postures, increasing apparent size and exaggerating movements. Paired birds engage in Triumph Ceremony similar to Greylag Goose. This has 2 phases: Rolling followed by Cackling, pair often alternating as swim, walk or run forward in parallel.

Pre-copulatory display in water usually, not always, initiated by ♂ who rhythmically holds head high, neck arched backward, then Dips head deeply below surface; sequence may be repeated many times. ♀ often seems to ignore; when responsive, allows ♂ to move alongside (often head to tail), then joins in Head-dipping. At high intensity leads to ♂ mounting ♀ at shoulder, grasping her neck feathers in bill. After copulation, ♀ bathes vigorously, ♂ stetches neck, points bill up, arches partly closed wings and often calls loudly, before also bathing (details in Fabricius and Radesäter 1972, Radesäter 1974).

Breeding and life cycle

Nesting may begin as early as mid Mar in south of range, not until late Apr in northern Ontario and mid May on Yukon delta, Alaska and McConnell River, Nunavut, 1st eggs being laid over period of *c* 9 days. Nest site selected by ♀, and laying begins shortly after construction starts. Eggs elliptical ovate; rough creamy white when laid, acquire polish and, often, staining from nest materials during incubation; dimensions vary from 74 × 49 for *minima* to 90 × 60 for *maxima*. Few wild records of mass; eggs of *moffitti* (87 × 59) weighed 145 when fresh and lost 24 g during incubation (Williams 1967). Captive laid eggs of *minima* weighed 98.6 (82.5–112.5) (*n* = 100), *leucopareia* 122.9 (*n* = 22), *parvipes* 125.6 (*n* = 77), *occidentalis* 150.4 (*n* = 53) and *maxima* 179 (*n* = 81). One egg laid per day, with days skipped once or twice; more skipping in south than north. Clutch 4–7 (1–8) eggs, larger numbers due to dumping by other ♀♀; mean clutches 5.34 for *moffitti*, 5.22 for *maxima*, 4.57 *interior*, 4.27 for *minima* (summary in Bellrose 1980). Incubation 26–27 (24–30) days, little latitudinal variation. ♀ alone incubates, ♂ on guard nearby usually accompanies her on occasional short feeding breaks; *hutchinsii* ♀ spends longer off nest than larger subspecies (Jarvis and Bromley 2000).

Goslings precocious and nidifugous, and cared for by both parents. Weight at hatching, *minima* 67.6 ± 1.17 (*n* = 23) and *maxima* 103.3 ± 0.44 (*n* = 55) (Smart 1965b). Brooded on nest for 24 h, then led to water. Crèching fairly normal amongst southern races. If threatened, both parents may feign injury while young dive. Parents moult wings while young still flightless; larger races fledge in 8–9 weeks, smallest in 6 (Palmer 1976, Bellrose 1980). Family migrates together. McWilliams and Raveling (1998) suggested that relatively weak family and pair associations of small *minima* during nonbreeding season may relate to high predation rates by eagles, which could select for gregarious behaviour by taking birds from small groups more easily.

Age at 1st breeding 3 (2–4) years. In North America, average annual survival rates for adults vary from 50–90%, strongly influenced by the management of harvest (Mowbray *et al.* 2002). Oldest ringed bird in UK 24.2 years (Clark *et al.* 2002).

Conservation and threats

Doing well, and increasing rapidly in abundance and range; however, conservation planning in North America needs to take great racial diversity into account. Maintenance of geographically distinct groups is function of fidelity to nesting sites, migratory stopovers, and winter areas, as well as strong family ties, and, at least for northern groups, tendency towards colonial or semi-colonial nesting (Mayr 1942, Delacour 1954–64, Raveling 1978a, Malecki and Trost 1998), all features tending to restrict gene flow amongst groups.

To focus conservation effort in face of such diversity, Canada Geese throughout North America have been grouped into management populations based on relatively distinct breeding ranges, migration routes and winter areas. Often these populations do not correspond exactly with subspecies. Birds of Eastern Prairie, Mississippi Valley, Southern James Bay and Atlantic Populations are all *interior*. But it is difficult to establish status of Shortgrass Prairie Population (SGPP), which includes both *parvipes* and *hutchinsii*, and breeds in northwestern part of Canadian Arctic, migrating through Saskatchewan and Alberta, and through Central Flyway of US. There has been a decline in winter counts over the past few years. Whether this represents a decline in one or both races is not known, because they cannot be distinguished during surveys. *leucopareia* delisted from Endangered Species Act following successful long-term conservation programme in Aleutians—including eradication of introduced foxes from breeding islands, and a re-establishment programme on the Semidi Islands (Callaghan and Green 1993). Dusky Canada race *occidentalis* listed as Vulnerable by Threatened Waterfowl Specialist Group (2001).

Now so many temperate-breeding geese that conflicts with human activities have increased steadily. In recreational areas, may cause fouling of parks, golf courses and local water areas. So far, little evidence that human health affected by goose faeces, or by disease. Temperate-breeding geese, or staging migrants of other subspecies, often in conflict with agriculture; crop damage in spring mainly involves destruction of winter wheat crops and haylands, and in autumn of unharvested grains. Federal wildlife agencies in Canada and US can issue permits allowing farmers to scare and, in some instances, to kill geese. Municipalities with nuisance problems can request permits that allow destruction of nests and eggs. Formerly, translocation of geese caught while flightless was widespread, but this added to conflict with humans, rather than solving problem.

In Europe, similar difficulties occur in management of conflict (Andersson *et al.* 1999); these mainly solved by issuing shooting permits to farmers, and abandonment of translocations. In southern Sweden, where problems widespread, shooting on fields permitted during special extensions before and after regular hunting season. Additional difficulty in Europe is that of competition with native species, which can involve direct aggression, or competition for food.

The annual kill in Sweden rose from 17 000 in 1990 to 20 000–25 000 in 1996; in mid 1990s *c* 3500 were shot in Norway, 1000 in Denmark and < 100 in Germany. Although spread in Britain was intended to encourage shooting, no good estimates of UK kill. Canada Geese are not legal quarry in The Netherlands or Belgium.

Hugh Boyd and Kathryn Dickson

Hawaiian Goose (Nene) *Branta sandvicensis*
PLATE 7

Anser sandvicensis Vigors, 1833, List Animals Gardens Zool. Soc., London, ed. 3, p. 4
Hawaiian Islands

Etymology: *sandvicensis* because Captain James Cook called Hawaii the Sandwich Islands, in honour of John Montague 4th Earl of Sandwich (1718–92) of the British Admiralty.

Other names: Nene. French: Bernache néné. Previously in genus *Nesochen* in North America.

Variation: no subspecies. Analysis of DNA divergence suggests evolved on Hawaii in < 500 000 years (Paxinos *et al.* 2002a) and derived from a small Canada Goose ancestor. Much genetic variability lost before recent population decline (Paxinos *et al.* 2002b). Genetic variation in few goslings manifested as sparse down lacking some plumules (Kear and Berger 1980).

Description

ADULT: sexes alike; ♂ slightly larger and heavier. Has black face and crown; neck particularly striking, with black waves and furrows in tan plumage. Below black ring at base of neck, feathers of chest, back and sides brown. Black band, tipped with white line found at top of wing coverts and secondary feathers. Underparts, below legs and tail coverts white. Primary and tail feathers black. Bill black; legs and feet black; eyes brown.

MOULT: single moult of body feathers annually. Wing feathers moulted simultaneously after breeding.

IMMATURE: duller than adult with browner head and neck, and scaled rather than barred plumage markings. As adult after 1st moult.

GOSLING: short, velvety brownish grey down, with olive-grey feet only partially webbed. Dark crown and ear-spot; large eye surrounded by pale grey ring and dark mask (Nelson 1993).

MEASUREMENTS AND WEIGHT: data from captivity at WWT, Slimbridge, ♂ wing ($n = 30$), 351–404 (378); skull length ($n = 31$), 90.2–98.8 (93.5); bill ($n = 30$), 36.0–43.1 (39.4); tarsus ($n = 31$), 76.0–89.6 (85.0); weight, 1695–3050 (2165). ♀ wing ($n = 30$), 347–368 (361); skull length ($n = 30$), 84.8–94.5 (89.2); bill ($n = 44$), 31.9–40.0 (37.0); tarsus ($n = 31$), 73.8–82.9 (78.0); weight, 1525–2560 (1930) (Kear and Berger 1980).

Field characters

Medium-sized goose, 560–710 mm long, with partially webbed, black feet. Distinguishable from Canada Goose by striking neck plumage and lack of white cheek patch. Instead of black neck of

Canada Goose, has unique tan plumage with black waves and furrows. Some individuals have thin ring of white plumage around eye, i.e. an eye-ring.

Voice

Kear and Berger (1980) noted low murmuring *nay* or *nay-nay*, given with bill closed, as probable origin of Polynesian name. This commonly heard throughout year between contented pairs and feeding flocks, presumably functioning as short distance contact call that helps maintain proximity between pairs and family members. ♀ also produces soft purring when in contented situation. Another soft, guttural sound made on approach to food items. Louder calls consist of trumpeted sound, slightly double syllable in structure, often followed by series of shorter, more staccato notes and ending with painful-sounding moan (produced with sharps and flats). Voice not melodious at close quarters, but high in lava fields, where pairs call their territorial challenges, acquires unique quality. This loud crying probably also functions as long distance contact call that enables mates to locate one another if separated. Similar, but discrete, calls produced in flight.

As breeding season approaches, calls become louder and more strident. Pairs, especially ♂♂, call with open bills and outstretched necks directing movement at mate. Depending on circumstance, ♀ may join in with high-pitched repetitive note making duet with ♂. This display referred to as Triumph Ceremony. Sonogram of adult call in Kear and Berger (1980), and of gosling's distress and sleepy calls in Kear (1968).

Range and status

Endemic to Hawaiian Islands, originally occurring on most major islands, became extinct on all but largest island, Hawaii, where 30 birds survived in 1950s (Baldwin 1945, Smith 1952). After extensive reintroduction programme, currently found on Hawaii, Maui and Kauai, numbering 885 individuals estimated in 1997 (Banko *et al.* 1999). Largest population on Hawaii occurs in and adjacent to Hawaii Volcanoes National Park at 500–2500 m elevation. Populations not permanently self-sustaining, and maintained by periodic releases of additional birds (Black and Banko 1994). Current subpopulations centred around release sites. Some movement occurs between sites, especially during periods of drought (Black *et al.* 1997). Seasonal movement probably common in past, but currently movements localized, within 25 km^2 area for sub-population at Volcanoes National Park (Stone *et al.* 1983).

Habitat and general habits

Black *et al.* (1994) provided detailed account of foraging behaviour on lava fields and pastures. Takes grass and leaves of other plants, berries, seeds, and flowers. Grass seedheads stripped at rate of 21 per min and grass leaves taken at rate of 62 per min. Berries taken at 25–75 per min depending on abundance on bush. ♀ apparently more selective in choosing plants on which to feed.

During daily incubation recesses, ♀ fed on pastures for 7 min and scrubland vegetation for 41 min. ♂♂ that flew to pastures with ♀♀ fed for only 2 min, as tended to remain vigilant. Within territory, while ♀ incubated, ♂ foraged for *c* 66 min per day (Black *et al.* 1994). Daily feeding time for those not attending nests in breeding season (nonbreeders, failed breeders and pre-breeders) amounted to 240 min for ♀♀ and 157 min for ♂♂ at Volcanoes National Park, and 415 min for ♀♀ and 226 min for ♂♂ at Haleakala National Park. During nonbreeding season, average time spent feeding during 11 h of daylight varied considerably between sexes and habitats; ♀ always fed more than ♂ (Black *et al.* 1994).

Diet consisted of 31 plant species identified from analysis of 257 droppings (Black *et al.* 1994). Most fragments were of grass leaves and seeds, followed by moderate amounts of berries and fewer herb leaves and flowers. Kikuyu Grass *Pennisetum clandestinum*, Yorkshire Fog *Holcus lanatus*, Broom Sedge *Andropogon virginicus*, Molasses Grass *Melinis minutiflora* and Pukiawe berries *Styphelia tameiameiae* predominated. Eats 4 different berry species, which occurred in 98.5% of droppings and made up 36.6% of overall diet of breeding birds, Pukiawe being most prevalent, although breeders at Haleakala National Park preferred Ohelo berries *Vaccinium reticulatum*. Diet, measured by abundance of each

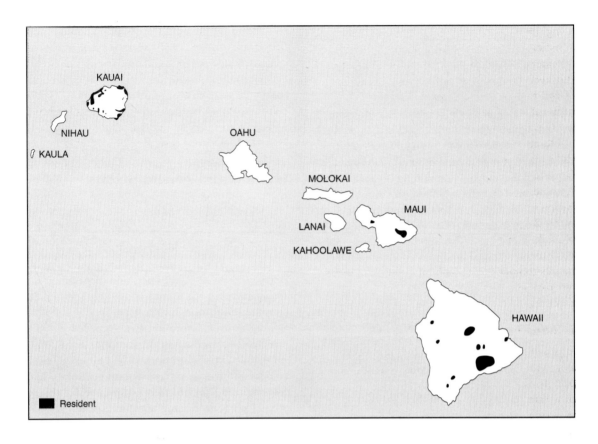

Resident

species, varied in relation to sex, bird-class, area and date.

Between 1938 and 1944, Baldwin (1947) identified 31 different plant species from 543 droppings from Kau Desert, Puu Waawaa, Mauna Loa (Volcanoes National Park), Humuula and Hualalai (all on Hawaii Island). Most abundant item found was endemic hairgrass *Deschampsia nubigena*. In 1992 study, this species identified only in droppings from Haleakala National Park. In droppings from Kau Desert, Baldwin found only 8 plant species, whereas Black *et al.* (1994) found 26. Changes possible in birds' behaviour and/or vegetation over last 50 years; latter more likely since endemic and indigenous plants out-competed by more vigorous, introduced plants resulting in decline in availability of former vegetation. Change in diet may have enabled Nene to make use of new areas, such as Kau Desert.

Goslings select for high protein herb, Gosmore *Hypochoeris radicata*, in excess of its abundance in habitat, and avoid less digestible grasses.

Displays and breeding behaviour

Pre-copulatory display similar to other geese, only not seen on water; ♂ performs head and neck dipping movements directed toward ground. Post-copulatory display also similar to other geese, where ♂ raises wings above back, neck held high and strutting. ♀ flaps her wings and preens (Johnsgard 1965a).

Pairbond members greet one another after temporary separation with loud calls and exaggerated head and neck movements in sideways and vertical fashion, as if towards opponent.

Encounters with flock members while foraging occur on regular but infrequent basis, consuming 1–3% of day (Black *et al.* 1994). Variety of threat displays used by aggressive Nene, most common being Bent-neck threat posture accompanied by vibrations of furrowed neck feathers. Goose faces opponent with neck and bill pointing to ground, and neck quivering obvious. Severe threats consist of run towards opponent while holding head and neck parallel with ground, and calling and/or hissing (Kear and Berger 1980).

Dominance rank related to number of individuals in social unit, where large families beat small families, all families beat pairs and pairs beat singles. Age and body size also explain outcome of disputes within social classes. Actual fights seldom occur; i.e. when 2 birds grab one another with bill at base of neck, pull towards one another and beat down with metacarpal bone on outer wing. Both pair members may chase birds that approach nesting territory; intruders attacked and chased in air well beyond terrestrial boundaries.

Breeding and life cycle

♀ apparently selects nest site, usually near natal area. Most parent-reared ♀♀ that fledged (without parents) from open-topped pens later nested inside or within 2 km of pen. ♀ typically nests within 1 km of previous nest but as far away as 12 km in subsequent years. Most pairs nest several km from nearest neighbours, while some congregate into loose associations. Closest spacing of simultaneously active nests 35 m in wild and 20 m in pens containing natural vegetation (Banko 1988). Laying in Hawaii may start as early as end Aug and continue until Apr (Woog 2002); at WWT Slimbridge at 52°N, presumably because need stimulation of short daylength, breeding initiated *c* 5 months later and season much shorter (Zillich and Black 2002).

Eggs white to creamy; immaculate when laid but somewhat soiled and stained during incubation; smooth, dull, occasionally with 1–2 calcarious bumps but rarely pitted. Measure in captivity 83.1 × 55.6 (68.2–98.1 × 49.0–64.3) (*n* = 300); characteristic of waterfowl endemic to remote islands, produces heavy eggs relative to adult weight; fresh egg weight, at *c* 150, 9% of post-breeding ♀ body weight (Banko *et al.* 1999). Eggs of 2nd clutches only slightly smaller than 1st. Clutch 3.1 (1–6) eggs (*n* = 552); wild clutch of 8 eggs and brood of 7 goslings suggests that

larger clutches occur, or more than one ♀ may lay in nest. Clutch size of 2nd nests similar. Range of annual variability within ♀♀, 0–2 eggs (Banko *et al.* 1999). Little or no down deposited in nest until day before last egg laid. At least 9% of wild ♀♀ re-nested after loss of 1st clutch or brood (Banko *et al.* 1999); replacements laid on 8 of 28 occasions when clutch or brood lost. Interval between clutches 49–81 days. Second nests initiated on 3 of 26 (12%) occasions when 1st brood survived to fledging (Banko *et al.* 1999).

Only ♀ incubates, starting almost as soon as last egg laid (Kear and Berger 1980). During incubation, ♀ has single brood patch on upper abdomen/lower breast. Incubation period longest of all anserine geese at 30 (29–32) days. ♂ typically guards from elevated spot within 15 m of nest; ♀ sometimes joins ♂ in defending nest but less vigorously and for less time. ♂ occasionally leaves ♀ unattended, and some spend much time away from nest area. Generally, recesses by incubating ♀ taken at sunrise, sunset, and once during night; average number in 24 h was 3.4. Average time off nest 99 min per day (Black *et al.* 1994). During 62% of recesses, ♀ stayed in immediate surroundings of nest; in other cases, ♀ flew off, usually accompanied by mate, to feed on grass pastures. Flight time between nesting territory and distant foraging area ranged 2–7 min. Goslings weigh 94–101 at hatching, *c* 775 at 3 weeks and, in wild, fledge in *c* 12 weeks (Kear and Berger 1980). Positive correlation between inbreeding coefficients and fertility of eggs and survival of young found in captive stock (Rave *et al.* 1995, Rave *et al.* 1998). Rave *et al.* (1995) also showed that, whereas Volcanoes National Park subpopulation consisted of least inbred birds, Kauai and Maui flocks were most inbred; translocation was suggested to remedy situation.

Based on short survey searching for parasites, Bailey and Black (1995) suggested that parasites probably did not limit recovery, but encouraged further research, especially on occurrence of avian pox-like lesions seen on some wild birds.

Before Polynesian colonization, no mammalian predators occurred in Hawaii, only avian ones. Polynesians brought Polynesian Rat *Rattus exulans*, dogs, and pigs, all of which may have predated eggs, goslings and adults, although only subfossil remains of rats occur where bird bones have accumulated. Hawaiians also kept Nene in semidomesticated state (Wilson and Evans 1893), and captured wild goslings and moulting adults (Henshaw 1902). Most serious predator today is Small Indian Mongoose, introduced to Hawaii Island in 1883 and sometime later to Maui, Molokai, and Oahu. Mongooses destroyed 34% of clutches and also killed incubating ♀♀ (Hoshide *et al.* 1989, Banko 1992). Other predators include domestic cats and Black Rat *R. rattus* that Europeans introduced after arrival in 1778.

Conservation and threats

Hunting major limiting factor until passage and enforcement of ban in 1907 (Henshaw 1902, Munro 1960). Poaching may occasionally occur today. Pre-human condition and suitability of lowland habitat (primary nesting areas) difficult to assess because of extensive burning and other agricultural activities by Polynesians during past 1500 years that may have enhanced or degraded conditions. During last 200 years of Western influence, lowlands altered (probably degraded) by ungulate grazing and browsing and domination by alien plants that generally provide unfavourable conditions for foraging and nesting unless maintained as lush pasture with low predator densities. Highland habitats (secondary nesting areas) still largely dominated by native species and somewhat less modified than lowlands but generally provide marginal conditions for foraging and nesting without predator control and availability of pastures. All habitats degraded by introduction and spread of mammalian predators, but Kauai currently free of Small Indian Mongoose. Spread of unpalatable alien grasses and other weeds also diminish foraging opportunities. Use of palatable grasses in some pasture lands, golf courses, lawns, and roadsides, allows occurrence where foraging opportunities otherwise limited, but mortality high in human modified habitats due to increased predation, collisions with motor vehicles and other accidents. Fire can enhance foraging and nesting opportunities for *c* 12 months, but repeated burning eventually results in loss of essential shrub cover.

One of most endangered wildfowl. Listed as Endangered by US Fish & Wildlife Service and State of Hawaii, and as Vulnerable by BirdLife International (2000). Early conservation efforts initiated primarily by Sir Peter Scott and Herbert Shipman, and conducted by Territory (State) of Hawaii biologists, emphasized captive breeding in Hawaii and England and release of large cohorts of juveniles on Hawaii and Maui from open-topped pens located in remote, highland sanctuaries with limited predator removal (Kear and Berger 1980, Banko and Elder 1990). After 1974, small numbers of parent or foster-reared birds released annually from open-topped pens in Volcanoes and Haleakala National Parks while fewer hand-reared birds released in highland sanctuaries.

Restoration programme, including release of captive-bred birds (2325 on Hawaii and Maui and 125 on Kauai to 1999 (Banko *et al.* 1999)), has not resulted in self-sustaining wild population, except possibly on Kauai. Results from capture–recapture analysis indicate that 3 factors affect mortality rates on Hawaii and Maui: year of release, age-class and method of release (Black *et al.* 1997). Estimated annual mortality ranged 0–87%. Comparisons between sites revealed unsuitability of upland sanctuaries on Hawaii as release sites, particularly during drought years. Birds made temporarily flightless, in order to contain them initially in release pens, survived less well than those released prior to fledging. Upland geese that did survive did so in areas other than release site. Research on captive rearing methods revealed that social skills learned from parents are useful to goslings prior to release (Marshall and Black 1992). Research on birds that became accustomed to wild (and their progeny) demonstrated that many pairs do not attempt nesting, and those that do then suffer high nest predation and extremely high gosling mortality, indicating that nutrition and predation were important limiting factors (Banko 1992).

After 1990, national park programmes emphasized restricting human activity and removing some predators by trapping and poisoning around nesting and rearing areas in addition to continuing limited captive propagation and release efforts. State programme consisted mainly of limited predator removal, supplemental feeding, and sporadic population monitoring at several sites. New population started on Kauai in 1985, when *c* 25 captives released (Banko *et al.* 1999); flock was augmented with further releases of captive-bred birds and totaled 256 individuals in 1997. WWT initiated research, management, and public education programme, inaugurated in 1990, to invigorate conservation efforts (Black *et al.* 1991b, Black 1995). Maintenance of lush pastures near scrubland nesting areas suggested as primary habitat management option to provide pre-breeding ♀♀ and young goslings with adequate nutrition (see Black and Banko 1994, Black *et al.* 1994, Black 1995). Predator control, especially of Small Indian Mongoose, also important (Banko *et al.* 1999). Rave *et al.* (1995) outlined programme to reduce degree of genetic similarity in various subpopulations.

Jeffery M. Black and Paul C. Banko

Brent Goose (Brant) *Branta bernicla*
PLATE 8

Anas Bernicla Linnaeus, 1758, Syst. Nat., ed. 10, p. 124.
Europe
    Etymology: *bernicla* L. for Barnacle Goose, with which once confused.
    Other names: Brant in North America. Danish: Knortegås; Dutch: Rotgans; French: Bernache cravant; German: Ringelgans; Icelandic: Margæs. Several subspecific names exist: *B. b. glaucogaster*, *B. b. hrota* Müller, 1776, *B. b. nigricans* Lawence, 1846, and *B. b. orientalis* Tugarinov, 1941, in addition to nominate *B. b. bernicla*, and vernacular names Atlantic, Black or Pacific, and dark- and light-bellied (or -breasted) applied to groups that differ in belly colour and extent of white markings on neck, and in distribution in summer or winter (Figure 9.10). No collection of names now in general use corresponds well with known distribution and separateness of existing breeding groups. Genetic analysis using mitochondrial DNA techniques (Shields 1990) began to unravel tangle in North America; until that analysis extended to Eurasian populations, seems best to use only binomial name, with temporary vernacular names corresponding to breeding ranges. See Madge and Burn (1988) for popular use of subspecific names.
    Variation: see above.

Description

ADULT: sexes alike, ♀ tending smaller at all ages. Has sooty black head and neck. On sides of neck, and sometimes encircling it, are patches of speckled white, due to white bases of feathers. Rest of upperparts black with grey bloom and brown tips (especially when worn); short central uppertail coverts black-brown; rest of uppertail coverts and sides of rump white. Sides of body and flanks brown-grey, feathers tipped brownish white; rest of breast and belly brown-grey to slate-grey; vent and undertail coverts white. Tail sooty-black. Axillaries and underwing coverts brown-grey; primaries and secondaries black, inner webs black-brown; primary coverts and alula hair-brown; other wing coverts sooty black, narrowly edged light brown. Bill black; tarsus and feet black, upper surface of toes tinged olive-green; iris dark brown.
    Darkest Brent, with largest neck collars, found on both sides of Bering Strait. Mean height and variability of collar of adult ♀♀ from Alaska and East Siberia and mean belly colour of adults nearly identical (Figure 9.10); but range of belly colour of Siberian specimens much greater. West Siberian Brent slightly browner with shorter collars. Brent from Parry Islands (western high Arctic), which Shields (1990) identified as genetically older group than neighbours, greyer, but resemble those dark stocks rather more than pale-bellied birds in rest of circumpolar range. Great variability within each breeding group ensures that many individuals cannot be assigned to 'correct' breeding group without knowing where were found. Most caught on western Queen Elizabeth Islands were from indigenous grey-bellied stock, but some catches included dark moult migrants from Alaska or

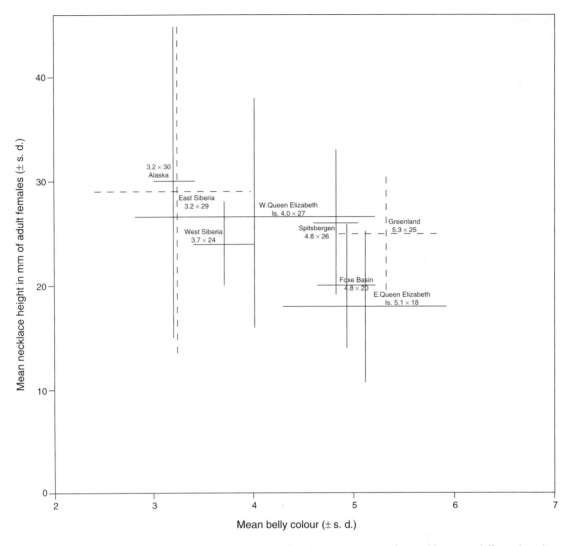

9.10 Variations in belly colour and white neck markings of adult Brent Geese within and between different breeding populations. Mean belly colour (± s.d.) is plotted against mean necklace height in mm of adult females (± s.d.). The belly colours were matched against chart 10YR of the Munsell Soil Color Chart and ranged from 2.5 (black-brown) to 7 (very pale grey). See Boyd and Maltby (1979) for more details, although this figure includes data from groups not dealt with by them.

Siberia. One collector on Prince Patrick Island believed 2 species involved; his series is strongly bimodal, that of second collector is not. Likely that breeders in eastern Siberia share appearance of Alaskan birds; some very dark ones, with massive necklaces, taken in winter in China, Japan and Korea in 19th century. New material needed to establish how many groups now breed in Siberia.

MOULT: no seasonal change in plumage, except from wear. Single body and wing moult annually.

IMMATURE: as adult but less, or no, white on sides of neck, upperparts duller and browner, underparts paler so that little contrast between tips and bases of feathers. Tail feathers may be tipped white. Wing as adult, but secondaries (in some, also primary and some median coverts) tipped white, rest of median and lesser coverts tipped ash-white. In many, most of 1st juvenile body feathers replaced during winter but replacements also narrower than those of adult. Some seem to retain juvenile plumage until following summer. All continue to show pale tips to secondaries and most coverts. Soft parts as adult, though legs and feet duller. Second year cannot be reliably distinguishable from older birds, though few retain vestiges of 1st year plumage.

GOSLING: grey-brown above, darker on crown and around eyes, pale grey underparts with brownish grey band across chest. Whitish spots on wings and flanks. Bill, legs and feet dark slate. Alaskan and east Siberian birds darker than other groups, crown nearly black—see Nelson (1993) who illustrates goslings from Southampton Island and from Alaska.

MEASUREMENTS AND WEIGHT: ♂ adult wing (*n* = 42), 325–353 (337), juv 1st winter (*n* = 4), 320–332 (325); adult bill from feathers (*n* = 247), 29–38 (32.3), juv (*n* = 183), 28–34 (31.0); adult tarsus (*n* = 247), 58–68 (62.6), juv (*n* = 183), 56–66 (61.2). ♀ adult wing (*n* = 29), 317–361 (328), juv 1st winter (*n* = 4), 310–331(320); adult bill from feathers (*n* = 213), 28–35 (30.5), juv (*n* = 33), 27–32 (29.5); adult tarsus (*n* = 212) 55–64 (59.6), juv (*n* = 33) 56–63 (59.3).

There seems no significant variation in size between different breeding stocks. Weight of adult in early June, at start of breeding ♂ (*n* = 22), 1280–1710 (1490), ♀ (*n* = 28), 1130–1730 (1340); during wing moult, Jul–Aug, in Queen Elizabeth Island ♂ (*n* = 403), 1080–1790 (1370), ♀ (*n* = 361), 880–1590 (1230); in Alaska ♂ (*n* = 277), 940–1760 (1260), ♀ (*n* = 285), 850–1330 (1080); in winter in British Columbia and California ♂ (*n* = 210), 1130–1810 (1460), ♀ (*n* = 195), 1080–1730 (1310); in winter in New Jersey ♂ (*n* = 327), 970–1170 (1530), ♀ (*n* = 284), 1140–1770 (1430). First winter on US Atlantic coast ♂ (*n* = 112), 1360, ♀ (*n* = 125), 1220; in moult, following summer, on Queen Elizabeth Is ♂ (*n* = 43), 910–1420 (1220), ♀ (*n* = 63), 920–1470 (1160).

Field characters

One of smallest geese, 560–660 mm long. On water, floats high, with cocked tail, black head and neck showing little contrast with dark brown upperparts, ventral region white. On land, usually in tightly packed fast moving flocks. Underparts vary from nearly black to very pale grey, depending on population involved. White necklace may only be visible at fairly close range. First winter birds have little, if any, white on neck and are duller, with pale transverse bars on wings. In flight, very dark, short-necked, with white rear end (black tail obscured by upper coverts), and dark underwings; pale flanks of *hrota*—see Madge and Burn (1988) for illustration of different forms. Usually fly in tight packs, highly manoeuvrable, except when low over sea. Wings narrow and appear to beat rapidly.

Voice

Icelandic name *hrota*, adopted by Müller as specific name, imitates characteristic rolling call, hard *raunk, raunk* and softer *ronk*, uttered in flight, on land and while swimming. At close range, other low conversational calls heard. Alarm call higher-pitched *wauk*, uttered also when attacked by neighbour. Difficulty of providing verbal equivalents illustrated by comparing Bergmann *et al.* (1994) for *bernicla* in Europe and Palmer (1976) for *hrota* in North America—Russian race uses *wok/wrok/rott, og-og, wa-ng* or *karng*; while Atlantic race apparently calls *cronk* or *car-r-up, gut-cronk, tarronk, cronnk, gurrr*, and *cut cut cut*; both authors record hissing as defensive. Whether vocabularies of several breeding groups differ substantially will be unclear until sonograms, given for *bernicla* in Bergmann *et al.* (1994), can be made for all.

Range and status

Dark-bellied nominate form *bernicla* breeds in western Siberia, on Kolguev Island, Severnaya Zemlya, eastern Taymyr Peninsula (most abundantly) and Lena delta. In 1997, 5 mixed colonies of *bernicla* and *nigricans* found breeding on low outer islands of Olenyok Delta and western Lena Delta. Status of breeders further east uncertain; darker-bellied birds occur from New Siberian Island and Jana delta to Wrangel Island and Anadyr Peninsula; opinions on

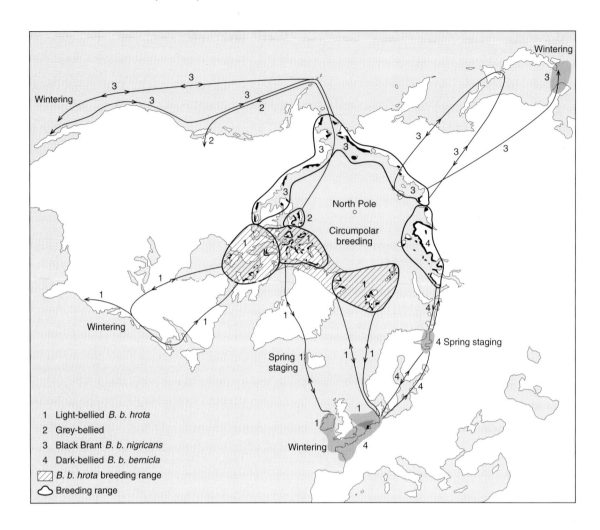

whether these differ in appearance and are reproductively isolated from those in Alaska have changed
many times. mtDNA analyses might enable differences to be settled. At present, Wetlands International recognizes two wholly Asian groups: part of
nigricans, wintering in Kamchatka and Japan, and *ori-
entalis*, wintering in Korea and China.

In North America, at least 4 distinct breeding
groups: (a) large group of *c* 180 000 dark-bellied birds
breeding in low and mid-arctic Alaska (Yukon-
Kuskokwim Delta holding >80%) and in smaller
numbers east to Banks Island and coastal islands of
Queen Maud Gulf; (b) much less numerous Western
High Arctic group (7000–15 000) of grey-bellied
birds nesting on Parry Islands (Prince Patrick, Eglin-

ton and Melville); (c) pale-bellied Eastern High
Arctic group (15 000–24 000) breeding in eastern
Queen Elizabeth Islands; (d) large pale-bellied
mid-arctic group (100 000–150 000) centred around
Foxe Basin—largest known colonies on Southamp-
ton Island and northwest and southwest Baffin
Island, though where most of population nests still
unknown.

Small group of dark-bellied 'Lawrence's Brant',
that probably bred in eastern Canada, are represented in collections in Smithsonian Institution by
3 specimens, including type of *nigricans*, taken on
US Atlantic coast in mid 19th century (Delacour
and Zimmer 1951), and were reportedly familiar to
fowlers there and in eastern Canada until well into

20th century; 2 specimens in Canadian Museum of Nature, taken in Labrador 3 June 1928, may be this form. Smithsonian skins have caused prolonged controversy, especially amongst those who have not examined them; which might be resolved by mtDNA analysis.

Final distinct breeding group consists of *c* 4000 light-bellied geese breeding in Svalbard, with few in Franz Josef Land; < 1000 breeding in Kronprins Christian Land, north Greenland, belong with them, as shown by radio-telemetry of birds marked in Denmark in spring 1997 (Clausen and Bustnes 1998). Early in 20th century, were more numerous and occupied wider range in Greenland than today; breeding birds in British Museum (Nat. Hist.) were collected in northwest Greenland in June 1876.

In winter, West Siberian Brent are in northwest Europe, from Denmark through The Netherlands and England (chiefly southeast coast) to northwest France, where most numerous when winter cold around North Sea (Ward 2004). About 4000 dark-bellied Brent winter in China and Japan, but most of those from northeast Siberia thought to join those from Alaska, which winter on Pacific coast of North America, now chiefly in Mexico. They begin northward migration as early as late Jan, when increasing numbers found in California, Washington and British Columbia. Few overwinter in southern Alaska and Queen Charlotte Islands. Most grey-bellied Western high arctic Brent winter in Padilla and Samish bays, Puget Sound, Washington, though few reach Mexico. Pale eastern high arctic Brent winter almost entirely in Ireland, with very small numbers on Channel Islands and in northwest France. Some stop briefly in Inner Hebrides in early spring, *en route* to Iceland, their major staging area. Pale Foxe Basin Brent winter on US Atlantic coast, from Massachusetts to North Carolina, though chiefly off New Jersey, Long Island and Virginia. Those from Svalbard winter around southern North Sea, from Denmark to The Netherlands and northeast England, returning to Denmark in spring (Denny *et al.* 2004).

All travel long distances (2500–9000 km) between breeding and wintering places. These long journeys explain why Brent are exceptional amongst geese for flying efficiency, and why they accumulate proportionately large fat reserves before migrating.

Brent from Parry Islands make 2 long flights in autumn. Radio-marking shows them travelling at least 2500 km to reach Izembek Lagoon on southwest coast of Alaska, where join (though remaining somewhat apart from) great majority of darker-bellied Brent from Alaska and eastern Siberia. Then fly at least 2400 km over Pacific Ocean to reach Padilla Bay, Washington; some then join those Alaskan Brent that have stopped in Washington and Oregon in flying similar distance further south to Baja California.

Dark-bellied Brent from Queen Maud Gulf also head west to Izembek Bay in autumn (travelling at least 3000 km, much more if, as seems probable, they fly around Alaskan coast, rather than overland). After spending *c* 7 weeks at Izembek, head for Baja California (4800 km), most apparently without stopping. Seem usually to leave when tail winds available to assist them. On return in spring, some of Mackenzie Brent (and from Parry Islands?) fly overland across Yukon, without long detour to Izembek. Other high arctic Brent also make long migratory journeys. Those from Svalbard believed to fly directly to western Denmark in autumn (> 2500 km) and to return non-stop in spring. Routes followed by Brent travelling from eastern Queen Elizabeth Island to Ireland not yet clear, though ringed birds have been shot in central parts of West Greenland 16 Aug–22 Oct, most in early Sept, while recoveries in Iceland range 6 Sept–9 Nov, most 6–20 Sept. In late Apr or early May, these fly about 1500 km from Ireland to west coast of Iceland, where stay until late May or early June. Then cross Denmark Strait (500 km) before flying another 800–900 km over Greenland icecap, > 2500 m high, to reach west coast. After stopping for 3–4 days (dates of local shooting 28 May–6 June), fly another 1200–2100 km to nesting areas, i.e. 4000–5000 km in all. Radio-tracking shows (Guðmundsson *et al.* 1995) that icecap crossing stretches geese close to physiological limits; some marked birds made several stops during climb up eastern face. Movements between western Europe and Taymyr Peninsula, though long (4600 km), are topographically less demanding; yet Ebbinge (1989) showed, in some years, flying into head winds depleted reserves of migrants sufficiently to affect breeding performance. Staging areas on south shore of White Sea, *c* 2300 km from Denmark, found recently. Migration from US Atlantic coast to Foxe Basin, often with brief stop on St Lawrence or Ottawa rivers (1300 km), and with stay of 2–3 weeks on southeast coast of Hudson Bay (> 1100 km to Southampton Island) relatively easy as well adapted and (in most years) well prepared for long-distance flying. Yet, after severe winters and cold springs (notably 1976–77, when US Atlantic coast population reduced by starvation from 110 000 in Nov to 36 000 in Mar), many survivors arrive in breeding areas in poor condition unable to nest. Formerly, most of these took more easterly route, stopping in Maritimes and Gulf of St Lawrence before travelling across Québec and Labrador to Ungava Bay, but few do so now.

Habitat and general habits

Most breeding in Siberia and Alaska, and many of those in mid arctic Canada, nest in colonies, varying widely in density, chiefly in, or very close to, wet coastal meadows with abundant graminoid vegetation. Small islands in lakes or rivers favoured nest sites, especially if nesting Sabine's Gulls *Larus sabini*, Snowy Owls *Nyctea scandiaca* or large raptors present to deter predators; on Wrangel Island, said to breed only in association with Snowy Owls such is predation pressure from foxes (Litvin *et al.* 1985). In Alaska *Puccinellia phryganoides, Carex subspathacea, Dupontia fischeri* and *Triglochin palustris* preferred food plants.

High-arctic Brent not colonial, because habitat unsuitable. Some breed on small islands in lakes and rivers, but these provide little protection where ice remains into July. Most nests widely scattered over tundra, often well away from water, presumably to reduce vulnerability of nesting ♀ and eggs to Arctic Foxes, Polar Bears *Ursus maritimus* and other predators, including gulls, skuas and Ravens. Many nest alongside boulders, where snow clears first. After young hatched, families move to join moulting nonbreeders on coastal wet meadows where sedges, grasses and other food plants most plentiful, and can escape predators by swimming into lakes, rivers or sea. Of necessity, high arctic Brent make more use of mosses and upland forbs, such as *Saxifraga*, than do those nesting at lower latitudes, as well as taking sedges, e.g. *Juncus biglumis*.

Among more southerly-breeding groups, concentrations of moult migrants (mostly pre-breeders) sometimes found well away from nesting areas. In north, moulting geese seem to remain near breeding birds, and rarely found in large flocks.

Away from breeding grounds, usually roosts on estuaries and shallow muddy bays, where feeds on plants in intertidal zone. *Zostera* preferred food, and widespread scarcity in 1930s, due to disease, thought largely responsible for great reductions in most stocks of Brent at that time. *Ulva lactuca* and (in Alaska) *U. fenestrata* also important. Other marine plants taken regularly include *Ruppia maritima, Enteromorpha, Phyllospadix, Spartina alterniflora, Salicornia* and *Triglochin maritima*.

In spring, early in northward migrations, some stocks have long used saltmarsh and other coastal grasslands, although others stop only in areas where *Zostera* abundant. In winter, used to remain almost entirely below high-water mark. During last 20 years or so, most wintering groups make increasing use of improved grassland and winter cereals. This greatly extends potential 'carrying capacity' of some wintering places, and also provides conflict with agriculture for first time.

Displays and breeding behaviour

While nesting, ♂♂ in colonies are more aggressive than those of other species, and continue to be so during incubation and brood rearing. Forward threat posture, shared with other geese, enhanced by raising neck feathers so that white collar appears to surround black head and bill; impressive at Brent eye-level. Before incubation begins, both members of pair defend nest site against other geese and predatory birds, and ♂ defends territory, first around mate and then nest. These defended areas usually much larger at high Arctic sites than in colonies at lower latitudes. ♂ stays near nest during incubation and often flies in pursuit of intruders. Incubating ♀♀ make themselves inconspicuous by crouching low, with neck stretched flat along ground. ♀♀ often allow close approach, before joining mate at a distance; vigorous defence of nest unusual.

Most sexual activity (and pair formation) takes place in winter and at spring staging areas, where copulations also occur. Pair formation difficult to study, except in small groups of marked birds, so that little yet known about occurrence in wild. In large flocks, most obvious manifestation is in 3-bird flights, low and fast close pursuits, which usually involve 2nd ♂ attempting to break up mated pair, though sometimes seen as 2 ♂♂ pursuing ♀. These flights infrequent, though occasionally prolonged, and seen in all months Oct–May.

Monogamous and arrive in breeding areas already paired. Although most copulations probably occur before pairs reach nesting places, copulation between ♀ and ♂ that were not paired accounted for 7 of 28 seen at colony in Yukon-Kuskokwim Delta, Alaska. If this frequency of extra-pair copulation general in colonies, may be of reproductive and genetic importance. Little recorded about whether pairs may be accompanied by young of previous year; some families remain intact in Iceland in May.

Breeding and life cycle

Substantial differences in timing of nesting between different breeding groups (see Table 9.11). As expected, arrives later at high latitudes, where tends to begin laying after shorter interval than in Alaska or Foxe Basin, but much variation from year to year in timing of main arrivals and in period before

laying begins. No evidence of substantial difference between stocks in egg dimensions: 71.6×47.1 ($n = 1233$); weight 78.9 (69–91) ($n = 245$); of shell only 6.7 (5.1–9.5) ($n = 251$). Flint and Sediger (1992) measured volume of 3478 eggs, mean $84.0\,cm^2$ (s.e. 5.7); sources of variation included: larger clutches had larger eggs, older females laid larger eggs, early clutches had larger eggs, the first egg was usually the smallest, size increasing through the laying sequence, and there were variations between years.

Clutch size 3–5 (1–7). On Southampton Island in 1950s, mean 3.94 ($n = 853$); on Yukon-Kuskokwim Delta in 1970s mean 3.27 ($n = 130$). Because of wide inter-annual variation and small samples from other areas, no other clear evidence of differences between breeding groups. Incubation starts with 2nd egg of clutch. Little recorded variation in incubation period of 23–24 days. Because lack sufficient reserves, ♀♀ less attentive than most geese, leaving nest to feed 6–7 times daily, except just prior to hatching. Frequent lengthy absences do not harm eggs because nest down unusually abundant and of high insulating efficiency. ♂ often very close to nest when ♀ absent, but not known to incubate. Hatching tends to be spread over 10–14 days, with occasional very late clutches not emerging until early Aug. Eggs hatch nearly simultaneously. Young led away 8–60 h, usually 12–36 h, after hatching. Gosling mass at hatching 43.6, 315–398 at 14 days

9.11 Average timing of nesting events in breeding ranges of separate groups of Brent Geese.

Region	°N	Arrival		Length of laying period (days)	Peak hatch
		Early	Peak		
W. Siberia	77	14 June	17–20 June	3–5	mid July
E. Siberia	66–70	29 May–4 June	10 June	7–10	12 July
Alaska	61	mid May	late May	9–11	late June
Mackenzie	69	25 May–2 June	6–9 June	7–11	early July
Parry Islands (W. High Arctic)	76	6 June	12–17 June	?	10–15 July
E. High Arctic	77	3–5 June	10–15 June	7–10	mid July
Foxe Basin	64	7–10 June	20 June	7–16	mid July
N.E. Greenland	81	early June	14–20 June	3–5	mid July
Svalbard	78	end May	9 June	10	10–15 July

and about 967 at 32 days. In Alaska, early hatched young grew faster than those hatched late.

Nesting success highly variable from place to place, year to year, and over longer periods, from various combinations of causes, relative importance of which hotly disputed. In sequence, these include adult condition before embarking on spring migration, loss of condition due to adverse conditions (especially strong headwinds) during migration, timing of snow melt and abundance of predators in breeding areas, availability of alternative prey (notably Norwegian Lemming *Lemmus lemmus* and Collared Lemming *Dicrostonyx torquatus*). Prey-switching hypothesis—that predation on birds and eggs especially high in years following peak in lemming cycle—gained some academic popularity in late 1980s, but does not account for many observed fluctuations in nesting and rearing success, especially in high Arctic where lemmings, if present, not clearly cyclic, and where gulls, skuas and Polar Bears can be more important predators than Arctic Foxes. Goslings closely guarded by both parents and brooded frequently by ♀, especially in cold, wet weather, until 10–16 days. Later, rest close to parents. Parents lead young to feeding sites, ♂ vigilant and threatening predators and intruding neighbours more often than ♀. Goslings fed for *c* 13 h every day in Svalbard, 14 h in Alaska. In Alaska, about 20% of parents lose entire brood. Broods usually remain distinct during 1st 2 weeks, but brood size often seen to increase later, suggesting some amalgamation, though isolated goslings not usually accepted by parents, and may join other young to form gangs. Young fly at 40–45 days: no strong evidence of regional variation. In high Arctic, families leave rearing areas about 2 weeks after young fledge; in low Arctic may remain for 5–6 weeks before leaving.

Adult survival rates of ♀♀ investigated over several years in Alaska, 2 on Yukon-Kuskokwim Delta and one on arctic coast. Survival slightly higher in Arctic (0.90 ± 0.036) than in Tutakoke River (0.85 ± 0.004) or Kokechik Bay (0.86 ± 0.011). Thus estimates did not support hypothesis that cost of longer migration, or harvest experienced by arctic Brant, reduced annual survival relative to Yukon-Kuskokwim Delta (Sedinger *et al.* 2002). Longevity

record of UK-ringed bird 28.2 years (Clark *et al.* 2002).

Conservation and threats

Different stocks fall into 2 classes. Several are very small and will always require special care, while 3 groups are large enough to be agricultural nuisances in some wintering areas. Yet 2 of those large stocks were small not long ago. Dark-bellied Brent breeding on Taymyr peninsula and wintering on south coast of North Sea, > 200 000 strong early in 20th century, were reduced to < 20 000 by late 1950s. Heavy shooting, particularly in Denmark, seemed major cause. It took 20 years to secure total legal protection from shooting in nearly all parts of their range and, from 1970s onwards, increased to > 250 000, despite breeding failure in years when snow melt delayed and Arctic Foxes and predators numerous. Increase accompanied, and presumably encouraged, shift from feeding in intertidal zone in winter and (in spring) on saltmarsh, to extensive use of agricultural crops, including winter wheat as well as improved grasslands.

Pale-bellied Brent breeding around Foxe Basin and wintering along US Atlantic coast, usually numbering 100 000–150 000, suffered 2 severe mishaps in 1970s. Unusual conditions exposed them to very heavy losses from shooting in 1972; hunting was banned and recovery began. Then cold winter of 1976–77, with freezing of intertidal zone, led to widespread starvation and vulnerability to shooting. By spring 1977, < 40 000 remained of autumn population of > 130 000. Two of next 3 winters along Atlantic coast were also cold. Ban on hunting remained in effect for several years and there was rapid recovery to former level. During cold winters, some moved inland to feed on improved grasslands, including golf courses; this habit persisted, turning geese into nuisances, rather than causing severe damage to crops.

Third large stock, Black Brant breeding in Alaska and northwest Canada and wintering along Pacific coast, declined in 1930s, when most were wintering in California. They found own solution, by moving south to spend much of winter along west coast of Mexico, where food supplies seem more reliable and hunting was, and remains, much less, apart from incursions by American hunters attracted by lack of bag limits. Field feeding seems no problem.

Little known of problems facing 2 (or more?) very small groups breeding in eastern Siberia and wintering in Kamchatka and Japan (*c* 4000 in autumn, fewer in midwinter) and in Korea and China (probably <2000). What could be done to help them is unclear, but they should not be forgotten. Their genetic relationships to other groups are of considerable interest (some look distinctive). More importantly, no extremely small remnant stocks should be abandoned simply because few know of them. Other small groups are quite closely monitored. Pale-bellied birds breeding in Svalbard and northeast Greenland and wintering around North Sea, particularly in Denmark, are protected from hunting and seem to hold their own, despite falling so low as 4000. They were most numerous breeding geese in Svalbard in 19th century, but replaced by Barnacle Geese in many places. Another pale-bellied group, breeding in eastern Queen Elizabeth Islands (and formerly, though probably no longer, in northwest

Greenland) winters primarily in Ireland, where well provided with refuge areas and public concern. Some graze sports fields in Dublin, where regarded as a nuisance, not a menace.

Grey-bellied group breeding in western Queen Elizabeth Islands and wintering in Puget Sound pose perhaps most awkward conservation problem among North American geese, both because it is taking many years to convince American agencies of their distinctiveness and antiquity, and because they remain in Puget Sound throughout winter while Black Brant pass through in autumn, exposing them to prolonged hunting. Would probably receive better treatment if bred in Alaska, not in Canada. Disparity in numbers of different groups, members of single species totalling over half a million, exemplifies general problem in conservation—at what taxonomic level should 'safety mechanisms' be put in place? In this case, concentrating on readily identifiable subspecies would miss many of groups most in need of special care.

Hugh Boyd

Barnacle Goose *Branta leucopsis*
PLATE 7

Anas leucopsis Bechstein, 1803, Ornith. Taschenbuch Deutschland, **2**, p. 424
Germany

Etymology: *leucopsis* means white-headed. 'Barnacle' derives from legend of Geraldus, *c* 1185 and perhaps older, that birds emerged from shellfish known as goose barnacles.

Other names: Norwegian: Kvitkinngås or white-cheeked goose. Danish: Bramgås; French: Bernache nonnette (meaning nun goose, as appears to have hood over white face); German: Weisswangengans; Icelandic: Helsingi.

Variation: no subspecies, despite huge breeding range. No recognized morphological (and hence no taxonomic) variation in 4 populations (Owen 1980), although Swedish flock does behave differently in that nests and moults month earlier than other populations.

Description

ADULT: sexes alike. Neck, chest, primary and tail feathers black, and back greyish with white and black bands on each wing covert. Head white or cream except for black crown and variable amount of black around eye and base of bill. Underparts white, flanks pale grey, and bill, legs and eye black (Owen 1980).

MOULT: no seasonal change in plumage; one body moult annually and one wing and tail moult after breeding.

IMMATURE: can be distinguished at close quarters until spring. Paler version of adult, chest and neck greyish black and back brownish with pale grey rather than white margin to wing coverts. Usually more black on head, especially around eye and above base of bill. In 2nd summer, retains few brown feathers on wing coverts, and can be distinguished reliably in hand at least until Aug. Reach full adult size in 2nd year.

GOSLING: short dense down; white or yellowish below and grey on top of head, on wings and on back. Black bill and feet (Nelson 1993).

MEASUREMENTS AND WEIGHT: ♂ wing 412; tarsus 72. ♀ wing 389; tarsus 68 (Owen 1980). Weight 1700–2400. ♂ substantially heavier (on average 180 g more) and larger than ♀ and adult heavier and larger than gosling and yearling. Body size (i.e. skull and tarsus) in Svalbard study decreased over last 20 years; in some areas by *c* 2% per year, possibly due to increased competition for limited amount of food during 1st 8 weeks of life. Feeding performance during this early age linked with final body size in many goose populations (Black *et al.* 1998).

Field characters

Largest of black geese of Europe, 580–710 mm long. Distinguishable from Canada Goose by grey and black, rather than brown, plumage on back. Cheek patch extends right around head, beyond eye and over forehead, while that of Canada Goose normally restricted to cheek and under throat.

Voice

Short, sharp bark, not unlike yap of small dog. Bark repeated in rapid series of notes especially on warm days in spring and during breeding season. During Triumph Ceremony (greeting between paired birds) high pitched *yip* of ♀ overlaps with loud calls of ♂ producing duet (Hausberger and Black 1990). Variation in calls caused by how wide mouth opens during production of sound. Bird opens mouth to same extent every time, thus producing unique call, detectable by sonographic analyses and presumably by geese themselves (Hausberger *et al.* 1991).

Studies of semi-captive flock at WWT Slimbridge showed that proportion of different types of call given by pair changed with increasing age and pairbond duration (varying 1–14 years). As pair duration increased, proportion of soft calls declined, medium intensity calls increased slightly and louder calls increased most. Soft contact calls thought to help maintain contact between partners at close range, while louder calls often precede aggressive interactions and maintain long-range contact (Black *et al.* 1996).

Range and status

Four populations distributed in 3 polar and one temperate region in summer and 3 major wintering areas in western Europe. These include Greenland population that winters in Ireland and western Scotland, Svalbard population wintering in northern UK, and Russian (Novaya Zemlya) and Swedish populations, both of which winter on North Sea coast in Germany and The Netherlands (Owen 1980, Larsson *et al.* 1988). Breeding occurred in 9 localities in Baltic Sea. Most colonies consist of fewer than 6 pairs, except Swedish colonies which, since 1971, breed in Gotland area; this flock, which now consists of > 1000 pairs, may not have established if man's management of islands had not made habitat suitable for breeding geese. Occasional stragglers venture to and from all 4 populations. Also several naturalized flocks in UK and Norway (Delany 1992).

Currently 12 000 in Sweden, 13 700 in Svalbard, 32 000 in Greenland and 120 000 in Russia. Before 1960, few individuals of any population ringed; only 40 recoveries received before 1959, of which 6 were from range of Svalbard population. Nevertheless, recovery pattern clear-cut and indicated geographical isolation of different breeding groups in winter (Boyd 1961). Position clarified in 1960s when > 1000 of Svalbard population ringed, plus substantial numbers from range of Greenland and Russian breeders. More than 9000 from Svalbard population individually marked by WWT, and confirmed discreteness of populations, with only 0.1% emigration and no recorded immigration (Owen and Black 1991).

In early parts of last century, said to be common on northern Solway Firth, with flocks of 6000; however, drastic decline occurred by 1930s, and

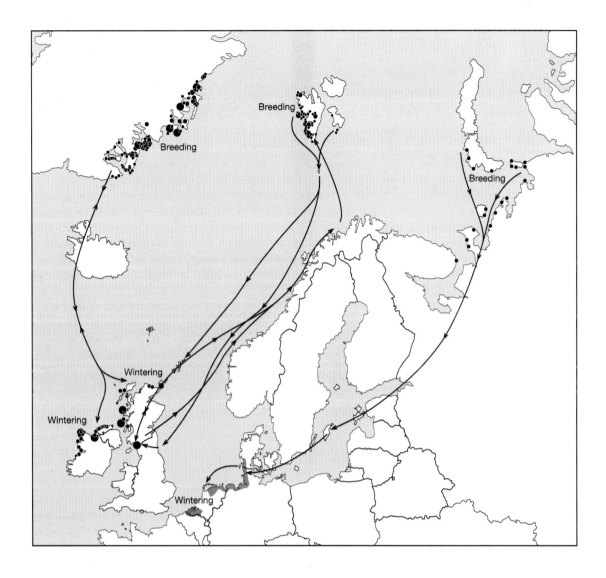

unusual to see > 500 during that decade (Berry 1939). In latter part of 19th century, Svalbard well visited but few geese recorded, and many currently important breeding areas had few or no geese (Løvenskiold 1964, Norderhaug 1970). From incidence of leucistic gene in population, Owen and Shimmings (1992) suggested that population established recently from few founders. Possible that large flocks on Solway in early years came from Greenland, and decrease at start of last century due to geese 'short-stopping' in Hebrides, particularly

on Islay, as conditions improved with intensifying agriculture (Owen *et al.* 1995).

Celebrated recovery of Svalbard population depicted in Figure 9.12. In mid 1940s, considerable disturbance on wintering grounds from wartime activities and heavy shooting meant lowest ever count in 1948, when only 300 found on Solway (Owen and Norderhaug 1977). Partly protected from shooting in UK in 1954 and in Svalbard in 1955 and this, with establishment of National Nature Reserve (NNR) at Caerlaverock in 1957,

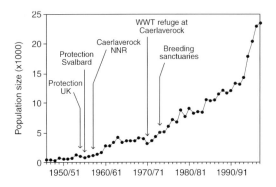

9.12 The increase in the Svalbard Barnacle Goose population from the 1940s to the 1990s and the conservation measures responsible for the changes.

led to recovery in numbers, to 3000–4000 in 1960s. Further increases, to 25 750 (Musgrove *et al.* 2001), followed establishment of WWT reserve at Caerlaverock in 1970, and declaration of breeding sanctuaries on main island sites in Svalbard in 1973.

Habitat and general habits

Generally present on breeding grounds in May/June–Aug/Sept, autumn staging areas in Sept, wintering grounds from late Sept–Apr/May and spring staging areas Apr–May.

Many individuals capable of breeding immediately on arrival in arctic breeding grounds but snow cover may delay nesting for several weeks. In late years, makes use of vegetation on south-facing mountain slopes, fertilized by droppings of cliff nesting seabirds. Moves down to breeding areas as soon as snowfree patches appear on tundra. Main habitats in summer consist of fjellmark (polar semidesert tundra), wet moss-meadows and mudflats. Diet in summer varied, comprising 52 plant species (Prop *et al.* 1980). In Svalbard, main foods *Cerastium arcticum, Saxifraga oppositifolia, S. caespitosa, Equisetum, Cochlearia officianalis, Polygonum viviparum, Salix, Puccinellia, Dupontia* and *Carex*. In addition, mosses form virtually inexhaustible food supply (Prop and de Vries 1993).

After hatching, families disperse to vegetated areas surrounding tundra lakes and along rivers; family groups tend to separate from flocks of nonbreeders in same general area. After moult, return to forage fertilized mountain slopes prior to departure.

During autumn migration, many from Svalbard population stop on Bear Island *c* 500 km to south of main islands of Svalbard (i.e. Spitsbergen). Little of island vegetated, so gather on few patches of vegetation in river valleys and headlands on coast where gulls rest in large numbers, fertilizing tundra with droppings (Owen and Gullestad 1984). Departure from island depends on weather conditions; do not leave until winds northerly and favourable for migration. Analyses of weather in Bjørnoya, and mass arrival pattern at Caerlaverock in Scotland indicate that journey takes *c* 48 h.

Wintering areas in The Netherlands, Germany and Scotland fairly similar and consist of mudflats, saltmarsh and improved pastures (Owen and Kerbes 1971, Ebbinge *et al.* 1975, Owen *et al.* 1987). Rarely flies more than 5 km from roost on mudflats. When on saltmarsh, stolons of White Clover *Trifolium repens* primary food in autumn, supplemented by grass and herbs such as *Puccinellia maritima, Festuca rubra* and *Triglochin maritima*. On pasture, eats *Lolium perenne* or *Holcus lanatus*, main constituent of sown sward in wintering areas. In early autumn, also visits stubble fields, gleaning spilt grain.

Leaves wintering grounds mid Apr on, and arrives at spring staging areas *c* 24 h later. Geese present in staging areas for 20–30 days, and individuals for 2–3 weeks (Gullestad *et al.* 1984). Greenland birds stage in Iceland, and Svalbard ones in Helgeland, Norway, where spread across range of habitat types, from coastal areas dominated by *Festuca rubra*, to improved pastures. Part of Russian population stage on coast with *Festuca* and *Agrostis stolonifera* and improved pastures on Gotland, Sweden, breeding location of Swedish population. Studies of behaviour and feeding ecology of spring staging geese reveal that those using agricultural habitats subsequently become fatter and breed better than those using less nutritious habitats (Black *et al.* 1991a).

After departing Helgeland, Norway, in Spring, Svalbard geese travelling to northernmost breeding colonies in Kongsfjorden, spend 14–31 days in transit; may stop during migration or spend some time in southern parts of Svalbard for refuelling (Tombre *et al.* 1996).

Displays and breeding behaviour

Pre-copulatory display similar to other geese (Johnsgard 1965a). Post-copulatory display also as other geese, where ♂ raises wings above back, neck held high and strutting. ♀ flaps wings and preens. Numerous displays performed while potential mates assess one another during pair-formation process (Black and Owen 1988, Hausberger and Black 1990). Pairbond members greet one another after temporary separation with loud calls and exaggerated head and neck movements in sideways and vertical fashion, as if towards opponent; this ceremony linked with increasing aggressive effort during long spring days prior to migration from wintering ground (Black and Owen 1988).

Flock and colonial living costly in creating numerous conflicts with neighbours. Most aggressive encounters solved according to number of individuals in social unit where large families dominate small families, all families dominate pairs and pairs dominate singles (Black and Owen 1989a). Gosling aggressiveness shaped by learning paternal behaviour, and genetic predisposition gained from both parents (Black and Owen 1987); thus, aggressive parents produce aggressive offspring. More aggressive geese tend to have access to best food (Black and Owen 1989b, Black *et al.* 1992) and have largest territories (Owen and Wells 1979). Time that goslings remain with parents in 1st year may also influence acquired aggressiveness (Black and Owen 1989b). Adult aggressiveness/dominance also influenced to some extent by body size, age and reproductive history (Black and Owen 1987, 1989a). Actual battles often solved with minimum of fighting/threatening and aggressive effort tuned according to perceived level of success. Dominant birds win encounters against subordinate ones with mildest threat, but 2 dominants may escalate towards actual grappling and wing-beating (Black and Owen 1989b).

Breeding and life cycle

Whereas majority in Russian and Greenland population nest colonially on steep cliffs, those in Svalbard and Swedish populations nest on islands to lessen risk of predation. Traditionally, nests in Svalbard also on cliffs and hillsides in larger valleys but, in recent decades, nesting on coastal islands common (Norderhaug 1970). Data indicate that 87% of nests are on islands, 6.5% on other coastal sites and 6.5% on cliffs and canyons (Prestrud *et al.* 1989). Main ground predators are Arctic Fox and Polar Bear. Aerial predators include large gulls, skuas, falcons and eagles.

Nest made in shallow depression and, typically, ♀ deposits thick layer of droppings around rim during incubation. Eggs white; 75.7 × 50.2 (68–82 × 46–54) ($n = 75$) (Schönwetter 1960–66) and weigh 104.8 (77.0–125.0) ($n = 100$) in captivity or 107 calculated (Schönwetter 1960–66). Clutch size > 4 (2–7) eggs, majority 3–5. ♀ exclusively incubates for 24–25 days and ♂ stands guard. Extra-pair copulation, where eggs fertilized by another ♂, rare, but intraspecific nest parasitism frequent in form of egg dumping and adoptions (Choudhury *et al.* 1993, Larsson *et al.* 1995). Parasitic ♀♀ dump eggs before and during host ♀'s incubation period (Forslund and Larsson 1995); process lasts *c* 30 minutes during which host ♀ continuously attacks parasitic ♀, while host ♂ usually passively stands by.

Typically when ♀ leaves nest during incubation, ♂ remains rather than accompany her, defending nest against large gulls that breed locally. On islands some distance from shore, that lack food for incubating birds, predation rates high because both partners forced to leave together. In 1986, nesting success (at least one egg hatching) was 84% in Svalbard colony where food supply available on islands themselves, compared with 21% on island with no food and 1.5 km from adjacent coast, which itself provided poor feeding. In area (Nordenskiøldkysten) with islands without food, but close to good mainland feeding, success was intermediate at 60%.

Studies on Nordenskiøldkysten, Svalbard, showed that nest success varied according to ability of ♀ to gain sufficient food of right quality during short absences off nest (Prop *et al.* 1984). Extended absences by 'poor' ♀♀ led to egg predation. Also depending on season, so nest success varied in same area 18–74% in different years (Prop *et al.* 1984,

Prop and de Vries 1993). Goslings at hatching weigh 63.4 (48.4–71.5) ($n = 12$) (Smart 1965b) or 67.9 ($n = 10$) in captivity. Adoptions mainly due to brood mixing shortly after hatch, but may occur with goslings up to 12 weeks, when filial imprinting complete (Choudhury *et al.* 1993). Fledge in 6–7 weeks.

Studies of individual performance indicate much variation in productivity; best 10% produce > third of young, and half of next generation's recruits produced by only 15% (Owen and Black 1989a). Breeding success increases with age, with most productive period 6–11 years; thereafter productivity decreases. Improvement at young age attributed to ♀ benefiting from experience in pre-breeding fattening and nesting; decline in old age attributed to ♂'s declining ability to establish and defend nesting territory and to compete for feeding opportunities for family (Black and Owen 1995).

Tend to mate for life; only 2% of 5974 pair-years ended in divorce. Remaining with same mate seems most successful option available, given energetically expensive lifestyles and limited time in which to breed in arctic (Black *et al.* 1996). Choosing appropriate mate can influence reproductive success; e.g. small ♀ more successful if paired with small ♂, and large with large (Choudhury *et al.* 1996). Possible that mismatch in body size can affect ♀'s ability to cope with more aggressive nature of ♂. ♀'s build-up of fat reserves, which influence breeding potential, apparently related to effort mate puts into providing space in flock in which she can feed without interruption (Black and Owen 1988, 1989b, Black *et al.* 1991a). Highest breeding performance achieved by middle-aged ♂ paired to middle-aged ♀. Young ♀♀ and old ♂♂ had consistently low brood success, irrespective of mate's age. On other hand, young ♂♂ and old ♀♀ could improve reproductive success by pairing with

middle-aged mates. This suggests that many should be attempting to gain prime, middle-aged mates in order to improve own reproductive performance (Black *et al.* 1996).

Longevity record of ringed Svalbard bird 18 years 9 months (Toms and Clark 1998).

Conservation and threats

Historically, nesting wildfowl exploited by humans, largely for eggs and down (Kear 1990). Barnacle Goose eggs and down were collected in Novaya Zemlya and numbers there declined drastically as consequence (Dementiev and Gladkov 1952). Whalers and explorers in Svalbard also havested geese and eggs (Løvenskiold 1964, Norderhaug 1970). Shooting during migration and on wintering grounds was also allowed during autumn, though Pink-footed Goose was more accessible to hunters and preferred quarry. Today, fully protected throughout range. Treated as whole, species ranked Safe, with favourable conservation status, according to IUCN (Mace and Collar 1995) and BirdLife International classification criteria (Tucker and Heath 1994). Swedish, Svalbard and Greenland populations, however, treated as separate entities, would be categorized as Vulnerable in IUCN Red List due to small population size and restricted range during migration and winter. Populations classified as such should receive highest priority for conservation and management under African Eurasian Waterbird Agreement of Bonn Convention.

Benefits from an international flyway agreement and network of well-managed reserves on winter grounds and sanctuaries on breeding grounds (Black 1995). In Scotland and Norway, new payment and grazing schemes reduce potential conflict with farmers and provide safe havens.

Myrfyn Owen and Jeff Black

Red-breasted Goose *Branta ruficollis*
PLATE 8

Anser ruficollis Pallas, 1769, Spicilegia Zool., fasc. 6, p. 21, pl. 4
lower Ob, Siberia

Etymology: *ruficollis* L. *rufus* meaning red, plus *collis* necked.

Other names: Red-necked Goose. French: Bernache à cou roux; Spanish: Barnacla cuellirroja. Known as *Rufibrenta ruficollis* in Russia and former Soviet states (Borodin 1984); also referred to as *Bernicla ruficollis* (Astley 1917).

Variation: no subspecies.

Description

ADULT: sexes similar. Chestnut-red patches on sides of head, on foreneck and breast. Crown, mane, back, wings, tail, belly, bill and legs black. White barring on wing coverts and flanks, and red cheek and neck areas bordered by white. Lores white. Broad white band along flank, and ventral region white.

MOULT: single annual body moult, so no seasonal differences. Wing moult takes place on or near breeding grounds, sometimes with Whitefronts and Bean Geese. Groups usually 25–500 (mean 116), though flock of 1500 observed. May moult in association with birds of prey for protection during flightless stage (Naumov 1931); however, no relationship found between distribution of moulting geese and birds of prey. Flightless stage lasts 15–20 days, mid July–late Aug, nonbreeders moult 2 weeks earlier (Uspenski 1965).

IMMATURE: duller than adult; cheek patch smaller and more grey than red, back not so dark, less barring on flanks.

GOSLING: crown and upperparts sepia tinged greenish, forehead, nape and wing tip yellowish, underparts pale greenish yellow (Witherby *et al.* 1952).

MEASUREMENTS AND WEIGHT: vary dependent on source. ♂ wing (*n* = 5 wild, 8 skins), 345–361 (367); tail (*n* = 5 wild, *n* = 8 skins), 99–109 (109); bill (*n* = 5 wild, 9 skins), 24–26 (24.9); tarsus (*n* = 5 wild, 8 skins),(52–58 (61.3); weight (*n* = 5), 1200–1625 (1375). ♀ wing (*n* = 7 skins), 342–357 (343); tail (*n* = 8 skins), 96–107 (102); bill (*n* = 8 skins), 23–27 (24.2); tarsus (*n* = 8 skins), 54–61 (57.1); weight (*n* = 2), 1058–1130 (1094); data from wild (Witherby *et al.* 1952), skins (Cramp and Simmons 1977), weights (Bauer and Glutz 1968). Measurements from Alferaki (1904), sexes combined, noticeably larger (see also egg dimensions), wing, 350–360; tail, 153–154; bill, 25–28.

Field characters

Probably most striking of all geese; small with small head and bill and short neck; recognized by rounded shape and bright coloration. Length 530–560 mm (Cramp and Simmons 1977), 540–560 mm (Alferaki 1904). At distance, and in flight, white band along flank remains visible, although head and neck markings less distinguishable. On nest, bright parts mostly obscured, leaving only head and black back visible, thus allowing goose to blend with surroundings. In adult ♂, forehead rises from top of bill more vertically than in ♀ and, with experience, feature can be used to sex birds in field (Kostin 1985).

Voice

Sexes similar; short, shrill, staccato call of two disjointed syllables, second syllable slightly longer and lower in tone than first: *kee-kwa, kik-wik* or *ē-e*. Sonogram in Cramp and Simmons (1977). Uses hiss in aggression. Gosling vocalizations begin to change at about one month and attain adult characteristics at 2.5–3 months (Kostin 1985).

Range and status

Breeds on arctic tundra of Russia, between Arctic Circle and 78°N, on Taimyr, Yamal and Gydan peninsulas, with 70% nesting on Taimyr. Range appears to have extended northwards in recent years to Pyasina delta, and eastwards to Bikada reserve, though may be traditional nesting sites previously little documented. In autumn, migrates southwest along narrow corridor to wintering grounds, staging at 4 major areas in Russia and Kazakhstan. Wintering range changed dramatically within last 30 years (Hunter and Black 1996), and traditional wintering site of Azerbaijan coast of Caspian Sea abandoned for western coast of Black Sea. In early 1990s, 90% of world population wintered in Bulgaria and Romania. Suggestion that geese were forced from Azerbaijan when cotton, vineyards and market gardening replaced steppe and brackish marsh habitat where they foraged on grasses *Potamogeton fluitans*, seeds of *Galium* and *Bolboschoenus maritimus* plus *Salicornia europaea* (Cramp and Simmons 1977). Small flocks winter on north and northwestern Black Sea coasts of Ukraine, while others may visit Greece. Whether Azerbaijan still used by small flocks uncertain (Hunter and

Black 1996). Occasional small numbers reach Hungary, Turkey, Iraq and Iran. Accidental in UK, Belgium, The Netherlands (Hustings *et al.* 1998), Norway, Sweden, Denmark, Finland, Germany, France, Poland, Czech Republic, Slovakia, Austria, Italy, Spain, Albania, Serbia, Israel, Cyprus, Egypt and southeast China (Cramp and Simmons 1977). Extensive distribution of accidental flocks suggests that geese once ranged more widely; features on 6000-year-old Egyptian friezes (Kohl 1958).

Population stable with slight increase within traditional breeding area. Comprehensive midwinter counts (1991–93) in Bulgaria and Romania estimated 70 000–75 000 (Hunter and Black 1996), and world population may be 88 000 (Wetlands International 2002).

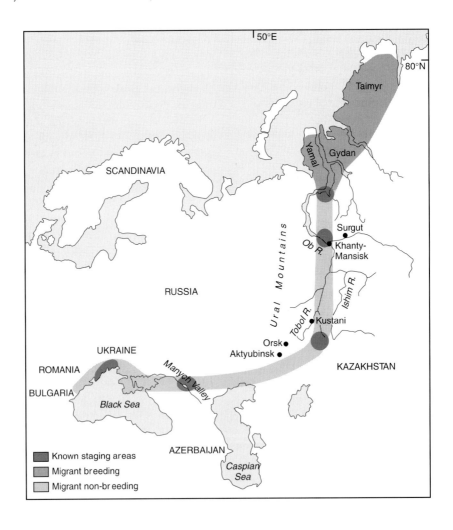

Habitat and general habits

Spring migration starts Mar. In early May, geese reach Kazakh uplands and, by early June, are on breeding ground. Little information on habitat use in staging areas, though probable that diet consists of grass shoots supplemented with tubers and rhizomes (Dementiev and Gladkov 1952). Usually migrates in association with White-fronted Geese.

Nests mostly in tundra and sometimes open parts of northern shrub tundra. Favours high and dry situations on steep river banks and precipices, low hills, rock outcrops and rocky islands, mud/clay ridges and outcrops and, less commonly, low islands in lowland areas (Krechmar and Leonovich 1967, Kostin 1985). Cover usually thin and includes dwarf birch *Betula*, willow *Salix* and dead grass (Cramp and Simmons 1977). Grass leaves and shoots of cottongrasses *Eriophorum angustifolium* and *E. scheuchzeri* make up bulk of diet (Uspenski 1965, Zharkova and Borzhonov 1972), with *Carex* and *Equisetum* also important. Usually nests close to eyries of birds of prey, or within gull and tern colonies, and near water that provides refuge for young during early life (Cramp and Simmons 1977, Kostin 1985).

Autumn migration starts mid Sept, with birds reaching Kazakhstan by end of Sept (Cramp and Simmons 1977, Owen 1980). Few may continue south to Aral Sea, while majority travel southwest towards Caspian. Small flocks may remain to winter on Caspian Sea coast in Azerbaijan and some individuals continue south to Iran and Iraq. Most (90% of population), however, travel to western Black Sea coast, arriving Oct–Nov usually with White-fronted Geese. In severe weather, small numbers visit Greece from main wintering grounds in Bulgaria and Romania. On western Black Sea coast, feeds on agricultural land, diet consisting of winter wheat, barley, maize, some pasture grasses, grass shoots on ploughed land, and spilt grain (Sutherland and Crockford 1993). Almost always feeds with other larger geese such as White-fronted Goose. Throughout day, flies to coastal and freshwater lakes to drink. Some of these lakes also used as night roosts, where utilizes middle of lake or remoter shallow areas and muddy and sandy beaches with low aquatic vegetation. When lakes freeze, roosts on ice and sea if calm (Hunter and Black 1996).

Does not usually fly in V formation characteristic of other migratory geese, but rather like starlings *Sturnus*, densely grouped and turning simultaneously (Madge and Burn 1988); small size may be one factor that allows flight in this unusual manner. Apparently lacks specialized pre-flight movements typical of Canada and Barnacle Geese (Johnsgard 1965a), although pre-flight head-shake seen in captive birds.

Displays and breeding behaviour

Aggression shown by quivering of mane feathers, lowered head and stretched neck while honking and sometimes hissing. Pre-copulatory display consists of erect posture and raised tail—unlike other black geese, but similar to some grey geese (Johnsgard 1965a). Non-territorial.

Breeding and life cycle

Arrives on breeding grounds early June, as tundra snow melts. Nests in colonies of 5–6 pairs, although up to 37 observed, and usually within 6 m of one another (Kostin and Mooij 1995, Uspenski 1966). Nests often in hollows and fissures in ground, up to 150 mm deep, though usually 50–80 mm deep and 200 mm in diameter. Nests lined with dark-grey down and grass with which ♀ covers eggs when she leaves. Same site may be used for several years (Witherby *et al.* 1952, Krechmar and Leonovich 1967). Laying begins 2nd half of June. Eggs blunt oval, creamy white with greenish tinge, and slightly glossy (Popham 1897, Naumov 1931); 67.9 × 44.7 (63–74.4 × 42.1–47.8) (n = 68), or 69–72 × 45–55 (Alferaki 1904); weight 76.4 (69.9–81.45). Clutch 3–10 eggs, most commonly 5–6. ♀ incubates for 25 days while ♂ remains nearby. When flushed from nest, pair moves to water or circles overhead calling (Krechmar and Leonovich 1967). Most clutches hatch mid July. Weight of captive goslings at day old 49.5 (45.8–52.9) (n = 14) (Smart 1965b); wild goslings few days old weighed 52 ± 0.3 (n = 3 broods) (Kostin 1985). ♀ continues to sit immediately after hatching. Once goslings have left nest, mostly 24–36 hours after hatching, both parents remain close, leading brood to water and grassy feeding sites, up to several km from colony (Kretschmar and Leonovich 1967). Goslings achieve 70% of adult mass at 30 days, faster than many goose species. Fledging occurs late Aug–early Sept at 35–42 days of age (Kostin 1985, Owen 1980). Single-brooded.

On average, 24.4% (7–54%) of population breeds in any season (1977–83). Success fluctuates and depends mainly on condition on arrival at breeding ground, as well as climate, predation and population levels of birds of prey. Clutch loss averages 15.4% (5–32%), and 4.5 goslings per breeding pair leave colony (Kostin and Mooij 1995). Severe climatic conditions can inhibit all recruitment (Hunter and Black 1996). Arctic Foxes thought to be main predators, Herring Gulls *Larus argentatus* and skuas to lesser extent, and Snowy Owls occasionally. Nest predation varies 7–59%, depending on cyclical variation of lemmings that are fox's main prey (see Brent Goose account and Chapter 5), and proximity of nests to those of Peregrine Falcons, Rough-legged Buzzards and Herring Gulls, which are thought to provide protection (Kostin and Mooij 1995, Quinn *et al.* 2003). Nesting within colonies of Arctic Terns *Sterna paradisaea* also observed. Terns might provide some protection from raiding skuas and gulls. Goose nests usually not more than 100 m from bird of prey's nest, usually within 10–30 m (but see Alison 1975). Nineteen of 20 falcon nests investigated had colonies of Red-breasted Geese in immediate vicinity (Krechmar 1965). Numbers and distribution of geese in association with birds of prey, gulls and terns probably varies between years and areas. Goose nests not attacked by birds of prey and gulls (Ratcliffe 1993), perhaps because communal nesting advantageous to both for detecting potential predators and competitors (Kostin 1985); however, when hatched goslings leave 'safe' zone, they become vulnerable and must seek relative safety of water. Some goslings may be taken at this time.

Captive birds will nest in 2nd year but 3rd and 4th years most productive (Anon 1972). No data on rearing success or adult survival. Two captive individuals lived for 21 years (Hillgarth *et al.* 1983).

Conservation and threats

Given Vulnerable status by BirdLife International (2000, 2001). In 1950–60, numbers estimated 50 000–60 000. From 1969–89, however, totals did not exceed 30 000. Population may have crashed when forced from traditional wintering area on Caspian Sea, from exploitation, overhunting and/or effects of DDT on populations of birds of prey. Apparent increase in numbers (from 30 000 in 1980s–70 000 in early 1990s) perhaps due to improved monitoring, but also to improved conservation effort in breeding and wintering ranges and, possibly, coincidental recovery of numbers of birds of prey (Hunter and Black 1996, Quinn and Kokorev 2000).

Current threats include probable change to wintering habitat in Bulgaria and Romania; recent privatization of agricultural land leads to changes from cereal to cash crops which geese do not use, and intensification may cause conflict between farmers and geese. Also, in contrast to former collective farming, greater economic significance of losses to individual farmers. Is illegally hunted through most of range, and disturbance caused by increased hunting of closely associated goose species on wintering grounds—e.g. at least 1000 shot annually during legal hunting of White-fronted Geese in Ukraine (Rusev and Korzukov 2001)—may limit feeding opportunities and subsequent breeding success (Hunter and Black 1996). Because of popularity with collectors and aviculturists, trade in eggs and adults taken from wild significant problem before export ban declared in 1970.

However, prospects improve. Protected now through most of range, international Action Plan should help conservation status, and breeding and wintering habitat (Hunter and Black 1996). Major wintering areas in Bulgaria now have Ramsar status. Current efforts to conserve Peregrine Falcon (Eastham *et al.* 2000) may improve situation further.

Janet Hunter

Freckled Duck

Taxonomy

The Freckled Duck is the only member of the Stictonettinae subfamily, and is not recorded in the fossil record. Although it resembles superficially the dabbling ducks (Anatini) because it has short legs, it exhibits many primitive characters including a simple syrinx without a bulla, non-metallic plumage, lack (almost) of sexual dimorphism, reticulated tarsi and, in particular, a recurved bill (Delacour and Mayr 1945, Johnsgard 1960a, Wolfenden 1961, Olson and Fedducia 1980a, Livezey 1986) (Figure 2.8 in Chapter 2). Its affinities are confusing; indeed, authors have linked it with the whistling-ducks (Wolfenden 1961), dabbling ducks (Delacour and Mayr 1945, Delacour 1954–56), shelducks (Peters 1931, Boetticher 1942) and stifftails (Fullagar *et al.* 1990, Marchant and Higgins 1990); however, most regard it as a distant relative of the geese and swans (Verheyen 1961, Frith 1964a, 1964b, Johnsgard 1965a, 1978, Jacob and Glazer 1975, Brush 1976). It obviously has no very near relatives. The red base to its bill perhaps suggests an association with the Black-headed Duck.

Des Callaghan

Freckled Duck *Stictonetta naevosa*
PLATE 8

Anas naevosa Gould, 1841, Proc. Zool. Soc. London (1840) p. 177
Western Australia.
Stictonetta Reichenbach, 1853

Etymology: *stictonetta* Gr. *stiktos* means spotted and *netta* duck; *naevosa* L. for abundantly spotted.

Other names: Speckled, Monkey, Grey, Oatmeal and Diamantina Duck, Gadwall, Canvas-back. Australian Aboriginal: Gnall-gnall, Keimul, Koodnapina, Korneock, Nal-nal; French: Stictonette tachetée; Dutch: Stippeleend; German: Affengans; Spanish: Pata Pecoso.

Variation: no subspecies.

Description

ADULT: sexes alike. Whole body speckled and vermiculated on dark grey-brown (appearing almost black at distance). Belly distinctly paler with undertail coverts buff to warm brown. Primaries dark brown; upperwing coverts and secondaries speckled as on body; no speculum. Tail speckled. Underwings mostly whitish or speckled whitish on coverts. ♂ generally darker than ♀ at all times, particularly in head region which becomes almost unspeckled on forehead, lores and chin in best plumage examples. Base of ♂ upper mandible becomes bright red during breeding season. Upper mandible of nonbreeding ♂ fades to dull orange-red, with remainder of bill slate grey; legs dull slate grey (scales on front of legs reticulate); iris dark brown in both sexes. ♀ shows no difference between breeding and nonbreeding plumage and bill colour remains slate grey at all times.

MOULT: no ♂ eclipse plumage. Moult sequence variable and timing in wild little understood. In captivity, adults undergo full post-breeding moult, including flight feathers (flightless 4 weeks) but some drop wing feathers synchronously in spring, some in autumn, and some at both times. Immatures have complete moult, usually but not always including simultaneous moult of flight feathers at *c* 6 months. Body feathers replaced continuously with peak moult late summer–winter when facial feathers of sexually mature ♂ darken due to reduction in density of freckles. Feathers of nonbreeders fade to brownish tones and become worn (Marchant and Higgins 1990). Observations on moult in wild mostly based on samples taken in late summer (Norman and Norris 1982) but agree with studies on captive breeding birds.

IMMATURE: resembles adult ♀ although appearance neater with freckled pattern finer and warmer in tone. ♂ begins to show bill coloration after 6 months but never brighter than nonbreeding adult. ♂ head often appears longer than ♀.

DUCKLING: uniformly light grey, slightly paler below with pale grey legs; bill grey-blue initially, losing blueness well before fledging at 7 weeks; iris black-brown. Superficially resembles tiny cygnet. First feathers appear at 4 weeks.

MEASUREMENTS AND WEIGHT: from wild birds, ♂ wing (*n* = 62), 186–258 (232); tail (*n* = 13), 65–77 (69); bill (*n* = 63), 50–59 (54); tarsus (*n* = 13), 41–49 (48); weight (*n* = 63), 747–1130 (969). ♀ wing (*n* = 31), 205–236 (224); tail (*n* = 12), 64–71 (66); bill (*n* = 29), 46–53 (52); tarsus (*n* = 13), 42–47 (44); weight (*n* = 31), 691–985 (842) (Marchant and Higgins 1990). Another sample gave mean values ♂ (*n* = 97) wing, 234; bill, 57; tarsus, 48; weight, 994. ♀ (*n* = 83) wing, 222; bill, 51; tarsus, 45; weight, 839 (Norman and Norris 1982).

Field characters

Medium-sized, dark coloured duck, 510–560 mm long. In silhouette, large head with slight crest, long neck and narrow, retroussé heavy-based bill diagnostic. No marked wing pattern in flight. Sexes not easily separated in field if ♂ lacks red on bill. May appear similar to Pacific Black Duck but slower to rise from water and, with neck and head carried low in flight, giving hunchback appearance. Swims buoyantly, sitting high on water, and takes off after short run with slow climb but can rise rapidly if pressed. Wingbeat fast but does not manoeuvre acutely in flight. Lands rather heavily on outstretched feet from shallow approach. When loafing ashore, often sits in extreme upright stance with bill tucked below scapulars. Most easily confused with Hardhead (particularly when loafing) but lacks white patch undertail and white wing stripe visible in flight.

Voice

Generally silent and calls usually difficult to detect in field. Most adult calls deep Roars, best described as between soft growl and snorting hiss. Raucous Roar given by both sexes, uttered with bill open, somewhat querulous and vibrant. Axle-grind call of ♂ sounds like rapid double squeaky note (actually more complex but see details in Fullagar *et al.* 1990, Marchant and Higgins 1990). Head-Raised-Chin-Lift call of ♀ throaty chuckle. Defence call of ♀ at nest or with brood explosive version of Roar and similar or identical to distress call. Alarm call of ♀ loud clipped version of Roar. Greeting calls seem feeble versions of Roar but constantly uttered soft call of ♀ often heard at close range.

Call of newly hatched duckling cricket-like trill that functions as appeasement, distress and alarm in contact with ♀ parent and siblings. This call continues to be given in gradually modified form to well beyond time young feathered. Syringeal bulla absent, and trachea of adult ♂ not looped (*contra* Frith 1982). Further details on development of Axle-grind call in maturing ♂ illustrated by sonograms in Fullagar *et al.* (1990) and sonograms for most known calls in Marchant and Higgins (1990).

Range and status

Endemic and restricted to continental Australia; rare in Tasmania but common at times on Kangaroo Island. No extra-limital records. Stronghold in Murray-Darling watershed but also found in southwestern Australia and vagrant elsewhere. High densities in northeast of South Australia and southwest

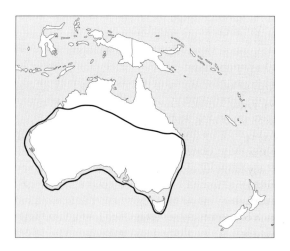

corner of Queensland (Kingsford and Porter 1994). Distribution follows changing environmental patterns; dry season or drought conditions cause high concentration on what little water remains, and erratic distribution to more permanent wetlands, mainly to coastal swamps. Population difficult to census, and numbers vary considerably. Martindale (1984, 1986) estimated 19 000. Aerial surveys conducted over southeastern Australia 1983–99 indicated abundance varied, with no significant decline over period (Kingsford *et al.* 2000). Estimates of total population suggest 5000–120 000 during last 30 years.

Habitat and general habits

In nonbreeding range prefers coastal swamps or large permanent open waters, often saline, which may have little or no emergent vegetation. In breeding range prefers freshwater vegetated with lignum *Muehlenbeckia* or canegrass *Eragrostis*. Breeding restricted to small areas in southwest Western Australia (occasionally) and widely within Murray-Darling catchment of southeast Australia. Evidence to suggest that irruptions occur irregularly but particularly following extensive flooding inland. Breeding takes place if suitable nesting habitat available but, as floods recede, concentrates and eventually disperses when inland wetlands become dry. Some details on such events 1876–1989 summarized in Marchant and Higgins (1990).

Frequently gregarious. Often found loafing ashore during daytime. Can be found on variety of waterbodies from coastal swamps to floodplains associated with Murray-Darling catchment and channel country of Diamentina and Cooper. Utilization of open, fresh and hypersaline lakes (Halse and Jaensch 1989) frequent, although few breed on saline lakes. Not found in marine or estuarine habitats. Dives only when bathing or to escape. Walks easily on land, though shuffles onto perches from water in clumsy fashion.

Specialist filter feeder (Crome 1985). Feeds by scything from side to side as advances, either walking or swimming, but all time 'suzzling' rapidly at surface or on bottom; if necessary will up-end to reach bottom. Feeds at any time but usually crepuscular or nocturnal. Takes particularly invertebrates

from shallow wetland margins, and filters around algae-covered objects in water. Seeds and other vegetable matter often ingested as by-catch (Briggs 1982). Details of feeding method and diet summarized in Marchant and Higgins (1990).

Displays and breeding behaviour

Comprehensive study of display, based on captive specimens supported by field observation from northwest of New South Wales including Paroo River system where wild birds bred (Fullagar *et al.* 1990). Pre-flight signal vertical Head-pumping without calling (Fullagar *et al.* 1990). In wild, pair-bond seasonal, short-term, sequential and monogamous but, in captivity in Australia and England, pairs maintained or reformed in following year. Some evidence of polygamous matings in captivity and possibly in wild. Gregarious during nonbreeding season, lives in well-dispersed pairs or small groups during reproductive periods. Bond formed during receptive period and lasts until clutch laid. At least early in incubation, ♂ may accompany ♀. ♂♂ play no part in brood rearing. Breeding displays and vocalizations not spectacular and easily overlooked. ♂ nest-builds using movements exactly like those of ♀, and ♂ often prepares presentable platform before ♀ adopts site for nest. ♂ sometimes guards site even when 1st eggs laid, defending site uttering Raucous Roar. Dominance indicated by thrusting head forward with bill slightly open while giving short hiss-like Raucous Roar. Also vigorous tail wags, used by both sexes, indicative of dominance. Sometimes clash and briefly spar face to face accompanied by much Raucous Roaring leading occasionally to fights with both attempting to jab at other's bill, head or neck (more details in Marchant and Higgins 1990). ♀ defends nest site and small young with forward thrusts while giving loud growls. Injury-feigning by ♀ with brood takes form of wing flailing across surface. ♂ advertising display appears to be communal courtship centred around receptive ♀. Only ♂ advertising display is Axle-grind mostly performed on water. While swimming, bill of ♂ points down and quickly flicks from side to side, head then stretched forward and Axle-grind call uttered; as head reaches outstretched position, noticeable throbbing of upper throat occurs; final part of display simultaneous return of head to normal position and brief tail wag (details and illustrations in Fullagar *et al.* 1990, Marchant and Higgins 1990). ♀ response to Axle-grind is to give Head-Raised-Chin-Lift (HRCL) signal in which head raised and bill flicked upwards slowly and irregularly through small arc at same time giving distinctive throaty chuckle. Once partnership formed, ♂ tends to defend mate by swimming with her or using Raucous Roar and outstretched neck and head towards all intruding ♂♂, thus reinforcing bond until egg-laying. Upward Nod by ducklings (from time of hatching) similar to HRCL of ♀. No obvious submissive displays known at any age. Copulation brief and performed on water and not introduced or followed by any elaborate display. After coitus and dismount, long 100 mm pseudopenis may temporarily connect partners. Male then usually preens vent region as organ retracts within cloaca. Copulation not repeated frequently (more details in Marchant and Higgins 1990). Comfort movements similar to other dabbling ducks (Marchant and Higgins 1990).

Breeding and life cycle

Breeding season broadly June–Dec. In captivity in Australia, clutches laid in most months but at WWT, Slimbridge has laid as early as Jan although main bulk of egg-laying Apr–late July. Sites in wild well constructed, usually of fine sticks or debris and close to water level; often well dispersed. Nest requires horizontal support and easy access (details in Marchant and Higgins 1990). Does not lay in elevated holes in trees. In captivity, incubating ♀ defends site vigorously. Nests usually found in Lignum *Muehlenbeckia cunninghamii*, but paperbarks and ti-tree *Melaleuca* used in some areas and sometimes uses concealed site in other types of thick cover (e.g. debris on banks of streams or billabongs) and often takes over nest of other waterbirds, particularly coot *Fulica*.

Eggs pale creamy white, thick shelled, smooth and lustrous, glossy or greasy to touch and oval; 63×47 ($n = 81$) (Frith 1982) or 62.4×45.3 ($n = 19$) (Braithwaite 1976b); in captivity 64.2×46.3 ($n = 20$); weight 75.9 ($n = 39$); clutch in wild probably 5–7 but records complicated by dumping; average clutch in captivity 4.8 ($n = 15$). Wispy light grey down added by ♀ before completion of clutch with quantity variable. Down easily dislodged and often insufficient to cover eggs when ♀ absent. In captivity, egg usually laid daily, in early morning, with occasional gaps. Random egg dumping frequent in captivity and found in wild. Usually occurs before incubation commences, but new eggs found in well incubated clutches, and would naturally be abandoned. Evidence reviewed in detail in Marchant and Higgins (1990) does not suggest strategic pattern of dumping by certain ♀♀. Incubation, by ♀ alone, 28 days (Frith 1982) and data from captivity support this, although eggs may hatch day earlier or later. During incubation, ♀ leaves nest in late afternoon or early evening, and again at dawn and, on these occasions, ♀ sometimes accompanied ♂ during recess. ♂ otherwise loafs near nest site during most of day.

After hatching, ♀ broods ducklings on nest for 24 h and, on 2nd day, leads them to water. Brooding occurs on nest for few nights in captivity, although this not reported in wild (Braithwaite 1976b). ♀ intensely defensive of brood for up to 5 weeks. Weight at hatching probably 40–50 (Frith 1982). Young able to fly at 7 weeks. Details of growth, based on observations in captivity, in Marchant and Higgins (1990). No data on breeding success in wild, adult survival nor on longevity.

Conservation and threats

Has full protection throughout Australia. Tends to be abundant on inland wetlands well distant from main hunting areas (Marchant and Higgins 1990, Norman *et al.* 1994) but may occur on hunting areas during dry periods. Historically frequent on coastal wetlands when these wetlands more extensive, but loss of coastal habitat affected distribution. Formerly bred on many coastal swamps, particularly seasonally ephemeral ones (Marchant and Higgins 1990). Occurs in relatively low numbers that fluctuate widely and, at times, has undoubtedly declined to very low numbers in surviving population (Frith 1982, Marchant and Higgins 1990, Norman and Horton 1993). Improved monitoring and programme to educate hunters in proper identification reduced hunting hazard in Victoria (Holmes 1994). Closure of wetlands occupied by significant numbers during hunting seasons is effective management option (Kingsford *et al.* 2000).

Most Australian authorities agree should be placed in Near Threatened or Vulnerable category. Recently, captive breeding colonies established in UK and North America following export of 4 birds in 1985 and 10 more in 1992. Whilst these overseas colonies have expanded successfully, few birds now held in captivity in Australia and captive breeding is insecure.

Peter Fullagar, Chris Davey,
Phil Shepherd and Clive Peters

The stiff-tailed ducks and their allies

The most aquatic of all ducks are the stifftails. They have short, rounded wings and most have long stiffened tail feathers. Their tails are often lifted and carried at an angle to the surface, and are much used in display. Specialized divers, they have legs placed so far back on their bodies that walking is difficult; the three forward toes are large and fully webbed and the hind toe, like that of other diving ducks, is lobed. Their diet contains both small animals and seeds which are strained from the bottom ooze of muddy ponds; chironomid larvae are a favourite food. At about six months of age, stifftails undergo a full post-juvenile body-moult that includes the wings and the tail; thereafter wing and tail feathers are moulted twice per year. The tail feathers, which are used to change direction under water, probably wear out rapidly and need to be replaced more than once a year. The mechanisms whereby the tail and wing quills are shed are not thoroughly understood, but may be physiologically linked so that one cannot be moulted without the other. The phenomenon of a double tail moult perhaps could not have evolved if two annual periods of flightlessness had been an enormous disadvantage but, presumably, to these most water-adapted of ducks, any such drawback is negligible in comparison with the potential loss of an effective rudder (Murton and Kear 1978). More research is needed.

All stifftails are sexually dimorphic in breeding plumage, and typically the males have a dull female-like plumage that lasts for quite a long period of the year. They acquire their ruddy colours, and their bright bills, shortly before the nesting season starts. There is evidence, especially from captivity, that this bright nuptial dress can be suppressed in subordinate males by dominant brightly coloured ones living on the same pond. Sexual maturity can be reached in 12 months. All male ducks, geese and swans have intromittant organs (equivalent to a penis) for the transfer of sperm to the female's oviduct, but those of stifftails are remarkably large and elaborate (McCracken *et al.* 2001b) and may be involved in sperm competition, since their size seems related to the frequency of forced copulation (Coker *et al.* 2002).

Since stifftails have little need to fly, except during migration, their courtship lacks the aerial displays and pursuit flights that are so common in ducks less specialized as divers. The males frequently produce sounds, not from the windpipe like other ducks, but by using inflatable air sacs under the skin of the throat, or by slapping their feet on the water. Despite elaborate courtship displays (Tail-cocking, Bill-dipping, various surface Rushes, and Sousing— see later) (Johnsgard 1961a, 1965a, 1978, Johnsgard and Carbonell 1996), pairbonds are short or nonexistent, and males take no part in parental care. Females also lack the Decrescendo and Inciting calls that characterize the dabbling ducks (Livezey 1995b).

Nests are built over water by the female—often the old nest of a coot will be used—without the copious quantities of down typical of most wildfowl. Eggs are large, proportionately the largest of all the ducks; for example, the White-headed Duck lays an egg that, at 96 g, is over 15% of her own weight, and she typically produces six in a clutch. From these hatch active, diving, well-insulated young that need relatively little care, even from their mother; so much is this the case, that stifftails regularly lay eggs in the nests of other birds, leaving their ducklings to be reared by surrogate parents. The only obligate brood parasite among the ducks is the Black-headed Duck, the offspring of which receive no attention from any adult bird beyond incubation (Rees and Hillgarth 1984).

Janet Kear

Taxonomy

Stiff-tailed ducks of the subfamily Oxyurinae are among the most distinctive wildfowl. Most authors agree that they diverged relatively early from other ducks (Delacour and Mayr 1945, Johnsgard 1965a, 1978, Raikow 1970, Bottjer 1983, Patton and Avise 1986, Madsen *et al.* 1988, Sibley and Ahlquist 1990, Harshman 1996, Sraml *et al.* 1996). However, Brush (1976) and Livezey (1986a, 1995b) believed them to be the sister group of seaducks.

The earliest known stifftail fossil is a Masked Duck-like bird, *Oxyura* cf. *Dominica*, from the late Miocene of Florida, US (Becker 1987). The distribution of Holocene species covers fresh and brackish waters of most of the Americas and Australia, and limited areas of Eurasia and Africa. Species diversity is highest in the southern hemisphere, particularly South America (Figure 9.13).

Stiff-tailed ducks traditionally were composed of four groups: (a) Black-headed Duck; (b) Masked Duck; (c) *Oxyura* species; and (d) Musk Duck (which we have removed to a separate position). The Black-headed Duck was considered a link between the stifftails and surface-feeding ducks (Delacour and Mayr 1945, Johnsgard 1961a, Raikow 1970, Brush 1976, Livezey 1995b), and mitochondrial DNA sequencing studies supported a relatively early divergence before that of the Masked Duck and *Oxyura* (McCracken *et al.* 1999). The Black-headed Duck is unusual as a stifftail since it feeds primarily by dabbling, shows only weak sexual dichromatism,

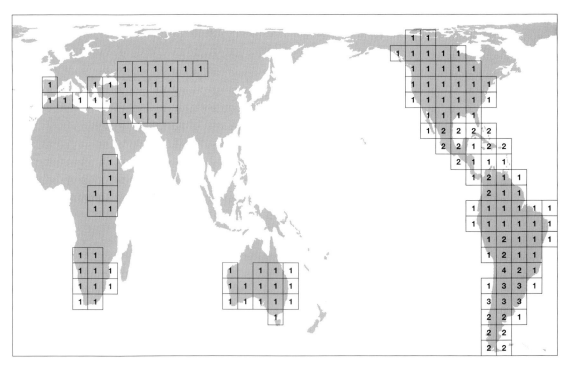

9.13 Species diversity of stiff-tailed ducks (Oxyurini) that survived into the Holocene. The number of species that occur (or occurred) within each grid-cell is indicated.

and retains many non-stifftail-like characters in the duckling (Weller 1967c, 1968a, Rees and Hillgarth 1984, Livezey 1986, 1995b, Johnsgard and Carbonell 1996). It is also the only obligate nest parasite within anseriforms (Rees and Hillgarth 1984, Johnsgard and Carbonell 1996).

Of the typical stifftails (i.e. *Nomonyx*, *Oxyura*), the Masked Duck is the sister of the rest (Phillips 1922–26, Delacour and Mayr 1945, Johnsgard 1961a, 1978, McCracken *et al.* 1999) (Figure 9.14). Masked Ducks exhibit several characters unusual to stifftails, for example, a shiny speculum on the wing, ability to take-off from the water vertically, a less recurved bill nail, and several characters of the skeleton (Delacour 1954–64, Livezey 1986a, Johnsgard and Carbonell 1996). Taxonomists have disagreed about whether or not Masked Duck should be classified in the same genus as the *Oxyura* stifftails. Ridgway (1880) split it

into the genus *Nomonyx* on the basis of its less recurved bill nail. Delacour and Mayr (1945) subsequently dropped *Nomonyx*, which was reinstated by Woolfenden (1961). Livezey (1995b) also recognized *Nomonyx* as a separate genus, but Johnsgard and Carbonell (1996) did not. McCracken *et al.* (1999) demonstrated that *Nomonyx* is the sister group to *Oxyura* and recommended retaining the genus *Nomonyx* based on the large genetic distance between *Nomonyx* and *Oxyura*.

Oxyura species have been classified traditionally into two geographically distinct groups: (a) the northern species—Ruddy Duck (including *O. j. andina* and *O. j. ferruginea*) and White-headed Duck; and (b) the southern black-headed species, the Blue-billed Duck, Maccoa, and Argentine Ruddy Duck (Phillips 1922–26, Delacour 1954–64, Johnsgard 1961a, 1965a, 1966a). The southern species

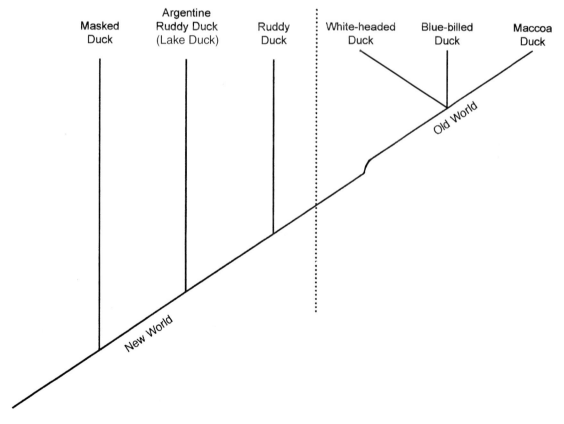

9.14 Evolutionary relationships of the stiff-tailed ducks (Oxyurini) (after McCracken and Sorenson 2004).

share a number of displays that are not performed by the northern ones (Johnsgard 1966a, Johnsgard and Nordeen 1981, Johnsgard and Carbonell 1996). However, Livezey (1995b) split *Oxyura* into three lineages: (a) Ruddy Duck (including *O. j. andina*); (b) Andean Ruddy Duck, Argentine Ruddy Duck and Blue-billed Duck; and (c) Maccoa and White-headed Duck. Molecular analyses (e.g. McCracken and Sorenson 2004) supported a different pattern. The two New World species, the Argentine Ruddy Duck and the Ruddy Duck, probably diverged first following the Masked Duck. The Colombian Ruddy Duck (*O. j. andina*) and Andean Ruddy Duck (*O. j. ferruginea*) are close relatives of the Ruddy Duck *O. j. jamaicensis*. *O. j. andina* shares

mtDNA haplotypes with *O. j. jamaicensis* and *O. j. ferruginea*, but *O. j. ferruginea* appears to be monophyletic, sister to either *O. j. jamaicensis* or nested within *O. j. jamaicensis*. Todd (1979) and Fjeldså (1986) suggested that *O. j. andina* represents an intergrade or a relic Pleistocene population involving *O. j. jamaicensis* and *O. j. ferruginea*, with males approaching one or the other phenotype. The Old World species, the Blue-billed Duck, White-headed Duck and Maccoa Duck, are more recently diverged but the order in which they diverged remains unclear (McCracken and Sorenson 2004). The Old World species probably diversified rapidly.

Des Callaghan and Kevin McCracken

Black-headed Duck *Heteronetta atricapilla*
PLATE 30

Anas melanocephala Vieillot, 1816
Anas atricapilla Merrem, 1841, in Ersch and Gruber, Allgemeine Encycl. Wissen. Künste, sec. 1, **35**, p. 26 Buenos Aires
Heteronetta Salvadori, 1865

Etymology: *Heteronetta* Gr. *hetero* different plus *netta* duck, in reference to parasitic breeding habit; *atricapilla* L. for black *ater* and *ceps* head.

Other names: none in English. French: Canard à tete noire de l'Argentine; German: Schwarzkopfente; Spanish: Pato sapo, Pato riconero, Pato de color pardo; Pato cabeza negra (Argentina and Uruguay).

Variation: no subspecies.

Description

ADULT: slightly dimorphic, ♀ somewhat larger than ♂. ♂ head and neck black, chin whitish. Upperparts largely black, flecked and vermiculated rufous, contrasting with rufous brown breast and flanks, flecked darker. Undertail coverts reddish brown while remainder of underparts silvery white. Speculum lacking, but thin white wing bars on edges of greater coverts and secondaries. Flight feathers blackish, upperwing coverts grey brown, underwing coverts and axillaries white. Bill blue-grey with black tip and nail, bright red in breeding plumage, paler in nonbreeding season; legs and feet grey-brown with

darker webs (lacks strong lobed hind toe typical of *Oxyura*); iris dark brown. ♀ lacks black head and neck, otherwise resembles paler, drabber version of ♂. Mantle, back and uppertail blackish brown, underparts more buff. Dark brown crown, nape and eye-stripe, remainder of cheeks and neck buffish, flecked darker. Wing as ♂. Bill as ♂ but instead of red base has tinge of yellowish orange; iris brown.

MOULT: plumage similar in breeding and non-breeding periods, but somewhat brighter in former.

IMMATURE: as ♀, but with cheek feathers edged yellowish.

DUCKLING: blackish brown above and dark yellow below. Dark facial stripe below eye from bill to cheeks and pale superciliary stripe. Two dark yellow patches on back and small patch on each wing (Johnsgard and Carbonell 1996).

MEASUREMENTS AND WEIGHT: ♂ wing ($n = 71$), 157–178 (168); tail ($n = 70$), 44–57 (49); culmen ($n = 67$), 40.7–47.0 (44.1); tarsus ($n = 71$), 30.0–34.5 (32.0); weight ($n = 11$), 434–580 (513). ♀ wing ($n = 62$), 154–182 (172); tail ($n = 62$), 44–59 (52); culmen ($n = 57$), 41.0–48.1 (45.0); tarsus ($n = 63$), 28.0–35.0 (32.3); weight ($n = 13$), 470–630 (565) (Johnsgard and Carbonell 1996).

Field characters

'Jizz' more like dabbling duck than stifftail. Both sexes immediately recognizable by combination of elongate body, 350–380 mm long, short tail, small head, short thick neck, and bill with concave culmen. Also tends to swim somewhat front-heavy in water, with head forward and breast submerged. ♂ unlike other waterbirds with similar distribution. Argentine Ruddy Duck also has black head, but can be separated by typical stifftail 'jizz' (short, rounded body, relatively large head and long tail), bright chestnut breeding plumage and blue bill. Black-headed Ducks can also take off vertically from water rather than having to patter across surface to gain speed for lift-off. ♀♀ superficially resemble ♀ Cinnamon Teal, but have more rufous flanks and more uniform plumage coloration, lacking scalloped flank feathers, speculum and/or coloured wing coverts of ♀ ducks of South America.

Voice

Generally silent. ♀♀ do not quack, but give low clucking contact calls. ♂♂ utter 3 faint croaks followed by low piping calls during courtship. Ducklings uniquely lack piercing distress calls typical of waterfowl, presumably because of parasitic nesting habits and loss of parental care.

Range and status

Resident in central Chile and central Argentina, from Andean foothills to Buenos Aires. Probably breeds in southern Uruguay, but rare in southern Brazil, Bolivia and Paraguay. Mostly resident, but southern breeders may migrate north in nonbreeding season. Locally common, population estimated at 100 000–1 000 000 individuals (Rose and Scott 1997), but latter figure probably too high (Todd 1996).

Habitat and general habits

Generally shy and retiring, frequenting aquatic habitats surrounded by emergent vegetation, particularly bulrush (Weller 1967). Usually found in pairs or small groups on enclosed habitats during breeding season, but gregarious in winter, often mixing with other species on large, open water bodies. Will dive to feed, but prefers to dabble or up-end. While dabbling, may follow one another in manner of Shovelers. In contrast to other stifftails, mainly herbivorous,

Resident common
Resident less common

with bulrush seeds predominating in one diet study (Weller 1968), though animal matter commonly taken during breeding season.

Displays and breeding behaviour

Lacks elaborate courtship displays. Apart from ritualized Head and Wing-shaking, ♂♂ have one major, rather fleeting, display sequence—Toad Call (figures in Johnsgard and Carbonell 1996), analogous to Head-pumping display of other stifftails, and may be performed during courtship or aggressive encounters. ♂ inflates neck and cheeks, lifts tail and wings, then lowers tail while raising head. As wings and head fully raised, bill withdrawn and wings lowered. Head then lowered and pulled back quickly while wings raised once more. ♂ shakes tail and assumes normal swimming posture. This Head-pumping sequence, which lasts seconds, accompanies barely audible croaks and piping calls. ♀♀ have few displays and no Inciting behaviour, but mutual Head-pumping occurs prior to copulation.

Unique among waterfowl in being obligate brood parasite; does not build or incubate, and reproduces by laying in other birds' nests. At least 18 species parasitized (Todd 1996), most commonly Red-fronted Coot *Fulica rufifrons* and Rosy-billed Pochard, but also unsuitable hosts such as Brown-hooded Gull *Larus maculipennis* and Chimango Caracaras *Milvago chimango*. ♀ appears less selective in choice of host than in choice of nesting habitat, preferring to lay in nests located in dense emergent vegetation. Pairbond formed, but promiscuity and mate switching common. Few wild birds remain paired beyond egg-laying. As might be expected of obligate brood parasite, territoriality absent.

Breeding and life cycle

Breeding, which in Argentina extends Sept–Dec, protracted in common with other stifftails, and probably necessitated by poor duckling production resulting from parasitic nesting. Adults spend much time searching for host nests, concentrating egg-laying activity in early morning and late evening. ♀ targets hosts that are egg-laying, mostly entering nests to lay when host absent, but will force ♀♀ from nest (Rees and Hillgarth 1984). Number of eggs laid by individual ♀ poorly known, but reported 5–16 (Todd 1996) when host nests hold 1–8 eggs, with 1–2 norm (Weller 1968a, Peña 1976, Nores and Yzurieta 1980). In common with other stifftails, eggs large, weighing up to 20% of ♀'s body weight, but incubated for only 22–25 days (Johnsgard and Carbonell 1996), shorter than incubation of most host species, thus maximizing chances of hatching successfully. Eggshells not thicker nor rounder than other nonparasitic ducks (Mallory 2000); 60.0 × 43.6 (55.3–61.7 × 40.2– 45.1) (*n* = 21); weight 60.9 (57.9–65.1) (*n* = 4) (Carbonell 1983).

Ducklings, weighing 36.9 (30.5–41.5) on hatching (Carbonell 1983), leave nest after 24 h and usually desert surrogate family within few days. Survive to fledging at 10 weeks without parental care. As means of maximizing survival chances, are relatively large and have thicker down than other stifftails (Todd 1996); nevertheless, proportion of young surviving to fledging apparently low (Johnsgard and Carbonell 1996), perhaps explaining need for large clutch size and extended breeding season. Little information from wild populations on survival rates nor on prevalence of disease, although captives at 52°N particularly susceptible to pneumonia (Hillgarth and Kear 1982b).

Little information on predators, but Long-winged Harrier *Circus buffoni* and Cinereous Harrier *C. cinereus*, both common in marshland habitat, may take young and adults, while Crested Caracara and Chimango Caracaras may predate eggs.

Conservation and threats

Population reportedly stable (Rose and Scott 1997) but could be threatened by wetland loss, degradation and pollution. Reduction in hunting pressure and establishment of reserve areas needed. May be relatively more vulnerable than sympatric wetland birds because of reliance on other species for incubation.

Baz Hughes

Masked Duck *Nomonyx dominicus*
PLATE 29

Anas dominica Linnaeus, 1766, Syst. Nat., ed. 12, **1**, p. 201
South America = Santo Domingo
Nomonyx Ridgeway, 1880

Etymology: *onux* Gr. means nail or claw, plus *nomos* regular or orderly, and refers to distinctive nail on upper mandible; *dominicus* means of Dominica. Common name from ♂'s facial 'mask'.

Other names: many, including White-winged Lake Duck and Squat Duck. French: Canard masqué; Spanish: Pato Agostero, Pato Timido, plus other names in various South American countries (see Johnsgard and Carbonell 1996).

Variation: no subspecies.

Description

ADULT: dimorphic. ♂ black face mask extending to rear crown and neck, but nape same rufous red-brown as remainder of upperparts and flanks. Upperparts distinctly scalloped blackish, less so underparts.

Belly and breast have whitish wash, but less so than other stifftails. Tail and wings blackish, noticeable white speculum on secondaries, median and greater coverts. Underwing blackish with white axillaries. Bill bright but pale blue, fading slightly towards base and towards broad black tip, black line on culmen from nostrils to nail; legs and feet greyish or grey-green; eye dark brown with pale bluish eye-ring. ♀ characteristic narrow double dark stripe on pale buff cheeks. Body plumage rufous brown, heavily streaked dark brown, more so on upperparts. Cheeks, throat and upperneck buff. Tail and wings as ♂, but slightly paler underwings and less extensive white speculum, especially on median coverts. Bill slate grey with blackish nail; feet and legs greyish; eye dark brown.

MOULT: ♂ in eclipse resembles ♀, but with larger white wing patch, less contrasting face pattern, wider lower cheek stripe and paler, more contrasting flanks. ♀ in eclipse has body plumage lacking rufous tones, becoming paler sandy buff thus contrasting more with dark brown streaking. As other stifftails, both sexes undergo 2 body and wing moults annually, spaced at *c* equal intervals (Palmer 1976), and tail feathers moulted gradually rather than simultaneously.

IMMATURE: no detailed information. As ♀, but with more uniform underparts, darker crown, and more extensive pale barring to upperparts. As in all stifftails, tail feathers have notched tips and are narrower and slightly paler than in subsequent generations.

DUCKLING: blackish above and yellowish brown below. Face quite yellow, unlike most *Oxyura*. Crown sepia, with 2 yellowish superciliary and upper cheek bands separated by 2 dark brown stripes; 2 pairs of small yellow patches on either side of back (illustration and description in Nelson 1993). Long stiff tail feathers obvious.

MEASUREMENTS AND WEIGHT: although samples small, morphological sexual dimorphism appears less than in *Oxyura* species, with ♂ and ♀ probably not significantly different in size or weight. ♂

($n = 5$) wing, 136–138 (137); tail, 75–79 (77); culmen, 31.1–33.9 (32.0); tarsus, ($n = 5$) 26.1–27.6 (27.0); weight ($n = 19$), 359–449 (385). ♀ wing ($n = 5$), 132–139 (136); tail ($n = 4$), 74–79 (77); culmen ($n = 5$), 30.8–34.2 (32.0); tarsus ($n = 5$), 25.7–27.9 (26.9); weight ($n = 17$), 275–445 (346) (Johnsgard and Carbonell 1996). ♂ ($n = 12$) wing, 142–148 (145); tail, 81–85 (82); culmen, 31–33.9 (32.8); tarsus, 26–29 (27.6). ♀ ($n = 12$) wing, 136–148 (143); tail, 74–86 (80); culmen, 32–35 (33.8); tarsus, 27–28 (27.4) (Palmer 1976).

Field characters

Likely confused only with other stifftails (North American Ruddy Duck in North America, and Argentine Ruddy Duck in northern Argentina), but distinctive in inhabiting more enclosed waterbodies with dense emergent vegetation. Also smaller, 300–350 mm long, with larger head, longer tail (though this rarely held aloft), shorter, stubbier, less spatulate bill with broad black tip and less recurved nail. Body plumage characteristically scalloped black in ♂ (other ♂ stifftails reddish chestnut). ♀ has characteristic double dark cheek stripes and more contrasting plumage than ♀ *Oxyura*. White wing patches distinctive in flight, as is ability to take flight directly from water rather than running along surface to gain momentum. Subtle differences from other stifftails in posture and 'jizz' include thicker neck, flatter crown and larger eyes. When alert, may hold bill upwards and, when loafing, may sit with head further back, as White-backed Duck.

Voice

♂ utters distinctive *kirri-kirroo kirri-kirroo kirroo kirroo kirroo*, and dull *oo-oo-oo*, low in throat (Palmer 1976), likened to call of domestic pigeon (Johnsgard and Carbonell 1996). Quiet puffing sounds produced during Golf-Ball display apparently non-vocal (Palmer 1976). ♀ silent, but hisses like other ♀ stifftails when disturbed. Ducklings have high-pitched peeping voices typical of downy waterfowl (Johnsgard and Hagemeyer 1969).

Range and status

Mainly resident throughout West Indies and most of South America; absent only from eastern and

Resident common
Resident less common

lilies and Water Hyacinth *Eicchornia crassipes* (Wetmore 1918, Gómez-Dallmeier and Cringan 1990). Often seen in company of jacanas *Jacana* and Least Grebes *Podiceps dominicus* (Gómez-Dallmeier and Cringan 1990, Johnsgard and Carbonell 1996), presumably through similar habitat preferences. Dives when approached, subsequently emerging among water-lilies with only heads protruding from water (Renssen 1974). Apparently more vegetarian than other stifftails; however, detailed information lacking. Feeds mainly on seeds of smartweeds and wild millet (Weller 1968b, Crider *in* Johnsgard and Carbonell 1996), although invertebrates taken (Palmer 1976). Not active during day, small parties leaving late afternoon to feed elsewhere (Renssen 1974). Prefers to feed in relatively shallow water with dive times 20–30 sec in water 2 m deep (Jenni 1969, Johnsgard 1975). Foraging dives not preceded by forward leap as other stifftails (Eitniear 1999).

Displays and breeding behaviour

Little information. Johnsgard and Carbonell (1996) described and illustrated Golf-Ball display in which ♂ inflates upper neck to golf ball size while uttering low cooing noise; seems similar to Toad Call display of Black-headed Duck, but without associated Head-bobbing. Head-bobbing occurs when disturbed (Palmer 1976). Palmer (1976) described display similar to North American Ruddy Duck's Ringing-rush, in which ♂ rushes over water surface with head held forward; however, unclear whether courtship or aggressive behaviour involved. Tail raising, common in most *Oxyura* courtship, but absent in Black-headed Duck, unrecorded. Limited information suggests courtship display intermediate between Black-headed Duck and *Oxyura*, and perhaps more like former.

Scant information on mating systems and, indeed, on breeding biology. No evidence of territoriality, and pairbond probably of short duration.

Breeding and life cycle

Breeds apparently during wet season, although records of broods and of ♂♂ in breeding plumage throughout year. In south of range, nests primarily Nov–Dec (Todd 1996), while in West Indies and Venezuela, breeding peaks June–Oct (Downer and Sutton 1990, Gómez-Dallmeier and Cringan 1990).

southern areas where Peruvian Ruddy Duck and Argentine Ruddy Duck occur. Most common in Cuba, northern Argentina and Uruguay (Scott and Carbonell 1986). Uncommon along gulf coast of Mexico into southern Texas where numbers in winter increase following wet summers and tropical storms, with some remaining to breed. World population crudely guessed at 25 000–100 000 individuals, though Wetlands International (2002) made no estimate. Texas population estimated at 3800 (Eitniear 1999).

Habitat and general habits

Can be tame; Todd (1996) described 3 pairs in Texas in Apr 1996 approachable within 2 m. Usually, however, encountered infrequently due to secretive nature, gathering in pairs or small groups, less commonly in small flocks of up to 40 individuals, especially in nonbreeding season. Characteristically inhabits lowland lakes, swamps and forested rivers with dense cover of emergent vegetation, such as

Like other stifftails, uses little feather down in nest constructed by ♀ from emergent vegetation (reeds or sometimes rice stems), over water and often covered with domes of vegetation. Buffy white eggs lack chalky shell of other stifftails, smoother and smaller; 53.7–55.6 × 40.0–41.6 (*n* = 5) (Bond 1958); clutch of 4–6 (Wetmore 1965, Palmer 1976), laid one per day, but dump nesting and parasitic laying result in larger clutches, individual nests holding up to 27 eggs (Johnsgard and Carbonell 1996). Incubation perhaps overestimated at 28 days (Johnsgard and Carbonell 1996), during which time ♀ covers eggs before leaving nest (unlike other stifftails). Brood of 4 ducklings in Texas fledged in 45 days accompanied by 2 ♀-like birds, could indicate cooperative breeding (Eitniear 1999), but perhaps represents ♂ accompaniment of brood, since Palmer (1976) stated that ♂♂ attain ♀-like nonbreeding plumage while young still growing. Renssen (1974) also noted both ♂ and ♀ present with 4 half-grown young in Surinam in Nov. Predators of eggs include Crested Caracara, and nests may be parasitized by Black-headed Ducks (Johnsgard and Carbonell 1996).

Basically similar to stifftails in general structure, appearance, and biology, including important traits such as occurrence of twice yearly wing moult, and dump nesting. Reported 'playful stick-throwing behaviour' (Todd 1996), however, decidedly unstifftail-like! In many respects, resembles Black-headed Duck in agility on land, flying directly from water, having sexes not different in size, and smallish eggs lacking chalky appearance.

No data on duckling survival, adult survival nor on longevity.

Conservation and threats

Among least known of non-threatened wildfowl; many aspects of general biology still undocumented. No data on long-term population trends. Wetland drainage and human disturbance pose threats, although secretive habits make these difficult to quantify. Legally hunted in Texas with daily bag limit of 6 birds (Lockwood 1997). Existence there threatened by wetland loss and degradation through invasion of aquatic weeds. Radio-tracking studies planned in Texas to provide data on movements and help document reproductive behaviour and ecology (Eitniear 1999).

Baz Hughes

Ruddy Duck *Oxyura jamaicensis*
PLATE 29

Anas jamaicensis Gmelin, 1789, Syst. Nat., **1**, p. 519 Jamaica
Oxyura Bonaparte, 1828

Etymology: *oxus* Gr. for sharp or pointed, plus *oura* tail, in reference to stiff tail; *jamaicensis* from Caribbean island of Jamaica where type specimen taken.

Other names: North American Ruddy Duck, plus *c* 100 colloquial names, including Butterball, Bumblebee Buzzer, Fool Duck, Hardhead, Noddy Paddy, Sleepy Head, and Tough Head (Kortright 1942); many relate to lack of daytime activity and to reputation among hunters of being easy to approach and shoot, but difficult to kill. French: Erismature or canard roux; German: Schwarzkopf Ruderente; Spanish: Malvasia canela, Pato rojizo alioscuro (see also Johnsgard and Carbonell 1996).

Variation: 3 subspecies recognized here: nominate North American Ruddy Duck *O. j. jamaicensis*; Peruvian Ruddy Duck *O. j. ferruginea* Eyton, 1838; and Colombian Ruddy Duck *O. j. andina* Lehmann, 1946. Some authors treat Peruvian Ruddy as full species (e.g. Livezey 1995), but not adopted here due to similarity of ♂ courtship and lack of unique display sequences. Colombian Ruddy Duck considered either intergrade between North American Ruddy Duck and Peruvian Ruddy Duck or hybrid between 2; high degree of variability in cheek plumage of ♂ apparently favours latter view (Fjeldså 1986). Phillips (1922–26) and Palmer (1976) followed separation of mainland and West Indian populations into 2 races *O. j. rubida* Wilson, 1814 and *O. j. jamaicensis*, respectively, but these doubtfully distinct.

Description

ADULT: dimorphic. ♂ distinctive in alternate plumage with bright cobalt blue bill, glossy black crown and nape, white cheeks and bright reddish chestnut body plumage. Darker chestnut brown upper breast with silvery white lower breast and belly. Undertail coverts strikingly white against dark brownish black tail. Legs and feet bluish grey; iris reddish brown. ♀ in alternate plumage, crown dark rufous brown. Cheeks and neck buff, mottled darker with pronounced dark brown stripe running from base of upper mandible back through pale cheek patch. Rest of upperparts dark brownish, barred and vermiculated lighter brown and often suffused chestnut. Lower breast and belly silvery white. Bill slaty often with blue patches; legs slaty black to dark brown, webs black; iris brown.

ferruginea ♂ in alternate plumage similar to nominate race but darker reddish chestnut body plumage and wholly black head. ♂ in basic plumage and ♀ similar to nominate form but with darker, blackish plumage and less pronounced cheek stripe.

andina similar to nominate race in all plumages, but ♀ shows variable amount of black on white cheeks, from almost wholly white to completely black (Fjeldså 1986); also has slightly stouter bill.

MOULT: ♂ in basic plumage, cheeks, tail and undertail coverts similar to alternate, but reddish chestnut body replaced by dark brown mantle and grey-brown neck, breast and flanks. Crown black/brown and bill blackish. ♀ in basic plumage has facial stripe more diffuse, chestnut tones lacking and bill lacking blue areas, but otherwise similar to alternate plumage. Data from captivity in UK and US suggest that all stifftails have 2 complete moults of wing and tail annually rather than one; however, recent isotope analysis of wild Ruddy Ducks suggests may not be norm for wild birds (Hobson *et al.* 2000). Plumage cycle also differs from most other waterfowl as nonbreeding feathers worn for ext-ended period from autumn through spring rather than for just month of late summer. Reasons for any double wing moult unclear, although see page 343. Full description of plumages and moult sequences in Johnsgard and Carbonell (1996).

IMMATURE: juvenile plumage retained until late winter. As basic ♀, but with paler cheeks giving more dark-capped appearance and more barred upperparts, especially flanks and rump. Sexes generally inseparable in field until prebasic moult when ♂ acquires white cheeks and blackish crown.

DUCKLING: sooty black with greyish white shoulder spots, breast, underparts and cheeks split by black-brown cheek stripe (illustrated and described in Nelson 1993). Stiff spiny tail, spatulate high-bridged bill, thick tarsi and short round body characteristic.

MEASUREMENTS AND WEIGHT: wild in UK, ♂ wing ($n = 62$), 144–158 (152); tail ($n = 78$), 70–84 (78); culmen ($n = 60$), 39.0–44.9 (41.9); tarsus ($n = 62$), 30.3–35.2 (32.9); weight ($n = 37$), 530–700 (588). ♀ ($n = 26$) wing, 142–153 (147); tail, 72–82 (77); culmen, 39.2–42.9 (41.1); tarsus, 29.5–33.6 (31.9); weight ($n = 22$), 450–845 (571). Linear measures from freshly dead ducks collected May–Aug 1993–94; weights from WWT Ringing Station at Abberton Reservoir, Mar–Sept 1981–88; ♀ weight includes laying birds, winter weights typically less than 600.

Field characters

Usually only observed on water where small size (length 350–430 mm) and long, often erect tail distinguish members of stifftail family. White cheeks and dark crown of ♂ separate from other stifftails, but ♀ may be confused with Masked Duck in Americas and White-headed Duck in Europe. Single, rather than double, cheek stripe and white supercilium best features to distinguish from ♀ Masked Duck, while smaller size, shorter tail, thinner cheek stripe and concave bill profile allow separation from ♀ White-headed Duck.

Voice

Both sexes generally silent except in breeding season. Bubbling display of ♂ begins with series of popping sounds as bill slapped on breast and ends with bi-syllabic Burp. Sequence best described as *tick-tick-tickety quo-ack* (Wetmore 1917) or *tick-tick-tick-tickety quek* (Wetmore 1920). Popping noise produced during Display-flight non-vocal, and results from feet slapping water surface (Miller *et al.* 1977). ♀ gives variety of hissing and squeaking noises when engaged in aggressive encounters. Ducklings utter variety of high-pitched *pee-pee* notes typical of most young waterfowl (Nelson

1993). Sonogram of duckling distress call in Kear (1968).

Range and status

North American population of *jamaicensis* thought to number *c* 500 000 birds (Wetlands International

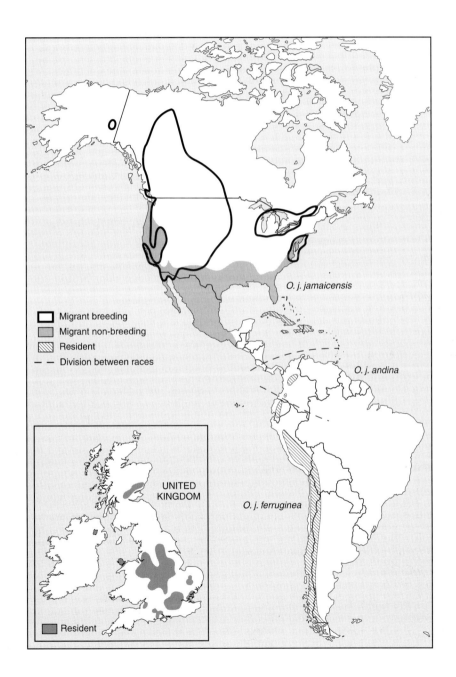

2002). Breeding range centres on northern prairies, extending southwards into inter-mountain basins and valleys of western US, but small numbers breed throughout North and Central America from Alaska to Mexico and Guatemala. Most winter on Pacific coast and west coast of Mexico (55%) and Atlantic coast (25%), remainder inland in southern US (Bellrose 1980). Stable population of some thousands resident in West Indies. Introduced population in UK (*c* 5000 in Jan 2000) nests mainly in central and northern England, moving south to winter; small numbers also attempt to breed annually in France, Belgium, The Netherlands, Morocco and Spain. In mid 1990s, Iceland held 10–15 breeders, thought to originate in UK.

andina, resident in Andes of central and eastern Colombia at 2500–4000 m, estimated at <10 000 birds. *ferruginea*, with total population of 25 000–100 000 birds (Wetlands International 2002), has more extensive distribution and occurs throughout eastern South America, from southern Andes to Tierra del Fuego and across lowlands of southern Argentina and Chile, where sympatric with Argentine Ruddy Duck.

Habitat and general habits

Disperses widely to breed on freshwater marshes, but congregates in winter in large flocks on coast or on large inland waterbodies. On freshwater habitats mainly carnivorous, feeding on invertebrate larvae throughout year (Gray 1980, Woodin and Swanson 1989); however, wide variety of animal or plant matter taken depending on availability. Forages mainly at night, especially during winter, but breeders may feed by day (Bergan *et al.* 1989, Tome 1991, Hughes 1992).

Displays and breeding behaviour

Highly charismatic ♂ courtship. Lowest intensity of major displays is Tail-flash in which ♂ manoeuvres himself, with tail cocked, in attempt to display white undertail coverts constantly to ♀. After aggressive encounters with other ♂♂, he often returns to ♀ in Surf-boarding posture: swimming with rear of body submerged, tracheal sac inflated, scapulars raised, neck drawn back and bill on breast. In Display-flight or Ringing-rush, ♂ assumes alert posture before suddenly snapping down tail and rushing across surface in Hunched posture, flapping wings

and slapping feet on water. Highest intensity display is Bubbling, in which ♂ assumes alert posture before beating breast with bill 6–12 times in increasing tempo, each beat accompanied by muffled popping sound. Display ends as ♂ stretches neck forward, lowers tail, opens bill and utters bi-syllabic *que-eck* call. These major displays often accompanied by variety of ritualized behaviours, such as Bill-flicking, Rolling-cheeks-on-back, Tail-shaking, Wing-shaking and Diving.

♀ does not perform courtship display, but often incites ♂ in aggressive manner, including by bodily assault. ♀ may perform variants of ♂ Bubbling display, but usually only in association with aggressive interactions. ♀ highly aggressive during short brood-rearing period, exhibiting highest interaction initiation rate of any waterbird (Hughes 1992). Pairbond short-lived, probably only lasting to confirm paternity of clutch.

Breeding and life cycle

Has protracted breeding season with eggs laid Apr–May and broods observed through summer, mainly Jun–Aug, but often until Sept or Oct (Cramp and Simmons 1977). Nest building by ♀, although both sexes build nest platforms before laying begins (Siegfried 1973a). Nests suspended over water in emergent vegetation. Onset of breeding controlled mainly by nutrient availability (Alisauskas and Ankney 1994b). Mean clutch usually 7 white eggs (Alisauskas and Ankney 1994a); large relative to ♀ size at 14.3%; 62.3 × 45.6 (59.4–67.6 × 42.6–48.0) (*n* = 80) (Bent 1925); calculated weight 73.0, based on dimensions of *n* = 110 (Schönwetter 1960–66), 73.3 (*n* = 56) in captivity in England (Johnsgard and Carbonell 1996), or in wild 74.1 ± 4.3 (60.5–83.8) (Pelayo and Clark 2002); laid at one per day, 95% at night or early morning (Alisauskas and Ankney 1994a). If conditions unsuitable for breeding, ♀ may dump eggs without attempting to incubate; dump nests in US may contain up to 80 eggs (Palmer 1976). Also lays parasitically in nests of other Ruddy Ducks or other species, although proportion of young reared from parasitically laid eggs low (Joyner 1983); ♀ incubates for 24 days, and adds little down to nest. If clutch lost, may re-nest at least once per season in wild (Tome 1987) and up to 4 times in captivity (Murton and Kear 1978). Extended breeding season beyond midsummer may allow ♀ to rear 2 broods a year (Palmer 1976).

Usually has high nesting success, with *c* 70% of nests producing young (Bellrose 1980), although Brua (1999) noted Mayfield nest success of 41%. Ducklings large, weighing 42.5 (*n* = 15) (Siegfried 1973b), or 48.6 ± 4.0 (38.2–55.3) (*n* = 50); in captivity, 44.4 (*n* = 72). Achieve independence quickly, as deserted by ♀ at *c* 3 weeks of age, some 4 weeks prior to fledging. ♂ sometimes seen with ♀ and brood.

Adults have no major predators during winter, except hunters—Johnsgard and Carbonell (1996) suggested that 15–20% of population might be harvested every year—but aggressive reaction or escape response towards certain species, notably large gulls and herons, suggests that predation occurs, as in White-headed Duck (Fox *et al.* 1994b). During breeding season, main predators of eggs are corvids, foxes, skunks *Mephitis* and Raccoons (Johnsgard and Carbonell 1996). Brown Rat *R. norvegicus* and American Mink *Mustela vison* prey on eggs and even on nesting ♀♀, who will fight rather than desert clutch (Low 1941). Gulls and herons main avian predators of ducklings, and fish such as pike and bass also hazardous. Avian botulism can be major cause of mortality in wild (Joyner 1975). Captive adults in England died mainly of tuberculosis, trauma and enteritis, ♀♀ also of egg peritonitis, perhaps reflecting large egg size (Hillgarth and Kear 1982b).

♀ capable of breeding at 1 year, although many may breed for 1st time at age 2. Adult survival rates unknown, but ringed individuals known to survive 13 years in wild, although majority die < 2 years after ringing.

Conservation and threats

Population now stable after earlier declines attributed to habitat loss, hunting pressure and oil spills on wintering grounds. West Indian population of nominate race, thought stable, but Colombian and Peruvian subspecies perhaps declining due to wetland loss (Callaghan and Green 1993, Wetlands International 2002), and listed as Endangered by Threatened Waterfowl Specialist Group (2003).

Main conservation concern is that introduced population thought to threaten European White-headed Duck with extinction through hybridization and competition (Hughes 1996a); see White-headed Duck account.

Baz Hughes

Argentine Ruddy Duck (Lake Duck) *Oxyura vittata*
PLATE 29

Erismatura vittata Philippi, 1860, Archiv Naturgeschichte **26**, pt. 1, p. 26
Chile

Etymology: *vittata* L. for banded or striped

Other names: Lake Duck, Argentine Blue-billed Duck. Spanish: Pato zambullidor, Pato toro (see Johnsgard and Carbonell 1996).

Variation: no subspecies. Although sympatric with Peruvian Ruddy Duck in Chile and Argentina, no hybrids reported, suggesting evolution of reproductive isolation mechanisms.

Description

ADULT: dimorphic. ♂ in breeding plumage, head and neck black reaching upper mantle on hind neck. Upperparts, breast and flanks rich, dark chestnut lacking reddish tones of North American Ruddy Duck. Underparts also chestnut, but with silvery white wash on centre of breast and on belly. Undertail coverts chestnut tipped greyish white. Wings dark brown above, greyish white below with pure white axillaries. Tail dark brown. Bill deep cobalt blue, pinkish yellow along cutting edge of mandible; legs olive grey to olive brown; iris dark brown. ♀ has tiger-barred plumage, crown and nape dark brown barred gingery brown. Chin, throat and cheeks whitish with narrow horizontal dark brown stripe, flecked paler. Mantle and uppertail coverts dark brown with fine buffish bars and vermiculations. Breast and underparts brown barred buffish white. Dark brown vertical bars on whitish flanks give characteristic barred appearance. Wing and tail as ♂. Bill slate grey; legs and feet bluish grey.

MOULT: eclipse ♂ as ♀, but with greyer head, whiter throat and more rufous body plumage with scattered chestnut feathers (Weller 1968b, Johnsgard and Carbonell 1996). ♀ in eclipse lacks warm brown plumage tones.

IMMATURE: as ♀, but paler above, browner below and with buff rather than whitish feather edging. Has typical narrow notched tail feathers until post-juvenile moult.

DUCKLING: dark blackish brown with no white except for line below eye and on chin and sides of neck; underparts whitish. No white markings on back; downy tail feathers dark brown and stiff; bill, legs and feet black (Johnsgard and Carbonell 1996).

MEASUREMENTS AND WEIGHT: captive birds, ♂ wing (*n* = 3), 142–168 (156); culmen (*n* = 16), 36–42 (39); tarsus (*n* = 4), 29.7–35.5 (33.2). ♀ wing (*n* = 4), 137–147 (144); culmen unrecorded; tarsus (*n* = 4), 31.8–33.9 (32.9) (Carbonell 1983). Weight, wild birds, ♂ (*n* = 3), 623–850 (718), ♀ (*n* = 1), 623 (Humphrey *et al.* 1970); captive birds, breeding ♀ (*n* = 4), 510–700 (585) (Carbonell 1983); ♂ in breeding condition, Nov, Rio Negro, Argentina (*n* = 5), 630 ± 24 (600–650) McCracken (2000).

Field characters

Typical stifftail 'jizz', 400–460 mm long. Similar to Peruvian Ruddy Duck, but ♂ can be separated by smaller size, proportionally longer, more graduated tail, shorter, stubbier, less spatulate bill and darker chestnut body plumage. Black head also extends further down neck, often onto upper mantle. ♀♀ easier to separate on plumage, since Argentine Ruddy Ducks sport characteristic barred flanks and upperparts, whiter cheeks with narrower, better defined cheek stripe, and more gingery plumage. ♀ Peruvian Ruddy Ducks have much darker, blackish rather than brown plumage, with less contrasting and diffuse cheek stripe. Masked Ducks smaller, with less concave bill profile and white wing patch in flight. ♂ Masked Ducks also have less extensive black head and dark markings on chestnut body plumage, while ♀ has characteristic dark cheek stripe.

Voice

Generally silent; displaying ♂ drums and produces mechanical rustling noises during Wing-shaking. ♀ more vocal than other ♀ stifftails, giving characteristic high-pitched, squeaking call when involved in aggressive encounters or when irritated by attentions of ♂. ♀♀ also hiss at intruders when disturbed, especially during incubation.

Range and status

Resident in Chilean lowlands from Atacama to Chiloe Island. East of Andes, resident in Uruguay and throughout Argentina to Tierra del Fuego. Some northward seasonal movements occur to Paraguay and central Brazil (Johnsgard and Carbonell 1996, Todd 1996). Argentine droughts can induce long-distance movements, such as in 1916–17 when Argentine Ruddy Ducks appeared on Falkland Islands and on Deception Island, 500 miles south of Cape Horn (Todd 1997). Only common in northern Argentina, total population crudely estimated at 10 000–100 000 birds (Ellis-Joseph *et al.* 1992, Rose and Scott 1997).

☐ Resident
☐ Areas of higher density

Habitat and general habits

Usually found on lowland waterbodies surrounded by emergent vegetation, but can occur up to 1200 m (Johnsgard and Carbonell 1996). Feeds mainly on benthic invertebrates and also aquatic vegetation, such as duckweed.

Displays and breeding behaviour

Nerk-jerking characteristic display (Johnsgard and Nordeen 1981, illustrated in Johnsgard and Carbonell 1996), in which ♂ rapidly bobs head up and down usually 6, but as many as 29, times. Onus is on upward thrust, performed much faster than downward movement. ♂'s most intense display is Sousing, in which assumes head-high posture, then raises tail to vertical position while uttering *prrr-prrr* call. Head then pumped 4–10 times as breast inflated and tail brought forward over back. This Head-pumping then develops into rocking motion until ♂ reaches upright posture with breast out of water and neck feathers fully erect, at which point he quickly splashes into water and begins series of 3–17 convulsive Chokes. These involve alternating hunched Neck-down, Bill-up-and-neck-up, Bill-down movements synchronized with drumming call. In common with other stifftails, ♂♂ perform as display ritualized versions of comfort movements, namely Bill-dipping, Cheek-rolling, Head-dipping, Dab-preening, and Wing-shaking accompanied by mechanical rustling noise.

Flotilla-swimming occurs in which groups of both sexes parade, swimming faster than normal while holding tails flat along water surface, ♂♂ uttering *prrr-prrr* noise. ♂♂ constantly jockey for position close to ♀♀, regularly Wing-shaking, and often becoming so engrossed that they seem oblivious to surroundings, even to presence of humans. Aggression between ♂♂ common, and sparring ♂♂ often square up, face-to-face, rearing vertically out of water and rapidly circling one another in comical synchronized dance. ♂♂ also rush over water surface in less ritualized, less extreme version of Surf-boarding display of Maccoa and North American Ruddy Duck, and similar to Motor-boating display of Australian Bluebill. ♀♀ appear uninterested in ♂ courtship, only reacting to threaten or attack displaying ♂♂.

Like other stifftails, disperse to breed, then congregate in flocks during nonbreeding season. Both sexes highly aggressive when breeding. Mating system apparently more monogamous than other stifftails (Johnsgard and Carbonell 1996), but promiscuity and forced extra-pair copulation common in captives (Todd 1996). Breeding ♂ possesses extraordinary intromittent organ, equal in length to that of Ostrich at *c* 223 ± 21 (190–245) mm, with surface covered in dense spines. Peculiarities of penile size, ornamentation and potential for sperm displacement may have evolved in conjunction with promiscuous, group display system where pairbond lasts only for copulation and ♀ guarding (McCracken 2000, Coker *et al.* 2002). ♂ defends ♀ from other ♂♂, but does not defend breeding territory.

Breeding and life cycle

Breeding occurs Oct–Jan in Argentina (Weller 1967b); however, in Chile, 2 nesting peaks reported though not defined (Johnson 1965).

Nests, built in emergent vegetation over water and without down, perhaps less elaborate than those of other stifftails. Many captive ♀♀ at Slimbridge site faithful, nesting in identical locations every year. Large white eggs (15.4% of ♀ body size); 66.7 × 47.5 (66.1–74.3 × 45.7–49.7) (*n* = 67); weight 82.6 (74.8–89.6) (*n* = 26) (Carbonell 1983), have chalky appearance of other stifftail eggs, but clutch size (3–5) typically smaller. Nest parasitism common, producing mixed clutches of up to 12 eggs. Incubation 23–24 days, and large independent ducklings, weighing 48.4 (43–58) (*n* = 24) at hatch (Carbonell 1983) tended by ♀ alone, but deserted after few weeks (Weller 1967b), surviving alone until fledging at 8–9 weeks. Although no data available from wild, most ♀♀ probably lay at 2 years. No data on breeding success, survival nor on longevity.

Conservation and threats

Population reportedly stable (Ellis-Joseph *et al.* 1992), although widespread surveys required. Hunting pressure apparently low, but may be threatened by wetland loss, and destruction of aquatic vegetation by cattle or by fishermen (del Hoyo *et al.* 1992, Todd 1996).

Baz Hughes

Blue-billed Duck *Oxyura australis*
PLATE 29

Oxyura Australis Gould, 1836, Proc. Zool. Soc. London, p. 85

Swan River, Western Australia

Etymology: *australis* L. means southern, or of Australia.

Other names: Australian Ruddy Duck, Little Musk Duck, Spiny-tailed or Stiff-tailed Duck, Bluebill, Stifftail, Spinetail, Diving Duck, Diver. Australian Aboriginal: Bood-doo, Bo-ta, Buata, Pukenjeri, Quut-tyaa-aqq, Teeriep; Dutch: Australische Stekelstaarteend; French: Erismature australe; German: Schwartzkinn-Ruderente; Spanish: Malvasía Australiana.

Variation: no subspecies.

Description

ADULT: dimorphic. ♂ has glossy jet-black head with most of body chestnut; only lower breast and belly silver-grey with undertail silvery white. Wings dark brown above, no speculum, mottled off white below. Bill conspicuous sky-blue; legs and feet mid grey; iris dark brown. ♀ uniformly medium grey with fine barring or vermiculation except for paler underparts. Faint pale stripe behind eye. Bill dark horn; legs, feet and iris as ♂.

MOULT: ♂ has seasonal plumage changes but not always obvious. Full eclipse ♂ plumage and bill colour similar to plumage and bill of adult ♀, but bill usually dark green with horn blotching at tip and head darker. Often bill colour fades to dull grey in ♂, and partially eclipsed plumage occurs when chestnut of body, especially on mantle, becomes mixed with dull ♀-like feathering. Most adults replace wing and tail feathers at intervals of *c* 6 months. Body moults more or less continuous with major plumage replacement post-breeding. Evidence, from captivity, that full expression of plumage colour of subordinate ♂♂ suppressed by presence of dominant birds in flock (Marchant and Higgins 1990).

IMMATURE: like ♀, and has complete body moult at 2–3 months. ♂ assumes adult colour at 6–10 months

depending on time of hatching (later hatched ♂♂ assume adult plumage earlier); this complete post-juvenile moult takes 1–2 months during which time blue bill of ♂ develops. At 6 months, 1st wing and tail moult occurs.

DUCKLING: dark grey to black, whitish on chin and underparts with indistinct paler spots on rump and wings, and faint pale stripe behind eye. Bill greyish black; legs and feet dark grey to greenish flesh with darker webs; iris blackish brown (Johnsgard and Carbonell 1996).

MEASUREMENTS AND WEIGHT: ♂ wing (*n* = 222), 150–173 (160); tail (*n* = 13), 64–71 (66.5); bill (*n* = 231), 37–48 (41); tarsus (*n* = 16), 35.4–39.2 (37.3); weight (*n* = 241), 610–965 (812). ♀ wing (*n* =153), 142–163 (153); tail (*n* = 7), 57–68 (64.6); bill (*n* = 122), 32–47 (41); tarsus (*n* = 8), 35.5–37.9 (37.1); weight (*n* = 140), 476–1300 (852) (Frith 1982, tail and tarsus from Marchant and Higgins 1990). ♀ especially heavy before egg-laying (Briggs 1988). Johnsgard and Carbonell (1996) suggested that ♂ to ♀ mass ratio normally 1.1:1, ♂ being slightly larger than ♀.

Field characters

Small compact duck, 350–440 mm long, with large rounded head and short neck. Bill prominent, broad with concave ridge. Conspicuous stiff tail often flat on water but distinctive if partly raised when loafing; held vertical when alarmed and, in ♂, during some courtship displays. In Australia, likely to be confused only with Musk Duck but much smaller and colours of adult ♂ usually unmistakable. Plumages, especially of breeding ♂, like those of Maccoa of South Africa, Argentine Bluebill and Peruvian and Andean subspecies of Ruddy Duck of Americas. Australian Blue-billed Duck does not overlap in range with any of these, but confusion can occur in captivity (Madge and Burn 1988, Johnsgard and Carbonell 1996). ♀ plumage darker and greyer than other ♀ stifftails, vermiculations reminiscent of Musk Duck and lacking pale cheeks. Low swimming profile characteristic of stifftails. Bluebills often rest on water with heads turned back and bill tucked below scapulars, and frequently roll over partly exposing undersides.

Voice

Generally silent and vocalizations rarely heard in field. ♂ makes several non-vocal sounds during courtship, often at dusk and at night. Thrashing sounds produced by rapid lateral tail wagging by ♂ (Whisking) and much louder rhythmic rippling noise also made by ♂ when smacking water with large feet during other dramatic performances. Latter sounds often audible at up to 1 km under still conditions. In some courtship displays, ♂ noisily expels air from bill dipped in water, and water often splashed about. ♂ has deep, low frequency throbbing *dunk-dunk-dunk* vocalization used before or during several courtship displays, and another soft wheezy scold-like call *chee-chee-che-chee-chee-* or *chit-chit-chit-* given with Look-each-way-and-dive display. ♀ almost always silent except for occasional soft, nasal, repeated call. Details of vocalizations and other sounds, plus sonograms, in Marchant and Higgins (1990).

Range and status

Endemic to Australia. Present in coastal regions of Western Australia, mainly in far southwest but has been recorded as far north as Pilbara and east to Esperance. In southeast, widespread throughout New South Wales and Victoria; rare in Tasmania. In South Australia, present mostly in southeast coastal region but range extends inland at times to northeastern parts of that state and to southern parts of Queensland. Eastern population mostly confined to Murray-Darling Basin but, at times of flood, found on some inland river systems flowing towards Lake Eyre from southwest Queensland. In Victoria, mostly present on coastal and near coastal wetlands in south. Widespread dispersal follows exceptional flooding events but otherwise generally sedentary especially on permanent wetlands where only minor short-distance seasonal movements occur (Marchant and Higgins 1990).

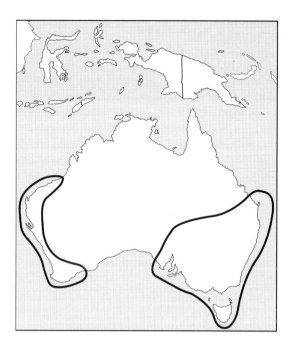

No reliable figures on population size, but counts suggest that world population unlikely to exceed 10 000 (some details summarized in Marchant and Higgins 1990).

Habitat and general habits

Wholly aquatic, and distribution restricted to terrestrial wetlands where prefers deeper, permanent freshwater; also found on saline wetlands and salt lakes but not on marine waters (Marchant and Higgins 1990). Usually remains far from shoreline and reluctant to fly in daytime, preferring to dive if alarmed. Rarely seen out of water or walking on land. Breeds on vegetated wetlands, nesting at or close to water level along shorelines, on small islands or in clumps of vegetation surrounded by water. Typically loafs on water during much of day, but periodically dives. Obtains food almost entirely by diving; diet includes range of aquatic animals (mostly invertebrates such as chironomid larvae) and plant material (details summarized in Marchant and Higgins 1990).

Generally gregarious, often forming large, loose flocks when not breeding, although these flocks break into smaller groups or into scattered pairs during breeding season.

Displays and breeding behaviour

Display repertoire probably most elaborate of all stifftails (Carbonell 1983, Marchant and Higgins 1990, Johnsgard and Carbonell 1996). ♂ generally aggressive towards other ♂♂ when breeding, but not so at other times. Chases occur with ruffled head and neck feathers and bill tucked low onto breast. Confrontations lead to Dab-preening in which spread tips of tail touch water, head held erect and bill pressed onto breast and rapidly vibrated sideways. Head raised jerkily and tilted forwards every time bill pulled into breast. Often this display followed by Bill-dip and Head-flick and Exhaling-into-water displays. Dab-preen performed by ♂ to other ♂♂ and sometimes reciprocated, but usually pursued ♂ dives to escape. Occasionally these confrontations lead to short fights, contestants briefly submerging locked together (Marchant and Higgins 1990). Dab-preening also performed by ♂ to ♀ and occasionally by ♀ to other ♀♀ and sometimes by ♀ to ♂♂. Threat in both sexes signalled by Gaping. In this posture, neck tucked in, head lowered and bill tilted upwards while bill held open. Body size inflated with feathers fluffed and wings slightly lifted. ♂ may give sharp grunt while gaping and ♀ often gives repeated soft bark call when gaping in defence of nest site or brood and to repel advances by ♂♂. Rapid Head-Pumping used to signal intention to dive and possibly also used as pre-flight signal.

Courtship displays often performed socially with several ♂♂ interacting with ♀♀; may occur at dusk or dawn and sometimes continue into early evening; accompanied by throbbing calls from ♂♂ and much splashing of water. ♂ shows intention to display in several ways—by head and body posture, fanning tail on water, cocking tail upright, and, particularly, by frequent dipping of bill into water and exhaling air or splashing water with rapid upward shaking action (Bill-dip-head-flick). Some or all of several other postures (most of which seem to be preening actions) may then follow in vanguard to more formal display, although seem to be used in no particular order: Head-shake, General Shake, Wing-ruffle, Wing-flaps, Head-pumping, Preen-dorsally, Swimming-low-and-flat, Hunch and High-head. Prominent action, termed Flotilla, involves several ♂♂ and ♀♀ (but often ♂♂ only) in which birds swim rapidly about, side by side with heads raised, seeming to jockey for position. Main display by ♂ involves Rolling-cheek-on-back (often to alternating sides), Dab-preening, Lurching (becomes rigid, paddles furiously to throw water over back while moving backwards slightly with bill in water then blows bubbles into water and lurches forwards by suddenly kicking feet causing plonk sound and water splash), Whisking (with head held low, tail rapidly shaken laterally on surface, causing soft thrashing sound, followed by rapid backwards kick, dipping bill into water and blowing and then raising body to give vibrant series of wing flaps), Look-each-way-and-dive (♂ close and facing ♀ with head up and half-open bill pointed down, sharp call given then head switched rapidly from side to side before ♂ plop-dives momentarily, emerging almost at point of entry). Ultimate stages of ♂ courtship involves 3 distinctive actions—complex but typical stifftail Sousing display with distended neck and constant utterance of low throbbing sound, Motor-boating (when he suddenly rears on water and dashes forwards creating bow-wave while planing over surface with rapidly thrashing feet), and Flutter-display (Display flights or Ringing Rush) when he Motor-boats but uses wings in shallow flight thus allowing feet to smack water more loudly. Sound of this display and of Motor-boating can be heard at distance (> 1 km) in calm conditions, and especially if displaying after dark (Marchant and Higgins 1990).

Copulates submerged after intensive chasing by ♂, with frequent dives; on surfacing, ♂ has extraordinarily long (80–100 mm) coiled pseudopenis everted and trailing in water. ♂ will preen vigorously, in particular half-rolling onto back and prodding at vent region while slowly retracting intromittent organ. Short term pairbond only for duration of copulation and laying. Polygamous. ♂ may re-unite with ♀ for re-nesting (Marchant and Higgins 1990).

Breeding and life cycle

Continuous opportunistic breeding probably normal (Marchant and Higgins 1990) but spring and summer most frequent season. Usually solitary nester with site concealed in vegetation at edge of water or surrounded by water. Nest platform and shallow nest bowl sparsely lined with down and sometimes no down present. Nest site becomes almost domed with continued weaving of surrounding materials by ♀ during incubation. ♀ gains considerable pre-laying weight (Briggs 1988), resulting in large eggs in proportion to body size. Eggs oval, coarse textured and lustreless, slightly pale green when fresh but becoming stained; 66 × 48 (64–72 × 45–51) (*n* = 62 from 12 clutches) (Frith 1982); estimated to weigh 84 (Johnsgard and Carbonell 1996); laid at 48 h intervals. Clutch probably 5 or 6 (3–7), but few reliable data and propensity for dump laying makes interpretation of observed larger clutches difficult. Re-laying occurs after loss of clutch or brood, and ♀ can rear 2 or more broods in season. ♀ alone incubates for 24 days (Marchant and Higgins 1990), leaving once a day to forage. Captive ducklings weigh 48.0 (*n* = 4) (Johnsgard and Carbonell 1996) at hatching. Brood attended by ♀; ♂ sometimes attends, but only to display to ♀. ♀ defends brood vigorously for *c* 12 days; ducklings probably remain close to ♀ for 28–35 days after hatching and become increasingly independent; fully independent at fledging by Day 60. Some data on growth rates given in Marchant and Higgins (1990) but little quantitative information on broods and fledging in wild. Most ♀♀ probably breed as yearlings but ♂ and ♀ capable of breeding at less than one year old (Marchant and Higgins 1990). No information on adult survival nor on longevity in wild.

Conservation and threats

Range restricted to southern parts of Australia where habitat requirements determine local distribution. Loss of suitable coastal wetlands might eventually be critical. Not gamebird in any State (Frith 1982). Not abundant, but currently in no danger, although population probably less than 10 000.

Peter Fullagar

Maccoa Duck *Oxyura maccoa*
PLATE 29

Erismatura maccoa Eyton, 1838, Monogr. Anatidae, p. 169
Indian Isles = South Africa

Etymology: *maccoa* may derive from African word *kacouw* or *macou* meaning goose (Johnsgard and Carbonell 1996).

Other names: none in common use, except Maccoa. Afrikaans: Makou-eend; French: Erismature maccoa; German: Maccoa-ente.

Variation: no subspecies.

Description

ADULT: dimorphic. ♂ in full breeding plumage, usually attained at 2 years, rarely at one, has sooty black head and upper neck, rich chestnut body plumage, cobalt blue bill and noticeable white eye-ring. Back and rump brownish, underparts grey-brown, tail coverts off-white. Tail and flight feathers blackish, upperwings grey-brown, underwings greyish white with white axillaries. Feet and legs greyish; iris dark brown. ♀ typical stifftail plumage, but with characteristic cheek bar somewhat broader than in other species. Head relatively larger and more rounded. Upperparts brownish grey with buff and white vermiculations, paler on flanks. In breeding plumage, upperparts warmer brown, especially on crown. Throat and chin greyish white grading to light brown on neck. Underparts grey brown washed silvery white on belly. Tail and wing as ♂, except upperwing coverts browner. Uppertail coverts brownish with off-white flecking. Bill dark grey with pale whitish tip; legs greyish.

MOULT: in nonbreeding plumage, worn May–July, ♂ resembles ♀, but has darker crown, and traces of chestnut may remain on upperparts (Siegfried 1968b). ♀ almost identical in nonbreeding plumage, but duller and lacking warm brown tones. Moult cycles similar to other stifftails, with adults replacing plumage twice a year and juveniles undergoing complete post-juvenile moult (Siegfried 1970).

IMMATURE: as ♀, but with darker crown, especially in ♂. Tail feathers narrower and with notched tips until post-juvenile moult.

DUCKLING: dark greyish brown above, with white line below eye less conspicuous than in North American Ruddy, and dark cheek markings that are larger and less distinct. Chin, throat, sides of neck and underparts off-white; white dorsal patches small. Dark brown tail with stiff shafts. Bill, legs and feet olive-grey to black; iris brown (Johnsgard and Carbonell 1996).

MEASUREMENTS AND WEIGHT: ♂ ($n - 4$) wing, 165–175 (171); tail, 64–71 (67); culmen, 38.5–42.0 (40.6). ♀ ($n = 5$) wing, 156–165 (161); tail, 64–71 (67); culmen, 35.5–40.0 (37.6) (Clancey 1967); ♂ tarsus ($n = 2$), 34 and 34, ♀ ($n = 1$), 31 (Maclean 1993). Weight ♂ ($n = 1$), 820; ♀ ($n = 3$), 516–580 (554) (Siegfried 1969, Brown *et al.* 1982); captive birds in England, ♂ ($n = 1$), 800, laying ♀ ($n = 11$), 580–720 (659) (Carbonell 1983).

Field characters

Only stifftail in Africa, can be identified by typical stifftail 'jizz' with large, thick-based bill, chunky body, 480–510 mm long, and long pointed tail often held aloft. Breeding ♂ unmistakeable with characteristic dark chestnut plumage, black head and cobalt blue bill. ♀, juvenile and eclipsed ♂ all have dusky brown body plumage, but swimming posture, distinctive horizontal dark brown cheek stripe and lack of vertical white face patches separate from Southern Pochard.

Voice

Both sexes relatively silent, but ♂ courtship and territorial display characterized by deep, bullfrog-like trumpeting and soft whistling. In threat display, either sex may utter soft grunting call.

Range and status

Two main populations in eastern and southern Africa. Northerly population fairly common in Ethiopia, Rwanda, Burundi, northern Tanzania and eastern Zaire, but less so in Kenya, Uganda, northern Tanzania and Sudan (Brown *et al.* 1982, Callaghan and Green 1993). Southern population most common in South Africa (Cape province and Transvaal highlands) and Namibia, less so in Zimbabwe, Lesotho, Malawi, Mozambique and Botswana. Total population estimated at 30 000–55 000 birds (Scott and Rose 1997), including 15 000–25 000 in east Africa where probably declining.

Habitat and general habits

Mainly sedentary, although local dispersal occurs during drought. Inhabits lowland waterbodies and dams through most of range, but may occur up to 3000 m in Ethiopia. In common with other stifftails, disperses to breed, but in nonbreeding season congregates in flocks of up to 1000. Prefers nutrient-rich, shallow, emergent fringed wetlands where feeds by diving, mainly on midge larvae and pupae from mud at lake bottom.

Displays and breeding behaviour

♂♂ do not display communally as other *Oxyura* but, along with 2 other black-headed southern hemisphere stifftails, have large repertoire of courtship display (Siegfried and van der Merwe 1975, Johnsgard 1968b, illustrated in Johnsgard and Carbonell 1996), many of which are ritualized versions of everyday behaviour.

Swimming-low-and-swift posture, in which head held low over water while swimming rapidly, used in many different contexts including territorial advertisement, aggressive encounters and on approaching ♀♀. ♂ shares 4 major displays with North American Ruddy Duck (Ringing-rush, Surf-boarding, Bill-dip-head-flick and Rolling-cheeks-on-back) and one with other black-headed stifftails (Sousing). However, 2 main displays are Vibrating trumpet call (VTC) and Independent vibrating trumpet call (IVTC); latter used in territorial advertisement, former in direct courtship of ♀♀. In VTC, which lasts for *c* 3 sec, ♂ starts in Swimming-low-and-swift posture, withdraws head then pushes it forward and downwards while inflating neck and erecting feather 'horns' on crown of

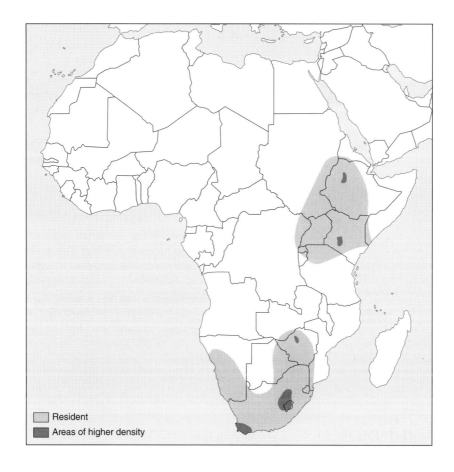

Resident
Areas of higher density

head. Tail then lifted vertically and bill lowered into water while uttering trumpeting or belching noise. In this display, ♂ presents himself sideways to ♀, but moves around her while performing. IVTC similar, but ♂ positions himself head-on to opponent, raises head vertically, stretches neck forward while raising tail at 45° angle before opening bill and uttering same bellowing noise as in VTC. This display also differs in that bill never touches water and tail does not reach vertical position.

Unlike most other waterfowl, ♂♂ highly territorial, aggressively defending patches of suitable breeding habitat for up to 3 months during breeding season (Clark 1964, Siegfried 1976c). These may extend for 80 m or more along front of emergent vegetation stands and encompass surface area of over 900 m². Polygynous and promiscuous mating system, and lack of pairbond, result in ♂♂ spending

much of day involved in reproductive behaviour—30% in total (15% in territorial defence and 15% in courtship display (Siegfried *et al.* 1976a)) compared to <5% in ♂ North American Ruddy Ducks (Hughes 1992). When not displaying, ♂ often rests in conspicuous position in order to promote territorial defence while conserving energy. Fitter ♂♂ defend larger or higher-quality territories in order to win access to more ♀♀, with up to 8 ♀♀ recorded in ♂'s territory (Siegfried 1976c). Dominance hierarchy exists in which only dominant ♂ acquires full breeding plumage (Siegfried 1985) and this is extreme when kept in close proximity in captivity. In captive enclosure in South Africa, ♂♂ in full colour rapidly moulted out breeding plumage on introduction of more dominant ♂. This even occurred when dominant birds of another species, African Black Duck, were introduced.

Breeding and life cycle

In South Africa, breeds during 10 months, July–Apr, with peak Oct–Nov, *c* 2 months later than dabbling ducks (Siegfried *et al.* 1976b). Nest, lacking feather down, built by ♀ in emergent vegetation over water; eggs 66.9 × 50.5 (63.0–72.5 × 46.7–52.5) (*n* = 54) (Brown *et al.* 1982); fresh mass 88 (73–98) (*n* = 8) (Siegfried 1969); laid at slightly less than one per day (Clark 1964). Clutch 6 (2–10) (mode 5) (*n* = 52); nests with more than 10 eggs probably parasitized by other ♀♀ (Clark 1964, Siegfried *et al.* 1976b) as, like other stifftails, regularly lays in nests of other birds, including Red-knobbed Coot *Fulica cristata* and Hottentot Teal (Dean 1970, Lees-May 1974). Such parasitic egg-laying and dump nesting especially common in years when availability of nesting cover reduced. Incubation, by ♀, 25–27 days, with newly hatched broods containing 3–4 large ducklings (Clark 1964) weighing on average 56 (Johnsgard and Carbonell 1996).

♂ does not attend ♀ after mating, and ♀ alone rears young to independence at 4–5 weeks (Clark 1964, Johnsgard and Carbonell 1996). ♀ aggressive during breeding season (Siegfried 1976c), regularly chasing other birds, such as cormorants *Phalacrocorax*, from brood (Siegfried *et al.* 1976b). Incubating ♀♀ at Slimbridge could even be lifted from nests after grasping sticks or fingers in their bills.

Like other stifftails, ♀ physiologically able to lay in 1st year (Siegfried 1985), but extent to which occurs in wild unknown. No data on breeding success, adult survival nor on longevity.

Conservation and threats

Total population reported to be stable, although numbers in southern Rift Valley declined sharply due to mortality in illegally set gill-nets (Callaghan and Green 1993). In contrast, increases occurred in Namibia and South Africa following construction of dams and sewage settlement lagoons. Not thought particularly threatened by hunting (del Hoyo *et al.* 1992).

Baz Hughes

White-headed Duck *Oxyura leucocephala*
PLATE 29

Anas leucocephala Scopoli, 1769, Annus I Hist.-Nat., p. 65
No locality given, but probably northern Italy. Type in Turin Museum.

Etymology: *leucocephala* Gr. for white *leukos* and head *kephalos*.

Other names: White-headed Stifftail, Spiny-tailed Duck, Ural Duck, Spanish Duck. French: Erismature à tête blanche; German: Ruderente; Russian: savka sinonossaia; Spanish: Malvasía cabeciblanca.

Variation: no subspecies recognized, although Amat and Sánchez (1982) reported differences in plumage coloration and bill dimensions between skins from western Mediterranean (Spain, Tunisia and Algeria) and populations further east. Amat and Sánchez (1982) found western birds had larger bills on average. Two colour phases (pale and dark) now occur in Spain, possibly associated with bottleneck suffered by tiny remaining population in 1970s (Urdiales and Pereira 1993, Torres and Morena-Arroyo 2000). Hybridizes to at least 3rd generation with North American Ruddy Duck (Figure 9.15), but genetic studies show these 2 species geographically isolated without gene flow for several million years (McCracken *et al.* 2000a).

Description

ADULT: dimorphic. ♂ in alternate plumage, white head with variable amount of black-brown on crown, varying from complete crown stripe in younger or subordinate ♂♂ to light speckling in dominant or older birds. Neck dark brown, contrasting with mid brown breast. Wings and mantle sandy rufous brown, vermiculated blackish. Back and rump grey-brown, uppertail coverts rich chestnut. Breast and belly chestnut, fading to grey-brown on central belly and to silvery grey on undertail coverts. Tail blackish.

9.15 Male Ruddy Duck displaying to a female White-headed Duck.

Upperwing grey-brown. Underwing silvery grey, with white axillaries. Bill pale blue; legs slaty grey; iris brown. Dark-phase ♂♂ in Spain have darker brown bellies and undertail coverts than pale ♂♂, and dark grey rather than mid grey underwing coverts. ♀ in alternate plumage, crown, hindneck and lower cheek stripe dark brown with rufous feather tips, cheeks buffish white freckled darker. Chin white. Breast and underparts rufous ochre finely barred darker. Undertail coverts grey-white. Flanks and scapulars chestnut brown finely barred darker. Back, rump and uppertail coverts brown-grey, barred darker. Bill and legs lead-grey; wings, tail, and eye as ♂. Dark-phase ♀♀ in Spain have darker cap and face stripe than pale ♀♀, with off-white cheeks more heavily mottled dark brown. Flanks, belly and undertail coverts also darker chestnut brown (barred black-grey), and underwing coverts dark rather than mid grey (Cramp and Simmons 1977, Amat and Sánchez 1982, Torres 1984, Torres and Ayala 1986, Madge and Burn 1988, Gantlett 1993, Urdiales and Pereira 1993, Johnsgard and Carbonell 1996).

MOULT: ♂ in basic plumage, similar to alternate plumage, but duller. Sides of neck pale grey barred darker rather than blackish. Sandy tones on upperparts and chestnut breast and rump replaced by grey-brown feathering. Dark mottling on crown and cheeks more extensive. Bill fades to grey-brown. ♀ in basic plumage, similar to alternate, but

chestnut tones replaced by duller, grey-brown. ♂♂ acquire blue bills and breeding plumage Dec–Mar, and lose them Aug–Sept (Amat and Sanchez 1982). Brightness of plumage and bill linked to dominance status with dominant ♂♂ in captivity brighter than nondominant birds. Furthermore, ♂ dominance hierarchies may change during season. In captivity, once dominant ♂♂ have bred, nondominant ♂♂ acquire brighter plumage and bills, become dominant and actively court ♀♀. Little information on moult available from wild. Flightless ♂♂ observed in winter in Pakistan and India (Finn 1909, Anstey 1989). Detailed studies of captives at Slimbridge suggest 2 complete (i.e. body, wing and tail) moults annually, in late winter and immediately post-breeding (Carbonell 1983); however, 5 of 19 captive birds in Spain underwent 3 wing moults in Apr, Aug and Dec. Dominant birds at Slimbridge wore alternate plumage for 2 months longer, moulting into and out of alternate plumage month before and after nondominant birds. First-year birds moulted into alternate plumage month later than adults. Post-breeding moult began with wing feathers and birds remained flightless for 2–3 weeks. Whilst flightless, tail feathers dropped, and blue bill colour faded before body moult began.

IMMATURE: resembles ♀, but no chestnut plumage tones, upperparts darker, and underparts buffer. Has more white on throat and neck than adult ♀, and paler cheeks give more striking cheek pattern. First basic ♂♂ resemble definitive basic ♂♂, but with less white on head. Full white head acquired in 2nd summer.

DUCKLING: head and neck black-brown, cheeks pale grey split by black-brown cheek stripe. Breast, upperparts and flanks dark brown, mantle and centre of chest greyer. Indistinct buff-grey shoulder spot. Chin, belly and vent white. Bill bluish grey with characteristic, swollen base; legs and feet deep grey; iris brown (Cramp and Simmons 1977, Fjeldså 1977).

MEASUREMENTS AND WEIGHT: ♂ wing ($n = 10$), 157–172 (152); tail ($n = 9$), 85–100 (92); culmen ($n = 17$), 43–48 (45.5); tarsus ($n = 17$), 35–38 (35.9) (Cramp and Simmons 1977). C. Violani and E. Grandi ($n = 37$) ♂ wing, 154–165 (159); tail, 82–109 (98); bill, 42–50 (46); tarsus, 34–43 (36). ♀ wing ($n = 6$), 148–167 (159); tail ($n = 5$), 75–93 (86); culmen ($n = 16$), 43–46 (44.5); tarsus ($n = 16$), 33–37 (34.9). Weight ♂ ($n = 9$), 553–865 (717); ♀ ($n = 9$), 510–900 (657) includes laying birds, winter weights usually < 650 (Cramp and Simmons 1977, Amat and Sánchez 1982, Torres 1984), ♀ Sept 575, 590; May 560; Jan 630, 655.

Field characters

Medium-sized, short-necked dumpy stifftail, 430–480 mm long. Both sexes distinguishable from other naturally occurring wetland species by bulbous base to bill, compact body, and characteristic long tail, often held aloft.

♂♂ can be separated from introduced North American Ruddy Duck by larger size, longer tail, greater extent of white on head, convex bill profile, chestnut rather than reddish upperparts and greyish buff, not white, undertail coverts. ♀ White-headed Ducks and Ruddy Ducks more difficult to separate. ♀ Ruddy Duck smaller, greyer, with shorter, often fanned tail, more buoyant body profile whilst swimming, and white undertail coverts. ♀ White-headed Duck more distinctly vermiculated plumage, and broader, darker cheek stripe contrasting more with paler cheeks. In field, convex bill profile and longer tail best identification features. During breeding season, ♂ can be separated on behaviour, ♂ Ruddy Duck

showing typical Bubbling display, and ♂ White-headed Duck performing Head-high-tail-cock, Kick-flap-sideways-piping and Sideways-hunch.

Although difficult to separate in field, Ruddy × White-headed Duck hybrids structurally intermediate between parent species: F_1 hybrids halfway, and F_2 backcross hybrids midway between F_1 and backcross. Thus F_2 hybrid from backcross to White-headed Duck structurally resembles White-headed Duck, whilst backcross to Ruddy resembles Ruddy Duck. F_1 hybrids can be identified by straight bill profile, shorter tail and more buoyant body profile whilst swimming. F_1 ♂ has White-headed Duck head pattern and Ruddy Duck body plumage (reddish back and flanks, silvery grey underparts and white undertail coverts). Ruddy Duck plumage coloration appears dominant, with ♂ F_2 ¾ White-headed Duck hybrids also possessing ♂ Ruddy Duck's body plumage. Behavioural features perhaps best clue to hybrid identification, with both F_1 and F_2 ♂♂ performing Bubbling display, but with only 4 chest beats in F_1 male, and one in F_2. ♀ hybrids very difficult to identify, F_1 hybrids can be separated on structural features mentioned above, greyer appearance and paler flanks, but F_2 hybrids are almost indistinguishable in field (Gantlett 1993, Urdiales and Pereira 1993).

Voice

Silent, except during aggression and courtship. During courtship, ♂♂ have 2 main vocalizations, rapid clicking noise or Tickering-purr which has been likened to sound of clockwork toy, and high-pitched, bi-syllabic, flutey piping noise during Sideways-piping display (Matthews and Evans 1974). Latter has same timbre as call of ♂ Common Scoter. During Flotilla-swimming both sexes recorded making quiet grunt or *gek* calls. Nesting ♀ may hiss and snort at intruders, or make low rattling purr as duckling contact call. Ducklings make high pitched, buzzing *weet weet* alarm call, less piercing than calls of other ducklings.

Range and status

Distribution highly fragmented, has become extinct last century as breeder in central Europe, Israel and Egypt (Anstey 1989, Green and Anstey

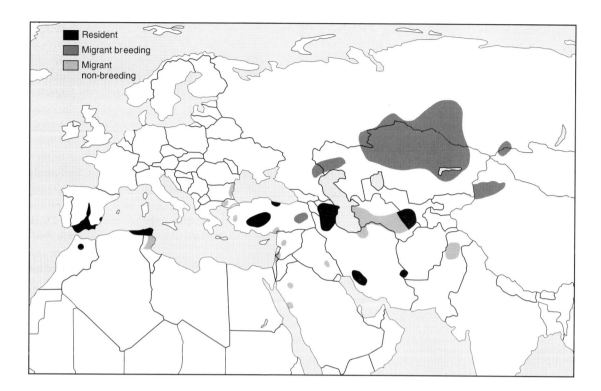

1992). Divisions between surviving biogeographical populations not understood (Scott and Rose 1996), but 4 major populations appear to remain—migratory central Asian population breeding in northern Kazakhstan and southern Russia and wintering as far west as Greece, migratory east Asian population breeding in southern Russia and Mongolia and wintering in Pakistan, population resident in Spain, and another in North Africa (Tunisia, northeast Algeria and Morocco).

Numbers in Asian populations declined markedly since 1930s, from around 100 000 to perhaps 10 000 (Green and Hunter 1996). This includes crash in numbers at main wintering site, Burdur Gölü in Turkey, from 11 000 in 1991 to fewer than 3000 since (Green *et al.* 1996, Green and Yarar 1996). Some may have relocated with recent high counts of 600–2500 wintering birds in Greece, Bulgaria, Romania, and Azerbaijan (Cranswick *et al.* 1998, Dimitrov *et al.* 2000, Munteanu 2000, Panayotopoulou and Green 2000), although lack of historical coverage and absence of ringing data precludes firm conclusions. Population wintering in

Pakistan fell from *c* 1000 in late 1960s to only 50 in 1995 (Chaudhry *et al.* 1997). Spanish population fell to low of 22 birds in 1977. Destruction of habitat and hunting main cause of these declines. Habitat preservation and protection from hunting in Spain increased numbers to 4500 in Sept 2000 (Torres and Moreno-Arroyo 2000).

Habitat and general habits

Highly gregarious outside breeding season, up to 11 000 birds recorded on one site in winter, although individual flock sizes usually < 500 (Dementiev and Gladkov 1952, Green *et al.* 1996, Lanovenko *et al.* 2000). Forms tight flocks whilst roosting but disperses to feed (Fox *et al.* 1994b, Green *et al.* 1999).

Prefers freshwater or brackish, alkaline, eutrophic lakes, which often have closed basin hydrology and are frequently semi-permanent or temporary. Breeding sites have dense emergent vegetation around fringes and are small or enclosed areas within larger wetland systems. Typically have extensive areas of 0.5–3.0 m depth (Matamala *et al.* 1994). Wintering sites generally larger, deeper, with little emergent vegetation (Anstey 1989). Wintering flocks often occur on saline inland lakes, such as Burdur Gölü, in coastal lakes in Greece and Black Sea countries, and in coastal waters of southern Caspian Sea, off Turkmenistan, Iran and Azerbaijan. Bulbous base to bill, containing large salt-excreting glands, thought to be adaptation to saline winter habitats.

Feeds entirely by diving, mainly at night (Amat 1984a, Green *et al.* 1999). In winter, diurnal feeding reduced on calm, sunny days when switch to roosting in tight flocks (Green *et al.* 1999). Benthic chironomid larvae major component of diet of adults and ducklings, but polychaetes (especially in coastal lakes used as wintering sites), amphipods and variety of other invertebrates eaten, as well as seeds and vegetative parts of *Potamogeton*, *Ruppia* and other aquatic plants (Torres and Arenas 1985, Anstey 1989, Green *et al.* 1999, Panayotopoulou and Green 2000, Sánchez *et al.* 2000). Availability of chironomid larvae key feature in habitat selection (Green *et al.* 1996, 1999). Highly aquatic, rarely seen on land or in flight.

Ducklings dive from 7 h old with mean dive times increasing from 5.9 ($n = 22$) to 11.5 ($n = 68$) sec over 1st week, and from 10.9 ($n = 745$) to 18.1 ($n = 85$) sec from 1–7 weeks (Matthews and Evans 1974). Adult dive times strongly depth dependent, varying 20–60 sec at Burdur Gölü where wintering birds dive to 10 m and ♂♂ have longest dive times (Green *et al.* 1993).

Displays and breeding behaviour

Four main displays recognized in increasing order of intensity: Flotilla swimming, Head-high-tail-cock, Sideways-hunch (Tickering-purr), and Kick-flap-sideways-piping. Flotilla swimming involves groups of both sexes swimming rapidly over water surface with heads stretched in front. This is often interspersed with ritualized movements such as Head-shaking, Dab-preening, diving and bathing. Head-high-tail-cock commonest low level display in which neck and tail stretched vertically at 90° to body. This often followed by primary display, of Sideways-hunch, in which ♂♂ approach ♀♀ side-on with heads low, scapulars raised, while vibrating tails spread flat on water. In this posture, ♂ utters mechanical Tickering-purr and paddles feet quickly. After holding position for few seconds, he continues Tickering-purr and either swims flank-first to present

opposite flank to another ♀, or turns through 180° to present other flank to same ♀. Highest level display, Kick-flap-sideways-piping, begins with Sideways-hunch; in rapid synchronized movement, he then sinks tail and head into water, while lifting scapulars, then kicks both feet (producing splashes) and flicks head and tail to point towards ♀. In side-on position, he vibrates tail, raises wings and opens bill whilst simultaneously uttering 7–23 high-pitched, bi-syllabic, flutey piping noises. Copulation occurs following high-intensity Kick-flap-sideways-piping, with ♂♂ moving closer to ♀♀ after each piping, until she assumes prone position and he mounts after 5–10 pipings. Copulation lasts 3–6 sec after which both sexes preen.

Courting ♂ and brood ♀ aggressive. Nine levels of aggressive display recorded for captive birds ranging from simple swimming at other birds, through various threat postures (hunched posture with feathers fluffed out and scapulars raised, and open-bill threat) to pursuit (attempted peck, hunched swim, hunched rush, flying hunched rush) and actual physical contact and fighting. While in courting groups, fighting between ♂♂ common, especially as dominance hierarchies established in spring (Matthews and Evans 1974, Amat and Sánchez 1982, Carbonell 1983, Torres *et al.* 1985, Johnsgard and Carbonell 1996).

Breeding and life cycle

On central Asian breeding ground, amongst last wildfowl species to arrive, being observed on passage late Apr–early May, and on breeding sites from mid May (Dementiev and Gladkov 1952, Gordienko *et al.* 1986). On Russian breeding ground, already paired (Dementiev and Gladkov 1952) and leave late Aug and arrive on wintering grounds Sept–Oct (Gordienko *et al.* 1986). Pre-breeding concentrations recorded on large lakes in Kazakhstan (e.g. 800 on Lake Tengiz Apr 1998, Cresswell *et al.* 1999) and post-breeding concentrations in Uzbekistan (2500 on Akushpa Lake on 21 Oct 1999, Kreuzberg-Mukhina and Lanovenko 2000). Migrate mainly at night (Gordienko *et al.* 1986). In Spain, although birds concentrate on certain sites in winter, no overall direction to seasonal movements, and location of major concentrations varies between years according to fluctuations in rainfall, wetland depth, etc. Court from late Mar and nesting starts Apr (Amat and Sánchez 1982). Broods hatch Apr–Sept, but mostly June–July.

Mating system requires further study. Unclear whether wild birds monogamous, polygynous, promiscuous or, as in Ruddy Duck (Gray 1980), mixture of three. In captivity, ♂♂ polygynous and form hierarchies in which dominant ♂♂ paired to 2 or more ♀♀ (Matthews and Evans 1974, Carbonell 1983). Evidence that this also case in wild in Spain (Torres *et al.* 1985).

♀♀ build nests over water in emergent vegetation, such as *Phragmites australis* and Bulrush *Typha dominguensis*, sometimes on top of old Common Coot *Fulica atra* nests (Amat and Sánchez 1982, Torres *et al.* 1985, Gordienko *et al.* 1986). In Kazakhstan, 12 of 15 nests located within gull and tern colonies (Gordienko *et al.* 1986). Nests made of whatever emergent vegetation found, and lined with sparse quantities of down. ♀♀ can breed at one year old although proportion doing so is unknown. ♀♀ lay 4–9 eggs, usually 5–6, at 1.5 day intervals, and re-lay if 1st clutch removed (Dementiev and Gladkov 1952, Matthews and Evans 1974, Johnsgard and Carbonell 1996); re-laying interval in captivity 17 days (Carbonell 1983). In Spain, North Africa and Russia, eggs laid late May–early July (Dementiev and Gladkov 1952, Amat and Sánchez 1982), with peak May–June. Large eggs white with thick, rough, granular shell characteristic of stifftails; dimensions 67.6 × 50.3 (60.4–75.9 × 46.3–53.3) (*n* = 185 eggs from captive birds at WWT Slimbridge, Johnsgard and Carbonell 1996), 69.1 ± 0.45 × 50.4 ± 0.34 (*n* = 21 in Spain, Amat and Sánchez 1982), 69.5 × 50.7 (66.0–73.0 × 49.0– 52.3) (*n* = 35) (Gordienko *et al.* 1986), and 67 × 51 (63–73 × 48–54) (*n* = 100) (Schönwetter1960–66); egg volume 85 (80–100) ml (*n* = 119) (Carbonell 1983); egg mass 91.4 (77.4–105.8) (*n* = 127) (Carbonell 1983), 96.4 ± 0.98 (*n* = 21, Amat and Sánchez 1982), 88.6–110.0 (Gordienko *et al.* 1986) or 96 (Schönwetter 1960–66). Total clutch mass approaches 100% of ♀'s nonbreeding body weight (Rohwer 1988). Incubation 24–26 days in captivity (Carbonell 1983), 22–24 days in wild (Gordienko *et al.* 1986). ♀ takes 2–3 nest recesses per day for 1.5–2 h (Borodin 1984). At one lake in Cadiz, most nests predated by Brown Rats. Newly-hatched young average 165 in length (Fjeldså 1977) and weigh 56 (47–65) (*n* = 35) (Johnsgard and Carbonell 1996).

At hatching, ducklings proportionally larger than other waterfowl; this may be related to semiparasitic breeding behaviour (with eggs laid in other birds' nests), and/or to fact that ducklings deserted by parents after only 15–20 days (Amat and Sánchez 1982). Following desertion, different-aged ducklings may amalgamate into crèches. Fledging period 8–10 weeks (Johnsgard and Carbonell 1996), somewhat longer than most ducks. In Cordoba, Spain, brood size at hatching 4.3 (*n* = 55) with 40% of ducklings surviving to fledging (Torres *et al.* 1989); in Seville and Cadiz, brood size at hatching 4.8 (*n* = 17) and survival to fledging 62% (Amat and Raya 1989); in Almeria, survival to fledging 80% (*n* = 336 ducklings, Castro *et al.* 1994). Brood size nationally 5.5 in 1995 (*n* = 49, Torres *et al.* 1996) but only 3.5 in 1996 (*n* = 84, Torres and Alcala-Zamora 1997). In El Hondo, brood size at hatch usually 6 (*n* = 25) or 5 (*n* = 18). Borodin (1984) reported brood sizes at fledging as 4.9 (4–7), but amalgamation makes this hard to interpret.

Adults predated by large gulls at Burdur Gölü. No data on adult survival, nor on longevity.

Conservation and threats

Action Plans produced at worldwide (Anstey 1989), European (Green and Hughes 1996) and national scale (Spain and Greece). Main threats for Asian populations are overhunting and habitat loss but, for species as a whole, hybridization and competition with introduced North American Ruddy Ducks, originating mainly from UK-released population, is crucial. Ruddy Duck records in Western Palearctic increased at 21% per year, 1976–96, with birds recorded in 19 countries and annual breeding season presence in 9 (Hughes *et al.* 1999). Ruddy Duck control programmes now operational in Spain, France, Portugal and UK. Lead poisoning major problem in some Spanish wetlands (Mateo *et al.* 2001), and by-catch in fishing nets important threat in Greece (Panayotopoulou and Green 2000), Iran and other countries. White-headed Duck reintroduction programmes ongoing in Spain (Majorca), France (Corsica) and Italy.

Baz Hughes and Andy J. Green

Blue Duck, Torrent Duck and steamer-ducks

Taxonomy

Analyses by Livezey (1986, 1996c) suggested a relationship between the Blue Duck, steamer-ducks and the Torrent Duck in a tribe Merganettini; however, he remained suspicious of the grouping, in part because of the effects of convergent life histories and analytical artifacts. None of the species is known to have produced interspecific hybrids (Johnsgard 1960b).

Both sexes are extremely territorial, which has led to the development of metacarpal wing-knobs (Eldridge 1979, 1986, Livezey and Humphrey 1985a). The steamer-ducks are large and marine, and consist of four species, three of which are flightless and more closely related to one another than any one of them is to the Flying Steamer-duck (Corbin *et al.* 1988). Most authors place them within the shelducks or in a separate tribe allied to the shelducks (Delacour and Mayr 1945, Delacour 1954, Johnsgard 1965a, 1978, Weller 1976, Livezey 1986, 1996c, Livezey and Humphrey 1992). However, Woolfenden (1961) put them within the dabbling ducks (Anatini), and DNA analyzis (Johnson and Sorenson 1999) has placed them as sister to three other South American dabblers, the Crested Duck, Bronze-winged Duck and Brazilian Teal.

Relationships of the Blue and Torrent Ducks are unclear. The former is a New Zealand river specialist and is often considered an ancient dabbling duck (Anatini) or of earlier origin, but with no close relative (Delacour and Mayr 1945, Wolfenden 1961, Johnsgard 1965a, 1978, Brush 1976, Sibley and Monroe 1990, Harshman 1996). The Torrent Duck is another river specialist, endemic to the Andes of South America (Johnsgard 1966a). It is frequently given tribal ranking (Merganettini) and considered relatively primitive (Woolfenden 1961, Brush 1976, Johnsgard 1978, Olson and Fedducia 1980). Links with Salvadori's Duck have been suggested (Kear 1975). Unlike the steamers or the Blue Duck, the Torrent Duck has pronounced sexual dichromatism with male and female plumages differing markedly.

If the composition and placement of this tribe is as Livezey (1996c) suggested, it is the first branch of the anseriforms that has scutellated or scaly legs.

Des Gallaghan

Blue Duck *Hymenolaimus malacorhynchos*
PLATE 14

Anas malacorhynchos Gmelin, 1789, Syst. Nat., **1**, p. 526
Dusky Sound, South Island, New Zealand
Hymenolaimus G.R. Gray, 1843

Etymology: *Hymenolaimus* Gr. *humenos* means membranous, plus *laimos* throat; *malakos* means soft and *rhunkhos*, bill.

Other names: Blue Mountain Duck. New Zealand Maori: Whio.

Variation: no subspecies recognized here. Modern listings of New Zealand birds (e.g. Turbott 1990) treat as monotypic and ignore Mathews's (1937) attempt to segregate North Island *H. m. hymenolaimus* and South Island *H. m. malacorhynchos* specimens at racial level; however, Marchant and Higgins (1990) have revived this debate.

Description

ADULT: sexes alike. General body colour slate blue with greenish gloss on head, neck and back, with breast covered in chestnut spots (denser and more extensive in ♂). Wings slate blue above and below, outer secondaries tipped with white and inner secondaries and tertials with thin black outer margin. Bill pink-white with black flap at tip; legs and feet dark grey with black at joints, webs black; eyes yellow.

MOULT: no ♂ eclipse plumage. Timing of body moults uncertain; wing moult follows breeding.

IMMATURE: similar to adult but with fewer and darker breast spots and no gloss on head and back. Bill grey; legs and feet as adult; eyes dark brown.

DUCKLING: upper surface dark grey with greenish gloss, under surface white. Face white with dark stripe from bill through eye to nape and with dark ear spot. Prominent rump spot dark chestnut in ♂, fawn in ♀. Bill grey-blue; legs and feet yellow-brown; eye dark brown.

MEASUREMENTS AND WEIGHT: from live birds, ♂ (*n* = 11) wing, 231–251 (242); tail, 99–117 (108); bill, 42.7–47.3 (45.8); tarsus, 48.8–54.3 (51.6); weight (*n* = 20), 820–1050 (903). ♀ (*n* = 10) wing, 204–240 (226); tail, 90–112 (99); bill, 41.0–45.3 (43.9); tarsus, 46.1–49.2 (47.4); weight (*n* = 20), 680–870 (767).

Field characters

Slate or blue-grey duck, 540 mm long, with pale bill, found on water course. Sits on water with prominent tail tilted upward, and moves easily in river current. Whistles.

Voice

♂ gives high-pitched, piercing, wheezy whistle as territorial or advertising call (phonetically described by Maori name *whio*) in characteristic posture with neck stretched forward and upper neck feathers raised. Also short *whi* call during interactions with territory intruders. ♀ utters long, low, rasping growl in response to disturbance or as threat. Also gives low-pitched staccato rasping during social interaction. Sonogram in Marchant and Higgins (1990).

Range and status

Now rare in both islands of New Zealand and generally restricted, with discontinuity, to forested headwater catchments along axial ranges. Prior to human settlement, inhabited lakes, and were widespread in upper, middle and lower sections of most rivers, almost reaching coast in some areas (e.g. Fiordland). May even have foraged on forest floor away from primary water courses (Worthy and Holdaway 1994). Widespread forest destruction and

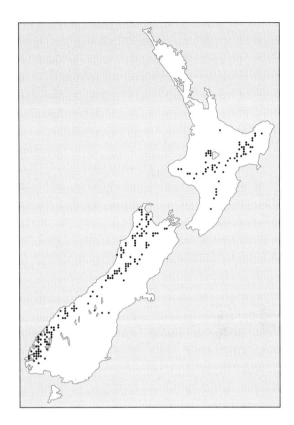

establishment of pasture to river edges caused total retreat from lowlands. Undergoing widespread decline in face of extensive mustelid predation on nesting ♀♀ and ducklings; breeding population estimated (in 2003) at 500 pairs.

Habitat and general habits

Most now confined to rivers of steep gradient in forested headwater catchments but extending downriver from these refugia wherever and for as far as riparian forest persists. Principal correlates of habitat presently occupied include stability of river channel, narrow stream widths, coarse riverbed substrata, and riparian forest (Collier *et al.* 1993). Also frequent alpine tarns and lakes, and occasionally farm ponds, but seem not to reside there.

Highly sedentary with adults establishing territories that they occupy, generally as pairs, year-round and throughout life (Williams 1991). When changes of pairings occur, either resulting from death or displacement of partner, rarely significant change in territory location. Juveniles more dispersive and may wander extensively within, and sometimes beyond, natal catchment during 1st year; however, most juveniles return to natal area and attempt to establish territory close by. Settlement beyond natal catchment seems very rare. DNA fingerprinting studies (Triggs *et al.* 1992) confirm little gene flow between neighbouring catchments, adjacent territorial pairs are often closely related, and sibling or cousin pairings common.

Territorial pairs have regular daily routine: birds roost overnight at river edge, usually under overhanging vegetation, in caves or amongst pile of logs and river debris; within 0.5 h of dawn, feed for 1.0–1.5 h; rest period of similar duration followed by another h of intensive feeding; by mid morning, retire to secluded riverside location where inactive through middle of day. From late afternoon, further bouts of prolonged feeding occur and pair generally roost at dusk. Feeding may occupy as little as 25% of active day (Veltman and Williams 1990). Nocturnal foraging occurs, particularly in rivers carrying high aggregate loads or where aquatic invertebrate densities generally low. Most feeding occurs in shallow water at margins of rivers where force of current dissipated by emergent rocks. Food collected by scraping bill tip over rock surface to remove invertebrates present, by probing between rocks on river bed, or by dabbling or pecking on water surface to collect floating insects. Bill has soft lateral flaps at tip which function to increase surface area from which food gathered and to protect bill from abrasion (Figure 9.16). Most feeding done by merely dipping head under water but occasionally birds dive in deeper and more swiftly flowing water.

Studies (Kear and Burton 1971, Collier *et al.* 1993, Wakelin 1993) confirm dominance of chironomid larvae and cased caddis larvae in diet and highlight extensive range of aquatic invertebrates taken. No convincing evidence of selective feeding though, in some instances, diet appears unrelated to abundance of prey items in river. In some rivers, food superabundant and less than 10 m^2 of rock surface may hold enough to provide daily energetic needs (Veltman *et al.* 1991). Berries of streamside plants recorded in diet of some alpine-dwelling ducks (Harding 1990). During floods, have been seen scraping sides of silt-covered rocks or riverside rock walls normally

9.16 Blue Duck adult and duckling.

beyond water margin, removing and consuming silt and periphyton. Droppings indicate that algae and mosses ingested but little affected by digestive process.

Ducklings feed on same foods as adults, particularly cased caddis larvae, and dive in shallow water when still downy.

Displays and breeding behaviour

Limited range of postures and calls (Eldridge 1985) that function both as agonistic displays and pair maintenance behaviour. Conspicuous Extended-neck posture adopted and *whio* call of ♂ given in response to birds overflying or landing in territory and to any sudden disturbance. Also adopted spontaneously by pairs, ♀ growling, in late evening, and perhaps functions as territorial advertisement. Threat displays include Swim-offs where resident constantly swims close to or displaces intruder, Upright posture in which resident stands tall, and Head-bobs with accompanying *whi* prior to fight. Pair maintenance displays include Rushing, mutual Head-bobbing and Lateral swimming (Eldridge 1985, Marchant and Higgins 1990). Pre-flight intention display is Head-flicking.

No obvious social courtship. Most new pairings result from physical displacement of already paired territory holder (Williams and McKinney 1996). Within small groups of juveniles, assembled at unoccupied river sections up to 6 months after fledging, pair associations established by means of physical dominance. Breeding is confined to territory holders and almost all attempt breeding every year (Williams 1991); those that do not are usually one year old. DNA fingerprinting confirms monogamous mating system (Triggs *et al.* 1991).

Breeding and life cycle

Eggs rarely laid before mid Aug and most 1st nests attempted by end Oct. Repeat laying following early loss of initial clutch may extend laying to early Dec and brood emergence to late Jan. Nests established close (< 30 m) to river edge in caves, hollow logs, holes in bank, within fern clumps, i.e. in sites that give shelter from above. Sites generally damp. Same site may be used in consecutive years; one ♀ used cave site for 7 years. Nest bowl shallow depression amongst ground debris; occasionally soft grass and twigs incorporated; some breast feathers and down provide scant cover in ♀'s absence. Eggs ovoid white; 64.5 × 44.8 (59.0–70.9 × 40.8–46.7) (*n* = 55); weight 62.3 (*n* = 25); clutch 6.0 (3–7) (*n* = 23). Eggs laid at more than 24 h intervals, e.g. clutch of 5 over 8 days, one of 6 in 10 days. Incubation by ♀ for 33–35 days. While mate on nest, ♂ spends 68–81% of daytime inactive and inconspicuous at river edge directly opposite nest site (Veltman and Williams 1990). Recesses by ♀ usually twice daily for 37–48 min; ♀ may not leave nest in 48 h prior to brood emergence. Of 61 nesting attempts, 33 (54%) successfully hatched ducklings, early laid nests being generally more successful (72%). In successful nests, 92% of eggs hatched. Nest failure results mainly from flooding and mammalian predation.

Both parents attend young through 70–82 day fledging period. ♀ remains close and maintains brood cohesion by soft vocalizations; ♂ maintains vigilance and ensures ducklings do not straggle. Full extent of territory used during brood rearing. In one study (Williams 1991), only 12% of 33 broods lost, and 60% of 55 ducklings reaching river survived to fledging. Break-up of brood and cessation of parental interest gradual, and marked by lack of synchrony in duckling and parental activities as adults start to moult and young commence roosting apart from parents.

Average annual productivity (Williams 1991) 1.3 fledglings per breeding pair (*n* = 58) but erratic between years (0–2.7 per pair). Also variability in reproductive output between pairs (0.25–2.3 young per year over 5–9 years) related mostly to quality of rearing habitat within territory. Mean annual survival of juveniles between fledging and settlement 0.44 (*n* = 50) and of territorial adults 0.86 (*n* = 116). Mean lifespan upon becoming territory holder 6.75 years. About 50% of birds holding territories as year-olds attempt breeding while remainder try in 2nd, or (rarely) 3rd year.

Conservation and threats

Endangered (IUCN 2002), with gradually declining range and population density. Recent rapid decline in South Island *Nothofagus* forest environments attributed to mustelid predation. Now largely confined to hitherto marginal habitat in catchment headwaters, whereas formally populations most dense and productive in warmer, less steep and more productive middle reaches of rivers. If lower altitude habitat with riparian forest cannot be colonized, duck will dwindle slowly to occupy 2 or 3 refugia in both islands of New Zealand.

Murray Williams

Torrent Duck *Merganetta armata*
PLATE 14

Merganetta armata Gould, 1842, Proc. Zool. Soc. London (1841), p. 95
Andes of Chile, 34°–35°S

Etymology: *Merganetta* L. *Mergus* merganser, plus Gr. *netta* duck; *armata* L. means armed, in reference to carpal spurs.

Other names: nominate form called Chilean Torrent Duck, *colombiana* Colombian Torrent Duck and *leucogenis* Argentine/Turner's/Bolivian/Peruvian Torrent Duck.

Variation: 3 subspecies recognized tentatively, *M. a. armata*, *M. a. colombiana* Des Murs, 1845 and *M. a. leucogenis* Tschudi, 1843, which some authorities regard as specifically distinct (e.g. Conover 1943). *M. a. turneri* P. L. Sclater and Salvin, 1869, *M. a. garleppi* Berlepsch, 1894 and *M. a. berlepschi* Hartert, 1909 may be colour morphs of *M. a. leucogenis* (Johnsgard 1966b), although uniform character expression in northern and southern parts of range might be treated as subspecies (*leucogenis* and *berlepschi*) separated by broad zone of intergradation.

Description

ADULT: dimorphic. ♂ head mostly white, with black crown stripe that extends from base of culmen to hind neck. Second black stripe extends from eye, and splits behind cheek, running down back and side of neck to base, forming white V on back of head. Feathers of mantle and scapulars long, pointed and black centred, with margins either white, buff or brown. Chest, flanks and underparts vary from black to light grey or ochraceous red streaked black. Lower back, rump and uppertail coverts finely lined with grey, white and black. Tail greyish brown. Wing coverts lead blue, primaries brown, and secondaries form brilliant green speculum anteriorly and posteriorly bordered white; there are prominent wing-spurs. Bill bright red, ridge brown or black; legs dull red and webs blackish; iris brown. ♀ upper head, hind neck and upperparts plumbeous grey, streaked black on mantle and scapulars. Lower head, fore neck and underparts cinnamon red to ochreous. Other parts as ♂, but wing-spur smaller.

armata ♂ has black band from eye (sometimes from crown) running down side of face to chin and down mid-throat to chest. Mantle almost pure white, and edges of scapulars and tertiaries white and comparatively wide. Chest black and rest of underparts ochreous red heavily streaked with black, which sometimes fuses to almost completely black underside. ♀ underparts cinnamon red, and grey colouring extends to just below eye and to middle of neck.

leucogenis ♂ very variable. Chest, flanks and under parts are streaked black to varying degrees, while background colour varies from buff white to ochreous or chestnut. Borders of scapulars and tertials vary from reddish brown to white. ♀ as *armata*.

columbiana ♂ has mantle brownish grey finely vermiculated with white. Dark shafts of breast feathers narrow and light grey, while borders of scapulars and tertials light brown. ♀ has paler underparts (ochreous) than *armata*, and grey terminates level with eye, not extending so far forward on neck (Phillips 1922–26, Wetmore 1926b, Conover 1943, Neithammer 1952, Delacour 1954–64, Johnsgard 1966b, 1978, Weller 1968c).

MOULT: no seasonal variation, so no evidence of well-defined non-nuptial plumage. First nuptial plumage acquired by 9–12 months. Has one complete annual moult in late summer (Jan–Feb) and probably partial spring moult (Weller 1968c).

IMMATURE: similar to ♀ but white below with side, flank and rump broadly barred black.

DUCKLING: blackish grey above and white below, with dark eyestripe and spot on ear coverts. White stripe runs along hind wing and horizontally across side of back, terminating just before tail. Large white spot on upper back, and tail tipped white.

MEASUREMENTS AND WEIGHT: ♂ (*n* = 48), wing, 142–185; tail, 108–124; culmen, 27–30; tarsus (*n* = 9), 37–44; weight, *c* 440. ♀ wing (*n* = 30), 136–174; tail (*n* = 28), 92–113; culmen (*n* = 23), 25–30; tarsus (*n* = 5) 35–38; weight, 315–340.

Field characters

Unmistakable, 400–430 mm long. Only duck inhabiting turbulent Andean streams. Long, narrow stiff tail, slim body, easily recognized by red bill and vivid plumage. In flight, plumbeous grey wings clearly show bronzy green speculum.

Voice

Commonest call of ♂ clear *wheet* and of ♀ throaty *queech*. In flight, call pattern ensures contact *queech-wheet . . . . wheet-queech . . . queech-wheet*. Both sexes stress similar frequency range (3–5 kHz), above sound of rapids (0–1.5 kHz) and clearly audible in field. During aggressive interactions, other calls emitted almost continuously, providing background noise; for ♂, these include *wheeow* call, warble (series of slightly ascending then descending notes), and whistle (highly variable series of clear notes), for ♀, include *gaga-brr* call (see Eldridge 1979 for sonograms). Distress call of ducklings, repeated single-noted peeping whistle (Johnsgard 1966b, Moffett 1970).

Range and status

Sedentary species scattered throughout most of Andes, *colombiana* south from North Merida Province (Venezuela) through Colombia and Ecuador to North Peru. *leucogenis* south from North Amazonas Province (Peru), reaching North Tarapacá

Province in Chile, and along east Andes of Bolivia and Argentina to northern La Rioja Province, and *armata* south from North Atacama Province (Chile) and central San Juan Province (Argentina) to southern Tierra del Fuego, with small isolated population on coastal massif of Nahuelbuta in Arauco (Goodall *et al.* 1951, Delacour 1954–64, Phelps and Phelps 1958, Johnson 1963, de Schauensee and Phelps 1978, Hilty and Brown 1986, Araya and Millie 1988, Gómez-Dallmeier and Cringan 1989, Fjeldså and Krabbe 1990, Canevari *et al.* 1991). *leucogenis* and *colombiana* may integrade, but arid diagonal from northern Chile to San Juan/Mendoza (Argentina) probably creates geographic barrier between *leucogenis* and *armata*. Population estimated at 20 000–35 000 and slowly declining (Callaghan 1997).

Johnson (1963) regarded *armata* as rare in northern part of range, commoner but very local at 33–38°S, reaching peak densities in lake district and declining again from *c* 42°S southwards. Population probably in region of 4000–10 000 individuals and relatively stable (Callaghan and Green 1993). Numbers of *leucogenis* unclear, but likely in range 9000–13 000 individuals and slowly declining. Remains locally common, while in other areas has disappeared. In Colombia and Venezuela, *colombiana* declining significantly and populations increasingly localized (Hilty and Brown 1986, Gómez-Dallmeier and Cringan 1989, Callaghan and Green 1993). Numbers probably in region of 7000–12 000 individuals and slowly declining (Callaghan 1997).

Habitat and general habits

Inhabits boulder strewn rivers and streams, where rapids and waterfalls separate more placid sections. River gradient varies from 1 in 200 to 1 in 10 (Johnsgard 1978). Both downy young and adults possess remarkable ability to negotiate most turbulent rapids. Range overlaps with diversity of vegetational zones, and rivers can be bordered with dense montane rainforest in north to barren grassland of sub-antarctic Patagonia in south. In northern part of range, are most frequent at 1000–4000 m, and even higher in driest parts, but in southern areas, occurs near sea level (Johnsgard 1966b, Moffet 1970).

Feeds mostly by dabbling in shallows or diving mid stream, methodically probing rocky substrate in search of invertebrates. Wide, shallow riffles favoured feeding area, since this where food most abundant (Eldridge 1986), as are more placid sections of rivers. Often dive repeatedly in strong currents for 16 (12–18) sec (*n* = 7) with inter-dive resting periods of 12.6 (9–18) sec (*n* = 7) (Johnsgard 1966b). Other foraging activities include swimming upstream with head submerged, apparently pecking food swept past, and up-ending (Johnsgard 1966b). The principal food items are trichopterans, ephemopterans, plecopterans (particularly *Rheophila*) and gastropods (Phillips 1922–26, Niethammer 1952, Johnson 1963). Vegetable matter occasionally consumed, probably unintentionally, and occasionally small fish taken (Johnsgard 1966b, Eldridge 1986).

When alarmed, dives and swims up to 40 m underwater, before emerging and either taking flight or continuing down stream with only head above water. Another frequent method of escaping danger is to hide within waterfalls. Birds fly reluctantly, but can spring from water with great agility, flying low with rapid (*c* 12 per sec), shallow

Resident

wing-beats along course of river (Wright 1965, Johnsgard 1966b, Moffett 1970). Tail used for manouvering, both under water and when swimming through rapids, and also for support while climbing rocks.

Displays and breeding behaviour

Exhibits complexity of displays, described and illustrated by Eldridge (1979), apparently similar for both sexes throughout range (Johnsgard 1966b, Eldridge 1986). During aggressive interactions, when either sex usually confronts intruders of same sex, displays include Pointing (evenly spaced horizontal thrusts of head and neck), Upright (erect stance with dropped wings), Barging (low or erect approach display), Bent-neck (slightly curved and rigidly extended neck with head and bill bent sharply downwards), Vertical-shake (arch forward and vertical leap out of water while head shaken), Mule-kick, Wing-flap, Shudder-shake (brief shudder to tight body rotation with Head-flick), Open-bill and Body-bend (lowering of breast in continuous motion while bill tilts upward until head rests against back and fanned tail lifted to vertical position). Well-developed, horny wing-spurs commonly shown in display postures, particularly by ♂ after performing Mule-kick, Wing-flap or Upright, and also used in rather infrequent fights (Phillips 1953, Scott 1954, Johnsgard 1966b, Moffett 1970, Eldridge 1979, 1986). Sex-specific reaction to intruders suggests that intruder threatens both territory and pairbond, and possible that both sexes can acquire territory by displacing paired territorial rival (Eldridge 1986).

Body-bend and Vertical-shake often associated with pair maintenance behaviour, although mutual defence of territory probably also form of pairbond maintenance. Other pair maintenance activities include Close-following, copulation weeks before and after egg-laying, and prolonged interactions between mates while nest searching (including Tail-wagging, Pointing and Body-bends). Pre-copulatory displays by ♂ include Barging and Vertical-shake, while he may approach ♀ in hunched posture performing Bill-dips and Head-shakes. ♀ pre-copulatory behaviour includes prone posture and Vertical-shake; post-copulatory behaviour includes bathing by ♀ and partial Body-bends by ♂ (Eldridge 1979, 1986).

Has strong, permanent pairbond, although forced copulations with intruders observed (Eldridge 1986). Pair strongly territorial, and usually defends length of river for 1–2 km (Johnsgard 1966b, Moffett 1970, Eldridge 1986). Remains on territory year-round, unless displaced by severe winter weather.

Breeding and life cycle

Near equator, breeding season protracted, and nesting occurs at almost any time. Further south, in southern Peru and Bolivia, limited data suggest breeding occurs during dry season June–Oct, while in southern Chile nesting recorded Nov, and ducklings Dec (Johnson 1963, Johnsgard 1966b, Hilty and Brown 1986). Before laying, ♀ feeds almost twice as much as mate, and searches for nest site *c* one month before egg-laying (Eldridge 1986). Nests usually located well above water, sometimes as high as 20 m, in holes in rock crevices, gravel banks and trees, and in abandoned burrows of Southern Ringed Kingfisher *Megaceryle torquata* (Johnson 1963, Moffett 1970, Eldridge 1986). Although information scarce, possible that laying interval long, reportedly 6–8 days (Johnson 1963, Moffett 1970, Eldridge 1986). Nest lined with quantity of mottled dark and whitish grey down suffused with faint brown tint. Eggs of *armata* elongate, pointed and creamy tan with smooth glossy surface; 62.6 × 41.6 (*n* = 11); weight 57.3 (*n* = 3); clutch 3.8 (3–5) (*n* = 6) (Johnson 1963, Moffett 1970, Eldridge 1986). Only ♀ incubates, leaving nest during early morning and afternoon for 2–3 h to feed. During feeding, accompanied by ♂ and seems to partition food resource by foraging at different depths using different techniques (Moffett 1970, Eldridge 1986). ♀ observed by Eldridge (1986) averaged only 7 h 26 minutes on nest during daylight hours in 2nd week of incubation, while Moffett (1970) suggested protracted incubation period of 43–44 days (longest of any wildfowl). Young jump from nest to river, where forage in shallows along river edge with heads submerged. Moffett (1970) recorded foraging bouts of ducklings at 78 (55–102) minutes amounting to 6 h 28 minutes during single day, concentrated along *c* 275 m of river. By Day 6, foraging time decreased, and able to dive for 6 sec. No known predators, and mortality of young primarily related to being swept away in torrents (see Moffett 1970).

Fledging period unclear, but thought to be protracted (see Weller 1968). Family groups observed for several weeks before youngsters disperse (Johnson 1963). Likely to reach sexual maturity within one year (Conover 1943). No data on adult survival nor on longevity.

Conservation and threats

Throughout range threatened by degradation of rivers, most frequently owing to mining activities, sewage discharge, hydroelectric developments, and siltation following deforestation. Sensitive to hunting, which may explain absence from some stretches of fine river habitat. Introduction of game fish to many rivers also poses potential threat (Humphrey et al. 1970, Eldridge 1986, Hilty and Brown 1986, Scott and Carbonell 1986, Madge and Burn 1988, Gómez-Dallmeier and Cringan 1989).

armata included in Chilean Red Data Book as Vulnerable (Rottmann and López-Calleja 1992), and well represented in protected areas both in Chile and Argentina (Scott and Carbonell 1986). *leucogenis* included in Peruvian Red Data Book as Vulnerable, moderately well represented in protected areas (Scott and Carbonell 1986, Pulido 1991, Callaghan and Green 1993, Callaghan 1997) and fairly high densities known from Lauca National Park (northern Chile) and Cotahuasi Valley (Arequipa, Peru). It is unclear how well *colombiana* is assisted by protected area network. Apparently, only specific conservation project was education programme in late 1980s aimed at local people in Macizo Colombiano (Colombia). Peruvian *leucogenis* and Columbian *columbiana* subspecies listed as Vulnerable by Threatened Waterfowl Specialist Group (2003).

Des Callaghan and Jon Fjeldså

Steamer-ducks

Steamer-ducks are massive, pugnacious diving ducks, predominately grey above and white below, with greenish to orange bills, and white secondary remiges and wing linings. The common name is descriptive of the turbulent surface locomotion used by all members of the genus *Tachyeres*, reminiscent of that of paddle-wheel ships (Livezey and Humphrey 1983). Steamer-ducks are noted for extreme territoriality that, at times, is directed at intruding birds of virtually all species, the evolutionary significance of which remains controversial (Livezey and Humphrey 1985a, 1985b, Nuechterlein and Storer 1985, Livezey 1987). All species show substantial sexual size dimorphism (Livezey and Humphrey 1984a), and all but one (the Magellanic Steamer) exhibit significant sexual dichromatism of the head and bill. Three species are completely flightless, and some males of the 'flying' species in marine localities also are incapable of flight (Humphrey and Livezey 1982a, Livezey and Humphrey 1986a). Dives are accomplished primarily through propulsion provided by strong, alternate strokes of the feet, with short strokes of the

half-folded wings limited to an ancillary role at submergence and during underwater manoeuvres (Livezey and Humphrey 1984b).

Bradley Livezey

Taxonomy

For more than a century the genus was considered to be monotypic and flightlessness a function of age (Livezey and Humphrey 1992); key works in the taxonomic controversy include Cunningham (1871), Oustalet (1891), Blaauw (1917), Brooks (1917), Phillips (1917, 1922–26), Bennett (1924), Lowe (1934), and Murphy (1936). Phylogenetic analyses (Livezey 1986a, 1996) supported their inclusion among the shelducks (Tadorninae), with limited dissension (Johnson and Sorenson 1999). Within the genus, the three flightless species appear to be monophyletic, among which the Falkland and White-headed Steamers are closest relatives (Livezey 1986b, Livezey et al. 1986, Corbin et al. 1988). All members can be devastatingly destructive to other birds if maintained together in captivity (Livezey and Humphrey 1985a, 1985b).

Four species are recognized currently: three flightless ones which are allopatric (not overlapping in range) and coastal, and one flying species which is widely distributed on sea coasts and inland lakes. The White-headed Steamer, endemic to coastal Chubut, Argentina and narrowly missed by the collecting expedition of R.M. Beck (Murphy 1936), is the most recently described wildfowl species (Humphrey and Thompson 1981). Although the three flightless species are mutually allopatric, confusion with the Flying Steamer-duck is likely in marine localities (unless the latter is seen in flight), particularly in the Falkland Islands and coastal Chubut (Livezey and Humphrey 1992). Identification to genus is straightforward, but differentiation of species in the field is challenging and the subtle interspecific differences do not lend themselves to the diagrammatic depictions characteristic of field guides. Diagnostic criteria for skin specimens of adults and downy young and skeletons are summarized by Livezey and Humphrey (1992). The genus is limited in distribution to southern Argentina, Chile and the Falkland Islands.

Bradley Livezey

Flying Steamer-duck *Tachyeres patachonicus*
PLATE 11

Micropterus patachonicus P.P. King, 1831, Proc. Comm. of Science and Correspondence of Zool. Soc. London, **1**, 1

Type locality designated by Murphy (1936) as western part of Strait of Magellan; by neotype, Estancia Viamonte, Isla Grande, Tierra del Fuego, Argentina (Livezey and Humphrey 1992). Regarding citation see Livezey (1989c) and Internat. Comm. Zool. Nomen. (1991).

Tachyeres Owen, 1875

Etymology: *Tachyeres* from Gr. for fast-rowing; *patachonicus* after Patagonia, southern plains region of Argentina.

Other names: Flying Loggerhead, Lesser Steamer-duck, Canvasback (Falkland Islands), Lake Logger. Argentina: Pato vapor volador; Chile: Quetru volador.

Variation: no subspecies; however, considerable variation in measurements of skins and skeletons among continental localities (differences particularly marked between southern, sedentary, marine and northern, migratory, freshwater populations), and few specimens from Falkland Islands also suggest significant differentiation from continental populations (Livezey 1986c, Livezey and Humphrey 1992).

Description

ADULT: ♂ head and neck white (supplemental plumage), or crown grey, cheek brown, with white post-ocular streak (alternate plumage), or brown with restricted white post-ocular streak (basic plumage); throat dark cinnamon (especially pronounced in supplemental plumage). Mantle, rump, breast, primary remiges, dorsal wing coverts, and tail battleship grey, with silvery central areas and browner margins of feathers producing scalloped appearance. Breast, scapulars, sides, and flanks with considerable chestnut. Lower breast and belly, undertail coverts, wing linings, and most secondary remiges white. Central tail feathers recurved, proportionately longer than those of flightless congeners. Bill bright yellow-orange (duller during pre-basic moult), with bluish green suffusion ventral to nostrils, and black nail; legs and feet yellow-orange; iris brown. ♀ like ♂, but in all definitive plumages head and neck brown with white post-ocular streak, and bill greenish yellow.

MOULT: most, if not all, populations have 3 moults and plumages per annual cycle, 3rd (supplemental) only conspicuous in ♂. Pre-basic moult, during which all tracts including remiges replaced, typically occurs after nesting season (i.e. in middle of austral summer Jan–Feb) but can be delayed in adults attending broods; basic plumage worn for undetermined period. Pre-alternate moult only affects head and neck, and occurs sometime between austral fall and next austral spring. Pre-supplemental moult, also limited to head and neck, occurs shortly before breeding season, i.e. during austral spring. Details concerning timing of moults and plumages may differ significantly among populations, and even in best-known populations (southern marine birds) remains complicated and incompletely understood (Humphrey and Livezey 1982b, Livezey and Humphrey 1992).

IMMATURE: like adult ♂ in basic plumage but post-ocular streak comparatively inconspicuous, chestnut and silvery tones of plumage less pronounced, and bill, tarsus, and feet dull greyish green. Subadult like adult ♂ in basic plumage or adult ♀, with orange tones of bill less pronounced, sex for sex.

DUCKLING: cheeks, lores, forehead, crown, nape, and upper eyelids dark brownish olive; lower eyelids and supraocular and supraloral patches whitish, the latter very narrow (especially anteriorly), and widely separated from the broad, whitish post-ocular streak. Bill black. Dorsum light fuscous, lower back and rump dark brownish olive. Upper breast brownish olive, lower breast and belly white (Humphrey and Livezey 1985, Livezey and Humphrey 1992).

MEASUREMENTS AND WEIGHT: based on recently collected birds and museum specimens from entire range, ♂ wing ($n = 54$), 282–325 (304); tail ($n = 31$), 93–119 (111); tarsus ($n = 65$), 53–66 (60); weight ($n = 54$), 2100–3600 (2958). ♀ wing ($n = 64$), 265–312 (287); tail ($n = 30$), 91–117 (104); tarsus ($n = 67$), 50–66 (56); weight ($n = 51$), 1665–3118 (2347) (Livezey and Humphrey 1992).

Field characters

Length 660–710 mm. Easily recognized as steamer by large size, massive build, and predominately grey and white plumage. Only steamer-duck expected on freshwater lakes more than few km inland, smallest member of genus and only one capable of sustained flight. In flight, white secondary remiges contrast with otherwise grey back. In marine localities, distinguishing from flightless congeners problematic, although discrimination of all species readily accomplished in hand (Livezey and Humphrey 1992). Under ideal conditions, can be told from flightless congeners by smaller size, more slender head and neck, and proportionately longer tail and absolutely longer wings. Relative wing length of steamer-ducks difficult to assess, even if wings flapped or otherwise extended; while swimming, remiges extend almost to base of tail, whereas in flightless species, remiges extend only to cranial half of rump. Within distributional range of *T. pteneres* (coastal Chile and Tierra del Fuego), paired adult Flying Steamer can be told by distinct sexual dichromatism of bill and head (*T. pteneres* essentially monochromatic with both sexes having orange bills). In coastal Chubut, Argentina, distinguishing *T. patachonicus* on water or land from *T. leucocephalus* difficult, although ♀ of latter has broader, more conspicuous post-ocular stripes. In marine habitats of Falkland Islands, telling comparatively uncommon Flying Steamer from abundant *T. brachypterus* is practically impossible in field, unless former is in flight.

Voice

♂ in territorial display makes repeated, mewing, descending whistles (Rasping Grunts and Sibilant Grunts), typically slightly higher in pitch than similar calls of ♂ of flightless species. ♂ also produces more rapid, simple *ticking* calls. Both these ♂ vocalizations often accompanied by shorter, deeper Grunts by ♀♀, sometimes in apparent synchrony (Moynihan 1958, Weller 1976, Nuechterlein and Storer 1985, Livezey and Humphrey 1992). Sonograms of ♂ and ♀ calls in Livezey and Humphrey 1992).

Range and status

Uncommon on marine coasts of Argentina (Rio Negro south), Chile (Ñuble south), and Falkland Islands; and uncommon and local on freshwater lakes throughout same region, northward to high-altitude lakes of southern Neuquen, Argentina. Sympatric with *T. pteneres* in coastal Chile and Tierra del Fuego, with *T. leucocephalus* in coastal Chubut, Argentina, and with *T. brachypterus* in coastal habitats of Falkland Islands. Contrary to several published accounts (e.g. Johnsgard 1978), is only

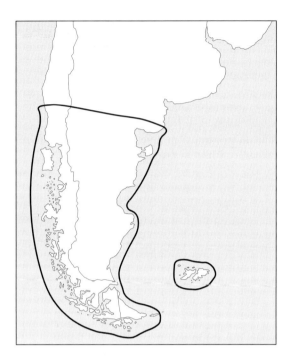

crabs Grapsidae most important crustacean. Diet also includes snails, limpets, and other bivalves; shrimp, insects, polychaetes, fish, and plants less frequently consumed; feeding intensity on saltwater strongly influenced by tidal rhythms (Livezey 1988).

When not feeding, found resting on shore, sometimes in large flocks of nonbreeders, or sleeping on water; members of breeding pairs often engaged in territorial defence (Nuechterlein and Storer 1985). Despite capacity of most birds to do so, flight uncommonly observed; flight can be elicited through pursuit in boats or gunfire, but other modes of escape (diving, steaming, semi-submerged swimming, or running) at least as common (Livezey and Humphrey 1982).

Displays and breeding behaviour

Intense territorial behaviour, frequently leading to combat and sometimes to death of one participant, characterizes breeding behaviour. Accordingly, described behaviours of Flying Steamer-ducks and other *Tachyeres* emphasize territorial display (Moynihan 1958, Johnsgard 1965a). Agonistic behaviour of ♂ includes False Drinking, Head-flagging, and conspicuous Short-high-and-broad posture, each generally performed while vocalizing. ♂ also uses Stretching postures and Triumph Ceremony towards ♀. ♀ also employs False Drinking and Stretch in agonistic contexts, often accompanied by vocalizations and in ritualized synchrony with displays by ♂.

Pre-copulatory display includes mutual Bill-dipping, Head-dipping, Ritualized Drinking and adoption of Alert posture. Copulation occurs on water surface. Post-copulatory displays include Alert posture, Grunting and Head-flagging (Moynihan 1958, Johnsgard 1965a).

Territorial attacks by either sex frequently commence with Submerged Sneak by aggressor toward intruder, often leading to complete submergence and grasping of victim from below surface with bill, and sometimes leading to drowning of target bird. Alternatively, combat by either sex can begin with Steaming surface rush, grasping of victim by neck or wing with bill, and pummelling of exposed body parts with rapid blows of carpal wing-knobs (Livezey and Humphrey 1985a, Nuechterlein and Storer 1985).

steamer-duck known to occur on Atlantic coast of Santa Cruz Province, Argentina. Vagrants found as far north as Buenos Aires Province, Argentina. Wetlands International (2002) suggested declining population of 1000–25 000 for mainland South America, and Woods and Woods (1997) estimated 200–400 pairs, or population of 600–1200, for Falkland Islands.

Habitat and general habits

On marine coastlines, preference given to rocky shores, protected bays and estuaries, and offshore islands. Evidently, birds breeding on freshwater lakes move to coastal habitats in winter. Like other members of genus, feeds primarily by diving to bottom to capture benthic invertebrates, with lesser reliance on surface feeding and foraging along waterline or on exposed tidal flats (Livezey 1988, Ryan *et al.* 1988). Most foraging occurs within 10 m of shore, with preference given to waters adjacent to rocky headlands or beds of kelp *Macrocystis pyrifera*. Average duration of dives 30 sec, but variation related to characteristics of habitat and sex significant. Molluscs and crustaceans most important prey items in birds collected on both salt and freshwater; in marine habitats, mussels were most important molluscan prey, and

Breeding and life cycle

Nesting typically occurs Oct–Jan. Typical nests shallow depressions in ground, thickly lined with down, and sometimes including lesser quantities of sticks or grass. Usually located close to water, often within few m of high tide level on marine coasts, although rarely placed as far as 400 m from water. Dense cover preferred, typically tangles of woody brush, dense grass, or other shoreline debris (Humphrey and Livezey 1985). Eggs rounded ovoid in shape, white to buff; 77.1 × 52.2 (73–84 × 51–55) from all localities (*n* = 40). Clutch size in 4 nests 6.2 (5–9). Incubation, by ♀, exceeds 30 days, with time to fledging estimated at *c* 12 weeks (Humphrey and Livezey 1985). Broods generally attended by both parents, and longevity of pairbond of this, and other non-migratory steamer-ducks, appears protracted and perhaps lifelong. No data on hatching success, adult survival nor longevity.

Conservation and threats

Prospects for continued existence improved in part by comparatively large distributional range. No evidence of extinction of any significant population to date, although considered rare in Falkland Islands and decidedly less common than its flightless congeners in areas of sympatry. Probably subject to limited pressure from hunters and egg collectors in some areas, potential damage to marine populations from oil spillage. Disturbance of nesting birds by human recreational activities on Andean lakes appears to be greater cause for concern.

Bradley Livezey

Magellanic Steamer-duck *Tachyeres pteneres*
PLATE 11

Anas pteneres J. R. Forster, 1844, Descr. Animal. Itinere Maris Australis Terras, p. 338
Tierra del Fuego; Isla Chiloé, Chile (Livezey and Humphrey (1992). Regarding citation see Livezey (1989c) and Internat. Comm. Zool. Nomen. (1991).

Etymology: *pteneres* Gr. *ptenos* meaning wing, *eretes* a rower, in reference to 'steaming' action of swimming bird.

Other names: Common Steamer, Flapping Loggerhead, Flightless Steamer-duck.

Variation: no subspecies recognized; modest latitudinal increase in body mass indicated.

Description

ADULT: sexes rather alike. ♂ crown light grey, rest of head and neck pale grey to greyish white (alternate plumage), or crown dark grey, rest of head and neck pale grey, with indistinct post-ocular streak (basic plumage); throat pale chestnut. Mantle, rump, breast, primary remiges, dorsal wing coverts, and tail battleship grey, feathers showing variable silvery wash or scalloped aspect. Lower breast and belly, undertail coverts, wing linings, and most secondary remiges white. Central tail feathers recurved and somewhat elongate, but tail shorter than in other steamer-ducks. Bill bright yellow-orange with black nail; legs and feet yellow-orange; iris brown. ♀ like ♂, with less sexual dichromatism than in other steamers (including similarly coloured bills) but, in all definitive plumages, head and neck darker grey, with less marked demarcation between crown and cheeks (alternate plumage) and more obvious whitish post-ocular streak, and bill often showing small bluish suffusion ventral to nares.

MOULT: present data indicate only 2 moults and plumages per annual cycle, with prebasic moult (affecting all feather tracts including remiges) typically occurring in late austral summer and fall, and pre-alternate moult (affecting only head and neck) occurring in early spring.

IMMATURE: like adult ♀ but post-ocular streak less pronounced (especially posteriorly), grey of head and neck darker, and bill, tarsus and feet greenish. Subadult like adult ♂ or adult ♀ in basic plumage, respectively, with grey of head and neck slightly darker and orange tones of bill less pronounced, sex for sex.

DUCKLING: cheeks, lores, forehead, crown, and nape dark brownish olive, becoming paler on the anterior forehead; upper eyelids blackish brown, lower eyelids whitish. Supraloral patch very small or absent; supraocular region blackish brown except for (in most specimens) small, whitish patch that is separated from whitish, 2-parted postocular streak. Bill black. Dorsum medium brownish olive, lower back and rump dark brownish olive. Upper breast brownish olive, lower breast and belly white (Humphrey and Livezey 1985, Livezey and Humphrey 1992).

MEASUREMENTS AND WEIGHT: based on recently collected birds and museum specimens, ♂ wing ($n = 38$), 243–294 (273), tail ($n = 14$), 83–112 (98); tarsus ($n = 37$), 65–79 (71); weight ($n = 16$), 4950–6500 (5394). ♀ wing ($n = 28$), 235–282 (262); tail ($n = 27$), 73–106 (87); tarsus ($n = 30$), 62–75 (68); weight ($n = 17$), 3400–5000 (4184) (Livezey and Humphrey 1992).

Field characters

Length 740–840 mm. Largest of genus, massive, flightless ducks of rugged seacoasts and cold waters. Does not occur with any other flightless duck; broadly sympatric, at least seasonally, with Flying Steamer-duck, from which can be told by larger size (almost twice as massive), heavy bill and neck, shorter wings and tail, much greyer body plumage, and virtual absence of sexual dichromatism (adults of both species having orange bills).

Voice

Calls similar to corresponding vocalizations of other steamers (Livezey and Humphrey 1992), but Grunting calls of both sexes considered more complex (Moynihan 1958) or lower and more slurred (Weller 1976). Sonograms of ♂ and ♀ calls in Livezey and Humphrey (1992).

Range and status

Locally common, permanent residents of marine coastlines from Isla Chiloé, Chile south to Tierra del Fuego, Argentina (including Isla de los Estados). Unconfirmed reports on Pacific coast as far north as Concepción, Chile (Olrog 1963), on freshwater Lago Fagnano, Isla Grande (Olrog 1948), and on Atlantic coast north of Rio Grande, Tierra del

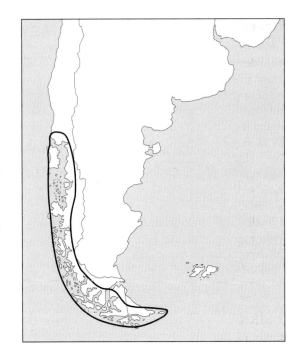

Fuego, Argentina (e.g. Murphy 1936, Olrog 1963, 1984, Johnsgard 1978); in absence of specimens, these reports presumably refer to either *T. patachonicus* or, on Atlantic coast, to *T. leucocephalus* (Livezey and Humphrey 1992). Wetlands International (2002) guessed at stable population of 25 000–100 000 in southern Chile and Tierra del Fuego.

Habitat and general habits

Feeds by deep water diving, up-ending in shallow water, and foraging at water's edge, and diet composed largely of molluscs and crustaceans (Weller 1976, Livezey 1988, Ryan *et al.* 1988). Preferred feeding grounds include rocky headlands, areas significantly more frequently defended by *T. pteneres* than smaller *T. patachonicus* in areas of sympatry (Livezey 1988).

Displays and breeding behaviour

Displays, most notably conspicuous territorial behaviour, similar to those of other, smaller congeners (Moynihan 1958, Weller 1976, Livezey and Humphrey 1985a). In most interspecific disputes, dominates Flying Steamer-duck and other wildfowl (Livezey and Humphrey 1985a, Livezey 1988).

Breeding and life cycle

Most nesting initiated in early austral spring, but considerable variation in nest dates reported, especially in northernmost parts of range (Humphrey and Livezey 1985). Most nests located close to high-tide level of saltwater and in heavy cover, although exceptional ones found several hundred m from sea or in exposed sites (Humphrey and Livezey 1985). Nests shallow depression often using sticks and grass, and typically lined with down. Eggs, all localities, 82.7 × 56.5 (78–88 × 52–61) (*n* = 32); in captivity weighed 137.25 (131–140) (*n* = 4) (Griswold 1968). Clutch 7 (4–8); incubation, by ♀, *c* 30 days; single captive duckling weighed 99 at hatching and 1360 at 35 days. 'Fledge' in *c* 12 weeks, attendance on broods typically biparental, and pairbond probably lifelong (Weller 1972, Humphrey and Livezey 1985). No data on breeding success, adult survival nor longevity.

Conservation and threats

Populations in most parts of range appear secure, although significant declines in some localities (e.g. northernmost part of range in Chile) indicated (Livezey and Humphrey 1992). As with all waterfowl and other birds inhabiting coastal environments of southern South America, principal threats to populations are destruction of habitat, most importantly development and pollution associated with petroleum industry.

Bradley Livezey

Falkland Steamer-duck *Tachyeres brachypterus*
PLATE 11

Anas brachyptera Latham, 1790, Index Ornith., p. 834
Falkland Islands; type locality Port Stanley, East Falkland Islands (Livezey and Humphrey 1992)

Etymology: *brachypterus* Gr. *brakhus* for short, plus *pteros* winged.

Other names: Loggerhead, Sea Logger, Logger, Logger Duck, Falkland Flightless Steamer-duck. Argentina: Pato vapor malvinero.

Variation: no subspecies and no geographic variation reported.

Description

ADULT: sexes rather alike, but usually distinguishable. ♂ head and neck white with variable greyish suffusion on crown in some individuals (supplemental plumage), or crown grey, cheeks brown, with white post-ocular streak (alternate plumage), or dark brown with faint whitish post-ocular streak (basic plumage); throat chestnut or cinnamon. Mantle, rump, breast, primary remiges, dorsal wing coverts, and tail battleship grey, feathers showing variable silvery wash and brown margins producing scalloped aspect. Breast, sides, and flanks with considerable chestnut. Lower breast and belly, undertail coverts, wing linings, and most secondary remiges white.

Central tail feathers recurved, proportionately elongate, intermediate in apparent length between longer rectrices of *T. patachonicus* and shorter ones of *T. pteneres*. Carpal joint orange. Bill bright yellow-orange (duller during pre-basic moult), with very limited or no bluish green suffusion ventral to nostrils, and black nail; legs and feet yellow-orange; iris brown. Breeding ♂♂ tend to become more white-headed with wear and exposure, and perhaps also with age and associated accumulation of scars and damage to head plumage from combat. ♀ like ♂, but in all definitive plumages, head and neck brown with comparatively narrow, white post-ocular streak, and bill greenish yellow.

MOULT: presence of 3 moults and plumages per annual cycle evidently identical in qualitative aspects to those of Atlantic-coastal Flying Steamer-duck (Livezey and Humphrey 1992). Prebasic moult affects all tracts including remiges, and typically occurs following nesting season or late austral summer (although reduced seasonality of Falkland Islands and associated variation in breeding schedules may render moulting schedules less predictable than in continental populations). Basic plumage worn for undetermined period of time, but pre-alternate moult (head and neck only) observed Oct–Feb. Details of schedule of pre-supplemental moult, also affecting only head and neck, not ascertained, but presumably occurs shortly before breeding season (Oct–Jan).

IMMATURE: like adult ♂ in basic plumage but post-ocular streak less pronounced (especially posteriorly), chestnut and silvery tones of plumage subdued, and bill, tarsus, and feet dull greyish green. Subadult like adult ♂ or ♀ in basic plumage, respectively, with orange tones of bill less pronounced, sex for sex.

DUCKLING: cheeks, lores, forehead, crown, nape, and upper eyelids medium fuscous; lower eyelids and supraocular and supraloral patches very pale smoke-grey and continuous, becoming very narrow at the junction with the whitish postocular streak. Bill black. Dorsum light fuscous, lower back and rump medium to dark fuscous. Upper breast fuscous, lower breast and belly white (Humphrey and Livezey 1985, Woods 1988, Livezey and Humphrey 1992).

MEASUREMENTS AND WEIGHT: based on recently collected birds and data from museum specimens, ♂ wing ($n = 24$), 238–296 (276); tail ($n = 15$), 92–110 (102); tarsus ($n = 25$), 60–72 (68); weight ($n = 12$), 3300–4800 (4228). ♀ wing ($n = 15$), 245–292 (268); tail ($n = 12$), 76–103 (96); tarsus ($n = 15$), 58–67 (64); weight ($n = 11$), 2900–4196 (3519) (Livezey and Humphrey 1992).

Field characters

Length 660–740 mm. Like all steamers, readily distinguished from other waterfowl by large size and predominately grey and white plumage; although only flightless duck in Falkland Islands, this character seldom useful for field identification. Primarily coastal in habitat, and rarely strays > 400 m inland. Virtually identical in plumage pattern and colour of soft parts to respective sex and age groups of Flying Steamer-duck (only congener with which sympatric), rendering separation of 2 species in Falklands most challenging problem of field identification of waterfowl in world. In Falkland Islands, unless steamer-duck seen in prolonged flight or observed on upland pond well inland, is most likely abundant *T. brachypterus*; confirmatory clues for

latter include heavier neck, relatively shorter wings and tail, stouter bill, and modally less pronounced sub-narial bluish area in adult ♂. In hand, specimens distinguished readily using measurements of skin or skeleton (Livezey and Humphrey 1992).

Voice

Similar to those of Flying Steamer. Calls of ♂, most typically used during nesting season and territorial encounters, include loud rasping whistles (intermediate in pitch between those of *T. patachonicus* and *T. pteneres*) and rapidly repeated, sharp ticking calls; ♀ produces series of deeper grunts, typically simultaneously with vocalizations of accompanying ♂ (Woods 1975, Weller 1976, Livezey and Humphrey 1992). Sonogram of ♂ calls in Livezey and Humphrey (1992).

Range and status

Endemic to Falkland Islands, where abundant in most low-lying coastal habitats, may also be found on ponds close to coast. Ranges northwest to Jason Islands where recorded on 7 islands during Striated Caracara *P. p. plancus* Survey of 1997, but apparently does not extend south to Beauchêne Island. Woods

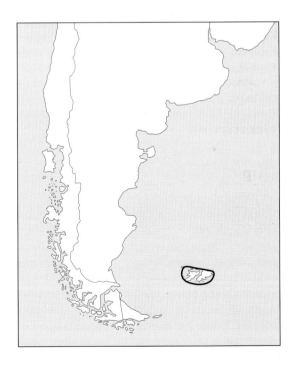

and Woods (1997) calculated average 12 200 (9000–16 000) breeding pairs; Wetlands International (2002) suggested population of 27 000–48 000.

Habitat and general habits

Similar to other coastal steamers in foraging behaviour and habitat, frequenting diversity of shorelines and showing a substantial variation in durations of dives and distances from shore during feeding; ♀♀ tend to remain submerged for shorter times than accompanying ♂♂. Where available in close proximity to marine shorelines, will walk or swim considerable distance to drink freshwater. In addition to diving, feeds near surface or searches for food along water's edge, activities showing strong associations with tidal rhythms. Composition of diet closely resembles that of marine *T. patachonicus*, with comparatively heavy consumption of bivalves and gastropods and lesser exploitation of crustaceans (Weller 1972, Livezey 1989c).

Preferred territories include rocky headlands, protected coves, and (near human habitation) breakwaters and sea-walls. Territorial pairs defend sections of coastline against encroachment by congeners and many other avian species (Livezey and Humphrey 1985a), and nonbreeders typically congregate in flocks in coastal areas or nearby lagoons not occupied by territorial adults. Although some remarkably tame (characteristic of most birds in Falkland Islands) and adults with broods known to charge humans, most move from human observers at distances of approximately 30 m (Humphrey *et al.* 1987), employing combination of walking, swimming, or (rarely, if pressed) diving and steaming.

Displays and breeding behaviour

Courtship and territorial displays similar to those of Flying Steamer-duck (Moynihan 1958), including methods of attack (often involving both sexes),

combat, anti-predator behaviour and specific displays. Agonistic behaviour includes Submerged Sneaks, Short-high-and-broad and Alert postures, and Stretch (Johnsgard 1965a, Pettingill 1965, Weller 1976).

Breeding and life cycle

Most nests initiated Sept–Dec, but nesting recorded throughout year (Pettingill 1965, Humphrey and Livezey 1985). Prefers heavy brush near high-tide level on marine shorelines, and not uncommonly uses abandoned burrows of Magellanic Penguins *Spheniscus magellanicus* for nest sites. Nests shallow depressions sometimes fortified with sticks or grass, typically heavily lined with down. Eggs, all localities, 81.8 × 56.6 (77–86 × 56–57) ($n = 11$); in captivity weigh 132 ($n = 19$). Clutch 6 (4–11); incubation, by ♀ alone, *c* 30 days. Captive ducklings weigh 82.7 ($n = 7$) on hatching, and 717 at 3 weeks ($n = 5$). Mortality among wild ducklings high, due to predation by Kelp or Southern Black-backed Gulls and Falkland Skuas *Catharacta antarctica antarctica*, but adults have no natural predators except seals (Woods and Woods 1997). Time to 'fledging' *c* 12 weeks, and attendance of brood typically biparental (Weller 1972, Humphrey and Livezey 1985). ♂ fertile in captivity at 16 months, and ♀ laid at 2 years. No data on breeding success, adult survival nor longevity in wild, although has lived for 20 years in captivity (Humphrey and Livezey 1985).

Conservation and threats

Common throughout Falkland Islands in suitable habitat (Woods and Woods 1997). Although birds in vicinity of Stanley reportedly suffered significant mortality during Falklands conflict, and maritime pollution oil spillage may pose threat in few places, keen affection and environmental sensitivity of locals bode well for continued abundance.

Bradley Livezey

White-headed Steamer-duck *Tachyeres leucocephalus*
PLATE 11

Tachyeres leucocephalus Humphrey and Thompson, 1981, University of Kansas, Museum of Natural History, Occasional Paper, **95**, 3
Puerto Melo, Chubut, Argentina
   Etymology: *leucocephalus* Gr. for white-headed.
   Other names: Chubut Steamer-duck.
   Variation: no subspecies.

Description

ADULT: sexes rather alike. ♂ head and neck white with variable amounts of greyish on crown, lores, and cheeks, with white post-ocular streak (alternate plumage), or dark brown with faint whitish post-ocular streak (basic plumage); throat chestnut or cinnamon. Mantle, rump, breast, primary remiges, dorsal wing coverts, and tail battleship grey, feathers showing variable silvery wash and brown margins producing scalloped aspect; feathers of breast, sides, and flanks comparatively chestnut. Lower breast and belly, undertail coverts, wing linings, and most secondary remiges white. Central tail feathers recurved, proportionately elongate, intermediate in apparent length between longer rectrices of *T. patachonicus* and shorter rectrices of *T. pteneres*. Bill bright yellow-orange (duller during pre-basic moult), with bluish green suffusion ventral to nostrils, and black nail; legs and feet yellow-orange; iris brown. ♀ like ♂, but in definitive plumages, head and neck brown, with white post-ocular streak broad (alternate plumage) or moderately broad (basic plumage), and greenish yellow bill.

MOULT: patterns of moult remain inadequately documented. Present data confirm presence of only 2 moults and plumages per annual cycle (although 3rd, supplemental plumage, remains possible): pre-basic moult which involves all feather tracts including remiges and typically occurs following nesting season (late austral summer) plus pre-alternate moult which only affects feathers of head and neck, and typically occurs several months after pre-basic moult but before following nesting season (by austral spring).

IMMATURE: like adult ♂ in basic plumage but head and neck dark brown with post-ocular streak obsolete, chestnut and silvery tones of plumage subdued, and bill, tarsus, and feet dull greyish green. Subadult like adult ♂ or ♀ in basic plumage, respectively, with orange tones of bill less pronounced, sex for sex.

DUCKLING: cheeks light to medium greyish brown, becoming paler caudoventrally; lores, forehead, crown, and nape medium to dark greyish brown; eyelids whitish to pale pearl grey. Supraloral patch broad, whitish or pearl grey, and continuous with the supraocular and postocular patches. Bill black. Dorsum light greyish brown, lower back and rump dark greyish fuscous. Upper breast medium greyish brown, lower breast and belly white (Humphrey and Livezey 1985, Livezey and Humphrey 1992).

MEASUREMENTS AND WEIGHT: based on recently collected birds and museum specimens, ♂ wing (*n* = 14), 262–295 (281); tail (*n* = 7), 78–109 (97); tarsus (*n* = 16), 61–69 (65); weight (*n* = 19), 2600–4400 (3808). ♀ wing (*n* = 13), 255–290 (273); tail (*n* = 7), 83–101 (94); tarsus (*n* = 13), 59–66 (63); weight (*n* = 16), 2450–3550 (3013) (Livezey and Humphrey 1992).

Field characters

Length 640–740 mm, readily recognized as steamer-duck by large size and predominately grey and white plumage; only flightless anseriform within range, inhabits coastal habitats within very limited range. Difficult to distinguish from corresponding sex-age groups of Flying Steamer-ducks, only other steamer with which even seasonally sympatric. Unless latter seen in prolonged flight or observed well inland, bird most likely abundant White-headed Steamer; on water, slightly larger size, heavier neck, relatively shorter wings and tail, stouter bill, and (in ♀) more pronounced post-ocular stripe characterize flightless species. In hand, specimens distinguished readily using measurements of skin or skeleton (Livezey and Humphrey 1992).

Voice

Similar to corresponding calls of sexes of Falkland Steamer and other congeners; sonograms in Livezey and Humphrey (1992).

Range and status

Locally common on marine coastlines of Chubut, Argentina, from Península Valdes south to northernmost parts of Golfo San Jorge. Wetlands International (2002) estimated stable population of < 10 000.

Habitat and general habits

Like other coastal *Tachyeres*, frequents diversity of shoreline habitats and employs range of (tidally influenced) foraging methods, including diving, dabbling and up-ending in shallow water, or searching substrate and water edge while walking. Composition of diet similar to congeners on saltwater, but with comparatively heavy consumption of crabs (Livezey 1989c).

Favourite resting places include shorelines of islands, with mainland sites including rocky headlands and protected coves. Territorial pairs exhibit pugnacity characteristic of genus (Livezey and Humphrey 1985a), although close proximity of nest sites on favourite islands suggests higher tolerance among incubating ♀♀ in certain conditions of congregation (Humphrey and Livezey 1985). Large flocks of nonbreeders found on beaches not occupied by territorial adults.

Displays and breeding behaviour

Least known of steamer-ducks. Preliminary observations indicate that courtship and territorial display correspond closely with those of Flying Steamer-ducks (Moynihan 1958) and Falkland Steamer-ducks (Johnsgard 1965a, Pettingill 1965, Weller 1976).

Breeding and life cycle

Most nests initiated Oct–Dec (Humphrey and Livezey 1985). Prefers heavy brush near high-tide level on marine shorelines, some sites accessible only through tunnels in brush. Strong preference for offshore islands evident, where aggregations of nests found. Nest shallow depressions variably adorned with sticks, grass, or litter, and typically heavily lined with down. Eggs, all localities, 81.2 × 54.2 (72–86 × 51–56) ($n = 15$). Clutch size 5 (3–6), incubation c 30 days by ♀, time to 'fledging' probably c 12 weeks, and generally both sexes care for brood (Humphrey and Livezey 1985). Predation of feeding ducks by Killer Whales *Orcinus orca* reported by Straneck *et al.* (1983). No data on breeding success, adult survival nor longevity.

Conservation and threats

Although likely that local residents take eggs and hunt adults for food, primary threats are oil spills and destructive impact of oil and other pollution related to commerce in region (Livezey and Humphrey 1992). Treated as Near-threatened by BirdLife International (2000).

Bradley Livezey

Spur-winged Goose and comb ducks

Taxonomy

The Plectropterini tribe consists of two distinct genera, the Spur-winged Goose *Plectropterus* of Africa and the comb ducks *Sarkidiornis* of South America, Africa and southern Asia. Only the former is known to have hybridized interspecifically (with the Muscovy Duck) (Johnsgard 1960c). All are polygamous without, usually, establishing significant pairbonds, and there is great difference in size between the sexes (Livezey 1996c).

The Spur-winged Goose was traditionally placed in the now obsolete 'perching duck' tribe (Cairininae or Cairinini) (Delacour and Mayr 1945, Boetticher 1952, Johnsgard 1965a, 1978). Livezey (1986a) re-assigned it to a monotypic subfamily (Plectropterinae) and placed the Comb Duck with the shelducks (Tadorninae). In a more thorough analysis (of 144 morphological characters), Livezey (1996c) proposed that the Spurwing and the comb ducks were related closely and re-assigned them to the Plectropterini; however, he noted that the assignment was tentative, and analytical artifacts might be responsible for showing such a relationship. Woolfenden (1961) concluded that the Spurwing was most similar to the shelducks, and Tyler (1964) found that the structure of their eggshells was intermediate between the goose and swan group and the shelducks. Mitochondrial cytochrome *b* data (Harshman 1996, Harvey 1999) show that neither species is close to the other nor to any other species. The spur-winged goose is suggested to be related to the shelducks, and the comb duck is suggested to be related to the dabblers, but support is ambiguous.

Des Callaghan

Spur-winged Goose *Plectropterus gambensis*
Plate 12

Anas gambensis Linneaus, 1766, Syst. Nat., ed. 12, **1**, p. 195
Gambia
Plectropterus Stephens, 1824

Etymology: *plectropterus* Gr. *plektron* means cock's spur plus *pteros* meaning winged

Other names: Spur-winged Duck. French: Oie-armée de Gambie, Canard armé; German: Sporengans; Spanish: Ganso espolonado; Dutch: Wildemakou; Zulu: iHoye.

Variation: 2 subspecies usually identified, Gambian Spur-winged Goose *P. g. gambensis* and Black Spur-winged Goose *P. g. niger* P. L. Sclater, 1877; however, not recognized by all authors due to individual plumage variation and overlap of body measurements (Clark 1979b, Halse and Skead 1983).

Description

ADULT: only slightly dimorphic, but ♀ smaller. Individual variation great, and intermediates between 2 races recorded and said to intergrade over wide area. ♂ has prominent knob formed by caruncles onto crown, with skin of bare face, knob, cheeks, and orbital ring bright pink to purplish to grey. Knob less pronounced or absent in *niger*. Ear coverts white, variable white feathering on face of *gambensis*, rest of head and upperparts black. White upperwing greater coverts form large patch. Upperwing lesser coverts and shoulder dark edged white, rest of wing black with coppery, green and pink-violet iridescence. Carpal spur on wing. Underwing coverts and axillaries brown and white. Chin, throat, front of neck, rest of underparts white. Small reddish pink caruncles visible along edge of white neck patch (*gambensis*). In *niger*, less white on face and underparts. Tail black with green iridescence, undertail coverts white. Bill deep pinkish red with whitish nail; legs and feet pink to red; iris dark brown. ♀ like ♂ with knob smaller or absent, and less extensive bare facial skin (bare parts and knob increase with age). Generally less iridescent, and white on wings not so extensive. In *niger*, white only on belly and undertail coverts.

MOULT: no data on body moults or their timing, but no seasonal plumage variation. Annual moult of flight feathers occurs mostly May–July in Transvaal (Dean 1978, Halse and Skead 1983). Mean date of initiation 3 weeks earlier in ♂ than ♀, with ♂ beginning wing moult 8 weeks and ♀ 6 weeks after breeding ends. Flightless for *c* 50 days. Moulting birds lose lipid and protein, and expend almost 30% more energy than non-moulting birds (Halse 1985a, Halse and Dobbs 1985). Moult of carpal spur occurs near end of annual flightless period (Zaloumis 1982).

IMMATURE: like adult but lacks bare facial skin and enlarged bill. Face and neck browner, body feathers fringed brown, less white on wing and underparts, with no white plumage in *niger*.

DUCKLING: yellow-brown above, buff below. Face light with indistinct brown eyestripe. Light band on sides of body, and light patches on wings and scapulars. Bill and legs blue-grey. Upper mandible slate blue 1st 6 weeks, rosy by 7 weeks, brownish red by 9 weeks.

MEASUREMENTS AND WEIGHT: ♂ wing ($n = 52$), 517 ± 22.2; wing-spur ($n = 59$), 29 ± 3.5; tail ($n = 48$), 220 ± 14.5; bill ($n = 52$), 69 ± 3.0; tarsus ($n = 60$), 115 ± 5.4; weight ($n = 58$), 5526 ± 635. ♀ wing ($n = 24$), 449 ± 15.7; wing-spur ($n = 27$), 22 ± 3.1; tail ($n = 22$), 192 ± 7.3; bill ($n = 23$), 62 ± 2.6; tarsus ($n = 28$), 96 ± 4.2; weight ($n = 34$), 3352 ± 489 (Halse and Skead 1983).

Field characters

Length 842–981 mm. Large black and white goose-like perching bird with knob on head and reddish pink bill and legs. Swims with hind end higher than shoulders. Feeds on land. In flight, long neck, broad wings with white shoulder patches, and white belly on an otherwise dark bird notable. Legs extend beyond wings in flight. Flocks fly in staggered lines, occasionally in V formation.

Voice

Weak, whistling voice. ♂ gives huffing *chu-chu*, soft, high-pitched *cherwit*, and repeated *tchic-tchic-tchic*

when threatened, and repeated *cherwit* in flight (Treca 1979, Brown *et al.* 1982). Squeaky *chi-chi-chi-chi* given by ♂ when approaching ♀ in courtship. ♀ silent except gives similar high-pitched *chi* calls with quick Bill-lifting movements when disturbed (Johnsgard 1965a). Sonogram of ♂ *cherwit* in Maclean (1993).

Range and status

gambensis occurs in Africa from Gambia, Senegal, Sudan, and Kenya south to Zambezi and Cunene Rivers; *niger* found south from Namibia and Zimbabwe in southern Africa. Does not breed in interior forest areas of central Africa and dry areas of southwestern Africa, but has occurred in Egypt, Oman, and Morocco (del Hoyo *et al.* 1992). Migratory over most of range, with marked seasonal movements of hundreds of km within continent. During dry season, large flocks gather at permanent water where often undergo wing moult in, e.g. Jan in Senegal, Feb in Lake Chad, Oct in Luangwa Valley, Zambia (Brown *et al.* 1982). Seasonally common to very common on most inland large waters. Most numerous on high veld of Transvaal, where population estimated to be 20 000 (Tarboton *et al.* 1987). Also 10 000 birds at times in Lac de Guiers, Senegal (Treca 1979). West African population estimated at 50 000 and decreasing due to desiccation of Sahel region, east African one stable at 200 000–300 000 and southern African population of *niger* stable at 50 000–100 000 (Rose and Scott 1997).

Habitat and general habits

Found in seasonal and permanent wetlands, including flooded grasslands, swamps, and pastures, often with Egyptian Geese. Regularly perches in trees to roost or loaf. Inhabits areas with open shorelines, islands, and sandbars when moulting. Wary. Feeds on farmland, and on water by picking at floating plant pieces, submerging head and neck or up-ending, and raking bottom with feet. Dives readily and swims underwater if pursued when flightless. In winter, rests by day and feeds in early morning, evening, or at night (Halse 1985a). Generally seen in small groups or pairs in wet season (breeding season) and in large flocks during nonbreeding season. For 68 birds collected over one year in Transvaal, diet consisted of 13 plant and 9 animal species, main food sources being crops

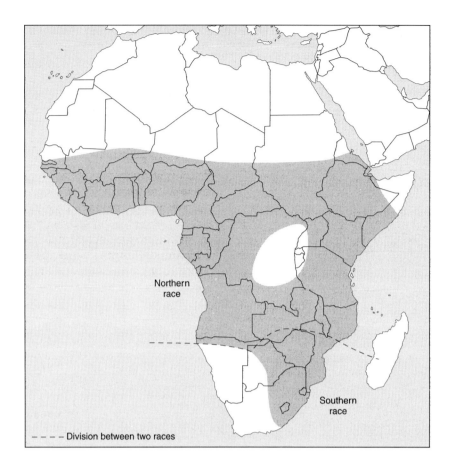

(primarily maize) 53%, weeds *Urochloa panicoides* 11%, lake plants *Potamogeton pectinatus* 34%, insects *Somaticus* 2%. Feeds on young grass when possible, noted feeding on figs some distance from water, and fond of sweet potatoes and ground nuts (Mackworth-Praed and Grant 1980). Changes in diet relate to changes in food availability and habitat use, and changes in digestive system noted during year, especially in gizzard (Halse 1985b). Ducklings mostly granivorous. Mean weight of grit in 97 adults 13.6 ± 0.71 g; most grit 2.8–1.7 mm long in adults (*n* = 31), 1.7–0.85 mm in ducklings (*n* = 3) (Halse 1983).

Displays and breeding behaviour

Displays not well documented. Pre-flight lateral Head-shakes and Chin-lifting. In courtship display, ♂ approaches ♀ with fluffed scapular feathers, shaking wings while uttering squeaky 4-syllable call. ♂ wings stretched to back, displaying spurs and white patches in wing, may function as simple threat display. ♂ attacks by running over ground with open bill, flapping wings and trying to strike intruder with wing-spurs. After attack, ♂ returns to ♀ and Wing-shakes with call, apparently simple Triumph Ceremony (Johnsgard 1965a). Copulation seen to occur once on water (Prozesky 1959). Suggested to be polygynous, with dominant ♂♂ accompanying more than one ♀ (Douthwaite 1978, Clark 1980). ♂ role in parental care variable; of 23 broods in South Africa, 17 attended by ♀ only, 6 by two adults (Clark 1980). Treca (1979) noted both parents with brood flying overhead, with ♂ giving *tchic-tchic-tchic* in reaction to danger, and young diving or hiding in reeds. In east Africa, both parents generally noted with young, perhaps in response to predation pressure (Pitman 1965).

Breeding and life cycle

Lays in ground and elevated nests near smaller, more secluded dams, pans, or marshes with emergent vegetation or fringing cover. In Senegal, uses tree sites 0.2–1.0 m high in acacia trees 3–4 m tall, generally on west or southwest side of tree, and occasionally with tunnel entrance through *Belanites aegyptiaca* thorns (Treca 1979). In South Africa, 20 of 32 nests on ground in dense grass near water (Clark 1980), and in Senegal, ground nests measured 400–450 mm across and 80–90 mm deep at centre of bowl (Treca 1979). In addition, nests found on termite heaps, tree boles, burrows, and on top of old nests of other birds (Pitman 1965, Clark 1980). ♀ grabs grass stems and sticks and adds them to nest bowl, gradually adding more materials from immediate surroundings as eggs laid and down plucked. Few Senegal nests re-used in subsequent year (Treca 1980). Generally breeds following onset of summer rains, but may breed in Zimbabwe in dry winter months and in other months of year. Eggs laid Aug–Jan in Nigeria, July and Sept in Uganda and Kenya, Aug–Oct in Cape Province, and Nov–Mar with majority (57%, $n = 97$) Jan–Feb in Transvaal (Clark 1980, Mackworth-Praed and Grant 1980, Tarboton *et al.* 1987). Eggs glossy ivory to pale brown, oval; 73.1 × 54.71 (66.2–76.7 × 55.2–58.5) ($n = 27$) (Treca 1979) and 75.2 × 55.4 (68.0–86.2 × 49.2–59.2) ($n = 93$) (Maclean 1993); weight 125 (104.4–135.3) ($n = 27$) (Treca 1979), 127 ($n = 93$) (Maclean 1993). Clutch size 17.5 (11–27) ($n = 11$) to 12.4 ($n = 17$) in Senegal (Treca 1979, 1980); 14.9 ± 6.2 ($n = 18$) in South Africa, 9.3 ± 3.0 ($n = 10$) in Zambia/Zimbabwe (Clark 1980); clutches of more than 14 probably laid by 2 ♀♀. Nest with 27 eggs incubated by 2 ♀♀; brood of 9 left with one ♀,

then brood of 5 left with other ♀ 15 days later (Treca 1979). ♀ obtains most nutrients for egg-laying from diet, with higher lipid and protein reserves during breeding than moulting (Halse and Dobbs 1985). Incubation by ♀ alone, 30–33 days (Treca 1980, Brown *et al.* 1982). Hatching success low in Senegal (4 of 27, 2 of 17 nests hatched) (Treca 1979, 1980), and brood size of only 6.3 ± 4.3 ($n = 31$) and 5.3 ± 2.9 ($n = 6$) noted in South Africa and Zambia/Zimbabwe, respectively (Clark 1980). Wing-spur *c* 3 mm long apparent at 4 weeks, 10 mm long by 10 weeks. Weight of young ♂ 90 and ♀ 87 on Day 5, rises to ♂ 3000 and ♀ 2451 by Day 70 (Brown *et al.* 1982). Young with parent(s) until dry season flocking period, and fledge at *c* 3 months. ♂ attendance on broods variable, and any pairbond may break during incubation. Some ♂♂ noted to accompany brood (Clark 1980) and call when danger near (Treca 1979). No data on breeding success, adult survival or longevity.

Conservation and threats

Not much valued as quarry, but can be sport target. Generally common to abundant, although northern populations may be affected by drought in Sahel (Scott and Rose 1996). On CITES III list in Ghana. Habit of feeding in cultivated land, sometimes in flocks of > 1000, causes consideration as pest (Tarboton *et al.* 1987); however, Halse (1984a) showed negligible reduction in maize yield by feeding geese. May have spread as result of dam building in southeastern Botswana. Potential adverse effect on moulting lakes if introduced fish affect availability of important aquatic food plants (Halse 1985a).

Gwenda L. Brewer

African Comb Duck *Sarkidiornis melanotos*
PLATE 12

Anser melanotos Pennant, 1769, Ind. Zool., p. 12, pl. 11 Ceylon (Sri Lanka)
Sarkidiornis Eyton, 1838

Etymology: Gr *sarx* flesh, plus *ornis* bird, referring to fleshy knob on ♂ bill. Gr *melas* means black, and *notos* backed.

Other names: Grey-sided Comb Duck, Knobbilled Duck or Goose. Afrikaans: Knobbeleend. French: Canard casque. Malagasy: Hara, Arosy. Hindi: Nakta.

Variation: no subspecies but species pair with *S. sylvicola* of South America.

Description

ADULT: dimorphic, mainly in size. ♂ back, wings and tail iridescent greenish black; breast, flanks and neck white. Rump grey with white head speckled black, although many individuals, particularly ♂♂, have black crown. ♂ acquires yellow 'wash' on head, neck and undertail coverts in breeding condition. Flanks grey, rather than blackish as in Neotropical *S. sylvicola*; however, ♂ photographed in Northern Kenya had black sides. ♂ has large fleshy black knob at base of upper mandible, reduced outside breeding season and absent in ♀; legs and feet dark grey; eyes dark brown. ♀ paler and considerably smaller.

MOULT: no ♂ eclipse, and no change in plumage except that yellow 'wash' acquired on head, neck and undertail of ♂ in breeding season; uncertain how change occurs, but probably due to moult, and colour intensity controlled by diet. No data on timing of body or wing moult.

IMMATURE: distinctive; upperparts and crown dark brown, head, neck and underparts buffish. Dark line through eye (Madge and Burn 1988).

DUCKLING: brown upperparts with large buffy yellow spots on sides and one on wing. Face and underparts buff yellow with small brown line through eyes (Delacour 1954–56).

MEASUREMENTS AND WEIGHT: in southern Africa, ♂ (n = 10) wing, 347–380 (360); tail, 117–150 (136); bill, 57–66 (62); tarsus, 56–67.5 (63.9). ♀ (n = 6) wing, 279–300 (286.6); tail, 100–120 (109); bill, 42.5–52 (46.6); tarsus, 42–50 (48.2) (Maclean 1993). In India (no sample size), ♂ wing, 339–406; tail, 139–153; bill, 63–70; tarsus, 64–75. ♀ wing, 280–309; bill, 59–66 (Ali and Ripley 1987).

Field characters

Length ♂ 790 mm, ♀ 640 mm. ♂ large stocky duck, often sitting high in water with head and neck held erect. Characteristic knob on bill and contrasting plumage make ♂ unmistakable throughout most of range. Smaller ♀ less conspicuous and may be confused, in Asia, with smaller Cotton Teal, which has similar plumage pattern. Further confusion can occur when associates with farmyard Muscovies; larger size and behaviour of domestics should facilitate identification. Caution needed where Comb Duck and White-winged Duck occur together; latter is larger and has darker breast and white wings. Are heavy flyers and move between roosts and feeding areas in 'goose-like' flocks, often flying in long lines or V formation. Large difference between sexes and knob of ♂ obvious in flight.

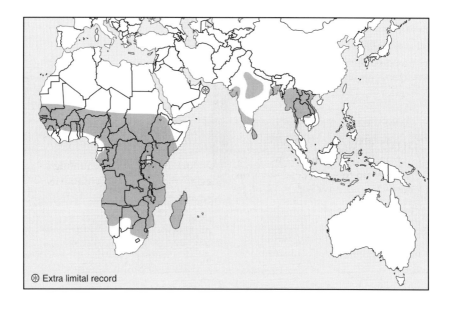

⊗ Extra limital record

Voice

Usually silent, may give soft wheezing hiss when flying. More vocal during display, when ♂♂ hiss and utter *guk-guk* calls. ♀ has soft clucking or melodious *karoo-oo* and harsher *krek-krek*. Sonogram of adult in Maclean (1993) and of young in Kear (1968).

Range and status

Widely distributed throughout sub-Saharan Africa, Madagascar and India. In Nepal, Myanmar (Burma) small numbers reported; in Thailand, Cambodia and Laos rare; no longer found in Pakistan and Sri Lanka (Miyabayashi and Mundkur 1999). In Africa migratory, arriving in breeding areas after onset of rain (Scott and Rose 1996); nearly 10% of those ringed in southern Africa travelled to sites north of equator (2000+ km) (Oatley and Prŷs-Jones 1986). Birds ringed in Zimbabwe recovered in Sudan (3600 km) and Chad (3880 km) (Brown *et al.* 1982). Large flocks of nonbreeders recorded in Senegal, Mali, Chad and Cameroon (Scott and Rose 1996). Vagrant to Oman.

Considered common but localized in places. In Asia, numbers estimated at 6000 and declining (Perennou *et al.* 1994); Wetlands International (2002) estimated 50 000-100 000 in western Africa, 100 000–500 000 in southern and eastern Africa, and declining population of 10 000–25 000 in Madagascar.

Habitat and general habits

Frequents marshes, floodplains, river deltas and forest-fringed wetlands. Utilizes temporary wetlands, flooded forest, pasture and rice paddies. Regularly perches, especially on dead trees in or near water.

Feeds by dabbling or up-ending and will graze on land and strip seeds from plants. Diet is seeds of aquatic plants, particularly grasses and water-lilies, rice, aquatic invertebrates and locusts.

Displays and breeding behaviour

Breeds in pairs, or in harems where one ♂ or 'harem master' may have up to 4 ♀♀, dependent on suitability of habitat. Polygyny rare or absent in Asia (Pitman 1965). Polygynous ♂♂ may breed with several ♀♀ in succession or simultaneously. Pairbond formed at breeding site. ♂♂ vigorously defend moving territory within home range.

♂ courtship includes Head-high, Supplant-bow, Body-shake, Breast-preen and exaggerated drinking and Turning-back-of-head displays. Head-down-end-up, given while swimming or standing, may be used as pre- or post-copulatory display: ♂ draws head in and holds bill pointing down against breast, wings slightly spread and raised posteriorly; posture held for several sec as ♂ aligns body laterally to ♀; if receptive, ♀ adopts prone posture with neck stretched forward on water. ♀ uses Inciting display aimed at desired ♂, and Going-away movement to encourage ♂ to follow. May use Wing-flap display, often from top of roost or nest tree (Siegfried 1978, Brown *et al.* 1982).

Breeding and life cycle

Breeding follows onset of rains, e.g. Nov–Dec in southern Africa, Dec–Apr in Zimbabwe, Nov–Mar in western Madagascar, and July–Sept in India and Nepal.

Nests in tree cavities or, less frequently, on ground where grass used as material; sometimes lays in old nests of Hammerkop *Scopus umbretta*. Nest trees usually in or near water. In harems, several ♀♀ occasionally lay in same nest and attempt to incubate clutch together. Eggs ovate, glossy white or yellowish; in southern Africa 58.6 × 43 (53–71 × 38.6–46.5) (*n* = 32) (Maclean 1993) or in India 61.8 × 43.3 (*n* = 100) (Ali and Ripley 1987); weight in southern Africa 46–56 (Maclean 1993), in captivity 47.0 (*n* = 29). Clutch *c* 8 (6–20) eggs; incubation, by ♀ alone, 28–30 days; hatch weight in captivity 28.7 (23.0–38.0) (*n* = 100). Ducklings can leave nest on mother's back. Fledge in 70 days (Brown *et al.* 1982). Age at 1st breeding uncertain.

No data on breeding success or mean adult survival, but oldest recorded in African ringing project recovered 3683 km north in Sudan, 21 years 6 months after ringing (Demey and Kirwan 2001).

Conservation and threats

Local populations threatened by hunting and habitat loss. Indiscriminate hunting in Madagascar has led to sharp declines. Considered quite threatened in Asia (Miyabayashi and Mundkur 1999). Protection of wetland habitat, prevention of pollution, and monitoring and control of hunting will maintain numbers. Dead trees with hollows suitable as nesting sites should be protected throughout range.

Glyn Young

South American Comb Duck *Sarkidiornis sylvicola*
PLATE 12

Sarkidiornis sylvicola Ihering and Ihering, 1907, in Mus. Paulista, São Paulo, Cat. Fauna Brazileira, **1**, p. 72 Iguapé, São Paulo, Brazil and Buenos Aires, Argentina

Etymology: *sylvicola* L. 'of woods or trees'.

Other names: Knob-billed Duck or Goose, Black-backed Goose.

Variation: no subspecies. Listed as *Sarkidiornis carunculata* by Phillips (1922–26), and regarded as race of African Comb Duck by some authors (Delacour and Mayr 1945, Delacour 1954–64, Johnsgard 1978).

Description

ADULT: dimorphic, mainly in size. ♂ head and neck white (usually tinged yellow in breeding season), variably spotted with black, more thickly on nape and hind neck. Upperparts metallic blue-green, secondaries bronzy, scapulars purple. Lower parts white, and flanks black. Undertail coverts white, becoming orange-yellow in breeding season. Bill black, with large fleshy protuberance or caruncle on mandible; legs dark grey; iris brown. ♀ similar to ♂ but much smaller, duller, less metallic above and no caruncle. Flanks dark grey. Undertail coverts white throughout year and no yellow tinge to nape and hind neck during breeding season (Delacour 1954–64, Johnsgard 1978).

MOULT: no great seasonal change except that yellow colour acquired on head, neck and undertail coverts of ♂ in breeding season; uncertain how change occurs, but probably due to moult, and colour intensity controlled by diet. No information on timing of wing moult.

IMMATURE: in 1st plumage has neck and underparts light buff brown, with dark brown crown and eyestripe, and dark brown spotting on flanks and breast. Mantle, tail and wings dark brown (Delacour 1954–64, Johnsgard 1978). Later, juvenile resembles ♀, but less glossy above and heavily barred with blackish on hind neck.

DUCKLING: crown, nape, hind neck and upperparts brown, with two large buff yellow spots on side of body (sometimes joined). Wings brown with posterior buff yellow edge. Face and underparts buff yellow with small brown line, often interrupted, through eye. Bill and legs grey (Delacour 1954–64).

MEASUREMENTS AND WEIGHT: ♂ wing ($n = 7$), 336; culmen (from back of caruncle), 55–57; weight ($n = 5$), 1863. ♀ wing, 283 ($n = 8$); weight ($n = 5$), 1069 (Delacour 1954–64, Gómez-Dallmeier and Cringan 1989).

Field characters

Goose-like duck that looks white-headed at distance, 550–630 mm long. Could be mistaken for domesticated forms of Muscovy, but lacks conspicuous white wing coverts (Hilty and Brown 1986).

Voice

Poorly documented, but usually silent (de Schauensee and Phelps 1978, Hilty and Brown 1986). ♂♂ utter faint, whistled *churr*, and ♀♀ weak quack or grunt (Fjeldså and Krabbe 1990). Vocalizations of African Comb Duck better studied and probably similar.

Range and status

Resident but somewhat nomadic in tropical and subtropical South America, from east Panama, locally throughout most of northern South America, to Paraguay, central Argentina and Uruguay.

Primarily occurs in lowlands but, on several occasions, recorded above 2000 m (up to 4080) in Andes (Fjeldså and Krabbe 1990). Although widespread, localized and generally scarce (Koepcke 1964, de Schauensee 1971, ffrench 1973, Hilty and Brown 1986, Narosky and Yzurieta 1987, Roth and Scott 1987, Fjeldså and Krabbe 1990, Menegheti *et al.* 1990, Dubs 1992, del Hoyo *et al.* 1992, Sick 1993). Indeed, sizeable populations currently known only from Venezuela (Apure, Guárico and Anzoátegui States) and northeast Brazil (Friedmann and Smith 1950, de Schauensee and Phelps 1978, B. Thomas 1979, Scott and Carbonell 1986, Gómez-Dallmeier and Cringan 1989, Bertonatti *et al.* 1991, Blanco and Canevari 1993). Venezuelan population estimated at 8000–40 000 (Gómez-Dallmeier and Cringan 1989), while highest number recorded was

Resident

Prefers areas where trees or other perching sites available, and usually encountered in pairs or small groups (♂ with several ♀♀ or parties of single sex); however, large groups occasionally gather during dry and wet seasons. Spends time on sandbars, mudflats or similar areas during middle of day, and restrict foraging to early morning and late afternoon. Primarily vegetarian, eating mostly seeds (including agricultural grains) and soft parts of aquatic plants, although invertebrates often consumed. Feeds in shallows along water edge, but also on land (de Schauensee and Phelps 1978, Gómez-Dallmeier and Cringan 1989).

Displays and breeding behaviour

Undocumented, but probably similar to African Comb Duck.

Breeding and life cycle

Nests not recorded from wild; indeed, almost nothing known of breeding period, but may correspond with wet season (Friedmann and Smith 1950, Gómez-Dallmeier and Cringan 1989).

Conservation and threats

Threats poorly known but, in Argentina, include overhunting, deforestation and indiscriminate poisoning of wildfowl in rice fields (Bertonatti et al. 1991). No indication of substantial decline in numbers, but considered near-threatened by del Hoyo et al. (1992), and listed (as *Sarkidiornis melanotus sylvatica*) as Near-threatened by Threatened Waterfowl Specialist Group (2001).

Des Callaghan

at Volta da Serra on east side of Sobradinho Lake (Bahia State, northeast Brazil) in 1992, when 5000 counted (Blanco and Canevari 1993). Total population estimated at 25 000–100 000 (Rose and Scott 1997), and declining.

Habitat and general habits

Occurs in variety of habitats, including freshwater marshes and lagoons, river deltas, inundated floodplains, forested rivers and rice fields, often associated with whistling-ducks and sometimes Orinoco Geese.

The shelducks and sheldgeese

Of the eight species of sheldgeese, all but two are restricted to South America. It is thought that they have only one moult of body feathers annually, so that they cannot appear different at different times of the year. However, male and female are often permanently unlike, and the most extreme examples of wildfowl sexual dimorphism are found here (Figure 9.17). Sheldgeese are grazers like the true geese but, unlike them, courtship is a conspicuous matter, and the functioning of sexual selection is obvious; females incite males—by voice and usually by pointing—to attack other males and select their mates on the basis of the male's reaction.

Shelducks are generally brightly coloured and unusually (because she does all the incubating) the ♀ is as conspicuous as the male. She nests under cover

9.17 Pair of Magellan Geese, the brown female on the left and the mainly white male on the right, illustrating the high level of sexual dimorphism in this species.

in mammal burrows, hollow trees, or rock crevices, and the down with which she lines her nest is light grey or white so that it is more easily seen in the dark. Shelducks moult their body feathers twice a year, so can change their colour with the seasons. They are generally sociable but highly territorial when breeding, displaying vigorously and noisily to other pairs before and during the nesting and rearing season, and giving a quarrelsome impression. Indeed, both sexes are aggressive, and the ♀ takes an active part in territorial defence which may be why, unlike most ducks, she is so boldly marked.

Except for the Ruddy and the Common Shelducks, the ranges of wild shelducks do not overlap, and none occurs in North or South America. Four of the six species—the Cape, Australian, Paradise and Ruddy—are clearly closely related. The first three are found in the southern hemisphere but possess a temperate type of breeding pattern in that egg-laying ceases before the long days of midsummer. It seems

probable, therefore, that the group evolved in the temperate latitudes, somewhere between 40° and 50°S. It has been supposed that the Ruddy Shelduck is a recent invader of the north. The ducklings of the Radjah Shelduck have a head pattern rather unlike other shelducks, and the windpipe of the male resembles that of surface-feeding ducks; the species has a protracted breeding season that suggests a long association with the tropics.

Sheldgeese and shelducks can live to a good age and, again unusually, females tend to outlive males. The pairbond is long-term and both parents look after the black and white ducklings (Kelp goslings are entirely white); nevertheless, the females seem to be the dominant partners and, in many non-breeding flocks, outnumber males. The juveniles in first plumage often resemble their fathers rather than their mothers—another feature in which the group differs from their relatives. Except for the Blue-winged Goose, the two sexes are unlike in voice; the males whistle and the females utter harsher quacks and growls.

Most tend to a vegetarian diet although Common and Radjah Shelducks eat molluscs and other invertebrates. Feeding frequently occurs at the coast or in saline lagoons, so that the birds take in salt with their food, and need nasal glands that extract the excess from the bloodstream. Feeding times on the shore are determined by the tides and, therefore, by the phases of the moon. Moult migrations to places of safety, where wing quills can be shed and replaced, are common after the young are independent.

Shelducks and geese are not generally considered good to eat and, perhaps because of this, tend not to be hunted for food. Since they breed at two years of age at the earliest, they are not ideal for harvesting by shooters anyway. However, like the true geese, the grazing habits of sheldgeese bring them into conflict with farming interests, and large numbers have been killed as pests. On the other hand, myths about the Ruddy Shelduck are common in Indian literature, where the bird's sacred status depends upon the saffron colour of its plumage resembling that of holy men.

Janet Kear

Taxonomy

Presently, the Tadornini tribe is composed of the shelducks *Tadorna* and sheldgeese *Cyanochen*, *Alopochen*, *Neochen* and *Chloephaga*. The sheldgeese were placed amongst the true geese (Anserini) by early taxonomists owing to superficial similarities (Sclater and Salvin 1876, Salvadori 1895, Phillips 1922–26, Peters 1931); however, it has since been established that the sheldgeese are closest to the shelducks, forming a group intermediate between the true geese (Anserini) and true ducks (Anatinae) (Delacour and Mayr 1945, Johnsgard 1965a, 1978, Livezey 1986, 1996c, 1997c). The Tadornini are distributed widely, though concentrated in the southern hemisphere, with diversity of Holocene species highest in South America and Africa (Figure 9.18).

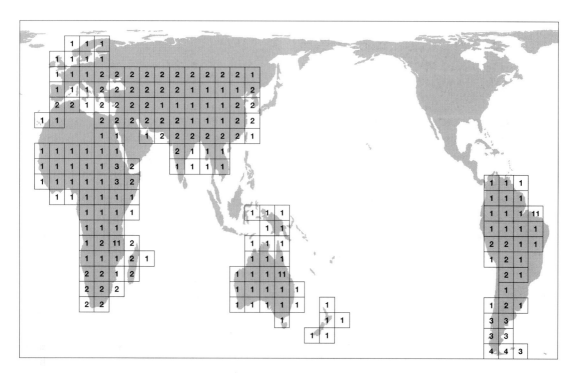

9.18 Species diversity of shelducks and sheldgeese (Tadornini) that survived into the Holocene. The number of species that occur (or occurred) within each grid-cell is indicated.

At least five species have become extinct during the Holocene, including four on the Mascarene Islands (*Alopochen sirabensis*, *A. mauritania*, *Centrornis majori* and *Mascarenachen kervazoi*) (Howard 1964a, Cheke 1987, Cowles 1994, Young *et al.* 1996, Mourer-Chauviré *et al.* 2000), and one on the Chatham Islands (*Pachyanas cathamica*) (Cassels 1984).

The oldest fossil Tadorninae is very similar to modern *Tadorna*, known from the mid Miocene of Germany (Feduccia 1996). In addition, fragmentary remains of a Tadornini are known from the mid Miocene of Maryland, US (Alvarez and Olson 1978). No tadorninesae are known from North America currently (Figure 9.18), but they did occur until at least the late Pleistocene, represented by, for example, the pygmy sheldgeese (*Anabernicula minuscula*, *A. gracilenta*, *A. robusta* and *A. oregonensis*) (Howard 1964b, Short 1970) and *Brantadorna downsi* (Brodkorb 1964). *Anabernicula* is in need of revision, since it may contain some species that belong in the Anserinae (Bickart 1990). Little is known of the life history of the extinct species. The pygmy sheldgeese seem to have inhabited aquatic habitats and may have shown sexual dimorphism in size (see Howard 1964b, Short 1970). The Chatham Island Shelduck *Pachyanas cathamica* was a marine bird that fed on molluscs and crustaceans (Holdaway 1989). It seems to have evolved large size, flightlessness, a diving habit and cavity nesting (see Cassels 1984, Holdaway 1989).

Sexual dichromatism has evolved at least twice within the group, in the Kelp and Magellan Geese, and in most of the shelducks; however, this has not been accompanied by changes from long-term to short-term pairbonds as is often the case in wildfowl (Livezey 1997c).

Relationships within the tribe were not studied comprehensively until the work of Livezey (1997c). In common with Johnsgard (1978), but in contrast to Delacour and Mayr (1945), Livezey (1997c) concluded that the sheldgeese had an earlier origin than the shelducks. Within the sheldgeese there seemed to be a consensus that the Blue-winged Goose is a sister to other living species (Johnsgard 1978, Bottjer 1983, Livezey 1997c); however, molecular evidence suggested that it might not be a sheldgoose at all, and may instead be related to pochards (Sorenson *et al.* 1999, Johnson and Sorenson 2000). The molecular data suggest that its closest relative within pochards is Hartlaub's Duck; both are African and both have unusual blue upper wings. Like most previous authors (Johnsgard 1965a, 1978, Sibley and Monroe 1990), Livezey (1997c) recognized a close relationship between Common and Rajah Shelducks.

Des Callaghan

Blue-winged Goose *Cyanochen cyanopterus*
PLATE 9

Bernicla cyanoptera Rüppell, 1845, Syst. Übersicht Vögel Nord-Ost-Afrika's, p. 129, pl. 47
Shoa, Ethiopia
Cyanochen Bonaparte, 1856
    Etymology: *Cyanochen* Gr. *kuanos* dark blue; *khen* the goose with blue, *pteros*, wings.
    Other names: Abyssinian Bluewing. Amharic: Kinfe-semayawi Ziy.
    Variation: no subspecies.

Description

ADULT: sexes similar but ♂ larger. ♂ head and neck brownish to ashy, paler on forehead, face and throat. Mantle and underparts mottled brown and pale grey. Back slate grey graduating to pale or darker brown on uppertail coverts. Vent and under tail coverts white. Tail rounded and black. Upperwing coverts pale slate to darker blue, primaries black, secondaries glossy with dark green sheen. Underwing coverts white. Bill, legs and feet black; eye dark brown. ♀ similar to ♂ but generally paler, especially head and neck, and considerably smaller.

MOULT: no seasonal change in plumage. Wing moult not described except that it takes place during heaviest part of long rainy season in Aug (Urban 1991). Uncertain how many annual body moults occur.

IMMATURE: similar to adult but duller.

GOSLING: brownish black above, marked with silvery white, underparts white; large black spot behind eye. Head tinged yellow which soon fades. Bill and legs black (Delacour 1954–64). Down long and silky as in Andean Goose.

MEASUREMENTS AND WEIGHT: ♂ (*n* unknown) wing, 368–374; tail, 160–164; bill, 32–33; tarsus, 70–73; weight (*n* = 3) 2000–2360 (2120). ♀ (*n* unknown) wing, 314–334; tail, 135–142; bill, 30–31; tarsus, 51–65; weight (*n* = 4) 1305–1520 (1444) (Delacour 1954–64, Lack 1968, Brown *et al.* 1982).

Field characters

Medium-sized, 600–750 mm long (similar to Ruddy Shelduck), and thick-necked grey-brown goose with conspicuous pale to darker blue innerwing patch in flight (Figure 9.19). White underwing coverts clear in flight. Distinctly rounded shortish black tail not projecting much behind body in flight. No risk of confusion with any other species of Anatidae in restricted range.

Voice

High-pitched and whistle-like, not so sexually different as in *Chloephaga* geese. Mild alarm call by ♂ weak *whew-whu-whu-whu*. Major alarm call on forced take-off nasal *penk-penk-penk* not continued in flight. ♂ display has repeated whistle *wheee-whu-whu-whu-whu*. Threat by both sexes *wi-wi-wi-wi-wi-wi* (Brown *et al.* 1982).

Range and status

Endemic to Ethiopian highlands from *c* 6–12°N latitude and 36–40°E longitude and usually

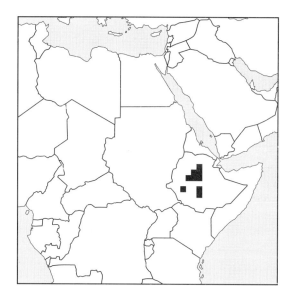

9.19 Blue-winged Goose in flight.

found above 2000 m with occasional records at lower altitudes (Figure 9.20).

Endemic, common, easily seen and conspicuous in preferred habitats at all times of year. Second in numerical importance of Afrotropical species only to Egyptian Goose and possibly Yellow-billed Duck. Surprisingly not recorded by James Bruce in late 18th century who stated there were no geese 'wild or tame' in Ethiopia except Egyptian Geese (Wilson 1992). Wetlands International (2002) estimated stable population of 5000–15 000 individuals.

Habitat and general habits

Main habitat marshy areas, shallow pools and river banks. In central part of range at altitudes of 2000– 3000 m, most common in areas of water-logged black cotton soils ('vertisols') with dense carpet of heavily grazed (by domestic livestock) short fine grasses and sedges. At higher altitudes in northern and southern parts of range, substrate granitic and grasses coarser and longer. Mainly grazer in marshy areas with grasses and sedges and some underground corms of sedges being bulk of diet. Probably also eats worms, insects and larvae and freshwater molluscs. Seldom swims.

Partially migratory (Figure 9.20), moving to higher alpine moorland in dry winter season where breeds, returning to lower altitudes during rains often in relatively large loose groups. Usually in pairs or family

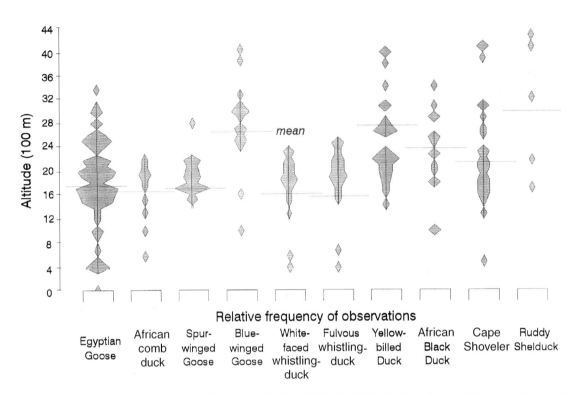

9.20 Altitudinal sightings of Blue-winged Goose and other wildfowl in Ethiopia (data abstracted from newsletters of the Ethiopian Wildlife and Natural History Society and reported by Wilson 1993).

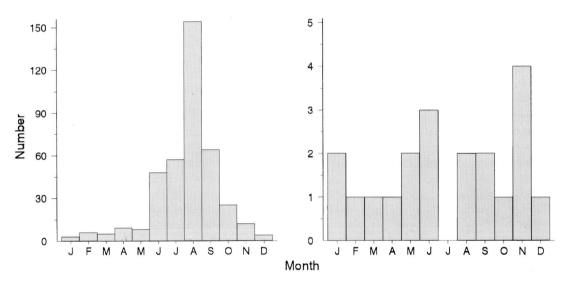

9.21 Monthly distribution of sightings of Blue-winged Goose (left hand histogram for Gaferssa Reservoir near Addis Ababa at 2600 m, from Urban 1991; right hand histogram as for Figure A covering whole range).

groups with young of year. Couples sometimes associate with others, especially at altitude in winter.

Displays and breeding behaviour

Aggressive towards other waterfowl, ♂♂ adopting threatening neck-out posture either standing or swimming. Following overt threat, ♂ and ♀ come together necks outstretched and heads close together. ♂ courts ♀ with head and neck bent over back and bill raised to sky, exposing wing patch and green secondaries and whistling rapidly and repeatedly. Territorial nester.

Breeding and life cycle

Little known; most data from captive studies. Estimated laying in short Mar–June dry season and towards end of long rains in Sept. Nest on or near ground probably constructed by ♀ and incubation solely by her but both birds defend young. Eggs elongated, cream; 70 × 50; weight 81.8 (73.0–94.0)

($n = 100$); clutch 4–9; incubation 30–34 days. Gosling hatches weighing 51.5 ($n = 21$) and reaches 88 by Day 5. Feathers start to emerge Day 21; almost fully feathered at Day 42, but wing feathers and coverts still short; fully fledged and almost adult size at Day 85. First moult starts *c* Day 176. No information from wild on nesting success, survival nor longevity.

Conservation and threats

Present in several national parks and conservation areas, most notably in Bale Mountains and Simien region. No other special protection measures in place and none appears needed, although designated Near-threatened by BirdLife International (2000). Not molested by local people, nor shy of humans, allowing close approach and slow to fly away. Must be some long-term concern for habitat over parts of range as human population and cultivation expand.

Trevor Wilson

Egyptian Goose *Alopochen aegyptiacus*
PLATE 11

Anas aegyptiaca Linnaeus, 1766, Syst. Nat., ed. 12, **1**, p. 197
Egypt
Alopochen Stejneger, 1885

Etymology: *Alopochen*, Gr. *alopos* fox-like, plus *khen* goose; *aegyptiacus* of Egypt.

Other names: African Sheldgoose. Afrikaans: Kolgans; French: Oie d'Egypte.

Variation: no subspecies; occupies monotypic genus with no close relative in Afrotropics. May have arisen out of Eurasian shelduck precursors that invaded Africa (Snow 1978). Relationship with extinct Indian Ocean *Cestrornis majori* and *Alopochen sirabensis* (Madagascar), *A. mauritiana* (Mauritius) and *Mascarenachen kervazoi* (Réunion) unclear (Young *et al.* 1997, Mourer-Chauviré *et al.* 1999).

Description

ADULT: sexes almost alike. ♂ forehead, lores and throat off-white. Crown, auriculars and neck dusky

brown (neck occasionally overlaid with indistinct chestnut spots). Dark brown circumorbital patch, frequently invading lores and chin. Chestnut brown collar at base of neck which broadens onto lower hind neck and upper mantle. Mantle and upper breast khaki to greyish with fine black vermiculations. Brown patch of irregular size and shape mid breast. Flanks greyish with narrow brown striations. Belly white and vent yellowish ochre. Back, rump and uppertail black. Wing coverts white but greater coverts transected by thin, diagnostic black stripe. Primaries and primary coverts blackish brown, speculum iridescent green and post-humerals rich chestnut. Underwing coverts of primaries black, rest of underwing coverts and axillaries white. Bill pink with edges and nail darkened; legs and feet fleshy pink becoming red in breeding season; eyes orange. Aberrant grey-mantled and leucistic individuals occur (Cramp and Simmons 1977, Campbell 1989). ♀ similar but smaller with narrower, less 'bullish' neck. Legs less intensely coloured in breeding season.

MOULT: no seasonal change in feather pattern; however, plumage attains brighter hue in breeding season, although mechanism not understood. Wing moult can occur throughout year (Dean 1978); in southern Africa, Geldenhuys (1975) suggested 2 main wing moult peaks, Jan–Feb and June–July, but Siegfried (1967), Dean (1978) and Milstein (1993) advocated one major moult in winter (Apr–June). Eltringham (1974) observed two apparent moulting peaks in Uganda. In Zambia, moults Feb–May (Douthwaite 1978). Brown *et al.* (1982) concluded that timing of moult corresponded with local breeding season and, consequently, varied geographically. During moult, primaries, secondaries, wing coverts and rectrices shed; remiges lost in *c* 4 days (Dean 1978) though this variable (Milstein 1993). New feathers take 30–35 days to grow and 3 days to harden, with *c* 40 days of flightlessness (Dean 1978). About 20–25% loss from pre-moult weight (Shewell 1959). Moulting localities usually little disturbed, have good visibility and minimal vegetation, with crop fields and grasslands adjacent (Maclean 1986). Capable divers when in moult, swimming adroitly beneath surface (Brickell 1988).

IMMATURE: duller, lacking eye and breast patches. Forewing panel dirty grey, black stripe less distinct. Eye-patch forms at 3–5 months and breast patch at 5 months (Maclean 1988).

GOSLING: upperparts dark brown relieved by whitish back and wing spots. Distinctive white supraorbital stripe present in otherwise umber forehead and crown. Sides of face, throat and underparts dull white. By 21 days, small brown cheek mark develops. Bill initially grey, turning greenish at 5 weeks and pallid pink at 7 weeks; legs and eyes greenish grey. Differentiating ♂ and ♀ goslings requires cloacal and tarsi length analyses (Milstein 1993).

MEASUREMENTS AND WEIGHT: ♂ wing ($n = 11$), 378–407 (396.1); tail ($n = 11$), 116–150 (131.6); culmen ($n = 12$), 45–55 (49.1); tarsus ($n = 12$), 74.5–95 (82.4); weight ($n = 41$), 2348. ♀ wing ($n = 12$), 340–390 (369.8); tail ($n = 11$), 111–145 (127.4); culmen ($n = 15$), 43–54 (49); tarsus ($n = 15$), 67–85 (76.7); weight ($n = 98$), 1872 (Halse and Skead 1982, Maclean 1993).

Field characters

Pale, upright, goose-like bird, 630–730 mm long. In most of Afrotropics, unmistakable; uniquely coloured, larger and more robust than sympatric buff-brown ducks. Within southern Africa, however, confusion possible with Cape Shelduck. Patches around eye and on breast, plus pinkish feet and bill, preclude misidentification. In flight, species resemble one another, and wing patterns similar; however, brown breast patch of Egyptian Goose distinctive, as is black line above speculum. Also resembles Ruddy Shelduck of north Africa and Europe, but rusty orange body of latter (without eye or breast patches) should distinguish. Vocalizations reliable method of separating sexes.

Voice

Sexually distinct. ♀ utters coarse, strident *hur-hur-hur*, whereas ♂ hisses hoarsely (Zimmerman *et al.* 1996); however, context and function affects pitch, duration and loudness of calls. On take-off, both sexes honk repeatedly (sonogram in Maclean 1993), and often Chin-lift (Cramp and Simmons 1977). Milstein (1993) defined Sky-call of Cramp and Simmons (1977) and Brown *et al.* (1982) as angry threat. Both sexes hiss when threatened (Maclean 1988). Goslings have soft whistled twitter (Milstein 1993); contact calls quick and high, in sequences of 6–7 notes, sonogram in Kear (1968).

Range and status

Afrotropical, with extensive sub-Saharan distribution, most numerous in eastern and southern Africa (Maclean 1988). Marginal in Palearctic; wild populations only extant in southern Egypt (Scott and Rose 1996).

Widespread and common in southern Africa, with Highveld, southern Cape, interior of KwaZulu-Natal, Mpumalanga and northern Botswana having highest reporting rates (Harrison *et al.* 1997). Largely absent from west and central Botswana, north, northeast and southwest margins of Namibia and interior of Lesotho. Milstein (1993) identified 'relatively temperate' areas of karoo and highveld (in southern Africa) as 'core' distribution areas. Most abundant waterfowl in national waterbird surveys; sometimes

> 4000 at dams and waterbodies (Taylor *et al.* 1999). Common in Zimbabwe, where has increased with growth of commercial agriculture and dam construction (Irwin 1981). Uncommon and localized in southern Mozambique; population estimated at 500 (Parker 1999). Had highest reporting rate of any southern African waterfowl during regional Atlas project (Maclean 1997). Population estimate of at least 30 000 birds for former Transvaal highveld (Tarboton *et al.* 1987). Wetlands International (2002) gave combined population estimates for eastern and southern Africa of 200 000–500 000.

Common throughout east Africa. Widespread and numerous in Kenya, Tanzania and Uganda (Britton 1980, Lewis and Pomeroy 1989, Zimmerman *et al.* 1996). Locally common to abundant in Ethiopia and Sudan (Nikolaus 1987, Scott and Rose 1996). Similarly numerous in east Democratic Republic of Congo, Zambia and Angola. Shuns equatorial

confines of Congo Basin and densely forested regions of Central and West Africa, but may penetrate larger rivers, e.g. lower Congo River (Snow 1978).

Locally common to sparse in West Africa from northern Senegal across to Cameroon and Central African Republic (Serle and Morel 1977). Rare south of 10° N, being vagrant to Ghana and Ivory Coast (Grimes 1987, Scott and Rose 1996). Perennou's (1991) West African estimate of 5000 birds considered too low by Rose and Scott (1997), who advocated 10 000–25 000.

Position in north Africa poorly known. Occasionally winters in Algeria and Tunisia (del Hoyo *et al.* 1992) but does not breed (Heim de Balsac and Mayaud 1962). Sporadic records from Morocco (Brickell 1988). Flocks of > 1000 not uncommon in southern Egypt, particularly at large waterbodies, e.g. Lake Nasser. Formerly present in northern Egypt, Middle East and along Danube River

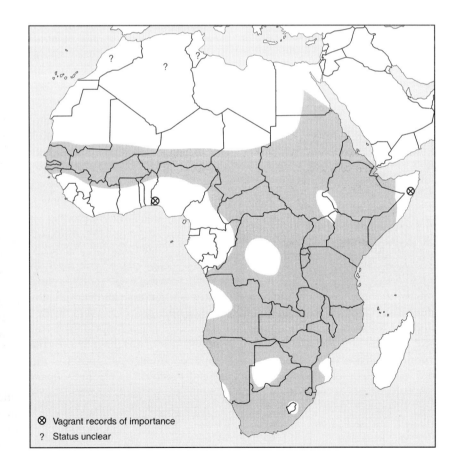

⊗   Vagrant records of importance

?   Status unclear

(Cramp and Simmons 1977, Scott and Rose 1996). Introduced into Britain (Sutherland and Allport 1991) where population estimated at 3–400 (Lever 1977), with 82 pairs recorded, principally in Norfolk, in 1998 (Ogilvie *et al.* 2000); also into The Netherlands, where *c* 1350 pairs breed (Lensink 1999), and Belgium where 100–150 pairs present by 1994. Isolated records in Europe usually considered escapes; however, Milstein (1993) maintained that many British and European records discarded erroneously, citing Morris (1855) who recorded 80 in Hampshire in 1824 following storms.

Habitat and general habits

Extensive use of aquatic environments such as dams, rivers, pans, lakes, estuaries, offshore islands, reservoirs, marshes, sewage works and large ponds (Brooke and Crowe 1982, Maclean 1993). In England, uses alder-willow swamp woodland and meadows (Cramp and Simmons 1977). In equatorial regions only occupies larger rivers (Maclean 1988). Absent from arid regions (Scott and Rose 1996). Recorded from sea level to 3810 m (Mt Karisimbi, Democratic Republic of Congo) and 4000 m (Ethiopia). Enters sea intermittently or forages along shoreline (Brickell 1988, Fraser and McMahon 1991, Sheppard and Sheppard 1991). Forages in crop fields and around periphery of

waterbody. Waterbodies with open shoreline, rich plant growth and proximity to commercial cereal production especially favoured in southern Africa (Geldenhuys 1975, Milstein 1993). Formerly probable inhabitant of floodplains and large rivers with broad sandbanks (Irwin 1981, Scott and Rose 1996).

Annual post-breeding moult migrations undertaken, large numbers assembling at selected waterbodies (Madge and Burn 1988). Nonbreeding flocks may consist of hundreds or thousands; in southern Africa these migrations occur in early winter (Milstein 1993). No traditional attachment to moulting water, present suitability main criterion, and recently built dams become new migratory destinations (Milstein 1993); however, yearlings (especially ♀♀) may return to hatching/rearing locales, albeit briefly (Siegfried 1965a).

Drying of ephemeral waterbodies causes nomadism and dispersion, especially in more arid regions (Maclean 1997, Underhill *et al.* 1999, Taylor *et al.* 1999), sometimes to permanent waterbodies, e.g. Lake Chad (Golding 1934). Seasonal rains cause further expansion to, e.g. Sahel region (Cramp and Simmons 1977). Stragglers to north Africa may represent wet season migration over larger distances (Brown *et al.* 1982). Migratory dispersal in southern Africa usually 70–800 km (Maclean 1997), but movements > 1000 km recorded (Cramp and Simmons 1977, Underhill *et al.* 1999). In southern Africa, ringing data (497 recoveries of 7008) indicate widespread movements within South Africa (Underhill *et al.* 1999), and some movement between southwestern Western Cape and southern Namibia (Underhill *et al.* 1999).

Grazers and grass-seed strippers (Milstein 1993), taking seeds, grasses, grain, shoots, leaves, aquatic plants and young crops (Brown *et al.* 1982, Maclean 1993). One stomach filled mostly with *Cyperus esculentus* corms (Taylor 1957); Halse (1985a), in South Africa, identified *Potomageton pectinatus* as important food plant, plus *Cyndon dactylon*. Frequently gathers in crop fields (maize, wheat, oats, lucerne, groundnuts and barley) to glean spilled material, sometimes considered pest (Clancey 1967, Halse 1984). Occasionally perches on and follows Hippopotamus *Hippopotamus amphibius*, feeding on disturbed plant and perhaps animal matter (Dean and Macdonald 1981). In Zambia, leaves of *Panicum repens* and *Echinochloa stagina*, ripening fruits of *P. subalbidum*, *P. repens* and *Brachiaria xantholeuca* favoured foods (Douthwaite 1978). At Barberspan in South Africa principally forages by flying to surrounding maize fields, also taking some *Potomageton pectinatus* but, when moulting, relies solely on aquatic algae *P. pectinatus* and *Cyndon dactylon* (Halse 1984). Strips seeds by seizing mid-stem, bending sideways and then passing seed-head through bill with rapid champs of lower mandible. In one study, 27% of food grazed, rest picked or nibbled (Halse 1985a). Invertebrates perhaps ingested by accident (Brown *et al.* 1982) but seen feeding actively on termite alates (Theron 1992). Foraging consists of dabbling and probing in shallow water or grazing singly, in pairs or flocks on land. Only *c* 7% of day dedicated to feeding in southern Africa (Maclean 1988). Goslings also feed on plants and, like most other waterfowl, not fed by parents.

In early morning, flies out to feed, returning after *c* 1.5 h; extended session of preening, resting and sleeping follows, and concludes with late-afternoon foraging sortie, birds returning after *c* 0.5 h (Halse 1985a) to several hours (Shewell 1959). In east Africa, Edroma and Jumbe (1983) saw feeding from 07.00–09.00 h, followed by rest and another feeding bout 11.00–13.00 h, inactivity in afternoon, and final feeding session 18.00–19.00 h. Halse (1985a) also recorded midday feeding. Clearly, local factors and seasonality affect daily activities.

Mainly terrestrial but roosts and nests in prominences. Perches in trees, on cliffs, buildings and lamp-posts. Returns to same roost in evening (Mackworth-Praed and Grant 1970). Wary and not easily approached. If threatened, resorts to water or walks away. When put to wing, flies strongly. Swims high in water and with facility; equally comfortable on land where walks easily, if slowly. Resting birds stand or lie down. In nonbreeding flocks, paired birds keep together, maintaining distance between themselves and other geese (Brown *et al.* 1982). Alarm indicated by erect posture with bill pointing skywards and feathers raised (Cramp and Simmons 1977). Aggressive towards other waterbirds and potential predators e.g. Crocodile *Crocodylus niloticus* (Shaw 1993), especially during breeding season. Implicated in displacing Little Grebe *Tachybaptus*

ruficollis from some waterbodies in Zimbabwe (Junor 1983).

Displays and breeding behaviour

Adaptable and versatile, generally proceeds through 3 phases of social organization: breeding season of strict monogamy, gregarious nonbreeding phase (often moulting), concluding with intermediate stage of paired birds moving in search of breeding territory (Milstein 1993). In Ethiopia, however, geese seen in flocks throughout year (Brown *et al.* 1982).

Courtship and pairbond formation poorly known but, 4 months prior to dispersal to breeding ground, courtship and aggressive activities initiated in nonbreeding flocks. Sexual display fairly rudimentary. ♀ usually assumes leading role, calling loudly to solicit ♂, head and neck extended in direction of mate, who responds with asthmatic call (Clancey 1967). ♀ also incites ♂ to attack other ♀♀ and ♂♂ (Cramp and Simmons 1977). Direct ♀ incitement of ♂ relates not only to pairbonding, but adjunct to territorial establishment and maintenance (Milstein 1993).

Courtship involves ♂ soliciting ♀ by performing Ceremonial-drinking or Swimming-high in water showing undertail coverts (Brown *et al.* 1982). If ♂ accepted, performs Triumph Ceremony, rhythmically craning neck back and forth with neck feathers erect, and flicking spread wings. ♀ may join in, uttering Inciting calls; both birds then point bills skyward, call vociferously, bow and cross necks. Wing-spread display (body upright and wings fully fanned) usual climax (Cramp and Simmons 1977). Milstein (1993) questioned whether these activities restricted to courting, concluding that pairbonds form gradually by mutual association. Cramp and Simmons (1977) noted that Triumph Ceremony used after altercations with intruders, and Brown *et al.* (1982) as greeting after pairs have been separated. Other courtship activities include Bill-dipping, ceremonial Wing-preening and aerial pursuits (Maclean 1988). Pre-copulatory display consists of Head-dipping and Water-flicking (Brown *et al.* 1982, Milstein 1993). Copulation initiated by either sex with ♀ sometimes simply adopting correct posture; generally occurs in shallow water, rarely in deeper water or on land (Milstein 1993). Process characterized by brevity, ♂ mounting quickly and grasping ♀'s neck. Eltringham (1974), in 2 observed copulations, noted calling in one, while Milstein (1993) recorded soft calling. Post-copulatory display consists of Wing-raising, predominantly by ♂. Contrary to Brown *et al.* (1982) and Cramp and Simmons (1977), far wing not necessarily raised, near wing or both can be lifted (Milstein 1993). Nor does ♂ retain hold of ♀'s nape after dismounting. Following copulation, birds usually bathe and preen (Milstein 1993).

During breeding season, both sexes intolerant of conspecifics within territory, resident ♂ being primary aggressor, although ♀ will confront intruders. Once incubation begins, territorial maintenance duty of ♂. His defence conducted from sentry post with good visibility and proximity to nest. Cramp and Simmons (1977) recognized Threat-display consisting of three parts: aggressive ♂ (and sometimes ♀) bends neck (with bill facing down) and fluffs up, producing 'coiled' posture (Milstein 1993); ♂ then exposes white forewings, flicking wings gently and sometimes strutting in either coiled or uncoiled posture; finally, with head and neck stretched, neck feathers fluffed, wings open and bill agape, ready to attack. Milstein (1993) recognized fourth threat posture, namely Triumph/ Wing-spread display of outstretched wings and fully elevated head undertaken in cases of severe provocation, which corresponds to Sky-call display of Brown *et al.* (1982). Wing-spread display (Cramp and Simmons 1977) occurs during territorial encounters with resident birds threatening intruders by stretching neck and head upwards, chest puffed out and wings fully spread. Milstein (1993) considered distinction between Wing-spread and Triumph display dubious. Threat display usually suffices to avoid combat, residents often repulsing intruders. Fighting between ♂♂ involves both birds biting and gripping one another mid-neck and striking repeatedly with carpal knobs. Fights can last longer than 5 min, usually take place in water (Milstein 1993) and frequently violent (Satchel and Satchel 2000).

Solitary nesters. Breeding pairs hold territory of up to 1 ha on suitable freshwater (Brown *et al.* 1982); adjoining pairs may undertake low-level flights over adjacent pair's territory, but such flights and incursions not serious in nature (Milstein 1993).

Breeding and life cycle

Breeding season in Kenya (Lake Turkana), Apr, May, Sept; in Kenya (rest), all months (no peak); in north Africa, Mar–Apr; in Sudan, June and Sept; in Ethiopia, July–Aug, probably also Feb–Apr; in Senegal, July–Oct; in Nigeria, Jan, Sept; in Uganda, Jan to Oct; in Tanzania, Jan–Dec; in Democratic Republic of Congo, June–Aug; in Angola, July–Oct; in Zambia, Jan–Nov; in Malawi, Jan, Aug; in Mozambique, July–Oct; in Zimbabwe, all months peaking May– Aug; in South Africa, all months peaking Aug–Sept; and in Britain, Mar–Apr (Brown *et al.* 1982, Brickell 1988).

Milstein (1993) in South Africa found 67.5% of nests on ground, and 32.5% in elevated positions up to 60 m high (*n* = 576); he noted predilection for nesting on small islands. Other sites include old Hammerkop nests, cliff ledges, reedy vegetation near water, tree holes (Figure 9.22), old crow *Corvus*, raptor (e.g. African Fish Eagle *Haliaeetus vocifer*), cormorant, waterfowl (e.g. Cape Teal, Brown and Gottschalk 1988) and heron nests, top of Sociable Weaver *Philetairus socius* communal nest, under bushes and trees near water, burrows, church steeples, caves and buildings (Brown *et al.* 1982, Maclean 1993). Most nests close to water, but up to 3 km distant. One tree nest site used for 5 consecutive years (Craib 1975). Site selection and construction undertaken by ♀, although ♂ may attend (Milstein 1993); if on ground, ♀ digs hollow with feet. Like other wildfowl, material such as grass, reeds and leaves collected by side-throwing action, and drawn in (Clancey 1967, Maclean 1993). Arboreal nests lined with down but no other material added. Siegfried (1964a) recorded 389–1632 down and 27–44 contour feathers in 4 nests. Nests 230–450 mm wide and 70–100 mm deep (Brown *et al.* 1982).

Single-brooded but may replace clutch, and breed twice in good years (Brown *et al.* 1982, Zaloumis 1987). Eggs white to creamy, laid at 24 h intervals, occasionally 48 h (Brickell 1988); 68.4 × 51.3 (57.9–75.8 × 46.0–57.7) (*n* = 277) (Maclean 1993) or 68.6 × 51.0 (62.0–76.7 × 46.0–57.9) (*n* = 240) (Milstein 1993); weight in captivity 97.5 (78.5–110.0) (*n* = 100) (Brown *et al.* 1982). Clutch 6.7 (5–11) (*n* = 654) (Maclean 1993) or 7.9 (*n* = 536) (Milstein 1993). Incubation by ♀ only, after last egg laid (Maclean 1986, Brickell 1988), 28–30 days (Maclean 1993). Old eggshells not removed nor hidden.

If nest elevated, goslings jump or slide down *c* 6 h after hatch, in response to vocal encouragement by

9.22 Female Egyptian Goose at her nest.

♀ (Maclean 1993); may be stunned on hitting ground but recover in *c* 4 min (Maclean 1986); weigh *c* 55 (Maclean 1986) or 53.2 (*n* = 22) in captivity. Brood size 5.8 (*n* = 718) (Milstein 1993). Fledge in *c* 55 (Maclean 1993) or 66–75 days (Brickell 1988). Goslings at 8 weeks have feathers too short for flight but practise, and can fly at 10–12 weeks, becoming proficient by 3 months (Siegfried 1965a). Goslings up to 9 weeks spend 42–51% of time foraging, 28–40% loafing and 8–21% evading predators (Milstein 1993).

Both parents lead goslings, ♂ usually in front (Milstein 1993); when leaving nest for waterbody, may be escorted past hazards, e.g. busy roads. If threatened, parents give alarm calls and summon young to water. Adults bold in defence of nest and young, e.g. adult attacked helicopter that flew close to arboreal nest (Ledger 1985); Baboon *Papio ursinus*, dogs, humans, African Fish Eagle and Secretarybird *Sagittarius serpentarius* may be attacked if close to nest or young (Craib 1975, du Toit 2001). Goslings that stray are called or fetched by ♀, who alone broods young. Of 106 goslings from 13 broods, 86 raised to dispersal, loss of 1.5 per brood (Milstein 1993); survival rates variable, ranging 5–80% (Eltringham 1974). Goslings killed by Baboon (du Toit 2001, Forbes 2001), African Fish Eagle (Howells 1982) and Wahlberg's Eagle *Aquila wahlbergi* (Butchart 2000). One nest (of 52 examined) parasitized by Maccoa in southwestern Western Cape (Siegfried 1964). Breeding success of introduced and increasing population in The Netherlands higher than in Uganda, or in Britain (Lensink 1999). Maturity attained at *c* 2 years (Maclean 1988).

No data on adult survival; maximum age reached in captivity 25 years (Johnsgard 1968a).

Conservation and threats

Population increased dramatically in South Africa over last century (Siegfried 1965, Brown *et al.* 1982); ability to colonize dams, and exploit expanding agriculture means under no threat and no conservation measures necessary (Maclean 1997, Taylor *et al.* 1999). Also common in east Africa and locally in west. Range contraction and local extinction occurred in north Africa, Middle East and southern Europe, but peripheral in Palearctic and populations probably ephemeral except at times of relatively warm winters and early springs.

Can become pest of crop farmers, causing damage and being shot or poisoned (Maclean 1993, Underhill *et al.* 1999, Mangnall and Crowe 2001); however, such measures have little effect on local populations. Is wily gamebird, sometimes shot by fowlers, but coarseness of meat makes such killing uncommon (Clancey 1967, Irwin 1981, Wynne-Jones 1993). Comprised < 5% of total waterfowl shot by licensed hunters in Zimbabwe during 1972–73 season (Woodall 1975). One of the 3 principal waterfowl species shot in 1980–81 in KwaZulu-Natal, South Africa but usually comprising < 30% of bag and influence on populations probably negligible (Colahan 1984).

Greg Davies

Orinoco Goose *Neochen jubata*
PLATE 11

Anser jubatus Spix, 1825, Avium Species Novae Itinere Brasiliam, **2**, p. 84, pl. 108
'Ad ripam fl. Solimoëns in insula Praya das Onças'
Neochen Oberholser, 1918

Etymology: *Neochen* Gr. for new goose, plus L. *jubata* for crested or maned.

Other names: Orinoco Sheldgoose. Spanish: Ganso de monte, Pato Carretero, Ganso del Orinoco; Portuguese: Pato-corredor, Marrecão-do-banhado; German: Orinokogans; French: Ouette d'Orénoque, Bernache de l'Orinoque.

Variation: no subspecies. Has hybridized in captivity with Egyptian Goose.

Description

ADULT: sexes alike. ♂ head, neck, and chest creamy or grey, darker on hind neck of ♂. Scapulars, flanks, and sides chestnut. Whitish area down breast midline to dark brown on vent. Black tail, wing coverts and linings, with glossy green on upper surfaces and broad white patch on secondaries. Knob on metacarpal joint. White undertail coverts. Red on lower edge of bill and most of lower mandible; red or salmon coloured legs (orange to pink); iris brown. ♀ smaller, and neck feathers not so long.

MOULT: no seasonal changes in plumage of either sex. Uncertain whether one or 2 annual moults of body feathers. Flightless birds seen Mar and May in Venezuela, but parents did not moult flight feathers while attending young.

IMMATURE: similar to adult but plumage colour less intense and bill and legs duller.

GOSLING: black with white markings and white underparts. Large dark spot on ear coverts. Narrow bands of dark brown to black and white extend down sides and back of neck. Broad white bands on wings and back.

MEASUREMENTS AND WEIGHT: ♂ (*n* = 7) wing, 305–333 (317.5); tail, 96–117 (107.1); bill, 35–43 (38.4); tarsus, 75–82; ♀ (*n* = 4) wing, 285–305 (295); tail, 108–112 (109.3); bill, 35–36 (35.7); tarsus, 70–72

(Blake 1977); weight, 1950 and 1700, and in captivity (*n* = 1) 1420. In Venezuela ♂ (*n* = 4) wing, 328–350 (339.5); bill, 37.0–42.6 (40.2); tarsus, 93.2–101.0 (96.6); ♀ (*n* = 5) wing, 300–320 (310.8); (*n* = 6) bill, 33.9–37.7 (36.6); (*n* = 6) tarsus, 84.3–90.6 (87.3); weight, 1250 (del Hoyo *et al.* 1992) and ♂ (*n* = 4), 1700–1950 (1800); ♀ (*n* = 6), 1200–1440 (1327).

Field characters

Length 610–660 mm. Only large goose-like bird in range and habitat. Upright stance, and usually perched. Creamy grey head, neck and centre of breast contrast with chestnut sides and upper back, and dark wings and tail. In flight, glossy green-black wings show broad white patch across secondaries, and white undertail coverts and reddish legs contrast with black tail.

Voice

Little information on wild birds. Calls in flight described as *shewit shewit* (♂) and *a-ohk* (♀) (Johnsgard 1965a). During sexual and aggressive display, ♂ gives whistling notes interrupted by wheezy *wi-chuff* and ♀ guttural honks or cackles. During fights, ♂ also gives loud honks. Pairs said to duet when perched. Wings rattle during take-off. Young ♂ has high-pitched whistle and young ♀ squawked when handled.

Range and status

Found in tropics east of Andes from Colombia, Venezuela, and Guianas south into east Ecuador, Peru, Bolivia, northwestern Argentina (Alto Rio Bermejo), Paraguay and Brazil, primarily along tributaries of Amazon and Orinoco. Recent photographic records from Barbados may indicate vagrancy or range extending north. Widespread but scarce in much of range, disappearing from navigable rivers. Non-migratory. Wetlands International (2002) suggested declining population of 25 000–100 000.

Habitat and general habits

Found along dense, lowland, jungle-lined rivers, streams and wooded islands. Also occurs in wetlands, in open grassland with scattered trees, especially llanos,

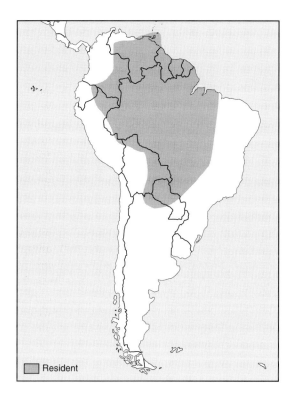

Resident

and on open, rocky river beaches in hottest regions of Brazil. Most arboreal of sheldgeese, frequently found perching in trees and rarely on water. Generally seen alone, in pairs or family groups. Groups of 50–300 noted in llanos of Venezuela in Apr, May and July. Sometimes found in large flocks (>100) during wing moult. Noted to be quite tame. Rather slow and deliberate flyers, but can lift directly from perches on trunks and branches. Feeds primarily on vegetation such as green stems, leaves and small seeds, but also aquatic plant tubers, berries, larvae, worms, small molluscs and insects (Delacour 1954–64).

Displays and breeding behaviour

Displays similar to other sheldgeese, but little information from wild. Both sexes give loud calls in flight and pairs duet from perches. Mutual preening of head region common, and may occur between birds not paired (same or opposite sex). In both sexes, elongated neck feathers erected as threat. ♂ also threatens by uttering whistles as neck stretched diagonally. During breeding season, ♂ engages in fierce battles, uttering constant guttural honking and using bill and

wings to attack. ♀ Inciting consists of calling loudly while extending neck and head low and walking around. In ♂ sexual display (like Puffing of other sheldgeese), body held erect with head back as far as possible, one or both wings extended showing white wing patch, and wheezy *wi-chuff* given with each forward movement of chest, interrupting constant whistling (Delacour 1954–64, Johnsgard 1965a).

Pairs inhabit well-spaced territories along river banks, defend them, or area around family group, at least during breeding season, and pair members appear together at other times of year.

Breeding and life cycle

Eggs laid Dec–Jan in Colombia (del Hoyo *et al.* 1992) and Venezuela, and nesting appears synchronized. Nests in cavities of hollow or broken off trees, or river banks (Bolivia), and rarely on ground at river edge, concealed in grass or bushes, with whitish nest down. Eggs, slightly glossy and pale brownish cream; 59–61 × 41–45 (Phillips 1922–26), 60.2 × 42.8 (58.0–62.0 × 40.9–46.5) (*n* = 16) (Schönwetter 1960–66), or 62.6 × 44.6 (57.5–69.4 × 38.7–47.0) (*n* = 118); weight 73.2 (64.0–86.0) (*n* = 68), in captivity 58.4 (*n* = 11), or calculated at 63 (Schönwetter 1960–66). Clutch size 6–10, although up to 19 observed due to nest parasitism. Incubation, by ♀ alone, 28–30 days (Phillips 1922–26), and possibly longer (32–34 days). Hatching success 8.3% from natural cavities (*n* = 12) and 20% from nest boxes (*n* = 24). ♂ joins ♀ after hatch, and both parents defend goslings. Families with as many as 12–13 goslings seen, and gosling survival appears high. No information on age at 1st breeding, adult survival nor longevity.

Conservation and threats

Listed by BirdLife International (2000) as Near-threatened. Said to be close to extinction in Peru, has vanished from areas of Colombia, but appears locally common in parts of Bolivia, Venezuela and Argentina (Callaghan and Green 1993, del Hoyo *et al.* 1992, Todd 1996). Hunting pressure and tropical rainforest destruction likely to continue as primary threats, especially as availability of nest cavities and brood habitat affected. Readily uses nestboxes.

Gwenda L. Brewer and Kenneth D. Kriese

Andean Goose *Chloephaga melanoptera*
PLATE 9

Anser melanopterus Eyton, 1838, Monogr. Anatidae, p. 93
Lake Titicaca
Chloëphaga Eyton, 1838

Etymology: *Chloephaga* Gr. for grass-eater; *melanoptera* Gr. for black-winged.

Other names: Andean Sheldgoose. South America: Piuquén, Guayata, Huallata, Huashua, Guallata, Avutarda de alas negras, Gancillo.

Variation: no subspecies.

Description

ADULT: ♂ and ♀ alike, although ♂ larger. Head, neck and body white; scapulars dark or white with dark centres giving spotted back; primaries and tertials glossy black; tail black. Greater coverts, or speculum, with iridescent purple sheen. Bill coral-red with black nail; legs and feet bright orange; iris dark brown (Goodall *et al.* 1951, Delacour 1954–64).

MOULT: no seasonal change in plumage. Wing and body moults undescribed.

IMMATURE: similar to adult but duller and off-white. Legs turn reddish from age 3 weeks; bill changes to adult colour from 3 months.

GOSLING: black and white, with black spot on ear coverts and on thighs; golden tinge to head. Bill and legs black (Delacour 1954–64). Down long and silky, as in other young wildfowl from high altitudes.

MEASUREMENTS AND WEIGHT: ♂ and ♀ (*n* = 6), wing, 392–450 (426); bill, 33–43 (37.7); tail, 142–171 (151) (Goodall *et al.* 1951); weight ♂ and ♀ 2730–3640 (Kolbe 1972), in captivity, ♂ (*n* = 1) 3130, ♀ (*n* = 1) 2580.

Field characters

Heavily built white goose, 750–800 mm long, with black back and tail, and short bill. Unlikely to be confused with other inhabitants of high Andes.

Voice

Sexually dimorphic. When alarmed, ♂ whistles shrilly and ♀ gives low grating *kuak-kuak* call (Goodall *et al.* 1951). Pair chatter together almost continuously, ♂ giving soft *huit-wit-wit* (Delacour 1954–64, Fjeldså and Krabbe 1990).

Range and status

Occurs in fertile valleys of high cordillera of Andes, above 3000 m in summer but may move to 2000 m in winter, from 10°S in Peru, through Bolivia and south to 35°S in Argentina and 38°S in Chile. Movements north and south along Andes may also take place (Casares 1934, Goodall *et al.* 1951, Johnson 1965). Occurs as pairs, small groups and in large flocks; e.g. 2000 at Laguna Pozuelos, Argentina and 1400 at Lake Junín, Peru (Summers and Castro 1988). Rose and Scott (1997) estimated population of 25 000–100 000 individuals.

Resident

Habitat and general habits

Occupies lake margins, river sides and marshes. Feeds by grazing fleshy-leaved bog marsh vegetation containing plants such as *Chara*, *Lilaeopsis*, *Myriophyllum* and *Nostoc*. During winter, early morning frosts delay onset of grazing which comprises 73% of diurnal activity budget. Daily food intake 208 g organic matter of herbage (Summers and Castro 1988). At night, roosts at lake margins.

Displays and breeding behaviour

Adults in captivity, kept with other birds, display elaborately (Delacour 1954–64). Antagonistic and sexual behaviour by ♀ involves Inciting, holding folded wings high off back, walking with high steps and calling *gack-gack-gack*. Aggressive ♂ threatens with Wing-flaps, Head-rolling and *wi wi* call with head outstretched, also Puffing while ♀ Incites (Johnsgard 1965a). Birds preen or nibble cheek region of mate. Territorial nester.

Breeding and life cycle

Nests in scrape on ground among sparse vegetation on hill slopes near water or on islets. Also on bare ground below snow line, or in hole in sandy cliff. Starts nesting Nov, laying 5–10 off-white eggs; 78.0 × 51.2 (76.2–80.3 × 50.5–51.7) ($n = 8$); weight in captivity 131.3 (115.0–144.5) ($n = 100$). Incubation by ♀ for 30 days while ♂ guards territory. At hatching in captivity weigh 78.0 ($n = 29$). Broods taken to waterside pasture Dec–Jan. Adults feign injury when goslings threatened. Fledge in *c* 12 weeks in captivity, and thought to mature at 2–3 years (Goodall *et al.* 1951, Johnson 1965, Johnsgard 1978). No data on nesting success, adult survival nor longevity.

Conservation and threats

Is hunted for food, especially goslings, and body parts used in local medicines; e.g. as cure for gout. Eggs also eaten (Casares 1934). In the past, type of bolas used to catch them (Koepcke and Koepcke 1965). Some wintering areas have changed in response to hunting pressure. Generally regarded as common.

Ron Summers

Magellan Goose *Chloephaga picta*
PLATE 9

Anas picta Gmelin, 1789, Syst. Nat., **1**, p. 504
Staten Island

Etymology: *picta* L. for painted. Vernacular name after the Straits of Magellan, themselves named after the Portuguese explorer and navigator Ferdinand Magellan (1480–1521).

Other names: Upland Goose, Upland Sheldgoose, White-winged Goose. South American Spanish: Avutarda, Ganso magallánico, Cauquén común, Caiquén, Kaiken.

Variation: 2 subspecies. *C. p. picta*, Lesser Magellan, found in southern Chile and Argentina, with ♂ in 2 colour phases. Barred phase breeds in Tierra del Fuego and southern Patagonia, and white breasted phase in northern Patagonia; interbreeding occurs between 2 phases in southern Patagonia (Plotnick 1961a). *C. p. leucoptera* Gmelin, 1789, Greater Magellan, is larger and inhabits Falkland Islands, ♂ always white breasted (Delacour 1950).

Description

ADULT: marked sexual dimorphism. *leucoptera* ♂ has head, neck, breast, belly and rump white. Back and flanks barred black and white, although thicker bars on flanks. Scapulars grey. Central tail feathers black with 3–4 outer ones white. Lesser and median coverts white and greater coverts, or speculum, metallic green. Secondaries white and primaries black. Carpal knob pale orange. Bill, legs and feet black; iris dark brown. ♀ head and neck red-brown though fades during year. Breast barred red-brown and black, grading to black and white barring on belly. Back barred buff, black and grey. Flanks thickly barred black and white. Tail black. Wing as ♂. Bill black, legs and feet yellow and carpal knob small. *picta* ♂ (white-breasted phase) as *leucoptera*. Barred phase has breast and belly barred black and white. Tail black and variable amounts of black and white on rump. Two phases interbreed leading to variable amounts of barring on breast and belly. ♀ as *leucoptera* but appears blacker and less brown on underparts due to thicker black bars.

MOULT: no seasonal change in plumage except by fading. In Falkland Islands, *leucoptera* gathers in flocks of up to several hundred at ponds or sheltered sea inlets to undertake moult of main wing feathers mid Nov–early Feb (Summers 1983b). Individuals flightless for 36 days. When disturbed, run to water, form compact raft and wait for disturbance to pass. Flocks composed of one-year-olds (14–50%), other non-breeders and failed breeders. Moult of one-year-olds more synchronized than in older birds. In contrast, most successful breeders stay with goslings and skip wing moulting. If this occurs over successive years, wing tips become exceedingly worn; however, some successful breeders, especially ♂♂, moult with family on territory (Summers 1983a). Moult-skipping also occurs in *picta* (Summers and Martin 1985). Moult of other feather tracts starts just before flightless moult and continues into autumn. Juveniles also undertake autumn body moult, losing juvenile plumage and resembling adult by 1st winter (Summers 1983b).

IMMATURE: *leucoptera* ♂ like adult but plumage off-white, breast and belly have thin dark brown bars. Other differences include lighter barring on flanks, sooty black rump, all black tail, and grey greater coverts instead of glossy green. Carpal knob absent. ♀ duller version of adult and wing similar to immature ♂. *picta* ♂ (barred phase) finer and paler bars than adult (Summers and McAdam 1993).

GOSLING: pale grey with usual sheldgoose markings in dark brown; *leucoptera* darker and more uniform above (Delacour 1954–64).

MEASUREMENTS AND WEIGHT: *picta* ♂ wing ($n = 10$), 411–447 (425); tail, 123–162 (146); bill, 34–40 (37.4); weight ($n = 8$), 2650–3560 (3170). ♀ wing ($n = 7$), 382–417 (396); tail, 125–163 (145); bill, 32–38 (34.8); weight ($n = 6$) 2470–3050 (2690) (Goodall *et al.* 1951). *leucoptera* ♂ wing ($n = 43$), 435–465 (456); bill, 41–47 (42.5); tarsus, 96–102 (98.8); weight ($n = 28$) 3450–4450 (3900). ♀ wing ($n = 39$), 415–440 (426); bill, 37–45 (41.0); tarsus, 85–94 (89.8); weight ($n = 21$), 2950–3450 (3190) (Summers and McAdam 1993).

Field characters

Length 600–650 mm, strongly dimorphic. ♂ white on head, neck and most of underparts; black legs distinguish from ♂ Kelp Goose. ♀ greyish brown recalling both Ashy-headed Goose and Ruddy-headed Goose; former has grey head, chestnut breast and whitish belly, Ruddyhead smaller and daintier with narrow white eye-ring (Madge and Burn 1988).

Voice

♂ has whistling *wheep* and ♀ low rattling *a-rrrr* (Woods 1975).

Range and status

White phase of *picta* mostly resident in northern Patagonia; however, white phase from southern Patagonia migrates north and east to winter in Buenos Aires province along with barred phase which leaves Tierra del Fuego late Apr–early May and flies along eastern Andes and east coast, mainly at night. Coastal route involves sea crossing over large gulfs (Plotnick 1961b). Two phases segregate partially in Buenos Aires province, barred phase being more coastal than white one. Magellan Geese comprised 88.0% and 93.8% of 4.1 and 4.5 sheldgeese per km in 1983 and 1984 (Martin *et al.* 1986). Spring migration takes place late Aug–Sept. Although *leucoptera* resident in Falkland Islands, some move long distances (up to 75 km); most, however, rarely move more than 5 km, usually when changing feeding areas or travelling to breeding territories and moulting areas (Summers 1985b).

In Argentine Tierra del Fuego (near Rio Grande), densities in Oct, Dec and Jan–Feb were 19–23, 21 and 12–38 per km^2 respectively (Martin *et al.* 1982). Population of Falklands probably 200 000, while Patagonian population estimated many times greater at 100 000–1 000 000 (Rose and Scott 1997). Sex ratio 1:1 in both populations (Siegfried *et al.* 1988, Summers and McAdam 1993).

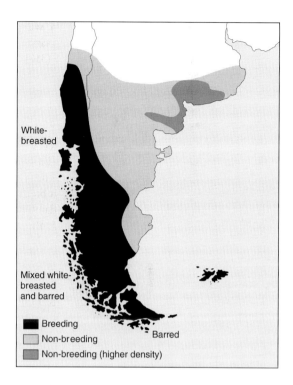

White-breasted

Mixed white-breasted and barred

Barred

- Breeding
- Non-breeding
- Non-breeding (higher density)

Habitat and general habits

Found in open grasslands, valleys, marshes, coastal greens and around farm settlements. Mean densities of *leucoptera* vary according to pasture type, highest around ponds (4.1 per ha) and *Poa* greens (7.8 per ha) and lowest (0.07 per ha) on *Cortaderia pilosa* grassland (Summers 1985a). Also high densities on reseeded pastures, especially in winter when *Poa* greens are less productive. Found as pairs that remain together throughout year, or in family parties, forming scattered flocks when large numbers congregate on favoured pastures. Flocking also occurs during flightless moult and at night when roosting on coastal inlets.

Herbivorous; in Patagonia, eats mainly *Arenaria, Trifolium repens, Plantago maritima, Eleocharis macrostachya, Holcus lanatus, Poa pratensis* and *Pucinellia glaucescens* (Martin 1984). In winter quarters in Buenos Aires province, selects grassland and stubbles of wheat, maize, sunflower and sorghum (Martin *et al.* 1986). In Falklands, grazes short greens composed of *Poa annua* and *P. pratensis,* consuming fragment lengths of only 8–15 mm. In autumn, eats ripe berries of Diddle-dee *Empetrum rubrum, Gunnera magellanica* and *Myrteola nummularia,* and strips seeds from grasses.

In winter, favours fertilized reseeded pastures composed of introduced European grasses, *Holcus lanatus, Dactylis glomerata* and *Agrostis.* If snow covers pastures, resorts to eating green seaweeds on shore (Summers and Grieve 1982). Digestive efficiency on grass diet low (38%), so grazes for much of day, 89% in winter and 71% in summer with noon lull (Summers and Grieve 1982). Total daily intake of grass, 253 g organic matter (Summers and Castro 1988).

Displays and breeding behaviour

Inciting by ♀ involves raising hind-quarters whilst walking or running to mate, Bowing and calling. ♂ responds in upright aggressive stance, with head held high, *wi-wi* calls given and carpal knobs held out from body. White lesser and median coverts, generally hidden when standing, exposed to reinforce signal of readiness to fight. Attack starts by running with head held low, and bill and wings used in fighting. Triumph Ceremony follows when pair re-unite (Johnsgard 1965a, Summers and McAdam 1993). Establishment of territorial boundaries between neighbouring ♂♂ involves pacing side by side with wing tips trailing and carpal knobs exposed; occasionally, ♂♂ face one another, grip necks and beat with their wings (Summers and McAdam 1993). Head-tossing occurs prior to flight.

Nests in territories defended by ♂, who is faithful to mate and territory.

Breeding and life cycle

Breeds around ponds, in valleys, on islands and along coast. Nests made on ground in grass or *Empetrum rubrum* late Sept–mid Nov (Falkland Islands). Eggs light-brown; *picta* measure 75.4 × 49.3 (Goodall *et al.* 1951) and weigh in captivity 113.6 ($n = 30$), *leucoptera* 81.5 × 53.4, weight 128 (120–135) ($n = 8$) (Summers and McAdam 1993) or 124 (83.5–146.0) ($n = 100$) in captivity. Laid every other day; in Falkland Islands clutch 6.1 ± 1.1 (3–8) ($n = 24$). Incubation, by ♀, 30 days, while she loses 12% of winter weight; during breaks in incubation covers eggs with down. Captive day-olds weigh *picta* 68.9 ($n = 10$) and *leucoptera* 77.3 ($n = 13$). Average brood size at hatching 5.1, at fledging, after 10 weeks, 3.9. Sex ratio at fledging 1:1. Broods sometimes combine, and Ruddy-headed goslings may also join crèches. About half breeding pairs fail and replacement clutches rare, so that annual productivity *c* 2 young per breeding pair (Summers 1983b). Despite sexual dimorphism of parents, goslings follow both, while preferring to stay with ♀. Losses attributed to predation by Antarctic Skua *Catharacta antarctica* and Kelp or Southern Black-backed Gulls in Falklands (Woods 1975), and by foxes *Pseudalopex culpaeus* and *P. griseus*, American Mink, caracaras and Grey Eagle-Buzzard *Geranoaetus melanoleucus* in Patagonia (Martin 1984). Intestinal parasites include nematodes *Amidostomum anseris* in gizzard and *Heterakis dispar* and *Trichostrongylus tenuis* in caeca. Hymenolepid cestodes occur in small intestine (Harradine 1982).

Families stay together until following spring when 1st year ♀♀ start pairing, but ♂♂ remain unpaired until at least 20 months old. ♀♀ breed initially at 2 years old.

Breeding adults have an annual survival of 82%, giving life expectancy of 5 years, though oldest ringing recovery was 12 years old (Summers 1983b), oldest in captivity 16 years (Hillgarth and Kear 1979b).

Conservation and threats

In Argentine Tierra del Fuego, has probably benefited from scrub clearance and perhaps extinction of Ona Indians and decrease in foxes as sheep farming developed (Crawshay 1907). Similarly, in Falkland Islands, browsing of Fachine *Chiliotrichum diffusum* and close-grazing of *Poa* grasses by sheep probably enhanced foraging conditions (Summers and McAdam 1993). Has long been regarded as pest by sheep farmers in Patagonia and Falkland Islands because reduces value of reseeded pastures (Douse 1987), and thought to compete with sheep for grass (Johnson 1965). In attempt at population reduction, 0.5 million killed in Falklands 1905–12, and bounty schemes meant that during 1975–80, *c* 25 000 killed annually and 10 000 eggs broken or collected (Summers and Dunnet 1984). Since war of 1982, and changes in land ownership, persecution has declined due to depopulation of farms, increase in fishing revenues and to slowly changing attitudes to wildlife. However, still listed as pest in 1999 Wildlife and Nature Ordinance. In wheat lands of Buenos Aires, wintering geese are driven out to sea by aircraft in attempts to kill them (Pergolani de Costa 1955).

Ron Summers

Kelp Goose *Chloephaga hybrida*
PLATE 9

Anas Hybrida Molina, 1782, Saggio Storia Nat. Chili, pp. 241, 344
Chiloé Island

Etymology: *hybrida* L. for hybrid; apparently Molina felt that the striking difference between the sexes made it appear that 2 species were hybridizing.

Other names: Antarctic Goose, Kelp Sheldgoose. Argentina: Cauquén caranca; Chile: Cagüe, Caranca. Also: Avutarda blanca, Carauco, Ganso del cachiyuyo, Avutarda de mar, Avutarda de las rocas.

Variation: 2 subspecies. *C. h. hybrida*, Patagonian Kelp Goose, found on mainland South America; *C. h. malvinarum* Phillips, 1916, Greater or Falkland Kelp Goose, occurs on Falkland Islands, and is larger than nominate race.

Description

ADULT: sexes markedly different. ♂ plumage entirely white; carpal knob yellow. Bill black with pink spot on top of upper mandible; legs and feet yellow; eyes brown. ♀ generally dark; brown mantle and head with pale brown crown. Thick black and white bars on breast and flanks. Undertail coverts, tail and back white. Wing like Magellan Goose. Bill pink; legs and feet yellow; iris dark brown and eye-ring white.

MOULT: no seasonal change in plumage, except caused by wear. Flocks of up to several hundred gather on coast to moult flight feathers late Nov–Feb, with ♂♂ moulting earlier than ♀♀ (Gladstone and Martell 1968). Also moults with Ashyheads in Patagonian fjords. Likely that moult-skipping occurs, judging by worn primaries (Pettingill 1965).

IMMATURE: similar to adult ♀ but no iridescent speculum, and dull greenish yellow legs and feet. ♂ has white on head; ♀ lacks light brown crown (Delacour 1954–64, Woods 1975).

GOSLING: fluffy and almost white with narrow black line around eye, except beneath, extending a little beyond. Base of down grey and faintly marked above with pale brown, as other *Chloephaga* goslings. Markings apparently stronger in ♀♀ than ♂♂, or 2 colour phases. Bill black with white nail; feet black (Delacour 1954–64).

MEASUREMENTS AND WEIGHT: *hybrida* ♂ wing (n = 12), 363–385 (370.5); tail, 127.5–139.0 (131.5); bill, 35.5–38.3 (36.7); tarsus, 66.3–71.1 (69.4). ♀ wing (n = 16) 334–359 (348.5); tail, 126.5–137.5 (130.2); bill, 34.6–38.6 (36.0); tarsus, 61.3–66.1 (63.7) (Murphy 1936). *malvinarum* ♂ wing (n = 3), 376–383 (380); bill, 39–40 (39.3); tarsus, 72–76 (74). ♀ wing (n = 5), 360–376 (366); bill, 36–38 (37.2); tarsus, 65–71 (67) (Phillips 1916). Weight *hybrida* ♂ (n = 2), 2540–2580; ♀ (n = 2), 2000–2020 (Ripley 1950, Humphrey *et al.* 1970); *malvinarum* ♂ (n = 5), 3250–3600 (3420); ♀ (n = 2), 2050–2800 (Summers and McAdam 1993).

Field characters

Stocky seashore goose, 550–650 mm long, sexes entirely unalike, ♂ white and ♀ chocolate coloured. Short-winged, and not strong fliers. In many places, shows no fear of humans.

Voice

♂ has *si-si-si* whistle and ♀ low honk *arnk-arnk*, or *ooer* and *ooeroo* calls (Woods 1975); sexual difference becomes apparent in goslings before feathers appear (Gladstone and Martell 1968). Young goslings have double-noted *cheep*.

Range and status

Continental *hybrida* found on coasts and islands of Chile from 42°S, Tierra del Fuego and north to 50°S in Argentina, with occasional northward movements to 33°S in Chile and 39°S in Argentina (Woods 1975). Short migrations undertaken by *hybrida*, arriving on east coast of Tierra del Fuego Mar and departing Sept (Ripley 1950). Densities of 0.46 birds/km of shore occur along Beagle

Channel, but >9 times this (4.36 birds/km) on Staten Island. Along Atlantic coast of Isla Grande de Tierra del Fuego, where birds from Beagle Channel and Staten Island winter, density in autumn of 2.14 birds/km (Raya Rey and Schiavini 2002). Falklands race *malvinarum* resident but may leave outlying coasts for sheltered inlets in winter; faithful both to winter and breeding areas (Woods 1975). Numbers stable; 25 000–100 000 estimated in mainland South America (Rose and Scott 1997) and 10 000–18 000 pairs on Falklands where population perhaps 25 000– 40 000 birds (Woods and Woods 1997).

Habitat and general habits

Common bird of rocky coasts, preferring wide intertidal zones protected by offshore kelp beds, and avoiding cliffs. Subsists largely on algae growing in rocky intertidal zone such as green seaweeds *Enteromorpha* and *Ulva*, and red seaweed *Porphyra umbilicalis* (Weller 1972). Small invertebrates accidentally ingested with weeds. Feeding pattern dictated by tides. When tide drops, may swim out and dip down to graze. Normally, however, walks intertidal rocks to

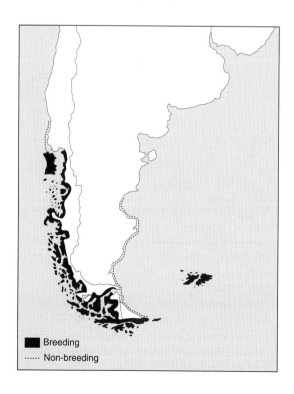

■ Breeding
‧‧‧‧‧ Non-breeding

graze at low tide. At high tide, often loafs (Weller 1972). May resort to inland feeding on grass and ripe berries of *Empetrum rubrum* and *Myrteola nummularia* (Sladen 1952, Woods 1975). High intake of salt balanced by regular drinking from freshwater streams, often at dawn (Gladstone and Martell 1968), but also has large nasal glands that excrete salt.

Displays and breeding behaviour

White plumage of ♂ conspicuous on dark rocky shores. Signals of territory occupation and defence reinforced by ♂'s upright aggressive stance when chest Puffed and high-pitched calls given. When Inciting, ♀ lowers head towards ♂ and raises tail (Johnsgard 1965a, Pettingill 1965). Both sexes defend territory; ♂♂ chase other ♂♂ and ♀♀, and ♀♀ other ♀♀. If fights develop, grapple with bills and flail wings at one another. Territories also defended against Magellan Geese, but not Ruddy-headed Geese. Territory length usually over 100 m of shore (Gladstone and Martell 1968).

Breeding and life cycle

Little known about breeding of nominate subspecies. In Chile and Tierra del Fuego, nesting takes place in long grass in Nov when 3–6 eggs laid; goslings appear Dec–early Jan (Goodall *et al.* 1951, Johnson 1965, Humphrey *et al.* 1970). In Falkland Islands, breeds along rocky coasts and on islands late Oct–Jan, most nests hatching Nov, somewhat later than Magellan. *hybrida* lays 3–6 creamy white eggs, measuring 79.1 × 52.0 (Goodall *et al.* 1951) and *malvinarum* clutch of 5.3 ± 0.8 (3–7) ($n = 44$); 82.5 × 55.6

(78–89 × 53–58) ($n - 48$); weight 139 (Gladstone and Martell 1968).

Nests usually within 10 m of shore, beside driftwood or large boulder, or among *Empetrum rubrum*, *Cortaderia pilosa* or 3 m high *Poa flabellata*. Nests tend to be in traditional areas and same site used over several years. White ♂ remains on territory while cryptic ♀ incubates for 30 days. During breaks, she covers eggs with grey down. Eggs hatch within 12–48 h and young leave together some hours after last egg hatches. Hatching success high (95%). Goslings cared for by both parents in territory but fledging success low (14%) due to stormy seas, predation by Kelp or Southern Black-backed Gulls and Antarctic Skuas. Only ♀ broods, but goslings imprint on both parents despite differences in colour and voice. Broods occasionally combine. Growth slow due to intermittent availability of food on intertidal zone. Fledge in 12–13 weeks (Gladstone and Martell 1968). Families stay together until midwinter at least, and pairs remain close throughout year (Woods 1975).

Nonbreeders occur in flocks, and pairing may occur during 1st year, before breeding at 2 years old (Pettingill 1965, Gladstone and Martell 1968, Weller 1972, Woods 1975). Single ringed bird at least 7 years 3 months when last seen (Woods 1975).

Conservation and threats

Status of no concern. Not hunted because flesh unpalatable (Pettingill 1965); eggs also unpleasant to eat (Delacour 1954–64). Protected status in Falklands.

Ron Summers

Ashy-headed Goose *Chloephaga poliocephala*
PLATE 9

Chloëphaga poliocephala P. L. Sclater, 1857, Proc. Zool. Soc. London, p. 128
Chiloé Island
  Etymology: *poliocephala* Gr. for grey-headed.
  Other names: Ashy-headed Sheldgoose, Coast Brant, White-breasted Brant. South American: Avutarda de cabeza gris, Cauquén cabecigris, Caiquén, Gansillo, Canquén, Avutarda.

Variation: no subspecies, but variation in breast barring of ♂.

Description

ADULT: sexes alike, but ♂ larger. Head and neck grey, breast chestnut-brown, belly white and flanks barred black and white; tail black. Wings like Magellan Goose. Bill black; legs and feet orange with dark markings; iris dark brown with small white eye-ring (Goodall *et al.* 1951, Delacour 1954–64).

MOULT: undescribed, no seasonal change in plumage; evidence of moult-skipping of wings (Summers 1983a). Moults with Kelp Geese in Patagonian fjords.

IMMATURE: duller and more finely barred than adults. No iridescent speculum. Adult plumage attained in 2nd year.

GOSLING: whitish with blackish grey markings; bill and legs black (Delacour 1954–64).

MEASUREMENTS AND WEIGHT: ♂ and ♀ wing (*n* = 7), 323–378 (350); bill, 29–32 (30.8); tail, 106–125 (118) (Goodall *et al.* 1951). Weight ♂ (*n* = 6), 1620–2040 (1890); ♀ (*n* = 2) 1470–1490 (1480) (Summers and McAdam 1993). Heavy weights (2240) in Tierra del Fuego in May indicate pre-migratory fattening (Ripley 1950).

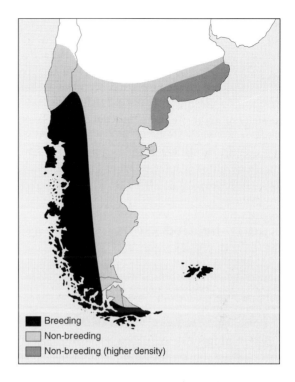

Breeding
Non-breeding
Non-breeding (higher density)

Field characters

Upright goose, 500–550 mm in length. Grey head, ruddy breast, fine barring of flanks and white belly distinguish from Ruddy-headed and Magellan Goose. Deep ruddy colour of breast noticeable when grazing. Wing pattern similar to Magellan in flight.

Voice

Sexually dimorphic. ♂ has soft whistle, 'wigeon-like' (Fjeldså and Krabbe 1990), and ♀ harsh cackle (Delacour 1954–64). Sonogram of contact call of gosling in Kear (1968).

Range and status

Breeds in Tierra del Fuego and Patagonia north to 37°S. In Argentine Tierra del Fuego, near Rio Grande, densities in Oct, Dec and Jan–Feb were 1.7–3.1, 0.7–2.3 and 0.4–0.7 per km² respectively (Martin *et al.* 1982). In winter, moves north in Argentina. In Buenos Aires province, joins Magellan and Ruddy-headed Geese, and comprises 6–12% of 4.1–4.5 sheldgeese per km along transects in 1983 and 1984 (Martin *et al.* 1986). Reaches Falkland Islands probably annually, where has bred (Woods 1975). Rose and Scott (1997) guess at declining population of 25 000–1 000 000.

Habitat and general habits

In summer, occurs on grasslands in river valleys, around lakes, marshes and by the sea. Compared with Magellan Goose, associates more with Andes and southern beech *Nothofagus* forests, where occurs in clearings, and less with flat grasslands of northern Tierra del Fuego and southern Magallanes. Diet undescribed in summer; in winter in Buenos Aires province, grazes young pastures and selects stubbles of wheat, maize, sunflower and sorghum (Martin *et al.* 1986).

Displays and breeding behaviour

♀ Incites by making rapid Bowing movements and calling, ♂ responds with aggressive upright stance, white belly enhancing aggressive display, calling *wi-wi* and holding carpal joints out ready to fight. During attack, head lowered during rush forward and wings used to beat opponent. After attack, ♂ returns to ♀ to perform Triumph Ceremony (Johnsgard 1965a). Territorial nester.

Breeding and life cycle

Limited information. Nests around marshes (mallines) and on islets, well-hidden in long grass;

occasionally in hollow dead trees (Johnson 1965) and on *Nothofagus* stumps, 1.2–4.0 m from ground (Schlatter *et al.* 2002). Breeds Nov–Mar in Tierra del Fuego (Humphrey *et al.* 1970). Eggs (4–6) brown; 72.3 × 48.4 ($n = 4$) (Summers and McAdam 1993); weight in captivity 97.1 (89.0–110.0) ($n = 100$). Incubation, by ♀, 30 days (Delacour 1954–64); at hatching in captivity weigh 64.3 ($n = 25$), at 21 days 504 ($n = 7$). Brood size 5–6, but up to 15 when broods amalgamate (Johnson 1965). Probably breeds

at 2 years. Oldest bird in captivity 16 years (Hillgarth and Kear 1979b). No data on breeding success nor adult survival in wild.

Conservation and threats

Not abundant. Subject to same persecution as other sheldgeese over apparent competition with grazing livestock.

Ron Summers

Ruddy-headed Goose *Chloephaga rubidiceps*
PLATE 9

Chloëphaga rubidiceps P. L. Sclater, 1861, Proc. Zool. Soc. London (1860), p. 387, pl. 173
Falkland Islands

Etymology: *rubidiceps* L. for red-headed.

Other names: Ruddy-headed Sheldgoose, Brent Goose, Brant. South America: Avutarda colorada, Avutarda de cabeza colorada, Canquén colorado, Cauquén colorado.

Variation: no subspecies or geographical variation.

Description

ADULT: sexes alike, but ♂ larger. Head and neck red-brown, although fades to grey-brown during inter-moult period; body grey and buff with brown bars; belly cinnamon and occasionally with white patches; tail black. Wing similar to Magellan Goose but small coverts often tinged pale yellow rather than white. Carpal knob orange and larger in ♂. Bill black; legs and feet orange with black blotches; iris dark brown with white eye-ring that varies in size.

MOULT: no seasonal change in plumage colour, except through fading. In Falkland Islands, flightless moult occurs mainly Dec–Jan. Up to several hundred gather at ponds or sheltered sea inlets, often with moulting Magellan Geese. Flocks composed of 30–40% one-year-olds; however, some individuals, thought to be successful breeders, skip annual wing moult (Summers 1983a). Movements to moulting sites only few km (Summers 1985b). In Tierra del Fuego and southern Patagonia, evidence of different moulting strategy; birds have wings with mixture of

old and new primaries, perhaps undergoing sequential partial moult, involving inner primaries at one period and outer primaries at another (Summers 1982).

IMMATURE: like adult but duller; greater coverts and large median coverts grey (Summers and McAdam 1993).

GOSLING: pale grey and dark grey. Legs and bill black.

MEASUREMENTS AND WEIGHT: ♂ ($n = 13$) wing, (357); tarsus, (67.8); bill, (29.4). ♀ ($n = 8$) wing, (332); tarsus, (61.6); bill (27.1) (Harradine 1977). Weight ♂ ($n = 4$) 1650–1850 (1750); ♀ ($n = 9$) 1200–1500 (1400) (Summers and McAdam 1993). Heavy weights (2020) in Tierra del Fuego in Apr suggest pre-migratory fattening (Ripley 1950).

Field characters

Smallest of *Chloephaga* geese, 450–500 mm long. Confusion with Ashyhead unlikely, and distinguished from ♀ Magellan Goose by smaller size, and paler plumage overall (Madge and Burn 1988).

Voice

Sexes differ. ♂ has short *seep* whistle and ♀ short rasping quack (Woods 1975).

Range and status

Resident in Falkland Islands. Individuals move up to 90 km, but most journeys less than 5 km to breeding, feeding and moulting areas (Summers

1985b). Variable turnover at feeding sites as birds move within home ranges (Summers *et al.* 1985).

In northern Tierra del Fuego, southern Santa Cruz province (Argentina) and Magallanes (Chile) arrives late Aug to breed. By Mar, gathers in flocks, abandons southern locations (San Juan River) (Matus *et al.* 2000), and departs Apr to winter in southern Buenos Aires province, coexisting with other sheldgeese.

In Falklands, mean densities highest around ponds (4.4 birds per ha), *Poa* greens (2.6 per ha) and reseeded pastures (Summers 1985a). Population of Falkland Islands estimated at 14 000– 27 000 pairs, so possible total of 35 000–60 000 (Woods and Woods 1997). Was numerous in Tierra del Fuego in 1950s (Scott 1954), but 20 years later had declined to small numbers (Rumboll 1975), perhaps due to introduced Grey Foxes *P. griseus*. Numbers remain small; in Buenos Aires province in winter, only 12 and 44 seen among 15 600 and 16 560 sheldgeese in 1983 and 1984 respectively (Martin *et al.* 1986). Rose and Scott (1997) suggested only 300 remained in mainland South America.

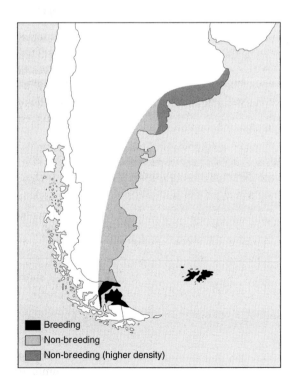

Breeding

Non-breeding

Non-breeding (higher density)

Habitat and general habits

In Falkland Islands, grazes on lush greens around farm settlements, at ponds, along valleys and coastal greens, eating primarily *Poa annua* and *P. pratensis*, also *Juncus scheuchzerioides*, *Aira praecox* and *Gunnera magellanica* berries. Foraging comprises 91% of time in winter and 69% in summer, with lull in middle of day. Daily intake 132 g organic matter (Summers and Grieve 1982). In Magallanes (Chile), forages on pampas wetlands (vegas and mallines) (Madsen *et al.* 2003). In winter quarters in Buenos Aires province, selects fields of young wheat, pastures and stubbles of maize, sunflower and sorghum (Martin *et al.* 1986).

Displays and breeding behaviour

Aggressive upright stance of ♂ and Inciting behaviour of ♀ similar to Ashy-headed Goose. Head-tosses prior to take-off. Territorial nester.

Breeding and life cycle

In the Falklands, breeds at ponds, along valleys and on coast, nesting in long grass or rushes, beneath rock outcrops and even in old Magellanic Penguin burrows. Lays late Sept–Nov (Woods 1975). On the continent, breeds on pampas wetlands; peak laying mid Oct (Madsen *et al.* 2003). Eggs laid at 2-day intervals (Rossi 1959); pale brown; 72.2 × 50.0 (*n* = 25) (Summers and McAdam 1993); weight in captivity 95.2 (74.0–106.0) (*n* = 100), similar in size to Ashyhead. Clutch size 5.0 (3–7); egg set of 11 suggests egg dumping. Incubation, by ♀, 30 days, and ♂ remains in territory. Captive goslings at day old weigh 64.1 (*n* = 18) and 540 at Day 21 (*n* = 6). Brood size drops to average 3.0 at fledging (Harradine 1977). Can breed at 2 years. No data on adult survival, but oldest ringing recovery was 14 years (Summers and McAdam 1993), and oldest in captivity 17 years (Hillgarth and Kear 1979b).

Conservation and threats

Rarest of *Chloephaga* geese. As with Magellan Goose, was killed for bounty money in Falkland Islands; however, now protected. In Tierra del Fuego, Grey Foxes introduced to control rabbits in early 50s possibly responsible for drastic fall in numbers and current low breeding success (Madsen *et al.* 2003).

Ron Summers

Common Shelduck *Tadorna tadorna*
PLATE 10

Anas Tadorna Linnaeus, 1758, Syst. Nat., ed. 10, p. 122
coasts of Europe
Tadorna Boie, 1822

Etymology:'tadorne' was Celtic for pied waterbird; 'sheld duck', which means variegated or pied duck, dates from *c* 1700, and was preceded by 'sheldrake'.

Other names: Northern Shelduck, Red-billed Shelduck, Burrow Duck. French: Tadorne de Belon; German: Brandgans; Icelandic: Brandgás; Dutch: Bergeend.

Variation: no subspecies, despite 2 separated populations that select somewhat different habitats.

Description

ADULT: slightly dimorphic. ♂ in breeding plumage has head and upperneck black with green sheen. Broad chestnut band encircles upperbody from breast to mantle. Rufous vent. Underparts otherwise white with blackish stripe from breast band to vent. Back, rump and wing coverts white, scapulars and remiges black, tertials with chestnut edging and secondaries with metallic green sheen. Tail white, tipped black. Bill bright waxy red, with large basal knob in spring (size of which varies with testis size); feet and legs pink; iris brown. ♀ similar, slightly smaller with white at base of bill, narrower chestnut breast band and blackish belly band and paler vent.

MOULT: 2 moults of body plumage and one of flight feathers annually. ♂ in eclipse has plumage of head, breast and belly bands less clear-cut and admixed with white. Frontal knob disappears and bill fades. Loss of primaries during wing moult, July–Oct, results in white appearance. Flightless for 25–31 days. Nonbreeding ♀ much as eclipsed ♂ but paler, with browner head, underparts occasionally becoming entirely white.

IMMATURE: underparts white, including face and forehead. Crown, hindneck and upperparts dark grey-brown. Bill, legs and feet pinkish grey.

DUCKLING: crown, eyestripe and hindneck dark brown, otherwise upperparts predominantly blackish brown and underparts white with blackish thigh patches. Bill and legs green-grey.

MEASUREMENTS AND WEIGHT: ♂ wing ($n = 33$), 312–350 (334); tail ($n = 27$), 6–115 (108); bill ($n = 37$), 50–58 (53.0); tarsus ($n = 34$), 52–60 (55.8). ♀ wing ($n = 28$), 284–316 (303); tail ($n = 27$), 89–106 (96.9); bill ($n = 36$), 44–50 (47.3); tarsus ($n = 36$), 46–54 (50.1). Weight ♂ Feb in SW Caspian ($n = ?$), 830–1500 (1180); Apr–May various ($n = 11$), 1100–1450 (1261); Jun–Aug various ($n = 7$), 1000–1350 (1167). ♀ Feb in SW Caspian ($n = ?$), 562–1085 (813); Apr–May various ($n = 5$), 926–1250 (1043); Jun–Aug various ($n = 5$), 850–1075 (952) (Cramp and Simmons 1977).

Field characters

Unmistakable large duck, 580–670 mm long, appearing white and black at distance. Juvenile superficially resembles young Egyptian Goose, from which separable by more contrasting plumage, especially much whiter underparts and darker head lacking dark eyepatch. Rises easily into flight (which rather goose-like) sometimes after short run. White tips to flight feathers of juvenile form trailing edge in flight. Moves freely on land and perches readily. Dependent young dive easily, adults only in emergency.

Voice

Quite vocal, especially just before and during breeding season. ♂ utters variety of whistling notes, most frequent being soft, clear *whee-chew* becoming urgent and frequent if danger threatens. Vocalizations of ♀ mostly louder and lower in pitch with cackling quality *gagagagaga* . . . , at rate of up to 12 notes per sec, often uttered in flight. Sonograms of ♂ and ♀ calls in Cramp and Simmons (1977). ♀ calls to hatching eggs, and ducklings imprint on her voice while in darkness of burrow. Ducklings utter high-pitched peeps when moving and feeding, and soft trills when in close contact. Sonogram of duckling distress call in Kear (1968).

Range and status

Numerous on estuaries and scarce on inland lowland lakes in northwest and Mediterranean Europe. Asiatic

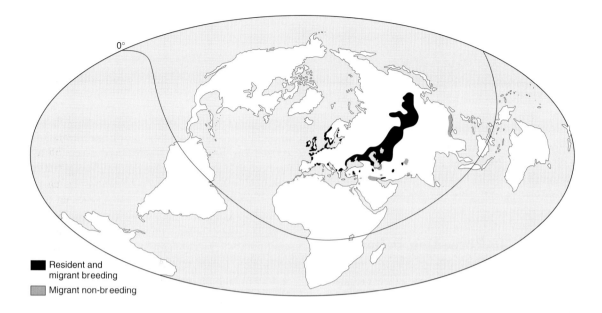

Resident and
migrant breeding

Migrant non-breeeding

population occupies rivers, and especially marshes and
lakes, in semi-desert and steppe, across fragmented
range from Turkey and north Black Sea coast through
central Asia to Mongolia and northern China, with
southern outliers in Iran and Afghanistan. Much of
European population undertakes moult migration to
northwest German coast, where 100 000 or more
gather at Heligoland Bight, June–Oct, on vast mudflats extending over 20 km offshore, that provide food
and protection from predators (Figure 9.23). Smaller
numbers moult at few large British estuaries, notably
Bridgwater Bay in southwest England, where 3000–
4000 gather, and at estuary of Rhine in The Netherlands. Asiatic birds appear to moult near breeding
grounds, but many migrate south to winter in
Caspian basin, and small numbers to north Africa,
Iraq, Pakistan, northern India, Bangladesh and southern China. Southeast European breeding population
mainly sedentary, flocking in winter.

Winter population estimates: northwest Europe,
300 000; Black Sea and Mediterranean, 75 000; west
Asia, Caspian Sea and Middle East, 80 000; central
and south Asia, 25 000–100 000; east Asia, 100 000–
150 000 (Wetlands International 2002). European
and Caspian populations apparently increasing; in
northwest Europe, rate of increase 1973–93 estimated at 50%, with indications of stabilization
between 1987 and 1996 (Delany *et al.* 1999).

9.23 Common Shelduck during wing moult.

Habitat and general habits

Favours semi-arid and mild maritime climates, governed by attachment to salt and brackish water
either on shallow coasts and muddy estuaries in the
west, or inland seas and lakes in the east (Cramp
and Simmons 1977). Adults and young feed on
variety of tiny invertebrates by digging, scything
and dabbling in muddy or sandy substrate, or head-
dipping and up-ending in water up to 400 mm
deep (Bryant and Leng 1975). Often marked tidal

rhythm of feeding by night and day, with 12 of 24 h spent feeding in winter. In northern and western Europe, small molluscs especially *Hydrobia*, predominate in diet; in southern Europe and Asia, small crustaceans and insect larvae apparently favoured. Small quantities of algae, seeds and grain also taken. One ♀, returning to incubate after feeding bout, contained 11 858 *Hydrobia* (Patterson 1982), whilst another individual in Russia (Dementiev and Gladkov 1952) contained (amazingly) 63 880 chironomid larvae. Ducklings partial to *Nereis* and *Corophium* mainly obtained by moving fast and pecking (Patterson 1982).

Displays and breeding behaviour

Breeding birds hold feeding territory from late winter until young hatch, otherwise gregarious, with nonbreeders remaining in flocks throughout year. Maximum concentrations occur during postbreeding moult, after which birds disperse and move back to breeding area, often in series of stages over several months. Nests inland of feeding territory, sometimes at high density in 'communes', where groups of off-duty adults form loose flocks (Hori 1964). Monogamous, with pairbond usually persisting from year to year, although ♂ and ♀ may migrate and winter separately. Fittest and heaviest birds succeed in competition for territories (Patterson 1982); those without territories do not breed.

Both sexes aggressive and threat displays enhanced by plumage pattern (Patterson 1982). ♂ diligent in defence of territory and ♀. Adults also defend young vigorously. Main threat display by ♂ Head-throwing, repeated rotary pumping movement of head, accompanied at high intensity by up and down rocking of body and agitated whistling. Both sexes run goose-like at opponent with head lowered and bill open, carrying attack through by biting if necessary. Sexual displays include Rest-intent (or High-and-erect) of ♂, where erect posture with raised nape feathers assumed while whistling and holding head still. Both sexes perform exaggerated Preen-behind-wing display on side towards mate. Copulation usually on water preceded by rapid swimming and Head-dipping. Courtship flights frequent in spring.

Breeding and life cycle

Well studied (Patterson 1982). Returns in stages to breeding ground, Oct–Mar, older birds returning earlier than younger ones, and breeds mid Apr–May. Nests in burrows (typically of European Rabbit *Oryctolagus cuniculus*), tree holes (up to 8 m high), under artificial objects such as hay bales, in nestboxes, occasionally in open or dense vegetation, up to 1 km from water. No material except abundant down in hole sites; elsewhere adds vegetation. Site chosen and cup formed by ♀; where sites abundant, ♀ tends not to use same one as previous year. Commune nests may be as close as 1 m apart.

Eggs creamy white; 65.6 × 47.3 (61–71 × 43–50) ($n = 175$) (Schönwetter 1960–66); weight 79.8 (65.5–92.5) ($n = 100$); laid daily; clutch 8.85 (3–12) ($n = 140$); egg dumping occurs. Incubation 29–31 days by ♀, who develops brood patch. She may leave 3–4 times daily to feed, bathe and preen, always during daylight; escorted back by ♂ (Patterson 1982). Hatching synchronous; ducklings precocial and nidifugous, weight of day-olds 48.8 ($n = 36$); at 21 days 715. High proportion (c 90%) of eggs hatch in successful nests, but hatching success of clutches laid in colonies low at 25–50%, perhaps associated with disturbance by other pairs. Both parents lead brood from nest to feeding, or nursery, area (up to 3 km), and may use Distraction display or 'tolling'—flying conspicuously while calling in vicinity of predator. ♀ broods young when small. One brood per season, and usually no re-laying after lost clutch. Some parents remain with young until fledging at 45–50 days; others depart on moult migration when young 15–20 days old, and crèches of up to 100 form, accompanied by one or more adults.

Dispersed populations shown to have significantly higher breeding success than crowded ones; Patterson (1982), in 13 years of study, found that c 35% of young fledged, and each pair, on crowded Ythan estuary in east Scotland, fledged one duckling annually. Predation by Great Black-backed *Larus marinus* and Herring Gulls, crows and foxes, and loss in poor weather, account for most early mortality. ♀ normally breeds at 2 years old, ♂ at 4–5, and ♂♂ show greater 1st year dispersal. Mean annual adult mortality 20%; life expectancy 4.5 years (Boyd 1962); oldest ringed bird c 14.5 years (Rydzewski 1974, Toms and Clark 1998).

Conservation and threats

Increases in numbers may be related to decrease in hunting pressure in 20th century. Human influence on nest sites considerable, from introduction (and control) of rabbits, to pollarding of willows and provision of hay bales. Principal threat now habitat change (e.g. barrage schemes) on often highly developed estuaries in Europe (e.g. Schekkerman *et al.* 1994) and associated with large-scale changes in land use in central Asia.

Simon Delany

Radjah Shelduck *Tadorna radjah*
PLATE 10

Anas radjah 'Garnot' Lesson, 1828, Man. Ornith., **2**, p. 417
Buru

Etymology: *radjah* is native name for bird on Buru Island in Moluccas.

Other names: White-headed Shelduck, Burdekin Duck. Australian Aboriginal: Co-mer-do, Dirrn-birrn, Karkiyal, Mahdo, Ngauaramo, Tjinborr.

Variation: 2 subspecies: *T. r. radjah*, Black-backed Shelduck, of New Guinea and Moluccas, *T. r. rufitergum*, Hartert, 1905, Red-backed Shelduck, of northern Australia.

Description

ADULT: sexes alike. Mostly white with dark back and breast band; flesh-coloured bill and legs; white eyes. Subspecies differ in size and plumage details (Madge and Burn 1988, Marchant and Higgins 1990); nominate *radjah* has blacker upperparts and breast band, while *rufitergum* has rich chestnut mantle and breast-band. Much individual variation, however, and inter-grades occur. Speculum marked in front by black line and behind by broad white border. ♀ smaller and lighter than ♂; breast band narrower.

MOULT: no seasonal plumage changes. No data on body and wing moult sequences.

IMMATURE: as adult but duller, grey and brown flecking to white plumage, especially on head. Iris dark brown.

DUCKLING: chestnut crown, otherwise as other shelduckling; nape, back and rump dark brown, underparts and face white; bill, legs and feet pink.

MEASUREMENTS AND WEIGHT: *rufitergum* in Australia ♂ wing (*n* = 4), 275–287 (282); tarsus (*n* = 5), 52.5–57.5 (54.9). ♀ wing (*n* = 4), 273–285 (279.2); tarsus (*n* = 6), 53.3–57.4 (55.5) (Marchant and Higgins 1990); ♂ weight (*n* = 46), 750–1101 (934); ♀ weight (*n* = 49), 600–1130 (839) (Frith 1982). Subadult ♀ *radjah* caught in Seram in Aug weighed 590, wing 194, tarsus 53.8.

Field characters

Small, dumpy shelduck, 485–555 mm long, usually seen in pairs and often perched. Cotton Teal also largely white with band at base of neck and dark upperparts, but much smaller with black cap and bill, and different wing pattern.

Voice

Very vocal, calling on land, in water and in flight. Calls differ between sexes, ♂ producing thin rattling whistle when displaying to ♀ who responds with harsh rattling note (Frith 1982). Calls often heard from flocks in flight or when Inciting. During day, roosting flocks quiet but squabbling may occur before leaving for feeding grounds. Sonogram of ♂ whistle in Marchant and Higgins (1990). Calls of young unrecorded.

Range and status

Only tropical shelduck. Nominate *radjah* widespread in coastal and near-coastal areas of New Guinea and Moluccas, *rufitergum* has disjunct distribution in northern Australia, in extreme northeast Western Australia and Northern Territory, and in Queensland. Birds from southern New Guinea

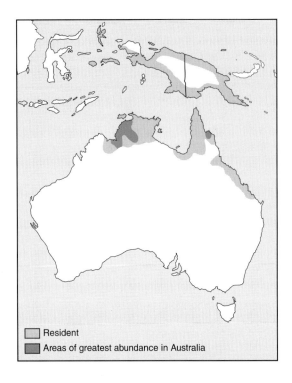

Resident

Areas of greatest abundance in Australia

intermediate between 2 forms (Frith 1982). Vagrant to Timor and Tanimbar in Lesser Sundas (White and Bruce 1986) and to New South Wales. Formerly more widespread in Australia, including Kimberley Division of Western Australia and northeast New South Wales; range contracted northwards in last century. Declined in Papua New Guinea where described as very uncommon in northern coastal regions and decidedly local along south coast (Madge and Burn 1988), although substantial population probably still exists here and in Irian Jaya. Still extant on some Moluccan islands, including Seram (Bowler and Taylor 1989), Bacan (Lambert 1994) and Obi (Linsley 1995), although populations probably not large. Considered to have declined last century on Buru where now rare (Jepson 1993). Wetlands International (2002) suggested declining population of 10 000–100 000 in New Guinea and Moluccas, and stable population of 150 000 in northern Australia.

Habitat and general habits

Selects terrestrial wetlands and estuarine and littoral habitats in monsoonal regions of Australia (Blakers

et al. 1984); tolerant of saline conditions. Restricted by strong preference for shallow water to complexes of shallow pools and mudbanks or fringes of deep wetlands. In dry season, mainly littoral, favouring mangrove-lined mudflats and rivers, fringing saline flats and beaches (Frith 1982, Erftemeijer *et al.* 1991), although in Seram more numerous during dry season on shallows and pools of gravel-lined riverbeds inland to 200 m altitude (Bowler 1993). Also in more permanent waterbodies on subcoastal floodplains of Northern Territories (Morton *et al.* 1990b) and in northeast Queensland (Marchant and Higgins 1990). Few birds in littoral habitat in wet season probably as unsuitable for nesting; mostly on fringes of extensive floodwaters on floodplains, retreating to small creeks and drainage lines as floods recede (Frith 1982, Morton *et al.* 1990b). Flight strong and fast, at low or moderate height above water, and weaves through, rather than over, canopy of trees. Regularly perches, and roosts by day on banks or in trees standing in or near water. Rarely swims but runs swiftly on land. Exhibits local movements between dispersed breeding territories and dry season pools or coast, e.g. numbers congregating in Alligator Rivers area during dry season greater than those breeding in wet season. Small numbers seen throughout year on isolated islands in Torres Strait suggest persistent but perhaps erratic movement between Australia and New Guinea (Draffan *et al.* 1983). Movements outside normal range in Australia usually at end of dry season. Can travel over 6 km from daytime roost to feeding territory (Frith 1982).

Feeds in early morning, evening and also at night, dabbling and up-ending in shallows or walking rapidly in shallow water scything bill from side to side, also sieves mud at water's edge and pecks for food on adjacent dry land (Veselovský 1976). Diet poorly known but probably molluscs, other aquatic invertebrates including insects and worms, and seeds (Marchant and Higgins 1990). In Northern Territory, 95% by volume of gizzard contents ($n = 21$) was animal matter, mostly molluscs and insects (29%), plants included *Cyperaceae* and algae (Frith 1982). In northern Queensland, 2 stomachs contained largely plants including *Ceratophyllum*,

Nymphoides, *Sida*, *Najas*, *Eleocharis* (37%), *Scirpus*, *Brachiara* and *Echinochloa* (Lavery 1971a).

In pairs or family groups during breeding season, small groups to large flocks (> 200) out of breeding season, on margins of coastal and subcoastal waters. All flocks appear to consist of pairs. ♂ intolerant of conspecifics, particularly during breeding season when noisily challenges and attacks newcomers near him or mate. Very active at roost before departure to feed, gathering in small groups at edge of cover. Birds fly short distance and settle on shallow water when disturbed. Generally confiding.

Displays and breeding behaviour

Both sexes involved in establishment and defence of breeding territory. Inciting display and territorial defence may be important in pairbond behaviour (Johnsgard 1978). Monogamous and pairbond probably lifelong (Frith 1982). White plumage may function in territorial defence (Johnsgard 1978). ♂ rushes at intruder with erect feathers and extended neck, ♀ may also rush at intruder whilst calling loudly. ♀ incites ♂ by repeated diagonal pumping movements in direction of opponent and raises folded wings revealing speculum. ♂ close by, responds with similar but more energetic movements and raises folded wings higher above back (Veselovský 1976). Triumph Ceremony takes form of mutual inciting display. Nest site chosen by flying to potentially suitable tree hollow, and intention to use it signalled by peering inside.

♂ dips head in front of ♀ in pre-copulatory display. Copulation on water. Post-copulatory display not well developed, includes ♂ vertically raising and lowering wing opposite ♀ (Johnsgard 1965a, 1978). Solitary nester.

Breeding and life cycle

Not well known. Sexual activity starts before, or at start of, wet season, clutches begun as floods begin to recede exposing bare mud and grass as good feeding habitat. Timing and duration differ in Australia, probably in relation to extent and intensity of wet season; egg-laying started Feb–May in Northern Territories (Frith and Davies 1961a), Nov–Jan in

Queensland (Marchant and Higgins 1990). Breeds Mar–July around Darwin (Goodfellow 2001). Nests in holes in trees near water. In Australia, cavities made by termites and other decay organisms such as fungal infections; same holes used annually, perhaps by same pair (Frith 1982). Nest composed largely of light grey down. Breeding territory, including nest site, feeding grounds and brood-rearing area defended vigorously. Territory size variable, pairs defended on average 3 km of river frontage on Adelaide River (Frith 1982), and 2.5 km on Wae Tuolorang river in Seram (Bowler 1993). Eggs in Australia swollen oval, smooth, lustrous and creamy white (Marchant and Higgins 1990); 59 × 41 (55–61 × 39–45) ($n = 52$) (Frith 1982); weight in captivity 49.5 ($n = 54$). Clutch size in wild unknown, likely *c* 9 (6–15) but egg dumping possible. Large broods may also involve amalgamation. No data on laying interval. Incubation 30 days (Frith 1982) probably based on captives (Marchant and Higgins 1990). Incubation by ♀ only (Johnsgard 1978); ♂ remains nearby and helps lead brood to water within breeding territory and assists with rearing. Young precocial and nidifugous; 9 captive day-old *rufitergum* weighed 25.1. In northern Australia, crocodiles *C. porosus* and Dingos *Canis dingo* take ducklings (Goodfellow 2001). Family group generally stays together during dry season, thus young accompanied by parents until fledged; however, broods may begin to break up prior to start of wet season (Bowler 1993). Families may stay on territory or move off to join flock (Marchant and Higgins 1990). No data on breeding success, adult survival nor longevity.

Conservation and threats

Range contracted northwards in Australia, local populations decline where settlements, agriculture and roads established, although uses artificial wetlands in developed areas. Introduction of rice growing into strongholds in monsoonal Northern Territory may be threat (Frith 1982), and considered least secure of northern Australian ducks (Blakers *et al.* 1984); however, large population of *rufitergum* estimated (30 000) in Alligator Rivers Region alone (Morton *et al.* 1990b) with total Australian population possibly several times higher.

Large population of *radjah* reported in Papua New Guinea and Irian Jaya of *c* 10 000 individuals. Confiding habits render vulnerable to exploitation by hunting in parts of range which may increase with current transmigration projects in Irian Jaya. In Seram and northern Australia considered bad eating on account of poor taste, and rarely hunted (Bowler 1993, Goodfellow 2001).

John Bowler

Ruddy Shelduck *Tadorna ferruginea*
PLATE 10

Anas ferruginea Pallas, 1764, in Vroeg, Cat. Raisonné Coll. Oiseaux, Adumbr., p. 5
no locality = Tartary (part of Russia and central and western Siberia)

Etymology: ferruginea L. means rusty or ruddy.

Other names: Ruddy Sheldrake. French: Tadorne casarca; India: Brahminy Duck.

Variation: no subspecies. Hybridizes readily with other shelduck to produce fertile offspring (Delacour 1954–64). Harrop (2002) stated ♀♀ from Siberia and other parts of Asian range lack white face patch; claim not investigated.

Description

ADULT: dimorphic. ♂ in breeding plumage has upperparts and underparts almost wholly rusty orange. Buff head and neck grading paler towards the stubby black bill and to orange-buff on the rear crown. Black neck collar from first breeding plumage. Rump, uppertail coverts, tail feathers, primaries and secondaries black. Extensive white upper and underwing coverts contrast with black flight feathers. Upperwing coverts washed buff. Speculum glossy metallic green. ♀ similar to ♂, but smaller, whiter on face and lacking black neck collar and buff wash to upperwing coverts (Johnsgard 1965a, Madge and Burn 1988).

MOULT: plumage similar all year-round, except black neck collar less distinct in eclipse. Partial pre-breeding moult (head, body and tertials) Sept–Oct, but may be arrested Dec–Feb. Breeding plumage attained Mar–Apr and retained until complete post-breeding moult June–July during which time flightless for *c* 4 weeks.

IMMATURE: juvenile similar to adult ♀, but duller with browner back. In 1st year has grey wash on upperwing coverts and scapulars (Cramp and Simmons 1977).

DUCKLING: like Common Shelduck, but down of crown and upperparts paler, dark olive-grey rather than dark brown. White patches on mantle and sides of rump generally smaller and small white spot above eye (present in most shelduck) usually absent. Dark spot on cheek also absent.

MEASUREMENTS AND WEIGHT: ♂ wing ($n = 30$), 333–402 (368); tail ($n = 8$), 116–135 (125); culmen ($n = 31$), 40–49 (44.1); tarsus ($n = 11$), 59–64 (61.5); weight (various months of year) ($n = 29$), 1200–1600. ♀ wing ($n = 36$), 321–371 (340); tail ($n = 6$), 112–122 (118); culmen ($n = 36$), 35–44 (40.1); tarsus ($n = 10$), 52–57 (54.6); weight ($n = 9$), 925–1500 (1100) (Cramp and Simmons 1977, Baker 1993).

Field characters

Unmistakable within native range. Large noisy duck, 610–170 mm long, with bright orange-chestnut plumage. White wing coverts contrast sharply with black flight feathers and tail. Similar to Cape Shelduck, ♂ of which can be distinguished by grey neck and head, ♀ by grey neck and white face patch.

Voice

Well known for incessant calling, especially when disturbed. Loud nasal honking *ang*, *ah-onk* or *chorr* call given, often in flight. Calls of sexes distinguishable,

those of ♀ being louder, deeper and harsher.
♀ calls predominantly *a* sound, and ♂♂ *o* quality
(Cramp and Simmons 1977); ♀ calls described as *ka-ha-ha* and ♂ as *ho-ho-ho* (Delacour 1954–64). Preflight
calls similar, and uttered in increasing tempo before
taking flight. ♂ also utters disyllabic *cho-hoo* call during courtship. Sonogram of Inciting ♀ in Cramp and
Simmons (1977).

Range and status

Second most numerous and widespread shelduck
(after Common Shelduck). Six geographical populations recognized, 2 small and mainly resident in
Africa and 4 migratory populations found largely
in Asia (Scott and Rose 1996, Rose and Scott
1997). In Africa, small group of 200–500 in
Ethiopia virtually restricted to Bale Mountains
National Park (Urban 1993, Scott and Rose 1996)

with at least 2500 in northwest Africa (Green *et al.*
2000). Asian populations much larger with *c* 20 000
breeding in Greece, west and central Turkey and
around Black Sea, and wintering in east Mediterranean south to Nile Delta; *c* 35 000 breeding from
eastern Turkey to Afghanistan and Central Asian
Republics, and wintering in Iran and Iraq; *c* 50 000
in central/ south/southeast Asian population and
another 50 000–100 000 (Miyabayashi and Mundkur 1999) in east Asian population. Asian populations move south to winter, but some from
northwest Africa went north to southern Spain
(Vielliard 1970) before recent population declines.
No trend data available for Ethiopian population.
Numbers in northwest African and Europe
declined markedly during last century, while Asian
populations either stable or increasing (Tucker and
Heath 1994); e.g. wintering population in Iran

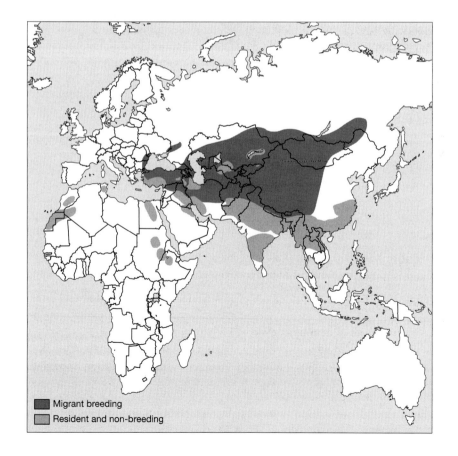

Migrant breeding

Resident and non-breeding

increased 5- or 6-fold 1970–90s (Perennou *et al.* 1994).

Bird ringed Kirghizstan recovered Poland. Numbers at many European locations may result from periodic invasion; however, large number of escaped birds complicates status (Vinicombe and Harrop 1999, Harrop 2002).

Habitat and general habits

Lives more inland than most shelduck, being found mainly on rivers, freshwater and brackish lakes rather than estuaries. Like other shelduck, generally shuns forested habitat. Relatively adaptable, making good use of reservoirs and similar artificial sites (Zubko and Popovkina 1999, Green 2000a). Omnivorous, feeding on grasses, grain, young shoots of terrestrial plants, submerged vegetation, aquatic and terrestrial invertebrates, using variety of techniques, including grazing on land, dabbling in lake and riverside shallows, up-ending in deeper water.

Aggressive during much of year, especially during breeding season, therefore often dispersed in pairs or small groups; however, autumn moult concentrations and wintering flocks may number thousands, e.g. 4000 birds at Kosi Barrage and Kosi Tappu Wildlife Reserve in Nepal in Feb 1981, and >10000 at Kulu Gölü in Turkey in July 1987 (Green *et al.* 1989). Inhabits range of open, inland habitats throughout year, from low-altitude salt lagoons to lakes in high plateau and mountainous regions up to 5000 m (Cramp and Simmons 1977). Thus among few waterfowl (along with Bar-headed Goose) encountered on high-altitude lakes of central Asia (Bishop *et al.* 1997). Migration to lower elevations usually takes place in winter, especially during periods of hard weather.

Generally wary, but approachable in Tibet, Mongolia and India where has sacred status and may even perch on house roofs.

Displays and breeding behaviour

Both sexes have limited courtship display, consisting mainly of ♀ Inciting ♂ by holding head low with neck outstretched, calling *gaaa* repeatedly, and making lateral pointing movements towards ♂. ♂ responds with honking *chorr* call or 2-note *cho-hoo*, often accompanied by jerking head back and lifting tail, thus assuming High-and-erect posture that exhibits undertail coverts. Copulation takes place in water, preceded by Head-dipping by both partners and by ♂ uttering *cho-hoo* call. Following copulation, ♀ begins to call before ♂. Before dismounting, ♂ calls while still holding ♀'s nape, then slightly lifts wing opposite ♀ before sliding off to one side in High-and-alert posture (Johnsgard 1965a). Both birds then bathe. Strong pairbond, assumed to pair for life (Delacour 1954–64).

Breeding and life cycle

Migrates to breeding areas Mar–Apr, in Central Asia often arriving at breeding sites before lakes icefree. In North Africa, may breed better in wet years (Vielliard 1970). In typical shelduck fashion, nests in cavities, including burrows, and holes in cliffs, trees and even buildings, often far from water. Eggs laid daily late Apr–early June in main Asian populations, and mid Mar–late Apr in North Africa. Eggs dull glossy white; 68 × 47 (62–72 × 45–50) (*n* = 110); weight 83 (69–99) (*n* = 70); clutch 8–9 (6–12) eggs, with incubation 28–29 (27–30) days beginning after last egg laid. Incubation solely by ♀ while ♂ stands guard nearby. As day-olds, 36 captive ducklings weighed 48.0 (42.5–55.0). Both parents tend young, but amalgamation of broods of mixed ages often seen in North Africa (Green 2000a). Fledge in *c* 55 days and family may remain together after fledging. In semi-wild population in Ukraine, clutch size 11.75 (*n* = 106), hatchability 56–72% and duckling survival 72–98% (Zubko and Popovkina 1999). Autumn migration occurs mainly Sept–Nov. First breeding probably takes place at 2 years old. No data on adult survival nor longevity.

Conservation and threats

Numbers in Central and East Asia thought to be either stable or increasing, with sacred status perhaps giving more security than western counterparts (plumage colour is associated with 'Yellow Hat' or Geluk Buddhist Sect headed by Dalai Lama). May also obtain protection in 9680 ha Pembo Black-necked Crane Reserve, established within Tibet's most important wintering area (Bishop *et al.* 1997).

Declines in western populations attributed mainly to wetland loss through drainage and over-abstraction, plus hunting, especially in southeast Europe where most sites still have no protection (Tucker and Heath 1994). Salt abstraction and overgrazing also mentioned as causal

factors of decline in Turkey. Site and species protection measures needed urgently over much of range; however, ability to exploit new wetland habitats, such as reservoirs, makes it less sensitive to habitat loss than many other waterbirds (Green *et al.* 2000).

Baz Hughes and Andy J. Green

Cape Shelduck *Tadorna cana*
PLATE 10

Anas cana Gmelin, 1789, Syst. Nat., **1**, p. 510
Cape of Good Hope (Western Cape Province, South Africa)

Etymology: *cana* L. means grey or hoary in reference to colour of ♂ head.

Other names: South African Shelduck. Afrikaans: Kopereend.

Variation: no subspecies. Variation in colour of ♀ head not geographic in origin.

Description

ADULT: dimorphic. ♂ in breeding plumage has head and neck grey, body largely rich russet; vent paler, tan coloured. Upper and underwing coverts white, showing as white patch in folded wing. Primaries and tail black, and secondaries tinged green above, resulting in green patch visible in folded wing. Bill, legs and feet black; iris dark brown. Some ♂♂ (18%) lack white tips to secondaries, but all ♀♀ have these white tipped. ♀ smaller with variable amount of white on face, dark brown head and neck, dark shading on greater wing coverts and sometimes grey or brown tinge to white middle and lesser wing coverts (Geldenhuys 1983). White face patterns identified by van Ee (1971); usually only facial area white but in 0.35% of individuals most or even all (0.08%), of head, upper neck and throat white. White patch may increase with age (Siegfried 1966) but unconfirmed from captives (van Ee 1971). ♀ usually (80%) has dark grey feet blotched light pink on inner sides of toes (Geldenhuys 1983).

MOULT: ♂ has brighter, finely vermiculated plumage during breeding season, and dull buff breast becomes bright creamy yellow (Geldenhuys 1981a). Seasonal changes in plumage more marked in ♂ than ♀; she assumes richer chestnut plumage during breeding season (Geldenhuys 1981a) but no change in face pattern. Wing moult occurs late Oct–end Feb (mainly Nov–Dec) when adults concentrate at large permanent freshwaters, preferring sites undisturbed by man (Taylor 1944, Shewell 1959, Dean 1978, Geldenhuys 1981a, 1983). Remiges shed within 1–6 days, starting with primaries (Shewell 1959, Dean 1978), and primary and secondary coverts few days later. Flightless for 28–40 days, during which 25–35% of weight lost, proportionally more in ♀ than ♂ (mean 28% v 26%) (Shewell 1959, Geldenhuys 1983). Shorter flightless period of ♀ (due to lighter body weight) may increase survival compared with ♂ and be responsible for skewed sex ratio (Shewell 1959). Geldenhuys (1983), however, suggested that weight loss has little effect on survival and minimal mortality seen in moulting flocks. Moulting birds spend day in deep water and only approach shallows and shoreline at night to feed (Shewell 1959); they swim low in water, are secretive, dive readily and sometimes hide amongst emergent vegetation (Dean 1978). Six large dams support huge numbers, and concentrations of *c* 5000 recorded (Brown *et al.* 1982). Shewell (1959) claimed tail moult gradual and occurs month after wing moult completed; Geldenhuys (1981a), however, found tail moult occurred immediately after breeding and suggested 2 annual tail moults. Body moult occurs twice yearly Mar–Oct (Geldenhuys 1981a).

IMMATURE: ♂ and ♀ resemble adult ♂ but duller, with browner head and neck, usually some white on eyebrows, and extensive dusky brown on white wing coverts (Shewell 1959). Sex of captives certain by Day 49 (i.e. before fledging) on basis of white rim around eyes and beak of ♀, regions uniformly grey in ♂ (Siegfried 1966); ♂ also has lighter-coloured breast. Differences not readily apparent in field (Geldenhuys 1980b). Juvenile ♀ with all-white head recorded.

DUCKLING: dusky brown upperparts, broken by white blotches, and underparts white. Forehead, crown, nape, back, and rump to tail dusky brown. White bar on wing and elongated white blotches on sides of back immediately behind base of wings. Two large white patches on rump near base of tail. Cheeks and sides of neck white, continuing without interruption to chin, throat and breast, and over abdomen to tail. Upper mandible blackish grey, tipped pale grey, and lower mandible blackish grey tinged olive and tipped pink; legs and feet buff brown, membranes and toes blackish grey; iris dusky brown (Siegfried 1966).

MEASUREMENTS AND WEIGHT: ♂ ($n = 5$) wing, 345–365 (355.8); tail, 120–136 (125.9); bill, 42–48 (45.2); tarsus, 56–60 (58); weight ($n = 1171$), 910–2200 (1357). ♀ ($n = 5$) wing, 315–335 (326.2); tail, 120–129 (124.5); bill, 39.5–45 (42.4); tarsus, 52–58 (56); weight ($n = 1092$) 700–1835 (1115) (Clancey 1967, Maclean 1993). Variations in body weight of both sexes largely due to weight loss during wing moult (Geldenhuys 1983).

Field characters

Larger than most sympatric wildfowl, 610–660 mm long; only Egyptian and Spur-winged geese and Comb Duck average larger. May be overlooked amongst Egyptian Geese but more richly coloured and lacks brown eye-patch, breast spot, grey underparts, pale bill and reddish legs; similar in flight but Shelduck has different head pattern, and no black

line through upperwing coverts. White face of ♀ can cause confusion with White-faced Whistling-duck which is darker and smaller, with long neck, long legs, and barred underparts. In flight, Whistling-duck has dark wing coverts.

Voice

Adults have loud nasal honk given when settled and, especially, in flight; ♂ usually lower pitched *honk* than ♀ *hank*, difference clear by Day 90 (Siegfried 1966). Pairs often duet in flight; both sexes screech during courtship and hiss loudly when alarmed (Taylor 1944). Chicks have cheeping alarm call (Taylor 1944). Sonogram in Maclean (1993).

Range and status

Endemic to southern Africa and occurs widely in South Africa, especially in west, Namibia, south-eastern Botswana and marginally, as nonbreeding visitor (Osborne and Tigar 1990), to lowlands of Lesotho, avoiding high massif (Maclean 1997). Single record from Zimbabwe (Webb 1973) and vagrant to northern Botswana and KwaZulu-Natal close to Mozambique border (Geldenhuys 1981b).

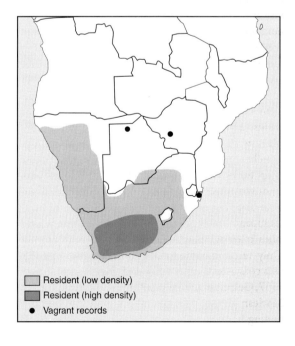

   ▢ Resident (low density)
   ▢ Resident (high density)
   ● Vagrant records

Core region, where particularly common, in western, eastern and northern Cape Provinces and southern Free State Province (Maclean 1997); range spans *c* 1.3 million km^2 and core region *c* 340 0000 km^2 (Geldenhuys 1981b, Maclean 1997). In places can be most abundant waterfowl and, at large irrigation dams in Free State, was commonest of 15 species after Egyptian Goose (Geldenhuys 1975, 1976a). At 23 moult localities in South Africa, 16 in Free State, 30 000 individuals occur, estimated at 70% of South African population (Geldenhuys 1981a). Population of former Transvaal Province estimated at *c* 5000 birds (Tarboton *et al.* 1987). Wetlands International (2002) suggested stable population of 50 000.

Over 9500 have been ringed producing 393 recoveries; longest movement, 1075 km from North-West Province to Western Cape, close to diameter of range. Further 12 recovered at distances > 900 km, and one crossed most of range in month (Underhill *et al.* 1999).

Habitat and general habits

Encompasses semi-arid region (< 600 mm annual rain) centred on Karoo (dwarf shrubland), and spans both summer and winter rainfall regions of southern Africa, although mainly nonbreeding summer visitor to latter (Winterbottom 1968). Mean temperature of coldest month, July (10 °C), when birds breed, correlated with distributional limits. Also found at edge of core range in fynbos/macchia (mesic shrubland), grassland and Kalahari (savanna). Avoids true desert of Namib. Occurs at dams, from small farm dams to extensive state impoundments, along rivers, and at pans and sewage works, many with brackish water. Prefers exposed muddy shorelines and extensive open shallows, avoiding deep water surrounded by tall emergents and wetlands with dense vegetation. Tolerates patchy, continuous, short grasses, herbs and sedges where visibility unimpaired. Preference for poorly vegetated wetlands may explain restriction to semi-arid regions. Only rarely recorded in marine environments but uses coastal lakes, estuaries and lagoons (Taylor 1944, 1957, Geldenhuys 1980b, 1981b, Hockey *et al.* 1989, Maclean 1993, 1997). For breeding, requires suitable nesting holes.

In Free State, breeding pairs widely scattered in south July–Sept, concentrate to moult at large central wetlands Nov–Dec, and disperse to temporary brackish pans in western areas for late summer and autumn (Geldenhuys 1975, 1976a, 1977, 1980b). Ringing recoveries show movements over entire range (Milstein 1975). Partial migrant to Namibia, being commonest in Damaraland in winter (Winterbottom 1971), but Maclean (1997) suggested mainly summer visitor to far north.

At wetland sites, forages in open muddy areas with scattered short aquatic plants. Diet includes algae, e.g. *Spirogyra* (Taylor 1944, 1957); only Branchiopida found in stomachs of 6 individuals, *Apus numidicus* (30–40 mm long) comprised 96% by volume along with sand grains and worn pebbles (Siegfried 1965b). Also feeds at night, especially when moulting (Shewell 1959), and frequently makes nocturnal flights (Taylor 1944). Flocks in crop fields tend to be larger than those eating aquatic foods. Study of diet in Free State (Geldenhuys 1977) found bird vegetarian in winter and spring, feeding on maize and sorghum seeds from harvested fields and soft aquatic plants, e.g. algae and *Lagarosiphon*.

During midsummer moult, flocks reliant on wheat seed, although individuals may fast while flightless. In late summer and autumn, takes both animal (chiefly crustacean and tendipedid larvae and pupae) and plant matter (submerged hydrophytes). Animal food consumed before breeding may be important in stimulating nesting (Geldenhuys 1980a). When on water, dabbling, scything and head dipping commonest foraging techniques, with up-ending occasionally seen, scything and digging used on exposed mud and pecking on dry ground (Geldenhuys 1977). Chicks feed largely on submerged aquatic vegetation, e.g. *Spirogyra* and *Lagarosiphon* (Geldenhuys 1980a).

Displays and breeding behaviour

Despite being monogamous, ♂♂ substantially outnumbered by ♀♀, i.e. 1:4.2 and 1:4.1 at sites in eastern Cape Province (Taylor 1944), 1:1.3 based on ringed birds (*n* = 209) and counts at Vogelvlei (Siegfried 1967), 1:2 in Goldfields area, Free State (*n* = 4224) (van Ee 1971) 1:1.2 in southern Free

State (Geldenhuys 1980b), and 1:1.5 based on ringed birds at Barberspan ($n = 375$) (Shewell 1959). In counts at Bloemfontein sewage works, however, ratio of 2:1 in favour of ♂♂ recorded ($n = 3019$) (van Ee 1971). Dean and Skead (1978) found that, although ratio significantly skewed to ♀♀ among ringed birds (1:1.1; $n = 822$), ratio from counts skewed towards ♂♂ (1.1:1; $n = 4103$), attributing this to visual confusion of juvenile ♀♀ with ♂♂. Unusual nesting habits might result in higher mortality of breeding ♀♀, although burrow-nesting should be less hazardous than ground-nesting (Siegfried 1976a). Perhaps competition for breeding territories, and need for vigorous defence, results in increased ♂ mortality (Siegfried 1976a). Information from ringed juveniles (Dean and Skead 1978), however, suggested that ratio biased before ♀ or ♂ attempt breeding.

Courtship occurs on land, water and in air, and is characterized by loud vocalizations. Initiated by either sex, usually by ♀, birds pursue mates, running at or around them in crouched posture with necks outstretched and bills almost touching ground, frequently raising heads to give shrill call. ♀ more likely to pursue mate, and similar chases and circling occur on water; ♂ Head-bobs in response. Copulation occurs on water and pair seen to fly to water to mate. ♂ initially swims around and mounts, submerging her except for head and neck (Taylor 1944). Copulation rapid, and both birds subsequently wash and preen. Shewell (1959) reported that, after mating, ♂ circled ♀ again and stiffly raised head and neck up and back, and then lowered it down and forward. Intrasexual fighting (chasing and pecking) common in both sexes and breeding pairs noisily drive off intruding pairs and individuals, with ♀ often taking lead (Taylor 1944). During incubation and rearing, however, territorial defence left largely to ♂ (Geldenhuys 1980b). Mated ♀♀ intolerant of ♀ intruders (Taylor 1944, Shewell 1959) and mated ♀♀, in flocks of close proximity, of unpaired ♀♀ (Geldenhuys 1980b). Sex ratio in favour of ♀♀ may be associated with active role in courtship (Siegfried 1976a) and ♀ aggression. In pre-breeding period (early winter), population splits into sedentary territorial pairs, nomadic non-territorial

pairs and flocks of nonbreeders; territorial adults made up 69.0% of birds at one site and 74.4% at another. Solitary individuals usually ♀.

Territories comprise 75–170 m of shoreline and space inward to centre of wetland of 50–80 m, or c 0.5 ha of water ($n = 24$) (Geldenhuys 1980b). On larger wetlands several territories may be adjacent. Social activity marked and occurs throughout day.

Breeding and life cycle

In eastern Cape, courtship lasts Feb–May; by June most pairs established; egg-laying occurs July–Oct, ducklings seen Aug–Nov (mainly Sept–Oct), and full-grown young with parents Oct–Dec (Taylor 1944, Taylor and Vincent 1949). Eggs, therefore, laid during midwinter dry period, and breeding restricted to permanent wetlands. In Free State, similar pattern noted, and egg-laying occurs during short period consistent between years, even when rainfall varies (Geldenhuys 1980a). Earliest laying date 17 May and latest 25 Sept, peaking last week of July, and 90% of clutches started 20 June–17 Aug ($n = 171$). Chicks feed largely on submerged aquatic plants in shallow water and such conditions optimal during dry winter, explaining timing of breeding season; in addition, shortage of littoral vegetation helps in predator detection. Curiously, breeds at same time of year in winter rainfall region of western Cape Province, when both rainfall and water levels high (Geldenhuys 1980a).

Breeds in isolated pairs, partly due to specialized requirements. Nests located in holes in ground made by mammals, especially Antbear or Aardvark *Orycteropus afer* which makes holes for feeding as well as dens. Nests 85–1700 m ($n = 9$) from territorial waters, typically associated with freshwater and artificial, rather than brackish or natural, wetlands (Geldenhuys 1980b) and occasionally among rocks (Horsburgh 1912). Of 14 nests, 11 were in Antbear burrows and 3 in smaller excavations of Springhaas or Cape Jumping Hare *Pedetes capensis* or South African or Cape Porcupine *Hystrix africaeaustralis* (Geldenhuys 1980b). One nest, about 9 m down an Antbear burrow, consisted of down and dry thistle weed, and had been used for several years (Edelsten 1932). Underground nesting probably related to sparse vegetation in wetlands chosen, and intolerance of high temperatures (Geldenhuys 1981b). ♀ leads in prospecting for nest site and ♂ largely responsible for defending area from other pairs (Geldenhuys 1980b). Choice of site may be implicated in largely xeric range.

Eggs white or cream, matt; 68.5×50.3 (64.5–72×48–52) ($n = 12$); weight 89.0 (74.5–99.5) ($n = 10$); clutch 8–10 but broods up to 21 recorded (Geldenhuys 1980a, Maclean 1993). Eggs laid daily; incubated for 30 days by ♀ (Siegfried 1976a), ♂ remaining close to burrow, away from aquatic breeding territory, and warning of predators by loud hissing (Geldenhuys 1980b). At Graaf-Reinet, up to 13 ducklings seen in brood, with mean 7.6 ($n = 15$) (Taylor 1944); in Free State, broods ($n = 139$) decreased from 7.4 in 1st week to 5.8 at fledging (70 days), excluding 7 broods lost entirely (Geldenhuys 1980b). Largest broods had lowest loss rate.

Captive day-olds ($n = 9$) weighed 52.0–61.5 (56.5) (Brown *et al.* 1982). First contour feathers appear at *c* Day 18 in flanks and tail of captives (Siegfried 1966); at 28 days still downy but feathers present on breast, flank, abdomen and scapulars, and remiges emerging. At 56 days, almost completely feathered, including wings, but nape feathers tipped with down. Growth virtually complete by 63 days. At 42 days, head and neck had grey feathers (as in adult ♂) and contrasted distinctly with tawny orange lower neck and breast. At 49 days, ♀ had narrow white rim around eyes and base of beak, regions uniformly grey in ♂, which had lighter-coloured breast. Between Days 49 and 77, white eye and beak rims of ♀ expanded, and by *c* Day 90, had merged to form white face patch of adult (Siegfried 1966).

Both parents lead ducklings to water, usually early in morning (Geldenhuys 1980b), and care for young. Brood kept in muddy shallow water, unless disturbed, when will take refuge in deeper water, and adults chase away large birds, e.g. herons and cormorants (Taylor 1944). While flightless, wild ducklings dive to escape predators (Taylor 1944). Flight possible in captives at *c* Day 70 (Siegfried 1966); wild ducklings take *c* 60–75 days to achieve flight and adult size (Taylor 1944).

Families apparently break up at *c* 90–120 days (Taylor 1957). Age at 1st breeding unknown.

Breeding success high in Free State (Geldenhuys 1980b), but not in Eastern Cape Province, where duckling mortality attributed to predation by freshwater Terrapin *Pelomedusa subrufa* (Taylor 1957). Survival to fledging slightly, but significantly, higher in Karoo study area (76.4%) compared with grassland study area (71.5%), due to higher mortality in 1st 2 weeks. Among territorial pairs, annual number of young successfully reared to fledging 5.0, with 86% of pairs breeding successfully. Success attributed to strong pairbond, territoriality and social hierarchy amongst age classes. Late broods no less successful than early ones but pairs that established territories earliest (but did not necessarily lay earliest) had larger broods, which also suffered lower rates of loss, than pairs establishing territories later (Geldenhuys 1980b). Birds captured for ringing ($n = 390$) at Barberspan only 4% juvenile, but figure unlikely to be representative of breeding success as site distant from main breeding areas; most juveniles avoid wing moulting sites and remain close to natal sites during 1st year (Shewell 1959). At Vogelvlei, 23% captured during post-breeding period were juvenile ($n = 209$), and little wing moulting occurs (Siegfried 1967). High density of breeding pairs present in wetter eastern parts of range suggests particular importance as major breeding ground relative to drier western regions (Geldenhuys 1980b).

Longest time elapsed between ringing and recovery, 13 years 11 months, and 5 further examples exceeding 10 years (Underhill *et al.* 1999). Oldest bird in captivity said to be 40 years (Hillgarth and Kear 1979b).

Conservation and threats

Populations remain relatively stable, despite annual variations in habitat availability and, in light of high breeding productivity, possible that adults suffer high mortality (Geldenhuys 1980b). Has recently increased twofold in range and now regular in Namibia, southeastern Botswana and KwaZulu-Natal. Has benefited from construction of dams, while reduction of wetland vegetation often advantageous (Geldenhuys 1976c, 1980b). Ability to exploit fallen grain also beneficial during moult, although habit may lead to hunting and intentional or accidental poisoning (Siegfried 1967, Geldenhuys 1977). Not subject to legal hunting; flesh apparently unpalatable and bird difficult to hit due to shy disposition and open nature of habitat (Horsbrugh 1912, Geldenhuys 1976c). Concentration of large proportion of population at few sites during wing moult potentially dangerous, although many sites protected (Geldenhuys 1981a); disturbance, e.g. from watersport enthusiasts, needs control (Dean 1978). Reliance on Antbears for nest sites of concern, as animal considered Threatened in South Africa (Geldenhuys 1980b), although still fairly numerous in semi-arid regions where low human density.

David G. Allan

Australian Shelduck *Tadorna tadornoides*
PLATE 10

Anas tadornoides Jardine and Selby, 1828, Illus. Ornith., pt. 4, pl. 62 and text
New South Wales

Etymology: *tadornoides* from Gr. *oides* meaning resembling, plus *tadorna* shelduck.

Other names: Mountain Duck, Chestnut, Chestnut-collared or Chestnut-breasted Shelduck or Sheldrake, Grunter. Origin of Mountain Duck misunderstood and mostly avoided in Australia, having no relevance to geographical features of that country; derives from German *Bergente. Berg* (mountain) referred colloquially to dunes as only 'mountains' on coasts of Holland and Germany, combined with *ente* (duck); Dune Duck, or equivalent in northeastern European languages, had wide vernacular usage for Common Shelduck. Australian Aboriginal: Bidjengal, Dibiyara, Gnarcoondull, Goon-de-mar, Goora-ga, Goor-a-go, Gnimeruk, Guraga, Karbunga, Kockadooroo, Kooracha, Nagundal, Niammaaraq, N-yuneruk, Perna, Pitjangul, Tarangkinji, Wanye. French: Tadorne d'Australie. German: Halsbandkasarka. Spanish: Tarro Australiano.

Variation: no subspecies.

Description

ADULT: dimorphic. ♂ in breeding plumage has chestnut-orange breast and all-dark head. Bill dark grey; legs and feet dark grey; eyes dark brown. ♀ smaller with irregular white eye-ring and white at base of bill. Both sexes have variable narrow white collar on lower neck, often less obvious or absent in ♀.

MOULT: plumage replaced twice annually; moult following breeding involves simultaneous replacement of flight feathers and often occurs when birds gather in flocks at suitable moulting areas. ♂ during latter part of breeding season assumes duller (eclipse) plumage. Pre-breeding body moult restores brightness to plumage, especially in ♂.

IMMATURE: like dull ♀.

DUCKLING: like ducklings of other shelduck; boldly patterned dark brown and white with conspicuous white cheeks.

MEASUREMENTS AND WEIGHT: ♂ (*n* = 4) wing, 376–391 (382); tail, 99–126 (113); bill, 43–50 (46); tarsus, 61–69 (65); weight (*n* = 67) 990–1980 (1559). ♀ (*n* = 4) wing, 323–353 (338); tail, 105–114 (110); bill, 42–44 (43); tarsus, 57–60 (59); weight (*n* = 185), 878–1850 (1291) (Frith 1982, Marchant and Higgins 1990).

Field characters

Large, stocky, boldly patterned shelduck, 550–720 mm long, with black head and neck, dark body with chestnut breast and tertials. In flight, conspicuous white forewings and green speculum; underwings mainly white. Erect stance and dark plumage unmistakable in Australia. Wing pattern in flight similar to smaller Radjah Shelduck which is much paler with all-white head and neck. Call also distinctive.

Voice

Generally noisy, particularly in flight, giving loud, resonant honking calls. Sexes differ in sound quality, with adult ♂ having large tracheal bulla. ♂ gives low pitched honks developing into wavering call during display when honks repeated in pairs with emphasis on first part of *ha-poo* (Johnsgard 1965a). Honks of ♀ softer and higher pitched, often less audible from pair in flight because of louder ♂ call. Further details, including sonograms, in Marchant and Higgins (1990).

Range and status

Endemic to Australia and widely distributed in south of continent, mostly south of 30°S, with disjunct distribution; one part restricted to southwest, other to southeast and Tasmania (Blakers *et al.* 1984). Although considerable movement documented within range, moult migrations, contrary to claims, do not occur regularly to specific wetlands. Known to disperse widely following flood and drought events, when occasionally reported in small numbers north of usual range both in west and east of continent but not breeding. In eastern Australia, Lachlan River, lower regions of Darling River and Murray

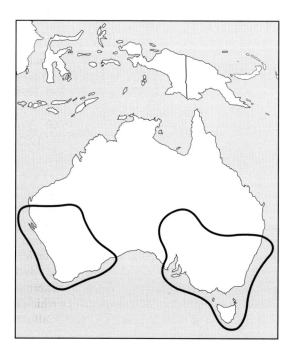

River define normal upper limit of breeding range. In Western Australia, normal range extends north to Gascoyne River and east to line from Lake Carnegie to Israelite Bay. Occasional vagrant to Norfolk Island, New Zealand and sub-antarctic islands. Counts in 1980s showed > 65 000 occurred at times on wetlands in southwest, and > 91 000 in Victoria. Similarly, aerial surveys in Oct (1983–92) across eastern Australian range (excluding Tasmania) showed numbers averaged 190 000 and sometimes almost reached a million. Over 17 years 1983–99, largest counts occurred in 1984 and again in 1990 (Marchant and Higgins 1990, Kingsford *et al.* 1999, 2000). Population > 300 000 in most years.

Habitat and general habits

Temperate, requiring freshwater, but found on grasslands and croplands as often as on terrestrial wetlands, estuaries and occasionally in wooded grasslands and on coastal islands. Grazes on dry-land plants or in shallow water, but also forages on mudflats or shore. Particularly favours flat terrain and large shallow waterbodies. Diet poorly known. Diverse range of vegetation and invertebrates taken. Uses wide range of feeding methods of which grazing, often some distance from water, most common. Frequently seen dabbling or up-ending in shallow water and often combing shoreline opportunistically. Walks fast and strongly. Further details on diet in Marchant and Higgins (1990).

Displays and breeding behaviour

Lateral-head-shaking and Chin-lifting used with calls as pre-flight signal. Pair formation involves Mock-preening, Preening-behind-wing and Chasing. On water, Head-dipping and Bathing by ♀ and Water-thrashing involving shallow dives and Mock-chases used by ♀. Inciting by ♀ involves typical shelduck lateral pointing with much calling. These activities can lead to Aerial-chases during pair formation. Inciting also used by paired ♀ to make partner drive off intruding pairs or individuals. After such incidents, ♂ returns to ♀ and performs Triumph Ceremony involving Mock-preens or Lateral-head-shaking and Chin-lifting, accompanied by loud honking in High-and-erect-posture.

Copulation follows pre-copulatory Preening with flashing of speculum by ♀ and mutual Water-thrashing before ♀ circles ♂ while calling, and Mock-attacks ♂ who responds by alternately dipping head and calling in Erect-posture with sleek head feathers. Eventually ♀ flattens on water and then adopts partly submerged prone posture in preparation for mounting by ♂. Post-copulatory display involves Raising-wing-opposite-partner in both birds with ♀ often calling. In this posture, white forewing and carpal joint held high above back. Details summarized in Marchant and Higgins (1990). Solitary nester.

Breeding and life cycle

Lays most often in tree hollows but also in holes in cliffs or ground. Good sites used repeatedly. Pairs select site together. Eggs laid mid June–late Sept; oval or round, fine grained, lustrous and glossy; pale creamy white to buff cream; 69 × 48 ($n = 147$); weight 88 ($n = 22$) (Riggert 1977); clutch 10.4 (5–14) ($n = 9$) (Frith 1982) with egg laid daily. On completion of clutch, plucked down forms bulk of nest. Only ♀ incubates, starting on completion of clutch, with early morning and late afternoon break; lasts 30–33 days (Delacour 1954–64). ♂ often accompanies ♀ back to site and frequently remains nearby. Ducklings drop from elevated sites with vocal encouragement from parents. Both parents care for brood, with ducklings led to brood territory, often some distance from nest, and defended vigorously by attacks on intruders or by feigning injury in Distraction display and flushing, while young dive and disperse, if on water, or remain concealed if on land. Young fly at *c* 10 weeks. Broods frequently remain with parents until flocks formed when families break up. Breeding age reached in 2nd year. For more detail see Marchant and Higgins (1990).

Conservation and threats

Not in any immediate danger with large numbers occurring in Western and southeast Australia. Considered unpalatable, with relatively few shot during past duck hunting season, partly because wary and leaves wetland following disturbance. Still hunted in South Australia, Victoria and Tasmania; recent cessation of hunting in Western Australia reduced risk, but still regarded in some districts as pest when large numbers present on pastures. Possible that land clearance and development has been of benefit (*cf* Australian Wood Duck). Steady decline in numbers detected in eastern Australia from mid 1980s to 1999, and decline shown to be significant long-term trend (Kingsford *et al.* 1999, 2000).

Peter Fullagar

Paradise Shelduck *Tadorna variegata*
PLATE 10

Anas variegata Gmelin, 1789, Syst. Nat., **1**, p. 505 Dusky Bay, South Island, New Zealand

Etymology: L. *variegatus* means variegated, in reference to different plumage of ♂ and ♀.

Other names: New Zealand Shelduck, Paradise Duck, Parrie, Rangitata Goose, Painted Duck. Maori: Putangitangi.

Variation: no subspecies.

Description

ADULT: dimorphic. ♂ in breeding plumage has head and neck black, rest of body black with yellow flecks, slightly lighter on abdomen. Undertail chestnut. Upper and lower wing coverts white, primaries black, secondaries metallic green, tertials rusty brown on outer vane. Underwing white. Bill black; legs and feet dark grey; eye black. ♀ in breeding plumage has head and neck white, back dark grey heavily flecked with yellow, rump and tail black, breast, abdomen, flanks and undertail bright chestnut, wings, bill, legs and eye as ♂. ♀ in nonbreeding plumage has feathers on underparts tipped black and interspersed with dark, heavily flecked feathers giving dark chestnut appearance.

MOULT: 2 body moults annually at one of which nonbreeding ♀, unusually, assumes eclipse plumage. From late Dec, gather in large flocks at traditional sites for annual wing moult. Nonbreeders first to assemble, followed by failed breeders and, lastly, successful breeders often accompanied by fledglings. Birds flightless for about 4 weeks (♂ takes longer to moult than ♀) but remain at flock site for at least 8 weeks (Williams 1979b).

IMMATURE: both sexes resemble adult ♂ except ♀ smaller with white patch at bill base. ♀ assumes white head during post-juvenal moult and breast and belly appear very dark chestnut. ♀ retains black ear-spot.

DUCKLING: white with brown stripe from crown to tail and brown mark on wings and flank. Eye, bill, legs, feet black.

MEASUREMENTS AND WEIGHT: from live birds. ♂ (*n* = 25) wing, 356–393 (374); tail, 110–145 (128); bill, 41.1–46.6 (43.7); tarsus, 63.8–70.7 (67.1); weight (*n* = 30), 1420–1980 (1689). ♀ (*n* = 31) wing, 320–368 (344); tail, 102–129 (117); bill, 36.3–42.6 (39.8); tarsus, 56.7–64.1 (60.7); weight (*n* = 31), 1060–1700 (1410).

Field characters

Small goose-like duck, 630–710 mm long, showing conspicuous white wing patches in flight, contrasting plumages of dark ♂ and chestnut bodied, white-headed ♀. Persistent noisy honkers.

Voice

♂ commonly gives goose-like honk; has longer disyllabic call as greeting to mate, and, when associated with High-and-erect posture, as threat. ♀ has loud high-pitched Inciting call repeated rapidly, also used as advertising and threat. Similar call, given more slowly and quietly, used as greeting. Both sexes have shrill Flock call for making contact with others in flock. Both also perform mutual Trumpeting or Triumph Ceremony after repelling territorial intruders, wherein ♀ gives high-pitched and rapidly repeated note and ♂ drawn-out disyllabic Triumph call. Sonogram of Inciting ♀ in Marchant and Higgins (1990).

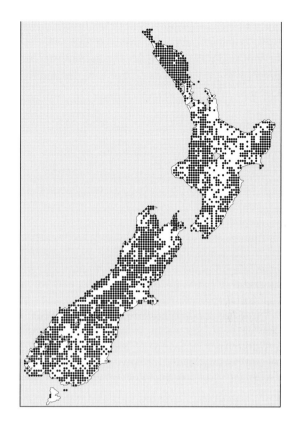

Range and status

Endemic to New Zealand with vagrants reaching east to Chatham Island and northwest to Lord Howe Island. In pre-human times, was limited predominantly to South Island grasslands and to estuaries, but uncommon north of 39° S (Williams 1971). Conversion of forests to pasture has greatly increased range and numbers, and now common on all farmland (McAllum 1965). Numbers and population densities still increasing despite being shot as game. Population (2001) in excess of 300 000.

Habitat and general habits

Selects grassland, especially pastoral farmland. Breeding territories established around small wetland, e.g. farm pond or swampy soak, giving clear view of surrounding area. Ponds and swamps in small gullies generally avoided. Nonbreeding flocks persist on flat grassland with nearby access to water, e.g. river, lake, large dam (Williams 1979a). Some birds inhabit coastal flats and estuaries; also common on river flats in alpine grasslands. From late Mar, adults begin to return to or near previous year's territory. During Mar–Apr, pairs re-unite on territory and for subsequent 3–4 months actively reinforce bond by means of vigorous defence against neighbours or previously non-territorial birds. Partnerships may be broken at this time. Breeding activity commences in late July with initial nest prospecting.

Territorial pairs sedentary, spending time in close company and generally restricting activities to confined area (territory), except when prospecting for nest sites. Territories vary in size, dependent on distribution of swampy grassland in which to feed, and on distance from open water which usually serves as focal point of range. Territory size not precisely known but, in pastoral hill country, may cover 1–20 ha.

Large flocks remaining at moulting sites gradually fragment into smaller groups as birds disperse to prime feeding areas nearby where they remain for rest of year. Birds in these flocks are almost exclusively one and two-year-olds; most ♀♀, but fewer ♂♂, bred locally. In late Sept, pairs commence forays to breeding areas to claim future breeding site; preliminary attachments are subjected to intense competition from other juvenile pairs within flock (Williams 1979a).

Adults primarily herbivorous, taking vegetative parts of range of grasses and weeds (Bisset 1976). Aquatic plants also eaten. Invertebrate foods consumed from swampy pasture or ponds include earthworms, snails, aquatic insect larvae and terrestrial insects. Duckling diet changes with age; predominantly insects when small but increasing plant material (vegetative parts and seeds) as feeding occurs beyond wetland areas (Williams 1979a). Diets of flock birds may be less varied than territorial pairs (Bisset 1976).

Displays and breeding behaviour

Within flocks, many birds associate as pairs and there is constant making, testing and breaking of temporary pairbond. Dominant ♀ courtship display is Inciting where she stretches head forward and down towards intruder or competitor, and then to and

from mate to elicit attack from him, accompanied by loud, repeated, high-pitched note uttered continuously. ♂ responds with High-and-erect posture (Williams 1979a), disyllabic calls and, perhaps, threat (head lowered) and charge. Chases that remove intruder usually followed by mutual Trumpeting by pair members. Success of ♂ in responding to ♀'s Inciting and Repulsing challenge may be basis of early pairbond maintenance. Mutual Trumpeting not always performed if ♂ fails to attack intruder, and absence may imply weakening of bond. Activity generally confined to all-purpose territory and most territorial pairs (87%) attempt to breed; however, nest site may be outside normal territory.

Breeding and life cycle

Nest-site prospecting may commence up to 2 months before egg-laying. First eggs usually laid early Aug with some clutches, especially of 1st time breeders, started as late as Oct. Peak laying late Aug, repeat clutches Sept–Oct. Nests, usually hidden from view above, inside hollow logs, in ground holes (burrows or beneath tree roots), tree holes up to 20 m above ground, under buildings, in hay barns, beneath fern and in drainage culverts. Most (79%, $n = 47$) established within 500 m of territory water area. Nest bowl, positioned to rear of cavity, comprises simple concavity on floor with few added breast feathers. Large amounts of down accumulate as incubation proceeds. Eggs white, and laid daily, usually in early morning; 67.2×48.6 (61.7–72.3×44.5–52.1) ($n = 223$); weight 84.5 (72.0–90.7) ($n = 10$); clutch 9.4 (5–15) ($n = 36$), most commonly 8–10. First time breeders lay fewer eggs 7.9 ($n = 7$); clutches of > 12 likely to result from dump-nesting, usually involving only 2 ♀♀. Incubation by ♀ alone and commencing just before laying of last egg. Incubation period in captivity 30 days ($n = 11$) and 32–33 days in wild ($n = 2$). ♀ leaves nest 2–3 times daily for about 1 h, ♂ accompanies her to nest and thereafter waits at centre of territory; she does not leave nest during last 2 days. Fertility of eggs 95% ($n = 267$) (Williams 1979a), 87% of which hatch. All eggs hatched in 31% of nests ($n = 29$), most failures being abandonment of last pipping egg. Ducklings weigh at hatching 49.0 (43.0–53.1) (*n* = 10), equivalent to 58% (50.0–63.2%) of fresh egg weight. Fledge in 55–65 days (*n* = 10).

♂ usually near nest when ducklings emerge and guards them as they follow ♀ to wetland nursery area. He maintains active guardian role throughout development whereas ♀ stays closer to brood. Brood rearing confined to territory, initially on water but more extensively on land as ducklings grow. Adults perform Broken-wing display to distract land predators. Breakup of brood occurs when parents depart for communal moulting sites. Some fledglings travel there with adults but others remain and gradually join other fledglings in vicinity of territory. From 54 broods in pastoral farmland study, 60.8% of 365 ducklings fledged, averaging 4.1 per brood; some 32–37% (*n* = 78) of territorial pairs failed to hatch ducklings so overall productivity 2.6–2.8 ducklings per pair. First year survival about 50%, and 55% in 2nd year. Breeding occurs from 2nd year, and annual adult survival 70% (57–82%), being slightly higher for ♂♂ (Williams 1979a). Adult survival in hunted populations 62–73% for ♀♀ and 64–70% for ♀♀ (Williams 1972, Duckworth 1986). Oldest ♀ in captivity was 15 years (Hillgarth and Kear 1979b).

Conservation and threats

Historically important gamebird, and now 2nd most numerous species in New Zealand hunter's bag (after Mallard) with total annual kill of 100 000 (2001). Former overexploitation by hunting led to severe restriction of range, but prolonged period of protection and light hunting in 1970s and 1980s has allowed bird to become numerous and support higher annual harvest. Hunting now carefully managed and monitored. In places, large flocks of pre-breeders or moulters cause extensive pasture fouling and calls from farmers for local population reductions.

Murray Williams

Crested Shelduck *Tadorna cristata*

Pseudotadorna cristata Nagamichi Kuroda, 1917, Tori, **I**, pp. 1, 2, fig.1
Naktung River near Fusan, Korea (Naktong River, South Korea)

Etymology: *cristata* L. means crested.

Other names: Korean Crested Shelduck, Korean Sheldrake, Korean Mandarin. Japanese: Kanmuri-tsukushi-gamo.

Variation: no subspecies. Sclater (1890) suggested was hybrid between Ruddy Shelduck and Falcated Duck 27 years before species described by Kuroda.

Description

ADULT: dimorphic. ♂ in presumed breeding plumage (Figure 9.24) had forehead, crown, nape and hindneck glossy greenish black, while rest of head and neck grey with brown vermiculations. Black patch on chin and long, drooping nuchal crest. Upper mantle and breast greenish black, and

9.24 A male of the extinct Crested Shelduck.

rump and tail black. Rest of body plumage grey, vermiculated white, except flanks, scapulars and undertail coverts cinnamon rufous. Upperwing coverts mostly white, but primary coverts black, glossed green. Secondaries form metallic green speculum that grades into black primaries. Tertials chestnut and entire underwing white. Feet and bill pinkish; iris brown. ♀ superficially resembles ♂, but grey of head and neck white and black line runs from in front of eye, below it and to hind-neck (producing spectacled appearance). Body plumage brown, and bill and feet paler (Delacour 1954–64, Labzyuk and Nazarov 1967). See also description in Kuroda (1924), summarized in Phillips (1922–26) with plates based on ♂ and ♀ type specimens.

MOULT: unknown.

IMMATURE: unknown.

DUCKLING: unknown.

MEASUREMENTS: ♂ (*n* = 1) wing, 320; tail, 117; culmen, 45; tarsus, 49.5. ♀ (*n* = 1) wing, 310; tail, 115; culmen, 41.5; tarsus, 47 (Delacour 1954–64). Weight unknown.

Field characters

Length 640 mm. Does not resemble any other bird in east Asia, although under poor visibility birds in flight may resemble Common Shelduck and Ruddy Shelduck, while crested appearance of Falcated Duck may also cause confusion.

Voice

Unknown.

Range and status

Historical range probably extended from southern limits of Far East of Russia south to southern Japan and eastern China (see Nowak 1984). Rare winter visitor to Japan, where became extinct during 19th century (Brazil 1991); seems extinct also in South Korea and Russia. Only 2 accepted records since 1950, in May 1964, when ♂ and

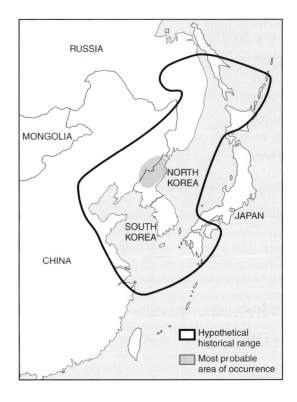

2 ♀♀ seen with small flock of Harlequin Ducks in sea off isolated Rimski-Korsakov Islands, southwest of Vladivostok (Russian Federation) (Labzyuk and Nazarov 1967), and in March 1971, when 2 ♂♂ and 4 ♀♀ were seen in mouth of River Pochon-gang (northeast North Korea) (Myong Sok 1984). Subsequent searches in former area have failed (Labzyuk 1972). In addition, however, many unconfirmed reports from eastern China in recent years, particularly on border with North Korea (Rank 1991, 1992, Green 1992b, Zhao 1993). Indeed, most likely area of persistence is in politically sensitive areas of Chang-bai Shan Mountains and Nangnim Sanmaek Mountains on North Korean/Chinese border, where large areas of remote habitat remain. If population does exist, probably < 100 individuals.

Habitat and general habits

Presumed to breed in mountainous, wooded areas, probably along rivers and streams, and possibly around lakes. In winter, observed most frequently on lower sections of rivers and in coastal areas (Nowak 1983, 1984). May feed at night.

Displays and breeding behaviour

Unknown. Pairbond probably long-term.

Breeding and life cycle

No nest, eggs or young recorded, but probably cavity nester like other shelduck, and may nest in hollows of trees, May–July. At least some birds seem to move to lower elevations during nonbreeding season and some migration south inferred (Nowak 1983, 1984).

Conservation and threats

Seems to have been rare for at least past 300 years (Nowak 1983). Some imported into Japan from Korea 1716–36 for aviculture, and further birds captured in Japan for this purpose at least until 1854 (Kakizawa and Sugawara 1989). Subsistence hunting and habitat degradation presumed to be principal threats to any that survive. Treated as Critically Endangered by BirdLife International (2001).

Des Callaghan

The true ducks, subfamily Anatinae
Pink-eared Duck and Salvadori's Duck

Taxonomy

Livezey (1996c, 1997b) considered, tentatively, that the tribe Malacorhynchini is composed of the Pink-eared Duck (endemic to Australia) and Salvadori's Duck (endemic to New Guinea), based on morphological similarities such as the black-and-white scalloping on the flanks and white barring on the mantle. A third species survived into the Holocene, *Malacorhynchus scarletti* of New Zealand, but became extinct following the arrival of the Polynesians (Olson 1977, Worthy 1995).

Both the Pink-eared and Salvadori's Ducks are usually treated as aberrant dabbling ducks, and are rarely considered to be related closely (Mayr 1931, Delacour and Mayr 1945, Boetticher 1952, Delacour 1956, Woolfenden 1961, Johnsgard 1965a, 1978, Frith 1967, Livezey 1986, 1991, 1997b, Mlíkovský 1989, Sibley and Monroe 1990, Christidis and Boles 1994). Some studies have suggested that the Pinkear is a shelduck (Tadorninae) (Livezey 1986), and others that it is of an ancient lineage, branching before most modern anseriforms (Brush 1976, Olson and Feduccia 1980a), a view that genetic analysis appears to support (Harshman 1996, Sraml *et al.* 1996). Duckling pattern and feather proteins differ greatly from typical dabbling ducks (Frith 1955, Brush 1976).

Salvadori's Duck is a river specialist, and has been linked with two other such specialists, the Blue Duck and Torrent Duck (Mayr 1931, Mlíkovský 1989). The three share many behavioural and morphological similarities, including long-term monogamous pairbonds, lack of eclipse plumage, highly territorial nature and associated wing-spurs, shared parental duties, downy plumage, the structure of the tracheal bullae, small clutches and large eggs (Kear 1975). Many of these features may, however, result from specialization for riverine habitats and are of limited taxonomic value (Livezey 1996c).

Des Callaghan

Pink-eared Duck *Malacorhynchus membranaceus*
PLATE 21

Anas membranacea Latham, 1801, Index Ornith., Suppl., p. 69
New South Wales
Malacorhynchus Swainson, 1831

Etymology: *malacorhynchus* Gr. *malakos* means soft, *rhunkhos* is bill; *membranaceus* L. for thin-skinned, both in reference to bill tipped with large membranous flaps.

Other names: Pink-ear, Pink-eyed Duck, Pinkeye or Pinkie, Zebra Duck or Zebra Teal, Whistling Teal or Whistler, Widgeon. Australian Aboriginal: Daula, Diwel-diwel, Gewallart, Korneok, Kumpanji, Tjupilpiti, Wrongi, Witjuwani, Wiwuldi, Wuya-wuya, Wymbin, Yukala; Dutch: Australische Lepelbekeend; French: Canard à orielles roses; German: Rosenohrente or Rotaugentente.

Variation: no subspecies. Together with Magpie Goose, Cape Barren Goose, Freckled Duck, Australian Wood Duck and Musk Duck, is 'old endemic component' of Australia's avifauna with no obvious close relatives elsewhere (e.g. Sraml *et al.* 1996).

Description

ADULT: sexes alike. Forehead and crown grey, white face with large dark brown eye-patch continuing as narrow stripe to nape then joining to form stripe down hind-neck. White ring circling eye. Small pink tuft above and behind eye at rear of eye-patch; underparts white with broad dark brown barring from upper breast to vent, becoming broader and bolder on flanks. Undertail coverts pale chestnut. Barred plumage continuous from upperbreast to mantle. Back and upperwings brown with fine pale vermiculations. Upperwings have narrow white trailing edges; no speculum. Rump white; uppertail coverts dark brown; tail brown with narrow white terminal band. Underwing surfaces white with pale barring on coverts merging to dark brown flight feathers. Bill leaden-grey square-tipped and spatulate with soft membranous flaps hanging from tip of upper mandible; legs and feet dark grey; eye brown. ♀ smaller and significantly lighter in weight, but difference not distinguishable in most circumstances.

MOULT: little information on sequence and timing of adult moult but assumed to be similar to that of most other Australian ducks. No seasonal plumage changes.

IMMATURE: paler and less barred than adult, forehead greyer and pink ear tufts absent until completion of 1st moult.

DUCKLING: pale coloured, grey-brown above, off-white below, with prominent dark brown eye-patch and eyestripe; from time of hatching, has characteristic bill flaps.

MEASUREMENTS AND WEIGHT: ♂ wing ($n = 46$), 172–213 (197); tail ($n = 7$), 60–62 (61); bill ($n = 82$), 44–74 (67); tarsus ($n = 12$), 33–37 (34); weight ($n = 77$), 290–480 (404). ♀ wing ($n = 67$), 152–200 (188); tail ($n = 5$), 57–64 (61); bill ($n = 83$), 53–67 (61); tarsus ($n = 14$), 32–35 (33); weight ($n = 81$), 272–423 (344) (Frith 1982, tail and tarsus from Marchant and Higgins 1990).

Field characters

Unmistakable small pale duck with oddly shaped bill, prominent eye-patch on white face, striped flanks, breast and lower neck, and dark grey-brown back. Length 380–400 mm. In flight, disproportionately large bill, dark tear drop eye-patch, pale undersides, white tipped tail, white rump patch and narrow white trailing edges on otherwise all dark wings characteristic. Twittering calls distinctive, especially from flocks in flight.

Voice

Calls generally chirruping or twittering. No obvious differences between calls of sexes; trachea of ♂ has no bulla. Four adult calls distinguished (Marchant and Higgins 1990): trilling, distinctive twittering *we-we-we-we-we-we-we-ooo* given at varying intensities from soft purring to louder almost frenzied versions, often rising and falling in pitch dominant sound heard from flocks in flight; ticking, sharp *tu-ick, puik* or *tick-uk* probably an alarm call; gronk, deep nasal *gronk* or *grunk* of unknown function; Trumpeting call, loud drawn out trumpeting whistle *whee-ooo* with rising and falling inflection given in characteristic upright pose with open bill tilting head upwards with each call, typically given especially by ♂♂ when defending partner, nest site or brood but probably uttered by both sexes without upright posture and tilting of bill. This or similar call given with greater intensity as drawn out note uttered during pair formation (Johnsgard 1965a). Further details and sonogram in Marchant and Higgins (1990). Ducklings give piping *shripp shripp* distress call and softer twittering *tititi* contentment call.

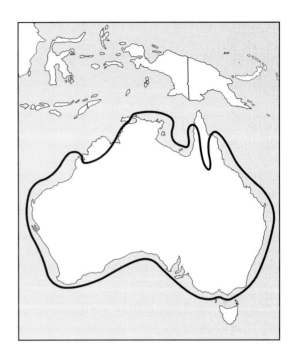

Range and status

Endemic to Australia and widespread on terrestrial wetlands through most of continent. Stronghold undoubtedly inland wetlands but regularly reaches coastal areas. Tends to concentrate on large shallow turbid floodwaters. Often breeds in huge concentrations, nesting over water in any available vegetation or tree hollow. Breeding frequently opportunistic following localized or more general flooding events. Numerous and highly mobile.

Aerial surveys in Oct (1983–92) in eastern Australia (excluding Tasmania) showed population size on average 370 000 and sometimes > 750 000 for that part of continent alone (Marchant and Higgins 1990, Kingsford *et al.* 1999, 2000). Surveys do not reveal any long-term trend over 17 years from early 1980s to 1999, but show wildly fluctuating nature of population occurring within eastern region from year to year (Kingsford *et al.* 1999, 2000). Taking into account wide distribution, certainly > 100 000 at most times and must often be > million, making

it next most abundant duck in Australia after Grey Teal.

Habitat and general habits

Feeds on invertebrates in abundant surface plankton (see Marchant and Higgins 1990 for details of diet), using specialized bill adaptations (Crome 1985b) and foraging techniques. Bill highly modified for efficient filtering of small organisms; food-laden water drawn in at bill tip and expelled between lamellae along sides of beak (Crome 1985b). Flaps highly sensitive (Kear and Burton 1971). Bill adaptation for filter-feeding fundamental characteristic of wildfowl, and Pink-eared Duck has most specialized form of this mechanism found among living wildfowl; only shovelers come close in similar adaptation for filter-feeding.

Forages in 3 ways—solitarily, in parallel or by spinning or 'vortexing' in pairs. Commonly feeds when swimming but also when walking on soft muds. On water, bill is thrust below surface to varying degrees; bill along surface to level of nostrils (which are placed high), head plunged below surface in short bouts and, finally, by frequent up-ending to limits of reach. Does not dive to feed. First method can be used to filter oozy muds while walking; often flocks seen feeding in formation, usually as loosely structured flotillas swimming on parallel courses. Common for birds to associate in couples when feeding on water, and the most elaborate form of cooperation demonstrated by vortexing method when pairs (rarely and briefly 3rd bird may join in) circle or spin constantly about central point. Two birds rotate in unison close together and almost head-to-tail but with bills turned inwards so that tips circumscribe much smaller area than propelling feet. This method presumably concentrates swarms of organisms into vortex created by constant rotational action. Vortexing birds can rotate in both directions and often switch.

Displays and breeding behaviour

Not well studied. Lateral Head-shaking used as pre-flight signal (Johnsgard 1965a). Conspicuous hostile Chin-lifting used as main threat signal. Upward Bill-tilting accompanied by Neck-stretching and series of whistle calls (trilling) is used by both sexes but specially by ♂ when defending ♀, nest site or brood. No lateral Inciting movements by ♀ observed (Johnsgard 1965a). Most common pair formation display seems to resemble threat signal; bill tossed rapidly up then lowered while giving Trumpeting call (Johnsgard 1965a, Marchant and Higgins 1990). Other displays seem to involve lateral Head-shakes with partly open bill followed by dorsal preening of scapulars (Johnsgard 1965a). Rapid shuffling of closed wings also observed; possibly mild threat signal indicative of social tension. Greeting signalled by loud trilling call. No special pre-copulatory displays known, and copulation rapid and followed by vigorous bathing and preening movements. Pairbond probably long-term.

Breeding and life cycle

Breeding occurs in most regions with no precise season, but in southeast Australia usually Aug–Feb following winter rainfall (Marchant and Higgins 1990). Likely that breeding driven by simple enrichment of food supply following floods (Crome 1986) and this will occur at any time of year in many drier parts of continent.

Nest site usually over water using hollow or crotch in tree, but often found in low shrub surrounded by water. Commonly occupy used nest sites of other waterbirds, especially coots, and will adopt suitable nestboxes. Frequently nests close together when breeding activity particularly intense. Grey down has distinctive 'tacky' feel, and copious amounts present forming tight springy mass surrounding sitting ♀. Clings so well that resistant to being blown away by strong winds; mass completely encloses clutch when ♀ leaves nest during incubation. Eggs oval, pointed, smooth, greasy and white to creamy-white (Marchant and Higgins 1990); 49 × 36 (45–53 × 34–38) ($n = 144$) from 21 clutches (Frith 1982); calculated weight 31 (Schönwetter 1960–66); clutch 7.3 (3–11) ($n = 120$), 6–8 typical (Frith 1982). Only ♀ incubates, for 26 days (Frith 1982). Brood attended by both sexes with ♂ showing strong parental care. Fledge in 45–60 days (Todd 1996). No data on growth. From 122 nests in New South Wales in 1956, a flood year, average 6.4 ducklings hatched, and 4.7 survived to fly (Frith 1982). Age at 1st breeding not studied, but almost certainly can occur in 1st year of life. No information on adult survival nor longevity.

Conservation and threats

Abundant, with no immediate threats to continued survival. Legal game in those states still permitting duck-hunting seasons.

Peter Fullagar

Salvadori's Duck *Salvadorina waigiuensis*
PLATE 14

Salvadorina waigiuensis Rothschild and Hartert, 1894, Novit. Zool., **1**, p. 683
Waigeo—although type specimen more likely taken in mountains of Vogelkop (Mayr 1941)

Etymology: *waigiuensis* from island of Waigeo, northwest of New Guinea, where type said to be collected. Conte A.T. Salvadori Paleotti (1835–1923) was an Italian ornithologist and collector.

Other names: Salvadori's Teal. Indonesian: Itik gunung.

Variation: no subspecies.

Description

ADULT: sexes alike. Head and neck hoary black, feathers with narrow pale edges particularly apparent on crown and throat; upperparts glossy black narrowly barred with white; wing bluish black with bright green speculum, two broad white bars and indication of spur on bend; 14 tail feathers are dull black narrowly bordered with white, generally barred with white in ♀ and young ♂; underparts pinkish buff, spotted with black on breast and abdomen, sides broadly barred black and buff, and flanks black barred with white; underwing coverts black and white; axillaries white (Delacour 1954–64). Bill and legs yellow; webs yellow and blackish; iris red in ♂, brown in ♀.

MOULT: no ♂ eclipse. ♂ reported in general body moult in Apr, Nov, June and July. ♂ in wing moult in Mar, and ♀ with young in wing moult in Sept (Kear 1975).

IMMATURE: as adult but duller and less distinctly marked; bill dark grey shading into olive on sides; feet pinkish grey in front with dusky streak in centre, blackish behind (Delacour 1954–64).

DUCKLING: black-dark brown and white. White patch on wing and two pairs of white spots on sides of back. Cheeks, throat and underparts white, with dark line from back of eye to neck, and darkish patch on ear coverts. Bill pink and grey (Kear 1975).

MEASUREMENTS AND WEIGHT: ♂ wing ($n = 18$), 185–207 (194); head ($n = 7$), 80.7–85.50 (83.0); bill ($n = 10$), 43.9–39.1 (37.2); tarsus ($n = 7$), 35.1–42.6 (39.7); weight ($n = 8$), 429–525 (462). ♀ wing ($n = 16$), 179–196 (185); head ($n = 4$), 76.4–81.0 (78.7); bill ($n = 7$), 34.0–37.8 (36.1); tarsus ($n = 4$), 36.0–40.7 (39.2); weight ($n = 7$), 420–520 (469) (Kear 1975).

Field characters

Small, slender, black-and-white striped duck, 430 mm long, with short, conspicuously yellow bill, pointed tail and forward-looking eyes. Found on water in pairs or family parties. Swims with curious jerking movement of head and, when alarmed, cocks tail to expose white underparts. Flies fast and low, following river.

Voice

Generally quiet. ♂ has whistle used in courtship but not in fights nor as territorial signal, and ♀ 2-syllabled quack. ♂ tracheal bulla not unlike that of dabbling ducks. Calls of ducklings also similar to dabblers. No sonogram published.

Range and status

Endemic to rivers of New Guinea at *c* 500–4000 m; found mainly at altitudes around 3700 m. Widespread but uncommon. Rose and Scott (1997) suggested declining population of 2500–10 000.

Habitat and general habits

Found in 3 habitat types: rushing mountain torrents, sluggish muddy streams and alpine lakes. Birds structurally adapted to, and at home in, turbulent water, but not confined to cascading rivers. Perhaps there was originally another waterfowl species in stiller waters that is no longer present, and Salvadori's Duck has taken its place or, since New Guinea was precipitous with no mountain lakes until recent geological time, may have adopted new calm water habitat because better adapted than other ducks to high altitudes.

Diet little studied. Caddis larvae, dragonfly nymphs, cladoceran water fleas, water beetles and

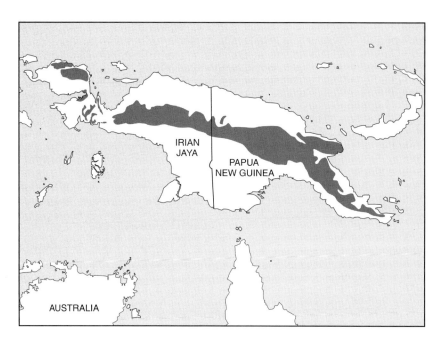

tadpoles suggested as available food. Often feeds in rapids, probing between rocks, dabbling, up-ending and diving. Dives smoothly, giving slight spring, for 12 sec (7–18) (*n* = 31) and, between dives, shakes and flaps wings, presumably to shed surplus water (Kear 1975).

Displays and breeding behaviour

Displays not well studied. In courtship, ♂ stretches neck, moves head slightly and whistles; ♀ incites with harsh *gak-gak* calls given with vertically directed pumping movements of neck (Johnsgard 1965a).

Highly territorial, with pairs occupying stretches of river apparently year-round. Pairbond assumed to be long-term. ♂♂ fight at territory boundaries using blunt spurs on wrists of wings. ♀ does not engage in combat but apparently incites mate by rushing about, giving up-and-down neck movements and double-noted quacks. Territories 160–1500 m long (Kear 1975).

Breeding and life cycle

Research needed into many aspects. Nesting prolonged, perhaps coinciding with dry season. Eggs laid May–mid Oct, and perhaps also Jan (Kear 1975). Ripley (1964) found ♂♂ in breeding condition Feb and Mar.

Nests never far from water and on ground; some on islands in depression concealed within grass or shrubs, or large boulder in stream may supply sufficient cover. Nest lined with grass and probably with down. Eggs large, 57.5 × 42.6 (55.5–61.5 × 41.1–44.8) (*n* = 4); 2 weighed 60 and 56, or about 13% of weight of ♀. Clutch size small at 3–4, and incubation lasts at least 28 days. Both parents care for young, and ducklings said to ride on back of ♀ (Kear 1975). Natural predators few; eels probably take ducklings, snakes rare at altitude of most ducks, but domestic dogs, which have gone wild in places, may be a hazard. Fledging, productivity, age at first breeding, adult survival and longevity unrecorded.

Conservation and threats

Listed in BirdLife International (2001) as Vulnerable. Officially protected since 1968, but probably continues to be hunted by primitive methods and, increasingly, with guns. More serious may be introduction (to improve protein content of human diets) into highland rivers of trout *Salmo* and other insectivorous fish that will compete for food. Greatest danger is increased human activity along river banks (Kear 1975) with consequent habitat degradation.

Janet Kear